6785
8/82

D1058614

Excerpts from Book Reviews

"It is extremely comprehensive – I am hard pressed to think of a performance evaluation technique that isn't discussed here. The emphasis is on practical techniques that could be used without a great deal of mathematical sophistication."
– Performance Evaluation Review

"I found that the pace of the material was very even, which makes this a particularly suitable text from which to teach."
– Computer Communications, UK

"IS managers, system buyers, or anyone who needs to compare two or more systems or products, understand the performance of existing systems, simulate future designs, or manage such projects will find this book helpful and entertaining."
– Capacity Management Review

"The frequent use of case studies was effective and sometimes entertaining."
– Computer Communication Review

"Although it's primarily written for the systems analyst, it's definitely a worthwhile addition to the marketing library."
– The Computer Marketing Newsletter

"Summary: A cyclopedia of the reasoning behind system performance evaluation."
– UnixWorld

"IS managers, system buyers, or anyone who needs to compare two or more systems or products, understand the performance of existing systems, simulate future designs, or manage such projects will find this book helpful and entertaining."
– Capacity Management Review

"Taken overall, the book is very impressive."
– ConneXions

"If you want to measure computer performance, whether to choose the best system to buy or to make your system the best, this is just about the only practical book available on the subject"

– Computer User

"It is certainly a very good introduction to a wide range of performance analysis topics, and if considered as a reference book, represents a breadth of topics that is unprecedented for this field."

– Operating Systems Review

"System designers and managers will appreciate the analytical simplicity they find here."

– IEEE Communications Magazine

"[This book] is a practical, rich and enjoyable addition to the library of anyone whose work includes performance evaluation, simulation of systems, or system testing."

– Simulation

THE ART OF COMPUTER SYSTEMS PERFORMANCE ANALYSIS

Techniques for Experimental Design, Measurement, Simulation, and Modeling

RAJ JAIN
Digital Equipment Corporation
Littleton, Massachusetts

JOHN WILEY & SONS, INC.

New York / Chichester / Brisbane / Toronto / Singapore

In recognition of the importance of preserving what has been written, it is a policy of John Wiley & Sons, Inc., to have books of enduring value published in the United States printed on acid-free paper, and we exert our best efforts to that end.

Copyright © 1991 by John Wiley & Sons, Inc.

All rights reserved. Published simultaneously in Canada.

Reproduction or translation of any part of this work beyond that permitted by Section 107 or 108 of the 1976 United States Copyright Act without the permission of the copyright owner is unlawful. Requests for permission or further information should be addressed to the Permissions Department, John Wiley & Sons, Inc.

Library of Congress Cataloging in Publication Data:

Jain, Raj.
    The art of computer systems performance analysis: techniques for experimental design, measurement, simulation, and modeling / Raj Jain.

      p. cm.
    Includes bibliographical references and index.
    ISBN 0-471-50336-3
    1. Electronic digital computers—Evaluation. I. Title.

QA76.9.E94J32   1991
004.2'4–dc20   90-45479
                                    CIP

Printed in the United States of America

10 9

To my mother, Sulochana Devi

PREFACE

This book is intended to be a comprehensive textbook for the computer professionals who design, procure, or use computer systems. These professionals may be proficient in their own field (design, procurement, application, and so forth) while knowing little about queueing theory, statistics, experimental design, or workload characterization. Performance analysis is a key step in the design and procurement of new computer systems including processors, languages, operating systems, networking architectures, or database systems. In all cases, it is necessary to compare performance of new computer systems with that of similar systems. This book provides these professionals with performance analysis techniques that are simple and straightforward and require a minimal level of statistical sophistication.

A computer systems performance analyst must understand computer systems as well as various analysis techniques such as statistics, probability theory, experimental design, simulation, and queueing theory. The purpose of this book is to give basic modeling, simulation, and analysis background to systems analysts so that they are able to understand performance terminology, correctly design performance experiments, use simple queueing or simulation models, and interpret results. Often performance analysts are of two basic types: those who can measure but cannot model and those who can model but cannot measure. In practice, one needs to use both measurement as well as modeling techniques to solve performance problems. This book stresses both aspects of the field.

There are many books on computer systems performance. These books discuss only one or two aspects of performance analysis, with a majority of the books being *queueing theoretic*. Queueing theory is admittedly a helpful tool, but the knowledge of simulation, measurement techniques, data analysis, and experimental design is invaluable. I wrote this book because there is no book available that emphasizes and integrates all these aspects of performance analysis. Experimental design techniques that help reduce analysis costs are currently a totally neglected area in performance analysis books. As a performance analyst with several design teams at Digital Equipment Corporation and as an instructor of a course on performance analysis at Massachusetts Institute of Technology, I have been involved in the performance analysis of a wide variety of computer systems and subsystems. This book is a compendium of the techniques that were used in these analyses.

Analytical simplicity is a valuable aspect of this book. Sophisticated queueing theoretic models and statistical techniques are of interest to *performance specialists*, but in the majority of cases simple analysis yields sufficiently useful results. Complex analyses are not feasible, for example, in an industrial environment where there are considerable time restraints and deadlines. Simple models and analyses that are easily understood expedite decisions and solutions within a design team that may be composed of team members of varying degree of analytical sophistication. In spite of my attempt to keep the mathematical rigor to a minimum, some portions, particularly those involving derivations or proofs of results, may be a bit too intricate for a few readers. In such cases, it is recommended that the reader skip the particular portion during the first pass, try to understand the examples illustrating the application of results, and then come back to the derivation, if necessary.

Another interesting aspect of this book is that it discusses common mistakes and games in various steps in performance studies. The book contains lists of common mistakes in performance evaluation, benchmarking, data presentation, data analysis, experimental design, and simulation. While most of these mistakes are a result of a lack of knowledge of proper techniques, there are a number of tricks that some analysts knowingly use to show the superiority of their systems. A knowledge of such tricks, called games, will help protect the readers from being victimized by such analysts. The book discusses several games including those in benchmarking, analyzing data, and presenting results.

The analysis techniques discussed in the book have been illustrated using examples and case studies—all from the field of computer systems. This is an important aspect of this book. Textbooks on statistics and experimental designs using examples from other fields such as agriculture do not interest computer scientists as much as this book does. The case studies are from *actual* computer system design projects. To illustrate the use and misuse of various techniques in the literature, several examples of analyses published in technical journals are also presented. Overall, there are more than 150 examples and case studies in the book.

Important techniques and results have been summarized in "boxes." There are more than 30 such boxes. It is expected that after a first reading, most readers would use these boxes for a quick reference.

The book consists of 36 chapters. Most chapters are organized so that each chapter can be presented in 45 minutes with some time left for discussion of exercises and their solutions in a typical 55-minute session of the class. This makes the book ideally suited for a one- or two-semester course. If the course is taught in one semester, some elementary material related to statistics and some of the advanced queueing techniques can be omitted or assigned for student reading. Most chapters also have exercises that can be assigned as homework.

Parts of this book were used as course notes in a graduate seminar on computer systems performance at the Massachusetts Institute of Technology. The students were *system oriented* with their primary goal being to design new computer systems. All of the students had previously taken courses in computer architectures, programming languages, and operating systems. Few had taken any advance courses on statistics, queueing theory, or probability. One of the course requirements included a project that required a performance analysis of their system. The projects were carried out on such diverse computer systems as LISP machines, data flow architectures, database querying packages, network protocols, and computer-aided design (CAD) tools.

Writing this book has been a monumental task. This being the first edition, many errors may have gone unnoticed. If you notice any errors or if you have any suggestions for improvement, please write to me care of the publisher.

RAJ JAIN

Littleton, Massachusetts

ACKNOWLEDGMENTS

I would like to thank my wife, Neelu, and my sons, Sameer and Amit, for enduring lonely evenings and weekends for the past seven years while I was preoccupied with this book. Neelu also helped in typing, editing, and correction.

I am indebted to Digital Equipment Corporation and Massachusetts Institute of Technology for supporting this effort. The seeds of this book were sown during my sabbatical at MIT in 1983-1984. The sabbatical was made possible by the encouragement and support of Linda Wright of DEC and Professor Jerry Saltzer of MIT. In later years, Bill Hawe of DEC and Professor Fernando Corbato of MIT encouraged me to teach the course and refine the class notes that resulted in this book.

A number of my colleagues read drafts and helped improve the readability of the text. Thanks are due to Katherin Winkler, Praduman Jain, Sandy Hsueh, Oliver Ibe, Dick Spencer, Sanjay Mithal, Yun-Cheng Liu, Jeff Dawson, Pete Kaiser, Brad Waters, Rich Pitkin, Vasmi Abidi, Tim Sager, Susan Owicki, Marc Greenwald, Kamesh Gargeya, Barbara Benton, George Cathey, Mark Dufresne, Bill Zahavi, Pete Benoit, Mike Peterson, Eugene Finkelstein, Mike Como, and Karen Dorhamer for their suggestions. Andrea Finger, Janice Wilkins, and Kathy Allen helped with typing and Kathy Colby helped in editing various parts of the book. The help by the staff of John Wiley & Sons is also appreciated. In particular, I enjoyed working with my editor, Diane Cerra, and production editor, Bob Hilbert.

Many of the case studies presented in this book were done by students as course projects at Massachusetts Institute of Technology. Thanks are due to Kirk Mousley (Case Study 11.1), J. P. Restivo (Case Studies 14.1 and 15.1), Andy Ayers (Case Study 18.1), Steve Hsu and John Wang (Case Study 19.1),

Andy Anderson (Example 21.1 and Case Studies 21.1 and 21.3), Henry Wu (Case Study 21.2), and Tomas Wanuga (Case Study 25.1).

The following trademarks have been used in the book. 68000 is a trademark of Motorola, Inc. 8086 is a trademark of Intel Corp. Z80 is a trademark of Zilog, Inc. PDP-11/70 and VAX-11/780 are trademarks of Digital Equipment Corp. TPC Benchmark is a trademark of the Transaction Processing Performance Council. PCjr is a trademark of International Business Machines, Corp. Macintosh is a trademark of Apple Computer, Inc. MS-DOS is a trademark of Microsoft Corp. UNIX is a registered trademark of Bell Laboratories.

CONTENTS

List of Boxes   **xxv**

List of Case Studies   **xxvii**

PART I   AN OVERVIEW OF PERFORMANCE EVALUATION   1

1   Introduction   3

     1.1   Outline of Topics, 3

     1.2   The Art of Performance Evaluation, 7

     1.3   Professional Organizations, Journals, and Conferences, 8

     1.4   Performance Projects, 11

             Exercise, 12

2   Common Mistakes and How to Avoid Them   14

     2.1   Common Mistakes in Performance Evaluation, 14

     2.2   A Systematic Approach to Performance Evaluation, 22

             Exercises, 28

3   Selection of Techniques and Metrics   30

    3.1   Selecting an Evaluation Technique, 30
    3.2   Selecting Performance Metrics, 33
    3.3   Commonly Used Performance Metrics, 37
    3.4   Utility Classification of Performance Metrics, 40
    3.5   Setting Performance Requirements, 41
         Exercises, 43

Further Reading for Part I   44

PART II   MEASUREMENT TECHNIQUES AND TOOLS   45

4   Types of Workloads   47

    4.1   Addition Instruction, 48
    4.2   Instruction Mixes, 48
    4.3   Kernels, 49
    4.4   Synthetic Programs, 50
    4.5   Application Benchmarks, 51
    4.6   Popular Benchmarks, 52
         Exercises, 59

5   The Art of Workload Selection   60

    5.1   Services Exercised, 60
    5.2   Level of Detail, 66
    5.3   Representativeness, 67
    5.4   Timeliness, 68
    5.5   Other Considerations in Workload Selection, 69
         Exercises, 69

6   Workload Characterization Techniques   71

    6.1   Terminology, 71
    6.2   Averaging, 73
    6.3   Specifying Dispersion, 73
    6.4   Single-Parameter Histograms, 75
    6.5   Multiparameter Histograms, 76
    6.6   Principal-Component Analysis, 76
    6.7   Markov Models, 81

6.8   Clustering, 83
       Exercises, 91

7 Monitors   **93**

7.1   Monitor Terminology, 94
7.2   Monitor Classification, 94
7.3   Software Monitors, 95
7.4   Hardware Monitors, 98
7.5   Software versus Hardware Monitors, 98
7.6   Firmware and Hybrid Monitors, 100
7.7   Distributed-System Monitors, 101
       Exercises, 109

8 Program Execution Monitors and Accounting Logs   **111**

8.1   Program Execution Monitors, 111
8.2   Techniques for Improving Program Performance, 114
8.3   Accounting Logs, 114
8.4   Analysis and Interpretation of Accounting Log Data, 117
8.5   Using Accounting Logs to Answer Commonly Asked
       Questions, 119
       Exercise, 122

9 Capacity Planning and Benchmarking   **123**

9.1   Steps in Capacity Planning and Management, 124
9.2   Problems in Capacity Planning, 125
9.3   Common Mistakes in Benchmarking, 127
9.4   Benchmarking Games, 130
9.5   Load Drivers, 131
9.6   Remote-Terminal Emulation, 132
9.7   Components of an RTE, 133
9.8   Limitations of Current RTEs, 136
       Exercises, 138

10 The Art of Data Presentation   **139**

10.1   Types of Variables, 140
10.2   Guidelines for Preparing Good Graphic Charts, 141
10.3   Common Mistakes in Preparing Charts, 144
10.4   Pictorial Games, 146

10.5   Gantt Charts, 150
10.6   Kiviat Graphs, 153
10.7   Schumacher Charts, 160
10.8   Decision Maker's Games, 161
       Exercises, 163

11 Ratio Games   **165**

11.1   Choosing an Appropriate Base System, 165
11.2   Using an Appropriate Ratio Metric, 167
11.3   Using Relative Performance Enhancement, 168
11.4   Ratio Games with Percentages, 169
11.5   Strategies for Winning a Ratio Game, 170
11.6   Correct Analysis, 174
       Exercises, 174

Further Reading for Part II   **175**

PART III   PROBABILITY THEORY AND STATISTICS   177

12 Summarizing Measured Data   **179**

12.1   Basic Probability and Statistics Concepts, 179
12.2   Summarizing Data by a Single Number, 182
12.3   Selecting among the Mean, Median, and Mode, 183
12.4   Common Misuses of Means, 186
12.5   Geometric Mean, 187
12.6   Harmonic Mean, 188
12.7   Mean of a Ratio, 189
12.8   Summarizing Variability, 192
12.9   Selecting the Index of Dispersion, 195
12.10 Determining Distribution of Data, 196
       Exercises, 200

13 Comparing Systems Using Sample Data   **203**

13.1   Sample versus Population, 203
13.2   Confidence Interval for the Mean, 204
13.3   Testing for a Zero Mean, 207
13.4   Comparing Two Alternatives, 208
13.5   What Confidence Level to Use, 212

13.6 Hypothesis Testing versus Confidence Intervals, 213
13.7 One-Sided Confidence Intervals, 214
13.8 Confidence Intervals for Proportions, 215
13.9 Determining Sample Size, 216
       Exercises, 218

14 Simple Linear Regression Models   221

14.1 Definition of a Good Model, 222
14.2 Estimation of Model Parameters, 223
14.3 Allocation of Variation, 226
14.4 Standard Deviation of Errors, 228
14.5 Confidence Intervals for Regression Parameters, 229
14.6 Confidence Intervals for Predictions, 232
14.7 Visual Tests for Verifying the Regression
       Assumptions, 234
       Exercises, 241

15 Other Regression Models   244

15.1 Multiple Linear Regression Models, 245
15.2 Regression with Categorical Predictors, 254
15.3 Curvilinear Regression, 257
15.4 Transformations, 259
15.5 Outliers, 265
15.6 Common Mistakes in Regression, 266
       Exercises, 270

Further Reading for Part III   272

PART IV EXPERIMENTAL DESIGN AND ANALYSIS   273

16 Introduction to Experimental Design   275

16.1 Terminology, 275
16.2 Common Mistakes in Experimentation, 278
16.3 Types of Experimental Designs, 279
       Exercise, 282

17 2^k Factorial Designs   **283**

   17.1 2^2 Factorial Designs, 284
   17.2   Computation of Effects, 285
   17.3   Sign Table Method for Calculating Effects, 286
   17.4   Allocation of Variation, 286
   17.5   General 2^k Factorial Designs, 291
           Exercise, 292

18 $2^k r$ Factorial Designs with Replications   **293**

   18.1 $2^2 r$ Factorial Designs, 293
   18.2   Computation of Effects, 294
   18.3   Estimation of Experimental Errors, 294
   18.4   Allocation of Variation, 295
   18.5   Confidence Intervals for Effects, 298
   18.6   Confidence Intervals for Predicted Responses, 299
   18.7   Visual Tests for Verifying the Assumptions, 302
   18.8   Multiplicative Models for $2^2 r$ Experiments, 303
   18.9   General $2^k r$ Factorial Design, 308
           Exercise, 313

19 2^{k-p} Fractional Factorial Designs   **314**

   19.1   Preparing the Sign Table for a 2^{k-p} Design, 316
   19.2   Confounding, 318
   19.3   Algebra of Confounding, 320
   19.4   Design Resolution, 321
           Exercises, 326

20 One-Factor Experiments   **327**

   20.1   Model, 327
   20.2   Computation of Effects, 328
   20.3   Estimating Experimental Errors, 330
   20.4   Allocation of Variation, 331
   20.5   Analysis of Variance, 332
   20.6   Visual Diagnostic Tests, 334
   20.7   Confidence Intervals for Effects, 335
   20.8   Unequal Sample Sizes, 337
           Exercise, 342

21 Two-Factor Full Factorial Design without Replications   **343**

21.1   Model, 344
21.2   Computation of Effects, 344
21.3   Estimating Experimental Errors, 346
21.4   Allocation of Variation, 347
21.5   Analysis of Variance, 348
21.6   Confidence Intervals for Effects, 351
21.7   Multiplicative Models for Two-Factor Experiments, 353
21.8   Missing Observations, 360
       Exercises, 367

22 Two-Factor Full Factorial Design with Replications   **368**

22.1   Model, 368
22.2   Computation of Effects, 369
22.3   Computation of Errors, 372
22.4   Allocation of Variation, 372
22.5   Analysis of Variance, 374
22.6   Confidence Intervals for Effects, 374
       Exercise, 379

23 General Full Factorial Designs with k Factors   **381**

23.1   Model, 381
23.2   Analysis of a General Design, 382
23.3   Informal Methods, 386
       Exercises, 389

Further Reading for Part IV   **390**

PART V   SIMULATION   **391**

24 Introduction to Simulation   **393**

24.1   Common Mistakes in Simulation, 394
24.2   Other Causes of Simulation Analysis Failure, 395
24.3   Terminology, 398
24.4   Selecting a Language for Simulation, 401
24.5   Types of Simulations, 403
24.6   Event-Set Algorithms, 408
       Exercises, 411

25 Analysis of Simulation Results   413

    25.1   Model Verification Techniques, 413
    25.2   Model Validation Techniques, 420
    25.3   Transient Removal, 423
    25.4   Terminating Simulations, 428
    25.5   Stopping Criteria: Variance Estimation, 430
    25.6   Variance Reduction, 436
           Exercises, 436

26 Random-Number Generation   437

    26.1   Desired Properties of a Good Generator, 437
    26.2   Linear-Congruential Generators, 439
    26.3   Tausworthe Generators, 444
    26.4   Extended Fibonacci Generators, 450
    26.5   Combined Generators, 450
    26.6   A Survey of Random-Number Generators, 452
    26.7   Seed Selection, 453
    26.8   Myths about Random-Number Generation, 455
           Exercises, 458

27 Testing Random-Number Generators   460

    27.1   Chi-Square Test, 461
    27.2   Kolmogorov-Smirnov Test, 462
    27.3   Serial-Correlation Test, 465
    27.4   Two-Level Tests, 466
    27.5 k-Dimensional Uniformity or k-Distributivity, 467
    27.6   Serial Test, 468
    27.7   Spectral Test, 470
           Exercises, 473

28 Random-Variate Generation   474

    28.1   Inverse Transformation, 474
    28.2   Rejection, 476
    28.3   Composition, 478
    28.4   Convolution, 479
    28.5   Characterization, 480
           Exercise, 482

29 Commonly Used Distributions   **483**

29.1   Bernoulli Distribution, 483

29.2   Beta Distribution, 484

29.3   Binomial Distribution, 485

29.4   Chi-Square Distribution, 486

29.5   Erlang Distribution, 487

29.6   Exponential Distribution, 488

29.7 F Distribution, 489

29.8   Gamma Distribution, 490

29.9   Geometric Distribution, 491

29.10   Lognormal Distribution, 492

29.11   Negative Binomial Distribution, 492

29.12   Normal Distribution, 493

29.13   Pareto Distribution, 495

29.14   Pascal Distribution, 495

29.15   Poisson Distribution, 496

29.16   Student's t Distribution, 497

29.17   Uniform Distribution (Continuous), 497

29.18   Uniform Distribution (Discrete), 498

29.19   Weibull Distribution, 499

29.20   Relationships among Distributions, 499
        Exercises, 501

Further Reading for Part V   **502**
        Current Areas of Research in Simulation, 503

PART VI   QUEUEING MODELS   **505**

30 Introduction to Queueing Theory   **507**

30.1   Queueing Notation, 507

30.2   Rules for All Queues, 510

30.3   Little's Law, 513

30.4   Types of Stochastic Processes, 515
        Exercises, 518

31 Analysis of a Single Queue   **519**

   31.1   Birth-Death Processes, 519
   31.2   M/M/1 Queue, 522
   31.3   M/M/m Queue, 527
   31.4   M/M/m/B Queue with Finite Buffers, 534
   31.5   Results for Other Queueing Systems, 540
           Exercises, 545

32 Queueing Networks   **547**

   32.1   Open and Closed Queueing Networks, 547
   32.2   Product Form Networks, 548
   32.3   Queueing Network Models of Computer Systems, 552
           Exercise, 554

33 Operational Laws   **555**

   33.1   Utilization Law, 556
   33.2   Forced Flow Law, 557
   33.3   Little's Law, 560
   33.4   General Response Time Law, 561
   33.5   Interactive Response Time Law, 563
   33.6   Bottleneck Analysis, 563
           Exercises, 568

34 Mean-Value Analysis and Related Techniques   **570**

   34.1   Analysis of Open Queueing Networks, 570
   34.2   Mean-Value Analysis, 575
   34.3   Approximate MVA, 579
   34.4   Balanced Job Bounds, 585
           Exercises, 591

35 Convolution Algorithm   **593**

   35.1   Distribution of Jobs in a System, 593
   35.2   Convolution Algorithm for Computing $G(N)$, 595
   35.3   Computing Performance Using $G(N)$, 598
   35.4   Timesharing Systems, 602
           Exercises, 607

36 Hierarchical Decomposition of Large Queueing Networks   608

36.1   Load-dependent Service Centers, 608
36.2   Hierarchical Decomposition, 613
36.3   Limitations of Queueing Theory, 620
        Exercises, 622

Further Reading for Part VI   624

        Symbols Frequently Used in Queueing Analysis, 624

Appendix A   Statistical Tables   627

A.1   Area of the Unit Normal Distribution, 628
A.2   Quantiles of the Unit Normal Distribution, 629
A.3   Commonly Used Normal Quantiles, 630
A.4   Quantiles of the t Distribution, 631
A.5   Quantiles of the Chi-Square Distribution, 632
A.6   90-Percentiles of the $F(n,m)$ Distribution, 634
A.7   95-Percentiles of the $F(n,m)$ Distribution, 635
A.8   99-Percentiles of the $F(n,m)$ Distribution, 636
A.9   Quantiles of the K–S Distribution, 637
A.10   Approximation Formulas for Statistical Tables, 638

Solutions to Selected Exercises   639

References   651

Author Index   661

Subject Index   665

LIST OF BOXES

2.1   Checklist for Avoiding Common Mistakes in Performance Evaluation, 22

2.2   Steps for a Performance Evaluation Study, 26

8.1   Techniques for Improving Program Performance, 115

10.1   Checklist for Good Graphics, 143

10.2   Reasons for Not Accepting the Results of an Analysis, 162

12.1   Summarizing Observations, 197

13.1   Confidence Intervals, 219

14.1   Simple Linear Regression, 240

15.1   Multiple Linear Regression, 246

15.2   Checklist for Regression Analyses, 269

18.1   Analysis of $2^k r$ Factorial Designs, 309

20.1   Analysis of One-Factor Experiments, 341

21.1   Analysis of Two-Factor Designs without Replications, 365

22.1   Analysis of Two-Factor Designs with Replications, 378

24.1   Checklist for Simulations, 398

31.1   M/M/1 Queue, 525

31.2   M/M/m Queue, 528

31.3   M/M/m/B Queue (B Buffers), 538

31.4   M/M/1/B Queue (B Buffers), 539

31.5   M/G/1 Queue, 540

31.6   M/G/1 Queue with Processor Sharing (PS), 541

31.7   M/D/1 Queue, 542

31.8   M/G/∞ Queue, 543

31.9   G/M/1 Queue, 543

31.10   G/G/m Queue, 544

33.1   Operational Laws, 567

34.1   Analysis of Open Queueing Networks, 572

34.2   MVA Algorithm, 577

34.3   MVA Algorithm Using Schweitzer's Approximation, 581

34.4   Balanced Job Bounds, 590

35.1   Convolution Algorithm, 606

36.1   MVA Including Load-dependent Centers, 610

LIST OF CASE STUDIES

2.1   Remote pipe and remote procedure call comparison, 25
3.1   Network congestion control algorithm comparison, 35
3.2   Performance requirements for a high-speed local-area network, 42
6.1   Program usage in educational environments, 74
8.1   Using accounting logs to characterize the workload, 121
11.1   Comparison of 6502 and 8080 on two workloads, 166
11.2   RISC performance evaluation using ratios, 166
12.1   Performance evaluation of a program optimizer, 191
14.1   Remote procedure call performance on UNIX and ARGUS, 230
15.1   RPC performance on UNIX and ARGUS using categorical predictors, 256
15.2   Garbage collection algorithm evaluation, 263
17.1   Comparison of two interconnection networks, 289
18.1   Garbage collection and memory management system evaluation, 311
19.1   Comparison of two text-formatting programs, 322
19.2   Design analysis of a scheduler for a WANG VS system, 324
21.1   Comparison of several cache design alternatives, 352
21.2   Comparison of Scheme and Spectrum RISC architectures, 354
21.3   Comparing four processors on five workloads, 357
21.4   Analysis of Intel iAPX 432 performance data, 358
21.5   Analysis of the RISC-I experiments, 360
23.1   Effect of various factors on the paging process, 382
25.1   Run length determination for an interconnection network simulation, 433

THE ART OF
COMPUTER SYSTEMS
PERFORMANCE ANALYSIS

PART I

AN OVERVIEW OF PERFORMANCE EVALUATION

Computer system users, administrators, and designers are all interested in performance evaluation since their goal is to obtain or provide the highest performance at the lowest cost. This goal has resulted in continuing evolution of higher performance and lower cost systems leading to today's proliferation of workstations and personal computers, many of which have better performance than earlier supercomputers. As the field of computer design matures, the computer industry is becoming more competitive, and it is more important than ever to ensure that the alternative selected provides the best cost-performance trade-off.

Performance evaluation is required at every stage in the life cycle of a computer system, including its design, manufacturing, sales/purchase, use, upgrade, and so on. A performance evaluation is required when a computer system designer wants to compare a number of alternative designs and find the best design. It is required when a system administrator wants to compare a number of systems and wants to decide which system is best for a given set of applications. Even if there are no alternatives, performance evaluation of the current system helps in determining how well it is performing and whether any improvements need to be made. Unfortunately, the types of applications of computers are so numerous that it is not possible to have a standard measure of performance, a standard measurement environment (application), or a standard technique for all cases. The first step in performance evaluation is to select the right measures of performance, the right measurement environments, and the right techniques. This part will help in making these selections.

This part provides a general introduction to the field of performance evaluation. It consists of three chapters. Chapter 1 provides an overview of the book and discusses why performance evaluation is an art. Mistakes commonly observed in performance evaluation projects and a proper methodology to avoid them are presented in Chapter 2. Selection of performance evaluation techniques and evaluation criteria are discussed in Chapter 3.

CHAPTER 1

━━━━━━━━━━━━━━━━━━━━━━━━━━━━━━━━━━━━━━

INTRODUCTION
──

I keep six honest serving men. They taught me all I knew. Their names are What and Why and When and How and Where and Who.

—Rudyard Kipling

Performance is a key criterion in the design, procurement, and use of computer systems. As such, the goal of computer systems engineers, scientists, analysts, and users is to get the highest performance for a given cost. To achieve that goal, computer systems professionals need, at least, a basic knowledge of performance evaluation terminology and techniques. Anyone associated with computer systems should be able to state the performance requirements of their systems and should be able to compare different alternatives to find the one that best meets their requirements.

1.1 OUTLINE OF TOPICS

The purpose of this book is to explain the performance evaluation terminology and techniques to computer systems designers and users. The goal is to emphasize simple techniques that help solve a majority of day-to-day problems. Examples of such problems are specifying performance requirements, evaluating design alternatives, comparing two or more systems, determining the optimal value of a parameter (system tuning), finding the performance bottleneck (bottleneck identification), characterizing the load on the system (workload characterization), determining the number and sizes of components (capacity planning), and predicting the performance at future loads (forecasting). Here, a **system** could be any collection of hardware, software, and firmware components. It could be a hardware component, for example, a central processing unit (CPU); a software system, such as a database system; or a network of several computers.

The following are examples of the types of problems that you should be able to solve after reading this book.

1. *Select appropriate evaluation techniques, performance metrics, and workloads for a system.* Later, in Chapters 2 and 3, the terms "evaluation techniques," "metrics," and "workload" are explained in detail. Briefly, the techniques that may be used for performance evaluation are measurement, simulation, and analytical modeling. The term **metrics** refers to the criteria used to evaluate the performance of the system. For example, **response time**—the time to service a request—could be used as a metric to compare two timesharing systems. Similarly, two transaction processing systems may be compared on the basis of their throughputs, which may be specified in transactions per second (**TPS**). The requests made by the users of the system are called **workloads**. For example, the CPU workload would consist of the instructions it is asked to execute. The workload of a database system would consist of queries and other requests it executes for users.

The issues related to the selection of metrics and evaluation techniques are discussed in Chapter 3. For example, after reading Part I you should be able to answer the following question.

Example 1.1   What performance metrics should be used to compare the performance of the following systems?

   (a) Two disk drives
   (b) Two transaction processing systems
   (c) Two packet retransmission algorithms   ☐

2. *Conduct performance measurements correctly.* To measure the performance of a computer system, you need at least two tools—a tool to load the system (**load generator**) and a tool to measure the results (**monitor**). There are several types of load generators and monitors. For example, to emulate several users of a timesharing system, one would use a load generator called a **remote terminal emulator** (RTE). The issues related to the design and selection of such tools are discussed in Part II. The following is an example of a problem that you should be able to answer after that part.

Example 1.2   Which type of monitor (software or hardware) would be more suitable for measuring each of the following quantities?

(a) Number of instructions executed by a processor

(b) Degree of multiprogramming on a timesharing system

(c) Response time of packets on a network ☐

3. *Use proper statistical techniques to compare several alternatives.* Most performance evaluation problems basically consist of finding the best among a number of alternatives. If a measurement or a simulation is repeated several times, generally the results would be slightly different each time. Simply comparing the average result of a number of repeated trials does not lead to correct conclusions, particularly if the variability of the result is high. The statistical techniques used to compare several alternatives are discussed in Part III. The following is an example of the type of question that you should be able to answer after reading that part.

Example 1.3 The number of packets lost on two links was measured for four file sizes as shown in Table 1.1.

TABLE 1.1 Packets Lost on Two Links

File Size	Link A	Link B
1000	5	10
1200	7	3
1300	3	0
50	0	1

Which link is better? ☐

4. *Design measurement and simulation experiments to provide the most information with the least effort.* Given a number of factors that affect the system performance, it is useful to separate out the effects of individual factors. In Part IV on experimental design, techniques to organize experiments to obtain maximum information with a minimum number of experiments are presented. The following is an example of an experimental design question that you should be able to answer after reading that part.

Example 1.4 The performance of a system depends on the following three factors:

(a) Garbage collection technique used: G1, G2, or none.

(b) Type of workload: editing, computing, or artificial intelligence (AI).

(c) Type of CPU: C1, C2, or C3.

How many experiments are needed? How does one estimate the perfor-
mance impact of each factor?   □

5. *Perform simulations correctly.* In designing a simulation model, one has to
   select a language for simulation, select seeds and algorithms for random-
   number generation, decide the length of simulation run, and analyze
   the simulation results. These issues are discussed in Part V on simulation. After reading that part, you should be able to answer the following
   simulation-related question.

   Example 1.5 In order to compare the performance of two cache replacement algorithms:

   (a) What type of simulation model should be used?
   (b) How long should the simulation be run?
   (c) What can be done to get the same accuracy with a shorter run?
   (d) How can one decide if the random-number generator in the simula-
       tion is a good generator?   □

6. *Use simple queueing models to analyze the performance of systems.* Queueing models are commonly used for analytical modeling of computer systems. In Part VI, different types of queues and networks of queues are
   discussed and and their use to answer commonly asked questions about
   system performance is described. The following is an exercise that you
   will be able to solve after reading that part.

   Example 1.6 The average response time of a database system is 3 seconds. During a 1-minute observation interval, the idle time on the system
   was 10 seconds. Using a queueing model for the system, determine the
   following:

   (a) System utilization
   (b) Average service time per query
   (c) Number of queries completed during the observation interval
   (d) Average number of jobs in the system
   (e) Probability of number of jobs in the system being greater than 10
   (f) 90-percentile response time
   (g) 90-percentile waiting time   □

The preceding six examples correspond to the six parts of this book.

The remainder of Part I explains the steps common to all performance
studies beginning with an example of the performance games people play to
show that their system is better. Some common mistakes that beginners make
are described. In addition, the key components of performance studies, in
particular, the selection of performance metrics and evaluation techniques,
are discussed.

1.2   THE ART OF PERFORMANCE EVALUATION

Contrary to common belief, performance evaluation is an art. Like a work of art, successful evaluation cannot be produced mechanically. Every evaluation requires an intimate knowledge of the system being modeled and a careful selection of the methodology, workload, and tools. When first presented to an analyst, most performance problems are expressed as an abstract feeling, like a rough sketch, by the end user. Defining the real problem and converting it to a form in which established tools and techniques can be used and where time and other constraints can be met is a major part of the analyst's "art."

Like an artist, each analyst has a unique style. Given the same problem, two analysts may choose different performance metrics and evaluation methodologies. In fact, given the same data, two analysts may interpret them differently. The following example shows a typical case for which, given the same measurements, two system designers can each prove that his/her system is better than that of the other.

Example 1.7   The throughputs of two systems A and B were measured in transactions per second. The results are shown in Table 1.2.

TABLE 1.2   Throughput in Transactions per Second

System	Workload 1	Workload 2
A	20	10
B	10	20

There are three ways to compare the performance of the two systems. The first way is to take the average of the performances on the two workloads. This leads to the analysis shown in Table 1.3. The conclusion in this case is that the two systems are equally good. The second way is to consider the ratio of the performances with system B as the base, as shown in Table 1.4. The conclusion in this case is that system A is better than B. The third way is to consider the performance ratio with system A as the base,

TABLE 1.3   Comparing the Average Throughput

System	Workload 1	Workload 2	Average
A	20	10	15
B	10	20	15

TABLE 1.4   Throughput with Respect to System B

System	Workload 1	Workload 2	Average
A	2	0.5	1.25
B	1	1	1

8

TABLE 1.5   **Throughput with Respect to System A**

System	Workload 1	Workload 2	Average
A	1	1	1
B	0.5	2	1.25

as shown in Table 1.5. The conclusion in this case is that system B is better than A. □

This example illustrates a technique known as the **ratio game**, which is discussed later in Chapter 11. Similar games can be played in selecting the workload, measuring the systems, and presenting the results. Some games are intentional, because the proponents of a system want to show the superiority of their proposed alternatives; others are simply a result of a lack of knowledge about performance evaluation techniques. A knowledge of common mistakes and games helps in understanding the importance of proper methodology. Therefore, such mistakes and games are discussed in many parts of this book.

1.3 PROFESSIONAL ORGANIZATIONS, JOURNALS, AND CONFERENCES

For those new to the field of performance evaluation, there are a number of ways to keep abreast of the new developments in this field. Some of the journals, professional organizations, conferences, and other subjects that a performance analyst would find useful are the topics of this section.

Computer systems performance analysts generally belong to at least two different types of professional organizations—one dealing with performance and the other dealing with the type of computer systems that interest them. For example, a performance analyst working on database system would belong to database organizations and performance organizations. Some of the organizations devoted exclusively to performance analysis are as follows:

1. *ACM SIGMETRICS*: The Association for Computing Machinery's Special Interest Group concerned with computer system performance is an organization for researchers engaged in developing methodologies and users seeking new or improved techniques for analysis of computer systems. It publishes a newsletter, *Performance Evaluation Review*, which is distributed quarterly to all members. For membership and other information contact ACM, 11 West 42nd Street, New York, NY 10036.

2. *IEEE Computer Society*: The Institute of Electrical and Electronic Engineers (IEEE) Computer Society has a number of technical committees. In particular, the technical committee on simulation may be of interest to performance analysts. For further information contact IEEE, 345 47th Street, New York, NY 10017-2394.

3. *ACM SIGSIM*: The ACM's special interest group on simulation publishes *Simulation Digest*, a quarterly newsletter in cooperation with IEEE Computer Society Technical Committee on Simulation.

4. *CMG*: The Computer Measurement Group, Inc. is oriented toward practical (as contrasted with theoretical) uses of computer performance measurement and evaluation tools and techniques. It publishes a quarterly journal called *CMG Transactions*, which contains articles on measurement, analysis, prediction, and management of computer systems performance. CMG has a number of regional groups in the United States and abroad that meet frequently to exchange information. The international regional groups include those in Australia, Canada, Japan, United Kingdom, Belgium, West Germany, France, and Italy. CMG headquarters are located at 111 E. Wacker Drive, Chicago, IL 60601.

5. *IFIP Working Group 7.3*: The International Federation for Information Processing is a multinational federation of technical societies concerned with information processing. The American Federation of Information Processing Societies (AFIPS) represents the United States. The Association for Computing Machinery (ACM), the IEEE, and other professional organizations are members of AFIPS. IFIP has several technical committees (TCs) and working groups (WGs). The WG 7.3 is devoted to computer systems modeling.

6. *The Society for Computer Simulation*: This is a society of professionals interested in computer simulation and mathematical modeling. The society sponsors regional meetings and national and international conferences and publishes a monthly technical journal, *Simulation*; the semiannual Simulation Series of hardbound books; and a quarterly journal, *Transactions of the Society for Computer Simulation*. The society has regional councils active in the continental United States, Canada, and the United Kingdom. SCS sponsors the Summer Computer Simulation Conference, the SCS Multiconference, the Eastern Simulation Conferences, the Winter Simulation Conference, and others. For membership information write to The Society for Computer Simulation, P.O. Box 17900, San Diego, CA 92117. Similar societies exist in many other countries, for example, Dutch Benelux Simulation Society, Gesellschaft fur Informatic—Arbeitsgemeinschaft fur Simulation, Japan Society for Simulation Technology, The Italian Society for Computer Simulation, Chinese System Simulation Council, and The International Marine Simulator Forum.

7. *SIAM*: The Society for Industrial and Applied Mathematics promotes basic research leading to the development of new mathematical techniques useful to industry and science. It publishes a number of journals on topics of interest to computer systems performance analysts. These include *SIAM Review, SIAM Journal on Control and Optimization, SIAM Journal on Numerical Analysis, SIAM Journal on Computing, SIAM Journal on Scientific and Statistical Computing*, and *Theory of Probability and*

Its Applications. For further information contact SIAM, Suite 1400, 117 South 17th Street, Philadelphia, PA 19103-5052.

8. *ORSA*: The Operations Research Society of America is an organization of professionals interested in operation research techniques including linear and dynamic programming, queueing theory, game theory, network analysis, replacement and inventory theories, scheduling, and simulation. The society holds semiannual national meetings jointly with The Institute of Management Sciences (TIMS). The society has a number of geographical sections, technical sections, special interest groups, and student sections throughout the United States. The society represents the United States in the International Federation of Operational Research Societies (INFORS). It publishes a number of journals of interest to performance analysts, including *Operations Research, ORSA Journal on Computing, Mathematics of Operations Research* (jointly with TIMS), *Operations Research Letters* (copublished with Elsevier/North-Holland), and *Stochastic Models* (copublished with Marcel Dekker). For further information contact ORSA Business Office, Mount Royal & Guilford Avenues, Baltimore, MD 21202.

Each of the organizations listed above organizes annual conferences. There are annual SIGMETRICS and CMG conferences. IFIP Working Group 7.3 sponsors conferences called "PERFORMANCE," which are scheduled every 18 months and are held alternately in Europe and in North America. Both SIGMETRICS and PERFORMANCE conferences carry high-quality papers describing new research in performance evaluation techniques. Proceedings of SIGMETRICS conferences generally appear as special issues of *Performance Evaluation Review*, the quarterly journal published by ACM SIGMETRICS. Applied Computer Research, a private business organization (address: P.O. Box 82266, Phoenix, AZ 85071) organizes annual conferences on EDP Performance and Capacity Management. ACM SIGSIM and IEEE Computer Society Technical Committee on Simulation jointly sponsor conferences on simulations. The University of Pittsburgh's School of Engineering and IEEE sponsor the Annual Pittsburgh Conference on Modeling and Simulation.

There are a number of journals devoted exclusively to computer systems performance evaluation. The papers in these journals are related to either performance techniques in general or their applications to computer systems. Of these, *Performance Evaluation Review, CMG Transactions, Simulation, Simulation Digest, SIAM Review,* and *Operations Research* have already been mentioned earlier. In addition, *Performance Evaluation* and *EDP Performance Review* should also be mentioned (published by private organizations). *Performance Evaluation* is published twice a year by Elsevier Science Publishers B.V. (North-Holland), P.O. Box 1991, 1000 BZ Amsterdam, The Netherlands. In the United States and Canada, it is distributed by Elsevier Science Publishing Company, 52 Vanderbilt Avenue, New York, NY 10017. *EDP Performance*

Review is published monthly by Applied Computer Research. The annual reference issue carries a survey of commercial performance-related hardware and software tools including monitoring, simulation, accounting, program analyzer, and others.

A vast majority of papers on performance appear in other computer science or statistics journals. For example, more papers dealing with distributed systems performance appear in journals on distributed systems than in the performance journals. In particular, many of the seminal papers on analytical modeling and simulation techniques initially appeared in *Communications of the ACM*. Other journals that publish papers on computer systems performance analysis are *IEEE Transactions on Software Engineering*, *IEEE Transactions on Computers*, and *ACM Transactions on Computers*.

Students interested in taking additional courses on performance evaluation techniques may consider courses on statistical inference, operations research, stochastic processes, decision theory, time series analysis, design of experiments, system simulation, queueing theory, and other related subjects.

1.4 PERFORMANCE PROJECTS

> *I hear and I forget. I see and I remember. I do and I understand.*
> —Chinese Proverb

The best way to learn a subject is to apply the concepts to a real system. This is specially true of computer systems performance evaluation because even though the techniques appear simple on the surface, their applications to real systems offer a different experience since the real systems do not behave in a simple manner.

It is recommended that courses on performance evaluation include at least one project where student teams are required to select a computer subsystem, for example, a network mail program, an operating system, a language compiler, a text editor, a processor, or a database. They should also be required to perform some measurements, analyze the collected data, simulate or analytically model the subsystem, predict its performance, and validate the model. Student teams are preferable to individual student projects since most real-life projects require coordination and communication with several other people.

Examples of some of the projects completed by students as part of a course on computer system performance analysis techniques based on the contents of this book are as follows:

1. Measure and compare the performance of window systems of two AI systems.
2. Simulate and compare the performance of two processor interconnection networks.

3. Measure and analyze the performance of two microprocessors.
4. Characterize the workload of a campus timesharing system.
5. Compute the effects of various factors and their interactions on the performance of two text-formatting programs.
6. Measure and analyze the performance of a distributed information system.
7. Simulate the communications controllers for an intelligent terminal system.
8. Measure and analyze the performance of a computer-aided design tool.
9. Measure and identify the factors that affect the performance of an experimental garbage collection algorithm.
10. Measure and compare the performance of remote procedure calls and remote pipe calls.
11. Analyze the effect of factors that impact the performance of two Reduced Instruction Set Computer (RISC) processor architectures.
12. Analyze the performance of a parallel compiler running on a multiprocessor system.
13. Develop a software monitor to observe the performance of a large multiprocessor system.
14. Analyze the performance of a distributed game program running on a network of AI systems.
15. Compare the performance of several robot control algorithms.

In each case, the goal was to provide an insight (or information) not obvious before the project. Most projects were real problems that the students were already required to solve as part of other courses, thesis work, or a job. As the course progressed and students learned new techniques, they attempted to apply the techniques to their particular problem. At the end of the course, the students presented the results to the class and discussed their findings and frustrations. The latter was especially enlightening since many techniques that worked in theory did not produce meaningful insights in practice.

At the end of many chapters in this book, there are exercises asking the reader to choose a computer system and apply the techniques of the chapter to that system. It is recommended that the students attempt to apply the techniques to the system of their project.

EXERCISE

1.1 The measured performance of two database systems on two different workloads is shown in Table 1.6. Compare the performance of the two systems

and show that
a. System A is better
b. System B is better

TABLE 1.6   Throughput in Queries per Second

System	Workload 1	Workload 2
A	30	10
B	10	30

CHAPTER 2

COMMON MISTAKES AND HOW TO AVOID THEM

Wise men learn by other men's mistakes, fools by their own.
—H. G. Wells

In order to motivate the use of proper methodology for performance evaluation, this chapter begins with a list of mistakes observed frequently in performance evaluation projects. This list then leads to the formulation of a systematic approach to performance evaluation. Various steps in correctly conducting a performance evaluation study and the order in which the steps should be carried out are presented.

2.1 COMMON MISTAKES IN PERFORMANCE EVALUATION

Unlike the games discussed in Section 1.2, most of the mistakes listed here are not intentional. Rather, they happen due to simple oversights, misconceptions, and lack of knowledge about performance evaluation techniques.

1. *No Goals*: Goals are an important part of all endeavors. Any endeavor without goals is bound to fail. Performance evaluation projects are no exception. The need for a goal may sound obvious, but many performance efforts are started without any clear goals. A performance analyst, for example, is routinely hired along with the design team. The analyst may then start modeling or simulating the design. When asked about the goals, the analyst's answer typically is that the model will help answer all design questions that may arise. A common claim is that the model will be flexible enough to be easily modified to solve different

problems. Experienced analysts know that there is no such thing as a general-purpose model. Each model must be developed with a particular goal in mind. The metrics, workloads, and methodology all depend upon the goal. The part of the system design that needs to be studied in the model varies from problem to problem. Therefore, before writing the first line of a simulation code or the first equation of an analytical model or before setting up a measurement experiment, it is important for the analyst to understand the system and identify the problem to be solved. This will help identify the correct metrics, workloads, and methodology.

Setting goals is not a trivial exercise. Since most performance problems are vague when first presented, understanding the problem sufficiently to write a set of goals is difficult. For example, a problem that was initially stated as one of finding a timeout algorithm for retransmissions on a network was later defined as a congestion control problem of finding out how the load on the network should be adjusted under packet loss. Once the problem is clear and the goals have been written down, finding the solution is often easier.

2. *Biased Goals*: Another common mistake is implicit or explicit bias in stating the goals. If, for example, the goal is "to show that OUR system is better than THEIRS," the problem becomes that of finding the metrics and workloads such that OUR system turns out better rather than that of finding the right metrics and workloads for comparing the two systems. One rule of professional etiquette for performance analysts is to be unbiased. *The performance analyst's role is like that of a jury.* Do not have any preconceived biases and base all conclusions on the results of the analysis rather than on pure beliefs.

3. *Unsystematic Approach*: Often analysts adopt an unsystematic approach whereby they select system parameters, factors, metrics, and workloads arbitrarily. This leads to inaccurate conclusions. The systematic approach to solving a performance problem is to identify a complete set of goals, system parameters, factors, metrics, and workloads. This is discussed in detail in Section 2.2.

4. *Analysis without Understanding the Problem*: Inexperienced analysts feel that nothing really has been achieved until a model has been constructed and some numerical results have been obtained. With experience, they learn that a large share of the analysis effort goes in to defining a problem. This share often takes up to 40% of the total effort. This supports the old saying: *A problem well stated is half solved.* Of the remaining 60%, a large share goes into designing alternatives, interpretation of the results, and presentation of conclusions. Development of the model itself is a small part of the problem-solving process. Just as cars and trains are a means of getting somewhere and not an end in themselves, models are a means of reaching conclusions and not

the final result. Analysts who are trained in modeling aspects of performance evaluation but not in problem definition or result presentation often find their models being ignored by the decision makers who are looking for guidance and not a model.

5. *Incorrect Performance Metrics*: A metric, as explained in Section 1.1, refers to the criterion used to quantify the performance of the system. Examples of commonly used performance metrics are throughput and response time. The choice of correct performance metrics depends upon the services provided by the system or subsystem being modeled. For example, the performance of Central Processing Units (CPUs) is compared on the basis of their throughput, which is often measured in terms of millions of instructions per second (**MIPS**). However, comparing the MIPS of two different CPU architectures, such as Reduced Instruction Set Computers (RISCs) and Complex Instruction Set Computers (CISCs), is meaningless since the instructions on the two computers are unequal. By manipulating the metrics, as shown in Chapter 11, it is possible to change the conclusions of a performance study. The considerations involved in selecting the right performance metrics are discussed in Section 3.2.

   A common mistake in selecting metrics is that analysts often choose those that can be easily computed or measured rather than the ones that are relevant. Metrics that are difficult to compute are ignored.

6. *Unrepresentative Workload*: The workload used to compare two systems should be representative of the actual usage of the systems in the field. For example, if the packets in networks are generally a mixture of two sizes—short and long—the workload to compare two networks should consist of short and long packet sizes.

   The choice of the workload has a significant impact on the results of a performance study. The wrong workload will lead to inaccurate conclusions. Workload selection is discussed in detail in Chapter 5. Benchmarking games that people play to show the superiority of their systems are discussed in Section 9.4.

7. *Wrong Evaluation Technique*: There are three evaluation techniques: measurement, simulation, and analytical modeling. Analysts often have a preference for one evaluation technique that they use for every performance evaluation problem. For example, those proficient in queueing theory will tend to change every performance problem to a queueing problem even if the system is too complex and is easily available for measurement. Those proficient in programming will tend to solve every problem by simulation. This marriage to a single technique leads to a model that they can best solve rather than to a model that can best solve the problem. The problem with these transformations is that they may introduce phenomena into the model that were not present in the original system or they may leave out some important phenomena that were in the original system.

An analyst should have a basic knowledge of all three techniques. There are a number of factors that should be considered in selecting the right technique. This topic is discussed further in Section 3.1.

8. *Overlooking Important Parameters*: It is a good idea to make a complete list of system and workload characteristics that affect the performance of the system. These characteristics are called parameters. For example, system parameters may include quantum size (for CPU allocation) or working set size (for memory allocation). Workload parameters may include the number of users, request arrival patterns, priority, and so on. The analyst can choose a set of values for each of these parameters; the final outcome of the study depends heavily upon those choices. Overlooking one or more important parameters may render the results useless.

9. *Ignoring Significant Factors*: Parameters that are varied in the study are called **factors**. For example, among the workload parameters listed above only the number of users may be chosen as a factor; other parameters may be fixed at their typical values. Not all parameters have an equal effect on the performance. It is important to identify those parameters, which, if varied, will make a significant impact on the performance. Unless there is reason to believe otherwise, these parameters should be used as factors in the performance study. For example, if packet arrival rate rather than packet size affects the response time of a network gateway, it would be better to use several different arrival rates in studying its performance.

   Factors that are under the control of the end user (or decision maker) and can be easily changed by the end user should be given preference over those that cannot be changed. Do not waste time comparing alternatives that the end user cannot adopt either because they involve actions that are unacceptable to the decision makers or because they are beyond their sphere of influence.

   It is important to understand the randomness of various system and workload parameters that affect the performance. Some of these parameters are better understood than others. For example, an analyst may know the distribution for page references in a computer system but have no idea of the distribution of disk references. In such a case, a common mistake would be to use the page reference distribution as a factor but ignore disk reference distribution even though the disk may be the bottleneck and may have more influence on performance than the page references. The choice of factors should be based on their relevance and not on the analyst's knowledge of the factors. Every attempt should be made to get realistic values of all relevant parameters and their distributions. For unknown parameters, a sensitivity analysis, which shows the effect of changing those parameters from their assumed values, should be done to quantify the impact of the uncertainty.

10. *Inappropriate Experimental Design*: Experimental design relates to the number of measurement or simulation experiments to be conducted and the parameter values used in each experiment. Proper selection of these values can lead to more information from the same number of experiments. Improper selection can result in a waste of the analyst's time and resources.

    In naive experimental design, each factor is changed one by one. As discussed in Chapter 16, this "simple design" may lead to wrong conclusions if the parameters interact such that the effect of one parameter depends upon the values of other parameters. Better alternatives are the use of the *full factorial experimental designs* and *fractional factorial designs* explained in Part IV.

11. *Inappropriate Level of Detail*: The level of detail used in modeling a system has a significant impact on the problem formulation. Avoid formulations that are either too narrow or too broad. For comparing alternatives that are slight variations of a common approach, a detailed model that incorporates the variations may be more useful than a high-level model. On the other hand, for comparing alternatives that are very different, simple high-level models may allow several alternatives to be analyzed rapidly and inexpensively. A common mistake is to take the detailed approach when a high-level model will do and vice versa. It is clear that the goals of a study have a significant impact on what is modeled and how it is analyzed.

12. *No Analysis*: One of the common problems with measurement projects is that they are often run by performance analysts who are good in measurement techniques but lack data analysis expertise. They collect enormous amounts of data but do not know how to analyze or interpret it. The result is a set of magnetic tapes (or disks) full of data without any summary. At best, the analyst may produce a thick report full of raw data and graphs without any explanation of how one can use the results. Therefore, it is better to have a team of performance analysts with measurement as well as analysis background.

13. *Erroneous Analysis*: There are a number of mistakes analysts commonly make in measurement, simulation, and analytical modeling, for example, taking the average of ratios and too short simulations. Lists of such mistakes are presented throughout this book during discussions on individual techniques.

14. *No Sensitivity Analysis*: Often analysts put too much emphasis on the results of their analysis, presenting it as fact rather than evidence. The fact that the results may be sensitive to the workload and system parameters is often overlooked. Without a sensitivity analysis, one cannot be sure if the conclusions would change if the analysis was done in a slightly different setting. Also, without a sensitivity analysis, it is difficult to access the relative importance of various parameters.

15. *Ignoring Errors in Input*: Often the parameters of interest cannot be measured. Instead, another variable that can be measured is used to estimate the parameter. For example, in one computer network device, the packets were stored in a linked list of buffers. Each buffer was 512 octets long. Given the number of buffers required to store packets, it was impossible to accurately predict the number of packets or the number of octets in the packets. Such situations introduce additional uncertainties in the input data. The analyst needs to adjust the level of confidence on the model output obtained from such data. Also, it may not be worthwhile to accurately model the packet sizes when the input can be off by as much as 512 octets. Another point illustrated by this example is the fact that input errors are not always equally distributed about the mean. In this case, the buffer space is always more than the actual number of octets transmitted on or received from the network. In other words, the input is biased.

16. *Improper Treatment of Outliers*: Values that are too high or too low compared to a majority of values in a set are called **outliers**. Outliers in the input or model output present a problem. If an outlier is not caused by a real system phenomenon, it should be ignored. Including it would produce an invalid model. On the other hand, if the outlier is a possible occurrence in a real system, it should be appropriately included in the model. Ignoring it would produce an invalid model. Deciding which outliers should be ignored and which should be included is part of the art of performance evaluation and requires careful understanding of the system being modeled.

17. *Assuming No Change in the Future*: It is often assumed that the future will be the same as the past. A model based on the workload and performance observed in the past is used to predict performance in the future. The future workload and system behavior is assumed to be the same as that already measured. The analyst and the decision makers should discuss this assumption and limit the amount of time into the future that predictions are made.

18. *Ignoring Variability*: It is common to analyze only the mean performance since determining variability is often difficult, if not impossible. If the variability is high, the mean alone may be misleading to the decision makers. For example, decisions based on the daily averages of computer demands may not be useful if the load demand has large hourly peaks, which adversely impact user performance.

19. *Too Complex Analysis*: Given two analyses leading to the same conclusion, one that is simpler and easier to explain is obviously preferable. Performance analysts should convey final conclusions in as simple a manner as possible. Some analysts start with complex models that cannot be solved or a measurement or simulation project with very ambitious goals that are never achieved. It is better to start with simple

models or experiments, get some results or insights, and then introduce the complications.

There is a significant difference in the types of models published in the literature and those used in the real world. The models published in the literature and, therefore, taught in schools are generally too complex. This is because trivial models, even when very illuminating, are not generally accepted for publication. For some reason, the ability to develop and solve a complex model is valued more highly in academic circles than the ability to draw conclusions from a simple model. However, in the industrial world, the decision makers are rarely interested in the modeling technique or its innovativeness. Their chief concern is the guidance that the model provides along with the time and cost to develop the model. The decision deadlines often lead to choosing simple models. Thus, a majority of day-to-day performance problems in the real world are solved by simple models. Complex models are rarely, if ever, used. Even if the time required to develop the model was not restricted, complex models are not easily understood by the decision makers, and therefore, the model results may be misbelieved. This causes frustrations for new graduates who are very well trained in complex modeling techniques but find few opportunities to use them in the real world.

20. *Improper Presentation of Results*: The eventual aim of every performance study is to help in decision making. An analysis that does not produce any useful results is a failure, as is the analysis with results that cannot be understood by the decision makers. The decision makers could be the designers of a system, the purchasers of a system, or the sponsors of a project. Conveying (or selling) the results of the analysis to decision makers is the responsibility of the analyst. This requires the prudent use of words, pictures, and graphs to explain the results and the analysis. *The right metric to measure the performance of an analyst is not the number of analyses performed but the number of analyses that helped the decision makers.*

21. *Ignoring Social Aspects*: Successful presentation of the analysis results requires two types of skills: social and substantive. Writing and speaking are social skills while modeling and data analysis are substantive skills. Most analysts have good substantive skills, but only those who have good social skills are successful in selling their results to the decision makers. Acceptance of the analysis results requires developing a trust between the decision makers and the analyst and presentation of the results to the decision makers in a manner understandable to them. If decision makers do not believe or understand the analysis, the analyst fails to make an impact on the final decision. Social skills are particularly important in presenting results that are counter to the decision makers' beliefs and values or that require a substantial change in the design.

Beginning analysts often fail to understand that social skills are often more important than substantive skills. High-quality analyses may be rejected simply because the analyst has not put enough effort and time into presenting the results. The decision makers are under time pressures and would like to get to the final results as soon as possible. They generally are not interested in the innovativeness of the approach or the approach itself. On the other hand, the analyst, having spent a considerable amount of time on the analysis, may be more interested in telling the decision makers about the innovativeness of the modeling approach than the final results. This disparity in viewpoint may lead to a report that is too long and fails to make an impact. The problem is compounded by the fact that the analyst also has to present the results to his/her peers who are analysts themselves and would like to know more about the approach than the final results. One solution, therefore, is to prepare two separate presentations (or reports) for the two audiences. The presentation to the decision makers should have minimal analysis jargon and emphasize the final results, while the presentation to other analysts should include all the details of the analysis techniques. Combining these two presentations into one could make it meaningless for both audiences.

Inexperienced analysts assume that the decision makers are like themselves and share the same beliefs, values, language, and jargon. This is often not true. The decision makers may be good at evaluating the results of the analysis but may not have a good understanding of the analysis itself. In their positions as decision makers, they have to weigh several factors that the analyst may not consider important, such as the political impact of the decision, the delay in the project schedule, or the availability of personnel to implement a particular decision. The analyst who makes an effort to understand the decision makers' concerns and incorporates these as much as possible into the presentation will have a better chance of "selling" the analysis than one who sees things only from his/her own point of view.

22. *Omitting Assumptions and Limitations*: Assumptions and limitations of the analysis are often omitted from the final report. This may lead the user to apply the analysis to another context where the assumptions will not be valid. Sometimes analysts list the assumptions at the beginning of the report but then forget the limitations at the end and make conclusions about environments to which the analysis does not apply.

The above discussion on common mistakes is summarized in Box 2.1, which presents a checklist of questions concerning performance analysis. All questions should be answered affirmatively. The list can also be used by the decision makers to review performance analyses presented to them.

Box 2.1   Checklist for Avoiding Common Mistakes in Performance Evaluation

1. Is the system correctly defined and the goals clearly stated?
2. Are the goals stated in an unbiased manner?
3. Have all the steps of the analysis followed systematically?
4. Is the problem clearly understood before analyzing it?
5. Are the performance metrics relevant for this problem?
6. Is the workload correct for this problem?
7. Is the evaluation technique appropriate?
8. Is the list of parameters that affect performance complete?
9. Have all parameters that affect performance been chosen as factors to be varied?
10. Is the experimental design efficient in terms of time and results?
11. Is the level of detail proper?
12. Is the measured data presented with analysis and interpretation?
13. Is the analysis statistically correct?
14. Has the sensitivity analysis been done?
15. Would errors in the input cause an insignificant change in the results?
16. Have the outliers in the input or output been treated properly?
17. Have the future changes in the system and workload been modeled?
18. Has the variance of input been taken into account?
19. Has the variance of the results been analyzed?
20. Is the analysis easy to explain?
21. Is the presentation style suitable for its audience?
22. Have the results been presented graphically as much as possible?
23. Are the assumptions and limitations of the analysis clearly documented?

2.2   A SYSTEMATIC APPROACH TO PERFORMANCE EVALUATION

Most performance problems are unique. The metrics, workload, and evaluation techniques used for one problem generally cannot be used for the next problem. Nevertheless, there are steps common to all performance evaluation projects that help you avoid the common mistakes listed in Section 2.1. These steps are as follows.

1. *State Goals and Define the System*: The first step in any performance evaluation project is to state the goals of the study and define what con-

stitutes the system by delineating system boundaries. Given the same set of hardware and software, the definition of the system may vary depending upon the goals of the study. Given two CPUs, for example, the goal may be to estimate their impact on the response time of interactive users. In this case, the system would consist of the timesharing system, and the conclusions of the study may depend significantly on components external to the CPU. On the other hand, if the two CPUs are basically similar except for their Arithmetic-Logic Units (ALUs) and the goal is to decide which ALU should be chosen, the CPUs may be considered the system's and only the components inside the CPU may be considered part of the system.

The choice of system boundaries affects the performance metrics as well as workloads used to compare the systems. Therefore, understanding the system boundaries is important. Although the key consideration in setting the system boundaries is the objective of the study, other considerations, such as administrative control of the sponsors of the study, may also need to be taken into account. If the sponsors do not have a control over some components, they may want to keep those components outside the system boundaries.

2. *List Services and Outcomes*: Each system provides a set of services. For example, a computer network allows its users to send packets to specified destinations. A database system responds to queries. A processor performs a number of different instructions. The next step in analyzing a system is to list these services. When a user requests any of these services, there are a number of possible outcomes. Some of these outcomes are desirable and some are not. For example, a database system may answer a query correctly, incorrectly (due to inconsistent updates), or not at all (due to deadlocks or some similar problems). A list of services and possible outcomes is useful later in selecting the right metrics and workloads.

3. *Select Metrics*: The next step is to select criteria to compare the performance. These criteria are called metrics. In general, the metrics are related to the speed, accuracy, and availability of services. The performance of a network, for example, is measured by the speed (throughput and delay), accuracy (error rate), and availability of the packets sent. The performance of a processor is measured by the speed of (time taken to execute) various instructions. The selection of the correct metrics is discussed in Section 3.2.

4. *List Parameters*: The next step in performance projects is to make a list of all the parameters that affect performance. The list can be divided into system parameters and workload parameters. System parameters include both hardware and software parameters, which generally do not vary among various installations of the system. Workload parameters are characteristics of users' requests, which vary from one installation to the next.

The list of parameters may not be complete. That is, after the first pass of the analysis, you may discover that there are additional parameters that affect the performance. You can then add these parameters to the list, but at all times keep the list as comprehensive as possible. This allows the analyst and decision makers to discuss the impact of various parameters and determine what data needs to be collected before or during the analysis.

5. *Select Factors to Study*: The list of parameters can be divided into two parts: those that will be varied during the evaluation and those that will not. The parameters to be varied are called **factors** and their values are called **levels**. In general, the list of factors, and their possible levels, is larger than what the available resources will allow. Otherwise, the list will keep growing until it becomes obvious that there are not enough resources to study the problem. It is better to start with a short list of factors and a small number of levels for each factor and to extend the list in the next phase of the project if the resources permit. For example, you may decide to have only two factors: quantum size and the number of users. For each of these two factors you may choose only two levels: small and large. The working set size and the type of workload may be fixed.

The parameters that are expected to have a high impact on the performance should be preferably selected as factors. Like metrics, a common mistake in selecting the factors is that the parameters that are easy to vary and measure are used as factors while other more influential parameters are ignored simply because of the difficulty involved.

In selecting factors, it is important to consider the economic, political, and technological constraints that exist as well as including the limitations imposed by the decision makers' control and the time available for the decision. This increases the chances of finding a solution that is acceptable and implementable.

6. *Select Evaluation Technique*: The three broad techniques for performance evaluation are analytical modeling, simulation, and measuring a real system. The selection of the right technique depends upon the time and resources available to solve the problem and the desired level of accuracy. The selection of evaluation techniques is discussed in Section 3.1.

7. *Select Workload*: The workload consists of a list of service requests to the system. For example, the workload for comparing several database systems may consist of a set of queries. Depending upon the evaluation technique chosen, the workload may be expressed in different forms. For analytical modeling, the workload is usually expressed as a probability of various requests. For simulation, one could use a trace of requests measured on a real system. For measurement, the workload may consist of user scripts to be executed on the systems. In all cases, it is essential that the workload be representative of the system usage

in real life. To produce representative workloads, one needs to measure and characterize the workload on existing systems. These and other issues related to workloads are discussed in Part II.

8. *Design Experiments*: Once you have a list of factors and their levels, you need to decide on a sequence of experiments that offer maximum information with minimal effort. In practice, it is useful to conduct an experiment in two phases. In the first phase, the number of factors may be large but the number of levels is small. The goal is to determine the relative effect of various factors. In most cases, this can be done with *fractional factorial experimental designs*, discussed in Part IV. In the second phase, the number of factors is reduced and the number of levels of those factors that have significant impact is increased.

9. *Analyze and Interpret Data*: It is important to recognize that the outcomes of measurements and simulations are random quantities in that the outcome would be different each time the experiment is repeated. In comparing two alternatives, it is necessary to take into account the variability of the results. Simply comparing the means can lead to inaccurate conclusions. The statistical techniques to compare two alternatives are described in Chapter 13.

   Interpreting the results of an analysis is a key part of the analyst's art. It must be understood that the analysis only produces results and not conclusions. The results provide the basis on which the analysts or decision makers can draw conclusions. When a number of analysts are given the same set of results, the conclusion drawn by each analyst may be different, as seen in Section 1.2.

10. *Present Results*: The final step of all performance projects is to communicate the results to other members of the decision-making team. It is important that the results be presented in a manner that is easily understood. This usually requires presenting the results in graphic form and without statistical jargon. The graphs should be appropriately scaled. The issue of correct graph plotting is discussed further in Chapter 10.

   Often at this point in the project the knowledge gained by the study may require the analyst to go back and reconsider some of the decisions made in the previous steps. For example, the analyst may want to redefine the system boundaries or include other factors and performance metrics that were not considered before. The complete project, therefore, consists of several cycles through the steps rather than a single sequential pass.

The steps for a performance evaluation study are summarized in Box 2.2 and illustrated in Case Study 2.1.

Case Study 2.1 Consider the problem of comparing remote pipes with remote procedure calls. In a procedure call, the calling program is blocked, control is passed to the called procedure along with a few parameters, and

Box 2.2   Steps for a Performance Evaluation Study

1. State the goals of the study and define the system boundaries.
2. List system services and possible outcomes.
3. Select performance metrics.
4. List system and workload parameters.
5. Select factors and their values.
6. Select evaluation techniques.
7. Select the workload.
8. Design the experiments.
9. Analyze and interpret the data.
10. Present the results. Start over, if necessary.

when the procedure is complete, the results as well as the control return to the calling program. A **remote procedure call** is an extension of this concept to a distributed computer system. A program on one computer system calls a procedure object on another system. The calling program waits until the procedure is complete and the result is returned. Remote pipes are also procedure like objects, but when called, the caller is not blocked. The execution of the pipe occurs concurrently with the continued execution of the caller. The results, if any, are later returned asynchronously.

The following project plan was written before starting the study.

1. *System Definition*: The goal of the case study is to compare the performance of applications using remote pipes to those of similar applications using remote procedure calls. The key component under study is the so-called channel. A **channel** can be either a procedure or a pipe. The system consists of two computers connected via a network as shown in Figure 2.1. The requests are sent via the channel from the client computer to the server computer. Only the subsets of the client

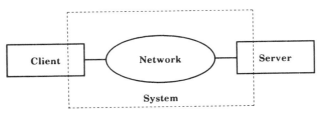

FIGURE 2.1   System definition for the study of remote procedure calls versus remote pipes.

and server computers that offer channel services is considered to be part of the system. The study will be conducted so that the effect of components outside the system is minimized.

2. *Services*: The services offered by the system are the two types of channel calls—remote procedure call and remote pipe. The resources used by the channel calls depend upon the number of parameters passed and the action required on those parameters. In this case study, data transfer is chosen as the application and the calls will be classified simply as small or large depending upon the amount of data to be transferred to the remote machine. In other words, the system offers only two services: small data transfer or large data transfer.

3. *Metrics*: Due to resource limitations, the errors and failures will not be studied. Thus, the study will be limited to correct operation only. For each service, the rate at which the service can be performed, the time taken for the service, and the resources consumed will be compared. The resources are the local computer (client), the remote computer (server), and the network link. This leads to the following performance metrics:

   (a) Elapsed time per call

   (b) Maximum call rate per unit of time, or equivalently, the time required to complete a block of n successive calls

   (c) Local CPU time per call

   (d) Remote CPU time per call

   (e) Number of bytes sent on the link per call

4. *Parameters:* The system parameters that affect the performance of a given application and data size are the following:

   (a) Speed of the local CPU

   (b) Speed of the remote CPU

   (c) Speed of the network

   (d) Operating system overhead for interfacing with the channels

   (e) Operating system overhead for interfacing with the networks

   (f) Reliability of the network affecting the number of retransmissions required

   The workload parameters that affect the performance are the following:

   (a) Time between successive calls

   (b) Number and sizes of the call parameters

   (c) Number and sizes of the results

   (d) Type of channel

   (e) Other loads on the local and remote CPUs

   (f) Other loads on the network

5. *Factors:* The key factors chosen for this study are the following:
   (a) Type of channel. Two types—remote pipes and remote procedure calls—will be compared.
   (b) Speed of the network. Two locations of the remote hosts will be used—short distance (in the campus) and long distance (across the country).
   (c) Sizes of the call parameters to be transferred. Two levels will be used—small and large.
   (d) Number n of consecutive calls. Eleven different values of n—$1, 2, 4, 8, 16, 32, \ldots, 512, 1024$—will be used.

   The factors have been selected based on resource availability and the interest of the sponsors. All other parameters will be fixed. Thus, the results will be valid only for the type of CPUs and operating systems used. The retransmissions due to network errors will be ignored (not included in the measurements). Experiments will be conducted when there is very little other load on the hosts and the network.

6. *Evaluation Technique:* Since prototypes of both types of channels have already been implemented, measurements will be used for evaluation. Analytical modeling will be used to justify the consistency of measured values for different parameters.

7. *Workload:* The workload will consist of a synthetic program generating the specified types of channel requests. This program will also monitor the resources consumed and log the measured results. Null channel requests with no actual work but with monitoring and logging activated will be used to determine the resources consumed in monitoring and logging.

8. *Experimental Design:* A full factorial experimental design with $2^3 \times 11 = 88$ experiments will be used for the initial study. The factorial experimental designs are explained in Chapter 16.

9. *Data Analysis:* Analysis of Variance (explained in Section 20.5) will be used to quantify the effects of the first three factors and regression (explained in Chapter 14) will be used to quantify the effects of the number n of successive calls.

10. *Data Presentation:* The final results will be plotted as a function of the block size n.

This case study was completed successfully and reported by Glasser (1987). □

EXERCISES

2.1 From published literature, select an article or a report that presents results of a performance evaluation study. Make a list of good and bad points of the study. What would you do different if you were asked to repeat the study.

2.2 Choose a system for performance study. Briefly describe the system and list

   a. Services

   b. Performance metrics

   c. System parameters

   d. Workload parameters

   e. Factors and their ranges

   f. Evaluation technique

   g. Workload

Justify your choices.

Suggestion: Each student should select a different system such as a network, database, processor, and so on, and then present the solution to the class.

CHAPTER 3

SELECTION OF TECHNIQUES AND METRICS

response time *n.* An unbounded, random variable T_r associated with a given TIMESHARING system and representing the putative time which elapses between T_s, the time of sending a message, and T_e, the time when the resulting error diagnostic is received.

—S. Kelly-Bootle
The Devil's DP Dictionary

Selecting an evaluation technique and selecting a metric are two key steps in all performance evaluation projects. There are many considerations that are involved in correct selection. These considerations are presented in the first two sections of this chapter. In addition, performance metrics that are commonly used are defined in Section 3.3. Finally, an approach to the problem of specifying the performance requirements is presented in Section 3.5.

3.1 SELECTING AN EVALUATION TECHNIQUE

The three techniques for performance evaluation are analytical modeling, simulation, and measurement. There are a number of considerations that help decide the technique to be used. These considerations are listed in Table 3.1. The list is ordered from most to least important.

The key consideration in deciding the evaluation technique is the life-cycle stage in which the system is. Measurements are possible only if something similar to the proposed system already exists, as when designing an improved

TABLE 3.1   Criteria for Selecting an Evaluation Technique

Criterion	Analytical Modeling	Simulation	Measurement
1. Stage	Any	Any	Postprototype
2. Time required	Small	Medium	Varies
3. Tools	Analysts	Computer languages	Instrumentation
4. Accuracy[a]	Low	Moderate	Varies
5. Trade-off evaluation	Easy	Moderate	Difficult
6. Cost	Small	Medium	High
7. Saleability	Low	Medium	High

[a]In all cases, result may be misleading or wrong.

version of a product. If it is a new concept, analytical modeling and simulation are the only techniques from which to choose. Analytical modeling and simulation can be used for situations where measurement is not possible, but in general it would be more convincing to others if the analytical modeling or simulation is based on previous measurement.

The next consideration is the time available for evaluation. In most situations, results are required *yesterday*. If that is really the case, then analytical modeling is probably the only choice. Simulations take a long time. Measurements generally take longer than analytical modeling but shorter than simulations. Murphy's law strikes measurements more often than other techniques. If anything can go wrong, it will. As a result, the time required for measurements is the most variable among the three techniques.

The next consideration is the availability of tools. The tools include modeling skills, simulation languages, and measurement instruments. Many performance analysts are skilled in modeling. They would not touch a real system at any cost. Others are not as proficient in queueing theory and prefer to measure or simulate. Lack of knowledge of the simulation languages and techniques keeps many analysts away from simulations.

Level of accuracy desired is another important consideration. In general, analytical modeling requires so many simplifications and assumptions that if the results turn out to be accurate, even the analysts are surprised. Simulations can incorporate more details and require less assumptions than analytical modeling and, thus, more often are closer to reality. Measurements, although they sound like the real thing, may not give accurate results simply because many of the environmental parameters, such as system configuration, type of workload, and time of the measurement, may be unique to the experiment. Also, the parameters may not represent the range of variables found in the real world. Thus, the accuracy of results can vary from very high to none when using the measurements technique.

It must be pointed out that level of accuracy and correctness of conclusions are not identical. A result that is correct up to the tenth decimal place may be misunderstood or misinterpreted; thus wrong conclusions can be drawn.

The goal of every performance study is either to compare different alternatives or to find the optimal parameter value. Analytical models generally provide the best insight into the effects of various parameters and their interactions. With simulations, it may be possible to search the space of parameter values for the optimal combination, but often it is not clear what the trade-off is among different parameters. Measurement is the least desirable technique in this respect. It is not easy to tell if the improved performance is a result of some random change in environment or due to the particular parameter setting.

Cost allocated for the project is also important. Measurement requires real equipment, instruments, and time. It is the most costly of the three techniques. Cost, along with the ease of being able to change configurations, is often the reason for developing simulations for expensive systems. Analytical modeling requires only paper and pencils (in addition to the analyst's time). Analytical modeling is therefore the cheapest alternative.

Saleability of results is probably the key justification when considering the expense and the labor of measurements. It is much easier to convince others if it is a real measurement. Most people are skeptical of analytical results simply because they do not understand the technique or the final result. In fact, people who develop new analytical modeling techniques often validate them by using simulations or actual measurements.

Sometimes it is helpful to use two or more techniques simultaneously. For example, you may use simulation and analytical modeling together to verify and validate the results of each one. Until proven guilty, every person should be presumed innocent. The performance counterpart of this statement is *until validated, all evaluation results are suspect*. This leads us to the following three rules of validation:

- Do not trust the results of a simulation model until they have been validated by analytical modeling or measurements.
- Do not trust the results of an analytical model until they have been validated by a simulation model or measurements.
- Do not trust the results of a measurement until they have been validated by simulation or analytical modeling.

In particular, the need for the third rule regarding validation of measurement results should be emphasized. This is the most commonly ignored of the three rules. Measurements are as susceptible to experimental errors and bugs as the other two techniques. The only requirement for validation is that the results should not be counterintuitive. This method of validation, called expert's intuition, is commonly used for simulation models. This and other validation methods can be used for measurement and analytical results and are discussed in Section 25.2.

Two or more techniques can also be used sequentially. For example, in one case, a simple analytical model was used to find the appropriate range for system parameters and a simulation was used later to study the performance in that range. This reduced the number of simulation runs considerably and resulted in a more productive use of resources.

3.2 SELECTING PERFORMANCE METRICS

For each performance study, a set of performance criteria or metrics must be chosen. One way to prepare this set is to list the services offered by the system. For each service request made to the system, there are several possible outcomes. Generally, these outcomes can be classified into three categories, as shown in Figure 3.1. The system may perform the service correctly, incorrectly, or refuse to perform the service. For example, a gateway in a computer network offers the service of forwarding packets to the specified destinations on heterogeneous networks. When presented with a packet, it may forward the packet correctly, it may forward it to the wrong destination, or it may be down, in which case it will not forward it at all. Similarly, a database offers the service of responding to queries. When presented with a query, it may answer correctly, it may answer incorrectly, or it may be down and not answer it at all.

If the system performs the service correctly, its performance is measured by the time taken to perform the service, the rate at which the service is

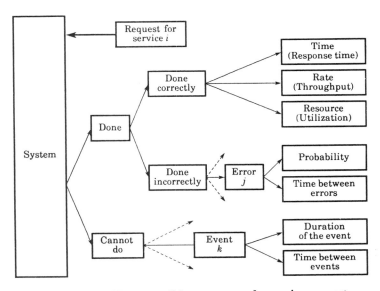

FIGURE 3.1   Three possible outcomes of a service request.

performed, and the resources consumed while performing the service. These three metrics related to **time-rate-resource** for successful performance are also called **responsiveness**, **productivity**, and **utilization** metrics, respectively. For example, the responsiveness of a network gateway is measured by its response time—the time interval between arrival of a packet and its successful delivery. The gateway's productivity is measured by its throughput—the number of packets forwarded per unit of time. The utilization gives an indication of the percentage of time the resources of the gateway are busy for the given load level. The resource with the highest utilization is called the **bottleneck**. Performance optimizations at this resource offer the highest payoff. Finding the utilization of various resources inside the system is thus an important part of performance evaluation.

If the system performs the service incorrectly, an **error** is said to have occurred. It is helpful to classify errors and to determine the probabilities of each class of errors. For example, in the case of the gateway, we may want to find the probability of single-bit errors, two-bit errors, and so on. We may also want to find the probability of a packet being partially delivered (fragment).

If the system does not perform the service, it is said to be *down, failed*, or *unavailable*. Once again, it is helpful to classify the failure modes and to determine the probabilities of each class. For example, the gateway may be unavailable 0.01% of the time due to processor failure and 0.03% due to software failure.

The metrics associated with the three outcomes, namely successful service, error, and unavailability, are also called **speed**, **reliability**, and **availability** metrics. It should be obvious that for each service offered by the system, one would have a number of speed metrics, a number of reliability metrics, and a number of availability metrics. Most systems offer more than one service, and thus the number of metrics grows proportionately.

For many metrics, the mean value is all that is important. However, do not overlook the effect of variability. For example, a high mean response time of a timesharing system as well as a high variability of the response time both may degrade the productivity significantly. If this is the case, you need to study both of these metrics.

In computer systems shared by many users, two types of performance metrics need to be considered: individual and global. Individual metrics reflect the utility of each user, while the global metrics reflect the systemwide utility. The resource utilization, reliability, and availability are global metrics, while response time and throughput may be measured for each individual as well as globally for the system. There are cases when the decision that optimizes individual metrics is different from the one that optimizes the system metric. For example, in computer networks, the performance is measured by throughput (packets per second). In a system where the total number of packets allowed in the network is kept constant, increasing the number of packets from one source may lead to increasing its throughput, but it may also decrease someone else's throughput. Thus, both the systemwide throughput and its distribution among individual users must be studied. Using only the system throughput or the individual throughput may lead to unfair situations.

Given a number of metrics, use the following considerations to select a subset: low variability, nonredundancy, and completeness. Low variability helps reduce the number of repetitions required to obtain a given level of statistical confidence. Confidence level is explained in Chapter 12. Metrics that are ratios of two variables generally have a larger variability than either of the two variables and should be avoided if possible.

If two metrics give essentially the same information, it is less confusing to study only one. This is not always obvious, however. For example, in computer networks, the average waiting time in a queue is equal to the quotient of the average queue length and the arrival rate. Studying the average queue lengths in addition to average waiting time may not provide any additional insights.

Finally, the set of metrics included in the study should be complete. All possible outcomes should be reflected in the set of performance metrics. For example, in a study comparing different protocols on a computer network, one protocol was chosen as the best until it was found that the best protocol led to the highest number of premature circuit disconnections. The *probability of disconnection* was then added to the set of performance metrics.

Case Study 3.1 Consider the problem of comparing two different congestion control algorithms for computer networks. A computer network consists of a number of **end systems** interconnected via a number of **intermediate systems**. The end systems send packets to other end systems on the network. The intermediate systems forward the packets along the right path. The problem of congestion occurs when the number of packets waiting at an intermediate system exceeds the system's buffering capacity and some of the packets have to be dropped.

The system in this case consists of the network, and the only service under consideration is that of packet forwarding. When a network user sends a block of packets to another end station called **destination**, there are four possible outcomes:

1. Some packets are delivered in order to the correct destination.
2. Some packets are delivered out of order to the destination.
3. Some packets are delivered more than once to the destination (duplicate packets).
4. Some packets are dropped on the way (lost packets).

For packets delivered in order, straightforward application of the time-rate-resource metrics produces the following list:

1. Response time: the delay inside the network for individual packets.
2. Throughput: the number of packets per unit of time.
3. Processor time per packet on the source end system.

4. Processor time per packet on the destination end systems.
5. Processor time per packet on the intermediate systems.

The response time determines the time that a packet has to be kept at the source end station using up its memory resources. Lower response time is considered better. The throughput is the performance as seen by the user. Larger throughput is considered better.

The variability of the response time is also important since a highly variant response results in unnecessary retransmissions. Thus, the variance of the response time became the sixth metric.

Out-of-order packets are undesirable since they cannot generally be delivered to the user immediately. In many systems, the out-of-order packets are discarded at the destination end systems. In others, they are stored in system buffers awaiting arrival of intervening packets. In either case, out-of-order arrivals cause additional overhead. Thus, the probability of out-of-order arrivals was the seventh metric.

Duplicate packets consume the network resources without any use. The probability of duplicate packets was therefore the eighth metric.

Lost packets are undesirable for obvious reasons. The probability of lost packets is the ninth metric. Excessive losses result in excessive retransmissions and could cause some user connections to be broken prematurely; thus the probability of disconnect was added as the tenth metric.

The network is a multiuser system. It is necessary that all users be treated fairly. Therefore, fairness was added as the eleventh metric. It is defined as a function of variability of throughput across users. For any given set of user throughputs $(x_1, x_2, \ldots, x_n)$, the following function can be used to assign a fairness index to the set:

$$f(x_1, x_2, \ldots, x_n) = \frac{\left(\sum_{i=1}^{n} x_i\right)^2}{n \sum_{i=1}^{n} x_i^2}$$

For all nonnegative values of x_i's, the fairness index always lies between 0 and 1. If all users receive equal throughput, the fairness index is 1. If only k of the n users receive equal throughput and the remaining $n - k$ users receive zero throughput, the fairness index is k/n. For other distributions also, the metric gives intuitive fairness values.

After a few experiments, it was clear that throughput and delay were really redundant metrics. All schemes that resulted in higher throughput also resulted in higher delay. Therefore, the two metrics were removed from the list and instead a combined metric called **power**, which is defined as the ratio of throughput to response time, was used. A higher power meant either a higher throughput or a lower delay; in either case it was considered better than a lower power.

The variance in response time was also dropped since it was redundant with the probability of duplication and the probability of disconnection. A higher variance resulted in a higher probability of duplication and a higher probability of premature disconnection.

Thus, in this study a set of nine metrics were used to compare different congestion control algorithms.   □

3.3 COMMONLY USED PERFORMANCE METRICS

This section defines and explains some of the commonly used performance metrics. In each case, the definition proposed is only one of many possibilities. Some definitions will need to be changed to suit certain applications.

Response time is defined as the interval between a user's request and the system response, as shown in Figure 3.2a. This definition, however, is simplistic since the requests as well as the responses are not instantaneous. The users spend time typing the request and the system takes time outputting the response, as shown in Figure 3.2b. There are two possible definitions of the response time in this case. It can be defined as either the interval between the end of a request submission and the beginning of the corresponding response from the system or as the interval between the end of a request submission and the end of the corresponding response from the system. Both definitions are acceptable as long as they are clearly specified. The second definition is preferable if the time between the beginning and the end of the response is

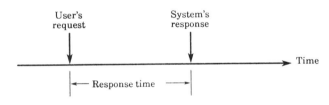

(a) Instantaneous request and reponse.

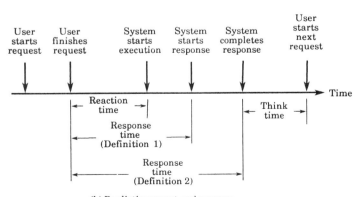

(b) Realistic request and reponse.

FIGURE 3.2 Response time definition.

long. Following this definition, the response time for interactive users in a timesharing system would be the interval between striking the last return (or enter) key and the receipt of the *last* character of the system's response.

For a batch stream, responsiveness is measured by **turnaround time**, which is the time between the submission of a batch job and the completion of its output. Notice that the time to read the input is included in the turnaround time.

The time between submission of a request and the beginning of its execution by the system is called the **reaction time**. To measure the reaction time, one has to able to monitor the actions inside a system since the beginning of the execution may not correspond to any externally visible event. For example, in timesharing systems, the interval between a user's last key stroke and the user's process receiving the first CPU quantum would be called reaction time.

The response time of a system generally increases as the load on the system increases. The ratio of response time at a particular load to that at the minimum load is called the **stretch factor**. For a timesharing system, for example, the stretch factor is defined as the ratio of the response time with multiprogramming to that without multiprogramming.

Throughput is defined as the rate (requests per unit of time) at which the requests can be serviced by the system. For batch streams, the throughput is measured in jobs per second. For interactive systems, the throughput is measured in requests per second. For CPUs, the throughput is measured in Millions of Instructions Per Second (**MIPS**), or Millions of Floating-Point Operations Per Second (**MFLOPS**). For networks, the throughput is measured in packets per second (**pps**) or bits per second (**bps**). For transactions processing systems, the throughput is measured in Transactions Per Second (**TPS**).

The throughput of a system generally increases as the load on the system initially increases. After a certain load, the throughput stops increasing; in most cases, it may even start decreasing, as shown in Figure 3.3. The maximum

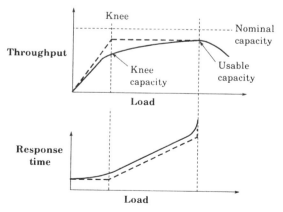

FIGURE 3.3   Capacity of a system.

achievable throughput under ideal workload conditions is called **nominal capacity** of the system. For computer networks, the nominal capacity is called the **bandwidth** and is usually expressed in bits per second. Often the response time at maximum throughput is too high to be acceptable. In such cases, it is more interesting to know the maximum throughput achievable without exceeding a prespecified response time limit. This may be called the **usable capacity** of the system. In many applications, the knee of the throughput or the response-time curve is considered the optimal operating point. As shown in Figure 3.3, this is the point beyond which the response time increases rapidly as a function of the load but the gain in throughput is small. Before the knee, the response time does not increase significantly but the throughput rises as the load increases. The throughput at the knee is called the **knee capacity** of the system. It is also common to measure capacity in terms of load, for example, the number of users rather than the throughput. Once again, it is a good idea to precisely define the metrics and their units before using them in a performance evaluation project.

The ratio of maximum achievable throughput (usable capacity) to nominal capacity is called the **efficiency**. For example, if the maximum throughput from a 100-Mbps (megabits per second) Local Area Network (LAN) is only 85 Mbps, its efficiency is 85%. The term efficiency is also used for multiprocessor systems. The ratio of the performance of an n-processor system to that of a one-processor system is its efficiency, as shown in Figure 3.4. The performance is usually measured in terms of MIPS or MFLOPS.

The **utilization** of a resource is measured as the fraction of time the resource is busy servicing requests. Thus this is the ratio of busy time and total elapsed time over a given period. The period during which a resource is not being used is called the **idle time**. System managers are often interested in balancing the load so that no one resource is utilized more than others. Of course, this is not always possible.

Some resources, such as processors, are always either busy or idle, so their utilization in terms of ratio of busy time to total time makes sense. For other

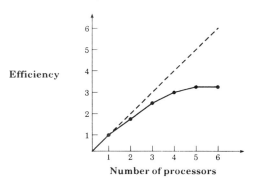

FIGURE 3.4 Efficiency of a multiprocessor system.

resources, such as memory, only a fraction of the resource may be used at a given time; their utilization is measured as the average fraction used over an interval.

The **reliability** of a system is usually measured by the probability of errors or by the mean time between errors. The latter is often specified as **error-free seconds**.

The **availability** of a system is defined as the fraction of the time the system is available to service users' requests. The time during which the system is not available is called **downtime**; the time during which the system is available is called **uptime**. Often the mean uptime, better known as the **Mean Time To Failure (MTTF)**, is a better indicator since a small downtime and a small uptime combination may result in a high-availability measure, but the users may not be able to get any service if the uptime is less than the time required to complete a service.

In system procurement studies, the **cost/performance ratio** is commonly used as a metric for comparing two or more systems. The cost includes the cost of hardware/software licensing, installation, and maintenance over a given number of years. The performance is measured in terms of throughput under a given response time constraint. For example, two transaction processing systems may be compared in terms of dollars per TPS.

3.4 UTILITY CLASSIFICATION OF PERFORMANCE METRICS

Depending upon the utility function of a performance metric, it can be categorized into three classes:

- *Higher is Better* or **HB**. System users and system managers prefer higher values of such metrics. System throughput is an example of an HB metric.

- *Lower is Better* or **LB**. System users and system managers prefer smaller values of such metrics. Response time is an example of an LB metric.

- *Nominal is Best* or **NB**. Both high and low values are undesirable. A particular value in the middle is considered the best. Utilization is an example of an NB characteristic. Very high utilization is considered bad by the users since their response times are high. Very low utilization is considered bad by system managers since the system resources are not being used. Some value in the range of 50 to 75% may be considered best by both users and system managers.

Figure 3.5 shows hypothetical graphs of utility of the three classes of metrics. The utility class of a metric is useful in data presentation, for example, in Kiviat graphs discussed later in Section 10.6.

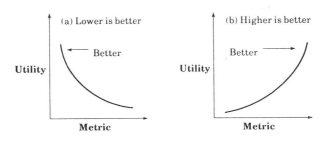

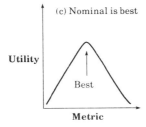

FIGURE 3.5   Types of metrics.

3.5   SETTING PERFORMANCE REQUIREMENTS

One problem performance analysts are faced with repeatedly is that of specifying performance requirements for a system to be acquired or designed. A
general method to specify such requirements is presented in this section and
is illustrated with a case study.

To begin, consider these typical requirement statements:

The system should be both processing and memory efficient. It should not
create excessive overhead.

There should be an extremely low probability that the network will duplicate a packet, deliver a packet to the wrong destination, or change the
data in a packet.

These requirement statements are unacceptable since they suffer from one
or more of the following problems:

1. *Nonspecific:* No clear numbers are specified. Qualitative words such as
low, high, rare, and extremely small are used instead.
2. *Nonmeasurable:* There is no way to measure a system and verify that it
meets the requirement.
3. *Nonacceptable:* Numerical values of requirements, if specified, are set
based upon what can be achieved or what looks good. If an attempt is

made to set the requirements realistically, they turn out to be so low that they become unacceptable.

4. *Nonrealizable:* Often, requirements are set high so that they look good. However, such requirements may not be realizable.

5. *Nonthorough:* No attempt is made to specify all possible outcomes.

What all these problems lack can be summarized in one word: **SMART**. That is, the requirements must be **S**pecific, **M**easurable, **A**cceptable, **R**ealizable, and **T**horough. Specificity precludes the use of words like "low probability" and "rare." Measurability requires verification that a given system meets the requirements. Acceptability and realizability demand new configuration limits or architectural decisions so that the requirements are high enough to be acceptable and low enough to be achievable. Thoroughness includes all possible outcomes and failure modes. As discussed in Section 3.2, every system provides a set of services. For every request for a service, there are three possible outcomes: successful performance, incorrect performance, and nonperformance. Thoroughness dictates that the requirements be set on all possible outcomes.

For the requirements to be meaningful, specify bounds, if any, on the configurations, workloads, and environments.

These ideas are illustrated in the following case study.

Case Study 3.2 Consider the problem of specifying the performance requirements for a high-speed LAN system. A LAN basically provides the service of transporting frames (or packets) to the specified destination station. Given a user request to send a frame to destination station D, there are three categories of outcomes: the frame is correctly delivered to D, incorrectly delivered (delivered to a wrong destination or with an error indication to D), or not delivered at all. The performance requirements for these three categories of outcomes were specified as follows:

1. *Speed*: If the packet is correctly delivered, the time taken to deliver it and the rate at which it is delivered are important. This leads to the following two requirements:

   (a) The access delay at any station should be less than 1 second.

   (b) Sustained throughput must be at least 80 Mbits/sec.

2. *Reliability*: Five different error modes were considered important. Each of these error modes causes a different amount of damage and, hence, has a different level of acceptability. The probability requirements for each of these error modes and their combined effect are specified as follows:

   (a) The probability of any bit being in error must be less than 10^{-7}.

   (b) The probability of any frame being in error (with error indication set) must be less than 1%.

   (c) The probability of a frame in error being delivered without error indication must be less than 10^{-15}.

(d) The probability of a frame being misdelivered due to an undetected error in the destination address must be less than 10^{-18}.

(e) The probability of a frame being delivered more than once (duplicate) must be less than 10^{-5}.

(f) The probability of losing a frame on the LAN (due to all sorts of errors) must be less than 1%.

3. *Availability*: Two fault modes were considered significant. The first was the time lost due to the network reinitializations, and the second was time lost due to permanent failures requiring field service calls. The requirements for frequency and duration of these fault modes were specified as follows:

(a) The mean time to initialize the LAN must be less than 15 milliseconds.

(b) The mean time between LAN initializations must be at least 1 minute.

(c) The mean time to repair a LAN must be less than 1 hour. (LAN partitions may be operational during this period.)

(d) The mean time between LAN partitioning must be at least half a week.

All of the numerical values specified above were checked for realizability by analytical modeling, which showed that LAN systems satisfying these requirements were feasible.   □

EXERCISES

3.1 What methodology would you choose?

  a. To select a personal computer for yourself

  b. To select 1000 workstations for your company

  c. To compare two spread sheet packages

  d. To compare two data-flow architectures, if the answer was required:

    i. Yesterday

    ii. Next quarter

    iii. Next year

3.2 Make a complete list of metrics to compare

  a. Two personal computers

  b. Two database systems

  c. Two disk drives

  d. Two window systems

FURTHER READING FOR PART I

There are a number of books on computer systems performance evaluation. However, most of these books emphasize only one of the three evaluation techniques.

The book by Lazowska et al. (1984) has an excellent treatment of queueing models. Lavenberg (1983) provides a good review of queueing models and simulation. Ferrari (1978), Ferrari, Serazzi, and Zeigner (1983), and Howard (1983) have good discussions of measurement techniques and their applications to a wide variety of performance problems, such as system tuning, workload characterization, program tuning, and others.

Other books on performance analysis and modeling are Gelenbe and Mitrani (1980), Kobayashi (1978), Leung (1987), McKerrow (1987), Molloy (1989), and Sauer and Chandy (1981).

Majone and Quade (1980) and Koopman (1956) have interesting discussions of common pitfalls of analysis.

The fairness definition presented in Case Study 3.1 is due to Jain, Chiu, and Hawe (1984). The complete case study is described in Jain (1985).

PART II

MEASUREMENT TECHNIQUES AND TOOLS

Computer system performance measurements involve monitoring the system while it is being subjected to a particular workload. In order to perform meaningful measurements, the workload should be carefully selected. To achieve that goal, the performance analyst needs to understand the following before performing the measurements:

1. What are the different types of workloads?
2. Which workloads are commonly used by other analysts?
3. How are the appropriate workload types selected?
4. How is the measured workload data summarized?
5. How is the system performance monitored?
6. How can the desired workload be placed on the system in a controlled manner?
7. How are the results of the evaluation presented?

The answers to these questions and related issues are discussed in this part.

CHAPTER 4

TYPES OF WORKLOADS

benchmark *v. trans.* To subject (a system) to a series of tests in order to obtain prearranged results not available on competitive systems.

—S. Kelly-Bootle
The Devil's DP Dictionary

This chapter describes workloads that have traditionally been used to compare computer systems. This description will familiarize you with workload-related names and terms that appear in performance reports. Most of these terms were developed for comparing processors and timesharing systems. In Chapter 5, the discussion is generalized to other computing systems such as database systems, network, and so forth.

The term **test workload** denotes any workload used in performance studies. A test workload can be real or synthetic. A **real workload** is one observed on a system being used for normal operations. It cannot be repeated, and therefore, is generally not suitable for use as a test workload. Instead, a **synthetic workload**, whose characteristics are similar to those of the real workload and can be applied repeatedly in a controlled manner, is developed and used for studies. The main reason for using a synthetic workload is that it is a representation or model of the real workload. Other reasons for using a synthetic workload are no real-world data files, which may be large and contain sensitive data, are required; the workload can be easily modified without affecting operation; it can be easily ported to different systems due to its small size; and it may have built-in measurement capabilities.

The following types of test workloads have been used to compare computer systems:

1. Addition instruction
2. Instruction mixes
3. Kernels
4. Synthetic programs
5. Application benchmarks

Each of these workloads is explained in this chapter, and the circumstances under which they may be appropriate are discussed.

4.1 ADDITION INSTRUCTION

Historically, when computer systems were first introduced, processors were the most expensive and most used components of the system. The performance of the computer system was synonymous with that of the processor. Initially, the computers had very few instructions. The most frequent is the addition instruction. Thus, as a first approximation, the computer with the faster addition instruction was considered to be the better performer. The addition instruction was the sole workload used, and the addition time was the sole performance metric.

4.2 INSTRUCTION MIXES

As the number and complexity of instructions supported by the processors grew, the addition instruction was no longer sufficient, and a more detailed workload description was required. This need led several people to measure the relative frequencies of various instructions on real systems and to use these as weighting factors to get an average instruction time.

An **instruction mix** is a specification of various instructions coupled with their usage frequency. Given different instruction timings, it is possible to compute an average instruction time for a given mix and use the average to compare different processors. Several instruction mixes are used in the computer industry; the most commonly quoted one is the Gibson mix.

The Gibson mix was developed by Jack C. Gibson in 1959 for use with IBM 704 systems. At that time, processor speeds were measured by memory cycle time, addition time, or an average of addition and multiplication times. The Gibson mix extended the averaging to 13 different classes of instructions, shown in Table 4.1. The average speed of a processor can be computed from the weighted average of the execution times of instructions in the 13 classes listed in the table. The weights are based on the relative frequency of operation codes as measured on a few IBM 704 and IBM 650 systems.

TABLE 4.1   Gibson Instruction Mix

1. Load and Store	31.2
2. Fixed-Point Add and Subtract	6.1
3. Compares	3.8
4. Branches	16.6
5. Floating Add and Subtract	6.9
6. Floating Multiply	3.8
7. Floating Divide	1.5
8. Fixed-Point Multiply	0.6
9. Fixed-Point Divide	0.2
10. Shifting	4.4
11. Logical, And, Or	1.6
12. Instructions not using registers	5.3
13. Indexing	<u>18.0</u>
	100.0

Instruction mixes have several disadvantages. Today's computers provide many more complex classes of instructions that are not reflected in the mixes. In modern computer systems, instruction time is highly variable depending upon addressing modes, cache hit rates, pipeline efficiency, and interference from other devices during processor-memory access cycles. The instruction times also vary according to parameter values such as frequency of zeros as a parameter, the distribution of zero digits in a multiplier, the average number of positions of preshift in floating-point add, and the number of times a conditional branch is taken. The mixes do not reflect the virtual addressing facilities (for example, page translation tables) that are provided by some processors.

Despite these limitations, instruction mixes do provide a single number for use in relative comparisons with other computers of similar architectures. Either this combined single time or a complete list of individual instruction times is useful in estimating the time required to execute key algorithms in applications and system programs. The inverse of average instruction time is commonly quoted as the MIPS (Millions of Instructions Per Second) or MFLOPS (Millions of Floating-Point Operations Per Second) rates for the processor.

It must be pointed that the instruction mixes only measure the speed of the processor. This may or may not have effect on the total system performance when the system consists of many other components. System performance is limited by the performance of the bottleneck component, and unless the processor is the bottleneck (that is, the usage is mostly compute bound), the MIPS rate of the processor does not reflect the system performance.

4.3 KERNELS

The introduction of pipelining, instruction caching, and various address translation mechanisms made computer instruction times highly variable. An individual instruction could no longer be considered in isolation. Instead, it became more appropriate to consider a set of instructions, which constitutes a higher level function, a *service* provided by the processors. Researchers started making a list of such functions and using the most frequent function as the workload. Such a function is called a **kernel**. Since most of the initial kernels did not make use of the input/output (I/O) devices and concentrated solely on the processor performance, this class of kernels could be called the **processing kernel**.

A kernel is a generalization of the instruction mix. The word *kernel* means nucleus. In some specialized applications, one can identify a set of common operations, for example, matrix inversion. Different processors can then be compared on the basis of their performance on this kernel operation. Some of the commonly used kernels are Sieve, Puzzle, Tree Searching, Ackermann's Function, Matrix Inversion, and Sorting. However, unlike instruction mixes, most kernels are not based on actual measurements of systems. Rather, they became popular after being used by a number of researchers trying to compare their processor architectures.

Most of the disadvantages of instruction mixes also apply to kernels, although some of the disadvantages related to parameter values, such as frequency of zeros and frequency of branches, no longer apply. The main disadvantage of kernels is that they do not typically make use of I/O devices, and thus, the kernel performance does not reflect the total system performance.

4.4 SYNTHETIC PROGRAMS

The processing kernels do not make use of any operating system services or I/O devices. As the applications of computer systems are proliferating, they are no longer used for processing-only applications. Input/output operations have become an important part of the real workloads. Initial attempts to measure I/O performance lead analysts to develop simple exerciser loops that make a specified number of service calls or I/O requests. This allows them to compute the average CPU time and elasped time for each service call. In order to maintain portability to different operating systems, such exercisers are usually written in high-level languages such as FORTRAN or Pascal.

The first exerciser loop was proposed by Buchholz (1969) who called it a synthetic program. A sample exerciser is shown in Figure 4.1. It makes a number of I/O requests. By adjusting the control parameters, one can control the number of times the request is made. Exerciser loops are also used to measure operating system services such as process creation, forking, and memory allocation.

The main advantage of exerciser loops is that they can be quickly developed and given to different vendors. It is not necessary to use real data files, which may contain proprietary information. The programs can be easily modified and ported to different systems. Further, most exercisers have built-in measurement capabilities. Thus, once developed, the measurement process is automated and can be repeated easily on successive versions of the operating systems to characterize the relative performance gains/losses.

```
        DIMENSION Record(500)
!Control parameters:
        Num_Computes=500        !Repeat count for computation
        Num_Reads=35            !Number of records read
        Num_Writes=40           !Number of records written
        Num_Iterations=1000     !Repeat count for the experiment
!Open files:
        OPEN(UNIT=1,NAME='In.dat',TYPE='Old',
       1FORM='Unformatted',ACCESS='Direct')
        OPEN(UNIT=2,NAME='Out.dat',TYPE='New',
       1FORM='unformatted',ACCESS='Direct')
        CALL Get_Time(CPU1,Elapsed1)    !Record starting time

        DO 500 Iteration=1,Num_Iterations

!Perform a number of read I/Os
        DO 100 i=1,Num_Reads
        READ(1'i),Record
100     CONTINUE
!Do computation
        DO 200 j=1,Num_Computes
        DO 200 i=1,500
200     Record(i)=1 + i + i*i + i*i*i
!Perform a number of write I/Os
        DO 300 i=1,Num_Writes
        WRITE(2'i),Record
300     CONTINUE
500     CONTINUE
        CALL Get_Time(CPU2,Elapsed2)    !Get ending time
!Close files:
        CLOSE(UNIT=1)
        CLOSE(UNIT=2)
        CPU_Time=(CPU2-CPU1)/Num_Iterations
        Elapsed_Time=(Elapsed2-Elapsed1)/Num_Iterations
        TYPE *,'CPU time per iteration is ',CPU_Time
        TYPE *,'Elasped time per iteration is ',Elapsed_Time
        STOP
        END
```

FIGURE 4.1 Synthetic workload generation program.

The disadvantages of exercisers are that they are generally too small and do not make representative memory or disk references. The mechanisms of page faults and disk cache may not be adequately exercised. The CPU-I/O overlap may not be representative. In particular, exercisers are not suitable for multiuser environments since the loops may create synchronizations, which may result in better or worse performance.

4.5 APPLICATION BENCHMARKS

If the computer systems to be compared are to be used for a particular application, such as banking or airline reservations, a representative subset of functions for that application may be used. Such benchmarks are generally described in terms of functions to be performed and make use of almost all resources in the system, including processors, I/O devices, networks, and databases.

An example of the application benchmark is the debit-credit benchmark described in Section 4.6.7.

4.6 POPULAR BENCHMARKS

In trade presses, the term *benchmark* is almost always used synonymously with workload. Kernels, synthetic programs, and application-level workloads, for example, are all called benchmarks. Although the instruction mixes are a type of workload, they have not been called benchmarks. Some authors have attempted to restrict the term benchmark to refer only to the set of programs taken from real workloads. This distinction, however, has mostly been ignored in the literature. Thus, the process of performance comparison for two or more systems by measurements is called **benchmarking**, and the workloads used in the measurements are called **benchmarks**. Some of the well-known benchmarks are described next.

4.6.1 Sieve

The sieve kernel has been used to compare microprocessors, personal computers, and high-level languages. It is based on Eratosthenes' sieve algorithm and is used to find all prime numbers below a given number n. The algorithm, in its manual form, consists of first writing down all integers from 1 to n and then striking out all multiples of k for $k = 2, 3, \ldots, \sqrt{n}$. For example, to find all prime numbers from 1 to 20, the steps are as follows:

1. Write down all numbers from 1 to 20. Mark all as prime:

   $\boxed{1}$ $\boxed{2}$ $\boxed{3}$ $\boxed{4}$ $\boxed{5}$ $\boxed{6}$ $\boxed{7}$ $\boxed{8}$ $\boxed{9}$ $\boxed{10}$ $\boxed{11}$
   $\boxed{12}$ $\boxed{13}$ $\boxed{14}$ $\boxed{15}$ $\boxed{16}$ $\boxed{17}$ $\boxed{18}$ $\boxed{19}$ $\boxed{20}$

2. Remove all multiples of 2 from the list of primes:

   $\boxed{1}$ $\boxed{2}$ $\boxed{3}$ 4 $\boxed{5}$ 6 $\boxed{7}$ 8 $\boxed{9}$ 10 $\boxed{11}$ 12 $\boxed{13}$ 14 $\boxed{15}$ 16 $\boxed{17}$ 18 $\boxed{19}$ 20

3. The next integer in the sequence is 3. Remove all multiples of 3:

   $\boxed{1}$ $\boxed{2}$ $\boxed{3}$ 4 $\boxed{5}$ 6 $\boxed{7}$ 8 9 10 $\boxed{11}$ 12 $\boxed{13}$ 14 15 16 $\boxed{17}$ 18 $\boxed{19}$ 20

4. The next integer in the sequence is 5, which is greater than the square root of 20. Hence, the remaining sequence consists of the desired prime numbers.

A Pascal program to implement the sieve kernel is given in Figure 4.2.

```
PROGRAM Prime (OUTPUT);
CONST
  MaxNum = 8191; (* Lists all primes up to MaxNum *)
  NumIterations = 10; (* Repeats procedure NumIterations times *)
VAR
  IsPrime : ARRAY [1..MaxNum] OF BOOLEAN;
  i,k,Iteration : INTEGER; (* Loop indexes *)
  NumPrimes : INTEGER; (* Number of primes found *)
BEGIN
  WRITELN('Using Eratosthenes Sieve to find primes up to ', MaxNum);
  WRITELN('Repeating it ',NumIterations,' times.');
  FOR Iteration := 1 TO NumIterations DO
    BEGIN      (* Initialize all numbers to be prime *)
      FOR i := 1 TO MaxNum DO
        IsPrime[i] := TRUE;
      i := 2;
      WHILE i*i <= MaxNum DO
        BEGIN
          IF IsPrime[i] THEN
            BEGIN (* Mark all multiples of i to be nonprime *)
              k := i + i;
              WHILE k <= MaxNum DO
                BEGIN
                  IsPrime[k] := FALSE;
                  k := k + i;
                END; (* of WHILE  k *)
            END; (* of If IsPrime *)
          i := i + 1;
        END; (* of WHILE i*i *)
    NumPrimes := 0;
    FOR i := 1 TO MaxNum DO (* Count the number of primes *)
      IF IsPrime[i] THEN NumPrimes := NumPrimes + 1;
      WRITELN(NumPrimes, ' primes');
    END; (* of FOR Iterations *)
  (* The following can be added during debugging to list primes. *)
  (* FOR i := 1 TO MaxNum DO IF IsPrime[i] THEN WRITELN(i); *)
END.
```

FIGURE 4.2   Pascal program to implement sieve workload.

4.6.2   Ackermann's Function

This kernel has been used to assess the efficiency of the procedure-calling mechanism in ALGOL-like languages. The function has two parameters and is defined recursively. The function Ackermann(3,n) is evaluated for values of n from 1 to 6. The average execution time per call, the number of instructions executed per call, and the amount of stack space required for each call are used to compare various systems.

A listing of the benchmark program in SIMULA is shown in Figure 4.3. The value of the function Ackermann(3,n) is $2^{n+3} - 3$. This knowledge is used

```
BEGIN
   INTEGER n;            !Loop index;
   INTEGER j;            !Function value;
   INTEGER num_calls;    !Number of recursive calls;
   INTEGER k;            !Contains 2**(n+3);
   INTEGER k1;           !Contains 4**(n-1);
   REAL t1,t2;           !CPU time values;

   INTEGER PROCEDURE Ackermann(m,n); VALUE m,n; INTEGER m,n;
      Ackermann := IF m=0 THEN n+1
                   ELSE IF n=0 THEN Ackermann(m-1,1)
                      ELSE Ackermann(m-1,Ackermann(m,n-1));
!Main Program;
   k := 16; K1 := 1;     !Initialize k and k1 for n=1;
   FOR n := 1 STEP 1 UNTIL 6 DO
      BEGIN
         t1 := CPUTIME;             !Beginning CPU time;
         j := Ackermann(3,n);       !Compute the function;
         t2 := CPUTIME;             !Ending CPU time;
         IF j <> k-3 THEN OUTTEXT("Wrong Value");
         OUTTEXT("Net CPU Time for Ackermann(3,");
         OUTINT(n,1); OUTTEXT(") is");
         OUTREAL(t2-t1,7,15); OUTIMAGE;
         Num_calls := (512*k1-15*k+9*n+37)/3;
         OUTTEXT("CPU Time per call:");
         OUTREAL((t2-t1)/num_calls,7,15);
         OUTIMAGE;
         k1 := 4*k1;       !Update k1 for the next n;
         k := 2*k;         !Update k for the next n;
      END
END
```

FIGURE 4.3 SIMULA program to implement Ackermann's function.

in the code to verify the implementation of the benchmark. The number of recursive calls in evaluating Ackermann(3,n) has been shown by Wichmann (1976) to be

$$(512 \times 4^{n-1} - 15 \times 2^{n+3} + 9n + 37)/3$$

This expression is used to compute the execution time per call. For Ackermann(3,n), the maximum depth of the procedure calls is $2^{n+3} - 4$. Hence, the amount of stack space required doubles when n is increased by 1.

4.6.3 Whetstone

Used at the British Central Computer Agency, the Whetstone kernel consists of a set of 11 modules designed to match observed dynamic frequency of operations used in 949 ALGOL programs. The kernel exercises such processor features as array addressing, fixed- and floating-point arithmetic, subroutine

calls, and parameter passing. It has been translated from ALGOL to FOR-
TRAN, PL/I, and other languages. A listing of the workload in ALGOL can
be found in Curnow and Wichmann (1975).

The results of the Whetstone benchmarks are measured in KWIPS (Kilo
Whetstone Instructions Per Second). There are many permutations of the
Whetstone benchmark, so it is important to ensure that comparisons across
various systems utilize the same source code and that the internal loop counter
is defined large enough to reduce timing variability.

Despite its synthetic mix of operations, Whetstone is generally considered
a floating-point benchmark and is mostly representative of small engineer-
ing/scientific applications that fit into cache memory.

The modules were designed to minimize the impact of known compiler
optimizations. Newer compiler optimization techniques can significantly affect the execution time of this workload on a processor. It suffers from other
problems of kernels in that there is no I/O and values of input parameters
significantly affect the measured performance.

4.6.4 LINPACK

Developed by Jack Dongarra (1983) of Argonne National Laboratory, this
benchmark consists of a number of programs that solve dense systems of linear
equations using the LINPACK subroutine package. LINPACK programs can
be characterized as having a high percentage of floating-point additions and
multiplications. Most of the time is consumed in a set of subroutines called
the Basic Linear Algebra Subprograms (BLAS), which are called repeatedly
throughout the benchmark.

The LINPACK benchmarks are compared based upon the execution rate
as measured in MFLOPS. The most popular variants solve a 100×100 system
of equations, either in single or double precision, and have become one of
the most widely used benchmarks to gauge engineering/scientific applications
performance. For example, many finite element, finite difference, simulation,
and regression analysis applications exploit LINPACK-like equation solvers.

LINPACK represents mechanical engineering applications on workstations.
These applications range from drafting to numerically controlled machines to
finite element analysis and call for both high computation speed and good
graphics processing.

4.6.5 Dhrystone

Developed in 1984 by Reinhold Weicker at Siemens, this kernel contains many
procedure calls and is considered to represent systems programming environments. It is available in three languages: C, Pascal, and Ada. However,
the C version is the most commonly used. The results are usually presented
in Dhrystone Instructions Per Second (DIPS). The benchmark documentation presents a set of ground rules for building and executing Dhrystone. The

benchmark has been updated several times, and it is important to specify the version number when the kernel is used. The kernel allegedly has a rather low dynamic nesting depth of the function calls, a low number of instructions per function call, and a large percentage of time spent in character-string copying and comparing. The benchmark is a popular measure of integer performance; it does not exercise floating-point or I/O processing.

4.6.6 Lawrence Livermore Loops

This workload consists of a set of 24 separate tests dominated by large scientific calculations that are largely vectorizable. They have been abstracted from the applications at Lawrence Livermore National Laboratories (see McMahon 1986) and run widely on systems from supercomputers to personal computers.

The results of this suite of benchmarks are rather complex to interpret because there is no attempt to reduce the results down to a single number. The results, given in MFLOPS (Millions of Floating-Point Operations Per Second), are reported for minimum, maximum, and three means: arithmetic, geometric, and harmonic.

A review of representative, large-scale computational science applications in the physics and chemistry fields reveals that 40 to 60% of the execution time, on average, is spent performing floating-point calculations both in single- and double-precision arithmetic. Large-scale computational fluid dynamics applications, such as those used in airplane design, weather modeling, and astrophysics, benefit from high, single-stream, floating-point performance, such as that provided by vector and RISC-based systems. Similarly, Monte Carlo simulations used in particle physics basic research and in computational chemistry as applied to chemical and drug design benefit from high scalar performance. The Lawrence Livermore FORTRAN kernels, which represent computational kernels extracted from actual applications developed and used in the National Laboratories, have become one de facto standard used to gauge the computational power of systems. As is common among large-scale computational science codes, a number of the kernels are highly resistant to vectorization but do benefit from high single- and double-precision floating-point performance.

4.6.7 Debit-Credit Benchmark

This application-level benchmark has become a de facto standard to compare transaction processing systems. Although several variations of the benchmark have been in use since 1973, it was first recorded in the published literature in an anonymous article by a group of two dozen computer professionals (see Anonymous et al. 1985). The benchmark represents a distributed banking network. As shown in Figure 4.4, a bank usually has several branch offices, each with several tellers. The customers arriving at the branch stand in a queue for the next available teller. Alternately, there may be a separate queue for each teller.

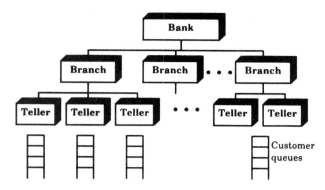

FIGURE 4.4   Banking environment.

The debit-credit benchmark came into being in 1973 when a large retail bank wanted to put its 1000 branches, 10,000 tellers, and 10,000,000 accounts on-line with a peak load of 100 Transactions Per Second (**TPS**). Smaller systems can be represented by suitably scaling these numbers. Each TPS requires 10 branches, 100 tellers, and 100,000 accounts. For example, systems claiming a performance of 50 TPS should run the benchmark with 500 branches, 5000 tellers, and 5,000,000 accounts.

Different systems are compared on the basis of a price-performance ratio. The performance is measured by throughput in terms of TPS such that 95% of all transactions provide 1 second or less response time. The response time is measured as the time interval between the arrival of the last bit from the communications line and the sending of the first bit to the communications line. The cost includes the total expenses for a 5-year period on purchase, installation, and maintenance of the hardware and software in the machine room. It does not include expenditures for terminals, communications, application development, or operations.

A pseudo-code definition of the debit-credit workload is given in Figure 4.5. There are four record types in the database: account, teller, branch, and history. History records are 50 bytes; others are 100 bytes. Each transaction consists of reading a 100-byte message from a block mode terminal connected via X.25. The system performs presentation services to map the input for a

```
Begin-Transaction
      Read message from the terminal (100 bytes)
      Rewrite account                 (100 bytes, random)
      Write history                   (50 bytes, sequential)
      Rewrite teller                  (100 bytes, random)
      Rewrite branch                  (100 bytes, random)
      Write message to the terminal   (200 bytes)
Commit-Transaction
```

FIGURE 4.5   Debit-credit transaction pseudo-code.

COBOL program, which in turn uses a database system to debit a bank account, do the standard double-entry bookkeeping, and then reply to the terminal. Fifteen percent of the transactions require access to remote branch databases; others are local.

Due to increased popularity of the transaction processing systems, an effort is underway to define transaction processing benchmarks more precisely. A council of several transaction processing system vendors, users, and consultants, called the *Transactions Processing Performance Council (TPC)*, was formed in August 1988. Its first benchmark, called TPC Benchmark A, is a variant of the debit–credit benchmark (see TPC 1989). In TPC benchmark, the throughput is measured in terms of TPS such that 90% of all transactions provide 2 seconds or less response time.

4.6.8 SPEC Benchmark Suite

The Systems Performance Evaluation Cooperative (SPEC) is a nonprofit corporation formed by leading computer vendors to develop a standardized set of benchmarks. Release 1.0 of the SPEC benchmark suite (see SPEC 1990) consists of the following 10 benchmarks drawn from various engineering and scientific applications:

1. *GCC*: The time for the GNU C Compiler to convert 19 preprocessed source files into assembly language output is measured. This benchmark is representative of a software engineering environment and measures the compiling efficiency of a system.

2. *Espresso*: Espresso is an Electronic Design Automation (EDA) tool that performs heuristic boolean function minimization for Programmable Logic Arrays (PLAs). The elapsed time to run a set of seven input models is measured.

3. *Spice 2g6*: Spice, another representative of the EDA environment, is a widely used analog circuit simulation tool. The time to simulate a bipolar circuit is measured.

4. *Doduc*: This is a synthetic benchmark that performs a Monte Carlo simulation of certain aspects of a nuclear reactor. Because of its iterative structure and abundance of short branches and compact loops, it tests the cache memory effectiveness.

5. *NASA7*: This is a collection of seven floating-point intensive kernels performing matrix operations on double-precision data.

6. *LI*: The elapsed time to solve the popular 9-queens problem by the LISP interpreter is measured.

7. *Eqntott*: This benchmark translates a logical representation of a boolean equation to a truth table.

8. *Matrix300*: This performs various matrix operations using several LINPACK routines on matrices of size 300×300. The code uses double-precision floating-point arithmetic and is highly vectorizable.

9. *Fpppp*: This is a quantum chemistry benchmark that performs two elec-
   tron integral derivatives using double-precision floating-point FOR-
   TRAN. It is difficult to vectorize.

10. *Tomcatv*: This is a vectorized mesh generation program using double-
    precision floating-point FORTRAN. Since it is highly vectorizable, sub-
    stantial speedups have been observed on several shared-memory multi-
    processor systems.

These benchmarks, which stress primarily the CPU, Floating Point Unit
(FPU), and to some extent the memory subsystem, are meant for comparing CPU speeds. Benchmarks to compare I/O and other subsystems may be
included in future releases.

The elapsed time to run two copies of a benchmark on each of the N
processors of a system (a total of 2N copies) is measured and compared with
the time to run two copies of the benchmark on a reference system (which is
VAX-11/780 for Release 1.0). For each benchmark, the ratio of the time on
the reference system and the system under test is reported as **SPECthruput**
using a notation of #CPU@Ratio. For example, a system with three CPUs
taking only 1/15th as long as the reference system on GCC benchmark has a
SPECthruput of 3@15. The ratio is a measure of the per processor throughput
relative to the reference system. The aggregate throughput for all processors of
a multiprocessor system can be obtained by multiplying the ratio by the
number of processors. For example, the aggregate throughput for the above
system is 45.

The geometric mean (discussed in Section 12.5) of the time ratios for single
copies of the 10 benchmarks is used to indicate the overall performance for the
suite and is called **SPECmark**. Again, the notation #CPU@Ratio is used to report the SPECmark.

The TPC and SPEC are the beginning of a new trend in the industry to
develop standard benchmarks for comparing all types of computer systems
including networks, image processing systems, and databases.

EXERCISES

4.1 Select an area of computer systems (for example, processor design, networks, operating systems, or databases), review articles on performance
evaluation in that area, and make a list of benchmarks used in those articles.

4.2 Implement the Sieve workload in a language of your choice, run it on
systems available to you, and report the results.

CHAPTER 5

THE ART OF WORKLOAD SELECTION

> *"Would you tell me, please, which way I ought to go from here?"*
> *"That depends a good deal on where you want to get to," said the Cat.*
> *"I don't much care where—" said Alice.*
> *"Then it doesn't matter which way you go," said the Cat.*
> —Lewis Carroll, *Alice's Adventures in Wonderland*

The workload is the most crucial part of any performance evaluation project. It is possible to reach misleading conclusions if the workload is not properly selected. When the conclusions of a study are found to be unacceptable, the inappropriateness of the workload is commonly used as a criticism of the study. Like other aspects of performance evaluation, proper selection of workloads requires many considerations and judgments by the analyst, which is a part of the art of performance evaluation that comes with experience. In this chapter, a number of considerations are described that will help you make the right selection and justify your choice.

The four major considerations in selecting the workload are the services exercised by the workload, the level of detail, representativeness, and timeliness. These are discussed in the next four sections. Other minor considerations, such as loading level, impact of other components, and repeatability, have been grouped together in Section 5.5.

5.1 SERVICES EXERCISED

The best way to start the workload selection is to view the system as a service provider. As discussed in Part I, each system provides a number of services, and making a list of services is one of the first steps in a systematic performance evaluation study. Often the term **System Under Test (SUT)** is used to denote the complete set of components that are being purchased or being designed by the organization. Sometimes there is one specific component in the SUT whose alternatives are being considered. This component is called **Component Under Study (CUS)** as shown in Figure 5.1. For example, a Central Processing Unit (CPU) design team might want to understand the impact of different Arithmetic-Logic Unit (ALU) organizations. In this case, the CPU is the SUT and the ALU is the CUS. Similarly, a bank purchasing a transaction processing system may want to compare different disk devices. In this case, the transaction processing system is the SUT and the disk devices are the CUS. Clearly, identifying the SUT and CUS is important since the workload as well as the performance metrics are determined primarily by the SUT. Confusing CUS with SUT and vice versa is a common mistake that leads to misleading results. In the remainder of this chapter, the word *system* will be used to mean SUT and the word *component* will be used to mean CUS.

The metrics chosen should reflect the performance of services provided at the system level and not at the component level. For example, the MIPS is a justifiable metric for comparing two CPUs, but it is not appropriate for comparing two timesharing systems. The CPU is only one component of the timesharing system. A timesharing system may provide services such as transaction processing, in which case the performance would be measured by transactions (as opposed to instructions) per second.

The basis for workload selection is also the system and not the component. For example, the services provided by the CPUs are the so-called instructions, and the CPU designers may want to use instruction frequency as a possible representation of workload. The services provided by the turn-key banking systems are generally called "transactions," and so the bank may use the transaction frequencies as the workload. Notice that using instruction frequencies to specify the workload of a banking system is not appropriate, since the performance of the banking system depends on several components in addition to that of the CPU. Similarly, using transactions to compare two CPUs may or may not be appropriate, since the performance may be affected by other components such as I/O devices. However, if a manufacturer offers two banking systems that are identical except for the CPUs, the two systems can be

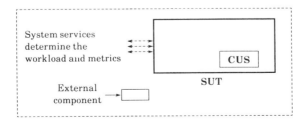

FIGURE 5.1 The SUT and CUS.

compared using transaction frequencies as the workload. This latter study may sometimes be inaccurately referred to as the comparison of the two CPUs.

If the system provides multiple services, the workload should exercise as complete a set of services as possible. Thus, it is inappropriate to measure the performance of an ALU that provides both floating and integer arithmetic by only using an integer workload. In this case, the workload does not exercise all the key services provided by the system.

In considering the services exercised, also take into account the purpose of the study. A workload may exercise the most efficient features of the system or the least efficient. For example, a graphics editor may not be an efficient text editor. Thus, a text-editing workload used to compare two editors may bring out the worst in the graphics editor and vice versa. A text-editing workload is not appropriate if the purpose of the study is to find an editor to be used primarily for graphics work.

To summarize the discussion so far, the requests at the service-interface level of the SUT should be used to specify or measure the workload, and one should carefully distinguish between the SUT and CUS since it is easy to confuse one for the other.

The types of workloads discussed in Chapter 4 can be shown to be an application of the principle outlined here. Figure 5.2 shows a hierarchical view of a timesharing system. A user typically types in a high-level request, for example, to make a withdrawal from a bank account. The application software may translate the transaction into a number of requests for the operating system. These requests in turn make a number of requests to be executed by various hardware components of the system, which may include a number of specialized processors, general purpose processors, I/O devices, and network links. The CPU requests may be translated into a number of instructions, each of which may make one or more requests to the ALU. Thus, as shown in Figure 5.2, there is a hierarchy of interfaces at which the requests are serviced. A single request at a higher level may result in one or more requests at the lower level. As shown in the figure, the interface levels are:

1. Arithmetic-logic unit
2. Central processing unit
3. Operating system
4. Applications

The workload could be described by summarizing the requests at any one of these interface levels, depending upon what constitutes the SUT. If two ALUs are being compared, that is, the ALUs are the systems, the arithmetic instructions constitute the services or requests. The appropriate workload in this case is to specify the frequency of various arithmetic instructions or to specify the most frequent arithmetic instruction, which may very well be the addition instruction.

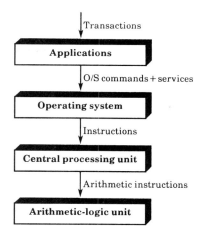

FIGURE 5.2   Hierarchical view of timesharing system.

If two CPUs are being compared, the instruction set of the processors constitutes the service provided. One possibility in this case is to use the instruction mix. However, if the performance of one instruction depends upon that of other neighboring instructions, the workload should be specified in terms of a set of instructions that are commonly used together. The popular kernels discussed in Section 4.6 are examples of such sets.

If two systems are being compared at the operating system level, the services provided by the operating systems, including the operating system commands and system services, should form the basis of the workload. In this case, synthetic programs discussed in Section 4.4 can be used.

If two turn-key transaction processing systems are being compared, the application interface is the SUT level and the requests at this level, namely, the transactions, would form the basis of workload. The workload could be described by specifying the frequency of various types of transactions or the most frequent transaction. The debit-credit workload described in Section 4.6.7 is an example of the workload to be used for such a study.

It should be obvious that the idea of a service interface level can be applied to other types of computer systems. The following example shows its application to computer networks.

Example 5.1   Consider the problem of selecting or designing the workload to compare two networks. In the literature, the term *network* is used loosely to mean anything from a cable between two computers to networking applications, such as mail, that allow communications between several computers. One way to represent the hierarchy of levels in this case is to use the seven layers identified by the ISO/OSI reference model as shown in Figure 5.3. These layers and the corresponding workloads are given next. Readers not familiar with networking terminology should see a networking textbook such as Tanenbaum (1988).

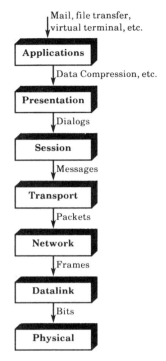

FIGURE 5.3 Workloads corresponding to the seven layers of the ISO/OSI reference model for computer networks.

1. *Physical Layer*: This layer deals with the transmission of individual bits over the physical medium, which may be a twisted-pair wire, a cable, or a fiber-optic link. The key service provided by this layer is the transmission of a bit. In some networks, the physical layer deals with a group of bits called symbols. Thus, the workload to compare two links should match the frequency of various symbols or bit patterns observed on real networks.

2. *Datalink Layer*: This layer deals with the transmission of frames over a single link. The workload to compare two datalink protocols would require specifying the characteristics of frames transmitted, such as their lengths and their arrival rates. On links that connect multiple stations, for example, on local-area networks, one would also want to specify the source-destination matrix.

3. *Network Layer*: This layer routes packets from a given source node to a given destination over multiple links. The workload in this case would require specifying the source-destination matrix, the distance between source and destination, and the characteristics of packets transmitted.

4. *Transport Layer*: This layer deals with the end-to-end aspects of communication between the source and the destination nodes. The services

provided include segmentation and reassembly of large messages. The workload would consist of specifying the frequency, sizes, and other characteristics of various messages.

5. *Session Layer*: The complete dialog between the user processes on the two end systems is called a session. The session layer provides services related to the initiation, maintenance, and disconnection of the sessions. The workload for the session layer would thus include the frequency and duration of various types of sessions.

6. *Presentation Layer*: This layer provides data compression and security. The workload for this layer would consist of specifying the frequency of various types of security and data compression requests.

7. *Application Layer*: This layer consists of user applications such as mail, file transfer, and virtual terminal. The workload at this layer would consist of specifying the frequency of various types of applications and their associated characteristics.

Thus, the choice of workload depends upon the layer at which the networks are being compared. While a typical mail session may be the right workload to compare two mail systems, it may not be appropriate to compare two fiber-optic links.   □

The following example illustrates the application of the services concepts to the analysis of an off-line backup storage system using magnetic tape drives.

Example 5.2   A magnetic tape backup system consists of several tape data systems, each containing several tape drives. The drives have separate read and write subsystems. Each subsystem makes use of magnetic heads. Thus, starting from a high level and moving down to lower levels, the services, factors, metrics, and workloads are as follows:

1. *Backup System*:
    (a) Services: Backup files, backup changed files, restore files, list backed-up files.
    (b) Factors: File system size, batch or background process, incremental or full backups.
    (c) Metrics: Backup time, restore time.
    (d) Workload: A computer system with files to be backed up. Vary frequency of backups.
2. *Tape Data System*:
    (a) Services: Read/write to the tape, read tape label, autoload tapes.
    (b) Factors: Type of tape drive.
    (c) Metrics: Speed, reliability, time between failures.
    (d) Workload: A synthetic program generating representative tape I/O requests.

3. *Tape Drives*:
   (a) Services: Read record, write record, rewind, find record, move to end of tape, move to beginning of tape.
   (b) Factors: Cartridge or reel tapes, drive size.
   (c) Metrics: Time for each type of service, for example, time to read record and to write record, speed (requests per unit time), noise, power dissipation.
   (d) Workload: A synthetic program exerciser generating various types of requests in a representative manner.

4. *Read/Write Subsystem*:
   (a) Services: Read data, write data (as digital signals).
   (b) Factors: Data-encoding technique, implementation technology (CMOS, TTL, and so forth).
   (c) Metrics: Coding density, I/O bandwidth (bits per second).
   (d) Workload: Read/write data streams with varying patterns of bits.

5. *Read/Write Heads*:
   (a) Services: Read signal, write signal (electrical signals).
   (b) Factors: Composition, interhead spacing, gap sizing, number of heads in parallel.
   (c) Metrics: Magnetic field strength, hysteresis.
   (d) Workload: Read/write currents of various amplitudes, tapes moving at various speeds. □

5.2 LEVEL OF DETAIL

After the service interface of the SUT has been identified and a list of services has been made, the next step in the workload selection is to choose the level of detail in recording (and thus reproducing) the requests for these services. A workload description may be as long as a time-stamped record of all requests or it can be as short as the single most commonly used request. A list of possibilities is as follows:

1. Most frequent request
2. Frequency of request types
3. Time-stamped sequence of requests
4. Average resource demand
5. Distribution of resource demands

The least detailed alternative is to select the most frequently requested service and use it as the workload. While this may not provide enough information about the system, this is commonly used as the initial workload. The addition instruction to compare early ALUs, various kernels to compare processors, and the debit-credit benchmark to compare transaction processing systems are examples of this approach. It is particularly valid if one type of service is requested much more often than others or is a major consumer of resources in the system.

The second alternative is to list various services, their characteristics, and frequency. The instruction mixes are examples of this approach. If the performance of a service depends upon the context, that is, on the services required in the past, the set of services that are expected to be context free are more appropriate than the individual services. History-sensitive mechanisms, such as caching in computer systems, often make this grouping necessary.

The third alternative is to get a time-stamped record (called a **trace**) of requests on a real system and use it as a workload. The problem with this alternative is that it may be too detailed. It is certainly inconvenient for analytical modeling. Also, for simulation it may require exact reproduction of component behavior to maintain the timing relationships. The advantages and disadvantages of trace-driven simulations are further discussed in Section 24.5.

In analytical modeling, the resource demands placed by the requests, rather than the requests themselves, are used as the workload. For example, the statement that each user has an average CPU time of 50 milliseconds and makes 20 I/O's per request may be a sufficient workload description for analytical modeling. In case of multiple services, several similar services can be grouped into a class, and each class may be characterized by its average resource demands.

The average demand may not be sufficient in some cases, and it may be necessary to specify the complete probability distribution for resource demands. This is particularly the case if there is a large variance in resource demands or if the distribution is different than that used in the model. Particularly, in simulations, it is easy to use different distributions. The analytical models are generally restricted to a given distribution.

The workload descriptions used for analytical and simulation modeling are also referred to as **nonexecutable** workloads since they are not in a form suitable for execution on a real system. On the other hand, a trace of user commands that can be executed directly on a system would be called an **executable** workload.

5.3 REPRESENTATIVENESS

A test workload should be representative of the real application. One definition of representativeness is that the test workload and the real application match in the following three respects:

1. *Arrival Rate*: The arrival rate of requests should be the same or proportional to that of the application.
2. *Resource Demands*: The total demands on each of the key resources should be the same or proportional to that of the application.

3. *Resource Usage Profile*: Resource usage profile relates to the sequence and the amounts in which different resources are used in an application. In a multiprogramming environment, it is important that the test workloads have a resource usage profile similar to that of the applications. Otherwise, it is possible that total resource demands of individual workloads may be representative of their respective applications, but when several workloads are run together, they may not produce results representative of combined applications.

5.4 TIMELINESS

Workloads should follow the changes in usage pattern in a timely fashion. User behavior has changed considerably over the years. For example, the trend has been to move away from machine languages toward higher level languages and from batch toward timesharing. Users change their usage pattern depending upon the services provided by the new systems. Thus, workloads become obsolete as soon as they become well understood. Nonetheless, these obsolete workloads keep getting used. The debit-credit workload used in transaction processing is an example of an outdated, but popular, workload. It is important that the workload represent the latest usage pattern.

Timeliness is a difficult goal to achieve. The main problem is that real user behavior is a moving and fuzzy target. Any observed user behavior applies to a specific environment for a specific system at a specific time. Users change their behavior with time, and any change in system performance prompts users to change their usage behavior. Users tend to change their demands to optimize the response for a given system, focusing on those features that the system can perform efficiently. For example, the processors that provide fast multiplication have a much higher frequency of multiplication instructions than the processors with slow multiplication instructions. Even on the same system, the usage pattern changes with time. Initially, computers were primarily used for scientific applications that required fast arithmetic operations. Today, some may argue that applications such as databases are I/O intensive, so the speed of I/O is more important than the speed of arithmetic operations.

This interdependence of system design and workload provides opportunity for debate at every performance evaluation presentation. This is particularly true for the evaluation of systems under design. A workload based on an existing system, even if modified for the new system features, cannot be guaranteed to be an accurate representation of future workloads. Furthermore, designs that are optimized on the basis of one or more workloads cannot be guaranteed to operate efficiently in other environments. It is therefore very important that the user's behavior be monitored on an ongoing basis and that the workload be based on recent measurements from a similar system.

5.5 OTHER CONSIDERATIONS IN WORKLOAD SELECTION

There are a few more issues, in addition to the services exercised and the level of detail, to consider in workload selection. These issues—loading level, impact of external components, and repeatability—are explained next.

1. *Loading Level*: A workload may exercise a system to its full capacity (best case), beyond its capacity (worst case), or at the load level observed in real workload (typical case). For procurement purposes, a workload measured in a similar existing environment may be good enough. However, for computer system design, you may have to identify all the environments where the system might be used and study performance under best, worst, and typical workloads. The correct choice of the loading level varies from case to case. For example, to measure the effectiveness of a congestion control scheme, the network should be exercised beyond its capacity, while the packet retransmission schemes should be tested for normal as well as heavy load, since the retransmissions may be required under both circumstances.

2. *Impact of External Components*: Sometimes components outside the system may have a significant impact on the system's performance. For example, the completion time of a synthetic program may depend heavily on I/O device performance. This is not a good workload to compare two processors. The speed difference between the processors may be masked completely by the I/O device. Ignoring this issue often leads to the conclusion that all alternatives in the system give equally good performance. The reason may be that the workload does not exercise the system or that there is a component external to the system that is the bottleneck. Therefore, either the workload should be modified to put less load on this other component, the system configuration should be modified to make this external component less significant, or the results should be analyzed to predict the performance of the system in the absence of the external bottleneck.

3. *Repeatability*: A workload should be such that the results can be easily reproduced without too much variance. Workloads that make a highly random demand on resources are less desirable since one would need to make many more runs to get a meaningful estimate of performance.

EXERCISES

5.1 Decide the metric and workload you would choose to compare the following:

   a. Two systems for very different applications: IBM PC versus Macintosh
   b. Two systems with identical functionality: IBM PC versus PCjr

  c. Two versions of the same operating systems: MS-DOS V1 versus MS-DOS V2

  d. Two hardware components: two floppy drives

  e. Two languages: C versus Pascal

5.2 Select an area of computer systems, for example, databases, networks, and processors. Prepare a table identifying increasing levels of services, components, factors, and workloads.

CHAPTER 6

WORKLOAD CHARACTERIZATION TECHNIQUES

> *Speed, quality, price. Pick any two.*
> —James M. Wallace

In order to test multiple alternatives under identical conditions, the workload should be repeatable. Since a real-user environment is generally not repeatable, it is necessary to study the real-user environments, observe the key characteristics, and develop a workload model that can be used repeatedly. This process is called **workload characterization**. Once a workload model is available, the effect of changes in the workload and system can be studied in a controlled manner by simply changing the parameters of the model. This chapter describes several techniques for workload characterization.

Workload characterization requires using several statistical techniques that are covered later in Part III of this book. You may skip this chapter during the first pass and come back to it after reading that part.

The discussion in this chapter requires a knowledge of basic probability theory and statistics. A brief introduction to the required concepts is presented in Chapter 12. Therefore, if you are not familiar with probability theory and statistics, you may skip this chapter and return to it after reading Part III.

6.1 TERMINOLOGY

The measured workload data consists of services requested or the resource demands of a number of users on the system. Here the term *user* denotes the entity that makes the service requests at the SUT interface (see Chapter 5 for a definition of SUT). The user may or may not be a human being. For example, if the SUT is a processor, the users may be various programs or batch jobs. Similarly, the users of a local-area network are the stations on the network. In workload characterization literature, the term **workload component** or **workload unit** is used instead of the user. The workload characterization consists of characterizing a typical user or workload component. Other examples of workload components are as follows:

- *Applications*: If one wants to characterize the behavior of various applications, such as mail, text editing, or program development, then each application may be considered a workload component and the average behavior of each application may be characterized.
- *Sites*: If one desires to characterize the workload at each of several locations of an organization, the sites may be used as workload components.
- *User Sessions*: Complete user sessions from login to logout may be monitored, and applications run during the session may be combined.

The key requirement for the selection of the workload component is that it be at the SUT interface. Another consideration is that each component should represent as homogeneous a group as possible. For example, if users at a site are very different, combining them into a site workload may not be meaningful. The purpose of the study and the domain of the control of the decision makers also affects the choice of components. For example, a mail system designer is more interested in determining a typical mail session than a typical user session combining many different applications.

The measured quantities, service requests, or resource demands, which are used to model or characterize the workload, are called **workload parameters** or **workload features**. Examples of workload parameters are transaction types, instructions, packet sizes, source destinations of a packet, and page reference pattern.

In choosing the parameters to characterize the workload, it is preferable to use those parameters that depend on the workload rather than on the system. For example, the elasped time (response time) for a transaction is not appropriate as a workload parameter, since it depends highly on the system on which the transaction is executed. This is one reason why the number of service requests rather than the amount of resource demanded is preferable as a workload parameter. For example, it is better to characterize a network mail session by the size of the message or the number of recipients rather than by the CPU time and the number of network messages, which will vary from one system to the next.

There are several characteristics of service requests (or resource demands) that are of interest. For example, arrival time, type of request or the resource demanded, duration of the request, and quantity of the resource demanded by each request may be represented in the workload model. Particularly those characteristics that have a significant impact on the performance should be included in the workload parameters, and those that have little impact should be excluded. For example, if the packet size has no impact on packet forwarding time at a router, it may be omitted from the list of workload parameters, and only the number of packets and arrival times of packets may be used instead.

The following techniques have been used in the past for workload characterization:

1. Averaging
2. Specifying dispersion
3. Single-parameter histograms
4. Multiparameter histograms
5. Principal-component analysis
6. Markov models
7. Clustering

These techniques will be discussed one by one.

6.2 AVERAGING

The simplest method to characterize a workload parameter is to present a single number that summarizes the parameter values observed. This single value is called average. If $\{x_1, x_2, \ldots, x_n\}$ are n observed values of of a workload parameter, the most common alternative is the arithmetic mean $\overline{x}$ given by

$$\overline{x} = \frac{1}{n} \sum_{i=1}^{n} x_i$$

There are cases, however, when arithmetic mean is inappropriate and the median, mode, geometric mean, or harmonic mean should be used instead. These alternatives and the conditions under which each one is appropriate are discussed in Chapter 12. In particular, if a parameter is categorical, then the most frequent value, called mode, should be used. For example, if the destination addresses of packets are A, B, and C, the sum of addresses or average address has no meaning. Instead, most frequent destination should be specified. Of course, if the frequency of the mode is not significantly different from other values, top-two, top-three, or top-n values may be specified.

6.3 SPECIFYING DISPERSION

The average alone is not sufficient if there is a large variability in the data. Variability is commonly specified by the variance. It is denoted by s^2 and is computed as follows:

$$s^2 = \frac{1}{n-1} \sum_{i=1}^{n} (x_i - \overline{x})^2$$

The standard deviation s, which is the square root of the variance, is often more meaningful because it is expressed in the same units as the mean. The ratio of the standard deviation to the mean is called the **Coefficient Of Variation (C.O.V.)**.

Other alternatives for specifying variability are range (minimum and maximum), 10- and 90-percentiles, semi-interquartile range, and the mean absolute deviation. These alternatives and the conditions under which they are appropriate are discussed in Section 12.8.

A zero C.O.V. implies zero variance and indicates that the measured parameter is a constant. In this case, the average value gives the same information as the complete set. A high C.O.V. indicates high variance, in which case the mean is not sufficient. In fact, if the C.O.V. is high, it may be useful to look at the complete histogram, as discussed in the next section. Another alternative is to divide the users into different classes and take averages only for those users that have similar parameters.

Case Study 6.1 The resource demands of various programs executed on six university sites were measured for 6 months. The average demand by each program is shown in Table 6.1. Notice that the C.O.V. of the measured values are rather high, indicating that combining all programs into one class is not a good idea. Programs should be divided into several classes. Table 6.2 shows the average demand for all editors in the same data. The C.O.V. are now much lower.

TABLE 6.1 Workload Characterization Using Average Values

Data	Average	Coefficient of Variation
CPU time (VAX-11/780)	2.19 seconds	40.23
Number of direct writes	8.20	53.59
Direct-write bytes	10.21 kbytes	82.41
Number of direct reads	22.64	25.65
Direct-read bytes	49.70 kbytes	21.01

TABLE 6.2 Characteristics of an Average Editing Session

Data	Average	Coefficient of Variation
CPU time (VAX-11/780)	2.57 seconds	3.54
Number of direct writes	19.74	4.33
Direct-write bytes	13.46 kbytes	3.87
Number of direct reads	37.77	3.73
Direct-read bytes	36.93 kbytes	3.16

6.4 SINGLE-PARAMETER HISTOGRAMS

A histogram shows the relative frequencies of various values of a parameter. For continuous-value parameters, this requires dividing the complete parameter range into several smaller subranges called *buckets* (or *cells*) and counting the observations that fall in each cell. An example is shown in Figure 6.1 for CPU time and disk I/O. The results can also be presented in tabular form, as shown in Table 6.3. This data can then be used in a measurement or simulation model to generate a test workload. In analytical modeling, histograms can be used to fit a probability distribution and to verify that the distribution used in the model is similar to that observed in the histogram. The quantile-quantile plots discussed in Section 12.10 and several statistical tests described in Chapter 27 may be useful in determining and verifying the distribution.

Given n buckets per histogram, m parameters per component, and k components, this method requires presenting nmk numerical values. This may be too much detail to be useful. Thus, this should be used only if the variance is high and the averages cannot be used.

The key problem with using individual-parameter histograms is that they ignore the correlation among different parameters. For example, short jobs (jobs with small elapsed time) may create a lower number of disk I/O and may take a smaller amount of CPU time than long jobs. A test workload based on the single-parameter histograms may generate a job with short CPU time and a large number of disk I/Os—a situation generally not possible in a real

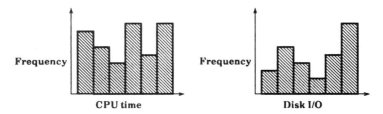

FIGURE 6.1   Single-parameter histograms of CPU time and disk I/O.

TABLE 6.3   Tabular Representation of a Single-Parameter Histogram

Program	CPU Time (milliseconds)				Number of Disk I/O			
	0–5	6–10	11–15	15+	0–20	21–40	41–60	60+
DOVERSEND	...	...	...	...	...	...	...	...
EMACS	...	...	...	...	...	...	...	...
MAIL	...	...	...	...	...	...	...	...
SCRIBE	...	...	...	...	...	...	...	...
PRESSIFY	...	...	...	...	...	...	...	...
DIRECTORY	...	...	...	...	...	...	...	...
TELNET	...	...	...	...	...	...	...	...

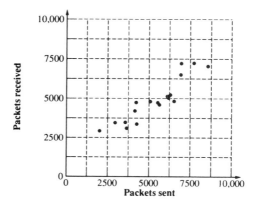

FIGURE 6.2   Two-parameter histogram.

workload. This problem is avoided by using multiparameter histograms, which are described next.

6.5   MULTIPARAMETER HISTOGRAMS

If there is a significant correlation between different workload parameters, the workload should be characterized using multiparameter histograms. An n-dimensional matrix (or histogram) is used to describe the distribution of n workload parameters.

Figure 6.2 shows an example of a simplistic plot of a two-parameter joint histogram. The number of frames sent and received by stations on a local-area network are plotted. Each dot in the figure represents a station. The number of dots in a square represents the number of stations that sent and received the frames in the range corresponding to the cell. Generally, the stations sending a large number of frames are also the ones that receive a large number of frames. Thus, there is a significant correlation between the two parameters.

It is difficult to plot joint histograms for more than two parameters. Also, as discussed before, even single-parameter histrograms are too detailed in some cases. Multiparameter histograms are even more detailed; they are therefore rarely used.

6.6   PRINCIPAL-COMPONENT ANALYSIS

One technique commonly used to classify workload components is by the weighted sum of their parameter values. Using a_j as weight for the jth parameter x_j, the weighted sum y is

$$y = \sum_{j=1}^{n} a_j x_j$$

This sum can then be used to classify the components into a number of classes such as low demand or medium demand. Although this technique is commonly used in performance analysis software, in most cases, the person running the software is asked to choose the weight. Without any concrete guidelines, the person may assign weights such that workload components with very different characteristics may be grouped together, and the mean characteristics of the group may not correspond to any member.

One method of determining the weights in such situations is to use the principal-component analysis, which allows finding the weights w_i's such that y_j's provide the maximum discrimination among the components. The quantity y_j is called the **principal factor**.[1] Statistically, given a set of n parameters $\{x_1, x_2, \ldots, x_n\}$, the principal-component analysis produces a set of **factors** $\{y_1, y_2, \ldots, y_n\}$ such that the following holds:

1. The y's are linear combinations of x's:

$$y_i = \sum_{j=1}^{n} a_{ij} x_j$$

Here a_{ij} is called the **loading** of variable x_j on factor y_i.
2. The y's form an orthogonal set, that is, their inner product is zero:

$$\langle y_i, y_j \rangle = \sum_k a_{ik} a_{kj} = 0$$

This is equivalent to stating that the y_i's are uncorrelated to each other.
3. The y's form an ordered set such that y_1 explains the highest percentage of the variance in resource demands, y_2 explains a lower percentage, y_3 explains a still lower percentage, and so forth. Thus, depending upon the level of detail required, only the first few factors can be used to classify the workload components.

Example 6.1 lists the key steps in finding principal factors and also illustrates them. The reader interested in further details of this technique should consult a book on factor analysis, for example, Harman (1976).

Example 6.1 The number of packets sent and received, denoted by x_s and x_r, respectively, by various stations on a local-area network were measured. The observed numbers are shown in the second and third columns of Table 6.4. A scatter plot of the data is shown in Figure 6.2. As seen from this figure, there is considerable correlation between the two variables. The steps in determining the principal factors are as follows:

---

[1] The correct term is principal component. However, to avoid confusion with workload components, the term *principal factor*, which has a slightly different meaning in factor analysis, is used here.

TABLE 6.4   Data for Principal-Component Analysis Example 6.1

Observation No.	Variables		Normalized Variables		Principal Factors	
	x_s	x_r	x_s'	x_r'	y_1	y_2
1	7718	7258	1.359	1.717	2.175	−0.253
2	6958	7232	0.922	1.698	1.853	−0.549
3	8551	7062	1.837	1.575	2.413	0.186
4	6924	6526	0.903	1.186	1.477	−0.200
5	6298	5251	0.543	0.262	0.570	0.199
6	6120	5158	0.441	0.195	0.450	0.174
7	6184	5051	0.478	0.117	0.421	0.255
8	6527	4850	0.675	−0.029	0.457	0.497
9	5081	4825	−0.156	−0.047	−0.143	−0.077
10	4216	4762	−0.652	−0.092	−0.527	−0.396
11	5532	4750	0.103	−0.101	0.002	0.145
12	5638	4620	0.164	−0.195	−0.022	0.254
13	4147	4229	−0.692	−0.479	−0.828	−0.151
14	3562	3497	−1.028	−1.009	−1.441	−0.013
15	2955	3480	−1.377	−1.022	−1.696	−0.251
16	4261	3392	−0.627	−1.085	−1.211	0.324
17	3644	3120	−0.981	−1.283	−1.601	0.213
18	2020	2946	−1.914	−1.409	−2.349	−0.357
$\sum x$	96,336	88,009	0.000	0.000	0.000	0.000
$\sum x^2$	567,119,488	462,661,024	17.000	17.000	32.565	1.435
Mean	5352.0	4889.4	0.000	0.000	0.000	0.000
Standard Deviation	1741.0	1379.5	1.000	1.000	1.384	0.290

1. *Compute the mean and standard deviations of the variables*:

$$\overline{x}_s = \frac{1}{n} \sum_{i=1}^{n} x_{si} = \frac{96{,}336}{18} = 5352.0$$

$$\overline{x}_r = \frac{1}{n} \sum_{i=1}^{n} x_{ri} = \frac{88{,}009}{18} = 4889.4$$

$$s_{x_s}^2 = \frac{1}{n-1} \sum_{i=1}^{n} (x_{si} - \overline{x}_s)^2$$

$$= \frac{1}{n-1} \left[\left(\sum_{i=1}^{n} x_{si}^2 \right) - n\overline{x}_s^2 \right]$$

$$= \frac{567{,}119{,}488 - 18 \times 5352^2}{17} = 1741.0$$

Similarly,

$$s_{x_r}^2 = \frac{462,661,024 - 18 \times 4889.4^2}{17} = 1379.5$$

2. *Normalize the variables to zero mean and unit standard deviation.* The normalized values x_s' and x_r' are given by

$$x_s' = \frac{x_s - \bar{x}_s}{s_{x_s}} = \frac{x_s - 5352}{1741}$$

$$x_r' = \frac{x_r - \bar{x}_r}{s_{x_r}} = \frac{x_r - 4889}{1380}$$

The normalized values are shown in the fourth and fifth columns of Table 6.4.

3. *Compute the correlation among the variables:*

$$R_{x_s,x_r} = \frac{(1/n)\sum_{i=1}^{n}(x_{si} - \bar{x}_s)(x_{ri} - \bar{x}_r)}{s_{x_s}s_{x_r}} = 0.916$$

4. *Prepare the correlation matrix:*

$$C = \begin{bmatrix} 1.000 & 0.916 \\ 0.916 & 1.000 \end{bmatrix}$$

5. *Compute the eigenvalues of the correlation matrix.* This is done by solving the characteristic equation. Using I to denote an identity matrix,

$$|\lambda I - C| = \begin{vmatrix} \lambda - 1 & -0.916 \\ -0.916 & \lambda - 1 \end{vmatrix} = 0$$

or

$$(\lambda - 1)^2 - 0.916^2 = 0$$

The eigenvalues are 1.916 and 0.084.

6. *Compute the eigenvectors of the correlation matrix.* The eigenvector q_1 corresponding to $\lambda_1 = 1.916$ is defined by the following relationship:

$$Cq_1 = \lambda_1 q_1$$

or

$$\begin{bmatrix} 1.000 & 0.916 \\ 0.916 & 1.000 \end{bmatrix} \times \begin{bmatrix} q_{11} \\ q_{21} \end{bmatrix} = 1.916 \begin{bmatrix} q_{11} \\ q_{21} \end{bmatrix}$$

or

$$q_{11} = q_{21}$$

Restricting the length of the eigenvector to 1, the following vector is the first eigenvector:

$$q_1 = \begin{bmatrix} \dfrac{1}{\sqrt{2}} \\ \dfrac{1}{\sqrt{2}} \end{bmatrix}$$

Similarly, the second eigenvector is

$$\mathbf{q}_2 = \begin{bmatrix} \dfrac{1}{\sqrt{2}} \\ -\dfrac{1}{\sqrt{2}} \end{bmatrix}$$

7. *Obtain principal factors by multiplying the eigenvectors by the normalized vectors:*

$$\begin{bmatrix} y_1 \\ y_2 \end{bmatrix} = \begin{bmatrix} \dfrac{1}{\sqrt{2}} & \dfrac{1}{\sqrt{2}} \\ \dfrac{1}{\sqrt{2}} & -\dfrac{1}{\sqrt{2}} \end{bmatrix} \begin{bmatrix} \dfrac{x_s - 5352}{1741} \\ \dfrac{x_r - 4889}{1380} \end{bmatrix}$$

8. *Compute the values of the principal factors.* These are shown in the last two columns of Table 6.4.

9. *Compute the sum and sum of squares of the principal factors.* The sum must be zero. The sum of squares give the percentage of variation explained. In this case, the sums of squares are 32.565 and 1.435. Thus, the first factor explains $32.565/(32.565 + 1.435)$, or 95.7%, of the variation. The second factor explains only 4.3% of the variation and can thus be ignored.

10. *Plot the values of principal factors.* The results are shown in Figure 6.3. Notice that most of the variation is along the first principal factor. The variation along the second factor is negligible.

The value of the factor y_1 can be used to classify the stations as low-, medium-, or high-load stations. Alternately, the pair (y_1, y_2) can be used to classify the stations, but the gain over using y_1 alone would be small.   □

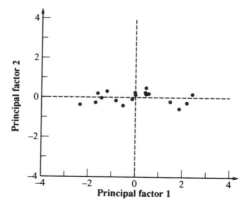

FIGURE 6.3 Packets sent and received data plotted along the principal-component axes.

6.7 MARKOV MODELS

Sometimes, it is important to have not only the number of service requests of each type but also their order. The next request is generally determined by the last few requests. If it is assumed that the next request depends only on the last request, then the requests follow a **Markov model**. Actually, the term is used in a more general sense of system states rather than for user requests. That is, if the next system state depends only on the current system state, the system follows a Markov model. Such models are commonly used in queueing analysis and are described in detail in Part VI. For now, it is sufficient to understand that such models can be described by a *transition matrix*, which gives the probabilities of the next state given the current state. For example, the transition probability matrix for a job's transition between the CPU, disk, and terminal is shown in Table 6.5. The corresponding state transition diagram is shown in Figure 6.4. After each visit to the CPU, the probability that the job will move to the disk is 0.3, the probability of it going to the terminal is 0.1, and so on.

Transition matrices are used not only for resource transitions but also for application transitions. For example, if the users in a software development environment run editors, compilers, linkers, and applications, a transition probability matrix can be used to characterize the probability of a user running software of type j after running the software of type i.

TABLE 6.5 Transition Probability Matrix

From/To	CPU	Disk	Terminal
CPU	0.6	0.3	0.1
Disk	0.9	0	0.1
Terminal	1	0	0

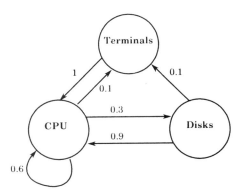

FIGURE 6.4 State transition diagram for a Markov model.

Transition matrices have also been used to specify page reference locality. In this case, the matrix entries specify the probability of the program referencing page (or module) i after referencing page (or module) j.

The transition probabilities give a more accurate picture of the order of requests than the frequency of requests. Given the same relative frequency of requests of different types, it is possible to realize the frequency with several different transition matrices. Each matrix may result in a different performance of the system. Therefore, in some cases it is important to measure the transition probabilities directly on the real system and to represent them in the workload model.

Example 6.2 Traffic monitoring on a computer network showed that most of the packets were of two sizes—small and large. The small packets constituted 80% of the traffic. A number of different transition probability matrices will result in an overall average of 80% of small packets. Two of the possibilities are as follows:

1. An average of four small packets are followed by an average of one big packet. A sample sequence, using s for small and b for big, is ssssb-ssssbssss. In this sequence, three of the four small packets are followed by another small packet. Also, every big packet is followed by a small packet. The corresponding transition probability matrix is

Current Packet	Next Packet	
	Small	Large
Small	0.75	0.25
Large	1	0

2. Another alternative is to generate a random number between 0 and 1. If the number is less than or equal to 0.8, generate a small packet; otherwise, generate a large packet. This assumes that the next packet size does not depend upon the current packet size. The transition probability matrix in this case is

Current Packet	Next Packet	
	Small	Large
Small	0.8	0.2
Large	0.8	0.2

If the performance of the network is affected by the order of the packet sizes, then measure the transition probabilities directly on the network along with the relative frequencies.   □

6.8 CLUSTERING

Generally, the measured workload consists of a large number of components. For example, several thousand user profiles may have been measured. For analysis purposes, it is useful to classify these components into a small number of classes or clusters such that the components within a cluster are very similar to each other. Later, one member from each cluster may be selected to represent the class and to study the effect of system design decisions on the entire class.

Figure 6.5 shows the CPU and disk I/O demands of 30 jobs. As shown, the jobs can be classified into five clusters. Thus, instead of using 30 jobs for each analysis, just 5 jobs can be used to represent the average resource demands of each cluster.

To characterize measured workload data using clustering, the steps are as follows:

1. Take a sample, that is, a subset of workload components.
2. Select workload parameters.
3. Transform parameters, if necessary.
4. Remove outliers.
5. Scale all observations.
6. Select a distance measure.
7. Perform clustering.
8. Interpret results.
9. Change parameters, or number of clusters, and repeat steps 3 to 7.
10. Select representative components from each cluster.

Each of these steps will now be discussed in detail.

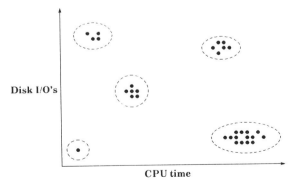

FIGURE 6.5 Hypothetical example of 30 jobs in five clusters.

6.8.1 Sampling

Generally, the number of components measured is too large to be used in the clustering analysis. Therefore, it is necessary to select a small subset. For example, several thousand user sessions may have been measured, but only a few hundred may be used in clustering analysis.

If sampling is done carefully, the components that were not used in clustering analysis will show behavior similar to those that were used in the analysis. In fact, at the end of the clustering exercise, one must try to assign each and every component to an appropriate cluster. The percentage of components not assignable to any cluster is a measure of sampling effectiveness.

One method of sampling is random selection. This results in a representative subset. However, if the goal of the workload characterization study is to design a workload for examining the impact of a particular device, for instance, a disk, only those components that are heavy consumers of the disk would provide meaningful information. Therefore, the components that top the list of consumers of that resource should be selected for workload characterization. Similarly, the most frequently used components should be selected if the goal of the study is to identify the components for better human interface and user training.

6.8.2 Parameter Selection

Each component has a large number of parameters (resource demands). Some of these parameters are important either because they belong to the bottleneck resource or to the most expensive resource. Less important parameters can be omitted from the clustering analysis, thereby reducing the analysis cost.

The two key criteria for selecting parameters are their impact on performance and their variance. Parameters that do not impact system performance should be omitted. For example, if the number of lines printed has no significant impact on the system performance, this parameter should be eliminated from the clustering analysis. The parameters that change little among clusters have no impact on clustering, and therefore, they can be omitted from the analysis.

One method to determine the minimum subset of parameters is to redo clustering with one less parameter and count the number of components that change their cluster membership. If the fraction of such components is small, the parameter can be removed from the list. Principal-component analysis, described in Section 6.6, can be used to identify the factors (and hence parameters) having the highest variance.

6.8.3 Transformation

If the distribution of a parameter is highly skewed, one should consider the possibility of replacing the parameter by a transformation or function of the parameter. For example, in one study, logarithmic transformation of CPU time was used because the analyst argued that two programs taking 1 and 2 seconds of CPU time are almost as different as those taking 1 and 2 milliseconds. Thus, the ratio of CPU time, rather than their difference, was considered more important. Several transformations and conditions under which they are appropriate are discussed in Section 15.4.

6.8.4 Outliers

The data points with extreme parameter values are called outliers, particularly if they lie far away from the majority of the other points. Such outliers can have a significant effect on the maximum or minimum values (or on the mean and variance) of parameters observed. Since these values are used in normalization (described next), their inclusion or exclusion may significantly affect the final results of clustering. Only those outlying components that do not consume a significant portion of the system resources should be excluded. Thus, for example, a disk backup program may make a number of disk I/O's that are an order of magnitude greater than these by other programs, so it cannot be excluded from a workload characterizing those sites where backups are done several times a day. On the other hand, it may be appropriate to exclude it if backups are done a few times per month.

6.8.5 Data Scaling

The final results of clustering depend heavily upon relative values and ranges of different parameters. It is therefore generally recommended that the parameter values be scaled so that their relative values and ranges are approximately equal. The four commonly used scaling techniques are as follows:

1. *Normalize to Zero Mean and Unit Variance*: Let $\{x_{1k}, x_{2k}, \ldots, x_{mk}\}$ be the measured values of the kth parameter. The scaled value x'_{ik} corresponding to x_{ik} is given by

$$x'_{ik} = \frac{x_{ik} - \overline{x}_k}{s_k}$$

   Here $\overline{x}_k$ and s_k are the measured mean and standard deviation of the kth parameter, respectively.

2. *Weights*:

$$x'_{ik} = w_k x_{ik}$$

   The weight w_k may be assigned depending upon the relative importance of the parameter or is inversely proportional to the standard deviation of the parameter values.

3. *Range Normalization*: The range is changed from $[x_{\min,k}, x_{\max,k}]$ to $[0,1]$. The scaling formula is

$$x'_{ik} = \frac{x_{ik} - x_{\min,k}}{x_{\max,k} - x_{\min,k}}$$

Here $x_{\min,k}$ and $x_{\max,k}$ are the minimum and maximum values, respectively, of the kth parameter. The main problem with this approach is that a few outliers can drastically impact $x_{\min,k}$ and $x_{\max,k}$ and hence the final outcome of clustering. This disadvantage is overcome by using percentiles rather than strict minimum and maximum, as discussed next.

4. *Percentile Normalization*: The data is scaled so that 95% of the values fall between 0 and 1:

$$x'_{ik} = \frac{x_{ik} - x_{2.5,k}}{x_{97.5,k} - x_{2.5,k}}$$

Here $x_{2.5,k}$ and $x_{97.5,k}$ are the 2.5- and 97.5-percentiles, respectively, of the kth parameter.

6.8.6 Distance Metric

Clustering analysis basically consists of mapping each component into an n-dimensional space and identifying components that are close to each other. Here n is the number of parameters. The closeness between two components is measured by defining a distance measure. Three methods that have been used are as follows:

1. *Euclidean Distance*: The distance d between two components $\{x_{i1}, x_{i2}, \ldots, x_{in}\}$ and $\{x_{j1}, x_{j2}, \ldots, x_{jn}\}$ is defined as

$$d = \left\{ \sum_{k=1}^{n} (x_{ik} - x_{jk})^2 \right\}^{0.5}$$

2. *Weighted Euclidean Distance*:

$$d = \sum_{k=1}^{n} \left\{ a_k (x_{ik} - x_{jk})^2 \right\}^{0.5}$$

Here a_k, $k = 1, 2, \ldots, n$, are suitably chosen weights for the n parameters.

3. *Chi-Square Distance*:

$$d = \sum_{k=1}^{n} \left\{ \frac{(x_{ik} - x_{jk})^2}{x_{ik}} \right\}$$

The Euclidean distance is the most commonly used distance metric. The weighted Euclidean is used if the parameters have not been scaled or if the parameters have significantly different levels of importance.

The chi-square distance is generally used in distribution fitting. In using this measure, it is important that the values x_k's be close to each other, that is, they have been normalized; otherwise, parameters with low values of x_k get higher weights.

6.8.7 Clustering Techniques

The basic aim of clustering is to partition the components into groups so the members of a group are as similar as possible and different groups are as dissimilar as possible. Statistically, this implies that the intragroup variance should be as small as possible and intergroup variance should be as large as possible. Fortunately, these two goals are redundant in the sense that achieving either one is sufficient. This is because

$$\text{Total variance} = \text{intragroup variance} + \text{intergroup variance}$$

Since the total variance is constant, minimizing intragroup variance automatically maximizes intergroup variance.

A number of clustering techniques have been described in the literature. These techniques fall into two classes: hierarchical and nonhierarchical. In nonhierarchical approaches, one starts with an arbitrary set of k clusters, and the members of the clusters are moved until the intragroup variance is minimum. There are two kinds of hierarchical approaches: agglomerative and divisive. In the agglomerative hierarchical approach, given n components, one starts with n clusters (each cluster having one component). Then neighboring clusters are merged successively until the desired number of clusters is obtained. In the divisive hierarchical approach, on the other hand, one starts with one cluster (of n components) and then divides the cluster successively into two, three, and so on, until the desired number of clusters is obtained. A popular technique known as minimum spanning tree method is described next.

6.8.8 Minimum Spanning Tree Method

This is an agglomerative hierarchical clustering technique, which starts with n clusters of one component each and successively joins the nearest clusters:

1. Start with $k = n$ clusters.
2. Find the centroid of the ith cluster, $i = 1, 2, ..., k$. The centroid has parameter values equal to the average of all points in the cluster.
3. Compute the intercluster distance matrix. Its (i, j)th element is the distance between the centroids of cluster i and j. Any distance measure described in Section 6.8.6 can be used.
4. Find the smallest nonzero element of the distance matrix. Let d_{lm}, the distance between clusters l and m, be the smallest. Merge clusters l and m. Also merge any other cluster pairs that have the same distance.
5. Repeat steps 2 to 4 until all components are part of one cluster.

Example 6.3 illustrates these steps.

Example 6.3 Consider a workload with five components and two parameters. The CPU time and the number of disk I/O's were measured for five programs. The parameter values after scaling are as shown in Table 6.6.

TABLE 6.6   Data for Clustering Example 6.3

Program	CPU Time	Disk I/O
A	2	4
B	3	5
C	1	6
D	4	3
E	5	2

Step 1: Consider five clusters with ith cluster consisting solely of the ith program.

Step 2: The centroids are $\{2,4\}$, $\{3,5\}$, $\{1,6\}$, $\{4,3\}$, and $\{5,2\}$. These are shown by the five points in Figure 6.6.

Step 3: Using the Euclidean distance measure, the distance matrix is

			Program		
Program	A	B	C	D	E
A	0	$\sqrt{2}$	$\sqrt{5}$	$\sqrt{5}$	$\sqrt{13}$
B		0	$\sqrt{5}$	$\sqrt{5}$	$\sqrt{13}$
C			0	$\sqrt{18}$	$\sqrt{32}$
D				0	$\sqrt{2}$
E					0

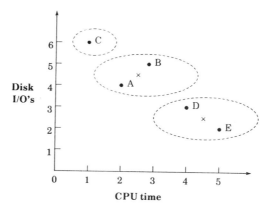

FIGURE 6.6   Clustering example.

Step 4: The minimum intercluster distance is $\sqrt{2}$ between A and B and between D and E. These two pairs are therefore merged.

Step 2: The centroid of cluster pair AB is $\{(2+3)\div2,(4+5)\div2\}$, that is, $\{2.5, 4.5\}$. Similarly, the centroid of pair DE is $\{4.5, 2.5\}$. The other centroids are the same as before.

Step 3: There are three clusters now, as shown in Figure 6.6, and the distance matrix is

	Program		
Program	AB	C	DE
AB	0	$\sqrt{4.5}$	$\sqrt{8}$
C		0	$\sqrt{24.5}$
DE			0

Step 4: The minimum intercluster distance is $\sqrt{4.5}$ between AB and C. These two clusters are therefore merged.

Step 2: The centroid of cluster ABC is $\{(2+3+1)\div3,(4+5+6)\div3\}$, that is, $\{2,5\}$.

Step 3: The distance matrix is

	Program	
Program	ABC	DE
ABC	0	$\sqrt{12.5}$
DE		0

Step 4: The minimum intercluster distance is $\sqrt{12.5}$. The merger of ABC and DE results in a single cluster ABCDE.   □

The results of the clustering process can be represented as a spanning tree called a **dendrogram**. Each branch of the tree represents a cluster and is drawn vertically to a height where the cluster merges with neighboring clusters. The spanning tree for Example 6.3 is shown in Figure 6.7. Components A and B merge at a height of $\sqrt{2}$. Components D and E also merge at the same height. The next merger is shown to occur at a height of $\sqrt{4.5}$ when AB merges with C. Finally, at $\sqrt{12.5}$ all five components merge into one cluster.

The purpose of drawing the spanning tree is to be able to obtain clusters for any given maximum allowable intracluster (or equivalently minimum allowable intercluster) distance. A horizontal line drawn at the specified height cuts the spanning tree at the desired clusters. For example, if the maximum allowable intracluster distance is 3, a horizontal line (shown broken in Figure 6.7) drawn

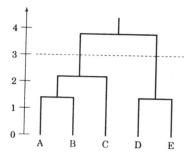

FIGURE 6.7   Dendrogram (spanning tree) for the clustering example.

at this height cuts the two branches of the tree representing clusters ABC and DE.

6.8.9   Cluster Interpretation

After obtaining the clusters, one should assign all measured components to the clusters. Clusters with very small populations can be discarded, particularly if the total resource demands of all members of the cluster have an insignificant impact on the system performance. Notice that the importance of the cluster is measured primarily by its total resource demands and not by the population size. A cluster having one component but using 50% of the system resources cannot be discarded regardless of its small size.

The next step is to interpret clusters in functional terms. If a majority of the components in a cluster belong to a single application environment, for example, a business application, it is helpful to name the cluster accordingly. Since the components of the cluster have similar resource demands, it is generally possible to label clusters by their resource demands, for example, CPU bound or I/O bound.

Finally, one or more representative components from each cluster are selected for use as a test workload in performance studies. The number of representatives can be proportional to the cluster size, to the total resource demands of the cluster, or to any combination of the two.

6.8.10   Problems with Clustering

Clustering has been used successfully to characterize workloads in many environments. However, unless it is done very carefully, it is possible to get conflicting conclusions from the same data.

The first problem with clustering is related to the definition of the goal itself. In general, the goal is to minimize the intracluster variance or maximize the intercluster variance. Figure 6.8 shows four different plots for two parameters. In each case, there are two natural clusters. However, in each case, minimization of variance would lead to final clusters that are quite different from those visible to the eye.

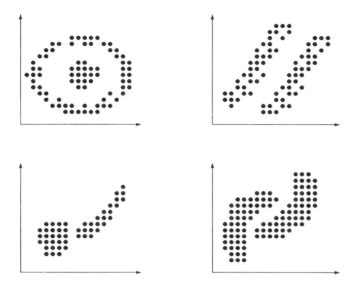

FIGURE 6.8 Problems with clustering.

Clustering is better than random selection of programs. However, the results of clustering are highly variable. There are no rules for selection of parameters, distance measure, or scaling. A different choice of any of these may lead to a totally different set of clusters and, hence, different conclusions.

Although the final step in clustering is to label each cluster by functionality, it is difficult in some cases. For example, in one study, editing programs appeared in 23 different clusters. It may have been more meaningful to characterize an average editing program rather than to characterize 23 clusters having no functional meaning.

Clustering is not very helpful if the goal is to compare the workload at different sites. Each site results in a different set of clusters, which cannot be compared with other sites.

Finally, clustering is a laborious process requiring many repetitions of the analysis and consuming a lot of system resources such as storage space.

EXERCISES

6.1 The CPU time and disk I/O's of seven programs are shown in Table 6.7. Determine the equation for principal factors.

6.2 Using a spanning-tree algorithm for cluster analysis, prepare a dendrogram for the data shown in Table 6.7. Interpret the result of your analysis.

TABLE 6.7   Data for Exercises 6.1 and 6.2

Program Name	Function	CPU Time	I/O's
TKB	Linker	14	2735
MAC	Assembler	13	253
COBOL	Compiler	8	27
BASIC	Compiler	6	27
Pascal	Compiler	6	12
EDT	Text editor	4	91
SOS	Text editor	1	33

CHAPTER 7

MONITORS

That which is monitored improves.
—Source unknown

A **monitor** is a tool used to observe the activities on a system. In general, monitors observe the performance of systems, collect performance statistics, analyze the data, and display results. Some also identify problem areas and suggest remedies.

Monitors are used not only by performance analysts but also by programmers and systems managers. Some of the reasons to monitor a system are as follows:

- A system programmer may use a monitor to find the frequently used segments of the software and optimize their performance.
- A systems manager may use a monitor to measure resource utilizations and to find the performance bottleneck.
- A systems manager may also use a monitor to tune the system. The system parameters can be adjusted to improve the performance.
- A systems analyst may use a monitor to characterize the workload. The results may be used for capacity planning and for creating test workloads.
- A systems analyst may use a monitor to find model parameters, to validate models, and to develop inputs for models.

In summary, monitoring is the first and key step in performance measurements.

7.1 MONITOR TERMINOLOGY

This section describes some of the monitor-related terms that are frequently used.

- **Event**: A change in the system state is called an event. Examples of events are process context switching, beginning of seek on a disk, and arrival of a packet.
- **Trace**: A trace is a log of events usually including the time of the event, the type of event, and other important parameters associated with the event.
- **Overhead**: Most monitors slightly perturb the system operation. They may consume system resources, such as CPU or storage. For example, the data collected by the monitor may be recorded on the secondary storage. This consumption of system resources is called overhead. One of the goals of monitor design is to minimize the overhead. Sometimes, the term **artifact** is also used to denote the overhead.
- **Domain**: The set of activities observable by the monitor is its domain. For example, accounting logs record information about CPU time; number of disks, terminals, networks, and paging I/O's; number of characters transferred among disks, terminals, networks, and paging device; and elasped time for each user session. These constitute the domain of the accounting logs.
- **Input Rate**: The maximum frequency of events that a monitor can correctly observe is called its input rate. Generally, two input rates are specified: burst mode and sustained. Burst-mode rate specifies the rate at which an event can occur for a short duration. It is higher than the sustained rate, which the monitor can tolerate for long durations.
- **Resolution**: The coarseness of the information observed is called the resolution. For example, a monitor may be able to record time only in units of 16 milliseconds. Similarly, the size of buckets used in a histogram may determine the resolution of the histogram.
- **Input Width**: The number of bits of information recorded on a event is called the input width. This, along with the input rate, determines the storage required to record the events.

7.2 MONITOR CLASSIFICATION

Monitors are classified based on a number of characteristics, such as the implementation level, trigger mechanism, and result displaying ability.

Depending upon the level at which a monitor is implemented, it is classified as a software monitor, hardware monitor, firmware monitor, or hybrid monitor. The hybrid is a combination of hardware, firmware, or software. This is the most common classification.

Depending upon the mechanism that triggers the monitor into action, a monitor may be classified as event driven or timer driven (sampling monitor). An **event-driven** monitor is activated only by the occurrence of certain events. Thus, there is no monitoring overhead if the event is rare. But if the event is frequent, it may cause too much overhead. The **sampling monitor** is activated at fixed time intervals by clock interrupts. Sampling monitors are ideal for observing frequent events. On activation, the monitor records device status registers and counters. The frequency of sampling is determined by the event frequency and the desired resolution.

Another way to classify monitors is according to their result displaying ability. **On-line monitors** display the system state either continuously or at frequent intervals. **Batch monitors,** on the other hand, collect data that can be analyzed later using a separate analysis program.

All three of the preceding classifications can be used together to characterize a monitor. For example, a particular monitor may be classified as a hybrid-sampling-batch monitor.

7.3 SOFTWARE MONITORS

Software monitors are used to monitor operating systems and higher level software such as networks and databases. At each activation, several instructions are executed, and therefore, they are suitable only if the input rate is low. For example, if the monitor executes 100 instructions per event, each activation would take 0.1 millisecond on a 1-MIPS machine. Thus, to limit the overhead to 1%, it should be activated at intervals of 10 milliseconds or more. That is, the input rate should be less than 100 events per second.

There are a few monitoring applications for which overhead is not an issue. For example, in an instruction-tracing monitor, every single-user instruction executed may be interrupted and followed by several hundred monitor instructions. This is acceptable if the increase in execution time does not have any impact on the path of execution or the instruction frequency. However, if the time between two successive instructions was being monitored, this type of monitor would not be appropriate.

Software monitors generally have lower input rates, lower resolutions, and higher overhead than hardware monitors. However, they have higher input widths and higher recording capacities than hardware monitors. They are easier to develop and easier to modify, if necessary.

7.3.1 Issues in Software Monitor Design

This section covers some of the design issues that occur during the design of software monitors.

1. *Activation Mechanism*: The first decision that a software monitor designer has to make is how to trigger the data collection routine. Three mechanisms have been used in the past:

(a) Trap instruction

(b) Trace mode

(c) Timer interrupt

The first mechanism is to instrument the system software with trap instructions at appropriate points in the code. The trap instruction is a software interrupt mechanism that transfers control to a data collection routine. The effect of the trap instruction is very similar to that of a subroutine call. In fact, if a trap instruction is not available on a processor, a call instruction would generally be used instead. The event-trace monitor described by Tolopka (1982) is an example of this approach. The monitor measures elapsed time for various operating system services using trap instructions at the beginning and at the end of the service code. Thus, to measure I/O service time, a trap instruction placed at the beginning of the I/O service-call-handling routine enables the monitor to record the time clock. After finishing the I/O, another trap instruction reads the clock, subtracts the beginning value, and thus obtains the time spent in the service routine.

The second mechanism is that of changing the processor to the trace mode. In this mode, which is available on many processors, the instruction execution is interrupted after every instruction, and the control is passed on to a data collection routine. This method has a very high overhead and is used only for those monitoring applications where time between events is not to be measured. For example, this approach can be used to develop an instruction-trace monitor to produce a program counter histogram (a histogram of instruction addresses). The monitor records the address (program counter) and returns control to the user program.

The final mechanism is that of a timer interrupt. A timer-interrupt service provided by the operating system is used to transfer control to a data collection routine at fixed intervals. This mechanism, called sampling, is specially suitable for frequent events since the overhead is independent of the event rate. The overhead per activation, input width, and rate of variation of the sampled quantity determine the desired sampling rate. If a counter is being sampled, the sampling should be done so that the probability of counter overflows between sampling is minimized.

2. *Buffer Size*: Most software monitors record data in buffers, which is later written onto disk or magnetic tape for storage. The size of the buffers should be large so that the frequency of writing onto the secondary storage is minimized. The size should be small so that the time lost per writing operation is not too large and so the effect of reduced memory available for system usage is not perceptible. Thus, the optimal buffer size is a function of the input rate, input width, and emptying rate.

3. *Number of Buffers*: Buffers are usually organized in a ring so that the recording (buffer-emptying) process follows the monitoring (buffer-

filling) process as closely as possible. If there is only one buffer, the two processes cannot proceed simultaneously, and monitoring may have to be stopped while recording is in progress. Thus, a minimum of two buffers is required for continuous, simultaneous operation. Generally, the number of buffers is much higher to allow for variation in the filling and emptying rate.

4. *Buffer Overflow*: In spite of multiple buffers per ring, there is always a finite probability that all buffers become full. The monitoring process is required to either overwrite a previously written buffer or stop monitoring until a buffer becomes available. In either case, some information is lost. If a buffer is overwritten, the relatively old information is lost. Whereas if the monitoring is blocked, new information is lost. Thus, the choice between the two alternatives depends upon the value of old versus new information. In either case, the fact that the buffer overflow occurred should be recorded.

A similar problem occurs when a counter (used to count the events) overflows. The choice is to keep the counter *stuck at* the highest value or to reinitialize it. The fact that counter overflow occurred should also be recorded.

5. *Data Compression or Analysis*: It is possible for the monitor to process the data as it is observed. This helps reduce the storage space required as the detailed data need not be stored. However, it adds to the monitor overhead.

6. *On/Off Switch*: Most hardware monitors have an on/off switch that enables/disables the monitoring operation. A software monitor should similarly have conditional (IF … THEN …) statements so that the monitoring can be enabled/disabled easily. Since monitoring does add to the system overhead, it should be possible to disable the monitor when it is not being used. Also, a software monitor usually requires modification of system codes, which may introduce bugs. The on/off switch helps during monitor development and debugging.

7. *Language*: Most monitors are written in a low-level system programming language, such as assembly, Bliss, or C, to keep the overhead at a minimum. Since a software monitor is usually a part of the system being monitored, it is better to write both in the same programming language.

8. *Priority*: If the monitor runs asynchronously, its priority should be low so that key system operations are least affected. However, if timely observation and recording of events is important, the priority should be high so that the delay in its execution does not cause a significant skew in the time values recorded.

9. *Abnormal-Events Monitoring*: A monitor should be able to observe normal as well as abnormal events on the system. Examples of abnormal events include system initialization, device failures, and program failures. In fact, if both cannot be accommodated, users may often prefer

to monitor abnormal events at a higher priority than normal events. This is because abnormal events occur at a lower rate and impose less monitoring overhead than normal events. The abnormal events also help the user take preventive action long before the system becomes unavailable.

7.4 HARDWARE MONITORS

A hardware monitor consists of separate pieces of equipment that are attached to the system being monitored via probes. No system resources are consumed in monitoring. Thus, hardware monitors generally have lower overhead than software monitors. Their input rate is also higher. Further, the probability of their introducing bugs into the system operation is generally lower than that of software monitors.

A number of general-purpose hardware monitors are available on the market. They consists of the following elements:

1. *Probes*: High-impedance probes are used to observe signals at desired points in the system hardware.
2. *Counters*: These are incremented whenever a particular event occurs.
3. *Logic Elements*: Signals from many probes can be combined using AND, OR, and other logic gates. The combinations are used to indicate events that may increment the counters.
4. *Comparators*: These can be used to compare counters or signal values with preset values.
5. *Mapping Hardware*: This allows histograms of observed quantities to be computed. It consists of multiple comparators and counters.
6. *Timer*: Used for time stamping or for triggering a sampling operation.
7. *Tape/Disk*: Most monitors have built-in tape/disk drives to store the data.

The monitor manufacturers also supply *probe-point libraries* for various systems that can be observed when using the monitor. Each library contains a list of points on the system where the probes can be attached and explains the signal that is observed.

Hardware monitors have gone through several generations of development. Originally, the monitors contained wired control logic. The next generation contained mapping hardware with memory and comparators. Today's monitors are intelligent in that they are programmable and contain their own processor, memory, and I/O devices.

7.5 SOFTWARE VERSUS HARDWARE MONITORS

Given a monitoring problem, should a hardware monitor or a software monitor be used? The choice is not as difficult as it may appear. For most applications, only one of the two types of monitors will be satisfactory.

The first step in selecting the monitor is to consider what needs to be measured. Hardware monitors can sense electrical signals on the busses and can accurately record them even at high speed. However, it is difficult for them to determine higher level information, such as queue lengths or current user, unless the information is easily available in a hardware register. Software monitors, conversely, can easily determine the higher level information but cannot easily observe low-level events, such as time to fetch an operation code for an instruction. Examples of variables that can be observed by both types of monitors are device utilizations and CPU-I/O overlap.

The second consideration is the input rate, the rate at which events have to be observed. Hardware monitors can record events very quickly. A software monitor, on the other hand, may require a few hundred instructions per observation and so cannot be used if the interevent time is small.

The time resolution required is the next consideration. A hardware monitor has a separate hardware clock and can provide time resolution in a few nanoseconds. The software monitors use the system clock, which typically has a resolution of a few milliseconds.

The expertise of the performance analyst also should be taken into consideration in selecting the monitor. Only an analyst with a good knowledge of the system hardware can correctly use a hardware monitor. A software monitor, on the other hand, requires an intimate knowledge of the system software to be instrumented.

The amount of data recorded directly affects the overhead of a software monitor. If the amount is expected to be huge, a hardware monitor with built-in secondary storage may be used.

A software monitor, by its nature, is sequential in that it cannot record several simultaneous events (unless the software is distributed). For example, if several devices request service from the processor and post an interrupt, the interrupts will be serviced sequentially and will be observed by the software monitor sequentially. Hardware monitors have several probes that can record simultaneous events.

Software monitors consume system resources that would otherwise be available to the users. A hardware monitor, on the other hand, consumes little, if any, of the system resources. Its presence may or may not be visible to the system.

Most hardware monitors are designed to be attached to a variety of systems. Thus, the same monitor can be used to monitor systems from different vendors or systems using different operating systems. Software monitors are developed specifically for a particular hardware and software base and cannot be easily ported across vendors.

A hardware monitor keeps observing the system even when it is malfunctioning, and thus, it can be used to debug the system. A software monitor may not be able to observe correctly during malfunctions, and it may not run at all when the system is down.

TABLE 7.1   Comparison of Hardware and Software Monitors

Criterion	Hardware Monitor	Software Monitor
Domain	Difficult to monitor operating system events.	Difficult to monitor hardware events unless recognizable by an instruction.
Input rate	Sampling rates of 10^5 per second possible.	Sampling rate limited by the processor MIPS and overhead required.
Time resolution	10 nanoseconds is possible.	Generally 10 to 16 milliseconds.
Expertise	Requires intimate knowledge of hardware.	Requires intimate knowledge of software.
Recording capacity	Limited by memory and secondary storage. Not a problem currently.	Limited by overhead desired.
Input width	Can record several simultaneous events.	Cannot record several simultaneous events unless there are multiple processors.
Monitor overhead	None	Overhead depends upon the input rate and input width. Less than 5% adequate and more than 100% possible.
Portability	Generally portable.	Specific to an operating system.
Availability	Monitoring continues even during system malfunction or failure.	Cannot monitor during system crash.
Errors	Possible to connect the probes to wrong points.	Once debugged, errors are rare.
Cost	High	Medium

Both hardware and software monitors can have bugs that can introduce errors into the measured data. However, with software monitors, once the software has been thoroughly debugged, errors are rare. With a fully debugged hardware monitor, it is possible to misplace probes.

Finally, and most importantly, hardware monitors are more expensive than software monitors. This fact alone may be sufficient to bias the choice in many cases.

The issues of hardware versus software monitors are summarized in Table 7.1.

7.6   FIRMWARE AND HYBRID MONITORS

Firmware monitors are implemented by modifying the processor microcode. These are useful for applications that fall between the software and hardware monitoring boundaries. In most respects, firmware monitors are similar to software monitors. However, since the microcode space is limited and there are tighter timing limitations, firmware monitors generally do very limited data reduction, if any. They are useful in applications where the timing considerations preclude the use of software monitors and inaccessability of probe points preclude the use of hardware monitors.

Firmware monitors have been used for network monitoring where existing network interfaces can be easily microprogrammed to monitor all traffic on the network. Another application suitable for firmware monitors is generating address profiles of microcode (micro-PC histograms). These profiles are used for optimizing the code.

A monitor using a combination of software, hardware, or firmware is a hybrid monitor. Software monitors have good data reduction capabilities, while hardware monitors have high resolution. Thus, a hybrid monitor, consisting of a hardware data-gathering component together with a software data reduction component, provides the best of both worlds.

An example of a hybrid monitor is the Diamond monitor described by Hughes (1980). The hardware part of the monitor consists of a board placed in the system cabinet. It can observe all traffic on the system bus. The software part can read instruction addresses, processor modes, and system and user identifications. The two parts can communicate through device status and control registers. The monitor has been used to generate address histograms, address traces, instruction traces, and others.

7.7 DISTRIBUTED-SYSTEM MONITORS

Most of the computer systems today are distributed and consist of many hardware and software components that work together separately and concurrently. Monitoring a distributed system is more difficult than monitoring a centralized system. In particular, the monitor itself must be distributed and should consist of several components that work separately and concurrently. In this section, the design issues and terminology related to such monitors are discussed. The discussion is based on an actual case study to design a network monitor. Although many of the examples in this section are from networks, the discussion is general and applies to all distributed systems, such as multicomputer systems and distributed database systems. Most of the discussion also aplies to nondistributed systems.

The easiest way to understand various components of a distributed-system monitor is to divide various functions in the monitor into a number of layers. Figure 7.1 shows such a layered view. Each layer makes use of the services provided by the lower layers and extends the available facilities to the upper layer. The layers are first briefly introduced. Later, each layer is discussed in detail. Proceeding from the bottom of Figure 7.1, the layers are as follows:

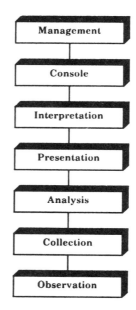

FIGURE 7.1   Layered view of a distributed-system monitor.

1. *Observation*: This layer gathers raw data on individual components of the system. Generally, each component may have an observer designed specifically for it. Thus, there may be several observers located on different subsystems.
2. *Collection*: This layer collects data from various observers. It is possible to have more than one collector on large systems.
3. *Analysis*: This layer analyzes the data gathered at various collectors. It may consist of various statistical routines to summarize the data characteristics. Simple analysis such as counting of events is done most efficiently in the observer and is not considered part of the analyzer.
4. *Presentation*: This component of the monitor deals with human user interface. It produces, for example, reports, displays, and alarms.
5. *Interpretation*: This refers to the intelligent entity (usually a human being or an expert system) that can make meaningful interpretations of the data. This generally requires multiple rules and trend analyses. Simple threshold-based alarms may be considered part of the presenter rather than of the interpreter, which usually requires the application of more sophisticated rules.
6. *Console*: This component provides an interface to control the system parameters and states. Strictly speaking, console is not a part of the monitor. However, the monitoring and control functions are often used

together, and it is desirable to allow system control as well as system observation facilities to be used together.

7. *Management*: The entity that makes the *decision* to set or change system parameters or configurations based on interpretation of monitored performance is called the **manager**. The manager implements its decision using a console. A software manager component exists only in monitors with automated monitoring and control facilities.

A monitor may consist of multiple (zero or more) components from each of the layers. Thus, as shown in Figure 7.2, it may consist of zero or more observers, collectors, analyzers, presenters, interpreters, consoles, and managers.

There is a *many-to-many* relationship between successive layers. For example, a single observer may send data to multiple collectors, and a single collector may gather data from multiple observers. Similar many-to-many relationships exist between collectors and analyzers, analyzers and presenters, presenters and interpreters, and so forth.

Most distributed-system monitors are hybrid and make use of software, hardware, and firmware as well as human beings. The observers may be implemented using software, hardware, or firmware. Collectors, analyzers, and pre-

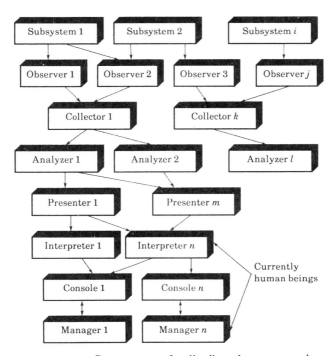

FIGURE 7.2 Components of a distributed-system monitor.

senters are usually implemented in software. The console may be a software package that can be called from any user workstation, or it can be a hardware component with special switches, knobs, and displays. The interpreters and managers are usually human beings, but as the system understanding improves, it should be possible to automate these functions.

The layers will now be described in more detail.

7.7.1 Observation

The bottom layer of the monitor, called **observation**, is concerned with raw-data gathering. Three commonly used data observation mechanisms are implicit spying, explicit instrumenting, and probing.

Implicit spying is the first and least intrusive monitoring technique. It requires promiscuously observing the activity on the system bus or network link. This technique is often used to monitor local-area networks in which all stations can hear all conversations, and one station is designated to be the observer. The advantage is that there is almost no impact on the performance of the system being monitored.

Implicit-spying observers are often accompanied by one or more *filters* that allow the monitor to decide which activities to record. Not all data observed in a system may be of interest at all times. The filters help decide whether to keep a record of an observed event or to ignore it. The filters generally consist of conditional expressions set by the monitor user. The conditions may be, for example, Boolean, arithmetic, or set membership.

Explicit instrumenting requires incorporating trace points, probe points, hooks, or counters in the system. This approach causes some overhead on the system and is used to augment the data obtained from implicit observing. Each component in the system that needs to be monitored may have to be instrumented differently. However, it helps to have a standard data-naming and reporting format so that other monitor components making use of this data can get it and use it in a device-independent manner.

Probing requires making "feeler" requests on the system to sense its current performance. For example, in a computer network, a specially marked packet sent to a given destination and looped back by the destination may provide information about queueing at the source, at intermediate bridges, the destination station, and back. This information is useful in determining the current load level on a path. It may also be used for diagnostic and reliability analysis.

Although there is considerable overlap in the domain of activities that can be observed using the three mechanisms, they are not totally redundant. There are activities that can be observed only by one of the three mechanisms. For example, requests to nonexistent devices may be observed only by implicit spying on the system bus. Explicit instrumentation is required to observe events internal to a component. Probing provides cumulative information about a number of components, which may be used by the feeler request. Therefore, in most systems, one would use a combination of the three data-observing mechanisms discussed above and pass the data to collectors, which are discussed next.

7.7.2 Collection

The data-gathering component of the monitor is called a collector. For example, in a computer system, separate data observers may be used for the processor, I/O, and networking devices. In a computer network, each computer may have its own observer. The collector provides a repository for the data collected at several observers.

In a distributed system, it is possible to have several users monitoring the system simultaneously. Each monitor may have its own collector. But all collectors share the same set of observers. Observing generally causes higher overhead as compared to collecting, so it is not desirable to have multiple observers per component. This is also the reason for separating the observation from the collection layer.

The problem of communication between m collectors and n observers is similar to the popular client-server problem. There are two well-known solutions to this problem. These are called **advertising** and **soliciting**, respectively. Advertising consists of observers sending the data on a system bus or a shared medium in such a form that all collectors can receive it. In tightly coupled systems, it is also possible to put it in a shared memory segment that can be accessed by all collectors and observers. Soliciting requires that each collector send queries to each observer and get the data individually. The queries may be sent periodically or only on occurrence of certain events.

Depending upon the level of hierarchy in the system being monitored, the collectors may operate at one or more layers. For example, in monitoring a large network, it is possible to divide the network into several subnetworks, each of which consists of several stations. The network collectors may obtain data from subnetwork collectors, which in turn may obtain data from observers on each station.

When collecting data from several observers, clock synchronization often becomes an important issue. Time stamps from different observers cannot be compared unless the observers' clocks are close to each other within some tolerance. The tolerance or maximum allowed clock skew is often related to the round-trip delay. In systems distributed over a large geographic area, the delay and hence the clock skews can be large. The monitored data should be used for performance analysis only if the data is aggregated over an interval that is much larger than the maximum skew. For example, if the maximum skew is a few milliseconds, per-second and per-minute summaries can be used.

In addition to gathering data from various observers, the collectors may store past data. Therefore, the various buffering and sampling issues discussed in Section 7.3.1 under software monitor design issues apply to collector design as well.

7.7.3 Analysis

The analyzer does somewhat more sophisticated analysis as compared to simple operations in the observer. The key criteria for determining which functions should be placed in the analysis layer are frequency, data required, complexity of the function, and the number of instances.

The frequency of events and the timeliness of an analysis dictate whether the analysis should be put in the observer or the analyzer. Operations such as time stamping and counting have to be done quickly in a short amount of time, particularly if the input rate (frequency of events) is high. Analyses that require too much time, for example, computation of means, variances, and standard deviation, should be done infrequently and, hence, in the analyzer.

The amount of data required for an analysis also dictates whether it should be in the observer or the analyzer. For example, to determine the link with the highest error rate, the errors at each and every link in a network should be observed. Errors observed at one station are not sufficient. This function, therefore, cannot be put in the observer. It has to be in the analyzer.

Complexity of the function limits the frequency with which it can be done. If a function is too complex, it may be better to simply record the events in the observer and analyze them later in the analyzer, if necessary.

The next criterion is the number of observers and analyzers. Many observer functions are always active, for example, counting of service requests received and number of errors detected. The analysis, on the other hand, is done infrequently. In most cases, the counters are hardly ever looked at. Also, there are more observers in a network than there are analyzers. Thus, the goal should be to simplify the observers as much as possible and to push complexity into the analyzer, which is invoked infrequently.

7.7.4 Presentation

The presentation layer deals with user interface. It is designed to allow the user to communicate its requests to the monitor and to make it easy for the user to understand the responses provided by the monitor. This layer is very closely tied to the applications for which the monitor is used. For example, it may be used for performance monitoring, configuration monitoring, or fault location. Individual applications are discussed later. First, issues that apply to more than one application are described. In particular, the issues of presentation frequency, hierarchical presentation, and alarm mode are discussed.

The first presentation issue in the design of a monitor is that of presentation frequency. The monitor user should be able to get a capsule summary of any specified interval in the past. In particular, the users should be able to get hourly, daily, weekly, and monthly summaries. These summaries should be organized such that a daily summary could be obtained from the hourly summaries, a weekly summary could be obtained from daily summaries, and so on. Thus, it would not be necessary to keep the detailed information on file. The summary kept in the monitor will, in general, be slightly more detailed than the one presented to the user.

The presentation should be structured in a manner similar to the structure of the system being monitored. For example, a network consists of many subnetworks, routers, and bridges. A subnetwork may consist of several segments with several stations on each segment. A user should be able to get a summary at any level of hierarchy. The user should be able to get a report for the whole network, for any subnetwork, for any router, for any segment, for any station, and so on. Again, it would be desirable to keep summaries in such a form that summaries for higher levels in the hierarchy can be obtained from those in the lower levels.

The alarm mode of presentation eases the task of system managers by notifying them only if a prespecified condition(s) occurs. Examples of such conditions are oversaturation of resources, error rates above a specified threshold, loss of key components, and security threats, for example, unidentified new nodes joining the network.

A general notification facility may activate a user-specified process if a performance or error threshold is exceeded or if a particular configuration change is detected. The user process can then ring a bell, send a message to a terminal, send a mail message, or automatically dial a telephone call.

The presentation layer would generally run on a user workstation. It may utilize interfaces, such as windows or menus, provided by the operating system. It is important to ensure that the presentation interface is portable and is independent of the operating system. A user should be able to use similar monitoring requests from any workstation.

The presentation layer determines the user friendliness of the monitor. It should be designed such that it expects minimum user intelligence. The user need not be aware of the current system configuration or even the current monitor configuration. The monitor should learn the system and the monitor configurations automatically, if possible.

The monitor should be able to run interactively or in the background mode. Most system managers want the system to be observed continuously and use the monitor interactively only when a problem is sensed. Thus, batch mode as well as interactive mode operation of the monitor should be possible.

Some monitors allow callable interfaces so that extensions can be easily built on top of the functions provided by the monitor.

The preceding issues are general and apply to all applications of the monitor. There are a number of presentation issues that apply to specific applications of a monitor. Three key applications of the monitor are related to the speed, accuracy, and availability of the services provided by the system. These are termed performance monitoring, error monitoring, and configuration monitoring, respectively. The presentation issues related to each of these applications will now be described.

1. *Performance Monitoring*: Performance monitoring helps to quantify the quality of service when the service is provided correctly. The users are generally interested in observing the system performance in terms of throughput, response time, and utilization of various resources. They may also be interested in seeing summary statistics of various events on the system. Depending upon the frequency of occurrence of each event and their importance, the summary statistics may consist of counts, class counts (or histograms), or a time-stamped trace.

   A monitor can simply count all service requests regardless of their type. It can categorize a request into several classes based on the type and then count the number for each class. This is called a class count or histogram. The monitor can sort these class counts in decreasing order and present only the top 10. It can present other statistical characteristics of the class counts, for example, average, standard deviation, and histogram. The monitor can also prepare a time-stamped trace of requests to be analyzed by other programs.

2. *Error Monitoring*: The error is defined as the "incorrect performance." The system appears to be operating, accepting user requests, and performing the service, but the end result is not what the user wanted. A monitor should provide the error statistics, counts, class counts, or traces in a manner similar to that described under performance statistics. The error statistics on various components of the system may be sorted to determine the unreliable parts of the system.

3. *Configuration Monitoring*: Configuration monitoring relates to the non-performance of the system components. It allows the user to determine which components are up. A monitor can determine this by promiscuous observation of traffic on the system bus or on the broadcast network medium by polling the components or by sending a marked packet. A monitor should record system initializations and any configuration changes due to components joining or leaving the configuration. The user can get a count, class count, or a trace of these events. The class count is generally that of interevent time—the interval for which the component was up or down.

   Often incremental configuration information is more useful than knowing the full configuration. Such information includes a list of subsystems that were added or dropped from the system. Also useful is the list of subsystems that are not on a list prepared by the system manager. This facility may be used, for example, on a network to identify unknown stations joining the network.

   The systems manager should be able to scope the configuration monitoring to any part of the system—the whole system, a single subsystem, or a set of subsystems.

7.7.5 Interpretation

The interpretation of data requires a set of rules on which the interpreter makes judgments about the probable state of the system. This requires building an expert system to warn the systems manager about probable faults before they occur or asking the manager to change system parameters.

7.7.6 Console Functions

Console functions allow the systems manager to change system parameters, reconfigure the system, and bring system components up or down. Remote console functions allow a remote diagnostic link to the system. Although console functions are not an essential part of a monitor, they are activated as a result of the data provided by the monitor. It is easier for the systems manager to be able to get feedback (monitor) and apply control (console) from the same location. Unfortunately, often consoles and monitors are designed and sold by different vendors, and their activation from the same workstation may not be possible.

EXERCISES

7.1 For each of the following measurements list the type of monitor that can and cannot be used. Which type of monitor would you prefer and why?

   a. Interrupt response time

   b. Instruction opcode frequency

   c. Program reference pattern

   d. Virtual memory reference pattern in a multiprogramming system

   e. CPU time required to send one packet on a network

   f. Response time for a database query

7.2 For each of the following environments, describe how you would implement a monitor to produce a program counter histogram:

   a. Using a hardware monitor

   b. Using a software monitor on an IBM PC with the CPU having a trace bit.

   c. Using a software monitor on a TRS-80 with the CPU not having a trace bit.

7.3 Choose a computer system or subsystem. Assume that prototypes of systems you selected already exist and you have decided to measure their performance. Make a list of quantities, if any, that you could measure using a

   a. Software monitor

   b. Hardware monitor

   c. Firmware monitor

In each case, describe how performance metrics of interest to you could be calculated using the quantities measured. Discuss how you would resolve some of the issues you would face in using or designing a monitor for your system.

CHAPTER 8

PROGRAM EXECUTION MONITORS AND ACCOUNTING LOGS

> *Measurements are not to provide numbers but insight.*
> —Ingrid Bucher

There are two monitors that deserve special discussion since they are used so frequently. Program execution monitors, also known as program optimizers or program execution analyzers, are software monitors designed to observe application software. They help improve the performance of the programs.

Most computer systems keep an accounting log where the resources used by the users and their processes are recorded. Although the primary aim of such logs is for accounting and billing, they are also a good source of information about resource usage.

The issues related to design and use of these two monitors are the topics of this chapter.

8.1 PROGRAM EXECUTION MONITORS

There are many reasons for monitoring the execution of a program. Some of these are the following:

- *Tracing*: To find the execution path of a program.
- *Timing*: To find the time spent in various modules of the program.
- *Tuning*: To find the most frequent or most time-consuming sections of the code.

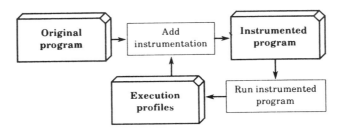

FIGURE 8.1   Steps in program execution monitoring.

- *Assertion Checking*: To verify the relationships assumed among the variables of a program.
- *Coverage Analysis*: To determine the adequacy of a test run.

Notice that not all applications of program execution monitors are related to the program's performance, although that may be the most common use of these monitors.

The programs to be monitored and improved should be chosen based on a number of criteria. The first criterion is the time criticality. Some programs are very time critical, and it is important to find out where the time is being spent so that the response can be improved. The second criterion is frequency of use. Programs used with high frequency should be optimized first. Finally, programs consuming the highest percentage of resources should be optimized. The resources include CPU time, I/O time, or elapsed (people) time. The most expensive resource should be optimized first. With the decreasing cost of computing resources, the people time is becoming the most expensive resource and may need to be optimized first.

Figure 8.1 shows the typical steps involved in program execution monitoring. First, instrumentation (or hooks) are added to the target program. The instrumented program is then run under the control of the execution monitor. Finally, the reports generated by the monitor are examined. Often the procedure is repeated several times and new instrumentation is added as more information about the execution profile of the program is obtained.

8.1.1   Issues in Designing a Program Execution Monitor

In designing an execution monitor, most of the issues to be considered are similar to those discussed in Section 7.3.1 on software monitor design. In addition, there are a number of issues that are specific to program execution monitors. These issues are as follows:

1. *Measurement Unit*: The execution monitor divides the program into smaller measurement units such as modules, subroutines, high-level language statements, or machine instructions. The data related to the execu-

tion of each unit is recorded and shown in the final report. The lower the level of the unit, the more the overhead of monitoring. Lower level reports (such as machine instruction execution profiles) may be too detailed for some applications. Some monitors use higher level language statements, such as COBOL or PL/I statements, as a measurement unit, but then they also become language dependent. As a result, a program written in a mix of languages may not be correctly observed by such monitors.

2. *Measurement Technique*: The two basic measurement techniques are tracing and sampling. Tracing can be performed by using either explicit hooks such as trap instructions or by the trace mode of the processor. Using the trace mode produces too much unwanted data and is suitable only for monitors operating at machine instruction level. The sampling monitors make use of the system timer facilities and record the program states at periodic intervals. The interval may be specified in terms of CPU time or in terms of elapsed time. If CPU time sampling is used, the program is always found in the execution state. On the other hand, if elasped time sampling is used, the program may be in a wait state, waiting for I/O completion or for some other event.

3. *Instrumentation Mechanism*: A program has to be compiled and linked before it can be executed. The instrumentation can be added before compilation, during compilation, after compilation (before linking), or during run time. In other words, a program can be instrumented by augmenting the source code, the compiler-generated object code, the run time environment, the operating system, or the hardware. Often, a combination of these techniques is used. Source code instrumentation requires the addition of high-level procedure call statements at strategic locations in the program. The call statements transfer control to the monitor routines, which collect the data. Run time instrumentation is accomplished by adding a sampling monitor to the run time environment of the program.

   Execution monitors may also make use of additional information. For example, the link-edit map produced by the linker is an excellent source of symbol-to-address map that is used by most execution monitors.

4. *Profile Report*: Most program monitors produce an execution profile showing a frequency and time histogram. For large programs, several summaries at different levels of hierarchy may be presented; for example, summaries by modules, and then for each module by procedures, and for each procedure by statements. The procedure profiles may distinguish between resources used directly by a procedure and those used by a subprocedure that was invoked by it. For CPU time, these resources are called **self-time** and **inherited time**, respectively. Many monitors have the ability to limit or expand (zoom in or zoom out) the amount of detail.

Having designed a program execution monitor and used it to monitor a set of critical programs, the next issue that an analyst may face is to suggest ways to improve the performance of the programs. This issue is discussed next.

8.2 TECHNIQUES FOR IMPROVING PROGRAM PERFORMANCE

The three common techniques of program optimization are code optimization, I/O optimization, and paging optimization. The code optimization consists of finding the dynamic frequency of execution of various program modules and optimizing the code of most frequently used modules. The I/O optimization usually consists of combining several I/O requests into larger records, changing the file access method, and caching or prefetching data. Paging optimization consists of observing the page reference pattern and reorganizing program segments so that the paging activity is minimized. Box 8.1 lists a number of techniques for writing high-performance programs and for improving the performance of existing programs.

8.3 ACCOUNTING LOGS

Accounting logs, although not primarily developed for monitoring, are classified as software monitors because they provide useful information about system usage and performance, and they can often be used as substitutes for monitors. Before starting to develop a monitor, one should look at the logging facilities built into the system. Often, a new monitor is not necessary.

The main advantage of accounting logs is that they are built in. No extra effort is required to develop them. Most of the data is already collected during normal operation. The overhead is generally small, so data collection can be performed for long periods of time. Further, the data reflects real-system usage.

The main disadvantage of accounting logs is that the log analysis programs are not usually supplied. Since the analysis needs are different in each case, most systems convert the log into a generally readable format or produce an overall summary. Additional analysis programs have to be written by the analysts themselves. A general-purpose statistical analysis package may be useful for detailed analysis.

The data in the logs may not be at the desired level of granularity. For example, a distribution of I/O sizes is generally not available from the logs. Only the total number of blocks read or written may be available. Further, often the only resource usages that are recorded are those charged to the user. For example, if terminal I/O's are not charged, a record of them may not be kept in the logs.

The accuracy of logs is also low. The resource usage not chargeable to any particular user is distributed either evenly among or randomly to users. For example, CPU time spent in servicing interrupts may be charged to the

Box 8.1   Techniques for Improving Program Performance

1. Optimize the common case. The most frequently used path should also be the most efficient. A procedure should handle all cases correctly and common cases efficiently.

2. Arrange a series of IF statements so that the most likely value is tested first.

3. Arrange a series of AND conditions so that the condition most likely to fail is tested first.

4. Arrange entries in a table so that the most frequently sought values are the first to be compared.

5. Structure the main line of the program so that it contains the most frequent path of the program. Errors and exceptions should be handled separately.

6. Question the necessity of each instruction in the main (time-critical or most frequent) path of the code.

7. Trade memory space for processor time wherever possible. If a function is computed more than once, compute it once and store the result. Some functions with parameters can be replaced by a table of precomputed values.

8. Use hints. Keeping a fast but possibly inaccurate hint along with a slow but robust algorithm may save time in most cases.

9. Cache the data that is accessed often. However, one must ensure that there is sufficient locality before using caches.

10. Unroll short loops. Save the cost of modifying and testing loop indexes.

11. Replace searches by direct indexing, wherever possible. In some cases, this may require more space than minimum.

12. Use the same size for data fields that need to be compared or added together.

13. Use the full word widths of the computer to evaluate expressions. For example, use 32 bits on a 32-bit computer even if you need only 31.

14. Align data fields on word boundaries, wherever possible.

15. Evaluate items only when needed, particularly if it is likely that it will not be needed.

16. Initialize data areas during run time only when used. Wherever possible, the values should be initialized at the compile time.

17. Use algebraic identities to simplify conditional expressions.

(Continued)

Box 8.1   Continued

18. Replace threshold tests on monotone (continuously nondecreasing or continuously nonincreasing) functions by tests on their parameters, thereby avoiding the evaluation of the function.

19. Evaluate variables not changing in a loop before entering the loop.

20. Combine two nearby loops if they use the same set of conditions.

21. Use shifts in place of multiplication and division by powers of 2.

22. Keep the code simple. Simpler programs are more efficient.

23. Block I/O requests together to reduce the number of I/O operations.

24. Preload small disk files into tables in memory.

25. Use multiple buffers for files to allow prefetching.

26. Link the most frequently used procedures together to maximize the locality of reference.

27. Reference data in the order stored. Arrays stored by columns should be referenced by columns.

28. Store data elements that are used concurrently together.

29. Store subroutines in sequence so that calling and called subroutines will be loaded together.

30. Align I/O buffers to page boundaries.

31. Open files that are used together in sequence so that buffers will be located together.

32. Pass simple subroutine arguments by value rather than by reference, wherever possible.

33. Pass large arrays and other data structures to subroutines by reference rather than value.

34. Separate read-only code areas from read-write data areas to minimize the number of page-writes.

user active at the time of the interrupt, even though the interrupt may be for another user not currently active.

Finally, most accounting logs contain no system-level information, such as queue lengths or device utilizations. The elapsed time includes service as well as queueing time at various resources along with the user think times. It is not possible to separate the effects of queueing (system-level phenomenon) from user service demands. Many programs, including most editors, frequently wait for user input throughout execution. The accounting logs do not record the time spent waiting for user inputs. Thus, there is no way to distinguish between this delay and queueing delay.

In spite of these disadvantages, accounting logs are used extensively for performance analysis.

TABLE 8.1   Typical Data Recorded by Accounting
Utilities

Name of the program
Program start time: date and time of the day
Program end time: date and time of the day
CPU time used by the program

Number of disk writes
Total disk write bytes
Number of disk reads
Total disk read bytes

Number of terminal writes
Total terminal write bytes
Number of terminal reads
Total terminal read bytes

Number of page-read I/O's to the paging device
Number of pages read from the paging device
Number of page faults

8.4   ANALYSIS AND INTERPRETATION OF ACCOUNTING LOG DATA

The data recorded in the logs consists primarily of resource usage: CPU time, elapsed time, number and total size of disk I/O, paging I/O's, terminal I/O's, network I/O's, and so forth. The data may consist of system wide resource usage, resources used by each program, or resources used by each user session. In addition, abnormal conditions such as security violations, abnormal job terminations, system restarts, downtimes, and device errors are also recorded in these logs.

Table 8.1 lists some of the workload parameters recorded in the accounting logs. In the table, the page faults and page-read I/O's are listed separately because in many operating systems, pages are prefetched and every page fault does not require an access to the paging device. It is possible to derive a number of other data items from these that can provide useful information about the workload. These data items and their usages are described in this section. This discussion assumes that the accounting log records data for each program activation. In other words, the workload unit or workload components are programs. The discussion is general and applies to other workload units such as users, jobs, sites, and applications.

For each program, many different data items can be calculated. In particular, all resource consumptions can be expressed in four ways:

• Per activation

• Percentage of total resources consumed by all programs

- Per-second resource consumption rate
- Per-CPU-second resource consumption

These derived quantities can then be interpreted as follows:

Per-activation data is the average resource consumption per activation of the program. This information is useful for performance analysts in modeling program behavior and in constructing synthetic workloads.

Percentage of total resource consumption is the resource consumed by all activations of a particular program, expressed as a percentage of the total resources consumed by all activations of all programs. For example, if the percentage of total disk I/O's for program A is 10%, it indicates that 10% of all disk I/O's on the system can be attributed to program A. To developers and product managers, the percentage of total data items shows the opportunity that different programs offer for reducing consumption of that resource. If the programs are sorted in order of decreasing percentage of total consumption of a particular resource, the programs on the top of the list will have a high impact and the programs on the bottom of the list will have little impact. Thus, if program A consumes only 0.01% of the total CPU, it may not be worthwhile to devote manpower to optimize this program for better CPU efficiency. Since elapsed time is also people time, programs with a high percentage of total elapsed time may provide high potential for improvements in worker productivity.

The percentage of total data items are also of interest to performance analysts. Analysts interested in analyzing a particular resource, for instance, a disk, should include in their workload programs consuming a high percentage of that resource. For example, an analyst interested in studying a remote-disk server should choose programs observed to consume a high percentage of disk I/O's. Programs consuming only, for instance, 0.01% of disk I/O's, even though performing poorly on a system with a remote-disk server, will have little impact on the total system performance. Similarly, programs with a high percentage of total CPU time should be used to analyze the impact of new CPUs. Similarly, programs with a high percentage of total terminal I/O's should be used to analyze the impact of new terminal devices, remote-terminal front ends, and network links connecting the terminals. Programs with a high percentage of total faults should be used to study new virtual memory schemes.

Per-second resource consumption rates are obtained by dividing the resource consumption by the elapsed time. These rates indicate the intensity of resource usage by the various programs. They can be used to calculate approximately the number of users that can be supported without making the resource a bottleneck. A higher number of users will increase the response time beyond the observed value. For example, disk I/O operations per second and disk I/O bytes per second determine the disk utilization or network link utilization in systems with remote-disk servers. System planners can use this information to determine the number and type of the disks required. Analysts and customers can use it to find out the programs that cause disks to become bottleneck. Similarly, a high CPU rate (CPU time per second) indicates highly compute-bound programs. A small number of highly compute-bound programs may saturate the CPU. Terminal I/O's per second and terminal I/O bytes per second indicate utilization of terminals, remote-terminal front ends, and network links to these front ends.

Per-CPU-second resource consumption is obtained by dividing the resource consumption by the CPU time consumed. Per-CPU-second consumption is less variable than per-second consumption. This is because the elapsed time depends heavily on the system load, which varies widely over time. Each CPU second represents the execution of a certain number of instructions. Per-CPU-second data, therefore, gives an idea of resource demand per instruction of the program. For example, "page faults per CPU second" gives the number of instructions per page fault. Similarly, "page-read operations per CPU second" indicates the number of instructions between successive page-read operations. Performance analysts can use this data to compare their synthetic workloads with those measured on the system.

Per-CPU-second resource consumption also represents the ratio of the resource demand to CPU demand. Programs with higher per-CPU-second resource consumptions tend to impose higher demands on the particular resource than the CPU, and they tend to make the resource the bottleneck. For these programs, therefore, the maximum number of simultaneous users is determined by the capacity of the corresponding resource. For example, the programs with high disk I/O per CPU second are generally disk bound; the maximum number of simultaneous users of such programs on a system is determined by the throughput of the disk.

Finally, a word about the number and amount of I/O's. Depending upon the I/O device, the number of I/O operations or the total bytes transferred may be more meaningful. For disk devices in which seeks take much longer than data transfer, which is the case with practically all disk devices, the disk time depends heavily on the number of I/O's and is not influenced by the size of the I/O. On the other hand, for some mass storage devices, setup (seek and rotational latency) time is less than the transfer time. In such cases, the number of bytes transferred provides more meaningful information than the number of I/O's. Similar arguments hold for terminal I/O's and paging operations.

8.5 USING ACCOUNTING LOGS TO ANSWER COMMONLY ASKED QUESTIONS

There are two ways to organize a doctor's prescription manual. One would be to list the diseases for each medicine. This is what has been done so far by describing how the data can be analyzed and what information can be obtained from each data item. Another alternative, probably a more useful one, is to list prescriptions for each disease. That is, given a performance question, which data items from the accounting log should be examined? This section, therefore, restates the information described in the previous section in a different manner. Given next are some examples of the commonly asked questions that can be answered using the accounting logs.

- *Which programs should the programmers be trained to use more efficiently? Or which programs provide the highest opportunity for better human interface?* The programs with a high percentage of total elapsed time provide the best opportunity for training as well as better human interface. For example, the data indicated that one-third of the active time in universities was being spent editing. The universities may be able to improve productivity by training their users in efficient use of the editors.

- *Which programs are good candidates for code optimization? Or which programs should be included in a workload to be used in analyzing a new CPU's performance?* The programs with a high percentage of total CPU time will have the highest impact on CPU usage. For developers, these programs offer the opportunity for code optimization. For analysts, these programs provide the programs to be included in their workloads for CPU analysis. In the observed data, the programs with a high percentage of total CPU time were mostly compilers and editors.

- *Which programs offer the highest opportunities for code restructuring to minimize the page faults?* The programs with a high percentage of total page faults, a high percentage of total page-read operations, or a high percentage of total pages read provide opportunities for the highest impact on page-read operations. These programs do not necessarily have poor paging behavior. However, even a small improvement in their paging behavior will have a significant impact on the system.

- *Which programs have a poor locality of reference?* The programs with high "page faults per CPU second" have a poor locality of reference. These programs might benefit from code restructuring. However, given a set of limited resources, greater benefits at the system level would be obtained by restructuring programs with a high percentage of total page faults.

- *How many jobs can run simultaneously without undue performance degradation?* The CPU rate (CPU time per second) as observed on a system with desired performance can be used to calculate the number of simultaneous users provided the program is compute bound. For non-compute-bound programs, the device with the highest utilization determines the number of supportable users.

- *Which programs are I/O bound?* The programs with high "disk I/O's per CPU second" generally impose more load on the disk than on the CPU. These programs are I/O bound, and their performance depends critically on the performance of the disk. Such programs are good candidates for I/O optimization.

The following case study illustrates the type of information that can be obtained from accounting logs.

Case Study 8.1   This case study illustrates the application of accounting logs. The data was collected at six different universities for a period of 6 months. There was a variety of types of installations: instructional, research, and administrative. Several installations had substantial use in more than one category. Two interesting observations from the data were as follows:

1. *There are more disk reads than writes. Similarly, there are more terminal writes than reads.* The ratios of reads to writes were as follows:

For Disk I/O		
Number of writes	to number of reads	1:3
Size of writes	to size of reads	1:2.5
Total write bytes	to total read bytes	1:7.5
For Terminal I/O		
Number of writes	to number of reads	2:1
Size of writes	to size of reads	4:1
Total write bytes	to total read bytes	8:1

Although the ratios may be different for other environments, the following inequalities should generally hold:

Number of disk writes < Number of disk reads

Size of disk writes < Size of disk reads

Number of terminal reads < Number of terminal writes

Size of terminal reads < Size of terminal writes

The argument is as follows. Disk reads are performed automatically by the computer. Disk writes, on the other hand, require either the creation of new information or modification of the old information. Human intervention is generally required. Humans read more and write less (be it a book or a memo or a data file). The creation of new information is therefore slow and always in smaller quantities than use of the old information. This reasoning, which is called the **law of slow creation,** explains why disk reads would be generally more frequent than disk writes and why disk reads would be larger in size than disk writes.

In the case of terminal reads and writes, a similar argument follows, although in reverse direction. Terminal writes are done automatically by the computer. Terminal reads, on the other hand, require human intervention. Thus, by the law of slow creation, terminal reads would be slower and smaller in size than terminal writes.

2. *About one-third of user time was spent on editors.* This clearly shows the importance of editing. At all installations, a substantial portion of the users' time and system resources were devoted to editing. At installations making use of full-screen editors, the resource usage was considerably greater than at those using line-oriented editors. Since there appears to be a strong trend toward more extensive use of full-screen editors, it seems safe to assume that editing will continue to be a major workload ingredient and will probably even increase in importance. The educational institutions should therefore give good training to the students in using the editors. This will have significant impact on user productivity.

□

EXERCISE

8.1 Using accounting log data, how would you answer the following questions:

a. Which programs should be used to analyze a new terminal concentrator?

b. How many program X users can be supported with a given disk device?

c. Is a benchmark representative?

d. Which programs should be chosen for I/O optimization?

CHAPTER 9

CAPACITY PLANNING AND BENCHMARKING

Do not plan a bridge capacity by counting the number
of people who swim across the river today.
—Heard at a presentation

One of the important problems for managers of data processing installations is **capacity planning**, which requires ensuring that adequate computer resources will be available to meet the future workload demands in a cost-effective manner while meeting the performance objectives. The term **capacity management** is used to denote the problem of ensuring that the currently available computing resources are used to provide the highest performance. Thus, capacity management is concerned with the present while capacity planning is concerned with the future.

The alternatives for capacity planning usually consist of procuring more computing resources, while the alternatives for capacity management consist of adjusting usage patterns, rearranging configuration, and changing system parameters to maximize the performance. The process of adjusting system parameters to optimize the performance is also called **performance tuning**.

To compare the performance of two competing systems in an objective manner, benchmarks are run on these systems using automatic load drivers. The mistakes and games of benchmarking as well as the issues related to load drivers are discussed in this chapter.

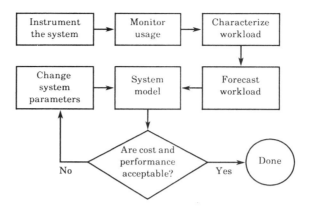

FIGURE 9.1   Steps in capacity planning process.

9.1   STEPS IN CAPACITY PLANNING AND MANAGEMENT

Figure 9.1 shows the steps in the capacity planning process. For planning as well as management, the steps are basically same:

1. Instrument the system.
2. Monitor system usage.
3. Characterize workload.
4. Predict performance under different alternatives.
5. Select the lowest cost, highest performance alternative.

The first step is to ensure that there are appropriate counters and hooks in the system to record current usage. In most cases, the counters already built in the operating systems, application software, and I/O devices are used. Use of accounting log data is probably the most popular method. The second step consists of monitoring the usage and characterizing the workload. This requires gathering data for a period of time and analyzing and summarizing it in a form so that it can be used as input to a system model for performance prediction.

For capacity management, the current configuration and workload are input into a tuning model that advises changes in a system parameter setting. This model is either a detailed simulation of the system or contains a set of rules developed specifically for the system. For example, one of the rules may be to advise balanced placement of files if a highly skewed usage of disk devices is seen.

For capacity planning, first the workload is forecasted based on long-term monitoring of the system. Then different configuration alternatives and future workloads are input to a model that predicts performance. This later step of equipment selection is also called **sizing**. The models for sizing are generally less detailed than tuning models. Often, analytic modeling techniques such as queueing models are used for sizing since the list of alternatives includes a wide variety of new hardware and software components for which detailed models may not yet exist. Thus, while the tuning models are detailed and system specific, the planning models are coarse and system independent or at least less system specific. In many sites, simple rules of thumb, such as demand increasing by a factor x every y years, are used for long-term planning. In many installations, the future workload is so unknown that more sophisticated prediction techniques may not be of great help.

9.2 PROBLEMS IN CAPACITY PLANNING

Most of the capacity planning literature deals with selecting performance metrics, monitoring techniques, workload characterization, forecasting, and modeling techniques. Since each of these issues is discussed in different parts of this book, the discussion here is limited to the list of problems faced by capacity planners. These problems are discussed next.

1. *There is no standard terminology.* Every vendor of capacity planning tools has a different definition of capacity management, capacity planning, sizing, tuning, and so on. Often one buys a capacity planning tool only to find out later that it does only tuning or sizing and has no workload measurement or characterization facilities. Some vendors use the term *capacity management* to include both capacity planning and tuning. Others use it to denote tuning only.

2. *There is no standard definition of capacity.* There are several possibilities. One definition of capacity, in terms of the maximum throughput, was presented in Section 3.3. Throughput is measured in requests per unit time, for example, jobs per second, Transactions Per Second (TPS), Instructions Per Second (MIPS), or bits per second (for network links). Another possibility is to define capacity as the maximum number of users that the system can support while meeting a specified performance objective. In this definition, *users* is only an example of what has been termed *workload unit*. Other workload units are sessions, tasks, activities, programs, jobs, accounts, projects, and so on, and the capacity is expressed in these units. Workload units are also called workload components.

3. *There are a number of different capacities for the same system.* In Section 3.3, three capacities—nominal capacity, usable capacity, and knee capacity—were described. Other capacity terms that have been used in the literature are practical capacity (usable capacity) and theoretical capacity (nominal capacity).

4. *There is no standard workload unit.* The problem with measuring capacity in workload units, such as users or sessions, is that it requires a

detailed characterization of the workload unit that varies from one environment to the next. It is because of this difficulty that the workload-independent capacity measures, such as MIPS, are still popular. System managers forecast and plan for their future in terms of their MIPS requirements.

5. *Forecasting future applications is difficult.* Most of the forecasting is based on the assumption that the future trend will be similar to the past. This assumption is violated if a new technology suddenly emerges. For example, many old predictions based on mainframe usage are no longer valid due to the introduction and popularity of low-cost workstations. A number of new applications have also become possible due to the high-performance computing capacity available at the desk.

6. *There is no uniformity among systems from different vendors.* The same workload takes different amounts of resources on different systems. This requires developing a vendor-independent benchmark and running it on different systems. Also, separate models (simulation or analytical) have to be developed for each system. It is possible to inadvertently introduce bias at any of these stages.

7. *Model inputs cannot always be measured.* Simulation or analytical models are used to predict the performance under different alternatives. Sometimes the inputs required for the model are not accurately measurable. For example, "think time" is commonly used in analytical models. In a real environment, the time between successive commands from the user may include thinking as well as other interruptions such as coffee breaks. It is almost impossible to correctly measure think time.

   Determining model inputs becomes even more difficult if the monitoring tool, workload analysis tool, and modeling tools are from different vendors. The output of one step may not be in a format usable by the next step.

8. *Validating model projections is difficult.* There are two types of model validations. The first type, **baseline validation**, requires using the current workload and configuration in the model and verifying that the model output matches the observed system performance. The second validation, called **projection validation**, requires changing the workload and configuration and verifying that the model output matches the changed real system's performance. While it is easy to change inputs to a model, it is difficult to control the workload and configurations on a real system. For this reason, projection validations are rarely performed. Without projection validations, the use of the model for capacity planning is suspect.

9. *Distributed environments are too complex to model.* Initial computer systems consisted of only a few components. Each component was expensive enough to justify the cost of accurately modeling its behavior.

Also, the number of users on the system was large. Thus, even though each user's behavior is highly variable, the aggregate performance of all users did not vary that much and could be modeled accurately. In distributed environments of today, the system consists of a large number of semi-autonomous clients, servers, network links, and I/O devices. Workstation usage is very different from others, and the interactions are also rather complex. Also, the cost of individual components is not high enough to justify accurate modeling.

10. *Performance is only a small part of the capacity planning problem.* The key issue in capacity planning is that of cost, which includes the cost of the equipment, software, installation, maintenance, personnel, floor space, power, and climate control (cooling, humidity control). Performance modeling helps only in sizing the equipment. However, as the cost of computer hardware is declining, these other costs are becoming dominant and have become a major consideration in capacity planning.

In spite of the problems listed above, capacity planning continues to be an important problem to be faced by a computer installation manager. Fortunately, a number of commercial capacity planning tools are available in the marketplace. Many of these tools have built-in models of specific systems and include workload analyzers that understand the accounting logs of the systems. Some also have built-in monitors.

9.3 COMMON MISTAKES IN BENCHMARKING

Benchmarking, the process of running benchmarks on different systems, is the most common method to compare the performance of two systems for capacity planning and procurements. Following is a list of mistakes that have been observed repeatedly in this process. Like mistakes discussed in other sections of this book, these mistakes are a result of inexperience or unawareness on the part of the analysts. The games, which are tricks played consciously by experienced analysts, are listed in Section 9.4.

1. *Only Average Behavior Represented in Test Workload*: A test workload is designed to be representative of the real workload. The workload designers ensure that the relative resource demands are similar to those observed in the real environments. However, only the average behavior is represented. The variance is ignored. For example, the average number of I/O's or average CPU time in the test workload may be similar to those in the real workload. A distribution, such as uniform, exponential, or constant, may be picked arbitrarily without any validation. Constant values are undesirable since they can cause synchronizations leading to faulty conclusions. In some cases, variance or even a more detailed representation of the resource demands is required.

2. *Skewness of Device Demands Ignored*: The I/O requests are commonly assumed to be evenly distributed among all I/O devices. In practice, the I/O requests may follow a train behavior such that all successive I/O's may access the same device leading to higher queueing times. Ignoring this skewness for I/O requests and for network requests leads to lower response time predictions and may not show device bottlenecks that may occur in real environments.

3. *Loading Level Controlled Inappropriately*: The test workloads have several parameters that can be changed to increase the load level on the system. For example, the number of users can be increased, the think time of the users can be decreased, or the resource demands per user can be increased. These three options do not have the same results. The most realistic way is to increase the number of users, but in measurements this requires more resources [more Remote-Terminal Emulators (RTEs) or more storage space in a simulation] and so the other two alternatives may be used. Changing the think time is the easiest alternative but is not equivalent to the first alternative since the order of requests to various devices is not changed; hence, the cache misses may be much lower than those in a system with more users. The third alternative changes the workload significantly, and it may no longer be representative of the real environment.

4. *Caching Effects Ignored*: Caches are very sensitive to the order of requests. In most workload characterization studies, the order information is totally lost. Even matching the average and variance of resource demands does not ensure that the cache performance will be similar to that in a real environment. In modern systems, caching is used for accesses to memory, disks, as well as networks. It has become more necessary than before to closely model the order of arrivals.

5. *Buffering Sizes Not Appropriate*: The buffer sizes have a significant impact on the performance of I/O and networking devices. For example, in some cases, a 1-byte change in the buffer size may double the number of network messages. The size and number of buffers are generally system parameters, and their values in experimental systems should represent the values used in production systems.

6. *Inaccuracies due to Sampling Ignored*: Some of the data collected for workload characterization is gathered using sampling, where in a number of state indicators the counters are read periodically. Sometimes, this can lead to significant errors in measurements, as shown in the following example.

Example 9.1   A device whose utilization is 1% is sampled every second for 10 minutes. During this period, the device's status would have been sensed 60×10 times, and the device is expected to be found busy $60 \times 10 \times 0.01$, or 6, times. In practice, since a random event is being sampled, the number of busy samples is expected to be binomially distributed with a mean of np

and a standard deviation of $\sqrt{np(1-p)}$, where n is the number of samples and p is the probability of the event. In this case, $n = 600$ and $p = 0.01$. The mean and standard deviations are 6 and 2.43. The probability of the number of busy samples being beyond the mean plus or minus one standard deviation (3.56 to 8.43) is approximately 32%. Thus, in 32% of the cases the utilization will be measured below 0.6% or over 1.4%. $\square$

Another example of inaccuracy due to sampling is that of program counter sampling. The addresses where a program makes I/O calls may be observed more often not because those addresses are visited more frequently but because a program may spend considerable time there waiting for I/O completions.

7. *Ignoring Monitoring Overhead*: The data collection mechanism or the software monitor used in measurement have overhead that introduces some error in the measured values. It may consume processor, storage, and I/O resources to keep and log the measurements. If the inaccuracy, for instance, is 10%, the model output may be more or less inaccurate, even if the model is precise.

8. *Not Validating Measurements*: This is a common mistake. While simulation and analytical models are routinely validated before use, validation of measured data is rarely thought of. Any errors in setting up the experiment may remain totally unnoticed. For example, in hardware monitors, it is easy to misplace a probe or have a loose probe. It is therefore necessary to cross check the measurements. All counterintuitive results should be explained. Any values that cannot be explained should be investigated. Automatic checks should be included in the measurements; for example, the total number of packets sent by all nodes in a network should be close to the total number received.

9. *Not Ensuring Same Initial Conditions*: Each run of the benchmark changes the state of the system. For example, the disk space available may be reduced. The data records may have different contents. Starting the next run on the changed system may make the experiment nonrepeatable. One solution is to ensure that all files created by a workload are deleted and those changed are reloaded to their original state. Another solution is to study the sensitivity of the results to such phenomena. If the results are very sensitive to the initial conditions, then more factors should be added to the workload model.

10. *Not Measuring Transient Performance*: Most measurement experiments, simulations, and analytical models are designed to predict the performance under stable conditions. During measurements, the system is allowed to reach a stable state before measurements are taken. For example, the caches are allowed to be filled in before starting the measurements. This is a valid approach in most cases. However, if the system is such that it takes a long time to reach steady state, then in

real environments it is expected to be often moving from one state to the next. In other words, the system is expected to be in a transient state more often than in a steady state. In this case, it is more realistic to study the transient performance of the system than the steady-state performance.

11. *Using Device Utilizations for Performance Comparisons*: Device utilizations are performance metrics in the sense that given the same workload, a lower utilization is preferred. However, their use to compare two systems may be meaningless sometimes. For example, in a closed environment requests are generated after a fixed think time interval after satisfying the old requests. Given two systems for such an environment, the system with faster response time will have more requests generated per unit time and will have higher device utilizations. Lower utilization for the same number of users should not be interpreted to mean a better system. The right metric to compare two systems in this case is to compare the throughput in terms of requests per second.

Another common mistake is to use utilizations for model validations. As shown in Chapter 33, utilizations can be determined easily from service times and the frequency of visits and can be matched easily even if the response times are very different. Matching utilizations predicted from a model to those measured in a real environment *does not* really validate the model.

12. *Collecting Too Much Data But Doing Very Little Analysis*: This is a common mistake. The data collection is the first step in benchmarking. The next step of data analysis may not get adequate attention for several reasons. First, the person doing the measurement may have little or no training in statistical techniques. The usual charts of resource demands and utilizations as a function of time may be prepared but no further insights may be drawn. Second, the data measurement may itself take so much time of the project that none is left for analysis. One way to avoid this pitfall is to form teams of analysts with measurement and analysis backgrounds, to carefully allocate analysis time during project planning, and to interweave the measurement and analysis activities. Often the measurement plans may have to be changed based on the results of the analysis.

The above list includes only those mistakes that an analyst may make inadvertently due to inexperience. The benchmarking tricks that have been used by experienced analysts to show the superiority of their systems are discussed in the next section.

9.4 BENCHMARKING GAMES

Benchmarking is the process of comparing two systems using standard well-known benchmarks. The process is not always carried out fairly. Some of the ways that the results of a benchmarking study may be misleading or biased are discussed next.

1. *Differing configurations may be used to run the same workload on two systems.* The configurations may have a different amount of memory, different disks, or different number of disks.

2. *The compilers may be wired to optimize the workload.* In one case, the compiler totally eliminated the main loop in the synthetic program, thereby giving infinitely better performance than other systems.

3. *Test specifications may be written so that they are biased toward one machine.* This may happen if the specifications are written based upon an existing environment without consideration to generalizing the requirements for different vendors.

4. *A synchronized job sequence may be used.* It is possible to manipulate a job sequence so that CPU-bound and I/O-bound steps synchronize to give a better overall performance.

5. *The workload may be arbitrarily picked.* Many of the well-known kernels, such as sieve and puzzle, have not been verified to be representative of the real-world applications.

6. *Very small benchmarks may be used.* Such benchmarks give 100% cache hits, thereby ignoring the inefficiency of memory and cache organizations. Small benchmarks may also not show the effect of I/O overhead and context switching. The results will depend mainly on the few instructions that occur in the inner loop. By judicious choice of instructions in the loop, the results can be skewed by any amount desired.

   Most real systems make use of a wide variety of workloads. To compare two systems, one should therefore use as many workloads as possible. By using only a few selected benchmarks, the results can be biased, as desired.

7. *Benchmarks may be manually translated to optimize the performance.* Often benchmarks need to be manually translated to make them runable on different systems. The performance may then depend more on the ability of the translator than on the system under test.

9.5 LOAD DRIVERS

In order to measure the performance of a computer system, it is necessary to have some means of putting loads on the system. Although our interest in load drivers here is purely for performance measurement, it must be pointed out that the same load drivers can also be used for other purposes, such as the following:

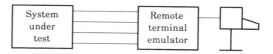

FIGURE 9.2   An RTE and a SUT.

- *Component Certification*: This requires rigorous testing of hardware and software components by imposing sequential and random combinations of workload demands.
- *System Integration*: This involves verifying that various hardware and software components of distributed systems work compatibly under different environments.
- *Stress-Load Analysis*: This requires putting high loads on the system to test for stable and error-free operation at these loads.
- *Regression Testing*: After every change in the system, the new version of the system should be tested to demonstrate that all previous capabilities are functional along with the new ones.

Three techniques that have been used for load driving are using internal drivers, live operators, or remote-terminal emulators.

The **internal-driver** method consists of loading programs directly into the memory and executing. If there is more than one program per user, then the whole sequence of commands is put in a disk file and run as a batch job. The main problem with the internal-driver method is that the effect of the terminal communication overhead is not visible. Also, the loading overhead may affect the system performance.

One way to account for terminal communication overhead is to have **live operators** utilize the system. To test a multiuser system, many people would need to sit down at their own terminal and execute a predetermined set of commands. This is a costly process and one that is difficult to control. The presence of the human element in the measurement increases the variance of the result. The increased variance means more trials are required to obtain a desired level of confidence.

The most desirable and popular method for putting the load on the system is to make use of computers. One computer can generally simulate many users in a very controlled and repeatable fashion. These computers are called **Remote-Terminal Emulators** (RTEs) (see Figure 9.2). The remainder of this chapter discusses the design and use of RTEs.

9.6   REMOTE-TERMINAL EMULATION

An RTE emulates the terminals, the terminal communication equipments, the operators, and the requests to be submitted to the System Under Test (SUT), as shown in Figure 9.3. In general, the RTE is a full-fledged computer that

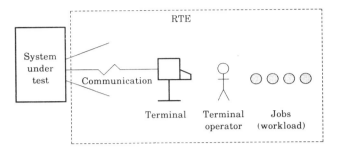

FIGURE 9.3   Components emulated by an RTE.

---

1. Take a directory of the user disk.
2. Print fifty files.
3. Run a number factoring program and factor numbers 1 through 50.

FIGURE 9.4   Sample scenario.

includes disks, magtapes, and at least one console terminal. In many cases, the RTE may be more powerful than the SUT. For example, super-minicomputers may be used to drive minicomputers and workstations. Most RTEs have their own operating system designed specifically for this real-time operation.

The RTE sends commands to the SUT at appropriate intervals. The user commands are read from a disk file called script. The script file contains user commands as well as other instructions for the RTE, such as when the RTE should send out a command.

Scripts written for one RTE system cannot be used on another RTE system because they may include an incompatible set of commands. For the same reason, scripts that are written for one SUT cannot be used on another SUT. To compare two incompatible SUTs, the workload should be first described in a manner independent of the SUT and RTE. This description is called a **scenario.** An example of a scenario is shown in Figure 9.4.

9.7 COMPONENTS OF AN RTE

The measurement operation using an RTE consists of three phases—preemulation, emulation, and postemulation. Correspondingly, RTEs also consist of three distinct components that are used in these phases. A sample design is shown in Figure 9.5. During the preemulation phase the system configuration and script are defined. Data is collected during the emulation phase, and data reduction occurs during the postemulation phase.

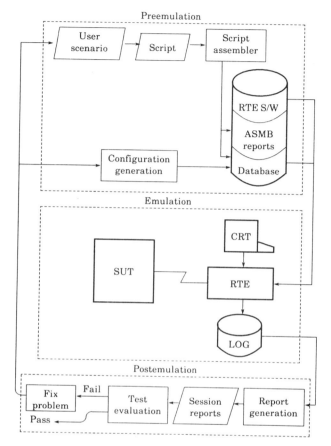

FIGURE 9.5   Three components of an RTE.

Defining the system configuration includes identifying specific characteristics of the terminals, users, and their programs. Terminal characteristics include I/O speed (baud rate) of the line and whether the line is synchronous or asynchronous. User characteristics include think time (the time between successive commands) and typing rate. Load characteristics include specifying the programs and the commands that will be executed.

The users can be started in a staggered manner. If, for example, the measurements are required for 40 users, it would not be a good idea to start out with all of these users on the system at the same time. Typically, users log in in a random sequence. In order to emulate this behavior, RTEs start each user after a prespecified starting delay.

Finally, a repetition count can be specified. The experiment is repeated as specified to get a specified level of statistical confidence.

```
**** Lines
Line #   Script   Input   Output   Think   Delay   Repeat   Random Set
    1    Test1      3       30       5       0       0       Think
    2    Test1      3       30       5       2       0       Think
    3    Test1      3       30       5       4       0       Think
    4    Test1      3       30       5       6       0       Think
    5    Test2      3       30       5       8       0       Think
    6    Test3      3       30       5      10       0       Think
    7    Test4      3       30       5      12       0       Think
   10    Test4      3       30       5      14       0       Think
   11    Test4      3       30       5      16       0       Think
   12    Test4      3       30       5      18       0       Think
10 lines are being simulated.
*
```

FIGURE 9.6 Sample RTE output after configuration definition phase.

A sample output from an RTE after the configuration definition phase is shown in Figure 9.6. The analyst has just defined 10 lines to be emulated. Line 1 is using the script labeled TEST1. The user is typing at a rate of 3 characters per second, and the terminal output rate is 30 characters per second. The user has a think time of 5 seconds and logs on the system immediately. The script will not be repeated again, and the think time will be randomly generated. Line 12 is similar to line 1, except that it has a different type of workload (script is TEST4) and starts 18 seconds after the first user.

The RTEs also allow the measurement of time for a particular operation, the repetition of an operation, the introduction of a random delay at any point, the enabling or disabling of a user's thinking, and forward or backward movement in the script. In essence, RTEs have their own programming language. A sample script with explanations is shown in Figure 9.7. It contains SUT commands as well as RTE commands. The RTE commands are enclosed in the symbol \\. All characters (including carriage returns) not enclosed in \\ are sent to the SUT. An RTE may have a complete programming language defined for it and may allow commands such as GOTO, GOSUB, and PAUSE.

Script	Explanation
\\TIME D1\\	RTE, Start a stopwatch timer named D1
DIR	SUT, Take a directory of the user's disk area
\\END TIME D1\\	RTE, Stop D1 and note the elapsed time
\\FOR I=50\\	RTE, Repeat the following 50 times
PRINT TIME.LST	SUT, Print the file named TIME.LST
\\NEXT I\\	RTE, End the "FOR" loop
\\DELAY 30\\	RTE, Introduce a delay of 30 seconds
RUN NUMBER	SUT, Run the "number" program
\\FOR I=50\\	RTE, Repeat the following 50 times
\\SEND I\\	RTE, Send the number "I" to the program
\\IGNORE N\\	RTE, Do not introduce think-time delay on the next N lines

FIGURE 9.7 Sample RTE script with explanations.

The emulation phase is the next phase of load driving. The data related to the system, terminals, users, and the users' workloads is input into the RTE during the preemulation phase. The experiment is then initiated. The emulation phase may continue for hours. During this phase, the operator can observe the system activities on the RTE's operator console. The system status may be displayed, which shows the number of active lines, number of characters sent, and elasped time on each line. It is also possible to monitor a particular line and watch everything that would have been presented to a real user sitting on that line. One can ask the RTE to change the experiment by activating or deactivating particular users. (This is one reason why, in the example shown in Figure 9.6, 12 lines were defined but only 10 were activated.) Characteristics of a user, a line, or the load can be changed. If the emulation completes successfully, the next phase of data reduction is begun.

The data gathered by the RTE is stored on magtapes or removable disk media. During the third phase, this data is transferred to another computer system for reduction and analysis. The system that was used as the RTE for measurement often may not be used for data reduction and analysis. This is because the measurements must be done on a dedicated system, and the system should not be interrupted by other tasks while the measurements are being done. Dedicated systems are hard to find. Only low-cost and, therefore, low-power machines can be justified for this purpose. This is why the definition as well as the data reduction are done on timeshared systems, which are not only more powerful but also have a more user-friendly operating system than that on the more primitive RTE. The RTE's operating system may not support all the statistical packages required for analysis.

The data reduction package that comes with an RTE supports common statistical analysis such as computing the average and standard deviation, plotting histograms, and fitting linear regressions. If the script contains time tests (stopwatches), the statistics on the time consumed are automatically presented during analysis. The analysis package may also convert the raw data into a format that can be understood by commercial statistical software for more sophisticated analysis.

9.8 LIMITATIONS OF CURRENT RTES

As the terminal communication is changing, the user's behavior in a real environment is changing, and RTEs need to be updated continuously to keep track of these changes. Many of these changes are difficult to emulate, and this limits the use of RTEs. Some of these limitations are as follows.

1. *The conditions for sending successive requests may not be realistic.* The issue is that of deciding when to send the next *n* lines of user input to the SUT. It should be representative of a real environment. In the real world, a user types in the next command based on several considerations. For example, the next request may be typed as follows:

(a) After a think time interval, which represents the time required to think about what should be done next.

(b) After a specified number of lines from the computer have been received. This represents waiting for all of the responses from the previous request.

(c) After a special character (for example, "?") has been sent by the SUT.

(d) After the SUT gives a specified prompt (for example, "A>").

(d) After the SUT gives one of a set of specified prompts.

Current RTEs do not allow all of these conditions to be emulated.

2. *It may not be possible to vary the input in successive repetitions.* In a real environment, successive requests are generally different. For example, in a sequence of reservation queries, the name of the reservation customer may need to be different in each query. If the same name is used in successive queries, the first query would require fetching the data from a remote site; all remaining queries for the same name may be satisfied from the local cache. Some RTEs, therefore, provide facilities for fetching input randomly from a table of inputs.

3. *The think time model may not be realistic.* The conclusions of RTE experiments are generally dependent upon the think time value used. Unfortunately, in most experiments the think time is not a measured value but a value simply taken "out of a hat." Few studies have been conducted that verify that the concept of think time is realistic. Do users really think before they link a program after compiling it? In most cases, users type "LINK" long before the computer comes back with the compilation errors. Should RTEs emulate these negative think times of type-ahead? It is also possible for think time to overlap with the previous command's execution. All of these alternatives are not modeled by current RTEs.

4. *Modern user interfaces are not emulated.* Progress in human interfacing techniques has also left RTEs behind the times. Today, many terminals are buffered and gather several characters before sending them to the user. Mouse input may be used along with or in place of the keyboard input. Function keys may be used to send predefined strings to the SUT. Graphics, such as a pie chart or a drawing with multiple colors and shades, may constitute the output instead of ASCII characters. Current RTEs do not allow such interfaces to be emulated or measured.

5. *Users are the shared resource.* With multiple screens on terminals, a user may be simultaneously thinking about several commands. Some windows may be waiting for the user input. Instead of the users waiting for the system response, the system may be waiting for the user's response. It is quite likely that the user is the bottleneck and also the most expensive resource. Such sharing of a user among many tasks is not currently emulated by RTEs.

6. *Modern communication technology is not emulated*. The RTEs attempt to include the communication overhead in the measurements. However, recent advances in communications technology have left RTEs behind. Terminals are no longer connected to the system directly. They are connected to a terminal concentrator on a local-area network. Another concentrator on the network is connected to the host system. Most RTEs do not yet allow emulation of this environment.

7. *Interfaces and definitions are different across RTEs*. Each RTE available on the market has its own script language. The scripts developed for one RTE cannot be run directly on another RTE. Even the definitions of the metrics used are different. Thus, for example, the response time measured on one RTE may not always be compared with that using another RTE.

8. *Workstation emulation is not provided*. Most RTEs emulate dumb synchronous or asynchronous terminals. All data processing is assumed to be done by the SUT. Delays inside the terminal are small and fixed. The introduction of workstations has changed the environment radically. Today, the workstations do most of the data processing; only tasks requiring large computations may be sent to the central host. A number of workstations may share a central pool of servers for file storage, computing, printing, and so on. In some cases, there is no clear server-client distinction. A workstation may be a server for some functions but may also act as a client and use other servers. Load-balancing schemes have been proposed that allow any idle workstation to be used for computation from any other workstation. Current RTEs cannot be used for load driving in such environments.

EXERCISES

9.1 Review a few articles or reports presenting results of performance measurements. Check if any of the mistakes listed in this chapter were made in the study.

9.2 Select an area or application of computer systems, for example, image processing, mail, networking, and medical diagnosis. List the characteristics of workloads that a load driver for that area should implement. Discuss how you would specify the required characteristics to the load driver and whether there are any difficulties in implementing it in a representative manner.

CHAPTER 10

THE ART OF DATA PRESENTATION

It is not what you say, but how you say it.

—A. Putt

One of the important steps in every performance evaluation study is the presentation of final results. The eventual aim of every performance analysis is to help in decision making. An analysis whose results cannot be understood by the decision makers is as good as one that was never performed. It is the responsibility of the analyst to ensure that results of the analysis are conveyed to the decision makers as clearly and simply as possible. This requires prudent use of words, pictures, and graphs to explain the results and the analysis.

Graphic charts such as line charts, bar charts, pie charts, and histograms are commonly used in presenting performance results. Guidelines for preparing such graphic charts are briefly discussed. In addition, a number of graphic charts that have been developed specifically for computer systems performance analysis are described. These are Gantt charts, Kiviat graphs, and Schumacher charts.

There are a number of reasons why a graphic chart may be used for data presentation in place of a textual explanation. First of all, a picture is worth a thousand words. A graphic chart saves readers' time and presents the same information more concisely. It can also be used to interest the reader. Most readers find it easier to look at the figures to quickly grasp the main points of the study and read the text only for details. A graphic chart is also a good way to emphasize or clarify a point, to reinforce a conclusion, and to summarize the results of a study.

10.1 TYPES OF VARIABLES

One important factor that affects the choice of a graphic chart is the type of variable to be displayed. Variables are of two types: quantitative and qualitative. **Qualitative variables**, also called **categorical variables**, have states, levels, or categories that are defined by a set of mutually exclusive and exhaustive subclasses. The subclasses, which are usually expressed in words, can be *ordered* or *unordered*. For instance, a computer type with three subclasses—supercomputers, minicomputers, and microcomputers—is an ordered qualitative variable. The variable workload type with three subclasses—scientific workload, engineering workload, and educational workload—is an unordered qualitative variable.

Quantitative variables are those whose levels are expressed numerically. There are two types of quantitative variables: discrete and continuous. For discrete variables, all values of the variable can be counted and put into a one-to-one correspondence with some subset or all of the set of positive integers. The number of values can be finite or infinite, but in either case the number is countable. Number of processors in a multiprocessor system, size of disks in blocks, number of peripherals in a system, are all examples of discrete quantitative variables.

Continuous variables can take uncountably infinite values. In many computer programming languages, they are called *real* variables. The response time of a job on a system, the weight of a portable computer, and the footprint (base area) of a workstation are all examples of continuous quantitative variables.

The hierarchy of various types of variables is summarized in Figure 10.1. Knowing the type of variable is important, since the type of graphic chart to be used depends upon the type of variable. A line chart is used to show the relationship between two continuous variables. A column chart or bar chart is used when the independent variable (also called *x*-variable) is a discrete or a qualitative variable.

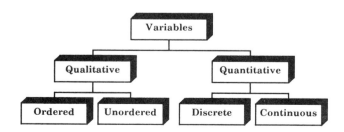

FIGURE 10.1 Types of variables.

10.2   GUIDELINES FOR PREPARING GOOD GRAPHIC CHARTS

The following guidelines will help you enhance your graphical presentations. Only the guidelines that apply to a large number of cases are discussed; application of these techniques to individual cases is an art which you will learn with experience. Remember, all of the following are guidelines, not rules.

1. *Require Minimum Effort from the Reader*: The single most important metric to measure the goodness of a graphic chart is the level of effort required to read and understand the chart, that is, to get the message. Given two representations of the same data, one can easily distinguish which one requires less effort, which is the preferable one.

   For example, consider the issue of deciding whether to use a legend box in a chart. There are two common ways of identifying different curves in a line chart: legends and direct labeling. Each curve corresponds to a different alternative and may be represented by a different line pattern. A *legend box*, as shown in Figure 10.2b, may be used to specify the correspondence between the patterns and the alternatives. This requires a little more effort on the part of reader than direct labeling of the curves, as shown in Figure 10.2a. Therefore, direct labeling is preferable particularly if the number of curves is large. Similarly, in a column chart, direct labeling of each column is preferable to a separate legend box.

2. *Maximize Information*: There should be sufficient information on the graph to make it self-sufficient. There are a number of ways to achieve this. Use key words in place of symbols since the symbols require extra access to the reader's memory to make sense. The axes labels should be as informative as possible. For example, if you are plotting daily CPU usage, "Daily CPU usage" is preferred over "CPU usage." Include units in the labels: "CPU time in seconds" is more informative than "CPU time."

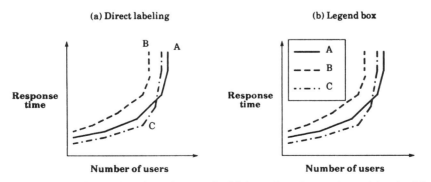

FIGURE 10.2   Direct labeling of curves in (a) is preferable to a legend box in (b).

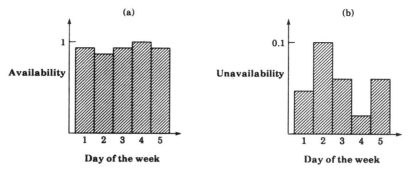

FIGURE 10.3   Two graphs from the same data. The second graph is more informative.

3. *Minimize Ink*: Present as much information as possible with as little ink as possible. The goal should be to maximize the information-to-ink ratio. Too much unnecessary information on a chart makes it cluttered and uninteresting. For example, grid lines on a graph should not be shown unless they are required to accurately read the values. Also, the chart that gives more information for the same data is preferable. For example, consider the two bar line charts in Figures 10.3a and 10.3b that show the availability and unavailability of a system. The unavailability is simply 1 minus the availability, but the second graph is more meaningful and informative than the first one.

4. *Use Commonly Accepted Practices*: Present what people expect. Most people expect the origin to be $(0,0)$, the independent variable or *cause* to be plotted along the x-axis, the dependent variable or *effect* to be plotted along the y-axis, scales to be linear, scales to increase left to right and bottom to top, and all scale divisions to be equal. Departures from these practices are permitted but require extra effort from the reader and should be used only when necessary.

5. *Avoid Ambiguity*: Show coordinate axes, scale divisions, and origin. Identify individual curves and bars. The graph should be easy to read. Do not plot multiple variables in the same chart.

The preceding list includes only a few of the possible guidelines. Box 10.1 presents a checklist to make it easier for you to check each of your graphs. The checklist is arranged so that a "yes" answer to each question, in general, leads to a better graph. However, in some cases an analyst may consciously decide not to follow a suggestion if it helps in conveying the intended message.

In practice, it is necessary to make several trials before arriving at the final graph. Several different scale ranges and x-y variable pairs should be tried, and the graph that presents the message most accurately, simply, concisely, and logically should be chosen.

Box 10.1   Checklist for Good Graphics

1. Are both coordinate axes shown and labeled?
2. Are the axes labels self-explanatory and concise?
3. Are the scales and divisions shown on both axes?
4. Are the minimum and maximum of the ranges shown on the axes appropriate to present the maximum information?
5. Is the number of curves reasonably small?
   (A line chart should generally have no more than six curves).
6. Do all graphs use the same scale?
   (Multiple scales on the same chart are confusing.)
7. Is there no curve that can be removed without reducing the information?
8. Are the curves on a line chart individually labeled?
9. Are the cells in a bar chart individually labeled?
10. Are all symbols on the graph accompanied by appropriate textual explanations?
11. If the curves cross, are the line patterns different to avoid confusion?
12. Are the units of measurement indicated?
13. Is the horizontal scale increasing from left to right?
14. Is the vertical scale increasing from bottom to top?
15. Are the grid lines aiding in reading the curves? (If not, the grid lines should not be shown.)
16. Does this whole chart add to information available to the reader?
17. Are the scales contiguous? (Breaks in the scale should be avoided or clearly shown.)
18. Is the order of bars in a bar chart systematic?
    (Alphabetic, temporal, or best-to-worst ordering is to be preferred over random placement.)
19. If the vertical axis represents a random quantity, are confidence intervals shown?
20. Are there no curves, symbols, or texts on the graph that can be removed without affecting the information?
21. Is there a title for the whole chart?
22. Is the chart title self-explanatory and concise?
23. For bar charts with unequal class interval, is the area and width representative of the frequency and interval, respectively?
24. Do the variables plotted on this chart give more information than other alternatives?
25. Does the chart clearly bring out the intended message?
26. Is the figure referenced and discussed in the text of the report?

10.3 COMMON MISTAKES IN PREPARING CHARTS

In this section, a number of mistakes seen frequently in performance reports and papers are discussed. It is easy to find charts with these mistakes even in articles published in technical journals.

1. *Presenting Too Many Alternatives on a Single Chart*: Regardless of which chart is used, the key goal of data presentation is to make the reader's task easier. Most readers cannot grasp more than five to seven messages at a time. Therefore, a chart with too many curves, bars, or components should be avoided. In general, a line chart should be limited to 6 curves. A column chart or bar chart should be limited to 10 bars. A pie chart should be limited to 8 components. The number of cells, and hence the number of bars, in a histogram should indicate that each cell has at least five data points. All these are rules of thumb and can be overridden if, in the judgment of the analyst, it would help to make the point.

2. *Presenting Many y-Variables on a Single Chart*: Figure 10.4 shows a line chart of response time, utilization, and throughput as a function of number of users. Plotting four y-variables saves space but leaves the task of associating the curves with the appropriate scales to the reader. It is difficult for the reader to get the intended message. Presenting four different graphs would have been more clear and logical. Combining unrelated graphs is commonly done to meet the length requirements of papers in journals.

3. *Using Symbols in Place of Text*: Figure 10.5 shows a line chart that is difficult to read since there is no text on the chart. The reader is left to flip through the report and search for what each symbol represents. While this may seem to have saved some time for the writer of the report, the writer's time was actually wasted since most readers are likely to skip the figure and the report as well.

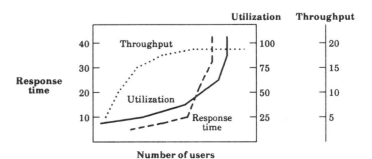

FIGURE 10.4 Too many variables plotted on a single chart make it difficult to read.

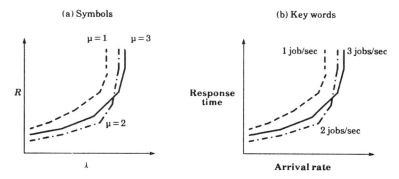

FIGURE 10.5   Keywords in place of symbols make a chart easier to read.

4. *Placing Extraneous Information on the Chart*: The goal of each figure is to convey a particular message to the reader. Any information that detracts the reader from getting the message is extraneous and should be removed. For example, grid lines on a line chart should be there only if the reader is expected to read the values precisely. Again, the granularity of the grid should be matched to the accuracy required.

5. *Selecting Scale Ranges Improperly*: Most graphs are prepared automatically by programs that have several built-in rules to select the scales based on the minimum and maximum values seen in the data. However, in practice it is often necessary to manually override this automatic selection and specify the ranges to be shown. This is particularly necessary if some part of the range does not add any further information.

6. *Using a Line Chart in Place of a Column Chart*: The lines joining successive points on a line chart signify the fact that the intermediate values can be approximately interpolated. Figure 10.6 shows an example of the misuse of a line chart. The performance in MIPS for various CPU types

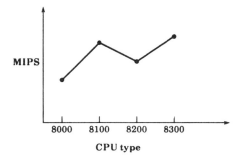

FIGURE 10.6   Line chart should not be used if intermediate values cannot be interpolated.

are plotted on the chart. Since the fractional values of CPU types have no meaning, a column or pie chart should have been used in this case.

10.4 PICTORIAL GAMES

Since a picture is worth a thousand words, one can deceive as much with a picture as would require at least a thousand words. In this section, a number of techniques that are known to have been used deliberately by analysts to hide the truth and to misguide the readers are presented. Unlike the mistakes discussed in Section 10.3, these are not a result of carelessness or inexperience of the analyst but a result of a careful plan to exaggerate the differences. Such pictorial games are more common in the trade press and in advertisements than in the technical literature.

1. *Using Nonzero Origins to Emphasize the Difference*: Normally both axes of a graph should meet at the origin, that is, at zero value of the x- and y-coordinates. By moving the origin and by appropriately scaling the graph, it is possible to magnify or reduce the perception of performance difference. In Figure 10.7, the same performance data is shown in two different graphs using different scales and origins. The two graphs lead to two different conclusions:

   (a) MINE is much much better than YOURS and
   (b) MINE and YOURS are almost the same.

   Which is the right graph? None of the two!
   The right way to scale a graph is to choose scales such that the vertical height of the highest point is at least three-quarters of the horizontal offset of the right-most point. This is known as the **three-quarter-high rule**. Also, the origin should be represented by $(0,0)$ on the two axes unless there is a justifiable reason to do otherwise. The performance data of Figure 10.7 is replotted in Figure 10.8 using the three-quarter-high rule.

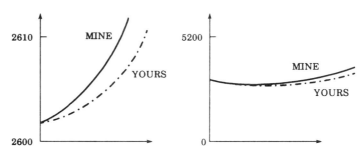

FIGURE 10.7 Inappropriate scaling can be used to emphasize or conceal the difference.

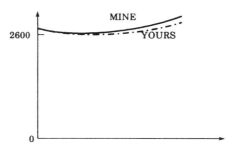

FIGURE 10.8 Three-quarter-high rule requires that the height of the highest point be at least three-quarters of the horizontal offset of the rightmost point.

2. *Using Double-Whammy Graph for Dramatization*: Two curves on the same graph can have twice as much impact as one. This can be used to amplify the goodness or badness of the information. If there are two metrics that are related, knowing one allows predicting the behavior of the other. Throughput and response time are examples of such metrics. For instance, as the response time to database queries goes up, the throughput in terms of transaction per second goes down. The news that the performance of YOUR system goes down steeply as the number of users is increased can be conveyed by plotting either of the two metrics. However, by plotting both (see Figure 10.9), impact is twice as much, because for an unguarded reader, YOUR system is losing on both metrics.

3. *Plotting Random Quantities without Showing Confidence Intervals*: Most performance measurements result in a *random* quantification of the performance. If the measurement were to be repeated, the result would not be exactly the same. In many cases the variance of results is high. This is particularly the case if there are many uncontrollable factors that impact the result. In such cases, it is necessary to repeat the experiment many times and to plot means. However, means alone are not enough

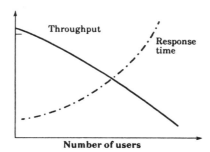

FIGURE 10.9 A double-whammy graph has twice as much impact.

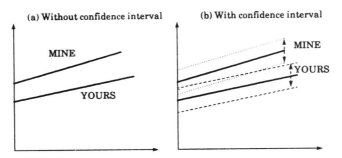

FIGURE 10.10   Confidence intervals should be shown for random quantities.

when comparing two random quantities. Overlapping confidence intervals are generally enough to deduce that the two random quantities are statistically indifferent. This is explained further in Chapter 13.

Figure 10.10 shows performance curves for two systems with and without confidence intervals. Figure 10.10a, without the confidence interval, leads one to believe that MINE is better than YOURS. Figure 10.10b, on the other hand, shows that the two systems cannot be differentiated with the current data. More repetitions would be required to claim superiority of one over the other.

4. *Pictograms Scaled by Height*: One way to depict difference in performance is to draw appropriately scaled pictures of systems. Figure 10.11 shows one such example. The performance of workstation MINE is twice that of YOURS. This is depicted using a picture of workstation MINE, which is twice as high and twice as wide as YOURS. The total area of MINE is four times that of YOURS, giving an impression of MINE being four times superior to YOURS. The correct way to scale a pictogram is by the area. For example, in Figure 10.11 the height and width of MINE should have been only 1.414 times those of YOURS so that the area of MINE would be twice that of YOURS.

5. *Using Inappropriate Cell Size in Histograms*: Selecting cell size for histograms is always a problem. Anyone who has tried plotting a histogram

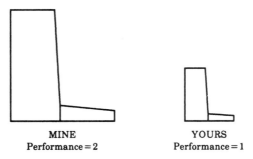

FIGURE 10.11   Pictograms scaled by height exaggerate the performance claims.

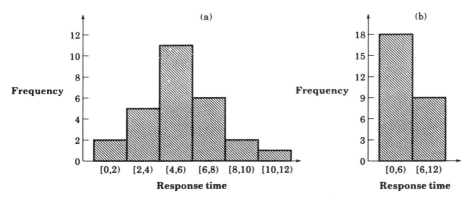

FIGURE 10.12 Inappropriate bucket sizes can result in a loss of information or in too much detail.

for real data knows that it requires more than one attempt. If cells are too large, all data points fall in a few cells. If the cells are too small, the histogram lacks smoothness. By appropriately selecting the cell size, one can get the data to look like the desired distribution.

Figure 10.12 shows two histograms for the same data. The first one looks more like a normal distribution while the second one looks like an exponential distribution. There are several statistical tests for determining whether the data fits the distribution under consideration. Most of these tests require that there be at least five observations in each cell. Nevertheless, given enough data points it is possible to statistically fit more than one distribution.

6. *Using Broken Scales in Column Charts*: An effect similar to that of non-zero origins discussed earlier is achieved in column charts and histograms by breaking the scale in the middle, as shown in Figure 10.13. It allows

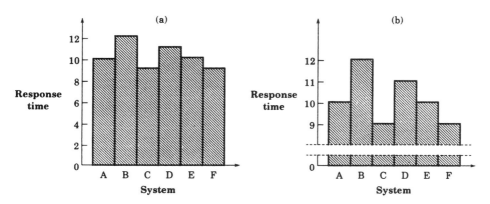

FIGURE 10.13 Histograms with a broken scale are often used to exaggerate small differences.

one to amplify negligible performance differences. In the figure, looking at chart (b) concludes that there are significant performance differences among systems, whereas chart (a) would be used to give the opposite message. Instead of a broken scale, the same effect can be achieved by using a nonzero origin.

This completes the discussion on general graphic charts. Next the charts designed specifically for performance analysts are discussed.

10.5 GANTT CHARTS

In data processing installations, computer performance evaluation (**CPE**) managers are often interested in ensuring that all resources of a system are utilized optimally. Any resource whose utilization is too high is a bottleneck and may degrade the performance. Similarly, a resource with very low utilization represents inefficiency in the system. For appropriate utilization of all resources, it is necessary that the workload represent a mix of jobs using different resources and that there be significant overlap in the use of resources. The overlap among resources can be shown by utilization profiles in a Gantt chart.

In general, a Gantt chart can be used to show the relative duration of any number of Boolean conditions—conditions that are either true or false. A resource being used or being idle is an example of a Boolean condition. Each condition is shown to be a set of horizontal line segments. The total length of the line segments represents the relative duration of the condition. The position of various segments is arranged such that the overlap between different lines represents the overlap between the conditions.

A sample Gantt chart is shown in Figure 10.14. The utilizations of three resources, CPU, I/O channel, and network link, are shown. The CPU utilization

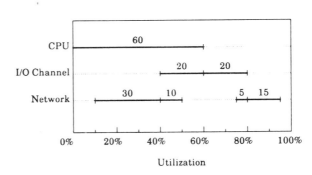

FIGURE 10.14 Sample Gantt chart.

TABLE 10.1   Data for Gantt Chart of Example 10.1

A	B	C	D	Time Used (%)
0	0	0	0	5
0	0	0	1	5
0	0	1	0	0
0	0	1	1	5
0	1	0	0	10
0	1	0	1	5
0	1	1	0	10
0	1	1	1	5
1	0	0	0	10
1	0	0	1	5
1	0	1	0	0
1	0	1	1	5
1	1	0	0	10
1	1	0	1	10
1	1	1	0	5
1	1	1	1	10
				100

is 60%. The I/O channel utilization is 40%. The overlap between the CPU and I/O channel is 20%. The network link utilization is 60% and is shown in four segments that add to 60%. The relative sizes and positions of the four segments are arranged so that the relative overlap among various devices can be read directly. During 30% of the time, the CPU and network but not the I/O channel are used. During 10% of the time all three resources are used. For 5% of the time, I/O and network are used but the CPU is idle. Network alone is used for 15% of the time.

The following example illustrates the procedure to develop a Gantt chart from raw data.

Example 10.1 For a system with four resources—CPU, two I/O channels, and a network link—the raw measured utilizations for 16 possible states are shown in Table 10.1. The resources are labeled A, B, C, and D, respectively, and a resource not being used is shown by a zero entry in the corresponding column.

The four resources are represented on four levels in the Gantt chart of Figure 10.15. The first level is divided into two parts representing A and $\overline{A}$. A dotted vertical line is drawn to divide all subsequent levels in two parts as well. The sum of eight entries with $A = 1$ is 55%. In the final chart, the division corresponding to A and $\overline{A}$ will have length proportional to 55 and 45, respectively. This is indicated by writing 55 and 45 below the labels A and $\overline{A}$.

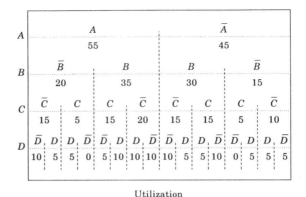

Utilization

FIGURE 10.15   Draft of the Gantt chart.

At the next level each of the two parts is subdivided into two parts, and the four parts so obtained are marked $\overline{B}$, B, B, and $\overline{B}$. These four parts correspond to $A\overline{B}$, AB, $\overline{A}B$, and $\overline{A}\,\overline{B}$, respectively.

The sum of four entries with $A = 1$ and $B = 0$ is 20%. This is the length of the division corresponding to $A\overline{B}$. Similarly, the length of the divisions corresponding to AB, $\overline{A}B$, and $\overline{A}\,\overline{B}$ is 35, 30, and 15, respectively. The lengths are written under the labels.

The dotted vertical lines showing the four divisions of this level are continued down to all subsequent levels. It must be pointed out that the order $\overline{B}$, B, B, and $\overline{B}$ is chosen to keep the two solid line segments corresponding to $B = 1$ together, thereby minimizing the number of segments.

The third level is divided into eight parts marked $\overline{C}$, C, C, $\overline{C}$, $\overline{C}$, C, C, and $\overline{C}$. These parts represent $A\overline{B}\,\overline{C}$, $A\overline{B}C$, ABC, $AB\overline{C}$, $\overline{A}B\overline{C}$, $\overline{A}BC$, $\overline{A}\,\overline{B}C$, and $\overline{A}\,\overline{B}\,\overline{C}$, respectively. For each division, the two corresponding entries in the table are added to determine the length of the divisions. Dotted vertical lines are drawn to divide the next level also into eight parts.

The fourth level is divided into 16 parts marked $\overline{D}$, D, D, $\overline{D}$, $\overline{D}$, D, D, $\overline{D}$, $\overline{D}$, D, D, $\overline{D}$, $\overline{D}$, D, D, and $\overline{D}$. The divisions correspond to $A\overline{B}\,\overline{C}\,\overline{D}$, $A\overline{B}\,\overline{C}D$, $A\overline{B}C D$, $A\overline{B}C\overline{D}$, $ABC\overline{D}$, $ABCD$, $AB\overline{C}D$, $AB\overline{C}\,\overline{D}$, $\overline{A}B\overline{C}\,\overline{D}$, $\overline{A}B\overline{C}D$, $\overline{A}BC D$, $\overline{A}BC\overline{D}$, $\overline{A}\,\overline{B}C\overline{D}$, $\overline{A}\,\overline{B}CD$, $\overline{A}\,\overline{B}\,\overline{C}D$, and $\overline{A}\,\overline{B}\,\overline{C}\,\overline{D}$. The single entry corresponding to each of these combinations is used to determine the length of the division. At this point, you can cross check that the lengths of divisions at level C correspond to the sum of its two subdivisions at level D. Similarly, lengths at level B and A can be verified.

Now the final chart is drawn with all segments drawn to scale. The segments corresponding to a "1" value, that is, $A = 1$, $B = 1$, $C = 1$, or $D = 1$, are drawn with solid lines. The final Gantt chart for this example is shown in Figure 10.16. Notice that the marking at each level is such that the number of line segments is minimized.   □

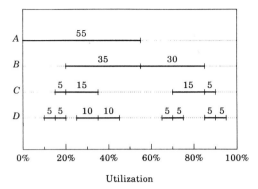

FIGURE 10.16   Final Gantt chart.

10.6   KIVIAT GRAPHS

A Kiviat graph is a visual device that helps system managers quickly recognize performance problems. It is a circular graph in which several different performance metrics are plotted along radial lines. In the most popular version of the graph, an even number of metrics are used. Half of these metrics are HB metrics (see Section 3.4) so that a higher value of the metric is considered better. The other half of the metrics measure are LB metrics, and a lower value is considered better. For example, CPU utilization is an HB metric because a higher utilization implies that the resource is being used. The percentage of time the CPU is waiting for I/O completion (CPU in a wait state) is an LB metric, and it would be better to have as little wait state time as possible. The HB and LB metrics are plotted along alternate radial lines in a Kiviat graph. In an ideal system, all HB metrics should be high and all LB metrics should be low. In other words, the Kiviat graph for an ideal system is a star. The following example illustrates the ideas discussed so far.

Example 10.2   Consider the Kiviat graph shown in Figure 10.17. Eight different metrics are plotted along eight radial lines. The metrics as shown represent the percentage of time spent in the following eight states:

1. CPU busy
2. CPU only busy
3. CPU and channel overlap
4. Channel only busy
5. Any channel busy
6. CPU wait
7. CPU in problem state
8. CPU in supervisor state

The first metric, percentage of time CPU is busy, or CPU utilization, is an HB metric in the sense that the resource is being used and not wasted. It

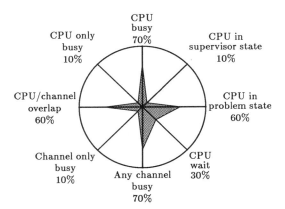

FIGURE 10.17 Kiviat graph for the sample data.

would be preferable to have as many resources simultaneously busy as possible so that there is a high parallelism in the resource usage. The second metric, percentage of time CPU only is busy, measures the fraction of time when only the CPU is used and none of the I/O channels are used. This is an LB metric since a low value of this metric is preferable. The third metric, CPU and channel overlap, measures the percentage of time the CPU is busy along with at least one I/O channel. It is preferable to have this value high and so this is an HB metric. The fourth metric, channel only busy, measures the time when the channel is being used but the CPU is idle. The CPU may be waiting for the I/O. This is again an LB metric. The fifth metric, any channel busy, is an HB metric since a high value would indicate the resource being put to use. The next three metrics measure the percentage of time CPU is in three different states as indicated by the processor status register. The CPU in the wait state indicates that it is waiting for I/O completion and represents wasted resource. The CPU in the problem state indicates the time used executing the user's program. A high value of this is considered good. Finally, the CPU in the supervisor state indicates the time spent in operating the system code. This represents the operating system overhead and is considered bad.

Notice that the good and the bad metrics alternate. All metrics in this example lie between 0 and 100%. The minimum value 0% is plotted as a point at the center of the circle, and the maximum value 100% is plotted along the periphery of the circle. The ideal desired graph is a star with all good metrics being at 100% and all bad metrics at 0%.

Figure 10.18 shows a Kiviat graph for a balanced well-utilized system. The CPU and I/O utilizations are both 95%, and the overlap is 90%. Most of the CPU time is spent in the problem state.

Although the set of metrics used in this example was one of the most popular sets in the early 1970s when the Kiviat graphs were first introduced

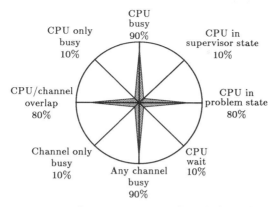

FIGURE 10.18 Star—Kiviat graph for a balanced system.

and almost all existing literature on Kiviat graphs uses these metrics for illustration, these metrics may not be good for all systems. One problem with this set is that the metrics are interrelated. There are only four independent metrics. Others can be obtained by the following relationships:

$$\text{CPU busy} = \text{problem state} + \text{supervisor state}$$

$$\text{CPU wait} = 100 - \text{CPU busy}$$

$$\text{Channel only} = \text{any channel} - \text{CPU/channel overlap}$$

$$\text{CPU only} = \text{CPU busy} - \text{CPU/channel overlap} \qquad \square$$

10.6.1 Shapes of Kiviat Graphs

The main reason for the popularity of Kiviat graphs over the popular Gantt chart form was the easy recognition of patterns by the system managers. In the 1970s, when the Kiviat graphs were first introduced, a number of commonly occurring shapes were given interesting names such as CPU keelboat, I/O arrow, and so forth. Figures 10.19 to 10.21 show these popular patterns. Figure 10.19 shows a CPU-bound system that has a high CPU utilization with very little I/O usage. The Kiviat graph for this system looks similar to a keelboat, and hence the pattern was dubbed CPU keelboat. Figure 10.20 shows an I/O-bound system with high I/O utilization and low CPU usage. Due to the wedge shape of the graph, it is called I/O wedge. Finally, Figure 10.21 shows the so-called I/O arrow and represents a system that uses considerable I/O as well as CPU.

Given two Kiviat graphs, it is easy to tell which system is more balanced by looking at their shapes. However, if a quantitative measure of the goodness of a graph can be designed, it will not be necessary to plot it. A number of such *figures of merit* have been proposed. The most popular one is due to Merrill (1974, 1975). He proposed that the LB axes be reversed so that 0% is

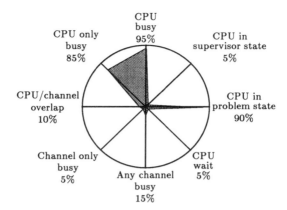

FIGURE 10.19   CPU keelboat—Kiviat graph for a CPU-bound system.

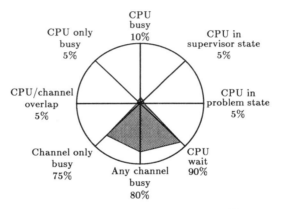

FIGURE 10.20   I/O wedge—Kiviat graph for an I/O-bound system.

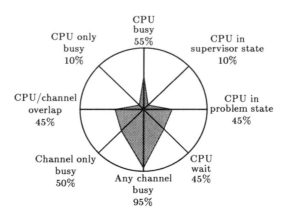

FIGURE 10.21   I/O arrow—Kiviat graph for a CPU- and I/O-bound system.

plotted along the circumference while 100% is plotted at the center; the square root of the area of this reversed Kiviat graph could be used to compare the overall goodness of systems. Consider a Kiviat graph with $2n$ axes. Let the percentage of performance values for a system be $\{x_1, x_2, x_3, \ldots, x_{2n}\}$, where the odd values $x_1, x_3, \ldots, x_{2n-1}$ represent good metrics and the even values $x_2, x_3, \ldots, x_{2n}$ represent bad metrics. All x_i's are percentages and lie between 0 and 100. Merrill's **Figure Of Merit (FOM)** is computed as follows:

$$\text{FOM} = \left[\frac{1}{2n} \sum_{i=1}^{n} (x_{2i-1} + x_{2i+1})(100 - x_{2i}) \right]^{1/2}$$

where x_{2n+1} is the same as x_1. The FOM always lies between 0 and 100, and its average value over a large number of systems is expected to be 50%. The following example illustrates the idea of FOM.

Example 10.3 The eight metrics of Example 10.2 were measured for two systems. The measured values are:

System	x_1	x_2	x_3	x_4	x_5	x_6	x_7	x_8
A	100	60	40	0	40	0	40	60
B	70	30	40	30	70	30	40	30

The Kiviat graphs for the two systems are shown in Figures 10.22 and 10.23, respectively. Notice that the Kiviat graph for System B is closer to a star shape than that of System A. The same conclusion can be obtained using FOM as shown next.

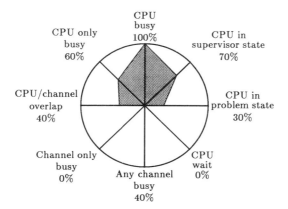

FIGURE 10.22 Kiviat graph for System A.

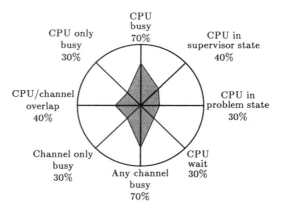

FIGURE 10.23   Kiviat graph for System B.

The FOM for System A is

$$\text{FOM}_A = \left[\tfrac{1}{8}\{(100+40)(100-60) + (40+40)(100-0)\right.$$
$$\left. + (40+40)(100-0) + (40+100)(100-60)\}\right]^{1/2}$$
$$= \left[\frac{5600 + 8000 + 8000 + 5600}{8}\right]^{1/2}$$
$$= \sqrt{\frac{27,200}{8}} = 58$$

Similarly, the FOM for System B is

$$\text{FOM}_B = \left[\tfrac{1}{8}\{(70+40)(100-30) + (40+70)(100-30)\right.$$
$$\left. + (70+40)(100-30) + (40+70)(100-30)\}\right]^{1/2}$$
$$= \left[\frac{7700 + 7700 + 7700 + 7700}{8}\right]^{1/2}$$
$$= \sqrt{\frac{30,800}{8}} = 62$$

System B has a higher figure of merit than System A, and hence, it is considered better.   □

This FOM has several known problems. Some examples follow.

1. All axes are considered equal. This may not always be the case. For example, 70% CPU utilization may not be considered as good as 70% I/O utilization in a system with an expensive I/O system and vice versa.

2. Extreme values are assumed to be better. The maximum value of a good metric is not always desirable. For example, 100% CPU utilization will lead to very high response times.
3. The utility of a system is not a linear function of FOM. A system with a FOM of 50% is not twice as good as a system with a FOM of 25%.
4. Two systems with the same FOM are not always equally good.
5. It is possible that a system with slightly lower FOM may at times be preferable to that with a slightly higher FOM. For example, a system of FOM 63 may be better than one of 64. It is recommended that FOM be computed only to the first significant digit.

10.6.2 Application of Kiviat Graphs to Other Systems

Although most of the literature on Kiviat graphs is on data processing systems, the idea of a Kiviat graph can be easily extended to networks, databases, and other types of computer systems. The following example illustrates their applications to computer networks.

Example 10.4 Table 10.2 shows HB and LB metrics that can be used to draw Kiviat graphs for computer networks. Six of these metrics are used in a sample Kiviat graph in Figure 10.24. □

TABLE 10.2 Metrics for Kiviat Graphs of Networks

HB Metrics	LB Metrics
Application throughput	Application response time
Link utilization	Link overhead
Router utilization	Routing overhead
Percentage of packets not requiring retransmission	Percentage of packets duplicated
Percentage of packets with implicit acknowledgment	Percentage of packets delivered with error

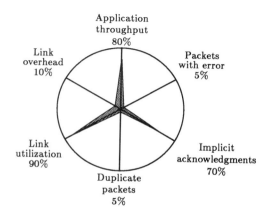

FIGURE 10.24 Kiviat graph for a computer network.

10.7 SCHUMACHER CHARTS

The Schumacher chart is another reporting format that has been suggested in literature. However, since this chart is not widely used, it is described only briefly. Like a Kiviat graph, a Schumacher chart can be used for periodic performance reporting to show daily, weekly, monthly, quarterly, or yearly resource usage. Any number of performance metrics can be plotted in tabular form, as shown in Figure 10.25. The values are normalized with respect to the long-term mean and standard deviations. Any observations that are beyond the mean plus or minus one standard deviation need to be explained. The performance metrics can also be grouped into several management categories and each category can be presented on a separate chart. Other information about the long-term behavior of the metrics can also be shown on the chart.

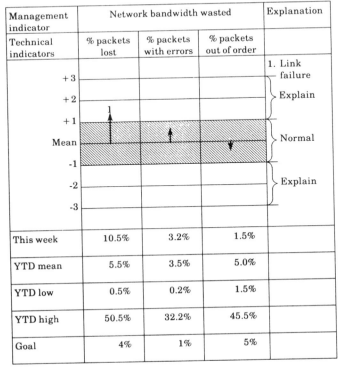

Management indicator	Network bandwidth wasted			Explanation
Technical indicators	% packets lost	% packets with errors	% packets out of order	
				1. Link failure / Explain / Normal / Explain
This week	10.5%	3.2%	1.5%	
YTD mean	5.5%	3.5%	5.0%	
YTD low	0.5%	0.2%	1.5%	
YTD high	50.5%	32.2%	45.5%	
Goal	4%	1%	5%	

FIGURE 10.25   Schumacher chart.

10.8 DECISION MAKER'S GAMES

Even if the performance analysis is correctly done and presented, it may not be enough to persuade your audience—the decision makers—to follow your recommendations. The list shown in Box 10.2 is a compilation of reasons for rejection heard at various performance analysis presentations. You can use the list by presenting it immediately and pointing out that the reason for rejection is not new and that the analysis deserves more consideration. Also, the list is helpful in getting the competing proposals rejected!

There is no clear end of an analysis. Any analysis can be rejected simply on the grounds that the problem needs more analysis. This is the first reason listed in Box 10.2. The second most common reason for rejection of an analysis and for endless debate is the workload. Since workloads are always based on the past measurements, their applicability to the current or future environment can always be questioned. Actually workload is one of the four areas of discussion that lead a performance presentation into an endless debate. These "rat holes" and their relative sizes in terms of time consumed are shown in Figure 10.26. Presenting this cartoon at the beginning of a presentation helps to avoid these areas.

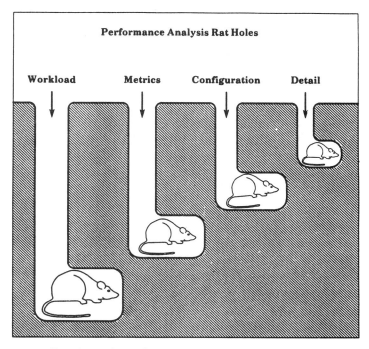

FIGURE 10.26 Four issues in performance presentations that commonly lead to endless discussion.

Box 10.2   Reasons for Not Accepting the Results of an Analysis

1. This needs more analysis.
2. You need a better understanding of the workload.
3. It improves performance only for long I/O's, packets, jobs, and files, and most of the I/O's, packets, jobs, and files are short.
4. It improves performance only for short I/O's, packets, jobs, and files, but who cares for the performance of short I/O's, packets, jobs, and files; its the long ones that impact the system.
5. It needs too much memory/CPU/bandwidth and memory/CPU/bandwidth isn't free.
6. It only saves us memory/CPU/bandwidth and memory/CPU/bandwidth is cheap.
7. There is no point in making the networks (similarly, CPUs/disks/...) faster; our CPUs/disks (any component other than the one being discussed) aren't fast enough to use them.
8. It improves the performance by a factor of x, but it doesn't really matter at the user level because everything else is so slow.
9. It is going to increase the complexity and cost.
10. Let us keep it simple stupid (and your idea is not stupid).
11. It is not simple. (Simplicity is in the eyes of the beholder.)
12. It requires too much state.
13. Nobody has ever done that before. (You have a new idea.)
14. It is not going to raise the price of our stock by even an eighth. (Nothing ever does, except rumors.)
15. This will violate the IEEE, ANSI, CCITT, or ISO standard.
16. It may violate some future standard.
17. The standard says nothing about this and so it must not be important.
18. Our competitors don't do it. If it was a good idea, they would have done it.
19. Our competition does it this way and you don't make money by copying others.
20. It will introduce randomness into the system and make debugging difficult.
21. It is too deterministic; it may lead the system into a cycle.
22. It's not interoperable.
23. This impacts hardware.
24. That's beyond today's technology.
25. It is not self-stabilizing.
26. Why change—it's working OK.

EXERCISES

10.1 What type of chart (line or bar) would you use to plot
   a. CPU usage for 12 months of the year
   b. CPU usage as a function of time in months
   c. Number of I/O's to three disk drives: A, B, and C
   d. Number of I/O's as a function of number of disk drives in a system
10.2 List the problems with the charts of Figure 10.27.
10.3 A system consists of three resources, called A, B, and C. The measured utilizations are shown in Table 10.3. A zero in a column indicates that the resource is not utilized. Draw a Gantt chart showing utilization profiles.
10.4 The measured values of the eight performance metrics listed in Example 10.2 for a system are 70, 10, 60, 20, 80, 30, 50, and 20%. Draw the Kiviat graph and compute its figure of merit.
10.5 For a computer system of your choice, list a number of HB and LB metrics and draw a typical Kiviat graph using data values of your choice.

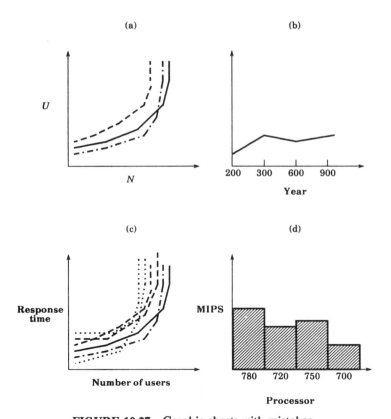

FIGURE 10.27 Graphic charts with mistakes.

TABLE 10.3   Data for Exercise 10.3

A	B	C	Time Used (%)
0	0	0	25
0	0	1	10
0	1	0	20
0	1	1	5
1	0	0	5
1	0	1	15
1	1	0	5
1	1	1	15
			100

CHAPTER 11

RATIO GAMES

> *If you can't convince them, confuse them.*
> —Truman's Law

Ratios provide good opportunities for playing performance games with competitors. Ratios have a numerator and a denominator. The denominator is also called a base. Two ratios with different bases are not comparable. There are, however, many examples in published literature where computer scientists have knowingly or unknowingly compared ratios with different bases. The technique of using ratios with incomparable bases and combining them to one's advantage is called a **ratio game**. There are many different ways in which ratios can be used. Some of these are explicit and others are implicit in the sense that it is not obvious that a ratio has been taken. Some of these techniques and the strategies that are used for winning such games are described in this chapter. Learning about such games is helpful, not because we recommend their usage, but because their knowledge will help us protect ourselves from being victimized by others.

11.1 CHOOSING AN APPROPRIATE BASE SYSTEM

The simplest way in which ratio games are played is by presenting the performance of two (or more) systems on a variety of workloads, taking a ratio of performance for each workload, and then using the average ratio to show that one's proposed system is better than the alternative.

An example of such a case was presented in Section 1.2, where three ways to average the performance of two systems A and B were compared. To recapitulate, these three ways are as follows:

- Take an average of each individual system's performance and then take a ratio.
- Normalize each system's performance on each workload by that of system A and then take an average of ratios.
- Normalize each system's performance on each workload by that of system B and then take an average of ratios.

It was shown that by appropriate choice of the base system one could reverse the conclusion about which of the two systems is better.

The following case study illustrates the game with real measurements.

Case Study 11.1   The performance of two processors, 6502 and 8080, was measured on two workloads called Block move and Sieve. The mean values of the 10 replications of each of the four experiments are shown in Table 11.1. The analysis of the data in using the average of totals, average of ratios with A as a base, and ratios with B as a base is also shown in the table. The three analyses lead to three different conclusions:

- *Ratio of Totals*: 6502 is worse. It takes 4.7% more time than 8080.
- *With 6502 as a Base*: 6502 is better. It takes 1% less time than 8080.
- *With 8080 as a Base*: 6502 is worse. It takes 6% more time.   □

TABLE 11.1   A Comparison of 6502 and 8080 Processors

| | Raw Measurements | | With 6502 as a Base | | With 8080 as a Base | |
| | System | | System | | System | |
Benchmark	6502	8080	6502	8080	6502	8080
Block	41.16	51.50	1.00	1.25	0.80	1.00
Sieve	63.17	48.08	1.00	0.76	1.31	1.00
Sum	104.33	99.58	2.00	2.01	2.11	2.00
Average	52.17	49.79	1.00	1.01	1.06	1.00

Ratio games can be played even when more than two systems or benchmarks are involved. The following case study illustrates one such case.

Case Study 11.2   Table 11.2 shows the measured code sizes for several workloads on a Reduced Instruction Set Computer (RISC) system and four other processors. This data has been adapted from those reported by Patterson and Sequin (1982). The sum of the code sizes is also shown in the table. RISC-I has the largest code size. The second processor, Z8002, requires 9% less code than RISC-I. Table 11.3 shows ratios of code sizes with

TABLE 11.2   Raw Data for the Code Size Comparison Study

Benchmark	Processor				
	RISC-I	Z8002	VAX-11/780	PDP-11/70	C/70
E-String Search	140	126	98	112	98
F-Bit Test	120	180	144	168	120
H-Linked List	176	141	211	299	141
K-Bit Matrix	288	374	288	374	317
I-Quick Sort	992	1,091	893	1,091	893
Ackermann(3,6)	144	302	72	86	86
Recursive Qsort	2,736	1,368	1,368	1,642	1,642
Puzzle (Subscript)	2,796	1,398	1,398	1,398	1,678
Puzzle (Pointer)	752	602	451	376	376
SED (Batch Editor)	17,720	17,720	10,632	8,860	8,860
Towers Hanoi (18)	96	240	77	96	67
Sum	25,960	23,542	15,632	14,502	14,278
Average	2,360	2,140.18	1,421.09	1,318.36	1,298

TABLE 11.3   Ratios with RISC-I as a Base for the Code Size Comparison Study

Benchmark	Processor				
	RISC-I	Z8002	VAX-11/780	PDP-11/70	C/70
E-String Search	1.00	0.90	0.70	0.80	0.70
F-Bit Test	1.00	1.50	1.20	1.40	1.00
H-Linked List	1.00	0.80	1.20	1.70	0.80
K-Bit Matrix	1.00	1.30	1.00	1.30	1.10
I-Quick Sort	1.00	1.10	0.90	1.10	0.90
Ackermann(3,6)	1.00	2.10	0.50	0.60	0.60
Recursive Qsort	1.00	0.50	0.50	0.60	0.60
Puzzle (Subscript)	1.00	0.50	0.50	0.50	0.60
Puzzle (Pointer)	1.00	0.80	0.60	0.50	0.50
SED (Batch Editor)	1.00	1.00	0.60	0.50	0.50
Towers Hanoi (18)	1.00	2.50	0.80	1.00	0.70
Sum	11.00	13.00	8.50	10.00	8.00
Average	1.00	1.18	0.77	0.91	0.73

RISC-I as a base. This table leads to the conclusion that Z8002 has the largest code size and that it takes 18% more code than RISC-I.   □

11.2   USING AN APPROPRIATE RATIO METRIC

Another form in which ratio games are used to show better performance is by choosing a suitable performance metric which is a ratio of two different metrics. The following example illustrates such a case.

TABLE 11.4   Performance of Two Network Architectures

Network	Throughput	Response
A	10	2
B	4	1

TABLE 11.5   Using a Ratio Metric

System	Throughput	Response	Power
A	10	2	5
B	4	1	4

Example 11.1   Throughput and response time were measured on two network architectures. The results are tabulated in Table 11.4. Notice that network A has higher throughput (an HB metric) but also has a higher response time (an LB metric).

The designers of network A suggest that the right metric to compare the networks is by power, which is defined as the ratio of throughput and response time. The transformed results are shown in Table 11.5. From this table, one would conclude that network A is better than network B.   □

11.3   USING RELATIVE PERFORMANCE ENHANCEMENT

Sometimes the performance metric is already specified. In this case, it is possible to show that relative increase in the performance is better using one type of enhancement than another provided the two are tried on different machines.

Example 11.2   Two floating-point accelerators A and B are to be compared. MFLOPS measured on two machines with and without the accelerators are tabulated in Table 11.6.

The right way to compare the two accelerators would be to try them out on a single machine. But since B seems to be a popular accelerator and A does not yet work on the same machine as B, the designers of A can exploit the technique of using incomparable bases, as shown in Table 11.7. *Conclusion*: A gives a higher improvement than B.   □

TABLE 11.6   MFLOPS of Two Processors with and without Accelerators

Alternative	Without	With
A on X	2	4
B on Y	3	5

TABLE 11.7 Improvement Due to an Accelerator

Alternative	Without	With	Ratio
A on X	2	4	2.00
B on Y	3	5	1.66

11.4 RATIO GAMES WITH PERCENTAGES

Percentages are basically ratios. They allow playing ratio games in ways that do not look like ratios.

Example 11.3 Two experiments were repeatedly conducted on two systems. Each experiment either passed or failed (system either met the specified performance goal or did not). The results are tabulated in the first two rows of Table 11.8.

One alternative to compare the two systems is to take each experiment individually, as shown in Figure 11.1a. The conclusion from this figure is that System B is better than System A in *both* experiments. Another alternative is to add the results of the two experiments as shown in the last row of Table 11.8 and plotted in Figure 11.1b. The conclusion in this case is that System A is better than system B.

Actually both alternatives have the problem of incomparable bases. In alternative 1, the base is the total number of times the experiment is repeated on a system, which is different for the two systems. In alternative 2,

TABLE 11.8 Two Tests on Two Systems

	System A				System B		
Test	Total	Pass	% Pass	Test	Total	Pass	% Pass
1	300	60	20	1	32	8	25
2	50	2	4	2	500	40	8
	350	62	20.6		532	48	9

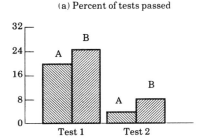

(a) Percent of tests passed

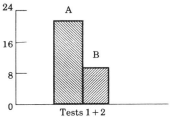

(b) Percent of total tests passed

FIGURE 11.1 Ratio games with percentages.

the base is the sum of repetitions of the two experiments together, which is also different for the two systems.   □

Percentages are misused in several other ways. For example, they can be used to have a psychological impact on the reader. Large numbers attract immediate attention. A 1000% improvement in performance sounds more impressive than an 11-time improvement. This is particularly useful when the performance before the improvement as well as the absolute increase in the performance are not impressive. Instead of saying that the network throughput improved from 1 packet per second to 11 packets per second (which are both unimpressive), it is better to say that the performance was improved by 1000%.

Small sample sizes can be neatly disguised by specifying the percentage. Saying that 83.3% of the universities in town use system X is more impressive than saying that five of the six universities use the system.

The base in the percentage should be the initial value—the value that comes first in the time order. Many people, particularly those trying to market a product aggressively, ignore this and specify percentages with respect to final values. For example, when they say that memory prices have gone down by 400%, it sounds like they are now paying you to buy memory. Actually, current prices are one-fifth of the original.

11.5 STRATEGIES FOR WINNING A RATIO GAME

Having seen several examples of ratio games, one obvious question is under what conditions can the conclusions be reversed by changing the base in a ratio game. This is the topic of this section. Only games involving the choice of a base system are considered. Application to other types of ratio games is straightforward. To win a ratio game, the guidelines are as follows:

1. *If one system is better on all benchmarks, contradicting conclusions cannot be drawn by any ratio game technique.* A contradicting conclusion means that one system is the best with one base and another is the best on some other base. Notice that in both case studies of the ratio games given in Section 11.1, the measurements were such that one system was better on some benchmark and worse on other benchmarks. If this is not the case, then the same system will come out the best using any base. For example, Table 11.9 shows the execution times of System A and System B on benchmarks I and J. The times relative to System A and System B are also shown in the table. In all three cases shown, System A is the better of the two systems.

2. *Even if one system is better than the other on all benchmarks, a better relative performance can be shown by selecting the appropriate base.* Thus, although the three analyses shown in Table 11.9 show System A to be

TABLE 11.9   An Example with One System Better on Both Metrics

Raw Measurements			With A as a Base			With B as a Base		
	System			System			System	
Benchmark	A	B	Benchmark	A	B	Benchmark	A	B
I	0.50	1.00	I	1.00	2.00	I	0.50	1.00
J	1.00	1.50	J	1.00	1.50	J	0.67	1.00
Average	0.75	1.25		1.00	1.75		0.58	1.00

better, System A is 40% better than System B using raw data, 43% better using system A as a base, and 42% better using System B as a base. The system A designers would prefer to use the raw-data averages.

3. *If a system is better on some benchmarks and worse on others, contradicting conclusions can be drawn in some cases.* In other words, contradicting conclusions cannot be drawn in all cases. The easiest way to verify whether a contradictory conclusion can be drawn for a particular data set is to try all possible bases. The following rules may help select the base.

4. *If the performance metric is an LB metric, it is better to use your system as the base.* The execution time is an LB metric, and as shown in Table 11.9, System A designers would be better off using System A as the base. System B designers would prefer to use System B as the base.

5. *If the performance metric is an HB metric, it is better to use your opponent as the base.* The throughputs, efficiency, MIPS, and MFLOPS are examples of HB metrics. In these cases, a higher average ratio would be obtained for System A if System B is used as a base.

6. *Those benchmarks that perform better on your system should be elongated and those that perform worse should be shortened.* The time duration of the benchmarks is often adjustable. For example, in the Sieve benchmark (described in Section 4.6), the number of prime numbers to be generated can be set by the experimenter. If System A performs better than system B on the Sieve benchmark, choosing to generate a larger number of prime numbers would make the results more favorable to System A designers if a ratio-of-totals technique is used to compare the two systems. This in effect increases the weight on the favorable benchmark. Shortening unfavorable benchmarks also has the same effect.

Once again, remember that taking an average of a ratio is not a correct way to analyze the data. Unfortunately, it is done so often that it is useful to know the rules for self-protection. The correct method to analyze such data is by using techniques to analyze experimental designs, as discussed later in Part IV of this book. For mathematically oriented readers, a derivation of these rules follows next.

TABLE 11.10 Derivation of the Rules

Raw Data			With A as a Base			With B as a Base		
	System			System			System	
Benchmark	A	B	Benchmark	A	B	Benchmark	A	B
I	a	ax	I	1	x	I	$\dfrac{1}{x}$	1
J	b	by	J	1	y	J	$\dfrac{1}{y}$	1
Average	$\dfrac{(a+b)}{2}$	$\dfrac{(ax+by)}{2}$		1	$\dfrac{(x+y)}{2}$		$\dfrac{1}{2}\left(\dfrac{1}{x}+\dfrac{1}{y}\right)$	1

Derivation 11.1 Assume the performance metric is an HB (higher is better) metric. The resulting LB metric can be derived in a manner similar to that presented here.

Consider the case of two systems A and B on two benchmarks I and J. Suppose the performance of System A on the two benchmarks is a and b, respectively. The relative performance of System B on the two benchmarks is x and y, respectively. This leads to the raw performance shown in Table 11.10. Using the raw data, System A is better if and only if

$$\frac{a+b}{2} > \frac{ax+by}{2}$$

or

$$y < -\frac{a}{b}x + \frac{a+b}{b} \tag{11.1}$$

Figure 11.2 shows a graphical representation of Equation (11.1). Both axes in the figure show the relative performance of System B with System A as a base. The horizontal axis shows x—relative performance of B on benchmark I. The vertical axis shows y—relative performance of B on benchmark J.

Equation (11.1) divides the possible space into two regions on the two sides of the line $y = -(a/b)x + (a+b)/b$. System A is better than system B below the line and worse above the line.

If System A is used as a base as shown in Table 11.10, System A will be considered better if and only if

$$\frac{x+y}{2} < 1$$

or

$$y < 2 - x \tag{11.2}$$

Graphically, the region below the line $y = 2 - x$ in Figure 11.2 represents the subspace in which System A will be considered better. Note that

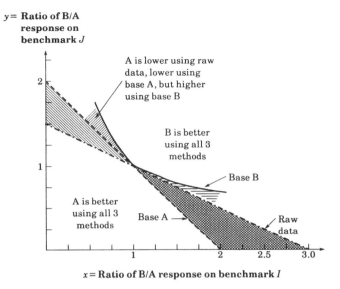

FIGURE 11.2 Strategies for ratio games. Contradictory conclusions can be obtained using different methods only in shaded regions.

this subspace is not identical to that given by Equation (11.1). The additional area covered by this equation is shown shaded in Figure 11.2. If the measurements fall in this shaded area, System A will be considered worse than System B using raw data but will be considered better using system A as the base. This is one possible region where ratio games will lead to contradictory conclusions. Notice that this region is a proper subset of the region $(x < 1, y > 1)$. That is, the performance of System B is better on one benchmark and worse on the other.

If System B is used as a base as shown in Table 11.10, System A will be considered better if and only if:

$$\frac{1}{2}\left(\frac{1}{x} + \frac{1}{y}\right) > 1$$

or

$$y < \frac{x}{2x - 1} \qquad (11.3)$$

Graphically, Equation (11.3) represents a hyperbola as shown in in Figure 11.2. In the region below this hyperbola, System A will be considered better. This region covers a bigger area for System A. Once again the region above the lines corresponding to Equations (11.1) and (11.2) and below this hyperbola represents the subspace in which contradictory results will be reached by using different bases and raw results.   □

11.6 CORRECT ANALYSIS

The main reason why the analysis of ratios, as presented so far, results in contradicting results is that the approach of taking a mean of the ratio is wrong. The approach completely ignores the fact that the performance is affected by several factors as well as by experimental errors. For example, in the case of execution time of a workload on a system, the two factors are the workload and the system. A statement about one factor, for example, the comparative power of systems involved, can be made only if the effects of different factors and errors are first isolated. The isolation requires developing a model of the way these factors and the experimental errors interact with each other. Techniques for this require knowledge of several probabilistic, statistical, and experimental design concepts. In parts III and IV of this book, these concepts are developed and explained. After reading these two parts, you will be able to correctly analyze the data presented in this chapter. In particular, taking means of ratios is discussed in Section 12.7, comparing two systems in the presence of variability is discussed in Chapter 13, and isolating effects of two factors is discussed in Chapters 16 to 23. An analysis of the code size comparison data of Table 11.2 is presented in Exercise 21.3.

EXERCISES

11.1 Table 11.11 shows execution times of three benchmarks I, J, and K on three systems A, B, and C. Use ratio game techniques to show the superiority of various systems.

TABLE 11.11   Raw Execution Times for Exercise 11.1

Benchmark	System A	System B	System C
I	50	100	150
J	100	150	50
K	150	50	100
Sum	300	300	300
Average	100	100	100

11.2 Derive conditions necessary for you to be able to use the the technique of combined percentages to your advantage.

FURTHER READING FOR PART II

Gibson Mix is described in Gibson (1970). Lucas, Jr. (1971) presents one of the earliest survey of test workloads. The articles by Hansen et al. (1982), Patterson (1982), and Levy and Clark (1982) argue the proper (or improper) use of kernels in comparing processors. Gilbreath (1981) describes the Sieve kernel and provides its listings in FORTRAN, C, PL/I, BASIC, FOURTH, and COBOL. Wright, Kohler, and Zahavi (1989) describe one interpreation of the debit-credit benchmark.

Surveys of workload characterization techniques can be found in Ferrari (1972), Agrawala et al. (1976), and Oed and Mertens (1981). The data presented in Tables 6.1 and 6.2 are from Jain and Turner (1982). Sreenivasan and Kleinman (1974) describe a case study of the the multiparameter histogram technique. Application of principal-component analysis techniques can be found in Serazzi (1981, 1985). Clustering analysis has been applied in numerous case studies. See, for example, Agrawala and Mohr (1977), Mamrak and Amer (1977), Artis (1978), Wight (1981), and Calzarossa and Ferrari (1986). For description of various clustering techniques see Everitt (1974), which also has a good discussion of problems with clustering.

Nutt (1975, 1979) and Svobodova (1976) present some of the earliest discussions on H/W and S/W monitors. Pinkerton (1977) describes common forms and mechanisms of software monitors. Ramage (1977) discusses various issues of software monitor design. Hughes (1980) presents the design of a hybrid monitor.

For a sample description of a commercially available hardware monitor, see COMTEN (1977). Howard (1983) presents a description of several commercially available performance analysis tools. Leavitt (1986b) has a more recent listing of commercially available monitors. EDP Performance Review publishes an annual issue listing all commercially available performance analysis tools. Plattner and Nievergelt (1981) describe performance measurements of programs.

Bouhana (1979) describes the issues related to use of accounting logs. The case study on accounting log usage is from Jain and Turner (1982).

Houghton, Jr. (1982) describes and compares four different ways to instrument a program. Power (1983) presents a survey of program execution monitoring and has an extensive bibiliography. Bentley (1982) discusses several techniques to improve the efficiency of programs.

The discussion on distributed monitoring is based on the features available in several commercially available network monitors. Joyce et al. (1987) present a case study of a distributed-monitor design.

For a survey of capacity planning issues, see the report prepared by Datametrics (1983) for the National Bureau of Standards. The report has an extensive bibliography. The CMG conference proceedings and EDP performance review regularly have articles on this topic. See also Strauss (1981). Leavitt (1986a) provides a list of commercial capacity planning products and vendor addresses.

For surveys of RTEs see Watkins and Abrams (1977a, 1977b) and Spiegel (1980). Figure 9.5 is based on Proppe and Wallack (1982). McGalliard and Theraja (1988) and Trehan (1978) discuss the problems of remote workstation emulation and describe the keyboard monitor emulation approach.

Many of the benchmarking mistakes discussed in this part are from Goldstein (1988), which has an interesting discussion of other issues related specifically to storage benchmarking.

Advice on preparing good graphic charts can be found in the books by Schmid and Schmid (1979), Lefferts (1981), Schmid (1983), Holmes (1984), and White (1984). Articles by Powell (1988), Finehirsh (1985), and MacKinnon (1987) also present additional information on graphic presentations.

The idea of Kiviat graphs was first proposed by Kolence (1973a). It immediately became a popular topic of discussion in *Performance Evaluation Review* for the next three years. Kolence and Kiviat (1973b) describe several common shapes. The paper by Morris (1974) gives an excellent history and classification of graphs. Merrill (1974) proposed a numerical figure of merit to compare Kiviat graphs, and a number of papers including those by Bahr (1975), Merrill (1975), Stevens (1975), and Calcagni (1976) subsequently proposed other alternative figures of merits. Schumacher charts are described in more detail in Morris and Roth (1982).

The data for Case Study 11.2 was adopted from Patterson and Sequin (1982). We have deleted one row and one column containing missing values.

The book by Ferrari, Serazzi, and Zeigner (1983) has an excellent treatment of many topics related to measurement and modeling of computer systems. Other books discussing performance measurements are Ferrari (1978), Barnes (1979), and McKerrow (1987).

PART III

PROBABILITY THEORY AND STATISTICS

This part introduces the basic concepts of probability theory and statistics. An understanding of these concepts will help you analyze and interpret data properly. After reading Part III, you will be able to answer questions such as the ones that follow.

1. How should you report the performance as a single number? Is specifying the mean the correct way to summarize a sequence of measurements?

2. How should you report the variability of measured quantities? What are the alternatives to variance and when are they appropriate?

3. How should you interpret the variability? How much confidence can you put on data with a large variability?

4. How many measurements are required to get a desired level of statistical confidence?

5. How should you summarize the results of several different workloads on a single computer system?

6. How should you compare two or more computer systems using several different workloads? Is comparing the mean performance sufficient?

7. What model best describes the relationship between two variables? Also, how good is the model?

Performance analysts and system designers face such questions frequently. Knowledge of techniques and concepts discussed in this part is required for understanding the simulation and queueing theory concepts discussed later in Parts V and VI of this book.

CHAPTER 12

SUMMARIZING MEASURED DATA

The object of statistics is to discover methods of condensing information concerning large groups of allied facts into brief and compendious expressions suitable for discussions.

—Francis Galton

Summarizing measured data is one of the most common problems faced by performance analysts. A measurement project may result in several hundred or millions of observations on a given variable. To present the measurements to the decision makers, it is necessary to summarize the data. Several alternative ways of summarizing data and the appropriateness of each alternative are discussed in this chapter.

12.1 BASIC PROBABILITY AND STATISTICS CONCEPTS

In this and all following chapters, it is assumed that you have an understanding of basic probability and statistics concepts. In particular, you should be familiar with the following terms:

1. **Independent Events**: Two events are called independent if the occurrence of one event does not in any way affect the probability of the other event. Thus, knowing that one event has occurred does not in any way change our estimate of the probability of the other event.
2. **Random Variable**: A variable is called a random variable if it takes one of a specified set of values with a specified probability.

179

3. **Cumulative Distribution Function**: The Cumulative Distribution Function (**CDF**) of a random variable maps a given value a to the probability of the variable taking a value less than or equal to a:

$$F_x(a) = P(x \leq a)$$

4. **Probability Density Function**: The derivative

$$f(x) = \frac{dF(x)}{dx}$$

of the CDF $F(x)$ is called the probability density function (**pdf**) of x. Given a pdf $f(x)$, the probability of x being in the interval (x_1, x_2) can also be computed by integration:

$$P(x_1 < x \leq x_2) = F(x_2) - F(x_1) = \int_{x_1}^{x_2} f(x)dx$$

5. **Probability Mass Function**: For discrete random variable, the CDF is not continuous and, therefore, not differentiable. In such cases, the probability mass function (**pmf**) is used in place of pdf. Consider a discrete random variable x that can take n distinct values $\{x_1, x_2, ..., x_n\}$ with probabilities $\{p_1, p_2, ..., p_n\}$ such that the probability of the ith value x_i is p_i. The pmf maps x_i to p_i:

$$f(x_i) = p_i$$

The probability of x being in the interval (x_1, x_2) can also be computed by summation:

$$P(x_1 < x \leq x_2) = F(x_2) - F(x_1) = \sum_{\substack{i \\ x_1 < x_i \leq x_2}} p_i$$

6. **Mean or Expected Value**:

$$\text{Mean } \mu = E(x) = \sum_{i=1}^{n} p_i x_i = \int_{-\infty}^{+\infty} x f(x)dx$$

Summation is used for discrete and integration for continuous variables, respectively.

7. **Variance**: The quantity $(x - \mu)^2$ represents the square of distance between x and its mean. The expected value of this quantity is called the variance x:

$$\text{Var}(x) = E[(x - \mu)^2] = \sum_{i=1}^{n} p_i(x_i - \mu)^2 = \int_{-\infty}^{+\infty} (x_i - \mu)^2 f(x)dx$$

The variance is traditionally denoted by σ^2. The square root of the variance is called the **standard deviation** and is denoted by σ.

8. **Coefficient of Variation**: The ratio of the standard deviation to the mean is called the Coefficient of Variation (**C.O.V.**):

$$\text{C.O.V.} = \frac{\text{standard deviation}}{\text{mean}} = \frac{\sigma}{\mu}$$

9. **Covariance**: Given two random variables x and y with means μ_x and μ_y, their covariance is

$$\text{Cov}(x,y) = \sigma_{xy}^2 = E[(x - \mu_x)(y - \mu_y)] = E(xy) - E(x)E(y)$$

For independent variables, the covariance is zero since

$$E(xy) = E(x)E(y)$$

Although independence always implies zero covariance, the reverse is not true. It is possible for two variables to be dependent and still have zero covariance.

10. **Correlation Coefficient**: The normalized value of covariance is called the correlation coefficient or simply the **correlation**

$$\text{Correlation}(x,y) = \rho_{xy} = \frac{\sigma_{xy}^2}{\sigma_x \sigma_y}$$

The correlation always lies between -1 and $+1$.

11. **Mean and Variance of Sums**: If $x_1, x_2, \ldots, x_k$ are k random variables and if $a_1, a_2, \ldots, a_k$ are k arbitrary constants (called weights), then

$$E(a_1 x_1 + a_2 x_2 + \cdots + a_k x_k) = a_1 E(x_1) + a_2 E(x_2) + \cdots + a_k E(x_k)$$

For independent variables,

$$\text{Var}(a_1 x_1 + a_2 x_2 + \cdots + a_k x_k) = a_1^2 \text{Var}(x_1) + a_2^2 \text{Var}(x_2) + \cdots + a_k^2 \text{Var}(x_k)$$

12. **Quantile**: The x value at which the CDF takes a value α is called the α-quantile or 100α-percentile. It is denoted by x_α and is such that the probability of x being less than or equal to x_α is α:

$$P(x \leq x_\alpha) = F(x_\alpha) = \alpha$$

13. **Median**: The 50-percentile (or 0.5-quantile) of a random variable is called its median.

14. **Mode**: The most likely value, that is, x_i, that has the highest probability p_i, or the x at which pdf is maximum, is called the mode of x.

15. **Normal Distribution**: This is the most commonly used distribution in data analysis. The sum of a large number of independent observations from any distribution has a normal distribution. Also known as Gaussian distribution, its pdf is given by

$$f(x) = \frac{1}{\sigma\sqrt{2\pi}} e^{-(x-\mu)^2/2\sigma^2}, \qquad -\infty \leq x \leq +\infty$$

There are two parameters μ and σ, which are also the mean and standard deviations of x. A normal variate is denoted by $N(\mu, \sigma)$. A normal distribution with zero mean and unit variance is called a **unit normal** or **standard normal distribution** and is denoted as $N(0, 1)$. In statistical modeling, you will frequently need to use quantiles of the unit normal distribution. An α-quantile of a unit normal variate $z \sim N(0, 1)$ is denoted by z_α. If a random variable x has a $N(\mu, \sigma)$ distribution, then $(x - \mu)/\sigma$ has a $N(0, 1)$ distribution. Thus,

$$P\left(\frac{x - \mu}{\sigma} \leq z_\alpha\right) = \alpha$$

or

$$P(x \leq \mu + z_\alpha \sigma) = \alpha$$

The areas under the unit normal pdf between 0 and z for various values of z are listed in Table A.1 of the Appendix.

There are two main reasons for the popularity of the normal distribution:

(a) *The sum of n independent normal variates is a normal variate.* If $x_i \sim N(\mu_i, \sigma_i)$, then $x = \sum_{i=1}^{n} a_i x_i$ has a normal distribution with mean $\mu = \sum_{i=1}^{n} a_i \mu_i$ and variance $\sigma^2 = \sum_{i=1}^{n} a_i^2 \sigma_i^2$. As a result of this linearity property, normal processes remain normal after passing through linear systems, which are popular in electrical engineering.

(b) *The sum of a large number of independent observations from any distribution tends to have a normal distribution.* This result, which is called the **central limit theorem**, is true for observations from all distributions. As a result of this property, experimental errors, which are contributed by many factors, are modeled with a normal distribution.

Exercises 12.1 to 12.7 have been designed to specifically test your understanding of the preceding concepts.

12.2 SUMMARIZING DATA BY A SINGLE NUMBER

In the most condensed form, a single number may be presented that gives the key characteristic of the data set. This single number is usually called an **average** of the data. To be meaningful, this average should be representative of a major part of the data set. Three popular alternatives to summarize a sample are to specify its mean, median, or mode. These measures are what statisticians call **indices of central tendencies**. The name is based on the fact that these measures specify the center of location of the distribution of the observations in the sample.

Sample mean is obtained by taking the sum of all observations and dividing this sum by the number of observations in the sample. **Sample median** is obtained by sorting the observations in an increasing order and taking the observation that is in the middle of the series. If the number of observations is even, the mean of the middle two values is used as a median. **Sample mode** is obtained by plotting a histogram and specifying the midpoint of the bucket where the histogram peaks. For categorical variables, mode is given by the category that occurs most frequently.

The word *sample* in the names of these indices signifies the fact that the values obtained are based on just one sample (see Section 13.1). However, if it is clear from the context that the discussion is about a single sample, and there is no ambiguity, the shorter names mean, median, and mode can be used.

Mean and median always exist and are unique. Given any set of observations, the mean and median can be determined. Mode, on the other hand, may not exist. An example of this would be if all observations were equal. In addition, even if modes exist, they may not be unique. There may be more than one mode, that is, there may be more than one local peak in the histogram.

The three indices are generally different. Figure 12.1 shows five different pdf's. Distribution (a) has a unimodal, symmetrical pdf. In this case, the mode exists with the mean, median, and mode being equal. Distribution (b) has a bimodal, symmetrical pdf. In this case, the mode is not unique. The median and mean are equal. Distribution (c) is a uniform density function. There is no mode and the mean and median are equal. Distribution (d) has a pdf skewed to the right (with a tail toward the right). For this distribution, the value of the mean is greater than the median, which in turn is greater than the mode. Finally, distribution (e) has a pdf skewed to the left; that is, it has a tail on the left. In this case, the mean is less than the median, which is less than the mode.

The main problem with the mean is that it is affected more by outliers than the median or mode. A single outlier can make a considerable change in the mean. This is particularly true for small samples. Median and mode are resistant to several outlying observations.

The mean gives equal weight to each observation and in this sense makes full use of the sample. Median and mode ignore a lot of the information.

The mean has an additivity or linearity property in that the mean of a sum is a sum of the means. This does not apply to the mode or median.

12.3 SELECTING AMONG THE MEAN, MEDIAN, AND MODE

A common mistake inexperienced analysts make is to specify the wrong index of central tendency. For example, it is common to specify the mean regardless of its validity in a particular situation.

The flow chart of Figure 12.2 shows a set of guidelines to select a proper index of central tendency. The first consideration is the type of variable. If the

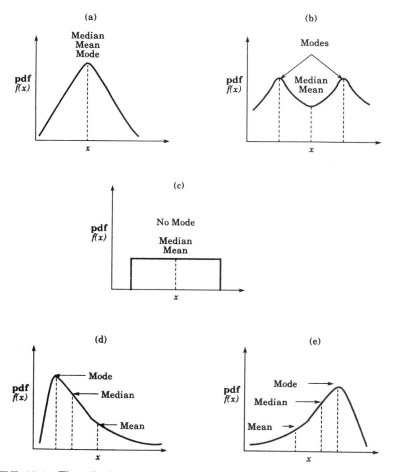

FIGURE 12.1 Five distributions showing relationships among mean, median, and mode.

variable is categorical, the mode is the proper single measure that best describes that data. An example of categorical data is the type of microprocessor in various workstations. A statement such as "the most frequent microprocessor used in workstations is the 68000" makes sense. The mean or median of the type of processor is meaningless.

The second consideration in selecting the index is to ask whether the total of all observations is of any interest. If yes, then the mean is a proper index of central tendency. For example, total CPU time for five queries is a meaningful number. On the other hand, if we count number of windows on the screen during each query, the total number of windows during five queries does not seem to be meaningful. If the total is of interest, specify the mean.

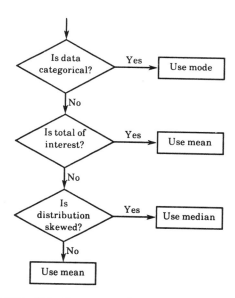

FIGURE 12.2   Selecting among the mean, meadian, and mode.

If the total is of no interest, one has to choose between median and mode. If the histogram is symmetrical and unimodal, the mean, median, and mode are all equal and it does not really matter which one is specified.

If the histogram is skewed, the median is more representative of a typical observation than the mean. For example, the number of disk drives on engineering workstations is expected to have skewed distribution, and therefore, it is appropriate to specify the median number. One simple to way to determine skewness for small samples is to examine the ratio of the maximum and minimum, y_{max}/y_{min}, of the observations. If the ratio is large, the data is skewed.

The following are examples of selections of indices of central tendencies:

- *Most Used Resource in a System*: Resources are categorical and hence the mode must be used.
- *Interarrival Time*: Total time is of interest and so the mean is the proper choice.
- *Load on a Computer*: The median is preferable due to a highly skewed distribution.
- *Average Configuration*: Medians of number devices, memory sizes, and number of processors are generally used to specify the configuration due to the skewness of the distribution.

12.4 COMMON MISUSES OF MEANS

The following is a list of some of the mistakes that are often committed by novices:

- *Using Mean of Significantly Different Values*: When the mean is the correct index of central tendency for a variable, it does not automatically imply that a mean of any set of that variable will be useful. Usefulness depends upon the number of values and the variance, not only on the type of the variable. For example, it is not very useful to say that the mean CPU time per query is 505 milliseconds when the two measurements come out to be 10 and 1000 milliseconds. An analysis based on 505 milliseconds would lead nowhere close to the two possibilities. In this particular example, the mean is the correct index but is useless.
- *Using Mean without Regard to the Skewness of Distribution*: Another example of misuse of means is shown in Table 12.1, where response times for two different systems have been tabulated. Both have mean response times of 10. In the first case, it is useful to know the mean because the variance is low and 10 is the typical value. In the second case, the typical value is 5; hence, using 10 for the mean does not give any useful result. The variability is too large in this case.
- *Multiplying Means To Get the Mean of a Product*: The mean of a product of two random variables is equal to the product of means if the two random variables are independent. If x and y are correlated,

$$E(xy) \neq E(x)E(y)$$

Example 12.1 On a timesharing system, the total number of users and the number of subprocesses for each user are monitored. The average number of users is 23. The average number of subprocesses per user is 2. What is the average number of subprocesses?

Is it 46? No! The number of subprocesses a user spawns depends upon how much load there is on the system. On an overloaded system (large

TABLE 12.1 System Response Times for 5 Days

	System A	System B
	10	5
	9	5
	11	5
	10	4
	10	31
Sum	50	50
Mean	10	10
Typical	10	5

number of users), users try to keep the number of subprocesses low, and on an underloaded system, users try to keep the number of subprocesses high. The two variables are correlated, and therefore, the mean of the product cannot be obtained by multiplying the means. The total number of subprocesses on the system should be continuously monitored and then averaged.

□

- *Taking a Mean of a Ratio with Different Bases*: This has already been discussed in Chapter 11 on ratio games and is discussed further in Section 12.7.

12.5 GEOMETRIC MEAN

The geometric mean of n values $x_1, x_2, \ldots, x_n$ is obtained by multiplying the values together and taking the nth root of the product:

$$\dot{x} = \left(\prod_{i=1}^{n} x_i \right)^{1/n}$$

The mean discussed in other sections is what should be termed the arithmetic mean. The arithmetic mean is used if the sum of the observations is a quantity that is of interest. Similarly, the geometric mean is used if the product of the observations is a quantity of interest.

Example 12.2   The performance improvements in the latest version of seven layers of a new networking protocol was measured separately for each layer. The observations are listed in Table 12.2. What is the average improvement per layer? The improvements in the seven layers work in a "multiplicative" manner, that is, doubling the performance of layer 1 and layer 2 shows up as four times the improvement in performance.

TABLE 12.2   Improvement in Each Layer of Network Protocol

Protocol Layer	Performance Improvement (%)
7	18
6	13
5	11
4	8
3	10
2	28
1	5

Average improvement per layer

$$= \{(1.18)(1.13)(1.11)(1.08)(1.10)(1.28)(1.05)\}^{1/7} - 1$$

$$= 0.13$$

Thus, the average improvement per layer is 13%. □

Other examples of metrics that work in a multiplicative manner are as follows:

- Cache hit ratios over several levels of caches
- Cache miss ratios
- Percentage performance improvement between successive versions
- Average error rate per hop on a multihop path in a network

The geometric mean can be considered as a function gm( ), which maps a set of responses $\{x_1, x_2, \ldots, x_n\}$ to a single number $\dot{x}$. It has the following multiplicativity property:

$$\mathrm{gm}\left(\frac{x_1}{y_1}, \frac{x_2}{y_2}, \ldots, \frac{x_n}{y_n}\right) = \frac{\mathrm{gm}(x_1, x_2, \ldots, x_n)}{\mathrm{gm}(y_1, y_2, \ldots, y_n)} = \frac{1}{\mathrm{gm}(y_1/x_1, y_2/x_2, \ldots, y_n/x_n)}$$

That is, the geometric mean of a ratio is the ratio of the geometric means of the numerator and denominator. Thus, the choice of the base does not change the conclusion. It is because of this property that sometimes the geometric mean is recommended for ratios. However, if the geometric mean of the numerator or denominator does not have any physical meaning, the geometric mean of their ratio is meaningless as well. Means of ratios are discussed further in Section 12.7.

12.6 HARMONIC MEAN

The harmonic mean $\ddot{x}$ of a sample $\{x_1, x_2, \ldots, x_n\}$ is defined as follows:

$$\ddot{x} = \frac{n}{1/x_1 + 1/x_2 + \cdots + 1/x_n}$$

A harmonic mean should be used whenever an arithmetic mean can be justified for $1/x_i$. For example, suppose repeated measurements are made for the elasped time of a benchmark on a processor. In the ith repetition, the benchmark takes t_i seconds. Now suppose the benchmark has m million instructions, the MIPS x_i computed from the ith repetition is

$$x_i = \frac{m}{t_i}$$

In Section 12.3, it was argued that t_i's should be summarized using the arithmetic mean since the sum of t_i has a physical meaning. For the same reasons,

x_i's should be summarized using the harmonic mean since the sum of $1/x_i$'s has a physical meaning. The average MIPS rate for the processor is

$$\ddot{x} = \frac{n}{\dfrac{1}{m/t_1} + \dfrac{1}{m/t_2} + \cdots + \dfrac{1}{m/t_n}}$$

$$= \frac{m}{(1/n)(t_1 + t_2 + \cdots + t_n)}$$

Notice, however, if x_i's represent the MIPS rate for n different benchmarks so that the ith benchmark has m_i million instructions, then the harmonic mean of n ratios m_i/t_i cannot be used since the sum of the t_i/m_i does not have any physical meaning. Instead, as shown later in Section 12.7, the quantity $\sum m_i / \sum t_i$ is a preferred average MIPS rate. This is a weighted harmonic mean of n observations. The weighted harmonic mean is defined as follows:

$$\ddot{x} = \frac{1}{w_1/x_1 + w_2/x_2 + \cdots + w_n/x_n}$$

where w_i's are weights that add up to 1:

$$w_1 + w_2 + \cdots + w_n = 1$$

The harmonic mean is a special case of the weighted harmonic mean with all weights being equal, that is, $w_i = 1/n$.

In the example of n observations of the MIPS rate, if the weights are chosen proportional to the size of the benchmark, that is,

$$w_i = \frac{m_i}{m_1 + m_2 + \cdots + m_n}$$

then the weighted harmonic mean would be

$$\ddot{x} = \frac{m_1 + m_2 + \cdots + m_n}{t_1 + t_2 + \cdots + t_n}$$

which is reasonable since the numerator represents the total size of all benchmarks and the denominator represents the total time on all benchmarks.

12.7 MEAN OF A RATIO

Given a set of n ratios, a common problem is to summarize them in a single number. This problem happens, as was discussed earlier in Section 12.6, when trying to summarize the MIPS rate for a processor from measurements of several different workloads. Considering the additivity of the numerator and denominator separately leads to the following rules for summarizing the ratios:

1. *If we take the sum of numerators and the sum of denominators and both have a physical meaning, the average of the ratio is the ratio of the averages.* For example, if $x_i = a_i/b_i$, the average ratio is given by

$$\text{Average}\left(\frac{a_1}{b_1}, \frac{a_2}{b_2}, \ldots, \frac{a_n}{b_n}\right) = \frac{a_1 + a_2 + \cdots + a_n}{b_1 + b_2 + \cdots + b_n}$$

$$= \frac{\sum_{i=1}^{n} a_i}{\sum_{i=1}^{n} b_i} = \frac{(1/n)\sum_{i=1}^{n} a_i}{(1/n)\sum_{i=1}^{n} b_i} = \frac{\bar{a}}{\bar{b}}$$

A common application of this guideline is in computing mean resource utilization as illustrated by the following example.

Example 12.3 The CPU utilization of a system as measured over five different intervals is tabulated in Table 12.3.

The average utilization is not 40% as it may appear. The base (denominators) of the ratios (total times) are not comparable. The mean utilization is obtained by calculating the total CPU busy time and total time and taking the ratio of the two.

$$\text{Mean CPU utilization} = \frac{\text{sum of CPU busy times}}{\text{sum of measurement durations}}$$

$$= \frac{0.45 + 0.45 + 0.45 + 0.45 + 20}{1 + 1 + 1 + 1 + 100} = 21\% \quad \square$$

Example 12.3 also disproves the myth that ratios should always be summarized by a geometric mean. A geometric mean of utilizations is useless. Two special cases of the preceding rule, which in some cases lead to justification for the arithmetic and harmonic mean, respectively, are as follows:

(a) *If the denominator is a constant, so that the ratio has been taken with respect to a base that is constant across all observations, and the sum of the numerator has a physical meaning, the arithmetic mean of the ratios can be used.* That is, if $b_i = b$ for all i's, then

$$\text{Average}\left(\frac{a_1}{b}, \frac{a_2}{b}, \ldots, \frac{a_n}{b}\right) = \frac{1}{n}\left(\frac{a_1}{b} + \frac{a_2}{b} + \cdots + \frac{a_n}{b}\right) = \frac{\sum_{i=1}^{n} a_i}{nb}$$

As an example of this guideline, consider again the problem of computing mean resource utilization. If n values of utilizations are all measured for the same interval of time, the average utilization can be computed using the straight arithmetic mean of n utilizations.

(b) *If the sum of the denominators has a physical meaning and the numerators are constant, then a harmonic mean of the ratio should be used to summarize them.* That is, if $a_i = a$ for all i's, then

$$\text{Average}\left(\frac{a}{b_1}, \frac{a}{b_2}, \ldots, \frac{a}{b_n}\right) = \frac{n}{b_1/a + b_2/a + \cdots + b_n/a} = \frac{na}{\sum_{i=1}^{n} b_i}$$

TABLE 12.3   CPU Utilization Measured over Five Intervals

Measurement Duration	CPU Busy (%)
1	45
1	45
1	45
1	45
100	20
Sum	200%
Mean	$\neq$ 200/5 or 40%

The problem of computing the mean MIPS rate for a processor using n observations of the same benchmark is an example of a case where this guideline can be used.

2. *If the numerator and the denominator are expected to follow a multiplicative property such that $a_i = cb_i$, where c is approximately a constant that is being estimated, then c can be estimated by the geometric mean of a_i/b_i.* The following case study illustrates the application of this guideline.

Case Study 12.1   A number of benchmarks were run through a program optimizer. The static size of the program as measured before and after the optimization are shown in Table 12.4. Also shown in the table are the ratios of sizes before and after the optimization.

In this case, the total sum of code sizes does make physical sense, and therefore, one would be tempted to argue that a ratio of sums should be used to estimate the average ratio. However, there are two problems with that argument. First, the workload sizes selected for this study are widely

TABLE 12.4   Program Optimizer Static Size Data

Program	Code Size		Ratio
	Before	After	
BubbleP	119	89	0.75
IntmmP	158	134	0.85
PermP	142	121	0.85
PuzzleP	8612	7579	0.88
QueenP	7133	7062	0.99
QuickP	184	112	0.61
SieveP	2908	2879	0.99
TowersP	433	307	0.71
Geometric mean			0.82

different. They cover a range of approximately two orders of magnitude. Thus, adding 119 (size of BubbleP) to 8612 (size of PuzzleP) could be justified only if it could be argued that the frequency of execution of these two workloads in a real user environment is equal; otherwise, the sizes should be weighted by their respective frequencies of usage. Since the frequency of usage is not known, the weights cannot be selected. Second, the sizes before and after the optimization are expected to follow the following multiplicative model:

$$a_i = c b_i$$

where b_i and a_i are the sizes before and after the program optimization and c is the effect of the optimization that is expected to be independent of the code size. As discussed later in Section 21.7 on multiplicative models for two-factor experiments, the best estimate of the effect c in this case is obtained by taking a log of the model:

$$\log a_i = \log c + \log b_i$$

or

$$\log c = \log b_i - \log a_i$$

and estimating $\log c$ as the arithmetic mean of $\log b_i - \log a_i$. This is equivalent to estimating c as the geometric mean of b_i / a_i. This geometric mean is 0.82 as shown in the Table 12.4. Notice that the assumption of the data following the multiplicative model is justified by the fact that the ratios b_i / a_i are all in the small range of 0.61 and 0.99. □

12.8 SUMMARIZING VARIABILITY

Then there is the man who drowned crossing a stream with an average depth of six inches.

—W. I. E. Gates

Given a data set, summarizing it by a single number is rarely enough. It is important to include a statement about its variability in any summary of the data. This is because given two systems with the same mean performance, one would generally prefer one whose performance does not vary much from the mean. For example, Figure 12.3 shows histograms of the response times of two systems. Both have the same mean response time of 2 seconds. In case (a), the response time is always close to its mean value, while in case (b), the response time can be 1 millisecond sometimes and 1 minute at other times. Which system would you prefer? Most people would prefer the system with low variability.

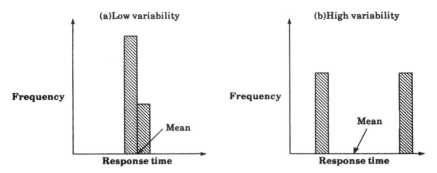

FIGURE 12.3   Histograms of response times of two systems.

Variability is specified using one of the following measures, which are called **indices of dispersion**:

- Range—minimum and maximum of the values observed
- Variance or standard deviation
- 10- and 90-percentiles
- Semi-interquantile range
- Mean absolute deviation

The **range** of a stream of values can be easily calculated by keeping track of the minimum and the maximum. The variability is measured by the difference between the maximum and the minimum. The larger the difference, the higher the variability. In most cases, the range is not very useful. The minimum often comes out to be zero and the maximum comes out to be an "outlier" far from typical values. Unless there is a reason for the variable to be bounded between two values, the maximum goes on increasing with the number of observations, the minimum goes on decreasing with the number of observations, and there is no "stable" point that gives a good indication of the actual range. The conclusion is that the range is useful if and only if there is a reason to believe that the variable is bounded. The range gives the best estimate of these bounds.

The variance of a sample of n observations $\{x_1, x_2, \ldots, x_n\}$ is calculated as follows:

$$s^2 = \frac{1}{n-1} \sum_{i=1}^{n} (x_i - \overline{x})^2 \qquad \text{where} \quad \overline{x} = \frac{1}{n} \sum_{i=1}^{n} x_i$$

The quantity s^2 is called the **sample variance** and its square root s is called the **sample standard deviation**. The word *sample* can be dropped if there is no ambiguity and it it is clear from the context that the quantities refer to just one sample. Notice that in computing the variance, the sum of squares $\sum(x_i - \overline{x})^2$ is divided by $n-1$ and not n. This is because only $n-1$ of the n differences

$(x_i - \bar{x})$ are independent. Given $n - 1$ differences, the nth difference can be computed since the sum of all n differences must be zero. The number of independent terms in a sum is also called its **degrees of freedom.**

In practice, the main problem with variance is that it is expressed in units that are the square of the units of the observations. For example, the variance of response time could be 4 seconds squared or 4,000,000 milliseconds squared. Changing the unit of measurement has a squared effect on the numerical magnitude of the variance. For this reason, it is preferable to use the standard deviation. It is in the same unit as the mean, which allows us to compare it with the mean. Thus, if the mean response time is 2 seconds and the standard deviation is 2 seconds, there is considerable variability. On the other hand, a standard deviation of 0.2 second for the same mean would be considered small. In fact, the ratio of standard deviation to the mean, or the coefficient of variation (C.O.V.), is even better because it takes the scale of measurement (unit of measurement) out of variability consideration. A C.O.V. of 5 is large, and a C.O.V. of 0.2 (or 20%) is small no matter what the unit is.

Percentiles are also a popular means of specifying dispersion. Specifying the 5-percentile and the 95-percentile of a variable has the same impact as specifying its minimum and maximum. However, it can be done for any variable, even for variables without bounds. When expressed as a fraction between 0 and 1 (instead of a percentage), the percentiles are also called quantiles. Thus 0.9-quantile is the same as 90-percentile. Another term used is **fractile,** which is synonymous with quantile. The percentiles at multiples of 10% are called **deciles.** Thus, the first decile is 10-percentile, the second decile is 20-percentile, and so on. **Quartiles** divide the data into four parts at 25, 50, and 75%. Thus, 25% of the observations are less than or equal to the first quartile Q_1, 50% of the observations are less than or equal to the second quartile Q_2, and 75% are less than or equal to the third quartile Q_3. Notice that the second quartile Q_2 is also the median. The α-quantiles can be estimated by sorting the observations and taking the $[(n - 1)\alpha + 1]$th element in the ordered set. Here, [.] is used to denote rounding to the nearest integer. For quantities exactly halfway between two integers, use the lower integer.

The range between Q_3 and Q_1 is called the **interquartile range** of the data. One half of this range is called **Semi-Interquartile Range (SIQR),** that is,

$$\text{SIQR} = \frac{Q_3 - Q_1}{2} = \frac{x_{0.75} - x_{0.25}}{2}$$

Another measure of dispersion is the **mean absolute deviation,** which is calculated as follows:

$$\text{Mean absolute deviation} = \frac{1}{n}\sum_{i=1}^{n}|x_i - \bar{x}|$$

The key advantage of the mean absolute deviation over the standard deviation is that no multiplication or square root is required.

Among the preceding indices of dispersion, the range is affected considerably by outliers. The sample variance is also affected by outliers, but the effect is less than that on the range. The mean absolute deviation is next in resistance to outliers. The semi-interquartile range is very resistant to outliers. It is preferred to the standard deviation for the same reasons that the median is preferred to the mean. Thus, if the distribution is highly skewed, outliers are highly likely and the SIQR is more representative of the spread in the data than the standard deviation. In general, the SIQR is used as an index of dispersion whenever the median is used as an index of central tendency.

Finally, it should be mentioned that all of the preceding indices of dispersion apply only for quantitative data. For qualitative (categorical) data, the dispersion can be specified by giving the number of most frequent categories that comprise the given percentile, for instance, the top 90%.

The following example illustrates the computation of percentiles and SIQRs.

Example 12.4   In an experiment, which was repeated 32 times, the measured CPU time was found to be {3.1, 4.2, 2.8, 5.1, 2.8, 4.4, 5.6, 3.9, 3.9, 2.7, 4.1, 3.6, 3.1, 4.5, 3.8, 2.9, 3.4, 3.3, 2.8, 4.5, 4.9, 5.3, 1.9, 3.7, 3.2, 4.1, 5.1, 3.2, 3.9, 4.8, 5.9, 4.2}. The sorted set is {1.9, 2.7, 2.8, 2.8, 2.8, 2.9, 3.1, 3.1, 3.2, 3.2, 3.3, 3.4, 3.6, 3.7, 3.8, 3.9, 3.9, 3.9, 4.1, 4.1, 4.2, 4.2, 4.4, 4.5, 4.5, 4.8, 4.9, 5.1, 5.1, 5.3, 5.6, 5.9}. Then

The 10-percentile is given by $[1 + (31)(0.10)] = $ 4th element $= 2.8$.
The 90-percentile is given by $[1 + (31)(0.90)] = $ 29th element $= 5.1$.
The first quartile Q_1 is given by $[1 + (31)(0.25)] = $ 9th element $= 3.2$.
The median Q_2 is given by $[1 + (31)(0.50)] = $ 16th element $= 3.9$.
The third quartile Q_3 is given by $[1 + (31)(0.75)] = $ 24th element $= 4.5$.

Thus,

$$\text{SIQR} = \frac{Q_3 - Q_1}{2} = \frac{4.5 - 3.2}{2} = 0.65 \qquad \square$$

12.9 SELECTING THE INDEX OF DISPERSION

In order to select the correct index among the four suggested in Section 12.8, the first question that should be asked is whether the variable is bounded. If so, then dispersion is best expressed by specifying the range. If there are no natural bounds, then check to see if the distribution is unimodal symmetric. If it is, then it makes sense to measure the average distance from the mean, that is, the variance, standard deviation, or coefficient of variation. If the distribution is nonsymmetric, percentiles are the best indices. These guidelines are summarized in Figure 12.4.

The decision rules given in Figure 12.4 are not hard and fast. In many cases, the quantity required for proper design and analysis is determined by

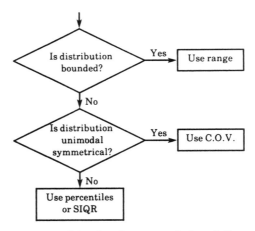

FIGURE 12.4   Selecting the correct index of dispersion.

other considerations. For example, a network designed for average traffic is grossly underdesigned. The network load is highly skewed. Networks are therefore designed to carry 95- to 99-percentile of the observed load levels. Thus, the dispersion of the load should be specified via range or percentiles. Power supplies are similarly designed to sustain peak demand rather than average demand.

One problem in using percentiles is that finding a percentile requires several passes through the data, and therefore, the observations have to be stored. On-the-fly display of percentiles as new observations are produced consumes considerable amount of computing and storage resources. Jain and Chlamtac (1985) have proposed a heuristic algorithm called P^2 that allows dynamic calculation of percentiles as the observations are generated. The observations are not stored; therefore, the algorithm has a very small and fixed storage requirement regardless of the number of observations. The algorithm has also been extended to allow histogram plotting.

Formulas for various indices of central tendencies and dispersion are summarized in Box 12.1.

12.10   DETERMINING DISTRIBUTION OF DATA

In the last two sections we discussed how a measured data set could be summarized by stating its average and variability. The next step in presenting a summary could be to state the type of distribution the data follows. For example, a statement that the number of disk I/O's are uniformly distributed between 1 and 25 is a more meaningful summary than to specify only that the mean is 13 and the variance is 48. The distribution information is also required if the summary has to be used later in simulation or analytical modeling.

Box 12.1   Summarizing Observations
Given: A sample $\{x_1, x_2, \ldots, x_n\}$ of n observations.

1. Sample arithmetic mean: $\bar{x} = \dfrac{1}{n}\displaystyle\sum_{i=1}^{n} x_i$

2. Sample geometric mean: $\dot{x} = \left(\displaystyle\prod_{i=1}^{n} x_i\right)^{1/n}$

3. Sample harmonic mean: $\ddot{x} = \dfrac{n}{\dfrac{1}{x_1} + \dfrac{1}{x_2} + \cdots + \dfrac{1}{x_n}}$

4. Sample median: $\begin{cases} x_{((n-1)/2)} & \text{if } n \text{ is odd} \\ 0.5(x_{(n/2)} + x_{((1+n)/2)}) & \text{otherwise} \end{cases}$

   Here $x_{(i)}$ is the ith observation in the sorted set.

5. Sample mode = observation with the highest frequency (for categorical data).

6. Sample variance: $s^2 = \dfrac{1}{n-1}\displaystyle\sum_{i=1}^{n}(x_i - \bar{x})^2$

7. Sample standard deviation: $s = \sqrt{\dfrac{1}{n-1}\displaystyle\sum_{i=1}^{n}(x_i - \bar{x})^2}$

8. Coefficient of variation $= s/\bar{x}$

9. Coefficient of skewness $= \dfrac{1}{ns^3}\displaystyle\sum_{i=1}^{n}(x_i - \bar{x})^3$

10. Range: Specify the minimum and maximum.

11. Percentiles: $100p$-percentile $x_p = x_{(\lfloor 1+(n-1)p\rfloor)}$.

12. Semi-interquartile range SIQR $= \dfrac{Q_3 - Q_1}{2} = \dfrac{x_{0.75} - x_{0.25}}{2}$

13. Mean absolute deviation $= \dfrac{1}{n}\displaystyle\sum_{i=1}^{n}|x_i - \bar{x}|$

The simplest way to determine the distribution is to plot a **histogram** of the observations. This requires determining the maximum and minimum of the values observed and dividing the range into a number of subranges called **cells** or **buckets**. The count of observations that fall into each cell is determined. The counts are normalized to cell frequencies by dividing by the total number of observations. The cell frequencies are plotted as a column chart.

The key problem in plotting histograms is determining the cell size. Small cells lead to very few observations per cell and a large variation in the number of observations per cell. Large cells result in less variation but the details of the distribution are completely lost. Given a data set, it is possible to reach very different conclusions about the distribution shape depending upon the cell size used. One guideline is that if any cell has less than five observations, the cell size should be increased or a variable cell histogram should be used.

A better technique for small samples is to plot the observed quantiles versus the theoretical quantile in a quantile-quantile plot. Suppose, $y_{(i)}$ is the observed q_ith quantile. Using the theoretical distribution, the q_ith quantile x_i is computed and a point is plotted at $(x_i, y_{(i)})$. If the observations do come from the given theoretical distribution, the quantile-quantile plot would be linear.

To determine the q_ith quantile x_i, we need to invert the cumulative distribution function. For example, if $F(x)$ is the CDF for the assumed distribution,

$$q_i = F(x_i)$$

or

$$x_i = F^{-1}(q_i)$$

For those distributions whose CDF can be inverted, determining the x-coordinate of points on a quantile-quantile plot is straightforward. Table 28.1 lists the inverse of CDF for a number of distributions.

For other distributions one can use tables and interpolate the values if necessary. For the unit normal distribution $N(0,1)$, the following approximation is often used:

$$x_i = 4.91[q_i^{0.14} - (1 - q_i)^{0.14}] \tag{12.1}$$

For $N(\mu, \sigma)$, the x_i values computed by Equation (12.1) are scaled to $\mu + \sigma x_i$ before plotting.

One advantage of a quantile-quantile plot is that often it is sufficient to know the name of the possible distribution. The parameter values are not required. This happens if the effect of the parameters is simply to scale the quantile. For example, in a normal quantile-quantile plot, x-coordinates can be obtained using the unit normal $N(0,1)$ distribution. The intercept and the slope of the resulting line give the values of location and shape parameters μ and σ.

Example 12.5 The difference between the values measured on a system and those predicted by a model is called modeling error. The modeling error for eight predictions of a model were found to be -0.04, -0.19, 0.14, -0.09, -0.14, 0.19, 0.04, and 0.09.

A normal quantile-quantile plot for the errors is shown in Figure 12.5. Computation of values plotted along the horizontal axis is shown in Table 12.5. The x_i's in the last column of the table are computed using Equa-

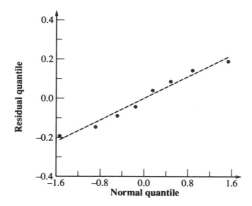

FIGURE 12.5   Normal quantile-quantile plot for the error data.

TABLE 12.5   Data for Normal Quantile-Quantile Plot Example

i	$q_i = \dfrac{i - 0.5}{n}$	y_i	x_i
1	0.0625	−0.19	−1.535
2	0.1875	−0.14	−0.885
3	0.3125	−0.09	−0.487
4	0.4375	−0.04	−0.157
5	0.5625	0.04	0.157
6	0.6875	0.09	0.487
7	0.8125	0.14	0.885
8	0.9375	0.19	1.535

tion (12.1). In the figure, a straight line that provides a linear least-squares fit to the points is also shown. From the figure, the errors do appear to be normally distributed.   □

Often it is found in a normal quantile-quantile plot that the data follows a straight line but departs from it at one or both ends. This is an indication of data having shorter or longer tails than the normal distribution. For example, Figure 12.6b shows data that has longer tails at both ends. An S-shaped normal quantile-quantile plot, such as the one shown in Figure 12.6c, indicates that the observations have a distribution that is more peaky and has shorter tails than a normal distribution. If the distribution is asymmetric so that it has a shorter tail on one end and a longer tail on the other, this will show up on the normal quantile-quantile plot as a combination of the two types of departures from normality just discussed. An example of asymmetric plot is shown in Figure 12.6d.

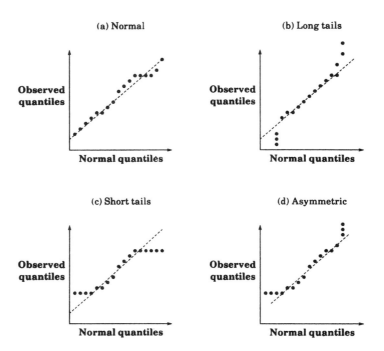

FIGURE 12.6 Interpretation of normal quantile-quantile plots.

EXERCISES

12.1 A distributed system has three file servers, which are chosen independently and with equal probabilities whenever a new file is created. The servers are named A, B, and C. Determine the probabilities of the following events:

a. Server A is selected

b. Server A or B is selected

c. Servers A and B are selected

d. Server A is not selected

e. Server A is selected twice in a row

f. Server selection sequence ABCABCABC is observed (in nine successive file creations)

12.2 The traffic arriving at a network gateway is bursty. The burst size x is geometrically distributed with the following pmf:

$$f(x) = (1 - p)^{x-1}p, \qquad x = 1, 2, \dots, \infty$$

Compute the mean, variance, standard deviation, and coefficient of variation of the burst size. Plot the pmf and CDF for $p = 0.2$.

12.3 The number of I/O requests received at a disk during a unit interval follows a Poisson distribution with the following mass function:

$$f(x) = \lambda^x \frac{e^{-\lambda x}}{x!}, \qquad x = 0, 1, 2, \ldots, \infty$$

Here, λ is a parameter. Determine the mean, variance, and coefficient of variation of the number. Plot the pmf and CDF for $\lambda = 8$.

12.4 Two Poisson streams (see Exercise 12.3) merge at a disk. The pmf for the two streams are as follows:

$$f(x) = \lambda^x \frac{e^{-\lambda x}}{x!}, \qquad x = 0, 1, 2, \ldots, \infty$$

$$f(y) = \lambda^y \frac{e^{-\lambda y}}{y!}, \qquad y = 0, 1, 2, \ldots, \infty$$

Determine the following:

a. Mean of $x + y$

b. Variance of $x + y$

c. Mean of $x - y$

d. Variance of $x - y$

e. Mean of $3x - 4y$

f. Coefficent of variation of $3x - 4y$

12.5 The response time of a computer system has an Erlang distribution with the following CDF:

$$F(x) = 1 - e^{-x/a} \left[\sum_{i=0}^{m-1} \frac{(x/a)^i}{i!} \right]$$

Find expressions for the pdf, mean, variance, mode, and coefficient of variation of the response time.

12.6 The CDF of a Pareto variate is given by

$$F(x) = 1 - x^{-a}, \qquad 1 \leq x \leq \infty$$

Find its pdf, mean, variance, mode, and coefficient of variation.

12.7 The execution times of queries on a database is normally distributed with a mean of 5 seconds and a standard deviation of 1 second. Determine the following:

a. What is the probability of the execution time being more than 8 seconds?

b. What is the probability of the execution time being less than 6 seconds?

c. What percentage of responses will take between 4 and 7 seconds?

d. What is the 95-percentile execution time?

12.8 What index of central tendency should be used to report

a. Response time (symmetrical pdf)

b. Number of packets per day (symmetrical pdf)

    c. Number of packets per second (skewed pdf)

    d. Frequency of keywords in a language

12.9 How would you summarize an average personal computer configuration:

    a. CPU type

    b. Memory size

    c. Disk type

    d. Number of peripherals

    e. Cost

12.10 The CPU times in milliseconds for 11 workloads on a processor are 0.74, 0.43, 0.24, 2.24, 262.08, 8960, 4720, 19740, 7360, 22,440, and 28,560. Which index of central tendency would you choose and why?

12.11 The number of disk I/O's performed by a number of programs were measured as follows: {23, 33, 14, 15, 42, 28, 33, 45, 23, 34, 39, 21, 36, 23, 34, 36, 25, 9, 11, 19, 35, 24, 31, 29, 16, 23, 34, 24, 38, 15, 13, 35, 28}. Which index of central tendency would you choose and why?

12.12 Choose a performance analysis problem. List all system performance metrics and workload parameters. For each metric/parameter discuss the following:

    a. Which index of central tendency would you use?

    b. Which index of dispersion would you use?

    Assume appropriate distributions, if necessary, and justify your assumptions. Include at least one example of each of the possible indices: mean, median, mode, geometric mean, range, variance, and percentiles. (This may require you to extend the problem or parameter list.)

12.13 For the data of Exercise 12.10, which index of dispersion would you choose and why?

12.14 For the data of Exercise 12.11, compute all possible indices of dispersion. Which index would you choose and why?

12.15 Plot a normal quantile-quantile plot for the following sample of errors:

−0.04444	−0.04439	−0.04165	−0.03268	−0.03235	−0.03182	0.02771	0.02650
−0.02569	−0.02358	0.02330	0.02305	0.02213	0.02128	0.01793	0.01668
−0.01565	−0.01509	0.01432	0.00978	0.00889	0.00687	0.00543	0.00084
−0.00083	−0.00048	0.00024	0.00079	0.00082	0.00106	0.00110	0.00132
0.00162	0.00181	0.00280	0.00379	0.00411	0.00424	0.00553	0.00865
0.01026	0.01085	0.01440	0.01562	0.01975	0.01996	0.02016	0.02078
0.02134	0.02252	0.02414	0.02568	0.02682	0.02855	0.02889	0.03072
0.03259	0.03754	0.04263	0.04276				

Are the errors normally distributed?

CHAPTER 13

COMPARING SYSTEMS USING SAMPLE DATA

Statistics are like alienists—they will testify for either side.
—Fiorello La Guardia

The English words *sample* and *example* both originated from an Old French word *essample*. Although the two words are now distinct, it is important to remember their common root. A sample is only an example. One example is often not enough to prove a theory. Similarly, one sample is often not enough to make a definite statement about all systems. Yet this distinction is often forgotten. We measure two systems on just 5 or 10 workloads and then declare one system definitely better than the other. The purpose of this chapter is to reinforce the distinction and to discuss how to use sample data to compare two or more systems.

The basic idea is that a definite statement cannot be made about the characteristics of all systems, but a probabilistic statement about the range in which the characteristics of most systems would lie can be made. The concept of confidence interval introduced in this chapter is one of the fundamental concepts that every performance analyst needs to understand well. In the remainder of this book, most conclusions drawn from samples are stated in terms of confidence intervals.

13.1 SAMPLE VERSUS POPULATION

Suppose we write a computer program to generate several million random numbers with a given property, for instance, mean μ and standard deviation σ. We now put these numbers in an urn and draw a sample of n observations.

Suppose the sample $\{x_1, x_2, \ldots, x_n\}$ has a sample mean $\bar{x}$. The sample mean $\bar{x}$ is likely to be different from μ. To distinguish between the two, $\bar{x}$ is called the sample mean and μ is called population mean. The word *population* denotes all the numbers inside the urn.

In most real-world problems, the population characteristics (for example, population mean) are unknown, and the goal of the analyst is to estimate these characteristics. For example, in our experiment of measuring a program's processor time, the sample mean obtained from a single sample of n observations is simply an estimate of the population mean. To determine the population mean exactly, we need to repeat the experiment infinitely many times, which is clearly impossible.

The population characteristics are called **parameters** while the sample estimates are called **statistics**. For example, the population mean is a parameter while the sample mean is a statistic. It is necessary to distinguish between the two because the parameters are fixed while the statistic is a random variable. For instance, if we draw two samples of size n from a normally distributed population with mean μ and standard deviation σ, the sample means $\bar{x}_1$ and $\bar{x}_2$ for the two samples would be different. In fact, we can draw many such samples and draw a distribution for the sample mean. No such distribution is possible for the population mean. It is fixed and can be determined only if we consider the entire population. Traditionally, the Greek letters such as μ and σ are used to denote the parameters, while the English letters such as $\bar{x}$ and s are used to denote the statistic.

13.2 CONFIDENCE INTERVAL FOR THE MEAN

Each sample mean is an estimate of the population mean. Given k samples, we have k estimates—all of them different. The next problem is to get a single estimate of the population mean from these k estimates.

In fact, it is not possible to get a perfect estimate of the population mean from any finite number of finite size samples. The best we can do is to get probabilistic bounds. Thus, we may be able to get two bounds, for instance, c_1 and c_2, such that there is a high probability, $1 - \alpha$, that the population mean is in the interval (c_1, c_2):

$$\text{Probability}\{c_1 \leq \mu \leq c_2\} = 1 - \alpha$$

The interval (c_1, c_2) is called the **confidence interval** for the population mean, α is called the **significance level**, $100(1 - \alpha)$ is called the **confidence level**, and $1 - \alpha$ is called the **confidence coefficient**. Notice that the confidence level is traditionally expressed as a percentage and is typically near 100%, for instance, 90 or 95%; while the significance level α is expressed as a fraction and is typically near zero, for instance, 0.05 or 0.1.

One way to determine the 90% confidence interval would be to use 5-percentile and 95-percentile of the sample means as the bounds. For example, we could take k samples, find sample means, sort them out in an increasing order, and take the $[1 + 0.05(k - 1)]$th and $[1 + 0.95(k - 1)]$th element of the sorted set.

Fortunately, it is not necessary to gather too many samples. It is possible to determine the confidence interval from just one sample. This is because of the central limit theorem, which allows us to determine the distribution of the sample mean. This theorem states that if the observations in a sample $\{x_1, x_2, \ldots, x_n\}$ are independent and come from the same population that has a mean μ and a standard deviation σ, then the sample mean for large samples is approximately normally distributed with mean μ and standard deviation $\sigma/\sqrt{n}$:

$$\bar{x} \sim N\left(\mu, \sigma/\sqrt{n}\right)$$

The standard deviation of the sample mean is called the **standard error**. Again, the standard error is different from the population standard deviation. If the population standard deviation is σ, the standard error is only $\sigma/\sqrt{n}$. From this expression, it is easy to see that as the sample size n increases, the standard error decreases.

Using the central limit theorem, a $100(1 - \alpha)\%$ confidence interval for the population mean is given by

$$\left(\bar{x} - z_{1-\alpha/2}s/\sqrt{n}, \ \bar{x} + z_{1-\alpha/2}s/\sqrt{n}\right)$$

Here, $\bar{x}$ is the sample mean, s is the sample standard deviation, n is the sample size, and $z_{1-\alpha/2}$ is the $(1 - \alpha/2)$-quantile of a unit normal variate. Since these quantiles are used very frequently, their values are listed in Table A.2 in the Appendix.

Example 13.1 For the sample of Example 12.4, the mean $\bar{x} = 3.90$, the standard deviation $s = 0.95$ and $n = 32$:

$$A\ 90\%\ \text{confidence interval for the mean} = 3.90 \mp (1.645)(0.95)/\sqrt{32}$$

$$= (3.62, 4.17)$$

We can state with 90% confidence that the population mean is between 3.62 and 4.17. The chance of error in this statement is 10%. That is, if we take 100 samples and construct a confidence interval for each sample as shown in Figure 13.1, in 90 cases the interval would include the population mean and in 10 cases the interval would not include the population mean. Similarly,

$$95\%\ \text{confidence interval for mean} = 3.90 \mp (1.960)(0.95)/\sqrt{32}$$

$$= (3.57, 4.23)$$

$$99\%\ \text{confidence interval for mean} = 3.90 \mp (2.576)(0.95)/\sqrt{32}$$

$$= (3.46, 4.33) \qquad \square$$

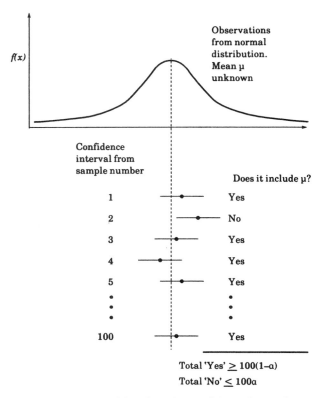

Total 'Yes' $\geq 100(1-\alpha)$

Total 'No' $\leq 100\alpha$

FIGURE 13.1 Meaning of a confidence interval.

The preceding confidence interval applies only for large samples, that is, for samples of size greater than 30. For smaller samples, confidence intervals can be constructed only if the observations come from a normally distributed population. For such samples, the $100(1-\alpha)\%$ confidence interval is given by

$$\left(\overline{x} - t_{[1-\alpha/2;n-1]}s/\sqrt{n}, \ \overline{x} + t_{[1-\alpha/2;n-1]}s/\sqrt{n}\right)$$

Here, $t_{[1-\alpha/2;n-1]}$ is the $(1-\alpha/2)$-quantile of a t-variate with $n-1$ degrees of freedom. These quantiles are listed in Table A.4 in the Appendix. The interval is based on the fact that for samples from a normal population $N(\mu,\sigma^2)$, $(\overline{x} - \mu)/(\sigma/\sqrt{n})$ has a $N(0,1)$ distribution and $(n-1)s^2/\sigma^2$ has a chi-square distribution with $n-1$ degrees of freedom, and therefore, $(\overline{x} - \mu)/\sqrt{s^2/n}$ has a t distribution with $n-1$ degrees of freedom (see Section 29.16 for a description of the t distribution). Figure 13.2 shows a sample t density function; the value $t_{[1-\alpha/2;n-1]}$ is such that the probability of the random variable being less than $-t_{[1-\alpha/2;n-1]}$ is $\alpha/2$. Similarly, the probability of the random variable being more than $t_{[1-\alpha/2;n-1]}$ is $\alpha/2$. The probability that the variable will lie between $\mp t_{[1-\alpha/2;n-1]}$ is $1-\alpha$.

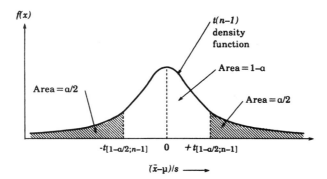

FIGURE 13.2   The ratio $(\bar{x} - \mu)/(s/\sqrt{n})$ for samples from normal populations follows a $t(n-1)$ distribution.

Example 13.2   Consider the error data of Example 12.5, which was shown to have a normal distribution. The eight error values are -0.04, -0.19, 0.14, -0.09, -0.14, 0.19, 0.04, and 0.09.

The mean of these values is zero and their sample standard deviation is 0.138. The $t_{[0.95;7]}$ from Table A.4 is 1.895. Thus, the confidence interval for the mean error is

$$0 \mp 1.895 \times 0.138/\sqrt{8} = 0 \mp 0.0926 = (-0.0926, 0.0926) \qquad \square$$

13.3   TESTING FOR A ZERO MEAN

A common use of confidence intervals is to check if a measured value is significantly different from zero. When comparing a random measurement with zero, the statements have to be made probabilistically, that is, at a desired level of confidence. If the measured value passes our test of difference with a probability greater than or equal to the specified level of confidence, $100(1 - \alpha)\%$, then the value is significantly different from zero.

The test consists of determining a confidence interval and simply checking if the interval includes zero. The four possibilities are shown in Figure 13.3, where CI is used as an abbreviation for confidence interval. The CI is shown

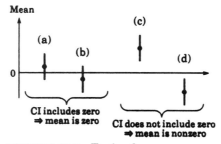

FIGURE 13.3   Testing for a zero mean.

by a vertical line stretching between the lower and upper confidence limits. The sample mean is indicated by a small circle. In cases (a) and (b), the confidence interval includes zero, and therefore, the measured values are not significantly different from zero. In cases (c) and (d), the confidence interval does not include zero, and therefore, the measured value is significantly different from zero.

Example 13.3   The difference in the processor times of two different implementations of the same algorithm was measured on seven similar workloads. The differences are $\{1.5, 2.6, -1.8, 1.3, -0.5, 1.7, 2.4\}$. Can we say with 99% confidence that one implementation is superior to the other?

$$\text{Sample size} = n = 7$$

$$\text{Mean} = 7.20/7 = 1.03$$

$$\text{Sample variance} = (22.84 - 7.20 * 7.20/7)/6 = 2.57$$

$$\text{Sample standard deviation} = \sqrt{2.57} = 1.60$$

$$\text{Confidence interval} = 1.03 \mp t \times 1.60/\sqrt{7} = 1.03 \mp 0.605t$$

$$100(1-\alpha) = 99, \qquad \alpha = 0.01, \qquad 1 - \alpha/2 = 0.995$$

From Table A.4 in the Appendix, the t-value at six degrees of freedom is $t_{[0.995;6]} = 3.707$, and

$$99\% \text{ confidence interval} = (-1.21, 3.27)$$

The confidence interval includes zero. Therefore, we cannot say with 99% confidence that the mean difference is significantly different from zero.   □

The procedure for testing for zero mean applies equally well to any other value as well. For example, to test if the mean is equal to a given value a, a confidence interval is constructed as before, and if the interval includes a, then the hypothesis that the mean is equal to a cannot be rejected at the given level of confidence. The following example illustrates this extension of the test.

Example 13.4   Consider again the data of Example 13.3. To test if the difference is equal to 1 at 99% confidence level, the confidence interval as determined in that example is $(-1.21, 3.27)$. The interval includes 1. Thus, a difference equal to 1 is also accepted at this confidence level.   □

13.4 COMPARING TWO ALTERNATIVES

A majority of performance analysis projects require comparing two or more systems and finding the best among them. This is the problem addressed in this section. The discussion, however, is limited to comparing just two systems on very similar workloads. If there are more than two systems or if the workloads are significantly different, the analysis of experimental design techniques discussed later in Part IV of this book should be used.

The statistical procedures to compare two systems are an extension of the test for a zero mean described earlier in Section 13.3. The procedure for paired and unpaired observations are different. These terms and the corresponding procedures are described next.

13.4.1 Paired Observations

If we conduct n experiments on each of the two systems such that there is a one-to-one correspondence between the ith test on system A and the ith test on system B, then the observations are called **paired**. For example, if x_i and y_i represent the performance on the ith workload, the observations would be called paired. If there is no correspondence between the two samples, the observations are called **unpaired**.

The analysis of paired observation is straightforward. The two samples are treated as one sample of n pairs. For each pair, the difference in performance can be computed. A confidence interval can be constructed for the difference. If the confidence interval includes zero, the systems are not significantly different.

Example 13.5 Six similar workloads were used on two systems. The observations are $\{(5.4, 19.1), (16.6, 3.5), (0.6, 3.4), (1.4, 2.5), (0.6, 3.6), (7.3, 1.7)\}$. Is one system better than the other?

The performance differences constitute a sample of six observations, $\{-13.7, 13.1, -2.8, -1.1, -3.0, 5.6\}$.

For this sample:

$$\text{Sample mean} = -0.32$$

$$\text{Sample variance} = 81.62$$

$$\text{Sample standard deviation} = 9.03$$

$$\text{Confidence interval for mean} = -0.32 \mp t\sqrt{(81.62/6)} = -0.32 \mp t(3.69)$$

The 0.95-quantile of a t-variate with five degrees of freedom is is 2.015:

$$90\% \text{ confidence interval} = -0.32 \mp (2.015)(3.69) = (-7.75, 7.11)$$

The confidence interval includes zero. Therefore, the two systems are not different.   □

13.4.2 Unpaired Observations

The analysis of unpaired observations is a bit more complicated than that of the paired observations. Suppose we have two samples of size n_a and n_b for alternatives A and B, respectively. The observations are unpaired in the sense that there is no correspondence between ith observations in the two samples. The steps to determine the confidence interval for the difference in mean performance requires making an estimate of the variance and an effective number of degrees of freedom. The procedure is as follows:

1. Compute the sample means:

$$\overline{x}_a = \frac{1}{n_a} \sum_{i=1}^{n_a} x_{ia}$$

$$\overline{x}_b = \frac{1}{n_b} \sum_{i=1}^{n_b} x_{ib}$$

2. Compute the sample standard deviations:

$$s_a = \left\{ \frac{\left(\sum_{i=1}^{n_a} x_{ia}^2\right) - n_a \overline{x}_a^2}{n_a - 1} \right\}^{1/2}$$

$$s_b = \left\{ \frac{\left(\sum_{i=1}^{n_b} x_{ib}^2\right) - n_b \overline{x}_b^2}{n_b - 1} \right\}^{1/2}$$

3. Compute the mean difference: $\overline{x}_a - \overline{x}_b$.
4. Compute the standard deviation of the mean difference:

$$s = \sqrt{\frac{s_a^2}{n_a} + \frac{s_b^2}{n_b}}$$

5. Compute the effective number of degrees of freedom:

$$\nu = \frac{\left(s_a^2/n_a + s_b^2/n_b\right)^2}{\dfrac{1}{n_a + 1}\left(\dfrac{s_a^2}{n_a}\right)^2 + \dfrac{1}{n_b + 1}\left(\dfrac{s_b^2}{n_b}\right)^2} - 2$$

6. Compute the confidence interval for the mean difference:

$$(\overline{x}_a - \overline{x}_b) \mp t_{[1-\alpha/2;\nu]}s$$

Here, $t_{[1-\alpha/2;\nu]}$ is the $(1 - \alpha/2)$-quantile of a t-variate with ν degrees of freedom.
7. If the confidence interval includes zero, the difference is not significant at $100(1 - \alpha)\%$ confidence level. If the confidence interval does not include zero, then the sign of the mean difference indicates which system is better.

This procedure is known as a t-**test**.

Example 13.6 The processor time required to execute a task was measured on two systems. The times on system A were {5.36, 16.57, 0.62, 1.41, 0.64, 7.26}. The times on system B were {19.12, 3.52, 3.38, 2.50, 3.60, 1.74}. Are the two systems significantly different?
For system A:

$$\text{Mean } \overline{x}_a = 5.31$$

$$\text{Variance } s_a^2 = 37.92$$

$$n_a = 6$$

For System B:

$$\text{Mean } \overline{x}_b = 5.64$$

$$\text{Variance } s_b^2 = 44.11$$

$$n_b = 6$$

Then

$$\text{Mean difference } \overline{x}_a - \overline{x}_b = -0.33$$

$$\text{Standard deviation of mean difference} = 3.698$$

$$\text{Effective number of degrees of freedom } f = 11.921$$

$$0.95\text{-quantile of } t\text{-variate with 12 degrees of freedom} = 1.71$$

$$90\% \text{ confidence interval for difference} = (-6.92, 6.26)$$

The confidence interval includes zero. Therefore, at this confidence level the two systems are not different.   □

13.4.3 Approximate Visual Test

A simpler visual test to compare two unpaired samples is to simply compute the confidence interval for each alternative separately as follows.
There are three possibilities as shown graphically in Figure 13.4:

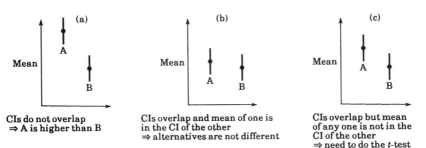

FIGURE 13.4 Comparing two alternatives.

1. The confidence intervals do not overlap. The alternative with higher sample mean is significantly better.
2. The confidence intervals overlap considerably such that the mean of one falls in the interval for the other. The two alternatives are equal with the desired confidence.
3. The confidence intervals overlap slightly such that the the mean of either is outside the confidence interval for the other. In this case, no visual conclusion can be drawn. We need to do the t-test as described previously.

Example 13.7 For the data of Example 13.6,

t-value at five degrees of freedom and 90% confidence $= 2.015$

90% confidence interval for mean of A $= 5.31 \mp (2.015)\sqrt{(37.92/6)}$

$$= (0.24, 10.38)$$

90% confidence interval for mean of B $= 5.64 \mp (2.015)\sqrt{(44.11/6)}$

$$= (0.18, 11.10)$$

The two confidence intervals overlap and the mean of one falls in the confidence interval for the other. Therefore, the two systems are not different at this level of confidence. □

13.5 WHAT CONFIDENCE LEVEL TO USE

Throughout this book, we use confidence levels of 90 or 95%. This should not lead one to believe that the confidence levels should always be that high. The choice of the confidence level is based on the loss one would sustain if the parameter is outside the range and the gain one would have if the parameter is inside the range. If the loss is high compared to the gain, the confidence levels should be high. If the loss is negligible compared to the gain, a lower confidence level is fine.

Consider, for example, a lottery in which a ticket costs one dollar but pays five million dollars to the winner. Suppose the probability of winning is 10^{-7} or one in ten million. To win the lottery with 90% confidence would require one to buy nine million tickets. It is clear that no one would be willing to spend that much for winning just five million. For most people, a very low confidence such as 0.01% would be fine in this case.

The system design decisions that computer systems performance analysts and designers face are not very different from those of the lottery. Although the loss (if the decision turns out wrong) and the gain (if the decision turns out correct) are not as widely different as in the case of the lottery, the risk level is decided essentially in the same manner.

The point is that if you come across a parameter that is significant only at 50% confidence level, do not automatically assume that the confidence is low and it is not worth making a decision based on that parameter. Similarly, even if a parameter is significant at 99% confidence level, it is possible for the decision makers to say that the confidence level is not high enough if the loss due to wrong decision is enormous.

13.6 HYPOTHESIS TESTING VERSUS CONFIDENCE INTERVALS

Most books on statistics have a chapter devoted to hypothesis testing. Here, we prefer an alternate method of doing the same thing. This alternate method makes use of confidence intervals and helps us to easily solve a few commonly encountered cases of hypothesis testing. Testing for zero mean is the first example in this book of a problem that can be solved by a hypothesis test as well as by a confidence interval. In practice, a confidence interval is preferable because it provides more information. A hypothesis test is usually a yes-no decision. We either reject a hypothesis or accept it. A confidence interval not only gives that answer; it also provides information about the possible range of values for the parameter. A narrow confidence interval indicates that the parameter has been estimated with a high degree of precision. A wide confidence interval, on the other hand, indicates that the precision is not high. Knowing the precision is often more helpful to decision makers than the simple yes-no answer from the hypothesis tests. For example, if the difference $A - B$ in the mean performance of two systems has a confidence interval for $(-100, 100)$, we can say that there is no difference between the systems since the interval includes a zero. On the other hand, if the interval was $(-1, 1)$, the conclusion is still "no difference" but we can now say it more loudly. Thus, confidence intervals tell us not only what to say but also how loudly to say it.

Confidence intervals are in general easier to understand and explain to decision makers than hypothesis tests. This is because the width of the interval is in the same units of measurements as the parameter being estimated. The decision makers find it easier to grasp. For example, it is more useful to know that a parameter is in the range, for instance, 100 to 200, than to know that the probability of the parameter being 110 is less than 3%.

13.7 ONE-SIDED CONFIDENCE INTERVALS

In all the tests so far, two-sided confidence intervals have been used. For such intervals, if the confidence level is $100(1 - \alpha)\%$, there is a $100\alpha/2\%$ chance that the difference will be more than the upper confidence limit. Similarly, there is a $100\alpha/2\%$ chance that the difference will be less than the lower confidence limit. For example, with a 90% two-sided confidence interval, there is a 5% chance that the difference will be less than the lower confidence limit.

Similarly, there is a 5% chance that the difference will be more than the upper confidence limit.

Sometimes only one-sided comparison is desired. For example, you may want to test the hypothesis that the mean is greater than a certain value. In this case, a one-sided lower confidence interval for μ is desired and it is given by

$$\left(\bar{x} - t_{[1-\alpha;n-1]} \frac{s}{\sqrt{n}}, \bar{x} \right)$$

Notice that the t-value is read at $1-\alpha$ confidence rather than at $1-\alpha/2$. Similarly, the one-sided upper confidence interval for the population mean is given by

$$\left(\bar{x}, \bar{x} + t_{[1-\alpha;n-1]} \frac{s}{\sqrt{n}} \right)$$

For large samples, z-values are used instead of t-values.

Example 13.8 Time between crashes was measured for two systems A and B. The mean and standard deviations of the time are listed in Table 13.1. To check if System A is more susceptible to failures than System B, we use the procedure of unpaired observations. The mean difference is

$$\bar{x}_A - \bar{x}_B = 124.10 - 141.47 = -17.37$$

The standard deviation of the difference is

$$s = \sqrt{\left(\frac{s_a^2}{n_a} + \frac{s_b^2}{n_b} \right)} = \sqrt{\frac{(198.20)^2}{972} + \frac{(226.11)^2}{153}} = 19.35$$

The effective number of degrees of freedom is

$$\nu = \frac{(s_a^2/n_a + s_b^2/n_b)^2}{\dfrac{1}{n_a+1}\left(\dfrac{s_a^2}{n_a}\right)^2 + \dfrac{1}{n_b+1}\left(\dfrac{s_b^2}{n_b}\right)^2} - 2$$

$$= \frac{\left((198.20)^2/972 + (226.11)^2/153\right)^2}{\dfrac{1}{972+1}\left((198.20)^2/972\right)^2 + \dfrac{1}{153+1}\left((226.11)^2/153\right)^2} - 2$$

$$= 191.05$$

TABLE 13.1 Time between System Crashes

System	Number	Mean	Standard deviation
A	972	124.10	198.20
B	153	141.47	226.11

Since the degrees of freedom are more than 30, we use the unit normal quantiles instead of t quantiles. Also, since this is a one-sided test, we use $z_{0.90} = 1.28$ for a 90% confidence interval, which is

$$(-17.37, -17.37 + 1.28 \times 19.35) = (-17.37, 7.402)$$

Since the confidence interval includes zero, we reject the hypothesis that System A is more susceptible to crashes than System B.   □

13.8 CONFIDENCE INTERVALS FOR PROPORTIONS

For categorical variables, the statistical data often consists of probabilities associated with various categories. Such probabilities are called **proportions**. Estimation of proportions is very similar to estimation of means. Each sample of n observations gives a sample proportion. We need to obtain a confidence interval to get a bound. Given that n_1 of n observations are of type 1, a confidence interval for the proportion is obtained as follows:

$$\text{Sample proportion} = p = \frac{n_1}{n}$$

$$\text{Confidence interval for proportion} = p \mp z_{1-\alpha/2}\sqrt{\frac{p(1-p)}{n}} \quad (13.1)$$

Here, $z_{1-\alpha/2}$ is the $(1-\alpha/2)$-quantile of a unit normal variate. Its values are listed in Table A.2 in the Appendix.

The previous formula for proportions is based on approximating binomial distribution (see Section 29.3) by a normal that is valid only if $np \geq 10$. If this condition is not satisfied, the computations are too complex to discuss here. They require using binomial tables. In particular, t-values cannot be used.

Example 13.9 If 10 of 1000 pages printed on a laser printer are illegible, then the proportion of illegible pages is characterized as follows:

$$\text{Sample proportion} = p = \frac{10}{1000} = 0.01$$

Since the condition $np \geq 10$ is satisfied, Equation (13.1) can be used:

$$\text{Confidence interval for the proportion} = p \mp z\sqrt{\frac{p(1-p)}{n}}$$

$$= 0.01 \mp z\sqrt{\frac{0.01(0.99)}{1000}}$$

$$= 0.01 \mp 0.003z$$

$$90\% \text{ confidence interval} = 0.01 \mp (1.645)(0.003) = (0.005, 0.015)$$

$$95\% \text{ confidence interval} = 0.01 \mp (1.960)(0.003) = (0.004, 0.016)$$

Thus, at 90% confidence we can state that 0.5 to 1.5% of the pages from the printer are illegible. The chance of error in this statement is 10%. If we want to minimize the chance of error to 5%, the 95% confidence numbers should be used.   □

The test for zero mean can be easily extended to test proportions, as shown by the following example.

Example 13.10 A single experiment was repeated on two systems 40 times. System A was found to be superior to system B in 26 repetitions. Can we state with 99% confidence that system A is superior?

$$p = \frac{26}{40} = 0.65$$

Standard deviation of estimated proportion $= \sqrt{p(1-p)/n} = 0.075$

99% confidence interval for proportion $= 0.65 \mp (2.576)(0.075)$

$$= (0.46, 0.84)$$

The confidence interval includes 0.5 (the point of equality). Therefore, we cannot say with 99% confidence that system A is superior.

Let us repeat the computations at 90% confidence.

90% confidence interval $= 0.65 \mp (1.645)(0.075) = (0.53, 0.77)$

The confidence interval does not include 0.5. Therefore, we can say with 90% confidence that system A is superior.   □

13.9 DETERMINING SAMPLE SIZE

The confidence level of conclusions drawn from a set of measured data depends upon the size of the data set. The larger the sample, the higher is the associated confidence. However, larger samples also require more effort and resources. Thus, the analyst's goal is to find the smallest sample size that will provide the desired confidence. In this section, we present formulas for determining the sample sizes required to achieve a given level of accuracy and confidence. Three different cases: single-system measurement, proportion determination, and two-system comparison are considered. In each case, a small set of preliminary measurements are done to estimate the variance, which is then used to determine the sample size required for the given accuracy.

13.9.1 Sample Size for Determining Mean

Suppose we want to estimate the mean performance of a system with an accuracy of $\pm r\%$ and a confidence level of $100(1-\alpha)\%$. The number of observations n required to achieve this goal can be determined as follows.

We know that for a sample of size n, the $100(1-\alpha)\%$ confidence interval of the population mean is

$$\bar{x} \mp z \frac{s}{\sqrt{n}}$$

The desired accuracy of r percent implies that the confidence interval should be $(\bar{x}(1 - r/100), \bar{x}(1 + r/100))$. Equating the desired interval with that obtained with n observations, we can determine n:

$$\bar{x} \mp z\frac{s}{\sqrt{n}} = \bar{x}\left(1 \mp \frac{r}{100}\right)$$

$$z\frac{s}{\sqrt{n}} = \bar{x}\frac{r}{100}$$

$$n = \left(\frac{100zs}{r\bar{x}}\right)^2$$

Here, z is the normal variate of the desired confidence level.

Example 13.11 Based on a preliminary test, the sample mean of the response time is 20 seconds, and the sample standard deviation is 5. How many repetitions are needed to get the response time accurate within 1 second at 95% confidence?

$$\text{Required accuracy} = 1 \text{ in } 20 = 5\%$$

Here, $\bar{x} = 20$, $s = 5$, $z = 1.960$, and $r = 5$,

$$n = \left(\frac{(100)(1.960)(5)}{(5)(20)}\right)^2 = (9.8)^2 = 96.04$$

A total of 97 observations are needed.   □

13.9.2 Sample Size for Determining Proportions

This technique can be extended to determination of proportions. The confidence interval for a proportion was shown in Section 13.8 to be

$$\text{Confidence interval for proportion} = p \mp z\sqrt{\frac{p(1-p)}{n}}$$

To get a half-width (accuracy of) r,

$$p \mp r = p \mp z\sqrt{\frac{p(1-p)}{n}}$$

$$r = z\sqrt{\frac{p(1-p)}{n}}$$

$$n = z^2\frac{p(1-p)}{r^2}$$

Example 13.12 A preliminary measurement of a laser printer showed an illegible print rate of 1 in 10,000. How many pages must be observed to get an accuracy of 1 per million at 95% confidence?

$$p = 1/10{,}000 = 10^{-4}, \qquad r = 10^{-6}, \qquad z = 1.960$$

$$n = (1.960)^2 \frac{10^{-4}(1 - 10^{-4})}{(10^{-6})^2} = 384{,}160{,}000$$

A total of 384.16 million pages must be observed.   □

13.9.3 Sample Size for Comparing Two Alternatives

The requirement of nonoverlapping confidence intervals allows us to compute the sample size required to compare two alternatives as shown by the following example.

Example 13.13   Two packet-forwarding algorithms were measured. Preliminary measurements showed that algorithm A loses 0.5% of packets and algorithm B loses 0.6%. How many packets do we need to observe to state with 95% confidence that algorithm A is better than the algorithm B?

$$\text{Confidence interval for algorithm A} = 0.005 \mp 1.960 \left(\frac{0.005(1 - 0.005)}{n} \right)^{1/2}$$

$$\text{Confidence interval for algorithm B} = 0.006 \mp 1.960 \left(\frac{0.006(1 - 0.006)}{n} \right)^{1/2}$$

For the two confidence intervals to be nonoverlapping, the upper edge of the lower confidence interval should be below the lower edge of the upper confidence interval:

$$0.005 \mp 1.960 \left(\frac{0.005(1 - 0.005)}{n} \right)^{1/2} \leq 0.006 \mp 1.960 \left(\frac{0.006(1 - 0.006)}{n} \right)^{1/2}$$

$$n \geq 84340$$

We need to observe 85,000 packets.   □

The formulas presented in this chapter are summarized in Box 13.1.

EXERCISES

13.1 Given two samples $\{x_1, x_2, \ldots, x_n\}$ and $\{y_1, y_2, \ldots, y_n\}$ from a normal population $N(\mu, 1)$, what is the distribution of
  a. Sample means: $\overline{x}, \overline{y}$
  b. Difference of the means: $\overline{x} - \overline{y}$
  c. Sum of the means: $\overline{x} + \overline{y}$
  d. Mean of the means: $(\overline{x} + \overline{y})/2$
  e. Normalized sample variances: s_x^2, s_y^2
  f. Sum of sample variances: $s_x^2 + s_y^2$

Box 13.1   Confidence Intervals

1. Given: A sample $\{x_1, x_2, \ldots, x_n\}$ of n observations.
   $\bar{x}$ = sample mean; s = sample standard deviation

   (a) Standard error of the sample mean: $\sigma_{\bar{x}} = \dfrac{s}{\sqrt{n}}$

   (b) $100(1-\alpha)\%$ two-sided confidence interval for the mean:
   $\bar{x} \mp z_{1-\alpha/2}s/\sqrt{n}$
   If $n \leq 30^\dagger$: $\bar{x} \mp t_{[1-\alpha/2;n-1]}s/\sqrt{n}$

   (c) $100(1-\alpha)\%$ one-sided confidence interval for the mean:
   $(\bar{x}, \bar{x} + z_{1-\alpha}s/\sqrt{n})$ or $(\bar{x} - z_{1-\alpha}s/\sqrt{n}, \bar{x})$
   If $n \leq 30^\dagger$: $(\bar{x}, \bar{x} + t_{[1-\alpha;n-1]}s/\sqrt{n})$ or $(\bar{x} - t_{[1-\alpha;n-1]}s/\sqrt{n}, \bar{x})$

2. To compare two systems using unpaired observations:

   (a) The standard error of the mean difference: $s = \sqrt{\dfrac{s_a^2}{n_a} + \dfrac{s_b^2}{n_b}}$

   (b) The effective number of degrees of freedom:

   $$\nu = \frac{(s_a^2/n_a + s_b^2/n_b)^2}{\dfrac{1}{n_a+1}\left(\dfrac{s_a^2}{n_a}\right)^2 + \dfrac{1}{n_b+1}\left(\dfrac{s_b^2}{n_b}\right)^2} - 2$$

   (c) The confidence interval for the mean difference:
   $(\bar{x}_a - \bar{x}_b) \mp t_{[1-\alpha/2;\nu]}s$

3. If n_1 of the n observations belong to a certain class, the following statistics can be reported for the class:

   (a) Proportion of the observations in the class: $p = \dfrac{n_1}{n}$

   (b) $100(1-\alpha)\%$ two-sided confidence interval for the proportion[‡]:
   $p \mp z_{1-\alpha/2}\sqrt{\dfrac{p(1-p)}{n}}$

   (c) $100(1-\alpha)\%$ one-sided confidence interval for the proportion[‡]:

   $$\left(p, p + z_{1-\alpha}\sqrt{\frac{p(1-p)}{n}}\right) \quad \text{or} \quad \left(p - z_{1-\alpha}\sqrt{\frac{p(1-p)}{n}}, p\right)$$

   [†] Only for samples from normal populations.
   [‡] Provided $np \geq 10$.

    g. Ratio of sample variances: s_x^2/s_y^2

    h. Ratio $(\bar{x} - \mu)/(s_x/\sqrt{n})$

13.2 Answer the following for the data of Exercise 12.11:

    a. What is the 10-percentile and 90-percentile from the sample?

    b. What is the mean number of disk I/O's per program?

    c. What is the 90% confidence interval for the mean?

    d. What fraction of programs make less than or equal to 25 I/O's and what is the 90% confidence interval for the fraction?

    e. What is the one-sided 90% confidence interval for the mean?

13.3 For the code size data of Table 11.2, find the confidence intervals for the average code sizes on various processors. Choose any two processors and answer the following:

    a. At what level of significance can you say that one is better than the other?

    b. How many workloads would you need to decide the superiority at 90% confidence?

    Note: Since the code sizes vary over several orders of magnitude, the arithmetic mean and its confidence interval are not very useful. Do not make any conclusions from the results of this exercise. This data is reconsidered in Chapter 21.

CHAPTER 14

SIMPLE LINEAR REGRESSION MODELS

Statistics is the art of lying by means of figures.
—Dr. Wilhelm Stekhel

Among the statistical models used by analysts, regression models are the most common. A regression model allows one to estimate or predict a random variable as a function of several other variables. The estimated variable is called the **response variable**, and the variables used to predict the response are called **predictor variables, predictors,** or **factors**. Regression analysis assumes that all predictor variables are quantitative so that arithmetic operations such as addition and multiplication are meaningful.

Most people are familiar with least-squares fitting of straight lines to data. Our objective in discussing regression models is twofold. First, we want to highlight the mistakes that analysts commonly make in using such models. Second, the concepts used in regression models, such as confidence intervals for the model parameters, are applicable to other types of models. In particular, a knowledge of these concepts is required to understand the analysis of experimental designs discussed in Part IV of this book. Although regression techniques can be used to develop a variety of linear and nonlinear models, their most common use is for finding the best linear model. Such models are called **linear regression models**. To simplify the problem, initially we limit our discussion to the case of a single predictor variable. Because of their simplicity, such models are called **simple linear regression models**.

14.1   DEFINITION OF A GOOD MODEL

The first issue in developing a regression model is to define what is meant by a good model and a bad model. Figure 14.1 shows three examples of measured data and attempted linear models. The measured data is shown by scattered points while the model is shown by a straight line. Most people would agree that the model in the first two cases looks reasonably close to the data while that for the third one does not appear to be a good model. What is good about the first two models? One possible answer is that the model line in the first two cases is close to more observations than in the third case. Thus, it is obvious that the goodness of the model should be measured by the distance between the observed points and the model line. The next issue, then, is how to measure the distance.

Regression models attempt to minimize the distance measured vertically between the observation point and the model line (or curve). The motivation for this is as follows. Given any value of the predictor variable x, we can estimate the corresponding response using the linear model by simply reading the y-value on the model line at the given x-value. The line segment joining this "predicted point" and the observed point is vertical since both points have the same x-coordinate. The length of the line segment is the difference between the observed response and the predicted response. This is called **residual, modeling error,** or simply **error.** The terms *residual* and *error* are used interchangeably.

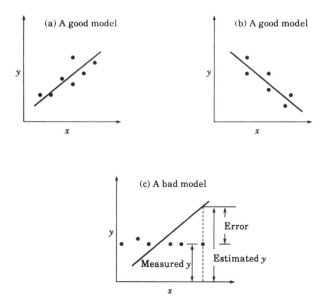

FIGURE 14.1   Good and bad regression models.

Some of the errors are positive because the estimated response is less than the observed response while others are negative. One obvious requirement would be to have zero overall error, that is, the negative and positive errors cancel out. Unfortunately, there are many lines that will satisfy this criterion. We need additional criteria. One such criterion could be to choose the line that minimizes the sum of squares of the errors. This criterion is called the **least-squares** criterion and is the criterion that is used to define the best model.

A mathematical definition of the least-squares criterion is as follows. Suppose the linear model is

$$\hat{y} = b_0 + b_1 x$$

where $\hat{y}$ is the predicted response when the predictor variable is x. The parameters b_0 and b_1 are fixed **regression parameters** to be determined from the data. Given n observation pairs $\{(x_1, y_1), \ldots, (x_n, y_n)\}$, the estimated response $\hat{y}_i$ for the ith observation is

$$\hat{y}_i = b_0 + b_1 x_i$$

The error is

$$e_i = y_i - \hat{y}_i$$

The best linear model is given by the regression parameter values, which minimizes the Sum of Squared Errors (**SSE**):

$$\sum_{i=1}^{n} e_i^2 = \sum_{i=1}^{n} (y_i - b_0 - b_1 x_i)^2$$

subject to the constraint that the mean error is zero:

$$\sum_{i=1}^{n} e_i = \sum_{i=1}^{n} (y_i - b_0 - b_1 x_i) = 0$$

It can be shown that this constrained minimization problem is equivalent to minimizing the variance of errors (see Exercise 14.1).

14.2 ESTIMATION OF MODEL PARAMETERS

As shown later, the regression parameters that give minimum error variance are

$$b_1 = \frac{\Sigma xy - n\bar{x}\bar{y}}{\Sigma x^2 - n(\bar{x})^2} \tag{14.1}$$

and

$$b_0 = \bar{y} - b_1 \bar{x} \tag{14.2}$$

where

$$\overline{x} = \text{mean of the values of predictor variables} = \frac{1}{n}\sum_{i=1}^{n} x_i$$

$$\overline{y} = \text{mean response} = \frac{1}{n}\sum_{i=1}^{n} y_i$$

$$\Sigma xy = \sum_{i=1}^{n} x_i y_i \qquad \Sigma x^2 = \sum_{i=1}^{n} x_i^2$$

Before deriving these expressions, let us look at an example that illustrates an application of these formulas.

Example 14.1   The number of disk I/O's and processor times of seven programs were measured as $\{(14, 2), (16, 5), (27, 7), (42, 9), (39, 10), (50, 13), (83, 20)\}$.

A linear model to predict CPU time as a function of disk I/O's can be developed as follows. Given the data $n = 7$, $\Sigma xy = 3375$, $\Sigma x = 271$, $\Sigma x^2 = 13,855$, $\Sigma y = 66$, $\Sigma y^2 = 828$, $\overline{x} = 38.71$, and $\overline{y} = 9.43$. Therefore,

$$b_1 = \frac{\Sigma xy - n\overline{x}\overline{y}}{\Sigma x^2 - n(\overline{x})^2} = \frac{3375 - 7 \times 38.71 \times 9.43}{13,855 - 7 \times (38.71)^2} = 0.2438$$

$$b_0 = \overline{y} - b_1\overline{x} = 9.43 - 0.2438 \times 38.71 = -0.0083$$

The desired linear model is

$$\text{CPU time} = -0.0083 + 0.2438(\text{number of disk I/O's})$$

A scatter plot of the data is shown in Figure 14.2. A straight line with intercept -0.0083 and slope 0.2438 is also shown in the figure. Notice that the line does give an estimate close to the observed values.

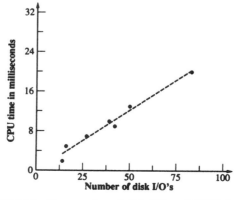

FIGURE 14.2   Scatter plot of disk I/O and CPU time data.

TABLE 14.1 Error Computation for Disk I/O's and CPU Time Data

Disk I/O's, x_i	CPU Time, y_i	Estimate, $\hat{y}_i = b_0 + b_1 x_i$	Error, $e_i = y_i - \hat{y}_i$	Error Squared, e_i^2
14	2	3.4043	−1.4043	1.9721
16	5	3.8918	1.1082	1.2281
27	7	6.5731	0.4269	0.1822
42	9	10.2295	−1.2295	1.5116
39	10	9.4982	0.5018	0.2518
50	13	12.1795	0.8205	0.6732
83	20	20.2235	−0.2235	0.0500
Σ 271	66	66.0000	0.0000	5.8690

In Table 14.1, we have listed the CPU time predicted by the model, the measured values, errors, and squared errors for each of the seven observations. The SSE is 5.869. This is the minimum possible SSE. Any other values of b_0 and b_1 would give a higher SSE. □

A derivation of the expressions for regression parameters now follows.

Derivation 14.1 The error in the ith observation is

$$e_i = y_i - \hat{y}_i = y_i - (b_0 + b_1 x_i)$$

For a sample of n observations, the mean error is

$$\bar{e} = \frac{1}{n}\sum_i e_i = \frac{1}{n}\sum_i \{y_i - (b_0 + b_1 x_i)\} = \bar{y} - b_0 - b_1\bar{x}$$

Setting the mean error to zero, we obtain

$$b_0 = \bar{y} - b_1\bar{x}$$

Substituting b_0 in the error expression, we get

$$e_i = y_i - \bar{y} + b_1\bar{x} - b_1 x_i = (y_i - \bar{y}) - b_1(x_i - \bar{x})$$

The sum of squared errors is

$$\text{SSE} = \sum_{i=1}^{n} e_i^2$$
$$= \sum_{i=1}^{n}\left[(y_i - \bar{y})^2 - 2b_1(y_i - \bar{y})(x_i - \bar{x}) + b_1^2(x_i - \bar{x})^2\right]$$

$$\frac{\text{SSE}}{n-1} = \frac{1}{n-1}\sum_{i=1}^{n}(y_i - \overline{y})^2 - 2b_1\frac{1}{n-1}\sum_{i=1}^{n}(y_i - \overline{y})(x_i - \overline{x})$$

$$+ b_1^2\frac{1}{n-1}\sum_{i=1}^{n}(x_i - \overline{x})^2$$

$$= s_y^2 - 2b_1 s_{xy}^2 + b_1^2 s_x^2$$

The value of b_1, which gives the minimum SSE, can be obtained by differentiating this equation with respect to b_1 and equating the result to zero:

$$\frac{1}{n-1}\frac{d(\text{SSE})}{db_1} = -2s_{xy}^2 + 2b_1 s_x^2 = 0$$

That is,

$$b_1 = \frac{s_{xy}^2}{s_x^2} = \frac{\Sigma xy - n\overline{x}\,\overline{y}}{\Sigma x^2 - n(\overline{x})^2}$$

This is Equation (14.1) presented earlier. □

14.3 ALLOCATION OF VARIATION

The purpose of a model is to be able to predict the response with minimum variability. Without a regression model, one can use the mean response as the predicted value for all values of the predictor variables. The errors in this case would be larger than those with the regression model. In fact, in this case, the error variance would be equal to the variance of the response, since

$$\text{Error} = \epsilon_i = \text{observed response} - \text{predicted response} = y_i - \overline{y}$$

and

$$\text{Variance of errors without regression} = \frac{1}{n-1}\sum_{i=1}^{n}\epsilon_i^2$$

$$= \frac{1}{n-1}\sum_{i=1}^{n}(y_i - \overline{y})^2$$

$$= \text{variance of } y$$

The SSE without regression would be

$$\sum_{i=1}^{n}(y_i - \overline{y})^2$$

This quantity is called the **total sum of squares** (SST). Although it is different from the variance of y (since we have not divided by $n-1$), it is a measure of y's variability and is called the **variation** of y.

The SST can be computed as follows:

$$\text{SST} = \sum_{i=1}^{n}(y_i - \bar{y})^2 = \left(\sum_{i=1}^{n} y_i^2\right) - n\bar{y}^2 = \text{SSY} - \text{SS0}$$

where **SSY** is the sum of squares of y (or Σy^2) and **SS0** is the sum of squares of $\bar{y}$ and is equal to $n\bar{y}^2$. The difference between SST and SSE is the sum of squares explained by the regression. It is called **SSR**:

$$\text{SSR} = \text{SST} - \text{SSE}$$

or

$$\text{SST} = \text{SSR} + \text{SSE}$$

Thus, the total variation SST can be divided into two parts. The SSE indicates the variation that was not explained by the regression, while SSR indicates the variation that was explained by the regression. The fraction of the variation that is explained determines the goodness of the regression and is called the **coefficient of determination, R^2**:

$$\text{Coefficient of determination} = R^2 = \frac{\text{SSR}}{\text{SST}} = \frac{\text{SST} - \text{SSE}}{\text{SST}}$$

The goodness of a regression is measured by R^2. The higher the value of R^2, the better the regression. If the regression model is perfect in the sense that all observed values are equal to those predicted by the model, that is, all errors are zero, SSE is zero and the coefficient of determination is 1. On the other hand, if the regression model is so bad that it does not reduce the error variance at all, SSE is equal to SST and the coefficient of determination is zero.

The coefficient of determination is denoted by R^2 because it is also the square of the sample correlation R_{xy} between the two variables:

$$\text{Sample correlation}(x, y) = R_{xy} = \frac{s_{xy}^2}{s_x s_y}$$

$$\text{Coefficient of determination} = \{\text{correlation coefficient}(x,y)\}^2$$

In computing R^2, it is helpful to compute SSE using the following shortcut formula:

$$\text{SSE} = \Sigma y^2 - b_0 \Sigma y - b_1 \Sigma xy$$

Example 14.2   For the disk I/O–CPU time data of Example 14.1 the coefficient of determination can be computed as follows:

$$SSE = \Sigma y^2 - b_0 \Sigma y - b_1 \Sigma xy = 828 + 0.0083 \times 66 - 0.2438 \times 3375 = 5.87$$

$$SST = SSY - SS0 = \Sigma y^2 - n(\bar{y})^2 = 828 - 7 \times (9.43)^2 = 205.71$$

$$SSR = SST - SSE = 205.71 - 5.87 = 199.84$$

$$R^2 = \frac{SSR}{SST} = \frac{199.84}{205.71} = 0.9715$$

Thus, the regression explains 97% of CPU time's variation.   □

14.4   STANDARD DEVIATION OF ERRORS

To compute the variance of errors, we need to divide the sum of squared errors (SSE) by its degrees of freedom, which are $n - 2$, since errors are obtained after calculating two regression parameters from the data. Thus, the variance estimate is

$$s_e^2 = \frac{SSE}{n - 2}$$

The quantity $SSE/(n - 2)$ is called the *mean squared error* (**MSE**). The standard deviation of errors is simply a square root of the MSE.

At this point it is interesting to point out the degrees of freedom for other sums of squares as well. The SSY has n degrees of freedom since it is obtained from n independent observations without estimating any parameters. The SS0 has just one degree of freedom since it can be computed simply from $\bar{y}$. The SST has $n - 1$ degrees of freedom since one parameter $\bar{y}$ must be calculated from the data before SST can be computed. The SSR, which is the difference between SST and SSE, has the remaining one degree of freedom. Thus, various sums and their associated degrees of freedom are as follows:

$$SST = SSY - SS0 = SSR + SSE$$

$$n - 1 = \quad n - 1 \quad = 1 + (n - 2)$$

Notice that the degrees of freedom add just the way the sums of squares do. This is an important property that we will use frequently in developing other statistical models.

Example 14.3   For the disk I/O-CPU data of Example 14.1, various sums of squares have already been computed in Example 14.2. The degrees of freedoms of the sums are

Sums of squares : $$SST = SSY - SS0 = SSR + SSE$$
$$205.71 = 828 - 622.29 = 199.84 + 5.87$$

Degrees of freedom : $$6 = 7 - 1 = 1 + 5$$

The mean squared error is

$$MSE = \frac{SSE}{\text{degrees of freedom for errors}} = \frac{5.87}{5} = 1.17$$

The standard deviation of errors is

$$s_e = \sqrt{MSE} = \sqrt{1.17} = 1.08 \qquad \square$$

14.5 CONFIDENCE INTERVALS FOR REGRESSION PARAMETERS

The regression coefficients b_0 and b_1 are estimates from a single sample of size n. Using another sample, the estimates may be different. Thus, the coefficients are random in the same manner as the sample mean or any other parameter computed from a sample. Using a single sample, only probabilistic statements can be made about true parameters β_0 and β_1 of the population. That is, the true model is

$$y = \beta_0 + \beta_1 x$$

and the computed coefficients b_0 and b_1 are "statistics" corresponding to the parameters β_0 and β_1, respectively.

The values of b_0 and b_1 obtained from Equations (14.2) and (14.1) are their mean values. Their standard deviations can be obtained from that of the error as follows:

$$s_{b_0} = s_e \left[\frac{1}{n} + \frac{\overline{x}^2}{\Sigma x^2 - n\overline{x}^2} \right]^{1/2}$$

$$s_{b_1} = \frac{s_e}{\left[\Sigma x^2 - n\overline{x}^2 \right]^{1/2}}$$

Here, s_e is the standard deviation of errors and $\overline{x}$ is the sample mean of x. The $100(1 - \alpha)\%$ confidence intervals for b_0 and b_1 can be be computed using $t_{[1-\alpha/2;n-2]}$—the $1 - \alpha/2$ quantile of a t variate with $n - 2$ degrees of freedom. The confidence intervals are

$$b_0 \mp t s_{b_0}$$

and

$$b_1 \mp t s_{b_1}$$

If a confidence interval includes zero, then the regression parameter cannot be considered different from zero at the $100(1 - \alpha)\%$ confidence level.

Example 14.4 For the disk I/O and CPU data of Example 14.1, we have $n = 7$, $\overline{x} = 38.71$, $\Sigma x^2 = 13,855$, and $s_e = 1.0834$. Using these values, the standard deviations of b_0 and b_1 are

$$s_{b_0} = s_e \left[\frac{1}{n} + \frac{\bar{x}^2}{\Sigma x^2 - n\bar{x}^2} \right]^{1/2}$$

$$= 1.0834 \left[\frac{1}{7} + \frac{(38.71)^2}{13,855 - 7 \times 38.71 \times 38.71} \right]^{1/2} = 0.8311$$

$$s_{b_1} = \frac{s_e}{\left[\Sigma x^2 - n\bar{x}^2 \right]^{1/2}}$$

$$= \frac{1.0834}{[13,855 - 7 \times 38.71 \times 38.71]^{1/2}} = 0.0187$$

From Table A.4 in the Appendix, the 0.95-quantile of a t-variate with five degrees of freedom is 2.015. Therefore, the 90% confidence interval for b_0 is

$$-0.0083 \mp (2.015)(0.8311) = -0.0083 \mp 1.6747 = (-1.6830, 1.6663)$$

Since the confidence interval includes zero, the hypothesis that this parameter is zero cannot be rejected at the 0.10 significance level. In simple terms, b_0 is essentially zero.

Similarly, the 90% confidence interval for b_1 is

$$0.2438 \mp (2.015)(0.0187) = 0.2438 \mp 0.0376 = (0.2061, 0.2814)$$

Since the confidence interval does not include zero, the slope b_1 is significantly different from zero at this confidence level. $\square$

Case Study 14.1 The performance of a remote procedure call (**RPC**) mechanism was compared on two operating systems named UNIX and AR-GUS. The performance metric was total elapsed time, which was measured for various data sizes. The measurements are shown in Table 14.2. The scatter diagrams of the two data sets along with the regression lines are shown in Figures 14.3 and 14.4 for UNIX and ARGUS, respectively. Notice that for large data sizes the variance of both data sets is large. This is because ARGUS measurements are affected by the garbage collection and UNIX measurements are affected by a page optimization technique that avoids copying of complete data pages by mapping the pages from the input buffer into the kernel instead of the normal copying. Ignoring this discrepancy for the moment, the best linear models are

$$\text{Time on UNIX} = 0.030 \ (\text{data size in bytes}) + 24$$

$$\text{Time on ARGUS} = 0.034 \ (\text{data size in bytes}) + 30$$

TABLE 14.2   Measured RPC Times on UNIX and ARGUS

UNIX		ARGUS	
Data Bytes	Time	Data Bytes	Time
64	26.4	92	32.8
64	26.4	92	34.2
64	26.4	92	32.4
64	26.2	92	34.4
234	33.8	348	41.4
590	41.6	604	51.2
846	50.0	860	76.0
1060	48.4	1074	80.8
1082	49.0	1074	79.8
1088	42.0	1088	58.6
1088	41.8	1088	57.6
1088	41.8	1088	59.8
1088	42.0	1088	57.4

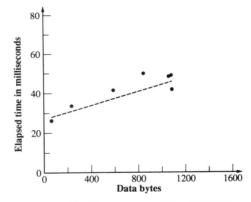

FIGURE 14.3   Scatter plot of the UNIX data.

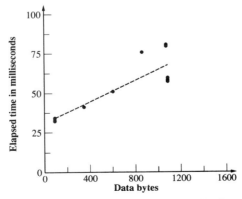

FIGURE 14.4   Scatter plot of the ARGUS data.

TABLE 14.3   Confidence Intervals for Regression Coefficients for RPC Study

UNIX				ARGUS			
Param- eter	Mean	Std. Dev.	Confidence Interval	Param- eter	Mean	Std. Dev.	Confidence Interval
b_0	26.898	2.005	(23.2968, 30.4988)	b_0	31.068	4.711	(22.6076, 39.5278)
b_1	0.017	0.003	(0.0128, 0.0219)	b_1	0.034	0.006	(0.0231, 0.0443)

The regressions explain 81 and 75% of the variation, respectively. Without considering the variance, one might be tempted to conclude that ARGUS takes larger time per byte as well as a larger setup time per call than UNIX. However, a careful analyst would make conclusions only after looking at the confidence intervals for the regression coefficients. The 90% confidence intervals are listed in Table 14.3.

Notice that intervals for intercepts overlap while those of the slopes do not. Thus, at this level of confidence, one can conclude that the setup times are not significantly different in the two systems while the per-byte times (slopes) are different. Even these conclusions are somewhat weak since the variance is not constant throughout the range of measurements. ☐

14.6 CONFIDENCE INTERVALS FOR PREDICTIONS

The purpose of developing regression usually is to predict the value of the response variable for those values of predictor variables that have not been measured. Given the regression equation, it is easy to predict the response $\hat{y}_p$ for any given value of predictor variable x_p:

$$\hat{y}_p = b_0 + b_1 x_p \tag{14.3}$$

This formula gives only the mean value of the predicted response based upon the sample. Like most of the other computations based on the sample, it is necessary to specify a confidence interval for this predicted mean. The formula for the standard deviation of the mean of a future sample of m observations is

$$s_{\hat{y}_{mp}} = s_e \left[\frac{1}{m} + \frac{1}{n} + \frac{(x_p - \bar{x})^2}{\Sigma x^2 - n\bar{x}^2} \right]^{1/2}$$

There are two special cases of this formula that are of interest. One case is for $m = 1$. This gives the standard deviation of a single future observation:

$$s_{\hat{y}_{1p}} = s_e \left[1 + \frac{1}{n} + \frac{(x_p - \bar{x})^2}{\Sigma x^2 - n\bar{x}^2} \right]^{1/2}$$

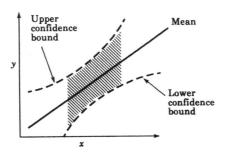

FIGURE 14.5 Confidence intervals for predictions from regression models.

The second case is for $m = \infty$. This gives the standard deviation of the mean of a large number of future observations at x_p:

$$s_{\hat{y}_p} = s_e \left[\frac{1}{n} + \frac{(x_p - \bar{x})^2}{\Sigma x^2 - n\bar{x}^2} \right]^{1/2}$$

Notice that the standard deviation for the mean of an infinite future sample is lower than that of finite samples since in the latter case the error associated with the future observations should also be accounted for.

In all cases discussed above, a $100(1 - \alpha)\%$ confidence interval for the mean can be constructed using a t quantile read at $n - 2$ degrees of freedom.

It is interesting to note from the above expressions that the standard deviation of the prediction is minimal at the center of the measured range (at $x = \bar{x}$) and it increases as we move away from the center. Since the goodness of any statistical prediction is indicated by its standard deviation, the goodness of the prediction decreases as we move away from the center. This is shown schematically in Figure 14.5. In particular, if we try to predict far beyond the measured range, the variance of the prediction will be large, the confidence interval will be wide, and the accuracy of the prediction will be low.

Example 14.5 Using the disk I/O and CPU time data of Example 14.1, let us estimate the CPU time for a program with 100 disk I/O's.

In this case, we have already seen that the regression equation is

CPU time $= -0.0083 + 0.2438$(number of disk I/O's)

Therefore, for a program with 100 disk I/O's, the mean CPU time is

CPU time $= -0.0083 + 0.2438(100) = 24.3674$

Standard deviation of errors $s_e = 1.0834$

The standard deviation of the predicted mean of a large number of observations is

$$s_{\hat{y}_p} = 1.0834 \left[\frac{1}{7} + \frac{(100 - 38.71)^2}{13,855 - 7(38.71)^2} \right]^{1/2} = 1.2159$$

From Table A.4 in the Appendix, the 0.95-quantile of the t-variate with five degrees of freedom is 2.015.

$$90\% \text{ confidence interval for predicted mean} = 24.3674 \mp (2.015)(1.2159)$$
$$= 24.3674 \mp 2.4500$$
$$= (21.9174, 26.8174)$$

Thus, we can say with 90% confidence that the mean CPU time for a program making 100 disk I/O's will be between 21.9 and 26.9 milliseconds. This prediction assumes that we will take a large number observations for such programs and then take a mean.

To set bounds on the CPU time of a single future program with 100 disk I/O's, the computation is as follows:

$$s_{\hat{y}_{1p}} = 1.0834 \left[1 + \frac{1}{7} + \frac{(100 - 38.71)^2}{13{,}855 - 7(38.71)^2} \right]^{1/2} = 1.6286$$

$$90\% \text{ confidence interval for single prediction} = 24.3674 \mp (2.015)(1.6286)$$
$$= 24.3674 \mp 3.2816$$
$$= (21.0858, 27.6489)$$

Notice that the confidence interval for the single prediction is wider than that for the mean of a large number of observations. □

14.7 VISUAL TESTS FOR VERIFYING THE REGRESSION ASSUMPTIONS

In deriving the expressions for regression parameters, we made the following assumptions:

1. The true relationship between the response variable y and the predictor variable x is linear.
2. The predictor variable x is nonstochastic and it is measured without any error.
3. The model errors are statistically independent.
4. The errors are normally distributed with zero mean and a constant standard deviation.

If any of the assumptions are violated, the conclusions based on the regression model would be misleading. In this section, we describe a number of visual techniques to verify that these assumptions hold. Unlike statistical tests, all visual techniques are approximate. However, we have found them useful for two reasons. First, they are easier to explain to decision makers who may not understand statistical tests. Second, they often provide more information than a simple "pass-fail" type answer obtained from a test. Often, using a visual test, one can also find the cause of the problem.

The assumptions, which can be visually tested, and the corresponding tests are as follows:

1. *Linear Relationship*: Prepare a scatter plot of y versus x. Any nonlinear relationship can be easily seen from this plot. Figure 14.6 shows a number of hypothetical possibilities. In case (a), the relationship appears to be linear and the linear model can be used. In case (b), there seems to be two different regions of operation, and the relationship is linear in both regions; thus, two separate linear regressions should be used. In case (c), there is one point, which is quite different from the remaining points. This may be due to some measurement error. The values must be rechecked, and if possible, measurements should also be made at other intermediate values. In case (d), the points appear to be related but the relationship is nonlinear; a curvilinear regression (discussed in Section 15.3) should be used in place of a linear regression.

2. *Independent Errors*: After the regression, compute errors and prepare a scatter plot of ϵ_i versus the predicted response $\hat{y}_i$. Any visible trends in the scatter plot would indicate a dependence of errors on the predictor variable. Figure 14.7 shows three hypothetical plots of error versus predicted response. In case (a), there is no visible trend or clustering of points, and therefore, the errors appear to be independent. In case (b), we see that the errors increase with increasing response. In case (c), the trend is nonlinear. Any such trend is indicative of an inappropriate

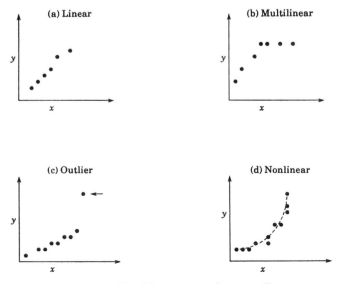

FIGURE 14.6 Possible patterns of scatter diagrams.

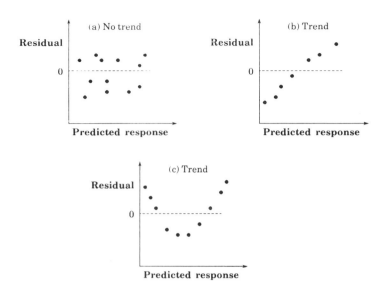

FIGURE 14.7   Possible patterns of residual versus predicted response graphs.

model. It is quite possible that a linear model is not appropriate for this case, and either the curvilinear model discussed in Section 15.4 or one of the transformations discussed in Section 15.4 should be tried.

You may also want to plot the residuals as a function of the experiment number where the experiments are numbered in the order they are conducted. As shown in Figure 14.8, any trend up or down in such a plot would indicate the presence of other factors, environmental conditions (temperature, humidity, and so on), or side effects (incorrect initializations) that varied from one experiment to the next and affected the response. The cause of such trends should be identified. If additional factors are found to affect the response, they also should be included in the analysis.

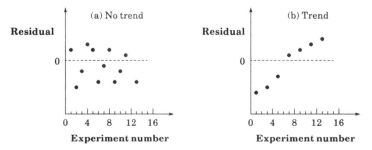

FIGURE 14.8   A trend in the residual versus experiment number may indicate side effects or incorrect initializations.

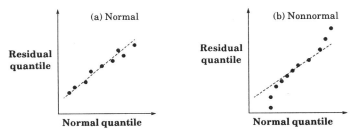

FIGURE 14.9   The normal quantile-quantile plots of the residuals should be a straight line.

We must point out that there is no foolproof test for independence. All tests for independence simply try to find dependence of one kind or the other. Thus, passing one test proves that the test was unable to find any dependence. This does not mean that another test will also not find any dependence. In other words, dependence can be proven in practice but independence cannot.

3. *Normally Distributed Errors*: Prepare a normal quantile-quantile plot of errors. If the plot is approximately linear, the assumption is satisfied. Figure 14.9 shows two hypothetical examples of such plots. In case (a), the plot is approximately linear, and so the assumption of normally distributed errors is valid. In case (b), there is no visible linearity and the errors do not seem to be normally distributed.

4. *Constant Standard Deviation of Errors*: This is also known as **homoscedasticity**. To verify it, observe the scatter plot of errors versus predicted response prepared for the independence test. If the spread in one part of the graph seems significantly different than that in other parts, then the assumption of constant variance is not valid.

Figure 14.10 shows two hypothetical examples. In case (a), the spread is homogeneous. In case (b), the spread appears to be increasing as the predicted response increases. This implies that the distribution of the errors still depends on the predictor variables. The regression model does not fully incorporate the effect of predictors. The linear model is not a

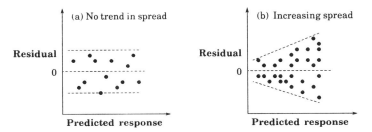

FIGURE 14.10   A trend in the spread of residuals as a function of the predicted response indicates a need for transformation or a nonlinear regression.

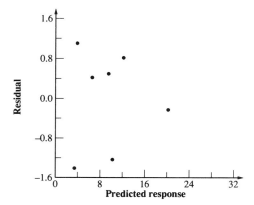

FIGURE 14.11   Graph of residual versus predicted response for the disk I/O and CPU time data.

good model in this case. A curvilinear regression should be tried instead. A transformation of the response, for example, using log(y) instead of y, may also help eliminate the problem. The transformations are discussed later in Section 15.4.

The following example illustrates the application of these tests.

Example 14.6   For the disk I/O and CPU time data of Example 14.1, a scatter plot of the data was shown in Figure 14.2. The plot does appear to satisfy a linear relationship. To check independence of errors, a plot of residuals as a function of the predicted CPU time (columns $\hat{y}_i$ and e_i in Table 14.1) is shown in Figure 14.11. There does not seem to be any definite trend in the plot. A plot of errors as a function of observation number is shown in Figure 14.12. This graph also does not show any trends.

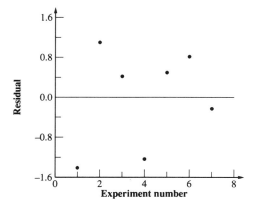

FIGURE 14.12   Residuals as a function of observation numbers for the disk I/O and CPU data.

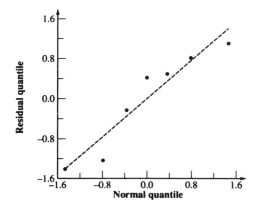

FIGURE 14.13 Normal quantile-quantile plot for the residuals of disk I/O and CPU time data.

To check whether the normality assumption is valid, a normal quantile-quantile plot of the errors is shown in Figure 14.13. The graph is reasonably close to a straight line, leading us to believe that the normality assumption is approximately valid in this case.

To check homoscedasticity, we notice that the errors do seem to have a larger spread toward the lower values of $\hat{y}$. It is difficult to make any judgments in this case due to a small number of observations. However, since the magnitude of errors is small relative to predictions, this is not a concern in this case.   □

Example 14.7 For the RPC performance study presented earlier in Case Study 14.1, a residual-versus-$\hat{y}$ plot for the ARGUS data is shown in Figure 14.14. The spread on the right side of the graph (at larger values of

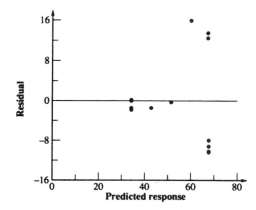

FIGURE 14.14 Graph of residual versus predicted response for the ARGUS data.

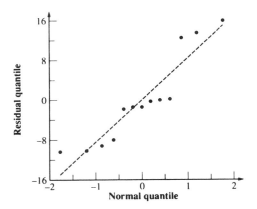

FIGURE 14.15   Normal quantile-quantile plot for the residuals of the ARGUS data.

$\hat{y}$) seems to be considerably higher than that on the left side. Since the magnitudes of errors are not negligible, this is a cause for concern.

A normal quantile-quantile plot for the same residuals is shown in Figure 14.15. Once again the departure from normality is high, at least in comparison to that in Figure 14.13.   □

The key results presented so far are summarized in Box 14.1.

Box 14.1   Simple Linear Regression

1. Model: $y_i = b_0 + b_1 x_i + e_i$

2. Parameter estimation: $b_1 = \dfrac{\Sigma xy - n\bar{x}\,\bar{y}}{\Sigma x^2 - n(\bar{x})^2}$

$$b_0 = \bar{y} - b_1\bar{x}$$

3. Allocation of variation: $\text{SSY} = \sum_{i=1}^{n} y_i^2$

$$\text{SS0} = n\bar{y}^2$$
$$\text{SST} = \text{SSY} - \text{SS0}$$
$$\text{SSE} = \Sigma y^2 - b_0 \Sigma y - b_1 \Sigma xy$$
$$\text{SSR} = \text{SST} - \text{SSE}$$

4. Coefficient of determination $R^2 = \dfrac{\text{SSR}}{\text{SST}} = \dfrac{\text{SST} - \text{SSE}}{\text{SST}}$

5. Standard deviation of errors $s_e = \sqrt{\dfrac{\text{SSE}}{n-2}}$

6. Degrees of freedoms: $\text{SST} = \text{SSY} - \text{SS0} = \text{SSR} + \text{SSE}$

$$n - 1 = \quad n \quad - \quad 1 \quad = \quad 1 \quad + (n - 2)$$

(Continued)

Box 14.1   Continued

7. Standard deviation of parameters: $s_{b_0} = s_e \left[\dfrac{1}{n} + \dfrac{\bar{x}^2}{\Sigma x^2 - n\bar{x}^2} \right]^{1/2}$

$$s_{b_1} = \frac{s_e}{\left[\Sigma x^2 - n\bar{x}^2\right]^{1/2}}$$

8. Prediction: Mean of future m observations:

$$\hat{y}_p = b_0 + b_1 x_p$$

$$s_{\hat{y}_p} = s_e \left[\frac{1}{m} + \frac{1}{n} + \frac{(x_p - \bar{x})^2}{\Sigma x^2 - n\bar{x}^2} \right]^{1/2}$$

9. All confidence intervals are computed using $t_{[1-\alpha/2;n-2]}$.

10. Model assumptions:

   (a) Errors are independent and identically distributed normal variates with zero mean.
   (b) Errors have the same variance for all values of x
   (c) Errors are additive.
   (d) x and y are linearly related.
   (e) x is nonstochastic and is measured without error.

11. Visual tests:

   (a) Scatter plot of y versus x should be linear.
   (b) Scatter plot of errors versus predicted responses should not have any trends.
   (c) The normal quantile-quantile plot of errors should be linear.

If any test fails or if the ratio y_{max}/y_{min} is large, curvilinear regressions and transformations should be investigated.

EXERCISES

14.1 Using the Lagrange multiplier technique, find the values of b_0 and b_1 that minimize the sum

$$\sum_{i=1}^{n} e_i^2 = \sum_{i=1}^{n} (y_i - b_0 - b_1 x_i)^2$$

subject to the constraint that the mean error is zero:

$$\sum_{i=1}^{n} e_i = \sum_{i=1}^{n} (y_i - b_0 - b_1 x_i) = 0$$

Verify that these values of b_0 and b_1 are the same as those obtained by the unconstrained minimization of error variance and presented in Equations (14.1) and (14.2).

14.2 For the disk I/O and CPU data in Example 14.1, find a linear formula to predict the number of disk I/O's given the CPU time. Answer the following questions about this regression:

a. Which parameters are significant?

b. What percentage of variation is explained by the regression?

c. What is the expected number of disk I/O's for a program with a CPU time of 40 milliseconds?

d. What bounds would you put on your answer in **c** if you wanted to take less than 10% chance of error on a single program to be measured tomorrow?

e. Repeat **d** for the case that you want to take a less than 10% chance of error on the mean of a large number of programs to be measured tomorrow?

14.3 The memory size of the seven programs mentioned in the disk I/O and CPU time data were also measured. The memory size (in kilobytes) and CPU time (in milliseconds) pairs observed are {(70, 2), (75, 5), (144, 7), (190, 9), (210, 10), (235, 13), (400, 20)}. Analyze the data using a simple regression model to predict CPU time as a function of the memory size.

14.4 The designers of a database information system that allows its users to search backward for several days wanted to develop a formula to predict the time it would take to search. Actual elapsed time was measured for several different values of days. The measured data is shown in Table 14.4. Prepare a simple regression model for this data to predict elapsed time as a function of the number of days and interpret results.

TABLE 14.4 Measured Performance of a Database Information System

Number of Days	Elapsed Time
1	0.65
2	0.79
4	1.36
8	2.26
16	3.59
25	5.39

14.5 In the second phase of Exercise 14.4, the analyst measured the elapsed time as a function of the complexity of the query. The complexity was measured by the number of keywords in the query. The number of disk-read operations were also measured, as shown in Table 14.5. For this data prepare regression models to predict the elapsed time as a function of number of keywords and interpret the results.

TABLE 14.5   Database Performance as a Function of Number of Keywords

Number of Keywords	Elapsed Time	Number of Disk Reads
1	0.75	3
2	0.70	6
4	0.80	7
8	1.28	78
16	1.60	92

14.6 Prepare a regression model to predict the number of disk I/O's as a function of the number of keywords for the data presented in Table 14.5.

14.7 The time to encrypt a k-byte record using an encryption technique is shown in Table 14.6. Fit a linear regression model to this data. Use visual tests to verify the regression assumptions.

TABLE 14.6   Measured Encryption Times for Various Record Sizes

Record Size	Observations		
	1	2	3
128	386	375	393
256	850	805	824
384	1,544	1,644	1,553
512	3,035	3,123	3,235
640	6,650	6,839	6,768
768	13,887	14,567	13,456
896	28,059	27,439	27,659
1,024	50,916	52,129	51,360

CHAPTER 15

OTHER REGRESSION MODELS

He uses statistics as a drunken man uses lamp-posts—for support rather than for illumination.

—Andrew Lang

The simple linear regression models discussed so far are restricted in three ways. First, only one predictor variable is allowed. Second, the predictor variables must be quantitative variables. Third, the response must be a linear function of the predictors. Sometimes, these restrictions cannot be met. In some of these cases the regression technique can still be used with a slight modification of the problem. Such special cases are the topic of this chapter. In particular, we describe techniques to handle the following cases:

- *Multiple Linear Regression*: More than one predictor variable is used.
- *Categorical Predictors*: The predictor variables are not quantitative but represent categories such as CPU type, disk type, and so on.
- *Curvilinear Regression*: The relationship between the response and predictors is nonlinear.
- *Transformations*: The errors are not normally distributed or the variance is not homogeneous.

In addition, the problem of outliers is discussed and a list of common mistakes in regression is presented in this chapter.

15.1 MULTIPLE LINEAR REGRESSION MODELS

A multiple linear regression model allows one to predict a response variable y as a function of k predictor variables $x_1, x_2, \ldots, x_k$ using a linear model of the following form:

$$y = b_0 + b_1 x_1 + b_2 x_2 + \cdots + b_k x_k + e$$

Here, $\{b_0, b_1, \ldots, b_k\}$ are $k + 1$ fixed parameters and e is the error term.

Given a sample $\{(x_{11}, x_{21}, \ldots, x_{k1}, y_1), \ldots, (x_{1n}, x_{2n}, \ldots, x_{kn}, y_n)\}$ of n observations, the model consists of the following n equations:

$$y_1 = b_0 + b_1 x_{11} + b_2 x_{21} + \cdots + b_k x_{k1} + e_1$$
$$y_2 = b_0 + b_1 x_{12} + b_2 x_{22} + \cdots + b_k x_{k2} + e_2$$
$$\vdots$$
$$y_n = b_0 + b_1 x_{1n} + b_2 x_{2n} + \cdots + b_k x_{kn} + e_n$$

In vector notation, we have:

$$
\begin{bmatrix} y_1 \\ y_2 \\ \cdot \\ \cdot \\ \cdot \\ y_n \end{bmatrix}
=
\begin{bmatrix}
1 & x_{11} & x_{21} & \cdots & x_{k1} \\
1 & x_{12} & x_{22} & \cdots & x_{k2} \\
\cdot & \cdot & \cdot & \cdot & \cdot \\
\cdot & \cdot & \cdot & \cdot & \cdot \\
\cdot & \cdot & \cdot & \cdot & \cdot \\
1 & x_{1n} & x_{2n} & \cdots & x_{kn}
\end{bmatrix}
\begin{bmatrix} b_0 \\ b_1 \\ \cdot \\ \cdot \\ \cdot \\ b_k \end{bmatrix}
+
\begin{bmatrix} e_1 \\ e_2 \\ \cdot \\ \cdot \\ \cdot \\ e_n \end{bmatrix}
$$

or

$$\mathbf{y} = \mathbf{Xb} + \mathbf{e}$$

where

$\mathbf{y}$ = a column vector of n observed values of y

$\quad = \{y_1, \ldots, y_n\}$

$\mathbf{X}$ = an n row by $k + 1$ column matrix whose

$\quad (i, j + 1)$th element $X_{i,j+1} = 1$ if $j = 0$ else x_{ij}

$\mathbf{b}$ = a column vector with $k + 1$ elements

$\quad = \{b_0, b_1, \ldots, b_k\}$

$\mathbf{e}$ = a column vector of n error terms

$\quad = \{e_1, \ldots, e_n\}$

Notice that all elements in the first column of $\mathbf{X}$ are 1.

The analysis of multiple regression is summarized in Box 15.1. Most of the expressions are similar to those for simple regression and are illustrated by the following example. The only considerations that have not been covered under simple linear regression are those of analysis of variance and the problem of multicollinearity. These are discussed in the sections following the example.

Box 15.1   Multiple Linear Regression

1. Model: $y_i = b_0 + b_1 x_{1i} + b_2 x_{2i} + \cdots + b_k x_{ki} + e_i$
   or in matrix notation: $\mathbf{y} = \mathbf{Xb} + \mathbf{e}$
   where $\mathbf{b} = $ A column vector with $k + 1$ elements $= \{b_0, b_1, \ldots, b_k\}$
   $\mathbf{y} = $ A column vector of n observed values of $y = \{y_1, \ldots, y_n\}$
   $\mathbf{X} = $ An n row by $k + 1$ column matrix whose
   $(i, j + 1)$th element $X_{i,j+1} = 1$ if $j = 0$ else x_{ij}

2. Parameter estimation: $\mathbf{b} = (\mathbf{X}^T\mathbf{X})^{-1}(\mathbf{X}^T\mathbf{y})$

3. Allocation of variation: $\text{SSY} = \sum_{i=1}^{n} y_i^2$ $\quad$ $\text{SS0} = n\bar{y}^2$
   $\text{SST} = \text{SSY} - \text{SS0}$ $\quad$ $\text{SSE} = \{\mathbf{y}^T\mathbf{y} - \mathbf{b}^T\mathbf{X}^T\mathbf{y}\}$
   $\text{SSR} = \text{SST} - \text{SSE}$

4. Coefficient of determination: $R^2 = \dfrac{\text{SSR}}{\text{SST}} = \dfrac{\text{SST} - \text{SSE}}{\text{SST}}$

5. Coefficient of multiple correlation $R = \sqrt{\dfrac{\text{SSR}}{\text{SST}}}$

6. Degrees of freedom:
   $\text{SST} = \text{SSY} - \text{SS0} = \text{SSR} + \quad \text{SSE}$
   $n - 1 = \quad n \quad - \quad 1 \quad = \quad k \quad + (n - k - 1)$

7. Analysis of variance: $\text{MSR} = \dfrac{\text{SSR}}{k}$; $\text{MSE} = \dfrac{\text{SSE}}{n - k - 1}$
   Regression is significant if MSR/MSE is greater than $F_{[1-\alpha;k,n-k-1]}$.

8. Standard deviation of errors: $s_e = \sqrt{\text{MSE}}$

9. Standard deviation of parameters: $s_{b_j} = s_e \sqrt{C_{jj}}$
   where C_{jj} is the jth diagonal term of $\mathbf{C} = (\mathbf{X}^T\mathbf{X})^{-1}$

10. Prediction: Mean of m future observations
    $\hat{y}_p = b_0 + b_1 x_{1p} + b_2 x_{2p} + \cdots + b_k x_{kp}$
    Or in vector notation: $\hat{y}_p = \mathbf{x}_p^T\mathbf{b}$; here, $\mathbf{x}_p^T = (1, x_{1p}, x_{2p}, \ldots, x_{kp})$

11. Standard deviation of predictions: $s_{\hat{y}_p} = s_e \sqrt{\left\{\dfrac{1}{m} + \mathbf{x}_p^T(\mathbf{X}^T\mathbf{X})^{-1}\mathbf{x}_p\right\}}$

12. All confidence intervals are computed using $t_{[1-\alpha/2;n-k-1]}$.

(Continued)

Box 15.1   Continued

13. Correlations among predictors:

$$R_{x_1 x_2} = \frac{\sum x_{1i} x_{2i} - n\bar{x}_1 \bar{x}_2}{\left[\sum x_{1i}^2 - n\bar{x}_1^2\right]^{1/2} \left[\sum x_{2i}^2 - n\bar{x}_2^2\right]^{1/2}}$$

14. Model assumptions:

(a) Errors are independent and identically distributed normal variates with zero mean.

(b) Errors have the same variance for all values of the predictors.

(c) Errors are additive.

(d) x_i's and y are linearly related.

(e) x_i's are nonstochastic and are measured without error.

15. Visual tests:

(a) Scatter plot of errors versus predicted responses should not have any trend.

(b) The normal quantile-quantile plot of errors should be linear.

Example 15.1   Seven programs were monitored to observe their resource demands. In particular, the number of disk I/O's, memory size (in kilobytes), and CPU time (in milliseconds) were observed. The data is shown in Table 15.1.

TABLE 15.1   Data on CPU Time, Disk I/O's, and Memory Size

CPU Time, y_i	Disk I/O's, x_{1i}	Memory Size, x_{2i}
2	14	70
5	16	75
7	27	144
9	42	190
10	39	210
13	50	235
20	83	400

We would like to find a linear function to estimate the CPU time:

CPU time $= b_0 + b_1$(number of disk I/O's) $+ b_2$(memory size)

In this case,

$$X = \begin{bmatrix} 1 & 14 & 70 \\ 1 & 16 & 75 \\ 1 & 27 & 144 \\ 1 & 42 & 190 \\ 1 & 39 & 210 \\ 1 & 50 & 235 \\ 1 & 83 & 400 \end{bmatrix}$$

$$X^TX = \begin{bmatrix} 7 & 271 & 1324 \\ 271 & 13855 & 67188 \\ 1324 & 67188 & 326686 \end{bmatrix}$$

$$C = (X^TX)^{-1} = \begin{bmatrix} 0.6297 & 0.0223 & -0.0071 \\ 0.0223 & 0.0280 & -0.0058 \\ -0.0071 & -0.0058 & 0.0012 \end{bmatrix}$$

$$X^Ty = \begin{bmatrix} 66 \\ 3,375 \\ 16,388 \end{bmatrix}$$

The regression parameters are:

$$b = (X^TX)^{-1}X^Ty = (-0.1614, 0.1182, 0.0265)^T$$

The regression equation is

CPU time $= -0.1614 + 0.1182$(number of disk I/O's) $+ 0.0265$(memory size)

Using this equation, we can estimate CPU time and compute the errors as shown in Table 15.2. From the table we see that

$$SSE = \sum e_i^2 = 5.3$$

An alternate method to compute SSE is

$$SSE = \{y^Ty - b^TX^Ty\}$$

For this data,

$$SSY = \sum y_i^2 = 828 \qquad SS0 = n\bar{y}^2 = 622.29$$

TABLE 15.2   Error Computation for the Disk-Memory-CPU Data

CPU Time, y_i	Disk I/O's, x_{1i}	Memory Size, x_{2i}	Estimated CPU time, $\hat{y}_i$	Error, e_i	Error Squared, e_i^2
2	14	70	3.3490	−1.3490	1.8198
5	16	75	3.7180	1.2820	1.6436
7	27	144	6.8472	0.1528	0.0233
9	42	190	9.8400	−0.8400	0.7053
10	39	210	10.0151	−0.0151	0.0002
13	50	235	11.9783	1.0217	1.0439
20	83	400	20.2529	−0.2529	0.0639
66	271	1324	66.0000	−0.0003	5.3000

Therefore,

$$SST = SSY - SS0 = 828 - 622.29 = 205.71$$
$$SSR = SST - SSE = 205.71 - 5.3 = 200.41$$

The coefficient of determination is

$$R^2 = \frac{SSR}{SST} = \frac{200.41}{205.71} = 0.97$$

Thus, the regression explains 97% of the variation of y.

The coefficient of multiple correlation is defined as the square root of the coefficient of determination. For this example, it is given by

$$R = \sqrt{0.97} = 0.99$$

The standard deviation of errors is

$$s_e = \sqrt{\frac{SSE}{n-3}} = \sqrt{5.3/4} = 1.2$$

The standard deviations of the regression parameters are

Estimated standard deviation of $b_0 = s_e\sqrt{c_{00}} = 1.2\sqrt{0.6297} = 0.9131$

Estimated standard deviation of $b_1 = s_e\sqrt{c_{11}} = 1.2\sqrt{0.0280} = 0.1925$

Estimated standard deviation of $b_2 = s_e\sqrt{c_{22}} = 1.2\sqrt{0.0012} = 0.0404$

The 0.95-quantile for a t-variate with four degrees of freedom is 2.132. The confidence intervals for the regression parameters are therefore

90% confidence interval of $b_0 = -0.1614 \mp (2.132)(0.9131) = (-2.11, 1.79)$

90% confidence interval of $b_1 = 0.1182 \mp (2.132)(0.1925) = (-0.29, 0.53)$

90% confidence interval of $b_2 = 0.0265 \mp (2.132)(0.0404) = (-0.06, 0.11)$

We see that none of the three parameters is significant at a 90% confidence level. In order to illustrate the applications of the prediction formula, let us predict a single future observation for programs with 100 disk I/O's and a memory size of 550. The predicted mean y_{1p} is given by

$$y_{1p} = b_0 + b_1 x_1 + b_2 x_2 = -0.1614 + 0.1182(100) + 0.0265(550) = 26.2375$$

The standard deviation of the predicted observation is

$$s_{y_{1p}} = s_e \sqrt{\{1 + \mathbf{x}^T (\mathbf{X}^T \mathbf{X})^{-1} \mathbf{x}\}} = 1.2\sqrt{1 + 7.4118} = 3.3435$$

The 90% confidence interval using the t-value of 2.132 is

$$26.2375 \mp (2.132)(3.3435) = (19.1096, 33.3363)$$

The standard deviation for a mean of a large number of observations is

$$s_{\bar{y}_p} = s_e \sqrt{\{\mathbf{x}^T (\mathbf{X}^T \mathbf{X})^{-1} \mathbf{x}\}} = 1.2\sqrt{7.4118} = 3.1385$$

The 90% confidence interval is

$$26.2375 \mp (2.132)(3.1385) = (19.5467, 32.9292) \qquad \square$$

15.1.1 Analysis of Variance

The partitioning of variation into an explained and unexplained part is useful in practice since it can be easily presented by the analyst to the decision makers. For example, it is easy for them to understand that a regression that explains only 70% of the variation is not as good as one that explains 90%. The next question is how much explained variation is good? A statistical answer to this question is obtained by the so-called **Analysis Of Variance (ANOVA)**. This analysis essentially tests the hypothesis that the SSR is less than or equal to the SSE.

Various sums of squares are related as follows:

$$\text{SST} = \text{SSY} - \text{SS0} = \text{SSR} + \text{SSE}$$

Each of the sums of squares has an associated degree of freedom that corresponds to the number of independent values required to compute them. The SSY has n degrees of freedom since each of its n observations can be independently chosen. The SSE has only $n - k - 1$ degrees of freedom since it is obtained after calculating $k + 1$ regression parameters from the data. Similarly, the SST has $n - 1$ degrees of freedom since one parameter $\bar{y}$ must be calculated from the data before the SST can be computed. The SSR, which is the difference between the SST and the SSE, has the remaining k degrees of freedom. Thus, various sums and their associated degrees of freedom are as follows:

$$\begin{aligned} \text{SST} &= \text{SSY} - \text{SS0} = \text{SSR} + \quad \text{SSE} \\ n-1 &= \quad n \quad - \quad 1 \;\; = \quad k \quad + (n-k-1) \end{aligned}$$

Notice that the degrees of freedom add in a manner similar to the sum of squares. This fact can be used to check if the degrees of freedoms have been assigned correctly.

Assuming that the errors are independent and normally distributed and that all of them are identically distributed (with the same mean and variance), it follows that the y's are also normally distributed since the x's are nonstochastic (they can be measured without errors). The sum of squares of normal variates has a chi-square distribution (see Section 29.4). Thus, various sums of squares have a chi-square distribution with the degrees of freedoms as given above.

Given two sums of squares SSi and SSj with ν_i and ν_j degrees of freedom, the ratio $(SSi/\nu_i)/(SSj/\nu_j)$ has an F distribution with ν_i numerator degrees of freedom and ν_j denominator degrees of freedom. This follows from the definition of the F distribution as explained in Section 29.7 The hypothesis that the sum SSi is less than or equal to SSj is rejected at the α significance level if the ratio is greater than the $1 - \alpha$ quantile of the F-variate. Thus, the computed ratio is compared with $F_{[1-\alpha;\nu_i,\nu_j]}$ obtained from the table of F quantiles (Tables A.6 to A.8 in the Appendix) and the sums of squares are considered significantly different if the computed F is more than that obtained from the table. This procedure is also known as in **F-test**.

The F-test can be used to check if the SSR is significantly higher than the SSE by computing the ratio $(SSR/\nu_R)/(SSE/\nu_e)$, where ν_R and ν_e are degrees of freedom for the SSR and SSE, respectively. The quantity SSR/ν_R is called the **mean square** of the regression (MSR). In general, any sum of squares divided by its degrees of freedom gives the corresponding mean square. Thus

$$MSR = \frac{SSR}{k}$$

and

$$MSE = \frac{SSE}{n - k - 1}$$

The ratio MSR/MSE has an $F[k, n-k-1]$ distribution, that is, an F distribution with k numerator degrees of freedom and $n - k - 1$ denominator degrees of freedom (see Section 29.7 for F distribution). If the computed ratio is greater than the value read from the F-table, the predictor variables are assumed to explain a significant fraction of the response variation. A convenient tabular arrangement to conduct the F-test is shown in Table 15.3. The table is arranged so that the computation can be done column by column from the left. As shown under the table, the standard deviation of errors can be estimated by taking a square root of MSE, which is an estimate of the error variance.

It must be pointed out that the F-test is also equivalent to testing the null hypothesis that y does not depend upon any x_j, that is

$$b_1 = b_2 = \cdots = b_k = 0$$

TABLE 15.3 ANOVA Table for Multiple Linear Regression

Component	Sum of Squares	Percentage of Variation	Degrees of Freedom	Mean Square	F-Computed	F-Table
y	$SSY = \Sigma y^2$		n			
$\bar{y}$	$SS0 = n\bar{y}^2$		1			
$y - \hat{y}$	$SST = SSY - SS0$	100	$n - 1$			
Regression	$SSR = SST - SSE$	$100\left(\dfrac{SSR}{SST}\right)$	k	$MSR = \dfrac{SSR}{k}$	$\dfrac{MSR}{MSE}$	$F_{[1-\alpha; \, k, n-k-1]}$
Errors	$SSE = y^Ty - b^TX^Ty$	$100\left(\dfrac{SSE}{SST}\right)$	$n - k - 1$	$MSE = \dfrac{SSE}{n-k-1}$		

$$s_e = \sqrt{MSE}$$

against an alternate hypothesis that y depends upon at least one x_j, and therefore, at least one $b_j \neq 0$. If the computed ratio is less than the value read from the table, the null hypothesis cannot be rejected at the stated significance level.

In simple regression models, there is only one predictor variable, and hence the F-test reduces to that of testing $b_1 = 0$. Thus, if the confidence interval of b_1 does not include zero, the parameter is nonzero, the regression explains a significant part of the response variation, and the F-test is not required.

Example 15.2 For the disk-memory-CPU data of Example 15.1, the analysis of variance is shown in Table 15.4. From the table we see that the computed F-ratio is more than that obtained from the table, and so the regression does explain a significant part of the variation. □

TABLE 15.4 ANOVA Table for the I/O's, Memory, and CPU Time Example

Component	Sum of Squares	Percentage of Variation	Degrees of Freedom	Mean Square	F-Computed	F-Table
y	828					
$\bar{y}$	622					
$y - \bar{y}$	206	100.0	6			
Regression	200	97.4	2	100.20	75.40	4.32
Errors	5.32	2.6	4	1.33		

$$s_e = \sqrt{MSE} = \sqrt{1.33} = 1.15$$

Notice that in example 15.2, the regression passed the F-test, indicating that the hypothesis of all parameters being zero cannot be accepted. However, none of the regression parameters are significantly different from zero. This apparent contradiction is due to the problem of multicollinearity, which is discussed next.

15.1.2 Problem of Multicollinearity

Two lines are said to be collinear if they have the same slope and same intercept. These two lines can be represented in just one dimension instead of the two dimensions required for lines that are not collinear. Two collinear lines are not independent. Similarly, when two predictor variables are linearly dependent, they are called collinear. The linear dependence between variables is measured by their correlation. Thus, if the correlation between two predictor variables is nonzero, they are collinear and the problem of linear dependence among many predictor variables is called the problem of multicollinearity. In particular, this problem may result in contradictory results from various significance tests.

To see if the problem of multicollinearity exists, we need to find the correlation between various x_i pairs. In cases where the correlation is relatively high, we might eliminate one of the x_i's from the regression and redo the computations with the remaining x-variables. If the significance of the regression as a whole improves, we can conclude that the correlation between the x's is causing the problem.

Example 15.3 We did get contradictory significance conclusions in Example 15.2. To see if this is due to correlation between the number of disk I/O's and the memory size, we compute the correlation coefficient between the two.

In this case, $n = 7$, $\Sigma x_{1i} = 271$, $\Sigma x_{2i} = 1324$, $\Sigma x_{1i}^2 = 1385$, $\Sigma x_{2i}^2 = 326{,}686$, $\Sigma x_{1i} x_{2i} = 67{,}188$:

$$\text{Correlation}(x_1, x_2) = R_{x_1 x_2}$$

$$= \frac{\sum x_{1i} x_{2i} - \dfrac{1}{n}\left(\sum x_{1i}\right)\left(\sum x_{2i}\right)}{\left[\sum x_{1i}^2 - \dfrac{1}{n}\left(\sum x_{1i}\right)\left(\sum x_{1i}\right)\right]^{1/2}\left[\sum x_{2i}^2 - \dfrac{1}{n}\left(\sum x_{2i}\right)\left(\sum x_{2i}\right)\right]^{1/2}}$$

$$= \frac{67{,}188 - \frac{1}{7}(271)(1324)}{\left[1385 - \frac{1}{7}(271)(271)\right]^{1/2}\left[326{,}686 - \frac{1}{7}(1324)(1324)\right]^{1/2}} = 0.9947$$

The correlation is in fact high. This may be due to large programs (programs with large memory sizes) doing more I/O's than small programs. To get a meaningful regression, we could try eliminating one of the two variables. In Example 14.1, we have already regressed CPU time on number of disk I/O's and found that the regression parameter was significant. Similarly, in Exercise 14.3, CPU time is regressed on the memory size, and the resulting regression parameters are found to be significant. Thus, either the number of I/O's or the memory size can be used to estimate CPU time, but not both. □

One important lesson to learn here is that adding a predictor variable does not always improve a regression. If the variable is correlated to other predictor variables, it may reduce the statistical accuracy of the regression.

If an analyst wants to choose the right subset of predictors from a set of k possible predictors, the simplest alternative is to try all 2^k possible subsets and choose the one that gives the best results with a small number of variables. Several different trade-offs may have to be made in selecting the subset. For example, some variables may be easier to measure and are better suited as predictors than others. With increasing availability of computing power, trying all 2^k subsets is usually not a problem for reasonable values of k and sample sizes. In any case, a correlation matrix for the subset chosen should be computed and checked to see that the correlation among the chosen predictors is low.

15.2 REGRESSION WITH CATEGORICAL PREDICTORS

Regression can also be used in one or more of the predictor variables as categorical variables—variables that are nonnumerical. For example, CPU type is a categorical variable. If you have performance data on three CPUs of types A, B, and C, you can use regression to model the data as discussed in this section.

Note: If all predictor variables are categorical, you should use one of the experimental design and analysis techniques described in Part IV of this book. Although the technique presented in this section can be used for several categorical predictors as well, statistically more precise (less variant) results will be obtained using factorial designs described in Part IV. Therefore, the use of the technique described in this section should be limited to the case of mixed predictors where most predictors are quantitative and only a few predictors are categorical.

To represent a categorical variable that can take only two values, we can define a binary variable, for instance, x_j, as follows. The advantage of this coding is that the regression parameter b_j represents the difference in the effect of the two alternatives. If the parameter is found to be statistically insignificant, the two alternatives can be assumed to provide similar performance.

The levels of the binary variable can also be -1 and $+1$. Thus,

$$x_j = \begin{cases} -1 \Rightarrow \text{first value} \\ +1 \Rightarrow \text{second value} \end{cases}$$

The parameter b_j in this case represents the difference from the average response for each level. The difference of the effects of the two levels is $2b_j$.

If the categorical variable takes three values, for instance, A, B, and C, the coding is not obvious. One alternative, which is undesirable, is to define a three-valued variable as follows:

$$x_1 = \begin{cases} 1 \Rightarrow \text{type A} \\ 2 \Rightarrow \text{type B} \\ 3 \Rightarrow \text{type C} \end{cases}$$

The problem with this coding is that it implies an order. It attempts to represent B halfway between A and C. In general, this is not true. The regression parameters, in this case, do not provide any meaningful information. The recommended coding is to use two predictor variables, for instance, x_1 and x_2, defined as follows:

$$x_1 = \begin{cases} 1 & \text{if type A} \\ 0 & \text{otherwise} \end{cases}$$

$$x_2 = \begin{cases} 1 & \text{if type B} \\ 0 & \text{otherwise} \end{cases}$$

Thus, the three types are represented by (x_1, x_2) pairs as follows:

$$(x_1, x_2) = (1,0) \Rightarrow \text{type A}$$
$$(x_1, x_2) = (0,1) \Rightarrow \text{type B}$$
$$(x_1, x_2) = (0,0) \Rightarrow \text{type C}$$

The coding does not imply any ordering among the types. Also, it provides an easy way to interpret the regression parameters. Suppose the regression model with this coding is

$$y = b_0 + b_1 x_1 + b_2 x_2 + e$$

The average responses for the three types are

$$\bar{y}_A = b_0 + b_1$$
$$\bar{y}_B = b_0 + b_2$$
$$\bar{y}_C = b_0$$

Thus, the parameter b_1 represents the difference between average responses with types A and C. The parameter b_2 represents the difference between average responses with types B and C. The parameter b_0 represents average response with type C.

In general, the number of values that a categorical variable can take is called its **level**. Thus, to represent a categorical variable with k levels (or k categories), we need to define $k - 1$ binary variables as follows:

$$x_j = \begin{cases} 1 & \text{if } j\text{th value} \\ 0 & \text{otherwise} \end{cases}$$

The kth value is defined by $x_1 = x_2 = \cdots = x_{k-1} = 0$. The regression parameter b_0 represents the average response with the kth alternative. The parameter

b_j represents the difference between the average responses with alternatives j and k.

Given k alternatives, if one of the alternatives represents the status quo or a standard against which other alternatives have to be measured, that alternative should be coded as the kth alternative since the differences from the kth response are directly available as regression parameters.

Case Study 15.1 Let us reconsider the RPC performance data of Case Study 14.1. One possible model for the data is to combine the samples on the two operating systems and use the following model:

$$y = b_0 + b_1 x_1 + b_2 x_2$$

where y is the elapsed time, x_1 is the data size, and x_2 is a binary variable representing UNIX or ARGUS as follows:

$$x_2 = \begin{cases} 1 \Rightarrow \text{UNIX} \\ 0 \Rightarrow \text{ARGUS} \end{cases}$$

The computed parameter values and their confidence intervals are shown in Table 15.5. All three parameters are significant. The regression explains 76.5% of the variation.

The model parameters are interpreted as follows. The per-byte processing cost (time) for both operating systems is 0.025 millisecond; the setup cost is 36.73 milliseconds on ARGUS, which is 14.927 milliseconds more than that with UNIX.

As an aside, notice that this model and its conclusions are different from those of the model used in Case Study 14.1 earlier. There we had concluded that there was no significant difference in the setup cost of the two operating systems. The per-byte costs were different. Which conclusion is correct? This is where system considerations help, and this is why statistical techniques applied without understanding the system can lead to a misleading result.

The model of Case Study 14.1 was based on the assumption that the processing as well as setup in the two operating systems are different. They were both modeled as separate parameters. Thus, there were four parameters in all. The data showed that the setup costs were numerically indistinguishable.

TABLE 15.5   Regression Coefficients for RPC Time on UNIX/ARGUS

Parameter	Mean	Standard Deviation	Confidence Interval
b_0	36.739	3.251	(31.1676, 42.3104)
b_1	0.025	0.004	(0.0192, 0.0313)
b_2	-14.927	3.165	$(-20.3509, -9.5024)$

The model used in this example is based on the assumption that the operating systems have no effect on per-byte processing. This will be true if the processing is identical on the two systems and does not involve the operating systems. Only setup requires operating system calls. If this is in fact true, then the regression coefficients estimated in the joint model of this example are more realistic estimates of the real world. On the other hand, if system programmers can show that the processing follows a different code path in the two systems, then the model of Case Study 14.1 would be more realistic. □

15.3 CURVILINEAR REGRESSION

A linear regression model can be used only if the relationship between the response and the predictor variables is linear. Therefore, the first step in developing a regression model is to plot a scatter diagram. If the relationship between the response variable y and the predictor variable x appears to be nonlinear or if it is known from other considerations that the relationship has a particular nonlinear form, then we need to use a nonlinear regression model. If the nonlinear function can be converted into a linear form, then the regression can be carried out using the simple or multiple linear regression techniques. Such a regression is called a curvilinear regression.

An example of a curvilinear regression is the exponential relationship

$$y = bx^a$$

Taking a logarithm of both sides, we get

$$\ln y = \ln b + a \ln x$$

Thus, $\ln x$ and $\ln y$ are linearly related. The values of $\ln b$ and a can be found by a linear regression of $\ln y$ on $\ln x$.

Other examples of curvilinear regression functions are

Nonlinear	Linear
$y = a + b/x$	$y = a + b(1/x)$
$y = 1/(a + bx)$	$(1/y) = a + bx$
$y = x/(a + bx)$	$(x/y) = a + bx$
$y = ab^x$	$\ln y = \ln a + (\ln b)x$
$y = a + bx^n$	$y = a + b(x^n)$

In curvilinear regressions, if a predictor variable appears in more than one transformed predictor variable, the transformed variables are likely to be correlated, causing the problem of multicollinearity. Therefore, the analyst should try regression using various possible subsets of the predictor variables to find a subset that gives significant parameters and explains a high percentage of the observed variation.

Example 15.4 Amdahl's law for I/O's in computer systems states that the I/O rate is proportional to the processor speed. For each instruction ex-

TABLE 15.6 Data for Amdahl's Law Study

System No.	MIPS Used	I/O Rate
1	19.63	288.60
2	5.45	117.30
3	2.63	64.60
4	8.24	356.40
5	14.00	373.20
6	9.87	281.10
7	11.27	149.60
8	10.13	120.60
9	1.01	31.10
10	1.26	23.70

ecuted there is one bit of I/O on the average. To validate the law, number of I/O's and processor utilizations were measured on a number of computer systems. Using the nominal MIPS rate for the system and its utilization, the rate of instructions usage (in MIPS) over a period of time and the I/O rate (in kilobytes per second) for the same period was computed. The data is shown in Table 15.6. Let us fit the following curvilinear model to this data:

$$\text{I/O rate} = \alpha(\text{MIPS rate})^{b_1}$$

Taking a log of both sides we get:

$$\log(\text{I/O rate}) = \log \alpha + b_1 \log(\text{MIPS Rate})$$

The parameters $b_0 = \log \alpha$ and b_1 can be estimated using the simple linear regression technique. The data after log transformation is shown in Table 15.7.

TABLE 15.7 Transformed Data for Amdahl's Law Study

Observation No.	x_1	y
1	1.293	2.460
2	0.736	2.069
3	0.420	1.810
4	0.916	2.552
5	1.146	2.572
6	0.994	2.449
7	1.052	2.175
8	1.006	2.081
9	0.004	1.493
10	0.100	1.375

TABLE 15.8 Regression Coefficients for Amdahl's Law Study

Parameter	Mean	Standard Deviation	Confidence Interval
b_0	1.423	0.119	$(1.20, 1.64)$
b_1	0.888	0.135	$(0.64, 1.14)$

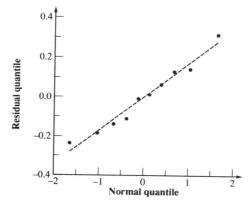

FIGURE 15.1   Normal quantile-quantile plot for the residuals in Amdahl's law study.

The parameters and their confidence intervals are shown in Table 15.8. Both coefficients are significant at the 90% confidence level. The regression explains 84% of the variation. Notice that at this confidence level we can accept the hypothesis that the relationship is linear since the confidence interval for b_1 includes 1.

A normal quantile-quantile plot of the residuals from the logarithmic model is shown in Figure 15.1. Notice that the errors in log(I/O rate) do seem to be normally distributed. ☐

15.4 TRANSFORMATIONS

The term *transformation* is generally used when some function of the measured response variable y is used in place of y in a model. For example, a square root transformation may be used in a multiple linear regression model to fit a model of the form

$$\sqrt{y} = b_0 + b_1 x_1 + b_2 x_2 + \cdots + b_k x_k + e$$

It may appear that transformation is a subset of the curvilinear regression. However, the ideas discussed in this section apply not only to the regression model but to other models as well, such as those used in factorial experimental designs discussed in Part IV. Thus, the discussion of transformations deserves a special section of its own.

There are three cases where a need for transformation should be investigated. First, a transformation should be used if it is known from physical considerations of the system that a function of the response rather than the response itself is a better variable to use in the model. For example, if an analyst has measured the interarrival times y for requests and it is known that the number of requests per unit time $(1/y)$ has a linear relationship to a certain predictor, then $1/y$ transformation should be used. We will see several such examples during experimental design and analysis. Second, a transformation should be investigated if the range of the data covers several orders of magnitude and the sample size is small. In other words, if y_{max}/y_{min} is large, a transformation of the response that reduces the range of variability should be investigated. Third, transformations are used if the homogeneous variance (homoscedasticity) assumption of the residuals is violated, as discussed next.

If a scatter plot of the residual versus predicted response ($\hat{y}$) shows that the spread in the residuals is not homogeneous, this indicates that the residuals are still functions of the predictor variables. The assumed linear model does completely describe the relationship, and a transformation of the response may help solve the problem. To find the transformation, compute the standard deviation of residuals at each value of $\hat{y}$ (assuming that there are more than one residuals at each value) and plot the standard deviation as a function of the mean $\hat{y}$. If there are several replicated measurements of response variable y for each given set of predictor variable values, then this plot can be prepared even before fitting a model. For each set of replicated observations, the standard deviation s and the mean $\bar{y}$ is computed and plotted on a scatter diagram. Suppose the relationship between the standard deviation s and the mean $\bar{y}$ is

$$s = g(\bar{y})$$

Then a transformation of the form

$$w = h(y)$$

may help solve the problem, where

$$h(y) = \int \frac{1}{g(y)} \, dy$$

A few transformations that have been found useful in practice are as follows:

- *Log Transformation*: If the standard deviation s is a linear function of the mean ($s = a\bar{y}$), as shown in Figure 15.2a, a logarithmic transformation of the form $w = \ln y$ may help stabilize the variance. This transformation was obtained as follows:

$$g(y) = ay$$

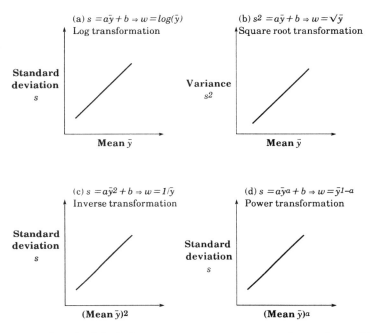

FIGURE 15.2   Standard deviation versus mean response graphs can be used to determine the transformation required.

and therefore

$$h(y) = \int \frac{1}{ay}\, dy = a \ln y$$

The logarithmic transformation is useful only if the ratio y_{max}/y_{min} is large. For a small range the log function is almost linear, and so the analysis of the transformed variable will be identical to that with the original variables.

- *Square Root Transformation*: A Poisson distributed variable has mean equal to the variance ($s = \sqrt{\bar{y}}$). A plot of variance versus mean for such a variable is a straight line, as shown in Figure 15.2b. Notice the we have shown s^2 on the vertical axis (instead of s). In this case, a transformation of the form $w = \sqrt{y}$ helps stabilize the variance.

- *Arc Sine*: If y is a proportion or percentage, a transformation of the type $\sin^{-1}\sqrt{y}$ may be helpful.

- *Omega Transformation*: This transformation is popularly used when the response y is a proportion. With this transformation, the transformed value w is obtained from original values of y as follows:

$$w = 10\log_{10}\left(\frac{y}{1-y}\right)$$

The transformed values of w are said to be in units of **dB** (decibels). The term comes from signaling theory, where the ratio of output power to input power is measured in decibels. Omega transformation converts fractions between 0 and 1 to values between $-\infty$ and $+\infty$. This transformation is particularly helpful if the fractions are very small or very large. If the fractions are close to 0.5, a transformation may not be required.

- *Power Transformation*: In this a power of the response variable, for instance, y^a, is regressed on the predictor variables. This transformation can be used if in testing the homogeneity of variance it is found that the standard deviation of residuals s_e is proportional to $\hat{y}^{1-a}$. This relationship is shown in Figures 15.2c and 15.2d for $a = -1$ and general a, respectively.

These transformations and a few others are listed in Table 15.9. In each case, y may also be shifted, and $y + c$ (with some suitable c) may be used in place of y. This shifting is useful if there are negative or zero values and if the transformation function is not defined for these values.

If the value of the exponent a in a power transformation is not known, the following transformation family, called **Box-Cox family of transformations**, can be used:

$$w = \begin{cases} \dfrac{y^a - 1}{ag^{a-1}} & a \neq 0 \\ (\ln y)g & a = 0 \end{cases}$$

Where g is the geometric mean of the responses:

$$g = (y_1 y_2 \cdots y_n)^{1/n}$$

TABLE 15.9 Transformations to Stabilize the Variance

Relationship between s and $\bar{y}$	Transformation
$s \propto \bar{y}$	$w = \ln y$ or $w = \ln(y + c)$
$s \propto \bar{y}^{1/2}$	$w = y^{1/2}$
$s \propto \bar{y}^a$	$w = y^{1-a}$ or $w = (y + c)^{1-a}$
$s \propto \bar{y}^2$	$w = \dfrac{1}{y}$
$s \propto 1 - \bar{y}^2$	$w = \ln\left(\dfrac{1+y}{1-y}\right)$
$s \propto \bar{y}(1 - \bar{y})$	$w = \ln\left(\dfrac{y}{1-y}\right)$
$s \propto (1 + \bar{y})\ \bar{\bar{y}}$	$w = \sin^{-1}\sqrt{y}$

The Box-Cox transformation has the property that w has the same units as the response y for all values of the exponent a. All real values of a, positive or negative, can be tried. The transformation is continuous even at zero, since:

$$\lim_{a \to 0} \frac{y^a - 1}{ag^{a-1}} = (\ln y)g$$

One way to determine the parameter a is to try regressions with several different values of a and to use the one that gives the smallest value of the sum of squared errors (SSE). A plot of the SSE versus a can be used to visually see the sensitivity of the SSE to a. Since the SSE generally varies by several orders of magnitude, a semilog plot with ln(SSE) on the vertical axis and a along the horizontal axis may be used.

In general, it is preferable to use simple values for a. For example, if $a = 0.52$ is found to give the minimum SSE and the SSE at $a = 0.5$ is not significantly higher, the latter value may be preferable. The $100(1 - \alpha)$ confidence interval for a includes all values of a for which the SSE is less than the following value:

$$\text{SSE}_{\min} \left(1 + \frac{t^2_{[1-\alpha/2;\nu]}}{\nu} \right)$$

where $\text{SSE}_{\min}$ is the minimum SSE and ν is the number of degrees of freedom for the errors. If the confidence interval for a includes the value $a = 1$, then the hypothesis that the relationship is linear cannot be rejected. In other words, there is no need for the transformation. The following case study illustrates the application of the Box-Cox family of transformation.

Case Study 15.2   The garbage collection time for a particular garbage collection algorithm was measured for various values of heap sizes, as shown in Table 15.10. The analyst hypothesizes that the square root of the time is linearly related to the inverse of the heap size. That is, the model is

$$(\text{Time})^{1/2} = b_0 + \frac{b_1}{\text{heap size}}$$

TABLE 15.10   Garbage Collection Times for Various Heap Sizes

Heap Size	Garbage Collection Time	Heap Size	Garbage Collection Time
500	594.34	1600	63.64
600	247.42	1800	1.00
800	114.24	2000	1.00
1000	85.64	2200	1.00
1200	49.60	2400	1.00
1400	50.30	2600	1.00

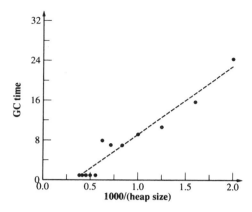

FIGURE 15.3 Scatter plot of the data for garbage collection study.

The transformed data along with the linear regression line is plotted in Figure 15.3. The points do not appear to be close to the straight line. Suppose we want to test the hypothesis that the exponent on time is different than a half. The Box-Cox family of transformation can be used for this purpose. Using several values of a ranging from -0.4 to 0.8, the SSE is computed for each value. Values of the SSE as a function of the exponent a are plotted in Figure 15.4. The minimum SSE of 2049 occurs at $a = 0.45$. Since 0.95-quantile of a t-variate with 10 degrees of freedom is 1.812, a horizontal line is drawn at

$$\text{SSE} = 2049 \left(1 + \frac{(1.812)^2}{10} \right) = 2721.8$$

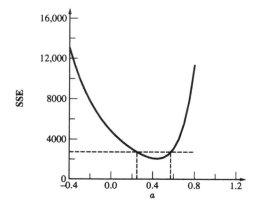

FIGURE 15.4 Plot of SSE versus the exponent a for the garbage collection study.

The line intersects the SSE curve at $a = 0.2465$ and $a = 0.5726$. Thus, the 90% confidence interval for a is $(0.2465, 0.5726)$. Since the interval includes 0.5, we cannot reject the hypothesis that the exponent is 0.5.   □

The Box-Cox family of transformation, as described here, cannot be used if there are some negative or zero values in the measured responses. The solution is to add a constant amount c to all y's replacing them with $y + c$. Thus, with a shift of c, the Box-Cox family of transformation becomes

$$w = \begin{cases} \dfrac{(y + c)^a - 1}{ag^{a-1}} & a \neq 0 \\ (\ln(y + c))g & a = 0 \end{cases}$$

where

$$g = \left(\prod_{i=1}^{n}(y_i + c) \right)^{1/n}$$

In this case, c becomes another parameter in addition to a, which needs to be estimated.

15.5 OUTLIERS

Any observation that is atypical of the remaining observations *may* be considered an outlier. Notice the emphasis on the word "may" in the last sentence. Including the outlier in the analysis may change the conclusions significantly. Excluding the outlier from the analysis may lead to a misleading conclusion if the outlier in fact represents a correct observation of the system behavior. A number of statistical tests have been proposed to test if a particular value is an outlier. Most of these tests assume a certain distribution for the observations. If the observations do not satisfy the assumed distribution, the results of the statistical test would be misleading. In practice, the easiest way to identify outliers is to look at the scatter plot of the data. Any value significantly away from the remaining observations should be investigated for possible experimental errors. Other experiments in the neighborhood of the outlying observation may be conducted to verify that the response is typical of the system behavior in that operating region. Once the possibility of errors in the experiment has been eliminated, the analyst may decide to include or exclude the suspected outlier based on intuition. One alternative is to repeat the analysis with and without the outlier and state the results separately. Another alternative is to divide the operating region into two (or more) subregions and obtain a separate model for each subregion.

15.6 COMMON MISTAKES IN REGRESSION

The following mistakes are common in regression analysis and often lead to misleading conclusions.

1. *Not Verifying That the Relationship Is Linear*: If the scatter diagram shows a highly nonlinear relationship or, if based on other considerations, it is known that the relationship is nonlinear, a curvilinear relationship should be used. A linear regression for variables that are nonlinearly related may lead to the misleading conclusion that they are not related, for example, if the regression parameters are zero.

2. *Relying on Automated Results without Visual Verification*: A visual check of the scatter diagram is an important step in regression analysis. Unfortunately, this step requires manual intervention and so it is often skipped. The analyst may use a measurement package, which automatically fits a regression model and presents the parameters. This may lead to misleading conclusions that could have been easily avoided by a visual check of the scatter diagram. For example, Figure 15.5 shows several scatter diagrams that will easily produce a regression with a high coefficient of determination but the model may not represent the system behavior. A quick look at the scatter diagram would have helped avoid the problem in each case.

3. *Attaching Importance to Numerical Values of Regression Parameters*: The absolute values of the regression parameters depend upon the dimensions of the corresponding predictor variable. For example, consider the following hypothetical example of predicting CPU time as a function of the number of disk I/O's and the memory size of a program:

CPU time in seconds = 0.01(number of disk I/O's)

+ 0.001(memory size in kilobytes)

Here, a careless analyst may conclude that the parameter 0.001 is too small, and therefore, the memory size can be ignored as compared to the number of disk I/O's. This is wrong, since the same relationship could have been written as either

CPU time in milliseconds = 10(number of disk I/O's)

+ 1(memory size in kilobytes)

or

CPU time in seconds = 0.01(number of disk I/O's)

+ 1(Memory size in bytes)

In either case, the analyst may not consider that the regression parameter value of 1 is too small. The lesson is that the absolute value of the

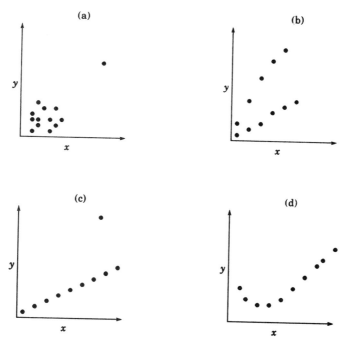

FIGURE 15.5 Examples of data that may give high coefficient of determination, but the linear model obtained may not represent the system correctly.

regression parameter depends upon the units in which it is measured, and two parameters measured in different units cannot be compared. The right way to compare the significance of a regression parameter is by its confidence interval.

4. *Not Specifying Confidence Intervals for the Regression Parameters*: Most analysts realize that the experiments need to be repeated, since observations are random variables. However, many analysts do not realize that all computations from a sample of n observations are also random. Therefore, a confidence interval should be specified that indicates the variability of the computation.

5. *Not Specifying the Coefficient of Determination*: Least-squares estimation is a well-known technique. Sometimes analysts compute the regression parameters, but they do not specify the coefficient of determination R^2. Without R^2, it is difficult to deduce the goodness of the regression. An F-test is used even more rarely. However, if R^2 is small, often we may not want to use the regression results anyway, and the F-test is not necessary.

6. *Confusing the Coefficient of Determination and the Coefficient of Correlation*: The coefficient of correlation is denoted by R and the coefficient of determination by R^2. The coefficient of determination gives

the percentage of explained variance; the coefficient of correlation does not. For example, if the coefficient of correlation is 0.8 ($R = 0.8$, $R^2 = 0.64$), the regression will explain only 64% of the variance and not 80%.

7. *Using Highly Correlated Variables as Predictor Variables*: Analysts often start a multilinear regression with as many predictor variables as possible. This may lead to severe multicollinearity problems. The correlations between predictor variables should be computed. Both variables of a correlated pair should be included in the regression only if this leads to a considerable increase in the significance of the regression.

8. *Using Regression to Predict Far Beyond the Measured Range*: A system may behave differently in different operating ranges. A regression relationship based on measurements in one operating range may not apply far outside the range. In particular, the statistical confidence decreases as we move outside the measured range. Inexperienced analysts, who may not be aware of this, often use small workloads or systems for measurement and then use the regression to predict the behavior for large workloads or systems. In such cases, it is necessary to verify that the relationship will apply beyond the measured range. Also, the predictions should be specified along with their confidence intervals so that the decision makers can decide whether they are willing to take the risk caused by inaccuracies of the predictions.

9. *Using Too Many Predictor Variables*: A common misconception among inexperienced analysts is that using more predictor variables increases the accuracy of predictions. We have already seen in Section 15.1.2 that adding a predictor variable that is correlated with others may decrease the statistical validity of the regression.

   Given a set of k measured predictor variables, there are $2^k - 1$ subsets that can be used. For example, given two variables A and B, we can try A only, B only, or both A and B. One can try all possible subsets and sort them in a decreasing order by the coefficient of determination R^2. Of course, the subset giving the maximum R^2 is the *best* subset. But other subsets that are close may be used instead for practical or engineering reasons. For example, if the second best has only one variable compared to five in the best, the second best may be the preferred model.

10. *Measuring Only a Small Subset of the Complete Range of Operation*: The measurements should cover as much of the typical operating range of a system as possible. For example, consider a computer system that supports up to 100 users. It is difficult to set up an experiment with a large number of users, and so the analysts will typically set up experiments with a small number of users, say, 10 or 20. Measurements in a limited range may result in a model that is quite different from that of the model that applies to the whole range. Figure 15.6 shows a hypothetical sample where the regression line that best fits the limited

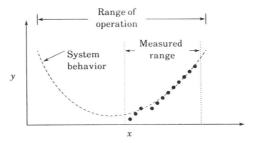

FIGURE 15.6 Measuring over only a portion of the range of operation may produce a model that does not apply to the whole range.

measured range is quite different from what would have been obtained if the whole range had been measured.

11. *Assuming That a Good Predictor Variable Is Also a Good Control Variable*: If two variables are highly correlated, one can be used to predict the other with a high precision. This is true even if one variable does not affect or control the other variable. A good regression model can be used to *predict* the performance, but if the goal of the study is to find what changes in the system will improve its performance, a regression model will be helpful only if the predictor variable is also a control variable. For example, a regression model of the disk I/O versus CPU time can be used to predict the number of disk I/O's for a program given its CPU time. However, reducing the CPU time by installing a faster CPU will not reduce the number of disk I/O's. In other words, CPU time is a predictor but not a controller of the number of disk I/O's.

If two variables w and y are both controlled by a third variable x, w and y may be highly correlated and would be good predictors for each other. The prediction works both ways: w can be used to predict y and vice versa. The control often works only one way: x controls y but y may not control x.

The list of mistakes presented in this section leads to the checklist presented in Box 15.2. The list is organized as a series of questions that should all be answered in the affirmative.

Box 15.2   Checklist For Regression Analyses

1. Have you plotted and visually verified that the relationship is linear?
2. Are all predictors in appropriate units so that regression coefficients are comparable?
3. Has the coefficient of determination been specified?
4. Is the coefficient of determination high enough?

(Continued)

Box 15.2   Continued

5. Have the confidence intervals for regression parameters been specified?
6. Are all regression parameters statistically significant?
7. If there are several predictors, has an F-test been performed?
8. Does the F-test show that regression parameters are statistically significant?
9. Has the correlation among predictor variables been computed?
10. Is the correlation negligible?
11. Is the regression being used for predictions close to the measured range?
12. Is the confidence interval for predictions specified?
13. Are all predictor variables required?
14. Has the normality assumption been verified using a quantile-quantile plot of errors?
15. Have all the outliers in the quantile-quantile plot of errors been explained?
16. If the quantile-quantile plot of errors is different from a straight line, have the transformations been investigated?
17. Has the homoscedasticity assumption been verified using an error versus predicted mean plot?

EXERCISES

15.1 The results of a multiple regression based on nine observations are shown in Table 15.11. Based on these results answer the following questions:

   a. What percentage of variance is explained by the regression?

TABLE 15.11   Results of a Multiple Regression Analysis

j	b_j	s_{b_j}
1	1.3	3.6
2	2.7	1.8
3	0.5	0.6
4	5.0	8.3

Intercept = 75.3
Coefficient of multiple correlation = 0.95
Standard deviation of errors = 12.0
F-value = 14.1

b. Is the regression significant at the 90% confidence level?

c. Which variable has the highest coefficient?

d. Which variable is most significant?

e. Which parameters are not significant at 90%?

f. What is the problem with this regression?

g. What would you try next?

15.2 The time to encrypt or decrypt a k-bit record was measured on a uniprocessor as well as on a multiprocessor. The times in milliseconds are shown in Table 15.12. Using a log transformation and the method for categorical predictors, fit a regression model and interpret the results.

TABLE 15.12   Time to Encrypt a k-bit Record

k	Uniprocessor	Multiprocessor
128	93	67
256	478	355
512	3,408	2,351
1024	25,410	17,022

FURTHER READING FOR PART III

There are a number of good books on statistics and probability theory. For example, see Levin (1981), Trivedi (1982), King and Julstrom (1982), and Papoulis (1965).

Those readers who want a basic nonmathematical treatment of statistics may want to read Haack (1981) or Runyon (1977).

Discussion on misuse of statistics can be found in Hooke (1983), Huff (1954), and Reichmann (1961).

For arguments in favor of geometric means, see Fleming and Wallace (1986). Smith (1988) refutes those arguments. Chambers et al. (1983) discuss quantile-quantile plots.

Natrella (1966) presents a variety of statistical tests and examples of their applications.

The formula for the general transformation technique using integration, first derived by Bartlett in 1947, is discussed in Das and Giri (1986).

The data for Case Study 12.1 is from Gross et al. (1988).

PART IV

EXPERIMENTAL DESIGN AND ANALYSIS

Performance often depends upon more than one factor such as the system and the workload. Proper analysis requires that the effects of each factor be isolated from those of others so that meaningful statements can be made about different levels of the factor, for instance, different systems. Such analysis is the main topic of this part. The techniques presented in this part will enable you to do the following:

- Design a proper set of experiments for measurement or simulation.
- Develop a model that best describes the data obtained.
- Estimate the contribution of each alternative (for example, each processor and each workload) to the performance.
- Isolate the measurement errors.
- Estimate confidence intervals for model parameters.
- Check if the alternatives are significantly different.
- Check if the model is adequate.

Chapter 16 introduces various types of experimental designs and defines several new terms. The remaining chapters in this part present techniques to analyze a number of popular designs.

INTRODUCTION TO EXPERIMENTAL DESIGN

The first ninety percent of the task takes ten percent of the time, and the last ten percent takes the other ninety percent.
—Ninety-ninety rule of project schedules

The goal of a proper experimental design is to obtain the maximum information with the minimum number of experiments. This saves considerable labor that would have been spent gathering data. A proper analysis of experiments also helps in separating out the effects of various factors that might affect the performance. Also, it allows determining if a factor has a significant effect or if the observed difference is simply due to random variations caused by measurement errors and parameters that were not controlled.

Several new terms that are used in experimental design and analysis are explained first in Section 16.1. There are numerous possible experimental designs. Some sample designs are briefly described in Section 16.3. Of these, some are more popular and generally applicable than others.

16.1 TERMINOLOGY

This section explains the terms that are used in experimental design and analysis. It does so by using the example of a personal workstation design study. The problem is to design a personal workstation, where several choices have to be made. First, a microprocessor has to be chosen for the CPU. The alternatives are the 68000, Z80, or 8086 microprocessor. Second, a memory size of 512 kbytes, 2 Mbytes, or 8 Mbytes has to be chosen. Third, the workstation could have one, two, three, or four disk drives. Fourth, the workload on the workstations could be one of three types—secretarial, managerial, or scientific. Performance also depends on user characteristics, such as whether users are at a high school, college, or postgraduate level.

The following terms are frequently used in the design and analysis of experiments:

- **Response Variable:** The outcome of an experiment is called the response variable. Generally the response variable is the measured performance of the system. For example, in the workstation design study the response variable could be the throughput expressed in tasks completed per unit time, or response time for tasks, or any other metric. Since the techniques of experimental design are applicable for any kind of measurements, not just performance measurements, the more general term *response* is used in place of performance.

- **Factors:** Each variable that affects the response variable and has several alternatives is called a factor. For example, there are five factors in the workstation design study. The factors are CPU type, memory size, number of disk drives, workload used, and user's educational level. The factors are also called **predictor variables** or **predictors**.

- **Levels:** The values that a factor can assume are called its levels. In other words, each factor level constitutes one alternative for that factor. For example, in the workstation design study the CPU type has three levels: 68000, 8080, or Z80. Memory size has three levels: 512 kbytes, 2 Mbytes, or 8 Mbytes. The number of disk drives has four levels: 1, 2, 3, or 4. The workload has three levels: secretarial, managerial, or scientific. Finally, users could be placed in one of three educational levels—high school graduates, college graduates, and postgraduates. An alternative term **treatment** is also used in experimental design literature in place of *levels*.

- **Primary Factors:** The factors whose effects need to be quantified are called primary factors. For example, in the workstation design study, one may be primarily interested in quantifying the effect of CPU type, memory size only, and number of disk drives. Thus, there are three primary factors in this case.

- **Secondary Factors:** Factors that impact the performance but whose impact we are not interested in quantifying are called secondary factors. For example, in the workstation study we may not be interested in determining whether performance with postgraduates is better than that with college graduates. Similarly, we do not want to quantify the difference between the three workloads. These are the secondary factors.

- **Replication:** Repetition of all or some experiments is called replication. For example, if all experiments in a study are repeated three times, the study is said to have three replications.

- **Design:** An experimental design consists of specifying the number of experiments, the factor level combinations for each experiment, and the number of replications of each experiment. For example, in the workstation design study, we could perform experiments corresponding to all possible combinations of levels of five factors. This would require $3 \times 3 \times 4 \times 3 \times 3$, or 324, experiments. We could repeat each experiment five times, leading to a total of 1215 observations. This is one possible experimental design. Later, in Section 16.3, several other possible experimental designs will be described.

- **Experimental Unit:** Any entity that is used for the experiment is called an experimental unit. Generally only those experimental units that are considered as one of the factors in the study are of interest. For example, in the workstation design study, the users hired to use the workstation while measurements are being performed could be considered the experimental unit. Other examples of experimental units are patients in medical experiments or land used in agricultural experiments. In all such cases, we are really not interested in comparing the experimental units, although they affect the response. Therefore, one goal of the experimental design is to minimize the impact of variation among the experimental units.

- **Interaction:** Two factors A and B are said to interact if the effect of one depends upon the level of the other. For example, Table 16.1 shows the performance of a system with two factors. As the factor A is changed from level A_1 to level A_2, the performance increases by 2 regardless of the level of factor B. In this case there is no interaction. Table 16.2 shows another possibility. In this case, as the factor A is changed from level A_1 to level A_2, the performance increases either by 2 or by 3 depending upon whether B is at level B_1 or level B_2, respectively. The two factors interact in this case. A graphical presentation of this example is given in Figure 16.1. In case (a), the lines are parallel, indicating no interaction. In the second case, the lines are not parallel, indicating interaction.

TABLE 16.1   Noninteracting Factors

	A_1	A_2
B_1	3	5
B_2	6	8

TABLE 16.2   Interacting Factors

	A_1	A_2
B_1	3	5
B_2	6	9

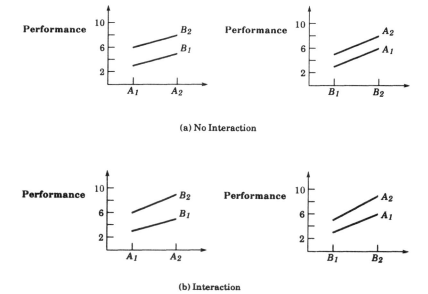

(a) No Interaction

(b) Interaction

FIGURE 16.1   Graphical presentation of interacting and noninteracting factors.

16.2 COMMON MISTAKES IN EXPERIMENTATION

Novice analysts who are not aware of the experimental design and analysis techniques often get misleading conclusions due to the following mistakes:

1. *The variation due to experimental error is ignored.* Every measured value is a random value. Each time it is repeated, the measured value would be slightly different even if all the controllable factors are kept at the same value. In making decisions based on measurements, it is important to isolate the effect of errors. The variation due to a factor must be compared with that due to errors before making a decision about its effect. Inexperienced analysts who are not aware of this assign all variation to the factors and completely ignore the errors.

2. *Important parameters are not controlled.* Earlier, in Section 2.2, it was pointed out that the list of parameters should include all workload, environment, and system parameters that affect the performance. Only some of these parameters are selected as factors and are varied. For example, when comparing two workstations, the user of the workstation has a significant effect on the measured performance. However, if the effect of users is not correctly accounted for, the results may not be meaningful.

3. *Effects of different factors are not isolated.* An analyst may vary several factors simultaneously and then may not be able to allocate the change in performance to any particular factor. To avoid this, some analysts

use very simple experimental designs that lead to the problem discussed next.

4. *Simple one-factor-at-a-time designs are used.* Such a design is wasteful of the resources. It requires too many experiments to get the same information. With proper experimental design, it is possible to get narrower confidence intervals for the effects with the same number of experiments.

5. *Interactions are ignored.* Often the effect of one factor depends on the level of other factors. For example, the effect of adding 1 kbyte of cache may depend on the size of the program. Such interactions cannot be estimated with one-factor-at-a-time designs.

6. *Too many experiments are conducted.* The number of experiments is a function of the number of factors and their levels. It is better to break up the project into several steps each using a small design rather than use one enormous design with too many factors and levels. In the first step, the number of factors and levels should be small. Such a design will help debug the experimental process and also help find out the factors that are not significant and need not be included in further designs. The first design will also tell whether the assumptions of the analysis are satisfied and whether any transformations of data are required. More factors and levels can then be added in the second and subsequent steps.

The experimental design and analysis techniques presented in this part help avoid these problems.

16.3 TYPES OF EXPERIMENTAL DESIGNS

There are numerous varieties of experimental designs. The three most frequently used designs are simple designs, full factorial designs, and fractional factorial designs. Explanations of these designs and their advantanges and disadvantages follow.

16.3.1 Simple Designs

In a simple design, we start with a typical configuration and vary one factor at a time to see how that factor affects performance.

For example, in the workstation design study discussed earlier in Section 16.1, a typical configuration might consist of a Z80 CPU with two disk drives running a managerial task by a college graduate. The performance of this configuration is measured first. Next, we vary the first factor—the CPU—and then performance is compared with other CPUs in the same configuration and workload. This will help us decide which CPU is the best. We then change the number of disk drives to one, three, and four, comparing performance so as to find the optimal number.

Given k factors, with the ith factor having n_i levels, a simple design requires only n experiments, where

$$n = 1 + \sum_{i=1}^{k} (n_i - 1)$$

However, this design does not make the best use of the effort spent. It is not statistically efficient. Also, if the factors have interaction, this design may lead to wrong conclusions. For example, if the effect of the CPU depends upon the size of the memory, the optimal combination cannot be determined until all possibilities are tried. This design, therefore, is not recommended.

16.3.2 Full Factorial Design

A full factorial design utilizes every possible combination at all levels of all factors. A performance study with k factors, with the ith factor having n_i levels, requires n experiments, where

$$n = \prod_{i=1}^{k} n_i$$

In the workstation design study, the number of experiments would be

$$n = (3 \text{ CPUs})(3 \text{ memory levels})(4 \text{ disk drives})$$

$$\times (3 \text{ workloads})(3 \text{ educational levels})$$

$$= 324 \text{ experiments}$$

The advantage of a full factorial design is that every possible combination of configuration and workload is examined. We can find the effect of every factor including the secondary factors and their interactions. The main problem is the cost of the study. It would take too much time and money to conduct these many experiments, especially when taking into account the possibility that each of these experiments may have to be repeated several times. There are three ways to reduce the number of experiments:

- Reduce the number of levels for each factor.
- Reduce the number of factors.
- Use fractional factorial designs.

The first alternative is specially recommended. In some cases, one can try just two levels of each factor and determine the relative importance of each factor. A full factorial design in which each of the k factors is used at two levels requires 2^k experiments. This is a very popular design and is called 2^k **design**. After the list of factors has been reduced substantially, one can try more levels per factor. The third alternative of fractional factorial design is described in the next section.

16.3.3 Fractional Factorial Designs

Sometimes the number of experiments required for a full factorial design is too large. This may happen if either the number of factors or their levels is large. It may not be possible to use a full factorial design due to the expense or the time required. In such cases, one can use only a fraction of the full factorial design. Later in Chapter 19 we discuss the procedure to design a specific class of fractional factorial designs. Here, we simply give an example.

> **Example 16.1** Consider only four of the five factors in the workstation study. Let us ignore the number of disk drives for this example. We have four factors, each at three levels. Therefore, the number of experiments required is
>
> $n = (3 \text{ CPUs})(3 \text{ memory levels})(3 \text{ workloads})(3 \text{ educational levels})$
>
> $= 81 \text{ experiments}$
>
> The full factorial design consisting of 81 experiments is the so-called 3^4 design. A 3^{4-2} fractional factorial design consisting of only nine experiments is shown in Table 16.3. Notice that each of the four factors is used three times at each of its three levels. □

TABLE 16.3 A Sample Fractional Factorial Design

Experiment Number	CPU	Memory Level	Workload Type	Educational Level
1	68000	512K	Managerial	High school
2	68000	2M	Scientific	Postgraduate
3	68000	8M	Secretarial	College
4	Z80	512K	Scientific	College
5	Z80	2M	Secretarial	High school
6	Z80	8M	Managerial	Postgraduate
7	8086	512K	Secretarial	Postgraduate
8	8086	2M	Managerial	College
9	8086	8M	Scientific	High school

For every advantage there is a corresponding disadvantage. Fractional factorial designs save time and expense when compared to full factorial designs. However, the information obtained from a fractional factorial design is less than that obtained from a full factorial design. For example, it may not be possible to get interactions among all factors. On the other hand, if some of the interactions are known to be negligible, this may not be considered a problem and the time and expense of a full factorial design may not be justified.

In the remainder of this book, we restrict our discussion to the full factorial and fractional factorial designs.

EXERCISE

16.1 The performance of a system being designed depends upon the following three factors:

a. CPU type: 68000, 8086, 80286

b. Operating system type: CPM, MS-DOS, UNIX

c. Disk drive type: A, B, C

How many experiments are required to analyze the performance if

a. There is significant interaction among factors.

b. There is no interaction among factors.

c. The interactions are small compared to main effects.

CHAPTER 17

2^k FACTORIAL DESIGNS

Twenty percent of the jobs account for 80% of the resource consumption.
— Pareto's Law

A 2^k experimental design is used to determine the effect of k factors, each of which have two alternatives or levels. This class of factorial design deserves special discussion because it is easy to analyze and helps in sorting out factors in the order of impact. At the beginning of a performance study, the number of factors and their levels is usually large. A full factorial design with such a large number of factors and levels may not be the best use of available effort. The first step should be to reduce the number of factors and to choose those factors that have significant impact on the performance.

Very often the effect of a factor is unidirectional, that is, the performance either continuously decreases or continuously increases as the factor is increased from minimum to maximum. For example, the performance is expected to improve as the memory size is increased or the number of disk drives is increased. In such cases we can begin by experimenting at the minimum and the maximum level of the factor. This will help us decide if the difference in performance is significant enough to justify detailed examination.

In order to explain the concepts of 2^k designs, it is helpful to start with a simple case of just two factors ($k = 2$). This special case is presented in the next few sections. After developing this case, we generalize the concepts to a larger number of factors.

17.1 2^2 **FACTORIAL DESIGNS**

A 2^2 experimental design is a special case of a 2^k factorial design with $k = 2$.
In this case, there are two factors each at two levels. Such a design can be
easily analyzed using a regression model as shown by the following example.

Example 17.1 Consider the problem of studying the impact of memory
size and cache size on the performance of a workstation being designed.
Two levels of each of these two factors are chosen for the initial simulation. The performance of the workstation in Million Instructions Per Second (MIPS) is listed in Table 17.1.

TABLE 17.1 Performance in MIPS

Cache Size (kbytes)	Memory Size 4 Mbytes	Memory Size 16 Mbytes
1	15	45
2	25	75

Let us define two variables x_A and x_B as follows:

$$x_A = \begin{cases} -1 & \text{if 4 Mbytes memory} \\ 1 & \text{if 16 Mbytes memory} \end{cases}$$

$$x_B = \begin{cases} -1 & \text{if 1 kbyte cache} \\ 1 & \text{if 2 kbytes cache} \end{cases}$$

The performance y in MIPS can now be regressed on x_A and x_B using a
nonlinear regression model of the form

$$y = q_0 + q_A x_A + q_B x_B + q_{AB} x_A x_B$$

Substituting the four observations in the model, we get the following four
equations:

$$15 = q_0 - q_A - q_B + q_{AB}$$
$$45 = q_0 + q_A - q_B - q_{AB}$$
$$25 = q_0 - q_A + q_B - q_{AB}$$
$$75 = q_0 + q_A + q_B + q_{AB}$$

These four equations can be solved uniquely for the four unknowns. The
regression equation is

$$y = 40 + 20x_A + 10x_B + 5x_A x_B$$

The result is interpreted as follows. The mean performance is 40 MIPS;
the effect of memory is 20 MIPS; the effect of cache is 10 MIPS; and the
interaction between memory and cache accounts for 5 MIPS. □

TABLE 17.2 Analysis of a 2^2 Design

Experiment	A	B	y
1	−1	−1	y_1
2	1	−1	y_2
3	−1	1	y_3
4	1	1	y_4

17.2 COMPUTATION OF EFFECTS

In general, any 2^2 design can be analyzed using the method of Example 17.1. In the general case, suppose y_1, y_2, y_3, and y_4 represent the four observed responses. The correspondence between the factor levels and the responses is shown in Table 17.2. The model for a 2^2 design is

$$y = q_0 + q_A x_A + q_B x_B + q_{AB} x_A x_B$$

Substituting the four observations in the model, we get

$$y_1 = q_0 - q_A - q_B + q_{AB}$$

$$y_2 = q_0 + q_A - q_B - q_{AB}$$

$$y_3 = q_0 - q_A + q_B - q_{AB}$$

$$y_4 = q_0 + q_A + q_B + q_{AB}$$

Solving these equations for q_i's, we get

$$q_0 = \tfrac{1}{4}(y_1 + y_2 + y_3 + y_4)$$

$$q_A = \tfrac{1}{4}(-y_1 + y_2 - y_3 + y_4)$$

$$q_B = \tfrac{1}{4}(-y_1 - y_2 + y_3 + y_4)$$

$$q_{AB} = \tfrac{1}{4}(y_1 - y_2 - y_3 + y_4)$$

Notice that the expressions for q_A, q_B, and q_{AB} are linear combinations of the responses such that the sum of the coefficients is zero. Such expressions are called **contrasts**.

Also notice that the coefficients of y_i's in the equation for q_A are identical to the levels of A listed in Table 17.2. Thus, q_A can be obtained by multiplying the columns A and y in the table. This is also true for q_B and q_{AB}, both of which can be obtained by multiplying the respective level columns with the response column. This observation leads us to the sign table method for calculating effects, which is described next.

TABLE 17.3 Sign Table Method of Calculating Effects in a 2^2 Design

I	A	B	AB	y
1	-1	-1	1	15
1	1	-1	-1	45
1	-1	1	-1	25
1	1	1	1	75
160	80	40	20	Total
40	20	10	5	Total/4

17.3 SIGN TABLE METHOD FOR CALCULATING EFFECTS

For a 2^2 design, the effects can be computed easily by preparing a 4×4 sign matrix as shown in Table 17.3. The first column of the matrix is labeled I, and it consists of all 1's. The next two columns, titled A and B, contain basically all possible combinations of -1 and 1. The fourth column, labeled AB, is the product of the entries in columns A and B. The four observations are now listed in a column vector next to this matrix. The column vector is labeled y and consists of the response corresponding to the factor levels listed under columns A and B.

The next step is to multiply the entries in column I by those in column y and put their sum under column I. The entries in column A are now multiplied by those in column y and the sum is entered under column A. This operation of column multiplication is repeated for the remaining two columns of the matrix.

The sums under each column are divided by 4 to give the corresponding coefficients of the regression model. Generally, 1 is not explicitly written out in the matrix entries. The plus or minus sign is enough to denote 1 or -1, respectively.

17.4 ALLOCATION OF VARIATION

The importance of a factor is measured by the proportion of the total variation in the response that is explained by the factor. Thus, if two factors explain 90 and 5% of the variation of the response, the second factor may be considered unimportant in many practical situations.

The sample variance of y can be computed as follows:

$$\text{Sample variance of } y = s_y^2 = \frac{\sum_{i=1}^{2^2}(y_i - \bar{y})^2}{2^2 - 1}$$

Here, $\bar{y}$ denotes the mean of responses from all four experiments. The numerator on the right-hand side of the above equation is called the **total variation** of y or **Sum of Squares Total (SST)**:

$$\text{Total variation of } y = \text{SST} = \sum_{i=1}^{2^2}(y_i - \bar{y})^2$$

For a 2^2 design, the variation can be divided into three parts:

$$\text{SST} = 2^2 q_A^2 + 2^2 q_B^2 + 2^2 q_{AB}^2 \qquad (17.1)$$

Before presenting a derivation of this equation, it is helpful to understand its meaning. The three parts on the right-hand side represent the portion of the total variation explained by the effect of A, B, and interaction AB, respectively. Thus, $2^2 q_A^2$ is the portion of SST that is explained by the factor A. It is called the sum of squares due to A and is denoted as SSA. Similarly, SSB is $2^2 q_B^2$ and SSAB (due to interaction AB) is $2^2 q_{AB}^2$. Thus,

$$\text{SST} = \text{SSA} + \text{SSB} + \text{SSAB}$$

These parts can be expressed as a fraction; for example,

$$\text{Fraction of variation explained by } A = \frac{\text{SSA}}{\text{SST}}$$

When expressed as a percentage, this fraction provides an easy way to gauge the importance of the factor A. The factors which explain a high percentage of variation are considered important.

It must be pointed out that *variation* is different from *variance*. Thus, a factor that explains 60% of the variation may or may not explain 60% of the total variance of y. The percentage of variance explained is rather difficult to compute. The percentage of variation, on the other hand, is easy to compute and easy to explain to decision makers.

A derivation of Equation (17.1) now follows. Readers not interested in mathematical details may skip to the example following the derivation.

Derivation 17.1 The model used in a 2^2 design is

$$y_i = q_0 + q_A x_{Ai} + q_B x_{Bi} + q_{AB} x_{Ai} x_{Bi}$$

Columns x_A, x_B, and $x_A x_B$ of the design matrix in Table 17.3 have the following properties:

1. The sum of entries in each column is zero:

$$\sum_{i=1}^{4} x_{Ai} = 0; \qquad \sum_{i=1}^{4} x_{Bi} = 0; \qquad \sum_{i=1}^{4} x_{Ai} x_{Bi} = 0$$

2. The sum of the squares of entries in each column is 4:

$$\sum_{i=1}^{4} x_{Ai}^2 = 4; \qquad \sum_{i=1}^{4} x_{Bi}^2 = 4; \qquad \sum_{i=1}^{4} (x_{Ai} x_{Bi})^2 = 4$$

3. The columns are orthogonal since the inner product of any two columns is zero:

$$\sum_{i=1}^{4} x_{Ai} x_{Bi} = 0; \qquad \sum_{i=1}^{4} x_{Ai}(x_{Ai}x_{Bi}) = 0; \qquad \sum_{i=1}^{4} x_{Bi}(x_{Ai}x_{Bi}) = 0$$

These properties allow us to compute the total variation as follows:

Sample mean $\bar{y} = \dfrac{1}{4}\sum_{i=1}^{4} y_i$

$$= \frac{1}{4}\sum_{i=1}^{4}(q_0 + q_A x_{Ai} + q_B x_{Bi} + q_{AB} x_{Ai} x_{Bi})$$

$$= \frac{1}{4}\sum_{i=1}^{4} q_0 + \frac{1}{4}q_A\sum_{i=1}^{4} x_{Ai} + q_B\frac{1}{4}\sum_{i=1}^{4} x_{Bi} + q_{AB}\frac{1}{4}\sum_{i=1}^{4} x_{Ai} x_{Bi}$$

$$= q_0$$

and

Total variation $= \displaystyle\sum_{i=1}^{4}(y_i - \bar{y})^2$

$$= \sum_{i=1}^{4}(q_A x_{Ai} + q_B x_{Bi} + q_{AB} x_{Ai} x_{Bi})^2$$

$$= \sum_{i=1}^{4}(q_A x_{Ai})^2 + \sum_{i=1}^{4}(q_B x_{Bi})^2 + \sum_{i=1}^{4}(q_{AB} x_{Ai} x_{Bi})^2$$

$$+ \text{ product terms}$$

$$= q_A^2\sum_{i=1}^{4}(x_{Ai})^2 + q_B^2\sum_{i=1}^{4}(x_{Bi})^2 + q_{AB}^2\sum_{i=1}^{4}(x_{Ai} x_{Bi})^2 + 0$$

$$= 4q_A^2 + 4q_B^2 + 4q_{AB}^2$$

The product terms in the preceding equation add to zero due to the orthogonality of the columns. □

Example 17.2 In the case of the memory-cache study

$$\bar{y} = \tfrac{1}{4}(15 + 55 + 25 + 75) = 40$$

$$\text{Total variation} = \sum_{i=1}^{4}(y_i - \bar{y})^2 = (25^2 + 15^2 + 15^2 + 35^2)$$

$$= 2100 = 4 \times 20^2 + 4 \times 10^2 + 4 \times 5^2$$

Thus the total variation is 2100, of which 1600 (76%) can be attributed to memory, 400 (19%) can be attributed to cache, and only 100 (5%) can be attributed to interaction. □

The percentage of variation helps the experimenter decide whether or not it is of value to further investigate a factor or interaction. For example, in the memory-cache study the 5% variation due to interaction seems negligible. The first factor worth exploring further is the memory size, which explains 76% of the variation. The cache is less important because it explains only 19% of the variation.

Case Study 17.1 Two memory interconnection networks called Omega and Crossbar were compared using simulation. Two different memory address reference patterns called *Random* and *Matrix* were used. As the name implies, Random reference pattern addresses the memory with a uniform probability of reference. The second pattern simulated a matrix multiplication problem in which each processor (of a multiprocessor system) is doing a part of the multiplication. To keep the analysis simple, many factors that were known to affect the performance of the interconnection networks were kept fixed at one level as follows:

1. Number of processors was fixed at 16.
2. Queued requests were not buffered but blocked.
3. Circuit switching was used instead of packet switching.
4. Random arbitration was used instead of round robin.
5. Infinite interleaving of memory was used so that there was no memory bank contention.

A 2^2 factorial experimental design was used. The symbol assignment is shown in Table 17.4. Three different performance metrics were computed using simulation: average throughput (T), 90% transit time in cycles (N), and average response time (R). The measured performance is shown in Table 17.5. The effects, computed using the sign table method, are shown in Table 17.6. The table also contains percentage of variation explained.

TABLE 17.4 Factors Used in the Interconnection Network Study

Symbol	Factor	Level −1	Level 1
A	Type of network	Crossbar	Omega
B	Address pattern used	Random	Matrix

TABLE 17.5 Measured Responses in the Interconnection Network Study

		Response		
A	B	T	N	R
−1	−1	0.6041	3	1.655
1	−1	0.4220	5	2.378
−1	1	0.7922	2	1.262
1	1	0.4717	4	2.190

TABLE 17.6 Mean Effects for the Interconnection Network Study

Parameter	Mean Estimate			Variation Explained (%)		
	T	N	R	T	N	R
q_0	0.5725	3.5	1.871			
q_A	0.0595	−0.5	−0.145	17.2	20	10.9
q_B	−0.1257	1.0	0.413	77.0	80	87.8
q_{AB}	−0.0346	0.0	0.051	5.8	0	1.3

The results are interpreted as follows:

- The average throughput is 0.5725. The throughput is mostly affected by the reference pattern, which makes a difference of ∓ 0.1257 and thus explains 77% of its variation. The network type contributes 0.0595 to the throughput. Omega networks give that much higher than the average, and crossbar networks give that much lower than the average. Thus, the net difference between the two types of networks is 0.119. The choice of the network is affected by the address pattern since there is a slight interaction. Depending upon the address pattern and network combination, the throughput can go up or down by 0.0346.
- The 90% transit time is also affected mostly by the address pattern. Since q_A is negative, the transit time is higher for $A = -1$ or the crossbar networks. This applies to both address patterns since there is no interaction between the address pattern and the network type.
- The response time also depends mostly on the address pattern. The interaction between the pattern and network type is low.

Thus, we notice that all three metrics are affected more by the address patterns than by the network type. This is because the address patterns chosen are very different.   □

17.5 GENERAL 2^k FACTORIAL DESIGNS

A 2^k experimental design is used to determine the effect of k factors, each of which have two alternatives or levels. We have already discussed the special case of two factors ($k = 2$) in the last two sections. Now we generalize the analysis to more than two factors.

The analysis techniques developed so far for 2^2 designs can be easily extended to a 2^k design. Given k factors at two levels each, a total of 2^k experiments are required. The analysis produces 2^k effects. These include k main effects, $\binom{k}{2}$ two-factor interactions, $\binom{k}{3}$ three-factor interactions, and so on. The sign table method of analyzing the results and allocating the variation is also valid. We illustrate this with an example.

Example 17.3 In designing a LISP machine, the three factors that need to be studied are: cache size, memory size, and whether one or two processors will be used. The three factors and their level assignments are shown in Table 17.7.

The 2^3 design and the measured performance in MIPS is shown in Table 17.8.

To analyze this, we prepare a sign table as shown in Table 17.9. As shown in the last row of this table, the effects of memory, cache, and processors are $q_A = 10$, $q_B = 5$, and $q_C = 20$, respectively. The three two-factor interactions are $q_{AB} = 5$, $q_{AC} = 2$, and $q_{BC} = 3$. The three-factor interaction q_{ABC} is 1. The portion of the variation explained by the various factors and interactions are proportional to the square of the effects. The SST can

TABLE 17.7 Factors and Levels in Example 17.3

Factor	Level −1	Level 1
Memory size, A	4 Mbytes	16 Mbytes
Cache size, B	1 kbyte	2 kbytes
Number of processors, C	1	2

TABLE 17.8 Results of a 2^3 Experiment

Cache Size (kbytes)	4 Mbytes		16 Mbytes	
	One Processor	Two Processors	One Processor	Two Processors
1	14	46	22	58
2	10	50	34	86

TABLE 17.9 An Example Sign Table

I	A	B	C	AB	AC	BC	ABC	y
1	−1	−1	−1	1	1	1	−1	14
1	1	−1	−1	−1	−1	i	1	22
1	−1	1	−1	−1	1	−1	1	10
1	1	1	−1	1	−1	−1	−1	34
1	−1	−1	1	1	−1	−1	1	46
1	1	−1	1	−1	1	−1	−1	58
1	−1	1	1	−1	−1	1	−1	50
1	1	1	1	1	1	1	1	86
320	80	40	160	40	16	24	9	Total
40	10	5	20	5	2	3	1	Total/8

be computed from the effects as follows:

$$\text{SST} = 2^3(q_A^2 + q_B^2 + q_C^2 + q_{AB}^2 + q_{AC}^2 + q_{BC}^2 + q_{ABC}^2)$$
$$= 8(10^2 + 5^2 + 20^2 + 5^2 + 2^2 + 3^2 + 1^2)$$
$$= 800 + 200 + 3200 + 200 + 32 + 72 + 8 = 4512$$

The portion of variation explained by the seven effects are 800/4512 (18%), 200/4512 (4%), 3200/4512 (71%), 200/4512 (4%), 32/4512 (1%), 72/4512 (2%), and 8/4512 (0%), respectively. □

EXERCISE

17.1 Analyze the 2^3 design shown in Table 17.10
   a. Quantify main effects and all interactions.
   b. Quantify percentages of variation explained.
   c. Sort the variables in the order of decreasing importance.

TABLE 17.10   A 2^3 Design

	A_1		A_2	
	C_1	C_2	C_1	C_2
B_1	100	15	120	10
B_2	40	30	20	50

CHAPTER 18

$2^k r$ FACTORIAL DESIGNS WITH REPLICATIONS

No experiment is ever a complete failure. It can always serve as a negative example.

—Arthur Bloch

One problem with 2^k factorial designs is that it is not possible to estimate experimental errors since no experiment is repeated. Experimental errors can be quantified by repeating the measurements under the same factor-level combinations. If each of the 2^k experiments in the 2^k design is repeated r times, we will have $2^k r$ observations. Such a design is called $2^k r$ design. Once again, it is helpful to start with a two-factor model, develop all the concepts, and then generalize them to a k-factor model.

18.1 $2^2 r$ FACTORIAL DESIGNS

A $2^2 r$ factorial design is used when there are two factors each at two levels and the analyst wants to isolate experimental errors. Each of the four experiments is repeated r times. Such a design allows us to add an error term to the model, which now becomes

$$y = q_0 + q_A x_A + q_B x_B + q_{AB} x_A x_B + e \qquad (18.1)$$

Here, e is the experimental error and the q's are the effects as before.

18.2 COMPUTATION OF EFFECTS

The easiest way to analyze a $2^2 r$ design is to use the sign table as before
except that in the y column we put the sample means of r measurements at
the given factor levels. The remaining analysis to compute the effects is the
same as before. This is illustrated by the following example.

Example 18.1 The memory-cache experiments were repeated three times
each. This resulted in the 12 observations shown in column y in Table 18.1.
The analysis is also shown in the table. We sum the individual observations
and divide by 3 (the number of replications) to get the sample means $\bar{y}$.
The first four columns in the table are sign columns as before. The entries
in each of the four columns are multiplied by those in column $\bar{y}$ and the
sum is entered under the column. The sums under each column are divided
by 4 to give the following effects:

$$q_0 = 41, \qquad q_A = 21.5, \qquad q_B = 9.5, \qquad q_{AB} = 5 \qquad \square$$

TABLE 18.1 Analysis of a $2^2 3$ Design

I	A	B	AB	y	Mean $\bar{y}$
1	-1	-1	1	(15, 18, 12)	15
1	1	-1	-1	(45, 48, 51)	48
1	-1	1	-1	(25, 28, 19)	24
1	1	1	1	(75, 75, 81)	77
164	86	38	20		Total
41	21.5	9.5	5		Total/4

18.3 ESTIMATION OF EXPERIMENTAL ERRORS

Once the effects have been computed in a $2^2 r$ design, the model can be used
to estimate the response for any given factor values (x-values) as follows:

$$\hat{y}_i = q_0 + q_A x_{Ai} + q_B x_{Bi} + q_{AB} x_{Ai} x_{Bi}$$

Here $\hat{y}_i$ is the estimated response when the factors A and B are at levels x_{Ai}
and x_{Bi}, respectively.

The difference between the estimate and the measured value y_{ij} in the jth
replication of the ith experiment represents the experimental errors:

$$e_{ij} = y_{ij} - \hat{y}_i = y_{ij} - q_0 - q_A x_{Ai} - q_B x_{Bi} - q_{AB} x_{Ai} x_{Bi}$$

We can compute the error in each of the $2^2 r$ observations. The sum of the
errors must be zero. The sum of the squared errors (SSE) can be used to estimate the variance of the errors and also to compute the confidence intervals

TABLE 18.2   Computation of Errors in Example 18.2

	Effect				Estimated Response,	Measured Responses			Errors		
	I	A	B	AB							
i	41	21.5	9.5	5	$\hat{y}_i$	y_{i1}	y_{i2}	y_{i3}	e_{i1}	e_{i2}	e_{i3}
1	1	−1	−1	1	15	15	18	12	0	3	−3
2	1	1	−1	−1	48	45	48	51	−3	0	3
3	1	−1	1	−1	24	25	28	19	1	4	−5
4	1	1	1	1	77	75	75	81	−2	−2	4

for the effects:

$$\text{SSE} = \sum_{i=1}^{2^2} \sum_{j=1}^{r} e_{ij}^2$$

Example 18.2   Consider the data of the memory-cache study of Example 18.1. The estimated response and the errors for each of the 12 observations are shown in Table 18.2. The estimated responses for each experiment are computed by adding the products of effects and the sign table entries for the experiment. For example, the estimated response for the first experiment is

$$\hat{y}_1 = q_0 - q_A - q_B + q_{AB} = 41 - 21.5 - 9.5 + 5 = 15$$

The experimental errors are computed by subtracting the estimated from the measured values. For example, for the first replication of the first experiment,

$$e_{11} = y_{11} - \hat{y}_1 = 15 - 15 = 0$$

Notice that the sum of the errors in each experiment is zero and hence the total sum of all errors is zero also. Thus

$$\text{SSE} = 0^2 + 3^2 + (-3)^2 + (-3)^2 + 0^2 + 3^2 + 1^2$$
$$+ 4^2 + (-5)^2 + (-2)^2 + (-2)^2 + 4^2$$
$$= 102 \qquad \qquad \square$$

18.4   ALLOCATION OF VARIATION

As in the 2^2 design, the percentage of variation explained by each factor is helpful in deciding whether a factor has a significant impact on the response. However, unlike the 2^2 design, now the variation due to experimental errors can also be isolated since we have multiple observations for each factor-level combination.

The total variation or Total Sum of Squares (SST) is given by

$$\text{SST} = \sum_{i,j}(y_{ij} - \bar{y}_{..})^2$$

Here, $\bar{y}_{..}$ denotes the mean of responses from all replications of all experiments. The dots in the subscript indicate the dimension along which the averaging is done. Thus, $\bar{y}_{i.}$ denotes the means of responses in all replications of the ith experiment and $\bar{y}_{.j}$ denotes the mean of responses in the jth replication of all experiments.

The SST can be divided into four parts as follows:

$$\sum_{i,j}(y_{ij} - \bar{y}_{..})^2 = 2^2 r q_A^2 + 2^2 r q_B^2 + 2^2 r q_{AB}^2 + \sum_{i,j} e_{ij}^2$$

$$\text{SST} \quad = \quad \text{SSA} + \text{SSB} + \text{SSAB} + \text{SSE}$$

where each SS (sum of square) corresponds to the expression above it. Thus, SSA, SSB, and SSAB are the variations explained by factors A, B, and interaction AB, respectively. The SSE is the unexplained variation attributed to the experimental errors.

A derivation of the division of the SST into four parts is as follows.

Derivation 18.1 The model for $2^2 r$ design is

$$y_{ij} = q_0 + q_A x_{Ai} + q_B x_{Bi} + q_{AB} x_{Ai} x_{Bi} + e_{ij}$$

Adding the terms of this equation across all $2^2 r$ observations, we get

$$\sum_{i,j} y_{ij} = \sum_{i,j} q_0 + \sum_{i,j} q_A x_{Ai} + \sum_{i,j} q_B x_{Bi} + \sum_{i,j} q_{AB} x_{Ai} x_{Bi} + \sum_{i,j} e_{ij}$$

Since the x's and their products as well as all errors add to zero, we have

$$\sum_{i,j} y_{ij} = \sum_{i,j} q_0 = 2^2 r q_0$$

The mean response is given by

$$\bar{y}_{..} = \frac{1}{2^2 r} \sum_{i,j} y_{ij} = \frac{1}{2^2 r} 2^2 r q_0 = q_0$$

The total variation is

$$SST = \sum_{i,j}(y_{ij} - \bar{y}_{..})^2$$

$$= \sum_{i,j} y_{ij}^2 - \sum_{i,j} \bar{y}_{..}^2$$

$$= \sum_{i,j} y_{ij}^2 - \sum_{i,j} q_0^2$$

$$= SSY - SS0$$

Here, SS0 represents the sum of squares of the mean. Squaring both sides of Equation (18.1) and ignoring the cross-product terms (since they add to zero), we have

$$\sum_{i,j} y_{ij}^2 = \sum_{i,j} q_0^2 + \sum_{i,j} q_A^2 x_{Ai}^2 + \sum_{i,j} q_B^2 x_{Bi}^2 + \sum_{i,j} q_{AB}^2 x_{Ai}^2 x_{Bi}^2 + \sum_{i,j} e_{ij}^2 \quad (18.2)$$

The terms of this equation correspond to various sums of squares, and we have

$$SSY = SS0 + SSA + SSB + SSAB + SSE$$

or

$$SST = SSY - SS0 = SSA + SSB + SSAB + SSE \qquad \square$$

Incidently, Equation (18.2) provides an easy way to compute SSE:

$$SSE = SSY - 2^2 r(q_0^2 + q_A^2 + q_b^2 + q_{AB}^2)$$

The following example illustrates the allocation of variation and computation of SSE.

Example 18.3   For memory-cache study of Example 18.1:

$$SSY = 15^2 + 18^2 + 12^2 + 45^2 + \cdots + 75^2 + 75^2 + 81^2 = 27,204$$
$$SS0 = 2^2 r q_0^2 = 12 \times 41^2 = 20,172$$
$$SSA = 2^2 r q_A^2 = 12 \times (21.5)^2 = 5547$$
$$SSB = 2^2 r q_B^2 = 12 \times (9.5)^2 = 1083$$
$$SSAB = 2^2 r q_{AB}^2 = 12 \times 5^2 = 300$$
$$SSE = 27,204 - 2^2 \times 3(41^2 + 21.5^2 + 9.5^2 + 5^2) = 102$$
$$SST = SSY - SS0 = 27,204 - 20,172 = 7032$$

Notice that the SSE computed here is the same as that obtained earlier in Example 18.2. Also, note that the sum of squares add up as follows:

$$SSA + SSB + SSAB + SSE = 5547 + 1083 + 300 + 102 = 7032 = SST$$

Thus, the total variation of 7032 can be divided into four parts. Factor A explains 5547/7032, or 78.88%, of the variation. Similarly, factor B explains 15.40%, and interaction AB explains 4.27% of the variation. The remaining 1.45% is unexplained and is attributed to errors. ☐

18.5 CONFIDENCE INTERVALS FOR EFFECTS

The effects computed from a sample are random variables and would be different if another set of experiments is conducted. The confidence intervals for the effects can be computed if the variance of the sample estimates are known.

If we assume that errors are normally distributed with zero mean and variance σ_e^2, then it follows from the model that the y_i's are also normally distributed with the same variance σ_e^2. Now consider an effect, for example, q_0:

$$q_0 = \frac{1}{2^2 r} \sum_{i,j} y_{ij}$$

Since q_0 is a linear combination of normally distributed variables, it is also normally distributed and its variance is $\sigma_e^2/(2^2 r)$.

The variance of errors can be estimated from the SSE as follows:

$$s_e^2 = \frac{\text{SSE}}{2^2(r-1)}$$

The quantity on the right side of this equation is called the **Mean Square of Errors (MSE)**. The denominator is $2^2(r-1)$, which is the number of independent terms in the SSE. This is because the r error terms corresponding to the r replications of an experiment should add up to zero. Thus, only $r-1$ of these terms can be independently chosen. Thus, the SSE has $2^2(r-1)$ degrees of freedom.

The estimated variance of q_0 is $s_{q_0}^2 = s_e^2/(2^2 r)$. The variance of other effects, q_A, q_B, and q_{AB}, can also be similarly shown to be $s_e^2/(2^2 r)$. In other words,

$$s_{q_0} = s_{q_A} = s_{q_B} = s_{q_{AB}} = \frac{s_e}{\sqrt{2^2 r}}$$

The confidence intervals for the effects are

$$q_i \mp t_{[1-\alpha/2; 2^2(r-1)]} s_{q_i}$$

The t-value is read at $2^2(r-1)$ degrees of freedom (which is the degrees of freedom associated with the experimental errors). Any effect whose confidence interval does not include a zero is significant. Some books on experimental design use an F-test (see Section 20.5) to determine the significance of effects. However, the F-test conclusions for a $2^k r$ design are always identical to those obtained using confidence intervals.

Example 18.4   Continuing the memory-cache study from Example 18.3, the standard deviation of errors is

$$s_e = \sqrt{\frac{\text{SSE}}{2^2(r-1)}} = \sqrt{\frac{102}{8}} = \sqrt{12.75} = 3.57$$

and the standard deviation of effects is

$$s_{q_i} = s_e/\sqrt{(2^2 r)} = 3.57/\sqrt{12} = 1.03$$

The t-value at eight degrees of freedom and 90% confidence is 1.86.

The confidence intervals for the parameters are $q_i \mp (1.86)(1.03) = q_i \mp 1.92$, that is, (39.08, 42.91), (19.58, 23.41), (7.58, 11.41), (3.08, 6.91) for q_0, q_A, q_B, q_{AB}, respectively. Since none of the intervals include a zero, all effects are significantly different from zero at this confidence level.   □

It is also possible to compute variance and confidence intervals for any contrast of effects. A contrast is any linear combination whose coefficients add up to zero. The variance of $\sum h_i q_i$, where $\sum h_i = 0$, is

$$s^2_{\sum h_i q_i} = \frac{s_e^2 \sum h_i^2}{2^2 r}$$

The $100(1-\alpha)\%$ confidence interval for $\sum h_i q_i$ can be computed using the $t_{[1-\alpha/2;2^2 r]}$ value from Table A.4 in the Appendix. This procedure for computing confidence intervals for linear combinations of effects can be used to compute confidence intervals for estimated response at any given factor levels.

Example 18.5   In the memory-cache study, the confidence interval for $u = q_A + q_B - 2q_{AB}$ is computed as follows.

Notice that u is a contrast with coefficients of 0, 1, 1, and -2. The mean of u is

$$\bar{u} = 21.5 + 9.5 - 2 \times 5 = 11$$

The variance of u is:

$$s_u^2 = \frac{s_e^2 \times 6}{2^2 \times 3} = 6.375$$

The standard deviation of u is

$$s_u = \sqrt{6.375} = 2.52$$

Since $t_{[0.95;8]}$ from Table A.4 in the Appendix is 1.86, the confidence interval for u is

$$\bar{u} \mp t s_u = 11 \mp 1.86 \times 2.52 = (6.31, 15.69)$$ □

18.6   CONFIDENCE INTERVALS FOR PREDICTED RESPONSES

It is also possible to compute confidence intervals for response y at a given combination of factors.

The mean response $\hat{y}$ can be easily computed for any given factor combination:

$$\hat{y} = q_0 + q_A x_A + q_B x_B + q_{AB} x_A x_B$$

Suppose we want to predict the mean of responses obtained from m repetitions of the experiment at the given factor combinations. The expression for the mean estimate is the same as above regardless of m. However, as m increases, the sample mean is expected to be closer to the predicted mean. In other words, the standard deviation of the estimate is a decreasing function of m. It can be shown to be

$$s_{\hat{y}_m} = s_e \left(\frac{1}{n_{\text{eff}}} + \frac{1}{m} \right)^{1/2}$$

Here, n_{eff} is the effective number of degrees of freedom (DFs), which is given by

$$n_{\text{eff}} = \frac{\text{total number of runs}}{1 + \text{sum of DFs of parameters used in } \hat{y}}$$

In a $2^2 r$ design, the total number of runs is $2^2 r$. The parameters q_0, q_A, q_B, and q_{AB} are used in estimating $\hat{y}$. Each of these parameters has one degree of freedom. Therefore,

$$n_{\text{eff}} = \frac{2^2 r}{5}$$

A $100(1 - \alpha)\%$ confidence interval for the mean response is given by

$$\hat{y} \mp t_{[1-\alpha/2;2^2(r-1)]} s_{\hat{y}_m}$$

The t-value is read at the degrees of freedom associated with the error.

Two special cases are of particular interest. First, if we want to predict the response for a single run ($m = 1$) of a confirmation experiment in the future, the standard error expression would be

$$s_{\hat{y}_1} = s_e \left(\frac{5}{2^2 r} + 1 \right)^{1/2}$$

Second, if we want to predict the population mean ($m = \infty$), the standard error expression would be

$$s_{\hat{y}} = s_e \left(\frac{5}{2^2 r} \right)^{1/2}$$

Example 18.6 For the memory-cache study, let us compute the confidence intervals for mean response with $x_A = -1$ and $x_B = -1$. Four different confidence intervals can be computed:

1. *Predicted Mean Response for a Future Confirmation Experiment*: The estimated mean response $\hat{y}_1$ is

$$\hat{y}_1 = q_0 - q_A - q_B + q_{AB} = 41 - 21.5 - 9.5 + 5 = 15$$

The standard deviation of the predicted observation is computed as follows:

$$s_{\hat{y}_1} = s_e \left(\frac{5}{2^2 r} + 1 \right)^{1/2} = 3.57 \sqrt{\frac{5}{12} + 1} = 4.25$$

Using $t_{[0.95;8]} = 1.86$, the 90% confidence interval is

$$15 \mp 1.86 \times 4.25 = (8.09, 22.91)$$

2. *Predicted Mean Response for Five Confirmation Experiments in Future*: In this case, the standard deviation of the predicted mean is

$$s_{\hat{y}_1} = s_e \left(\frac{5}{2^2 r} + \frac{1}{m} \right)^{1/2} = 3.57 \sqrt{\frac{5}{12} + \frac{1}{5}} = 2.80$$

The 90% confidence interval is

$$15 \mp 1.86 \times 2.80 = (9.79, 20.29)$$

3. *Predicted Mean Response for a Large Number of Experiments in Future*: In this case, the standard deviation of the predicted mean is

$$s_{\hat{y}_1} = s_e \left(\frac{5}{2^2 r} \right)^{1/2} = 3.57 \sqrt{\frac{5}{12}} = 2.30$$

The 90% confidence interval is

$$15 \mp 1.86 \times 2.30 = (10.72, 19.28)$$

4. *Current Mean Response*: This is not a case of predicting the results of future experiments. Here we simply want to get a confidence interval for $\hat{y}_1 = q_0 - q_A - q_B + q_{AB}$. This is a contrast of the effects. Using the formula for contrasts, we compute the standard deviation of $\hat{y}_1$ as follows:

$$s_{\hat{y}_1} = \sqrt{\frac{s_e^2 \sum h_i^2}{2^2 r}} = \sqrt{\frac{12.75 \times 4}{12}} = 2.06$$

The 90% confidence interval for the current mean response is

$$15 \mp 1.86 \times 2.06 = (11.17, 18.83)$$

Notice that the confidence intervals become narrower as we scan down the preceding list. The predictions always have a wider confidence or higher variance because the effect of errors in future experiments has to be added. As the number of future experiments increases, the confidence interval becomes narrower. Current mean response has an even narrower confidence interval.   □

18.7 VISUAL TESTS FOR VERIFYING THE ASSUMPTIONS

In deriving the expressions for effects, we made essentially the same assumptions as in regression analysis, namely:

1. The model errors are statistically independent.
2. The model errors are additive.
3. The errors are normally distributed.
4. The errors have a constant standard deviation σ_e.
5. The effects of factors are additive.

These assumptions lead to the observations being independent and normally distributed with constant variance.

Thus, the techniques for verifying the assumptions are also the same as those discussed earlier for regression in Section 14.7. The assumptions, which can be visually tested, and the corresponding tests are as follows:

1. *Independent Errors*: The model assumes that the errors are independently and identically distributed (**IID**). To verify this, after estimating the parameters, compute residuals and prepare a scatter plot of residuals versus the predicted response $\hat{y}_i$. Any visible trends in the scatter plot would indicate a dependence of errors on the factor levels. If the residuals are one or more orders of magnitude smaller than the predicted response, the trend, if any, can be ignored.

   One may also want to plot the residuals as a function of the experiment number where the experiments are numbered in the order they are conducted. Any trend up or down, as shown earlier in Figure 14.8, would indicate the presence of other factors or side effects (incorrect initializations) that varied from one experiment to the next and affected the response. The cause of such trends should be identified. If additional factors or covariates are found to affect the response, they should be included in the analysis.

2. *Normally Distributed Errors*: Prepare normal quantile-quantile plot of errors. If the plot is approximately linear, the assumption is satisfied.

3. *Constant Standard Deviation of Errors*: Prepare a scatter plot of y for various levels of the factor. The location along the horizontal axis can be chosen arbitrarily for each level. If the spread at one level seems significantly different than that at other levels, the assumption of constant variance is not valid. In this case, a transformation of the data, as discussed in Section 15.4, may help solve the problem.

The following example illustrates the application of these tests.

Example 18.7 Consider the memory-cache study of Example 18.1. A plot of the residuals versus predicted responses is shown in Figure 18.1. The

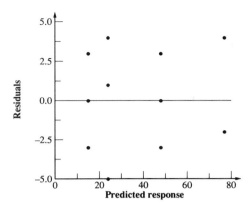

FIGURE 18.1 Plot of residuals versus predicted response for the memory-cache study.

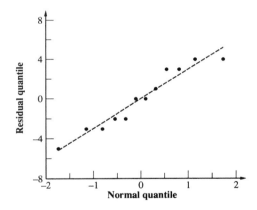

FIGURE 18.2 Normal quantile-quantile plot for residuals of the memory-cache study.

residuals are an order of magnitude smaller than the responses, and there does not appear to be any definite trend in the mean or spread of the residuals.

A normal quantile-quantile plot of the residuals is presented in Figure 18.2. Again, the residuals appear to be approximately normally distributed. Thus, the model appears to be valid for this case. ☐

18.8 MULTIPLICATIVE MODELS FOR $2^2 r$ EXPERIMENTS

In the analysis of $2^2 r$ experiments, the following additive model was assumed:

$$y_{ij} = q_0 + q_A x_A + q_B x_B + q_{AB} x_A x_B + e_{ij}$$

This model assumes that the effect of the factors, their interactions, and the errors are additive. Before using the model, the analyst must validate this assumption by carefully considering whether the effects are in fact additive. In many cases, this assumption is not valid. The most common example is that of performance of processors on different workloads. In this case, there are two factors: processors and workloads. If there are only two processors and two workloads, we can use a $2^2 r$ design. Suppose the measured response y_{ij} represents the time required to execute a workload of w_j instructions on a processor capable of executing v_i instructions per second. Then, if there are no errors or interactions, we know that the time would be

$$y_{ij} = v_i w_j$$

The effects of the two factors are not additive; they are multiplicative. In this case, if we take a logarithm of both sides, we get an additive model:

$$\log(y_{ij}) = \log(v_i) + \log(w_j)$$

Therefore, this is the correct model to use. In other words, we need to transform the measured responses to their logarithm and then use an additive model of the form

$$y'_{ij} = q_0 + q_A x_A + q_B x_B + q_{AB} x_A x_B + e_{ij}$$

Here, $y'_{ij} = \log(y_{ij})$ represents the transformed response. After the analysis, we can take an antilog of the additive effects q_A, q_B, and q_{AB} to produce multiplicative effects $u_A = 10^{q_A}$, $u_B = 10^{q_B}$, and $u_{AB} = 10^{q_{AB}}$.

The u_A so obtained would represent the ratio of the MIPS rating of the two processors. Similarly, u_B represents the ratio of the size of the two workloads. The antilog of additive mean q_0 produces the geometric mean of the responses:

$$\dot{y} = 10^{q_0} = (y_1 y_2 \cdots y_n)^{1/n} \qquad n = 2^2 r$$

The following example illustrates the application of multiplicative models.

Example 18.8 Consider the case of two processors A_1 and A_2 which were tested on two benchmarks B_1 and B_2. Each experiment was repeated three times. The measured execution times in seconds are listed in Table 18.3. A

TABLE 18.3 Analysis Using the Additive Model

I	A	B	AB	y	Mean $\bar{y}$
1	−1	−1	1	(85.10, 79.50, 147.90)	104.170
1	1	−1	−1	(0.891, 1.047, 1.072)	1.003
1	−1	1	−1	(0.955, 0.933, 1.122)	1.003
1	1	1	1	(0.0148, 0.0126, 0.0118)	0.013
106.19	−104.15	−104.15	102.17		Total
26.55	−26.04	−26.04	25.54		Total/4

straightforward analysis using the additive model is also shown in the table. We see that there is a large interaction between the processors and the benchmarks, which will lead us to conclude that the selection of processors would depend upon the benchmark. This is a misleading conclusion since this is really not true, as we show later.

There are several ways an experienced analyst would find out that the additive model does not represent the data. Among these are the following:

- The first and foremost is the physical consideration that a computer scientist can easily justify that the effects of workload and processors do not add. They multiply, as already argued.
- The range of values covered by y is large. The ratio y_{max}/y_{min} is 147.90/ 0.0118, or 12,534. Taking an arithmetic mean of 114.17 and 0.013 is inappropriate. This calls for a log transformation, as discussed earlier in Section 15.4.
- A plot of residuals versus predicted response is shown in Figure 18.3. Notice that the vertical and horizontal scales are of the same order of magnitude. The residuals are not small as compared to the response. Also, the spread of the residuals is large at larger value of the response. This is another indicator that calls for a log transformation.
- A normal quantile-quantile plot of the residuals is shown in Figure 18.4. Notice that the larger positive and negative residuals do not follow the same line as those in the middle. As was discussed earlier in Section 12.10, on a quantile-quantile plot, this indicates that the residuals have a distribution that has a longer tail than the normal. Thus, the normality assumption is violated.

Based on any one of these arguments, the analyst should at least try a multiplicative model and compare the results with those obtained using the

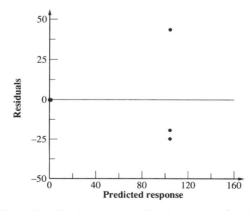

FIGURE 18.3 Plot of residuals versus predicted response for the additive model.

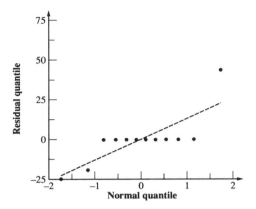

FIGURE 18.4 Normal quantile-quantile plot for residuals of the additive model.

additive model. The logarithm of responses and the corresponding analysis is shown in Table 18.4. The percentage of variation explained and the confidence intervals of effects of the two models are listed in Table 18.5. Notice that the interaction with a multiplicative model is almost zero. The two main effects explain 49.9% of the variation each. The unexplained variation is only 0.2%, which is 1/50th of the previous model.

TABLE 18.4 Transformed Data for Multiplicative Model Example

I	A	B	AB	y	Mean $\bar{y}$
1	−1	−1	1	(1.93, 1.90, 2.17)	2.00
1	1	−1	−1	(−0.05, 0.02, 0.03)	0.00
1	−1	1	−1	(−0.02, −0.03, 0.05)	0.00
1	1	1	1	(−1.83, −1.90, −1.93)	−1.89
0.11	−3.89	−3.89	0.11	Total	
0.03	−0.97	−0.97	0.03	Total/4	

TABLE 18.5 Percentage of Variation Explained by the Two Models

	Additive Model			Multiplicative Model		
Factor	Effect	Percentage of Variation	Confidence Interval	Effect	Percentage of Variation	Confidence Interval
I	26.55		(16.35, 36.74)	0.03		(−0.02, 0.07)[a]
A	−26.04	30.1	(−36.23, −15.84)	−0.97	49.9	(−1.02, −0.93)
B	−26.04	30.1	(−36.23, −15.84)	−0.97	49.9	(−1.02, −0.93)
AB	25.54	29.0	(15.35, 35.74)	0.03	0.0	(−0.02, 0.07)[a]
e		10.8			0.2	

[a] Not significant.

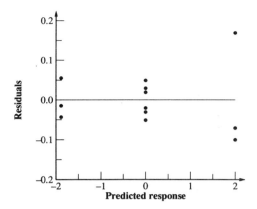

FIGURE 18.5 Plot of residuals versus predicted response for the multiplicative model.

A plot of residuals versus predicted response is shown in Figure 18.5. Notice that the residuals are an order of magnitude lower than the response and that there is no trend in the spread of the residuals. A normal quantile-quantile plot is shown in Figure 18.6. The distribution is satisfactorily normal. Overall the multiplicative model appears to be considerably better for this data than the additive model.

The results of the multiplicative model are interpreted as follows. The model is

$$\log(y) = q_0 + q_A x_A + q_B x_B + q_{AB} x_A x_B + e$$

or

$$y = 10^{q_0} 10^{q_A x_A} 10^{q_B x_B} 10^{q_{AB} x_A x_B} 10^{e}$$

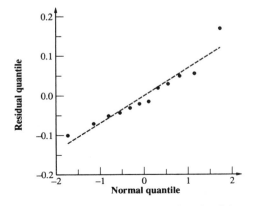

FIGURE 18.6 Normal quantile-quantile plot for residuals of the multiplicative model.

Substituting the model parameters, we obtain

$$y = 10^{0.03} 10^{-0.97 x_A} 10^{-0.97 x_B} 10^{0.03 x_A x_B} 10^e$$

or

$$y = 1.07 \times 0.107^{x_A} \times 0.107^{x_B} \times 1.07^{x_A x_B} 10^e$$

The time for an average processor on an average benchmark is 1.07. The time on processor A_1 is 9 times (0.107^{-1}) that on an average processor. The time on A_2 is one-ninth (0.107^1) that on an average processor. In other words, time on A_1 is 81 times that on A_2. Or equivalently, the MIPS rate for processor A_2 is 81 times that of A_1. Similarly, one can argue that the benchmark B_1 executes 81 times more instructions than B_2. The interaction is negligible. The results are therefore valid for all benchmark and processor combinations.   □

As was pointed out earlier in Section 15.4, the logarithmic transformation is useful only if the ratio y_{max}/y_{min} is large. For a small range the log function is almost linear, and so the analysis with the multiplicative model will produce results similar to that with the additive model.

Notice that a logarithm transformation resulting in a multiplicative model is just one of numerous other possible transformations. For example, the Box-Cox family of power transformations discussed in Section 15.4 can be used if a linear model is found inadequate and physical considerations allow their use.

Knowledge about the system behavior should always take precedence over statistical considerations. Statistics can help you find a suitable model if you have no other knowledge of the system. However, don't assume that the system is a black box when it isn't. In general, the system behavior known to the analyst should be used to come up with the model. Blindly using an additive linear regression model and ignoring system considerations is a frequent mistake.

18.9 GENERAL $2^k r$ FACTORIAL DESIGN

The $2^k r$ design with r replications of 2^k experiments is a straightforward extension of $2^2 r$ design. In all, there are 2^k effects including interactions and the overall mean. The expressions are summarized in Box 18.1 and are illustrated next by an example for a $2^3 3$ design and a case study for a $2^4 3$ design.

Example 18.9   Consider the data of Table 18.6 for a $2^3 3$ design. The table also shows estimation of effects. The SSE can be computed after computing other sums of squares. The values are listed in Table 18.7. The errors have

Box 18.1 Analysis of $2^k r$ Factorial Designs

1. Model: $y_{ij} = q_0 + q_A x_{Ai} + q_B x_{Bi} + q_{AB} x_{Ai} x_{Bi} + \cdots + e_{ij}$

2. Parameter estimation: $q_j = \dfrac{1}{2^k} \sum_{i=1}^{2^k} S_{ij} \bar{y}_i$; $S_{ij} = (i,j)$th entry in the sign table.

3. Sum of squares: $\text{SSY} = \sum_{i=1}^{2^k} \sum_{j=1}^{r} y_{ij}^2$
   $\text{SS0} = 2^k r q_0^2$
   $\text{SST} = \text{SSY} - \text{SS0}$
   $\text{SS}j = 2^k r q_j^2, \; j = 1, 2, \ldots, 2^k - 1$
   $\text{SSE} = \text{SST} - \sum_{j=1}^{2^k - 1} \text{SS}j$

4. Percentage of y's variation explained by the jth effect: $(\text{SS}j / \text{SST}) \times 100\%$

5. Standard deviation of errors: $s_e = \sqrt{\dfrac{\text{SSE}}{2^k(r-1)}}$

6. Standard deviation of effects: $s_{q_0} = s_{q_A} = s_{q_B} = s_{q_{AB}} = s_e / \sqrt{2^k r}$

7. Variance of contrast $\sum h_i q_i$, where $\sum h_i = 0$ is $s_{\sum h_i q_i}^2 = (s_e^2 \sum h_i^2)/2^k r$

8. Standard deviation of the mean of m future responses:

$$s_{\hat{y}_p} = s_e \left(\frac{1 + 2^k}{2^k r} + \frac{1}{m} \right)^{1/2}$$

9. Confidence intervals are calculated using $t_{[1-\alpha/2; 2^k(r-1)]}$.

10. Modeling assumptions:

    (a) Errors are IID normal variates with zero mean.
    (b) Errors have the same variance for all values of the predictors.
    (c) Effects of predictors and errors are additive.

11. Visual tests:

    (a) The scatter plot of errors versus predicted responses should not have any trend.
    (b) The normal quantile-quantile plot of errors should be linear.
    (c) Spread of y values in all experiments should be comparable.

    If any test fails or if the ratio $y_{\max}/y_{\min}$ is large, a multiplicative model should be investigated.

TABLE 18.6   Analysis of a $2^3 3$ Experimental Design

I	A	B	C	AB	AC	BC	ABC	y	Mean $\bar{y}$
1	−1	−1	−1	1	1	1	−1	(14, 16, 12)	14
1	1	−1	−1	−1	−1	1	1	(22, 18, 20)	20
1	−1	1	−1	−1	1	−1	1	(11, 15, 19)	15
1	1	1	−1	1	−1	−1	−1	(34, 30, 35)	33
1	−1	−1	1	1	−1	−1	1	(46, 42, 44)	44
1	1	−1	1	−1	1	−1	−1	(58, 62, 60)	60
1	−1	1	1	−1	−1	1	−1	(50, 55, 54)	53
1	1	1	1	1	1	1	1	(86, 80, 74)	80
319	67	43	155	23	19	15	−1	Total	
39.87	8.375	5.375	19.37	2.875	2.375	1.875	−0.125	Total/8	

TABLE 18.7   Sum of Squares for the $2^3 3$ Experimental Design

Component	Sum of Squares	Percentage of Variation
y	4.9×10^4	
$\bar{y}$	3.8×10^4	
$y - \bar{y}$	1.1×10^4	100.00
A	1683.0	14.06
B	693.3	5.79
C	9009.0	75.27
AB	198.3	1.66
AC	135.4	1.13
BC	84.4	0.70
ABC	0.4	0.00
Errors	164.0	1.37

$2^3(3-1)$, or 16, degrees of freedom. Therefore,

$$\text{Standard deviation of errors } s_e = \sqrt{\frac{\text{SSE}}{2^k(r-1)}} = \sqrt{\frac{164}{16}} = 3.20$$

$$\text{Standard deviation of effects } = s_{q_i} = s_e / \sqrt{(2^3 3)} = 3.20/\sqrt{24} = 0.654$$

The t-value at 16 degrees of freedom and 90% confidence is 1.337. The confidence intervals for the parameters are $q_i \mp (1.337)(0.654) = q_i \mp 0.874$, that is, (39.00, 40.74), (7.50, 9.25), (4.50, 6.25), (18.50, 20.24), (2.00, 3.75), (1.50, 3.25), (1.00, 2.75), (−1.00, 0.75) for q_0, q_A, q_B, q_C, q_{AB}, q_{AC}, q_{BC}, q_{ABC}, respectively. Only the last confidence interval includes zero. Thus all effects except q_{ABC} are significant.

The standard deviation of the mean predicted response in a single confirmation experiment ($m = 1$) is

$$s_{\hat{y}} = s_e \left(\frac{1 + 2^k}{2^k r} + \frac{1}{m} \right)^{1/2}$$

$$= 3.2 \left(\frac{9}{24} + 1 \right)^{1/2}$$

$$= 3.52$$

Assuming that the confirmation experiment will have factor levels corresponding to the first experiment in Table 18.6, the mean predicted response is 14 and a 90% confidence interval for the prediction is

$$14 \mp 1.337 \times 3.75 = 14 \mp 5.02 = (8.98, 19.02) \qquad \Box$$

Case Study 18.1 The garbage collection and memory management (GCMM) system for an object-oriented computer system is to be designed. The system allocates memory in small blocks called *chunks*. The memory is divided into two regions called local and permanent. The GCMM system tries to keep currently active objects in the fast local region and moves (exports) aged objects into permanent storage. Inactive objects are periodically reclaimed by the garbage collector and their storage put on a *free list*. The storage reclaimed by exportation is put on a *limbo* list. If an object in the permanent storage is referenced, the limbo list is checked first to see if the local storage corresponding to the last local copy has been reused. If not, a *cheap importation* can take place. The compiler can be modified to help garbage collection by explicitly *deallocating* objects no longer in use. The workload may consist of a single task or several parallel tasks. Thus, four factors—workload, compiler, limbo list, and chunk size—each at two levels were identified.

A 2^4 full factorial experimental design with repetition was used to quantify the main effects as well as interactions. The factor levels and their interpretations were as shown in Table 18.8. Six different metrics were measured: total run time, total number of garbage collection sweeps, total mark time, total sweep 1 time, total sweep 2 time (the mark and sweeps are phases of the garbage collection), and total garbage collection time (sum of

TABLE 18.8 Factors and Levels for the Garbage Collection Study

Variable	Factor	Level −1	Level 1
A	Workload	Single task	Several parallel tasks
B	Compiler	Simple	Deallocating
C	Limbo list	Enabled	Disabled
D	Chunk size	4 kbytes	16 kbytes

TABLE 18.9   Data for Garbage Collection Study

I	A	B	C	D	y	Mean $\bar{y}$
1	−1	−1	−1	−1	(97, 97, 97)	97.00
1	1	−1	−1	−1	(31, 31, 32)	31.33
1	−1	1	−1	−1	(97, 97, 97)	97.00
1	1	1	−1	−1	(31, 32, 31)	31.33
1	−1	−1	1	−1	(97, 97, 97)	97.00
1	1	−1	1	−1	(32, 32, 31)	31.67
1	−1	1	1	−1	(97, 97, 97)	97.00
1	1	1	1	−1	(32, 32, 32)	32.00
1	−1	−1	−1	1	(407, 407, 407)	407.00
1	1	−1	−1	1	(135, 136, 135)	135.33
1	−1	1	−1	1	(409, 409, 409)	409.00
1	1	1	−1	1	(135, 135, 136)	135.33
1	−1	−1	1	1	(407, 407, 407)	407.00
1	1	−1	1	1	(139, 140, 139)	139.33
1	−1	1	1	1	(409, 409, 409)	409.00
1	1	1	1	1	(139, 139, 140)	139.33
2695.67	−1344.33	4.33	9.00	1667.00		Total
168.48	−84.02	0.27	0.56	104.19		Total/8

TABLE 18.10   Effects and Variation Explained in Garbage Collection Study

Factor	Effect	Percentage of Variation	Confidence Interval
I	168.48	138.1	(168.386, 168.573)
A	−84.02	34.4	(−84.114, −83.927)
B	0.27	0.0	(0.177, 0.364)
C	0.56	0.0	(0.469, 0.656)
D	104.19	52.8	(104.094, 104.281)
AB	−0.23	0.0	(−0.323, −0.136)
AC	0.56	0.0	(0.469, 0.656)
AD	−51.31	12.8	(−51.406, −51.219)
BC	0.02	0.0	(−0.073, 0.114)[a]
BD	0.23	0.0	(0.136, 0.323)
CD	0.44	0.0	(0.344, 0.531)
ABC	0.02	0.0	(−0.073, 0.114)[a]
ABD	−0.27	0.0	(−0.364, −0.177)
ACD	0.44	0.0	(0.344, 0.531)
BCD	−0.02	0.0	(−0.114, 0.073)[a]
ABCD	−0.02	0.0	(−0.114, 0.073)[a]

[a] Not significant.

the three phases). Of these six we present only the garbage collection count data. The 16 experiments and the corresponding measurements are shown in Table 18.9. To save space, only the computation of main effects has been shown in the table. Other factors can be similarly computed. The mean value of effects, percentage of variation explained, and confidence intervals are shown in Table 18.10. It is seen that most of the variation is explained by factors A (workload), and D (chunk size) and the interaction AD between the two. Notice that several effects that explain less than 0.05% of the variation and hence are listed as 0.0% are statistically significant since the variation due to experimental error is small. This is why it is better to look at both the percentage of variation and the confidence intervals and select only those effects that have a practically significant as well as statistically significant contribution to the model. Only effects A, D, and AD satisfy both criteria.

EXERCISE

18.1 Table 18.11 lists measured CPU times for two processors on two workloads. Each experiment was repeated three times. Analyze the design.

TABLE 18.11   Data for $2^2 3$ Experimental Design Exercise

Workload	Processor A	Processor B
I	(41.16, 39.02, 42.56)	(63.17, 59.25, 64.23)
J	(51.50, 52.50, 50.50)	(48.08, 48.98, 47.10)

CHAPTER 19

2^{k-p} FRACTIONAL FACTORIAL DESIGNS

It is impossible to make anything foolproof because fools are so ingenious.
—Arthur Bloch

If the number of factors is large, a full factorial design may require a large number of experiments, which may be too expensive. In such cases, a fractional factorial design may be used, which requires considerably fewer experiments. For example, a 2^{k-p} design allows analyzing k two-level factors with only 2^{k-p} experiments, where p is a suitably chosen integer. A 2^{k-1} design requires only half as many experiments as a full factorial 2^k design. This design is therefore called a **half-replicate** of a 2^k design. Similarly, a 2^{k-2} design requires only one-quarter of the experiments required in a full factorial experiments.

Before discussing the theory of fractional factorial designs, it is helpful to look at an example and its result. A sample 2^{7-4} fractional factorial design is shown in Table 19.1. (The preparation of such a sign table is covered in Section 19.1.) A full factorial design in this case would have required 2^7, or 128, experiments. The design as shown allows us to study seven factors with only eight experiments. The first experiment consists of factors A, B, C, and G being at low level and D, E, and F being at high level. This is indicated by -1 and 1 under respective factors in the first row. The second experiment would consist of A, F, and G at high level and B, C, D and E at low level, and so on.

The key advantage of a 2^k full factorial design is the ease with which various effects could be calculated and their contributions to the total variation

314

TABLE 19.1 A 2^{7-4} Experimental Design

Experiment No.	A	B	C	D	E	F	G
1	−1	−1	−1	1	1	1	−1
2	1	−1	−1	−1	−1	1	1
3	−1	1	−1	−1	1	−1	1
4	1	1	−1	1	−1	−1	−1
5	−1	−1	1	1	−1	−1	1
6	1	−1	1	−1	1	−1	−1
7	−1	1	1	−1	−1	1	−1
8	1	1	1	1	1	1	1

could be explained. This advantage is the result of the orthogonality of sign vectors representing levels of various factors in different experiment. This advantage is maintained in 2^{k-p} designs by ensuring that the sign vectors are orthogonal. The factor levels (signs in the column) in Table 19.1 were very carefully chosen. Notice that the columns are mutually orthogonal, that is:

1. The sum of each column is zero:

$$\sum_i x_{ij} = 0 \quad \forall j$$

where x_{ij} represents the level of the jth variable in the ith experiment.

2. The sum of the products of any two columns is zero:

$$\sum_i x_{ij} x_{il} = 0 \quad \forall j \neq l$$

3. The sum of the squares of each column is 2^{7-4}, that is, 8:

$$\sum_i x_{ij}^2 = 8 \quad \forall j$$

The orthogonality allows us to compute the effects as well as their contributions to y's variation simply by computing inner products. For example, the particular design presented in Table 19.1 allows us to fit the following model to the data:

$$y = q_0 + q_A x_A + q_B x_B + q_C x_C + q_D x_D + q_E x_E + q_F x_F + q_G x_G$$

Using the orthogonality property of the factor levels chosen, it can be shown that

$$q_A = \sum_i y_i x_{Ai} = \frac{-y_1 + y_2 - y_3 + y_4 - y_5 + y_6 - y_7 + y_8}{8}$$

Similarly,

$$q_B = \sum_i y_i x_{Bi} = \frac{-y_1 - y_2 + y_3 + y_4 - y_5 - y_6 + y_7 + y_8}{8}$$

and so on.

Thus the effects can be easily computed using the inner product of the y-column and various x-columns as we did for the full factorial designs. The formulas for standard deviations of effects and confidence intervals are also similar to that for a full factorial design with $k - p$ factors. In all formulas, we simply need to replace 2^k by 2^{k-p}. The following example illustrates this.

Example 19.1 Consider the data shown in Table 19.2 for a seven-factor study.

TABLE 19.2   Data for a Seven-Factor Experimental Design

I	A	B	C	D	E	F	G	y
1	-1	-1	-1	1	1	1	-1	20
1	1	-1	-1	-1	-1	1	1	35
1	-1	1	-1	-1	1	-1	1	7
1	1	1	-1	1	-1	-1	-1	42
1	-1	-1	1	1	-1	-1	1	36
1	1	-1	1	-1	1	-1	-1	50
1	-1	1	1	-1	-1	1	-1	45
1	1	1	1	1	1	1	1	82
317	101	35	109	43	1	47	3	Total
39.62	12.62	4.37	13.62	5.37	0.125	5.87	0.37	Total/8

The effects of factors A through G are given in the last line of the table. The percentage of variation explained by each factor is proportional to the square of the corresponding effects. Thus, factors A through G explain 37.26, 4.74, 43.40, 6.75, 0, 8.06, and 0.03% variation, respectively. It is clear that further experimentation, if necessary, should be done using only factors C and A. Other factors explain very little variation.   □

Notice that in Example 19.1, we could obtain all main effects but we could not obtain any interactions. Thus, if the interactions are small or negligible, this design would save us a lot of experimental work.

19.1   PREPARING THE SIGN TABLE FOR A 2^{k-p} DESIGN

The next step in understanding 2^{k-p} designs is to learn to prepare tables with orthogonal columns. The procedure consists of the following two steps:

1. Choose $k - p$ factors and prepare a complete sign table for a full factorial design with $k - p$ factors. This will result in a table of 2^{k-p} rows and

2^{k-p} columns. The first column will be marked I and consists of all 1's. The next $k - p$ columns will be marked with the $k - p$ factors that were chosen. The remaining columns are simply products of these factors.

2. Of the $2^{k-p} - k + p - 1$ columns on the right, choose p columns and mark them with the p factors that were not chosen in step 1.

Example 19.2 To prepare a 2^{7-4} table, we start with a 2^3 design, shown in Table 19.3.

TABLE 19.3 A 2^3 Experimental Design

Experiment No.	A	B	C	AB	AC	BC	ABC
1	-1	-1	-1	1	1	1	-1
2	1	-1	-1	-1	-1	1	1
3	-1	1	-1	-1	1	-1	1
4	1	1	-1	1	-1	-1	-1
5	-1	-1	1	1	-1	-1	1
6	1	-1	1	-1	1	-1	-1
7	-1	1	1	-1	-1	1	-1
8	1	1	1	1	1	1	1

Now we mark the rightmost four columns with D, E, F, and G instead of AB, AC, BC, and ABC, respectively. This gives us the 2^{7-4} design shown in Table 19.1 earlier. □

Example 19.3 Let us prepare a 2^{4-1} design. Again we start with the 2^3 design shown in Table 19.3. From the four columns on the right, we arbitrarily pick the rightmost column and mark it D. This gives us the design shown in Table 19.4. This design will allow us to compute the main effects q_A, q_B, q_C, and q_D along with the interactions q_{AB}, q_{AC}, and q_{BC}. □

TABLE 19.4 A 2^{4-1} Experimental Design

Experiment No.	A	B	C	AB	AC	BC	D
1	-1	-1	-1	1	1	1	-1
2	1	-1	-1	-1	-1	1	1
3	-1	1	-1	-1	1	-1	1
4	1	1	-1	1	-1	-1	-1
5	-1	-1	1	1	-1	-1	1
6	1	-1	1	-1	1	-1	-1
7	-1	1	1	-1	-1	1	-1
8	1	1	1	1	1	1	1

19.2 CONFOUNDING

One problem with fractional factorial experiments is that some of the effects cannot be determined. Only the combined influence of two or more effects can be computed. This problem is known as **confounding** and the effects whose influence cannot be separated are said to be **confounded**. The following example makes the concept clear.

> **Example 19.4** Let us now analyze the design prepared in the previous example of 2^{4-1} design. If y_i represents the observed y-value in the ith experiment, then the effect of A can be obtained by taking the inner product of column A and column y and dividing the sum by 8. This gives
>
> $$q_A = \sum_i y_i x_{Ai} = \frac{-y_1 + y_2 - y_3 + y_4 - y_5 + y_6 - y_7 + y_8}{8}$$
>
> Similarly, the effect of D is given by
>
> $$q_D = \sum_i y_i x_{Di} = \frac{-y_1 + y_2 + y_3 - y_4 + y_5 - y_6 - y_7 + y_8}{8}$$
>
> The effect of the interaction ABC is obtained by multiplying the respective elements of columns A, B, C, and y. This gives
>
> $$q_{ABC} = \sum_i y_i x_{Ai} x_{Bi} x_{Ci} = \frac{-y_1 + y_2 + y_3 - y_4 + y_5 - y_6 - y_7 + y_8}{8}$$
>
> Notice that the expression for q_{ABC} is identical to that for q_D. In fact, the expression is neither q_D nor q_{ABC}; it is the sum of the two:
>
> $$q_D + q_{ABC} = \sum_i y_i x_{Ai} x_{Bi} x_{Ci} = \frac{-y_1 + y_2 + y_3 - y_4 + y_5 - y_6 - y_7 + y_8}{8}$$
>
> Without a full factorial design it is not possible to get separate estimates of D and ABC effects. In statistical terms the effects of D and ABC are confounded. This does not cause any serious problem, particularly if it is known prior to the experiments that the combined interaction of the factors A, B, and C is small compared to the effect of D. If that is the case, the preceding expression represents mostly q_D. $\square$

Thus, we see that if two or more effects are confounded, their computation uses the same linear combination of responses, with the possible exception of the sign.

For reasons that will become apparent soon, the confounding in Example 19.4 can be denoted as

$$D = ABC$$

In this design, D and ABC are not the only effects that are confounded. It is easy to see that the A and BCD effects are also confounded.

$$q_A = q_{BCD} = \sum_i y_i x_{Ai} = \frac{-y_1 + y_2 - y_3 + y_4 - y_5 + y_6 - y_7 + y_8}{8}$$

that is,

$$A = BCD$$

In fact, every column in the design represents a sum of 2 effects. With four variables, each at two levels, there are 16 effects (including the I column of mean responses). In a 2^{4-1} design, only eight quantities can be computed. Each quantity therefore represents a sum of 2 effects. The complete list of confoundings in this design is as follows:

$$A = BCD, \quad B = ACD, \quad C = ABD, \quad AB = CD$$
$$AC = BD, \quad BC = AD, \quad ABC = D, \quad I = ABCD$$

where $I = ABCD$ is used to denote the confounding of $ABCD$ with the mean.

A fractional factorial design is not unique. For the same number of factors k and the same number of experiments 2^{k-p}, there are 2^p possible different fractional factorial designs. One 2^{4-1} design was presented in Example 19.3. Another 2^{4-1} design is shown in Table 19.5. This design has the following confoundings:

$$I = ABD, \quad A = BD, \quad B = AD, \quad C = ABCD$$
$$D = AB, \quad AC = BCD, \quad BC = ACD, \quad ABC = CD.$$

This design is generally not considered as good as the previous design. In the previous design, the mean (I) was confounded with the fourth-order interaction, and the main effects were confounded with third-order interactions.

TABLE 19.5 Another 2^{4-1} Experimental Design

Experiment No.	A	B	C	D	AC	BC	ABC
1	−1	−1	−1	1	1	1	−1
2	1	−1	−1	−1	−1	1	1
3	−1	1	−1	−1	1	−1	1
4	1	1	−1	1	−1	−1	−1
5	−1	−1	1	1	−1	−1	1
6	1	−1	1	−1	1	−1	−1
7	−1	1	1	−1	−1	1	−1
8	1	1	1	1	1	1	1

In the second design, the mean is confounded with the third-order interaction, and the main effects (A, B, C, and D) are confounded with the second-order interactions. It is generally assumed that the higher order interactions are smaller than the lower order interactions. If this assumption is true, then the first design will give better estimates of main effects than the second design.

19.3   ALGEBRA OF CONFOUNDING

The fractional factorial design of Table 19.4 can be called the $I = ABCD$ design and that shown in Table 19.5 is the $I = ABC$ design. This is because given just one confounding, it is possible to list all other confoundings by multiplying the two sides of the confounding by different terms and using two simple rules:

1. The mean I is treated as unity. For example, I multiplied by A is A.
2. Any term with a power of 2 is erased. For example, AB^2C is the same as AC.

Let us illustrate this with the first design, which has

$$I = ABCD$$

Multiplying both sides by A, we get

$$A = A^2BCD = BCD$$

Multiplying both sides by B, C, D, and AB, we get

$$B = AB^2CD = ACD$$
$$C = ABC^2D = ABD$$
$$D = ABCD^2 = ABC$$
$$AB = A^2B^2CD = CD$$

and so on.

The polynomial $I = ABCD$ used to generate all confoundings for this design is called the **generator polynomial** for this design. Similarly, the generator polynomial for the second design is $I = ABC$.

In a 2^{k-1} design, 2^1 effects are confounded together. In a 2^{k-p} design, 2^p effects are confounded together. The generator polynomial has 2^p terms. For example, the 2^{7-4} design presented earlier in Table 19.1 was obtained from a 2^3 design by replacing columns AB, AC, BC, and ABC by D, E, F, and G, respectively. Thus, this design has the following confoundings:

$$D = AB, \qquad E = AC, \qquad F = BC, \qquad G = ABC$$

Multiplying each of the four equations by their left-hand sides, we get

$$I = ABD, \qquad I = ACE, \qquad I = BCF, \qquad I = ABCG$$

Or equivalently,

$$I = ABD = ACE = BCF = ABCG$$

The product of any subset of the preceding terms is also equal to I. Thus the complete generator polynomial is

$$I = ABD = ACE = BCF = ABCG = BCDE = ACDF$$
$$= CDG = ABEF = BEG = AFG = DEF = ADEG$$
$$= BDFG = ABDG = CEFG = ABCDEFG$$

Other confoundings for the design can be obtained by multiplying this equation by $A, B, \ldots$. For example,

$$A = BD = CE = ABCF = BCG = ABCDE = CDF$$
$$= ACDG = BEF = ABEG = FG = ADEF = DEG$$
$$= ABDFG = BDG = ACEFG = BCDEFG$$

19.4 DESIGN RESOLUTION

The resolution of a design is measured by the order of effects that are confounded. The order of an effect is the number of factors included in it. For example, $ABCD$ is of order 4, while I is of order 0. If an ith-order effect is confounded with a jth-order term, the confounding is said to be of order $i + j$. The minimum of orders of all confoundings of a design is called its resolution. In other words, a design is said to be of resolution r if no j factor effect is confounded with any effects containing fewer than $r - j$ factors.

By tradition, the resolution is denoted by the capital Roman letters. For example, a 2^{5-1} design with resolution of 3 is denoted as R_{III} design, resolution III design, or 2^{5-1}_{III} design. In such a design, the mean response I is confounded with third- or higher-order effects. The main effects are confounded with second- or higher-order effects.

To determine the resolution of a 2^{k-p} design, we only need to find the minimum of orders of the effects confounded with the mean response.

Example 19.5 Consider the 2^{4-1} design of Table 19.4 presented earlier. The generator polynomial for this design was $I = ABCD$. Its confoundings as determined earlier in Section 19.3 are

$$A = BCD, \qquad B = ACD, \qquad C = ABD, \qquad AB = CD$$
$$AC = BD, \qquad BC = AD, \qquad ABC = D, \qquad I = ABCD$$

Notice that the first-order effects $(j = 1)$ are confounded with the third-order effects. Second-order effects $(j = 2)$ are confounded only with second-order effects. The mean response I $(j = 0)$ is confounded with fourth-order effects. In each case, the sum of the order of confounded effects is greater than or equal to 4. Thus, this is a R_{IV} design.

We could have determined the order simply by looking at the generator polynomial $I = ABCD$. There is only one effect, namely, $ABCD$, that is confounded with the mean response. Its order is 4, and so the design resolution is IV. $\square$

Example 19.6 Consider the 2^{4-1} design of Table 19.5. The generator polynomial is $I = ABD$. The order of ABD is 3, and so this is an R_{III} design. $\square$

Example 19.7 In Section 19.3, the 2^{7-4} design of Table 19.1 was shown to have the following confoundings:

$$I = ABD = ACE = BCF = ABCG = BCDE = ACDF$$

$$= CDG = ABEF = BEG = AFG = DEF = ADEG$$

$$= BDFG = ABDG = CEFG = ABCDEFG$$

This is a resolution III design. $\square$

A design of higher resolution is considered a better design. This is because of the assumption that higher order interactions are smaller than lower order effects. This need not always be true. If this is true, then it is better to have higher order interactions confounded with main effects. For example, given a choice between the two designs $I = ABCD$ (an R_{IV} design) and $I = ABD$ (an R_{III} design) without any prior information about the relative magnitude of the interactions, it is preferable to use the R_{IV} design. On the other hand, if it is known that the ABD interaction is negligible, the $I = ABD$ design may be preferred even though it has a lower resolution.

Case Study 19.1 The CPU time taken by two text-formatting programs, called LaTeX and troff, was measured using synthetic files of various sizes and complexity levels. Six factors, each with two levels were chosen for the study. The first two factors were the text-formatting programs and size of the files. The remaining four factors were number of equations, floats, tables, and footnotes in the file. The assignment of factors and their levels is shown in Table 19.6. A 2^{6-1} fractional factorial design with the generator polynomial $I = BCDEF$ was used. The largest effects and interactions, computed by the sign table method, are shown in Table 19.7. The following conclusions can be reached from these results:

1. Over 90% of the variation is explained by the three factors Bytes, Program, and Equations and a second-order interaction.

TABLE 19.6   Factors and Levels for Text Formatting Programs

Symbol	Factor	Level -1	Level $+1$
A	Program	LaTeX	troff
B	Bytes	2100	25,000
C	Equations	0	10
D	Floats	0	10
E	Tables	0	10
F	Footnotes	0	10

TABLE 19.7   Effects for the Text Formatting Programs

Symbol	Factor	Effect	Percentage of Variation
B	Bytes	12.0	39.4
A	Program	9.4	24.4
C	Equations	7.5	15.6
AC	Program × Equations	7.2	14.4
E	Tables	3.5	3.4
F	Footnotes	1.6	0.7

2. The text file sizes (in bytes) in these experiments were significantly different, making the effect more than that of the text-formatting programs being compared.

3. The high percentage of variation explained by the "program × Equation" interaction indicates that the choice of the text-formatting program depends upon the number of equations in the text. If we consider only the programs and equations in isolation, the relative amount of CPU time for various combinations is shown in Table 19.8. This shows that troff takes too much CPU time if there are equations in the text.

4. The "Program × Bytes" interaction is low. This indicates that changing the file size affects both programs in a similar manner.

TABLE 19.8   CPU Time for Various Program × Equation Combinations

Program	Number of Equations $-1(0)$	$1(10)$
-1(LaTeX)	-9.7	-9.1
1(troff)	-5.3	24.1

5. If possible, the experiments should be redone with a reduced range of file sizes so that the programs rather than the workload come out as the most significant factor. Alternately, the number of levels of file sizes should be increased. ☐

Case Study 19.2 This case study concerns the design of a scheduler for a WANG VS system. The system allows word processing, data processing, and background data processing. The designers wanted to find out what type of scheduler should be used for each of these three environments and whether the same scheduler could be used for all three classes of jobs. The scheduling policies that were studied had five parameters:

• Whether the scheduler is preemptive or not.
• Whether the time slice (quantum size) is small or large.
• Whether to have one or two queues. The second queue would have a lower priority by assigning it a smaller time slice.
• How many job classes to keep and into what ready queue to place the task when it becomes runable due to events, such as I/O completion, intertask message received, system locks release, and so on.
• Whether any jobs waiting for too long should be given preference to improve fairness.

The five factors and their level assignments are summarized in Table 19.9. A 2^{5-1} fractional factorial design with 16 experiments was used to study the relative importance of these factors. The design was based on the generator $I = ABCDE$ or, equivalently, $E = ABCD$. The level assignments for the five factors in the 16 experiment and the measured throughput using three different synthetic workloads is shown in Table 19.10. In the table, columns T_W, T_I, and T_B denote throughput for word processing, interactive data processing, and batch data processing, respectively.

The mean effects and the percentage of variation explained for each the three workloads are listed in Table 19.11. The following conclusions can be drawn from this table:

• The ideal parameter setting for the three workloads is different. Looking at the percentage of variation explained, the effects that impact word

TABLE 19.9   Factors and Levels in the Scheduler Design Study

Symbol	Factor	Level −1	Level 1
A	Preemption	No	Yes
B	Time slice	Small	Large
C	Queue assignment	One queue	Two queues
D	Requeueing	Two queues	Five queues
E	Fairness	Off	On

TABLE 19.10 Measured Throughputs for Scheduler Design Study

Experiment No.	A	B	C	D	E	T_W	T_I	T_B
1	−1	−1	−1	−1	1	15.0	25.0	15.2
2	1	−1	−1	−1	−1	11.0	41.0	3.0
3	−1	1	−1	−1	−1	25.0	36.0	21.0
4	1	1	−1	−1	1	10.0	15.7	8.6
5	−1	−1	1	−1	−1	14.0	63.9	7.5
6	1	−1	1	−1	1	10.0	13.2	7.5
7	−1	1	1	−1	1	28.0	36.3	20.2
8	1	1	1	−1	−1	11.0	23.0	3.0
9	−1	−1	−1	1	−1	14.0	66.1	6.4
10	1	−1	−1	1	1	10.0	9.1	8.4
11	−1	1	−1	1	1	27.0	34.6	15.7
12	1	1	−1	1	−1	11.0	23.0	3.0
13	−1	−1	1	1	1	14.0	26.0	12.0
14	1	−1	1	1	−1	11.0	38.0	2.0
15	−1	1	1	1	−1	25.0	35.0	17.2
16	1	1	1	1	1	11.0	22.0	2.0

TABLE 19.11 Effects and Variation Explained in Scheduling Policy Comparison Study

Confounded Effects		T_W		T_I		T_B	
1	2	Estimate	% of Variation	Estimate	% of Variation	Estimate	% of Variation
I	$ABCDE$	15.44		31.74		9.54	
A	$BCDE$	−4.81	55.5	−8.62	31.0	−4.86	58.8
B	$ACDE$	3.06	22.5	−3.54	5.2	1.79	8.0
C	$ABDE$	0.06	0.0	0.43	0.1	−0.62	1.0
D	$ABCE$	−0.06	0.0	−0.02	0.0	−1.21	3.6
AB	CDE	−2.94	20.7	1.34	0.8	−2.33	13.5
AC	BDE	0.06	0.0	0.49	0.1	−0.44	0.5
AD	BCE	0.19	0.1	−0.08	0.0	0.37	0.3
BC	ADE	0.19	0.1	0.44	0.1	−0.12	0.0
BD	ACE	0.06	0.0	0.47	0.1	−0.66	1.1
CD	ABE	−0.19	0.1	−1.91	1.5	0.58	0.8
DE	ABC	−0.06	0.0	0.21	0.0	−0.47	0.5
CE	ABD	0.06	0.0	1.21	0.6	−0.16	0.1
BE	ACD	0.31	0.2	7.96	26.4	−1.37	4.7
AE	BCD	−0.56	0.8	0.88	0.3	0.28	0.2
E	$ABCD$	0.19	0.1	−9.01	33.8	1.66	6.8

processing throughput T_W are A (Preemption), B (Time slice), and AB. For interactive jobs, important factors are E (Fairness), A (preemption), BE, and B (Time slice). For background jobs, the important factors are A (Preemption), AB, B (Time slice), and E (Fairness). Thus, it might be worthwhile to have different policies for different classes of workloads.

- Factor C (Queue assignment) or any of its interactions do not have any significant impact on the throughput.
- Factor D (Requeuing) also is not very effective.
- Factor A (Preemption) impacts all three workloads significantly.
- Factor B (Time slice) has less impact than factor A.
- Factor E (Fairness) is important for interactive jobs and slightly important for background jobs.

We will reconsider this case study in Section 23.3, where we present further conclusions. □

EXERCISES

19.1 Analyze the 2^{4-1} design shown in Table 19.12.

TABLE 19.12   A 2^{4-1} Design

	$C_1 D_1$	$C_1 D_2$	$C_2 D_1$	$C_2 D_2$
$A_1 B_1$	—	40	15	—
$A_1 B_2$	—	20	10	—
$A_2 B_1$	100	—	—	30
$A_2 B_2$	120	—	—	50

- **a.** Quantify all main effects.
- **b.** Quantify percentages of variation explained.
- **c.** Sort the variables in the order of decreasing importance.
- **d.** List all confoundings.
- **e.** Can you propose a better design with the same number of experiments.
- **f.** What is the resolution of the design?

19.2 Is it possible to have a 2_{III}^{4-1} design? A 2_{II}^{4-1} design? A 2_{IV}^{4-1} design? If yes, give an example.

CHAPTER 20

ONE-FACTOR EXPERIMENTS

Experiments should be reproducible: they should all fail in the same way.
—Finagle's Rule

One-factor designs are used to compare several alternatives of a single categorical variable. For example, one could use such a design for comparing several processors, several computer systems, or several caching schemes. Techniques to analyze such designs are presented in this chapter. There is no limit on the number of levels that the factor can take. In particular, unlike the 2^k designs, the number of levels can be more than 2.

20.1 MODEL

The model used in single-factor designs is

$$y_{ij} = \mu + \alpha_j + e_{ij} \tag{20.1}$$

Here, y_{ij} is the ith response (or observation) with the factor at level j (that is, the jth alternative), μ is the mean response, α_j is the effect of alternative j, and e_{ij} is the error term. The effects are computed so that they add up to zero:

$$\sum \alpha_j = 0$$

20.2 COMPUTATION OF EFFECTS

The measured data in a one-factor design consists of r observations for each of the a alternatives. There are a total of ar observations, which are arranged in an $r \times a$ matrix so that r observations belonging to the jth alternative form a column vector. Let y_{ij} denote the ith entry in the jth column. If we substitute the observed responses in the model Equation (20.1), we obtain ar equations. Adding these equations, we get

$$\sum_{i=1}^{r}\sum_{j=1}^{a} y_{ij} = ar\mu + r\sum_{j=1}^{a}\alpha_j + \sum_{i=1}^{r}\sum_{j=1}^{a} e_{ij}$$

Since the effects α_j add up to zero (by design) and we want the mean error to be zero, the preceding equation becomes

$$\sum_{i=1}^{r}\sum_{j=1}^{a} y_{ij} = ar\mu + 0 + 0$$

The model parameter μ is therefore given by

$$\mu = \frac{1}{ar}\sum_{i=1}^{r}\sum_{j=1}^{a} y_{ij}$$

The quantity on the right-hand side is the so-called **grand mean** of all ar responses. It is denoted by $\overline{y}_{..}$. As explained earlier in Section 18.4, the two dots in the subscript indicate that the averaging is done along both dimensions (rows and columns) of the matrix. This should be distinguished from the **column means**, which are obtained by averaging responses belonging to a particular column (or alternative). The column mean for the jth column is denoted by $\overline{y}_{.j}$ and is computed as follows:

$$\overline{y}_{.j} = \frac{1}{r}\sum_{i=1}^{r} y_{ij}$$

Substituting $\mu + \alpha_j + e_{ij}$ for y_{ij}, we obtain

$$\overline{y}_{.j} = \frac{1}{r}\sum_{i=1}^{r}(\mu + \alpha_j + e_{ij})$$

$$= \frac{1}{r}\left(r\mu + r\alpha_j + \sum_{i=1}^{r} e_{ij}\right)$$

$$= \mu + \alpha_j$$

Here we have assumed that the error terms for r observations belonging to each alternative add up to zero. The parameter α_j can thus be estimated as follows:

$$\alpha_j = \overline{y}_{.j} - \mu = \overline{y}_{.j} - \overline{y}_{..}$$

TABLE 20.1 Data from a Code Size
Comparison Study

R	V	Z
144	101	130
120	144	180
176	211	141
288	288	374
144	72	302

This computation can be done easily in tabular form as illustrated in the following example.

Example 20.1 In a code size comparison study, the number of bytes required to code a workload on three different processors R, V, and Z was measured five times each (each time a different programmer was asked to code the same workload). The measured data is as shown in Table 20.1. In analyzing this data, the five observations are assumed to be for the same workload and the entries on a single row are considered unrelated. If the entries were related, a two-factor analysis, discussed in Chapter 21, would need to be used. *One-factor analysis, presented here, is valid only if the rows do not represent any additional factor.*

The analysis is shown in Table 20.2. Here, number of levels *a* is 3, and number of replications is 5. We sum each column to find the column sum and then add column sums to get the overall sum. The sums are divided by the respective number of observations to get the means. The differences between column means and the overall mean give the column effects. The results are interpreted as follows. An average processor requires 187.7 bytes

TABLE 20.2 Analysis of the Code Size Comparison Study

	R	V	Z	
	144	101	130	
	120	144	180	
	176	211	141	
	288	288	374	
	144	72	302	
Column sum	$\sum y_{.1} = 872$	$\sum y_{.2} = 816$	$\sum y_{.3} = 1127$	$\sum y_{..} = 2815$
Column mean	$\bar{y}_{.1} = 174.4$	$\bar{y}_{.2} = 163.2$	$\bar{y}_{.3} = 225.4$	$\mu = \bar{y}_{..}$ $= 187.7$
Column effect	$\alpha_1 = \bar{y}_{.1} - \bar{y}_{..}$ $= -13.3$	$\alpha_2 = \bar{y}_{.2} - \bar{y}_{..}$ $= -24.5$	$\alpha_3 = \bar{y}_{.3} - \bar{y}_{..}$ $= 37.7$	

of storage. The effects of the processors R, V, and Z are -13.3, -24.5, and 37.7, respectively. That is, R requires 13.3 bytes less than an average processor, V requires 24.5 bytes less than an average processor, and Z requires 37.7 bytes more than an average processor.   □

20.3 ESTIMATING EXPERIMENTAL ERRORS

Once the model parameters have been computed, we can estimate the response for each of a alternatives. The estimated response for the jth alternative is given by

$$\hat{y}_j = \mu + \alpha_j$$

The difference between the measured and the estimated response represents experimental error. If we compute experimental errors in each of the ar observations, the mean error should come out zero since the parameter values μ and α_j were computed assuming the sum of errors for each column was zero. The variance of the errors can be estimated from the Sum of Squared Errors (SSE):

$$\text{SSE} = \sum_{i=1}^{r} \sum_{j=1}^{a} e_{ij}^2$$

Example 20.2 Computation of errors for the code size comparison study of Example 20.1 is as follows:

$$
\begin{bmatrix}
144 & 101 & 130 \\
120 & 144 & 180 \\
176 & 211 & 141 \\
288 & 288 & 374 \\
144 & 72 & 302
\end{bmatrix}
=
\begin{bmatrix}
187.7 & 187.7 & 187.7 \\
187.7 & 187.7 & 187.7 \\
187.7 & 187.7 & 187.7 \\
187.7 & 187.7 & 187.7 \\
187.7 & 187.7 & 187.7
\end{bmatrix}
+
\begin{bmatrix}
-13.3 & -24.5 & 37.7 \\
-13.3 & -24.5 & 37.7 \\
-13.3 & -24.5 & 37.7 \\
-13.3 & -24.5 & 37.7 \\
-13.3 & -24.5 & 37.7
\end{bmatrix}
$$

$$
+
\begin{bmatrix}
-30.4 & -62.2 & -95.4 \\
-54.4 & -19.2 & -45.4 \\
1.6 & 47.8 & -84.4 \\
113.6 & 124.8 & 148.6 \\
-30.4 & -91.2 & 76.6
\end{bmatrix}
$$

Each observation has been broken into three parts: a grand mean μ, the processor effect α_j's, and the residuals. A matrix notation is used for all three parts. The sum of squares of entries in the residual matrix is

$$\text{SSE} = (-30.4)^2 + (-54.4)^2 + \cdots + (76.6)^2 = 94{,}365.20 \qquad □$$

20.4 ALLOCATION OF VARIATION

As in the case of $2^k r$ designs, the total variation of y in a one-factor experimental design can be allocated to the factor and errors. To do so, we square both sides of the model equation:

$$y_{ij}^2 = \mu^2 + \alpha_j^2 + e_{ij}^2 + 2\mu\alpha_j + 2\mu e_{ij} + 2\alpha_j e_{ij}$$

Adding corresponding terms of ar such equations, we obtain

$$\sum_{i,j} y_{ij}^2 = \sum_{i,j} \mu^2 + \sum_{i,j} \alpha_j^2 + \sum_{i,j} e_{ij}^2 + \text{cross-product terms}$$

The cross-product terms all add to zero due to the constraints that the effects add to zero ($\sum \alpha_j = 0$) and that the errors for each column add to zero ($\sum e_{ij} = 0$). The preceding equation, expressed in terms of sums of squares, can be written as

$$\text{SSY} = \text{SS0} + \text{SSA} + \text{SSE}$$

where SSY is the sum of squares of y, SS0 is the sum of squares of grand means, SSA is the sum of squares of effects, and SSE is the sum of square errors. Note that SS0 and SSA can be easily computed as follows:

$$\text{SS0} = \sum_{i=1}^{r}\sum_{j=1}^{a} \mu^2 = ar\mu^2$$

$$\text{SSA} = \sum_{i=1}^{r}\sum_{j=1}^{a} \alpha_j^2 = r\sum_{j=1}^{a} \alpha_j^2$$

Thus, SSE can be calculated easily from SSY without calculating individual errors.

The total variation of y (SST) is defined as

$$\text{SST} = \sum_{i,j}(y_{i,j} - \bar{y}_{..})^2 = \sum_{i,j} y_{ij}^2 - ar\bar{y}_{..}^2 = \text{SSY} - \text{SS0} = \text{SSA} + \text{SSE}$$

The total variation can therefore be divided into two parts, SSA and SSE, which represent the explained and the unexplained parts of the variation. They can be expressed as percentage of the total variation. A high percentage of explained variation indicates a good model.

Example 20.3   For the code size comparison study of Example 20.1,

$$SSY = 144^2 + 120^2 + \cdots + 302^2 = 633{,}639$$

$$SS0 = ar\mu^2 = 3 \times 5 \times (187.7)^2 = 528{,}281.7$$

$$SSA = r \sum_j \alpha_j^2 = 5[(-13.3)^2 + (-24.5)^2 + (37.6)^2] = 10{,}992.1$$

$$SST = SSY - SS0 = 633{,}639.0 - 528{,}281.7 = 105{,}357.3$$

$$SSE = SST - SSA = 105{,}357.3 - 10{,}992.1 = 94{,}365.2$$

$$\text{Percentage of variation explained by processors} = 100 \times \frac{10{,}992.13}{105{,}357.3}$$

$$= 10.4\%$$

The remaining 89.6% of the variation in code size is due to experimental errors, which in this case could be attributed to programmer differences. The issue of whether 10.4%—the processors's contribution to variation—is statistically significant is addressed in the next section.   □

20.5 ANALYSIS OF VARIANCE

In allocating the variation to different factors in Section 20.4, an informal approach was used that is very helpful in practice. In that approach, any factor that explained a high percentage of variation was considered important. This importance should be distinguished from *significance*, which is a statistical term. To determine if a factor has a significant effect on the response, statisticians compare its contribution to the variation with that of the errors. If unexplained variation (due to errors) is high, a factor explaining a large fraction of the variation may turn out to be statistically insignificant. The statistical procedure to analyze the significance of various factors is called **Analysis Of Variance** (**ANOVA**). The procedure for one-factor experiments is very similar to that explained earlier in Section 15.1.

To understand ANOVA, consider the sum of squares—SSY, SS0, SSA, and SSE. Each of the sums of squares has an associated degree of freedom that corresponds to the number of independent values required to compute them. The degrees of freedom for the sums are as follows:

$$SSY = SS0 + \quad SSA \quad + \quad SSE$$
$$ar \; = \; 1 \; + (a-1) + a(r-1)$$

The sum SSY consists of a sum of ar terms, all of which can be independently chosen. This therefore has ar degrees of freedom. The sum SS0 consists of a single term μ^2 that is repeated ar times. Once a value for μ has been chosen, SS0 can be computed. Thus, SS0 has one degree of freedom.

TABLE 20.3 ANOVA Table for One-Factor Experiments

Component	Sum of Squares	Percentage of Variation	Degrees of Freedom	Mean Square	F-Computed	F-Table
y	$SSY = \sum y_{ij}^2$		ar			
$\bar{y}_{..}$	$SS0 = ar\mu^2$		1			
$y - \bar{y}_{..}$	$SST = SSY - SS0$	100	$ar - 1$			
A	$SSA = r\sum \alpha_i^2$	$100\left(\dfrac{SSA}{SST}\right)$	$a - 1$	$MSA = \dfrac{SSA}{a-1}$	$\dfrac{MSA}{MSE}$	$F_{[1-\alpha;\,a-1,a(r-1)]}$
e	$SSE = SST - SSA$	$100\left(\dfrac{SSE}{SST}\right)$	$a(r-1)$	$MSE = \dfrac{SSE}{a(r-1)}$		

$$s_e = \sqrt{MSE}$$

The sum SSA contains a sum of a terms—α_j^2—but only $a - 1$ of these are indepdendent since the α_j's add up to zero. Therefore, SSA has $a - 1$ degrees of freedom. The sum SSE consists of ar error terms of which only $a(r - 1)$ can be independently chosen. This is because the r errors corresponding to r replications of each experiment must add up to zero. Thus, only $r - 1$ errors in each of a experiments are independent.

Notice that the degrees of freedom on the two sides of the preceding equations also add up. This verifies that the degrees of freedom have been correctly assigned.

The F-test, explained in Section 15.1, can now be used to check if SSA is significantly greater than SSE. Assuming that the errors are normally distributed, SSE and SSA have chi-square distributions. The ratio $(SSA/\nu_A)/(SSE/\nu_e)$, where $\nu_A = a - 1$ and $\nu_e = a(r - 1)$ are degrees of freedom (DF) for SSA and SSE, respectively, has an F distribution with ν_A numerator and ν_e denominator degrees of freedoms. If the computed ratio is greater than the quantile $F_{[1-\alpha;\nu_A,\nu_e]}$ obtained from the table of quantiles of F-variates (Tables A.6 to A.8 in the Appendix), SSA is considered significantly higher than SSE.

The quantity SSA/ν_A is called the **Mean Square** of A (MSA). Similary, SSE/ν_e is called the Mean Square of Errors (MSE). If the computed ratio MSA/MSE is greater than the value read from the table of quantiles of F-variates (Tables A.6 to A.8 in the Appendix), the factor is assumed to explain a significant fraction of the variation. A convenient tabular arrangement to conduct the F-test is shown in Table 20.3.

Example 20.4 The ANOVA for the code size comparison study of Example 20.1 is shown in Table 20.4. From the table we see that the computed F-value is less than that from the table, and therefore once again we conclude that the observed difference in the code sizes is mostly due to experimental errors and not to any significant difference among the processors. □

TABLE 20.4 ANOVA Table for the Code Size Comparison Study

Component	Sum of Squares	Percentage of Variation	Degrees of Freedom	Mean Square	F-Computed	F-Table
y	633,639.00					
$y_{..}$	528,281.69					
$y - y_{..}$	105,357.31	100.0	14			
A	10,992.13	10.4	2	5496.1	0.7	2.8
Errors	94,365.20	89.6	12	7863.8		

$$s_e = \sqrt{\text{MSE}} = \sqrt{7863.77} = 88.68$$

20.6 VISUAL DIAGNOSTIC TESTS

The analysis of one-factor experiments as presented here is based on the same set of assumptions as those discussed earlier in Section 14.7 for regression models and then in Section 18.7 for $2^k r$ experimental designs:

- The effects of various factors are additive.
- Errors are additive.
- Errors are independent of the factor levels.
- Errors are normally distributed.
- Errors have the same variance for all factor levels.

The visual tests to verify these assumptions are also the same as those discussed earlier. A normal quantile-quantile plot of the residuals should be prepared. If plot is approximately linear, normality can be assumed.

A scatter plot of residuals versus predicted response should be prepared and checked to see that there is no trend in the residuals or their spread. If the relative magnitude of errors is smaller than the response by an order of magnitude or more, the trends may be ignored.

Example 20.5 A scatter plot of residuals versus predicted response for the code size comparison study of Example 20.1 is shown in Figure 20.1. Notice that the residuals are not small. This is seen easily by comparing the ranges of scales along the vertical and horizontal axis. This reconfirms our previous conclusion that the variation due to factors, which is indicated by the spread along the horizontal axis, is small compared to the unexplained variation, which is indicated by the spread along the vertical axis. Notice, however, that the spread of errors is homogeneous and there is no visible trend in the errors.

A normal quantile-quantile plot for the residuals is shown in Figure 20.2. Notice that the plot is slightly S-shaped, which indicates that the distribution of residuals, although symmetrical, has slightly shorter tails than a normal distribution.   □

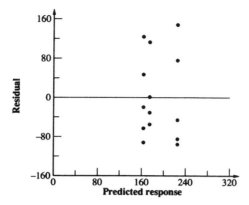

FIGURE 20.1 Plot of the residuals versus predicted response for the code size comparison study.

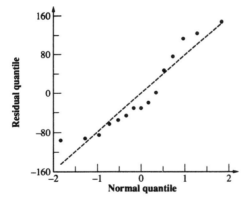

FIGURE 20.2 Normal quantile-quantile plot for the residuals of the code size comparison study.

20.7 CONFIDENCE INTERVALS FOR EFFECTS

The estimated values of the model parameters are random variables since they are based on one sample. The estimates obtained from another sample would be different. The variance of the model parameters can be estimated from that of the errors (see Exercise 20.1). These variances are listed in Table 20.5. The confidence intervals for the effects can be computed using t-values read at $r(a - 1)$ degrees of freedom (which are the degrees of freedom associated with errors).

In the table, we have also shown the estimates for linear combination of effects such as $\mu + \alpha_j$ and for contrasts $\sum h_j\alpha_j$. The former can be used to estimate confidence intervals for mean responses since

$$\hat{y}_j = \mu + \alpha_j$$

TABLE 20.5   Parameter Estimation from One-Factor Experiments

Parameter	Estimate	Variance
μ	$\overline{y}_{..}$	s_e^2/ar
α_j	$\overline{y}_{.j} - \overline{y}_{..}$	$s_e^2(a-1)/ar$
$\mu + \alpha_j$	$\overline{y}$	s_e^2/r
$\sum_{j=1}^{a} h_j\alpha_j$,		
$\sum_{j=1}^{a} h_j = 0$	$\sum_{j=1}^{a} h_j\overline{y}_{.j}$	$\sum_{j=1}^{a} s_e^2 h_j^2/ar$
s_e^2	$\sum e_{ij}^2/[a(r-1)]$	

Degrees of freedom for errors $= a(r-1)$

The contrasts can be used to compare any subset of effects. For example, the confidence interval for $\alpha_1 - \alpha_2$ can be used to check if there is a significant difference between alternatives 1 and 2.

Example 20.6   For the code size comparison study of Example 20.1

$$\text{Error variance} = s_e^2 = \frac{94,365.2}{12} = 7863.8$$

$$\text{Standard deviation of errors} = \sqrt{\text{variance of errors}} = 88.7$$

$$\text{Standard deviation of } \mu = s_e/\sqrt{ar} = 88.7/\sqrt{15} = 22.9$$

$$\text{Standard deviation of } \alpha_j = s_e\sqrt{[(a-1)/ar]} = 88.7\sqrt{\tfrac{2}{15}} = 32.4$$

For 90% confidence, the $t_{[0.95;12]}$ value read from Table A.4 in the Appendix is 1.782. The 90% confidence interval for various parameters are

$$\mu = 197.7 \mp (1.782)(22.9) = (146.9, 228.5)$$

$$\alpha_1 = -13.3 \mp (1.782)(32.4) = (-71.0, 44.4)$$

$$\alpha_2 = -24.5 \mp (1.782)(32.4) = (-82.2, 33.2)$$

$$\alpha_3 = 37.6 \mp (1.782)(32.4) = (-20.0, 95.4)$$

Notice that the code size on an average processor is significantly different from zero. However, none of the processor effects is significant.Therefore, we cannot say with 90% confidence that the processors have a significant effect on code size.

In order to compare processor R with processor V, we may compute the confidence intervals for $\alpha_1 - \alpha_2$, using the formula for $\Sigma h_j\alpha_j$. In this case,

$h_1 = 1$, $h_2 = -1$, $h_3 = 0$ (and we verify that $\sum h_j = 0$):

Mean value of $\alpha_1 - \alpha_2 = \bar{y}_{.1} - \bar{y}_{.2} = 174.4 - 163.2 = 11.2$

Standard deviation of $\alpha_1 - \alpha_2 = \dfrac{s_e}{\sqrt{\sum h_j^2 / ar)}} = \dfrac{88.7}{\sqrt{\frac{2}{15}}} = 56.1$

90% Confidence interval for $\alpha_1 - \alpha_2 = 11.2 \mp (1.782)(56.1)$

$$= (-88.7, 111.1)$$

The confidence interval for $\alpha_1 - \alpha_2$ includes zero, and therefore, we cannot confidently state that one is superior to the other. Similarly,

90% Confidence interval for $\alpha_1 - \alpha_3 = (174.4 - 225.4) \mp (1.782)(56.1)$

$$= (-150.9, 48.9)$$

90% Confidence interval for $\alpha_2 - \alpha_3 = (163.2 - 225.4) \mp (1.782)(56.1)$

$$= (-162.1, 37.7)$$

In both cases, the confidence intervals include zero, and therefore, any one processor is not superior to another. These conclusions based on $\alpha_i - \alpha_j$ are actually not surprising since the confidence intervals for α_j's have already shown that none of the processors are significantly different from an average processor. □

20.8 UNEQUAL SAMPLE SIZES

In the analysis presented so far we assumed that we have the same number of observations r at each of a levels of the factor. If the number of observations is different at different levels, the analysis has to be modified only slightly. The steps are essentially the same as discussed so far in this chapter. The modifications are described briefly here.

The model is still

$$y_{ij} = \mu + \alpha_j + e_{ij}$$

The effects α_j are defined so that

$$\sum_{j=1}^{a} r_j \alpha_j = 0$$

Here, r_j is the number of observations at the jth level. The expressions for the effects and their standard deviations are listed in Table 20.6. In the table, N denotes the total number of observations:

$$N = \sum_{j=1}^{a} r_j$$

TABLE 20.6 **Parameter Estimation from One-Factor Experiments with Unequal Sample Sizes**

Parameter	Estimate	Variance
μ	$\overline{y}_{..}$	s_e^2/N
α_j	$\overline{y}_{.j} - \overline{y}_{..}$	$s_e^2(N - r_j)/(N r_j)$
$\mu + \alpha_j$	$\overline{y}_{.j}$	s_e^2/r_j
$\sum h_j \alpha_j, \sum h_j = 0$	$h_j \overline{y}_{.j}$	$s_e^2 \sum_{j=1}^{a}(h_j^2/r_j)$
s_e^2	$\sum e_{ij}^2/(N - a)$	

Degrees of freedom for errors $= N - a$

TABLE 20.7 **ANOVA Table for One-Factor Experiments with Unequal Sample Sizes**

Compo-nent	Sum of Squares	Percentage of Variation	Degrees of Freedom	Mean Square	F-Computed	F-Table
y	$SSY = \sum y_{ij}^2$		N			
$\overline{y}_{..}$	$SS0 = N\mu^2$		1			
$y - \overline{y}_{..}$	$SST = SSY - SS0$	100	$N - 1$			
A	$SSA = \sum_{j=1}^{a} r_j \alpha_j^2$	$100\left(\dfrac{SSA}{SST}\right)$	$a - 1$	$MSA = \dfrac{SSA}{a-1}$	$\dfrac{MSA}{MSE}$	$F_{[1-\alpha;\ a-1,N-a]}$
e	$SSE = SST - SSA$	$100\left(\dfrac{SSE}{SST}\right)$	$N - a$	$MSE = \dfrac{SSE}{N-a}$		

$$s_e = \sqrt{MSE}$$

The ANOVA is shown in Table 20.7. It is easy to verify that if all sample sizes are indeed equal, so that $r_j = r$ for all j, the analysis does reduce to that for equal sample sizes.

Example 20.7 Consider again the code size comparison study of Example 20.1. Suppose after the measurements have been completed, it is discovered that three of the observations had not been done correctly and their observations should not be used in the analysis. Of the three incorrect observations, suppose one is for system V and two are for system Z. This is now a case of single-factor design with unequal sample sizes. The resulting data and its analysis is shown in Table 20.8. Column sums, obtained by adding all available observations in each column, are divided by the number of observations in that column to produce the column mean. The grand mean is 172.25 and is obtained by dividing the grand sum (2067, the total of column sums) by 12, which is the total number of observations. The column effects are 2.15, 13.75, and −21.92. A breakdown of the observations into

TABLE 20.8   Code Size Comparison Data with
Unequal Sample Sizes

	R	V	Z
	144	101	130
	120	144	180
	176	211	141
	288	288	
	144		
Column sum	872	744	451
Column mean	174.40	186.00	150.33
Column effect	2.15	13.75	−21.92

components corresponding to the grand mean, column effects, and residual
terms of the model is as follows:

$$
\begin{bmatrix}
144 & 101 & 130 \\
120 & 144 & 180 \\
176 & 211 & 141 \\
288 & 288 & \\
144 & &
\end{bmatrix}
=
\begin{bmatrix}
172.25 & 172.25 & 172.25 \\
172.25 & 172.25 & 172.25 \\
172.25 & 172.25 & 172.25 \\
172.25 & 172.25 & \\
172.25 & &
\end{bmatrix}
+
\begin{bmatrix}
2.15 & 13.75 & -21.92 \\
2.15 & 13.75 & -21.92 \\
2.15 & 13.75 & -21.92 \\
2.15 & 13.75 & \\
2.15 & &
\end{bmatrix}
$$

$$
+
\begin{bmatrix}
-30.40 & -85.00 & -20.33 \\
-54.40 & -42.00 & 29.67 \\
1.60 & 25.00 & -9.33 \\
113.60 & 102.00 & \\
-30.40 & &
\end{bmatrix}
$$

The sums of squares, obtained by squaring and adding the available
terms in each array, are

$$\text{SSY} = \sum y_{ij}^2 = 397{,}375$$

$$\text{SS0} = N\mu^2 = 356{,}040.75$$

$$\text{SSA} = 5\alpha_1^2 + 4\alpha_2^2 + 3\alpha_3^2 = 2220.38$$

$$\text{SSE} = (-30.40)^2 + (-54.40)^2 + \cdots + (-9.33)^2 = 39{,}113.87$$

$$\text{SST} = \text{SSY} - \text{SS0} = 41{,}334.25$$

By counting the number of independent terms in each array, the degrees of

TABLE 20.9 ANOVA Table for the Code Size Comparison Data

Component	Sum of Squares	Percentage of Variation	Degrees of Freedom	Mean Square	F-Computed	F-Table
y	397,375.00					
$\bar{y}_{..}$	356,040.75					
$y - \bar{y}_{..}$	41,334.25	100.00	11			
A	2,220.38	5.37	2	1110.19	0.26	3.01
Errors	39,113.87	94.63	9	4345.99		

$$s_e = \sqrt{\text{MSE}} = \sqrt{4345.99} = 65.92$$

freedom corresponding to various sums of square are

$$SSY = SS0 + SSA + SSE$$
$$N = 1 + (a-1) + N - a$$
$$12 = 1 + 2 + 9$$

The ANOVA is shown in Table 20.9. Notice that the variation due to processors is insignificant as compared to that due to modeling errors. Confidence intervals for processor effects can be obtained after computing their standard deviations using expressions given in Table 20.6. To understand how these expressions are derived, consider the effect of processor Z. Since,

$$\alpha_3 = \bar{y}_{.3} - \bar{y}_{..}$$
$$= \tfrac{1}{3}(y_{13} + y_{23} + y_{33}) - \tfrac{1}{12}(y_{11} + y_{21} + \cdots + y_{32} + y_{42} + y_{13} + y_{23} + y_{33})$$
$$= \left(\tfrac{1}{3} - \tfrac{1}{12}\right)(y_{13} + y_{23} + y_{33}) - \tfrac{1}{12}(y_{11} + y_{21} + \cdots + y_{32} + y_{42})$$
$$= \tfrac{1}{4}(y_{13} + y_{23} + y_{33}) - \tfrac{1}{12}(y_{11} + y_{21} + \cdots + y_{32} + y_{42})$$

The error in α_3 is the weighted sum of errors in the observations on the right-hand side of the preceding equation:

$$e_{\alpha_3} = \tfrac{1}{4}(e_{13} + e_{23} + e_{33}) - \tfrac{1}{12}(e_{11} + e_{21} + \cdots + e_{32} + e_{42})$$

Since e_{ij}'s are normally distributed with zero mean and an estimated variance of s_e^2, the variance of e_{α_3} (and hence that of α_3) is

$$s_{\alpha_3}^2 = \frac{1}{4^2} \times 3s_e^2 + \frac{1}{12^2} \times 9s_e^2$$
$$= 1086.36$$

It is easy to verify that the value computed here is the same as that obtained from the expression in Table 20.6. □

The key results related to the analysis of one-factor experiments are summarized in Box 20.1.

Box 20.1   Analysis of One-Factor Experiments

1. Model: $y_{ij} = \mu + \alpha_j + e_{ij}$; the effects are computed so that $\sum_{j=1}^{a} \alpha_j = 0$.

2. Effects: $\mu = \overline{y}_{..} = \sum_{j=1}^{a} \sum_{i=1}^{r} y_{ij}$
   $\alpha_j = \overline{y}_{.j} - \overline{y}_{..} = \sum_{i=1}^{r} y_{ij} - \overline{y}_{..}, \; j = 1, 2, \ldots, a$

3. Allocation of variation: SSE can be calculated after computing other terms below:

$$\sum_{ij} y_{ij}^2 = ar\mu^2 + r\sum_{j} \alpha_j^2 + \sum_{ijk} e_{ij}^2$$

$$\text{SSY} = \text{SS0} + \text{SSA} + \text{SSE}$$

4. Degrees of freedom: SSY = SS0 + SSA + SSE

$$ar = 1 + (a-1) + a(r-1)$$

5. Mean squares: MSA = SSA/(a − 1); MSE = SSE/[a(r − 1)]

6. Analysis of variance: MSA/MSE should be greater than $F_{[1-\alpha; a-1, a(r-1)]}$.

7. Standard deviation of errors: $s_e = \sqrt{\text{MSE}}$

8. Standard deviation of parameters: $s_\mu^2 = s_e^2/ar$; $s_{\alpha_j}^2 = s_e^2(a-1)/ar$

9. Contrast of effects $\sum_{j=1}^{a} h_j \alpha_j$, where $\sum_{j=1}^{a} h_j = 0$:

$$\text{Mean} = \sum_{j=1}^{a} h_j \overline{y}_{.j}; \quad \text{Variance} = \sum_{j=1}^{a} s_e^2 h_j^2/ar$$

10. All confidence intervals are computed using $t_{[1-\alpha/2; a(r-1)]}$.

11. Model assumptions:

   (a) Errors are IID normal variates with zero mean.
   (b) Errors have the same variance for all factor levels.
   (c) The effect of the factor and errors are additive.

12. Visual tests:

   (a) The scatter plot of errors versus predicted responses should not have any trend.
   (b) The normal quantile-quantile plot of errors should be linear.
   (c) Spread of y values for all levels of the factor should be comparable.

If any test fails or if the ratio y_{max}/y_{min} is large, multiplicative models or transformations should be investigated.

EXERCISE

20.1 For a single-factor design, suppose we want to write an expression for α_j in terms of y_{ij}'s:

$$\alpha_j = a_{11j}y_{11} + a_{12j}y_{12} + \cdots + a_{raj}y_{ra}$$

What are the values of the $a_{..j}$'s? From the preceding expression, the error in α_j is seen to be

$$e_{\alpha_j} = a_{11j}e_{11} + a_{12j}e_{12} + \cdots + a_{raj}e_{ra}$$

Assuming errors e_{ij} are normally distributed with zero mean and variance σ_e^2, write an expression for the variance of e_{α_j}. Verify that your answer matches that in Table 20.5.

CHAPTER 21

TWO-FACTOR FULL FACTORIAL DESIGN WITHOUT REPLICATIONS

*No amount of experimentation can ever prove me right;
a single experiment can prove me wrong.*
—Albert Einstein

A two-factor design is used when there are two parameters that are carefully controlled and varied to study their impact on the performance. For example, one would use a two-factor design to compare several processors using several workloads. In this case, processors are one factor and the workloads are another. In a full factorial design all combinations of processors and workloads will be experimented with. Another example of application of two-factor design is that of determining two configuration parameters, such as cache and memory sizes, number of disk drives and number of processors, and so on. It is assumed that the factors are categorical or they are being treated as such by the analyst. If the factors are quantitative, a regression model may be used instead.

A full factorial design with two factors A and B having a and b levels requires ab experiments. In this chapter, we consider the case where each experiment is conducted only once. The design with replications will be considered in Chapter 22.

Most of the concepts presented in this chapter are extensions of those presented earlier in Chapter 20 on one-factor designs. It is assumed that you have already read that chapter.

21.1 MODEL

The model for a two-factor design without replications is

$$y_{ij} = \mu + \alpha_j + \beta_i + e_{ij}$$

Here, y_{ij} is the observation in the experiment with the first factor A being at level j and the second factor B being at level i, μ is the mean response, α_j is the effect of factor A at level j, β_i is the effect of factor B at level i, and e_{ij} is the error term. The effects α_j and β_i are computed so that their sums are zero:

$$\sum \alpha_j = 0$$

$$\sum \beta_i = 0$$

Notice that it is assumed that the effects of the two factors add and the errors are additive. An alternative to these assumptions will be discussed later in Section 21.7.

21.2 COMPUTATION OF EFFECTS

The procedure to develop expressions for effects is similar to that used earlier in Section 20.2 for one-factor design. The observations are assumed to be arranged in a two-dimensional matrix of b rows and a columns such that the (i, j)th entry y_{ij} corresponds to the response in the experiment in which factor A is at level j and factor B is at level i. In other words, the columns correspond to the levels of A and rows correspond to levels of the factor B.

The values of model parameters μ, α_j's, and β_i's are computed such that the error has a zero mean. This means that the sum of error terms along each column and along each row is zero.

Averaging the jth column produces

$$\bar{y}_{.j} = \mu + \alpha_j + \frac{1}{b}\sum_i \beta_i + \frac{1}{b}\sum_i e_{ij}$$

Since the last two terms are zero, we have

$$\bar{y}_{.j} = \mu + \alpha_j$$

Similarly, averaging along rows produces

$$\bar{y}_{i.} = \mu + \beta_i$$

Averaging all observations produces

$$\bar{y}_{..} = \mu$$

TABLE 21.1 Measured Processor Times for the Cache
Comparison Study

Workload	Two Caches	One Cache	No Cache
ASM	54.0	55.0	106.0
TECO	60.0	60.0	123.0
SIEVE	43.0	43.0	120.0
DHRYSTONE	49.0	52.0	111.0
SORT	49.0	50.0	108.0

Thus, the estimates of the model parameters are

$$\mu = \overline{y}_{..}$$

$$\alpha_j = \overline{y}_{.j} - \overline{y}_{..}$$

$$\beta_i = \overline{y}_{i.} - \overline{y}_{..}$$

Computation of parameters can be easily carried out using a tabular arrangement of data as illustrated by the following example.

Example 21.1 In a study to compare three different cache choices, the processor times to execute five different workloads was measured on three different configurations of a processor. The three configurations differed only in their cache designs. The three cache options were to use two set associative caches, one set associative cache, or no cache. The measured times in milliseconds are shown in Table 21.1. The analysis to compute the effects of the caches and workloads is shown in Table 21.2. For each row (or column), we compute the mean of observations in that row (or column). Overall sum and means are also computed. The difference between a row (or column) mean and overall mean gives the row (or column) effect.

The results of the analysis are interpreted as follows. An average workload on an average processor requires 72.2 milliseconds of processor time.

TABLE 21.2 Computation of Effects for the Cache Comparison Study

Workload	Two Caches	One Cache	No Cache	Row Sum	Row Mean	Row Effect
ASM	54.0	55.0	106.0	215.0	71.7	−0.5
TECO	60.0	60.0	123.0	243.0	81.0	8.8
SIEVE	43.0	43.0	120.0	206.0	68.7	−3.5
DHRYSTONE	49.0	52.0	111.0	212.0	70.7	−1.5
SORT	49.0	50.0	108.0	207.0	69.0	−3.2
Column sum	255.0	260.0	568.0	1083.0		
Column mean	51.0	52.0	113.6		72.2	
Column effect	−21.2	−20.2	41.4			

The time with two caches is 21.2 milliseconds lower than that on an average processor, and the time with one cache is 20.2 milliseconds lower than that on an average processor. The time without a cache is 41.4 milliseconds higher than the average. This is equivalent to saying that the mean difference between a two-cache processor and a one-cache processor is 1 millisecond. Similarly, the difference between a one-cache processor and a no-cache processor is $41.4 - 20.2$, or 21.2, milliseconds.

The workloads also affect the processor time required. An average workload on an average processor takes 72.2 milliseconds. The ASM workload takes 0.5 millisecond less than the average. TECO takes 8.8 milliseconds higher than the average, and so on. □

21.3 ESTIMATING EXPERIMENTAL ERRORS

Having computed the model parameters, the estimated response in the (i, j)th experiment is given by

$$\hat{y}_{ij} = \mu + \alpha_j + \beta_i$$

The difference between the estimated response and the measured response y_{ij} is attributed to experimental errors. In other words,

$$e_{ij} = y_{ij} - \hat{y}_{ij} = y_{ij} - \mu - \alpha_j - \beta_i$$

The variance of errors can be estimated from the Sum of Squared Errors (SSE):

$$\text{SSE} = \sum_{i=1}^{b} \sum_{j=1}^{a} e_{ij}^2$$

Example 21.2 For the cache comparison study of Example 21.1, the errors in each of the 15 observations are shown in Table 21.3. To see how the entries are computed, consider the first experiment (with ASM workload on a two-cache processor). The estimated processor time is

$$\hat{y}_{11} = \mu + \alpha_1 + \beta_1 = 72.2 - 21.2 - 0.5 = 50.5$$

TABLE 21.3 Error Computation for the Cache Comparison Study

Workload	Two Caches	One Cache	No Cache
ASM	3.5	3.5	−7.1
TECO	0.2	−0.8	0.6
SIEVE	−4.5	−5.5	9.9
DHRYSTONE	−0.5	1.5	−1.1
SORT	1.2	1.2	−2.4

The measured processor time is 54 milliseconds. The difference $54 - 50.5 = 3.5$ is the error. The sum of squared errors is

$$\text{SSE} = (3.5)^2 + (0.2)^2 + \cdots + (-2.4)^2 = 2368.00 \qquad \square$$

21.4 ALLOCATION OF VARIATION

As in the case of one-factor designs and in $2^2 r$ designs, the total variation of y in a two-factor design can be allocated to the two factors and to the experimental errors. To do so, we square both sides of the model equation and add across all observations. The cross-product terms cancel, and we obtain

$$\sum_{ij} y_{ij}^2 = ab\mu^2 + b\sum_{j} \alpha_j^2 + a\sum_{i} \beta_i^2 + \sum_{ij} e_{ij}^2$$
$$\text{SSY} \; = \; \text{SS0} + \; \text{SSA} \; + \; \text{SSB} \; + \; \text{SSE}$$

where various sums of squares have been appropriately placed below their corresponding terms. The total variation (SST), as before, is

$$\text{SST} = \text{SSY} - \text{SS0} = \text{SSA} + \text{SSB} + \text{SSE}$$

Thus, the total variation can be divided into parts explained by factors A and B and an unexplained part due to experimental errors. This equation can also be used to compute SSE, since the other sums can be easily computed. The percentage of variation explained by a factor can be used to measure the importance of the factor.

Example 21.3 For the cache comparison study of Example 21.1, the sums of squares are

$$\text{SSY} = \sum_{ij} y_{ij}^2 = 91{,}595$$

$$\text{SS0} = ab\mu^2 = 3 \times 5 \times (72.2)^2 = 78{,}192.59$$

$$\text{SSA} = b\sum_{j} \alpha_j^2 = 5 \times [(-21.2)^2 + (-20.2)^2 + (41.4)^2] = 12{,}857.20$$

$$\text{SSB} = a\sum_{i} \beta_i^2 = 3 \times [(-0.5)^2 + (8.8)^2 + (-3.5)^2 + (-1.5)^2 + (3.2)^2]$$

$$= 308.40$$

$$\text{SST} = \text{SSY} - \text{SS0} = 91{,}595 - 78{,}192.59 = 13{,}402.41$$

$$\text{SSE} = \text{SST} - \text{SSA} - \text{SSB} = 13{,}402.41 - 12{,}857.20 - 308.40 = 236.80$$

The percentage of variation explained by the caches is

$$100 \times \frac{\text{SSA}}{\text{SST}} = 100 \times \frac{12{,}857.20}{13{,}402.41} = 95.9\%$$

The percentage of variation due to workloads is

$$100 \times \frac{\text{SSB}}{\text{SST}} = 100 \times \frac{308.40}{13,402.41} = 2.3\%$$

The unexplained variation is

$$100 \times \frac{\text{SSE}}{\text{SST}} = 100 \times \frac{236.80}{13,402.41} = 1.8\%$$

Looking at these percentages, we conclude that the choice of caches is an important parameter in the processor design. $\square$

21.5 ANALYSIS OF VARIANCE

To statistically test the significance of a factor, we divide the sum of squares by their corresponding degrees of freedom to get mean squares. The degrees of freedoms (DF) for various sums are as follows:

$$\text{SSY} = \text{SS0} + \text{SSA} + \text{SSB} + \text{SSE}$$
$$ab = 1 + (a-1) + (b-1) + (a-1)(b-1)$$

The errors have only $(a-1)(b-1)$ degrees of freedom since only $(a-1)(b-1)$ of the ab errors can be independently chosen. This is because the errors in each column should add to zero. Similarly, errors in each row should also add to zero. Once the errors in the first $a-1$ columns and first $b-1$ rows have been chosen, those in the last column and the last row can be computed using the constraints. The degrees of freedom for other sums can be similarly justified.

The mean squares are obtained by dividing the sum of squares by their corresponding degrees of freedom:

$$\text{MSA} = \frac{\text{SSA}}{a-1}$$
$$\text{MSB} = \frac{\text{SSB}}{b-1}$$
$$\text{MSE} = \frac{\text{SSE}}{(a-1)(b-1)}$$

The F-ratio to test the significance of the factor A is

$$F_A = \frac{\text{MSA}}{\text{MSE}}$$

This ratio has an F distribution with $a-1$ numerator degrees of freedom and $(a-1)(b-1)$ denominator degrees of freedom. Thus, the factor A is considered significant at level α if the computed ratio is more than $F_{[1-\alpha;a-1,(a-1)(b-1)]}$ obtained from the table of quantiles of F-variates (Tables A.6 to A.8 in the Appendix).

TABLE 21.4   ANOVA Table for Two Factors without Replications

Compo-nent	Sum of Squares	Percentage of Variation	Degrees of Freedom	Mean Square	F-Computed	F-Table
y	$\text{SSY} = \sum y_{ij}^2$		ab			
$\bar{y}_{..}$	$\text{SS0} = ab\mu^2$		1			
$y - \bar{y}_{..}$	$\text{SST} = \text{SSY} - \text{SS0}$	100	$ab - 1$			
A	$\text{SSA} = b\sum \alpha_j^2$	$100\left(\dfrac{\text{SSA}}{\text{SST}}\right)$	$a - 1$	$\text{MSA} = \dfrac{\text{SSA}}{a-1}$	$\dfrac{\text{MSA}}{\text{MSE}}$	$F_{[1-\alpha, a-1, (a-1)(b-1)]}$
B	$\text{SSB} = a\sum \beta_i^2$	$100\left(\dfrac{\text{SSB}}{\text{SST}}\right)$	$b - 1$	$\text{MSB} = \dfrac{\text{SSB}}{b-1}$	$\dfrac{\text{MSB}}{\text{MSE}}$	$F_{[1-\alpha, b-1, (a-1)(b-1)]}$
e	$\text{SSE} =$ $\text{SST} - (\text{SSA} + \text{SSB})$	$100\left(\dfrac{\text{SSE}}{\text{SST}}\right)$	$(a-1)$ $(b-1)$	$\text{MSE} = \dfrac{\text{SSE}}{(a-1)(b-1)}$		

$$s_e = \sqrt{\text{MSE}}$$

The F-ratio for factor B, similarly, is

$$F_B = \frac{\text{MSB}}{\text{MSE}}$$

A convenient tabular arrangement to conduct Analysis Of Variance (ANOVA) for a two factor design without replications is shown in Table 21.4.

Example 21.4   The ANOVA for the cache comparison study of Example 21.1 is shown in Table 21.5. Notice that the F-ratio for caches is more than that obtained from the table. This reconfirms our conclusion that the choice of the cache would make a significant difference in the performance of the processor. The F-ratio for the workloads is less than that obtained from the table. Thus, in this set of experiments, the workloads did not make any significant impact on the performance. Actually, this is a real case study

TABLE 21.5   ANOVA Table for the Cache Comparison Study

Compo-nent	Sum of Squares	Percentage of Variation	Degrees of Freedom	Mean Square	F-Computed	F-Table
y	91,595.00					
$\bar{y}_{..}$	78,192.59					
$y - \bar{y}_{..}$	13,402.41	100.0	14			
Caches	12,857.20	95.9	2	6428.60	217.2	3.1
Workloads	308.40	2.3	4	77.10	2.6	2.8
Errors	236.80	1.8	8	29.60		

$$s_e = \sqrt{\text{MSE}} = \sqrt{29.60} = 5.44$$

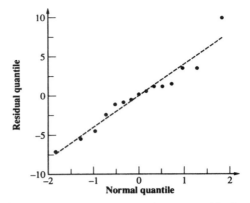

FIGURE 21.1 Normal quantile-quantile plot for the residuals of the cache design study.

in which the experimenter had taken precautions in choosing workloads that had comparable run times. This helped ensure that the effect of caches, if any, is not overshadowed by that due to differences in the workloads. This is an important point that is commonly missed by inexperienced analysts.

A normal quantile-quantile plot for residuals is shown in Figure 21.1. The plot is approximately linear, thereby verifying the applicability of the normality assumption in this case.

In order to check the homogeneity of the error variance, a scatter plot of residuals versus predicted response $\hat{y}$ was prepared and is shown in Figure 21.2. This plot is not very satisfactory since the spread in residuals is high at higher values of the response.   □

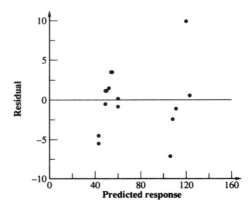

FIGURE 21.2 Plot of the residuals versus predicted response for the cache design study.

21.6   CONFIDENCE INTERVALS FOR EFFECTS

The expressions for variance of the model parameters are listed in Table 21.6. These can be derived in a manner similar to that for one-factor design (Exercise 20.1). The confidence intervals for the effects can be computed using t-values read at $(a - 1)(b - 1)$ degrees of freedom, which again is the degrees of freedom associated with errors. In the table, the estimates and variance for linear combination of effects, such as $\mu + \alpha_j$ and $\mu + \alpha_j + \beta_i$, are also shown along with those for contrasts of effects. The contrast formulas can be used to compute confidence intervals for differences such as $\alpha_1 - \alpha_2$ to see if there is a significant difference between the two levels of factor A.

TABLE 21.6   Parameter Estimation for Two Factors without Replications

Parameter	Estimate	Variance
μ	$\overline{y}_{..}$	s_e^2/ab
α_j	$\overline{y}_{.j} - \overline{y}_{..}$	$s_e^2(a - 1)/ab$
$\mu + \alpha_j$	$\overline{y}_{.j}$	s_e^2/b
β_i	$\overline{y}_{i.} - \overline{y}_{..}$	$s_e^2(b - 1)/ab$
$\mu + \alpha_j + \beta_i$	$\overline{y}_{.j} + \overline{y}_{i.} - \overline{y}_{..}$	$s_e^2(a + b - 1)/(ab)$
$\sum_{j=1}^a h_j \alpha_j,\ \sum_{j=1}^a h_j = 0$	$\sum_{j=1}^a h_j \overline{y}_{.j}$	$s_e^2 \sum_{j=1}^a h_j^2/b$
$\sum_{i=1}^b h_i \beta_i,\ \sum_{i=1}^b h_i = 0$	$\sum_{i=1}^b h_i \overline{y}_{i.}$	$s_e^2 \sum_{i=1}^b h_i^2/a$
s_e^2	$\left(\sum_{j=1}^a \sum_{i=1}^b e_{ij}^2\right) / [(a - 1)(b - 1)]$	

Degrees of freedom for errors $= (a - 1)(b - 1)$

Example 21.5   To compute the confidence intervals for the effects in the cache comparison study, we first compute the standard deviation of errors:

$$s_e = \sqrt{\text{MSE}} = \sqrt{29.60} = 5.4$$

The standard deviation of the grand mean μ is

$$s_\mu = s_e/\sqrt{ab} = 5.4/\sqrt{15} = 1.4$$

The standard deviation of α_j's is

$$s_{\alpha_j} = s_e \sqrt{(a - 1)/ab} = 5.4\sqrt{\tfrac{2}{15}} = 2.8$$

The standard deviation of β_i's is

$$s_{\beta_i} = s_e \sqrt{(b - 1)/ab} = 5.4\sqrt{\tfrac{4}{15}} = 2.0$$

The degrees of freedom for the errors are $(a - 1)(b - 1) = 8$. For 90% confidence interval, the $t_{[0.95;8]}$ read from Table A.4 in the Appendix is 1.86.

TABLE 21.7   Confidence Intervals for Effects in Cache Comparison Study

Parameter	Mean Effect	Standard Deviation	Confidence Interval
μ	72.2	1.4	(69.6, 74.8)
Caches			
Two caches	−21.2	2.8	(−24.9, −17.5)
One cache	−20.2	2.8	(−23.9, −16.5)
No cache	41.4	2.8	(37.7, 45.1)
Workloads			
ASM	−0.5	2.0	(−5.8, 4.7)[a]
TECO	8.8	2.0	(3.6, 14.0)
SIEVE	−3.5	2.0	(−8.8, 1.7)[a]
DHRYSTONE	−1.5	2.0	(−6.8, 3.7)[a]
SORT	−3.2	2.0	(−8.4, 2.0)[a]

[a] Not significant.

The confidence interval for the grand mean is

$$72.2 \mp 1.86 \times 1.4 = 72.2 \mp 2.6 = (69.6, 74.8)$$

Confidence intervals for other parameters can be similarly calculated and are shown in Table 21.7. From the table we see that all three cache alternatives are significantly different from the average. All workloads, except TECO, are similar to the average and hence to each other.

Using the formula for contrasts, we can also compare the caching alternatives in pairs. The confidence intervals for the differences of effects are shown in Table 21.8. From this table, we see that two-cache and one-cache alternatives are both significantly better than a no-cache alternative. However, there is no significant difference between two-cache and one-cache alternatives.   □

TABLE 21.8   Confidence Intervals for Differences of Cache Effects

	Two Caches	One Cache	No Cache
Two caches		(−7.4, 5.4)[a]	(−69.0, −56.2)
One cache			(−68.0, −55.2)

[a] Not significant.

Case Study 21.1   This case study is an extension of the cache comparison study that we presented in several preceding examples. In that study, it was concluded that two-cache and single-cache alternatives are not significantly different and so using one cache was the only cost-effective alternative. However, detailed investigation showed that each program that

TABLE 21.9   Processor Time for Cache Comparison Study in Multiprocess Environment

Workload	Two Caches	One Cache	No Cache
ASM5	231	262	489
TECO5	300	314	620
SIEVE5	213	214	604
DHRYSTONE5	245	263	564
ALL	229	242	551

was used as the workload could easily fit into one set of cache. In the next phase of the project, therefore, the measurements were repeated in a multiprocess environment. Five jobs were executed in parallel. The new measurements are shown in Table 21.9. The first four workloads are five processes of the same type. The last workload, labeled "ALL," consists of running five different programs ASM, TECO, SIEVE, DHRYSTONE, and SORT in parallel. The confidence intervals for differences of effects are shown in Table 21.10. Notice that even for this case the two caches do not produce statistically better performance.   □

TABLE 21.10   Confidence Intervals for Differences for Cache Comparison Study in Multiprocess Environment

	Two Caches	One Cache	No Cache
Two caches	—	$(-51.6, \ 20.8)^a$	$(-358.2, \ -285.8)$
One cache	—	—	$(-342.8, \ -270.4)$

^{a} Not significant.

21.7   MULTIPLICATIVE MODELS FOR TWO-FACTOR EXPERIMENTS

The multiplicative models discussed earlier in Section 18.8 on 2^2r designs can also be used in the analysis of two-factor experiments. In the analysis presented so far, the following additive model was assumed:

$$y_i = \mu + \alpha_j + \beta_i + e_{ij}$$

This model assumes that the effect of the factors are additive. It was argued in Section 18.8 that in many cases such as those involving processors and workloads, the effects are multiplicative rather than additive. In such cases, the log of the response follows an additive model. A need for logarithmic transformation is also indicated if the spread in the residuals increases with the mean response.

The following example illustrates a case where the multiplicative model (or log transformation) is useful.

Case Study 21.2   Two approaches to design high-speed processors are to use parallelism in time and parallelism in space. Parallelism in time is achieved by pipelining stages of execution in a single processor while parallelism in space is obtained by having several execution units that operate simultaneously. In this case study, to compare the two approaches, implementations of two architectures called Spectrum and Scheme86 were compared using several workloads. Spectrum is a Reduced Instruction Set Computer (RISC) architecture. One of its implementations, which is sold commercially as the HP9000/840 computer, is implemented with three pipelined stages. Each stage has a latency of 125 nanoseconds. The Scheme86 architecture uses a long instruction word with several independent execution units. It was designed at the Artificial Intelligence Laboratory at the Massachusetts Institute of Technology. A simulation model capable of executing any specified workloads on machines of the two architectures was used to compare their performance during design stages of Scheme86. Two different processor cycle times (125 and 62.5 nanoseconds) were used for Spectrum. They were compared with a Scheme86 implementation with 150-nanosecond technology. Execution times of the three implementations for five different workloads are listed in Table 21.11.

An analysis using an additive model (see Exercise 21.1) would conclude that there is no significant difference among the processors. This is clearly counterintuitive since it is easily seen from the data that Scheme86 is roughly two to three times faster than Spectrum125 for all workloads. (This was expected since Scheme86 has three execution units). Also, notice that Spectrum62.5 is twice as fast as Spectrum125. The reason for the misleading conclusion is that the right model for this problem is a multiplicative model. Also, statistically it is not appropriate to add observations that vary as much as those shown in Table 21.11. The ratio of y_{max}/y_{min} is over three orders of magnitude.

To analyze this data, we take a log of the execution times. Computation of effects using the transformed data is shown in Table 21.12 and the ANOVA is shown in Table 21.13. Notice that the effect of the processors is significant. The model explains 99.9% of the variation as compared to 88% in the additive model.

The confidence intervals for the difference in processor effects are listed in Table 21.14. We see that Scheme86 and Spectrum62.5 are of compara-

TABLE 21.11   Execution Times for the Scheme versus Spectrum Study

Workload	Scheme86	Spectrum125	Spectrum62.5
Garbage Collection	39.97	99.06	56.24
Pattern Match	0.958	1.672	1.252
Bignum Addition	0.01910	0.03175	0.01844
Bignum Multiplication	0.256	0.423	0.236
Fast Fourier Transform (1024)	10.21	20.28	10.14

TABLE 21.12   Computation of Effects for the Scheme versus Spectrum Study

Workload	Scheme 86	Spectrum 125	Spectrum 62.5	Row Sum	Row Mean	Row Effect
Garbage Collection	1.6017	1.9959	1.7500	5.3477	1.7826	1.6212
Pattern Match	−0.0186	0.2232	0.0976	0.3022	0.1007	−0.0607
Bignum Addition	−1.7212	−1.4949	−1.7447	−4.9608	−1.6536	−1.8150
Bignum Multiplication	−0.5918	−0.3737	−0.6271	−1.5925	−0.5308	−0.6922
Fast Fourier Transform (1024)	1.0090	1.3092	1.0060	3.3243	1.1081	0.9467
Column sum	0.2791	1.6598	0.4819	2.4208		
Column mean	0.0558	0.3320	0.0964		0.1614	
Column effect	−0.1056	0.1706	−0.0650			

TABLE 21.13   ANOVA Table for the Scheme versus Spectrum Study

Component	Sum of Squares	Percentage of Variation	Degrees of Freedom	Mean Square	F-Computed	F-Table
y	22.54					
$\bar{y}_{..}$	0.39					
$y - \bar{y}_{..}$	22.15	100.00	14			
Processors	0.22	1.00	2	0.11	39.29	3.11
Workloads	21.90	98.89	4	5.48	1935.48	2.81
Errors	0.02	0.10	8	0.0025		

$$s_e = \sqrt{\text{MSE}} = \sqrt{0.0025} = 0.05$$

TABLE 21.14   Confidence Intervals for Effect Differences in the Scheme versus Spectrum Study

	Scheme86	Spectrum125	Spectrum62.5
Scheme86		(−0.3387, −0.2136)	(−0.1031, 0.0220)[a]
Spectrum125			(0.1730, 0.2982)

[a] Not significant.

ble speed since the confidence interval of their difference includes a zero. Spectrum125 is significantly slower than the other two processors. On the original scale these intervals can be translated to say that Scheme86's time is 0.4584 to 0.6115 times that of Spectrum125 and 0.7886 to 1.0520 times that of Spectrum62.5. Similarly, the time on the Spectrum125 is 1.4894 to 1.9868 times that on the Spectrum62.5.

A scatter plot of residuals versus predicted response is shown in Figure 21.3. There is no visible trend in the residuals or their spread. A normal

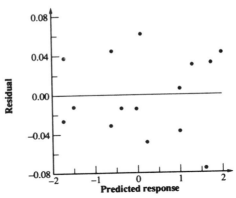

FIGURE 21.3 Plot of the residuals versus predicted response for the Scheme versus Spectrum study.

quantile-quantile plot is shown in Figure 21.4. The assumption of normality appears to be approximately valid.

The main problem with the data is that among the two factors used in the study, differences in the processors account for only 1% of the variation while differences in the workloads account for 99%. In general, such a widely different set of workloads is not recommended unless a large number of workloads is used to cover the range. In Chapter 5, it was pointed out that using a workload that makes a component other than the component under study a bottleneck would lead to the conclusion that the alternatives under study are not different. The problem here is similar. Using a small set of such widely different workloads would generally lead to the conclusion that the components under study are not different. Any set of

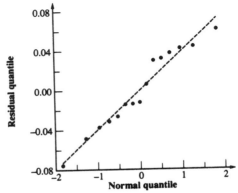

FIGURE 21.4 Normal quantile-quantile plot for the residuals of the Scheme versus Spectrum study.

experiments where primary factors explain more variation than secondary factors is considered a better set. □

A multiplicative model should be used whenever the physical considerations require it. However, the conclusions based on additive and multiplicative models are numerically different only if the numerical range covered by the observations is large. This is because the $\log(x)$ function is linear for small values of x. In the following case study, an explicit attempt was made to keep the range small by suitably scaling the workloads so that the times for all workloads on a processor were comparable.

Case Study 21.3 The elapsed times for five different workloads on four different processors are listed in Table 21.15. The workloads were scaled so that the total number of instructions on different workloads was comparable. From physical considerations it is clear that an additive model should not be used for this problem, but our purpose here is to see the difference between an additive model and a multiplicative model from statistical considerations.

An ANOVA for this data using an additive model is shown in Table 21.16. Notice that the differences in the workloads explains only 1.4% of the variation. Thus, the conclusions regarding processors using this data would be statistically more valid than one using data in which the workloads are

TABLE 21.15 Measured Elasped Times for the Processor Comparison Study

Workload	Processors			
	A	B	C	D
ASM	54	101	111	83
TECO	60	92	110	90
SIEVE	42	121	127	86
DHRYSTONE	49	97	122	81
SORT	52	100	107	82

TABLE 21.16 ANOVA Table for the Processors Comparison Study

Component	Sum of Squares	Percentage of Variation	Degrees of Freedom	Mean Square	F-Computed	F-Table
y	168,653.00					
$\bar{y}_{..}$	156,114.45					
$y - \bar{y}_{..}$	12,538.55	100.0	19			
Processors	11,522.15	91.9	3	3840.72	54.9	2.6
Workloads	176.30	1.4	4	44.07	0.6	2.5
Errors	840.10	6.7	12	70.01		

TABLE 21.17 ANOVA Table for the Processor Comparison Study

Component	Sum of Squares	Percentage of Variation	Degrees of Freedom	Mean Square	F-Computed	F-Table
y	74.56					
$y_{..}$	74.17					
$y - y_{..}$	0.39	100.00	19			
Processors	0.36	93.15	3	0.121	57.55	2.61
Workloads	0.00	0.37	4	0.000	0.17	2.48
Errors	0.03	6.47	12	0.002		

$$s_e = \sqrt{\text{MSE}} = \sqrt{0.002} = 0.05$$

responsible for a large part of the variation. Only 6.7% of the variation is unexplained.

The ANOVA using a multiplicative model is shown in Table 21.17. Processors explain about 93.2% variation, workloads explain only 0.4%, and the residuals account for the remaining 6.5%. Although not shown here, both models pass the visual tests equally well.

Thus, for a statistician looking at the two models, there is not much difference between the two. It is only the physical considerations that demand that a multiplicative model should be used. This is because it is more appropriate to say that processor B takes twice ($10^{\alpha_2 - \alpha_1}$) as much time as processor A than to say that processor B takes 50.7 milliseconds more than processor A. The second statement is valid only for the set of workloads used in the study. The first statement may apply more generally. Thus, simply because a model passes all statistical tests does not mean that it is a good model. It should be valid from the physical considerations as well. In fact, physical validity of the model is required before its statistical validity. □

Case Study 21.4 In an attempt to quantify the performance of the Intel iAPX 432 architecture, 12 different processor-operating system-language-word size combinations were measured on four different workloads. Measured execution times in milliseconds for the 12 systems are listed in Table 21.18. Physical considerations as well as the range of data dictate the necessity for a log transformation. The ANOVA is presented in Table 21.19. Notice that this is a good model since only 0.6% variation is unexplained. However, since the workloads explain a much larger percentage of variation than the systems, the workload selection is poor. The confidence intervals for the log system effects are shown in Figure 21.5. □

The logarithm transformation is just one of numerous other possible transformations. For a discussion of other possible transformations, see Chapter 15.

TABLE 21.18 Measured Execution Times for the Intel iAPX 432 Study

System No.	Processor	Language	Word Size	Workload Execution Times			
				484	Sieve	Puzzle	Acker
1	VAX-11/780	C	32	1.4	250.0	9,400.0	4,600.0
2		Pascal (UNIX)	32	1.6	220.0	11,900.0	7,800.0
3		Pascal (VMS)	32	1.4	259.0	11,530.0	9,850.0
4	68000 (8 MHz)	C	32	4.7	740.0	37,100.0	7,800.0
5		Pascal	16	5.3	810.0	32,470.0	11,480.0
6		Pascal	32	5.8	960.0	32,520.0	12,320.0
7	68000 (16 MHz)	Pascal	16	1.3	196.0	9,180.0	2,750.0
8		Pascal	32	1.5	246.0	9,200.0	3,080.0
9	8086 (5 MHz)	Pascal	16	7.3	764.0	44,000.0	11,100.0
10	432	Ada	16	35.0	3,200.0	350,000.0	260,000.0
11		Ada	16	14.2	3,200.0	165,000.0	260,000.0
12		Ada	32	16.1	3,200.0	180,000.0	260,000.0

Data from Hansen et al. (1982). Reprinted with permission.

TABLE 21.19 ANOVA Table for the Intel iAPX 432 Study

Component	Sum of Squares	Percentage of Variation	Degrees of Freedom	Mean Square	F- Computed	F- Table
y	576.64					
$y_{..}$	449.01					
$y - y_{..}$	127.63	100.0	47			
Workloads	113.01	88.5	3	37.7	1158.5	2.3
Systems	13.55	10.6	11	1.2	37.9	1.8
Errors	1.07	0.8	33	0.03		

$$s_e = \sqrt{\text{MSE}} = \sqrt{0.03} = 0.18$$

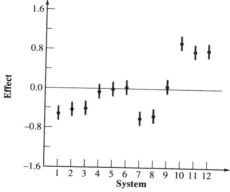

FIGURE 21.5 Confidence intervals for effects in the Intel iAPX 432 study.

21.8 MISSING OBSERVATIONS

If a few of the ab observations are missing in a design without replications, the methodology presented here can still be used. That is, the effects can be computed from the row (column) means and overall mean. Of course, the means should be obtained by dividing the sums by the respective number of observations added. The degrees of freedoms of sums of squares should also be adjusted accordingly. Further, the formulas for standard deviations of effects should be adjusted to reflect the number of observations present in the column or row.

Several other statistical alternatives have been proposed for missing values, and there is some controversy regarding their usefulness. One method, called the replacement method, requires that the missing value be replaced by an estimate $\hat{y}$ such that the residual for the missing experiment is zero. Another method, called the minimum residual variance method, requires that a symbol y be placed in the missing value cell and the SSE be written as a function of y. The value of y that minimizes the SSE is the desired missing value. The problem is that these two methods will result in different estimates of SSA and SSB and the conclusions using the two methods may be different.

Case Study 21.5   In order to quantify the performance gains from RISC architecture, several processors, including a RISC implementation called RISC-I designed at the University of California, Berkeley, were compared in terms of execution times of various benchmarks. The times for 11 different benchmarks on six different computers are listed in Table 21.20.

There are six missing values, which are indicated by a "dash" in the table. To analyze this data, we use a multiplicative model. The log of execution

TABLE 21.20   Measured Data for the RISC Execution Time Study

Workload	RISC-I	68000	Z8002	VAX-11/780	PDP-11/70	C/70
E-String Search	0.46	1.29	0.74	0.60	0.41	1.01
F-Bit Test	0.06	0.29	0.43	0.29	0.37	0.55
H-Linked List	0.10	0.16	0.24	0.12	0.19	0.25
K-Bit Matrix	0.43	1.72	2.24	1.29	1.72	4.00
I-Quick Sort	50.40	206.64	262.08	151.20	181.44	292.32
Ackermann(3,6)	3,200.00	—	8,960.00	5,120.00	5,120.00	—
Recursive Qsort	800.00	—	4,720.00	1,840.00	2,560.00	1,040.00
Puzzle (Subscript)	4,700.00	—	19,740.00	9,400.00	7,520.00	15,980.00
Puzzle (Pointer)	3,200.00	13,440.00	7,360.00	4,160.00	6,400.00	6,720.00
SED (Batch Editor)	5,100.00	—	22,440.00	5,610.00	5,610.00	13,260.00
Towers Hanoi (18)	6,800.00	—	28,560.00	12,240.00	15,640.00	10,880.00

Adapted with permission from Patterson and Sequin (1982).

TABLE 21.21 Computation of Effects for the RISC Execution Time Study

Workload	RISC-I	68000	Z8002	VAX-11/780	PDP-11/70	C/70	Row Sum	Row Mean	Row Effect
E-String Search	−0.34	0.11	−0.13	−0.22	−0.38	0.01	−0.96	−0.16	−2.16
F-Bit Test	−1.22	−0.54	−0.36	−0.54	−0.43	−0.26	−3.36	−0.56	−2.55
H-Linked List	−1.00	−0.80	−0.62	−0.92	−0.72	−0.60	−4.66	−0.78	−2.77
K-Bit Matrix	−0.37	0.24	0.35	0.11	0.24	0.60	1.17	0.19	−1.80
I-Quick Sort	1.70	2.32	2.42	2.18	2.26	2.47	13.34	2.22	0.23
Ackermann(3,6)	3.51	—	3.95	3.71	3.71	—	14.88	3.72	1.72
Recursive Qsort	2.90	—	3.67	3.26	3.41	3.02	16.27	3.25	1.26
Puzzle (Subscript)	3.67	—	4.30	3.97	3.88	4.20	20.02	4.00	2.01
Puzzle (Pointer)	3.51	4.13	3.87	3.62	3.81	3.83	22.75	3.79	1.80
SED (Batch Editor)	3.71	—	4.35	3.75	3.75	4.12	19.68	3.94	1.94
Towers Hanoi (18)	3.83	—	4.46	4.09	4.19	4.04	20.61	4.12	2.13
Column sum	19.90	5.45	26.25	23.01	23.70	21.42	119.73		
Column mean	1.81	0.91	2.39	2.09	2.15	2.14		2.00	
Column effect	−0.19	−1.09	0.39	0.10	0.16	0.15			

times as well as the analysis of effects is shown in Table 21.21. Various column sums are divided by the number of observations in that column to produce column mean. Row means are also similarly obtained. The grand mean is obtained by dividing the grand sum by the total number of observations, which in this case is 60. The column effects are simply the difference between the column means and the grand mean. Similarly, the row effect is the difference between the row mean and the grand mean.

TABLE 21.22 Error Computation in the RISC Execution Time Study

Workload	RISC-I	68000	Z8002	VAX-11/780	PDP-11/70	C/70
E-String Search	0.01	1.36	−0.36	−0.16	−0.38	0.02
F-Bit Test	−0.48	1.11	−0.20	−0.08	−0.03	0.15
H-Linked List	−0.04	1.07	−0.23	−0.24	−0.10	0.03
K-Bit Matrix	−0.37	1.13	−0.24	−0.18	−0.12	0.26
I-Quick Sort	−0.33	1.18	−0.20	−0.14	−0.12	0.10
Ackermann(3,6)	−0.03	—	−0.16	−0.11	−0.17	—
Recursive Qsort	−0.16	—	0.03	−0.08	—	−0.38
Puzzle (Subscript)	−0.15	—	−0.10	−0.13	−0.29	0.05
Puzzle (Pointer)	−0.10	1.42	−0.32	−0.27	−0.15	−0.11
SED (Batch Editor)	−0.04	—	0.02	−0.28	−0.35	0.04
Towers Hanoi (18)	−0.10	—	−0.06	−0.13	−0.09	−0.23

The modeling errors, that is, the differences between the model estimates and the measured values, are listed in Table 21.22. The sum of squared errors is

$$\text{SSE} = \sum_{i,j} e_{ij}^2 = 11.01$$

The errors have $60 - 1 - 5 - 10$, or 44, degrees of freedom since 16 independent parameters (μ, α_j, and β_i) have been computed. Notice that only 5 of 6 of the α_j's are independent. Similarly, only 10 of the 11 β_i's are independent. The mean square error is

$$\text{MSE} = \frac{\text{SSE}}{\nu_e} = \frac{11.01}{44} = 0.25$$

The standard deviation of errors is

$$s_e = \sqrt{\text{MSE}} = \sqrt{0.25} = 0.05$$

The standard deviation of α_j is obtained by expressing it as a weighted sum of the observations. The formula is

$$s_{\alpha_j} = s_e \sqrt{\frac{N - c_j}{N c_j}}$$

where c_j is the number of observations in column c_j. This formula can be derived by expressing α_j as a linear combination of e_{ij}'s and summing the variance of each term. The procedure is similar to that discussed in Section 20.8 on one-factor experiments with unequal sample sizes. Similarly, the standard deviation of the row effects is

$$s_{\beta_i} = s_e \sqrt{\frac{N - r_i}{N r_i}}$$

where r_i is the number of observations in the ith row. The confidence intervals for various processor effects are shown in Figure 21.6. The pairs

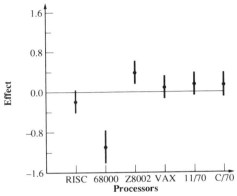

FIGURE 21.6 Confidence intervals for processor effects in the RISC execution time study.

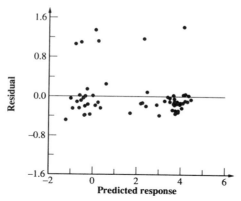

FIGURE 21.7 Plot of the residuals versus predicted response for the RISC execution time study.

that are significantly different from each other can be easily seen from this figure. Notice also that the 68000 processor has a larger confidence interval than other processors since there are fewer observations in its column.

A plot of residuals versus predicted response is shown in Figure 21.7. There are a few large positive errors. From Table 21.22, we notice that almost all large positive errors are in the second column (68000). This shows that the observations in this column do not follow the model. In general, *if a column (or row) has a large number of missing values, it is better to exclude the column. The procedure for missing values should be used only for one or two missing values.*

A normal quantile-quantile plot for the residuals is shown in Figure 21.8. Again, the large positive errors in the 68000 data are responsible for this deviation from normality.

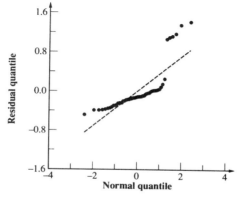

FIGURE 21.8 Normal quantile-quantile plot for the residuals of the RISC execution time study.

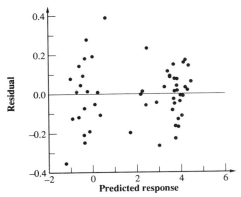

FIGURE 21.9   Plot of the residuals versus predicted response for the RISC execution time study without the 68000.

If we remove the 68000 column, the residual versus predicted response and the normal quantile-quantile plots based on the remaining data (which results in a model with different values of effects) are shown in Figures 21.9 and 21.10. These figures do not have the problems encountered in Figures 21.7 and 21.8.

In this case study, the code sizes for various processors were also measured. These sizes are listed in Table 21.23. Again, one can analyze the data using a multiplicative two-factor model with missing values (see Exercise 21.4). The confidence intervals for log effects of processors are shown in Figure 21.11.   □

The key results related to the analysis of two-factor full factorial designs without replications are summarized in Box 21.1.

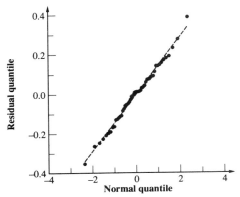

FIGURE 21.10   Normal quantile-quantile plot for the residuals of the RISC execution time study without the 68000.

TABLE 21.23 Measured Data for the RISC Code Size Study

Workload	RISC-I	68000	Z8002	VAX-11/780	PDP-11/70	C/70
E-String Search	140	112	126	98	112	98
F-Bit Test	120	144	180	144	168	120
H-Linked List	176	123	141	211	299	141
K-Bit Matrix	288	317	374	288	374	317
I-Quick Sort	992	694	1,091	893	1,091	893
Ackermann(3,6)	144	—	302	72	86	86
Recursive Qsort	2,736	—	1,368	1,368	1,642	1,642
Puzzle (Subscript)	2,796	2,516	1,398	1,398	1,398	1,678
Puzzle (Pointer)	752	—	602	451	376	376
SED (Batch Editor)	17,720	—	17,720	10,632	8,860	8,860
Towers Hanoi (18)	96	—	240	77	96	67

Adapted with permission from Patterson and Sequin (1982).

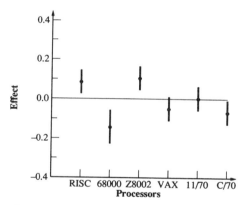

FIGURE 21.11 Confidence intervals for effects in the RISC code size study.

Box 21.1 Analysis of Two-Factor Designs without Replications

1. Model: $y_{ij} = \mu + \alpha_j + \beta_i + e_{ij}$; the effects are computed so that $\sum_{j=1}^{a} \alpha_j = 0$, $\sum_{i=1}^{b} \beta_i = 0$.

2. Effects: $\mu = \overline{y}_{..}$; $\alpha_j = \overline{y}_{.j} - \overline{y}_{..}$; $\beta_i = \overline{y}_{i.} - \overline{y}_{..}$

3. Allocation of variation: SSE can be calculated after computing other terms below:

$$\sum_{ij} y_{ij}^2 = ab\mu^2 + b\sum_{j} \alpha_j^2 + a\sum_{i} \beta_i^2 + \sum_{ijk} e_{ijk}^2$$

$$\text{SSY} = \text{SS0} + \text{SSA} + \text{SSB} + \text{SSE}$$

(Continued)

Box 21.1   Continued

4. Degrees of freedom:

$$SSY = SS0 + SSA + SSB + SSE$$
$$ab = 1 + (a-1) + (b-1) + (a-1)(b-1)$$

5. Mean squares:

$$MSA = \frac{SSA}{a-1}; \quad MSB = \frac{SSB}{b-1}; \quad MSE = \frac{SSE}{(a-1)(b-1)}$$

6. Analysis of variance:

MSA/MSE should be greater than $F_{[1-\alpha;a-1,(a-1)(b-1)]}$.

MSB/MSE should be greater than $F_{[1-\alpha;b-1,(a-1)(b-1)]}$.

7. Standard deviation of effects: $s_\mu^2 = s_e^2/ab$;
$s_{\alpha_j}^2 = s_e^2(a-1)/ab$; $s_{\beta_i}^2 = s_e^2(b-1)/ab$

8. Contrasts:
For $\sum_{j=1}^{a} h_j \alpha_j, \sum_{j=1}^{a} h_j = 0$: mean $= \sum_{j=1}^{a} h_j \bar{y}_{.j}$;
variance $= s_e^2 \sum_{j=1}^{a} h_j^2 / b$
For $\sum_{i=1}^{b} h_i \beta_i, \sum_{i=1}^{b} h_i = 0$: mean $= \sum_{i=1}^{b} h_i \bar{y}_{i.}$;
variance $= s_e^2 \sum_{i=1}^{b} h_i^2 / a$

9. All confidence intervals are calculated using $t_{[1-\alpha/2;(a-1)(b-1)]}$.

10. Model assumptions:

   (a) Errors are IID normal variates with zero mean.
   (b) Errors have the same variance for all factor levels.
   (c) The effects of various factors and errors are additive.

11. Visual tests:

   (a) The scatter plot of errors versus predicted responses should not have any trend.
   (b) The normal quantile-quantile plot of errors should be linear.

If any test fails or if the ratio y_{max}/y_{min} is large, multiplicative models or transformations should be investigated.

EXERCISES

21.1 Analyze the data of Case Study 21.2 using an additive model. Plot residuals as a function of predicted response. Also, plot a normal quantile-quantile plot for the residuals. Determine 90% confidence intervals for the paired differences. Are the processors significantly different? Discuss what indicators in the data, analysis, or plot would suggest that this is not a good model.

21.2 Analyze the data of Table 21.18 using a multiplicative model and verify your analysis with the results presented in Table 21.19.

21.3 Analyze the code size data of Table 21.23. Ignore the second column corresponding to the 68000 for this exercise. Answer the following:

   a. What percentage of variation is explained by the processor?

   b. What percentage of variation can be attributed to the workload?

   c. Is there a significant (at 90% confidence) difference between any two processors?

21.4 Repeat Exercise 21.3 with the 68000 column included.

CHAPTER 22

TWO-FACTOR FULL FACTORIAL DESIGN WITH REPLICATIONS

To estimate the time it takes to do a task: estimate the time you think it should take, multiply by 2, and change the unit of measure to the next highest unit. Thus, we allocate 2 days for a one-hour task.

—Westheimer's Rule

The two-factor full factorial design discussed in Chapter 21 helps estimate the effect of each of the two factors being varied. However, the interactions between the factors were assumed negligible and, hence, ignored as errors. Replicating a full factorial design allows separating out the interactions from experimental errors. Thus, if it is known that there is a significant interaction between the factors, the design with replications discussed in this chapter should be used.

22.1 MODEL

Consider a design with r replications of each of the ab experiments corresponding to the a levels of factor A and b levels of factor B. The model in this case is

$$y_{ijk} = \mu + \alpha_j + \beta_i + \gamma_{ij} + e_{ijk}$$

Here,

y_{ijk} = response (observation) in the kth replication of experiment with factor A at level j and factor B at level i

μ = mean response

α_j = effect of factor A at level j

β_i = effect of factor B at level i

γ_{ij} = effect of interaction between factor A at level j and
factor B at level i

e_{ijk} = experimental error

The effects are computed so that their sum is zero:

$$\sum_{j=1}^{a} \alpha_j = 0; \qquad \sum_{i=1}^{b} \beta_i = 0$$

The interactions are computed so that their row as well as column sums are zero:

$$\sum_{j=1}^{a} \gamma_{1j} = \sum_{j=1}^{a} \gamma_{2j} = \cdots = \sum_{j=1}^{a} \gamma_{bj} = 0$$

$$\sum_{i=1}^{b} \gamma_{i1} = \sum_{i=1}^{b} \gamma_{i2} = \cdots = \sum_{i=1}^{b} \gamma_{ia} = 0$$

The errors in each experiment add to zero:

$$\sum_{k=1}^{r} e_{ijk} = 0 \qquad \forall i, j$$

22.2 COMPUTATION OF EFFECTS

The expressions for effects can be obtained in a manner similar to that used in Section 21.2 for two-factor designs without replications. The observations are assumed to be arranged in ab cells arranged as a matrix of b rows and a columns. Each cell contains r observations belonging to the replications of one experiment. Averaging the observations in each cell produces

$$\bar{y}_{ij.} = \mu + \alpha_j + \beta_i + \gamma_{ij}$$

Similarly, averaging across columns and rows and over all observations produces

$$\bar{y}_{i..} = \mu + \beta_i$$
$$\bar{y}_{.j.} = \mu + \alpha_j$$
$$\bar{y}_{...} = \mu$$

From these equations, we obtain the following expressions for effects:

$$\mu = \bar{y}_{...}$$
$$\alpha_j = \bar{y}_{.j.} - \bar{y}_{...}$$
$$\beta_i = \bar{y}_{i..} - \bar{y}_{...}$$
$$\gamma_{ij} = \bar{y}_{ij.} - \bar{y}_{i..} - \bar{y}_{.j.} + \bar{y}_{...}$$

Computation of parameters can be easily carried out using a tabular arrangement similar to that used in Section 21.2 except that ab cell means are used in each cell to compute row and column effects.

Example 22.1 Consider the data of Table 22.1, which represents code sizes of five different workloads on four different computers. Three different programmers with similar backgrounds independently wrote the programs and so the sizes represent three replications of each experiment.

The physical considerations as well as the response range dictates the need for a multiplicative model for this problem. A log transformation of the data is shown in Table 22.2. The computation of row and column ef-

TABLE 22.1 Data for Code Size Study with Replications

Workload	W	X	Y	Z
I	7,006	12,042	29,061	9,903
	6,593	11,794	27,045	9,206
	7,302	13,074	30,057	10,035
J	3,207	5,123	8,960	4,153
	2,883	5,632	8,064	4,257
	3,523	4,608	9,677	4,065
K	4,707	9,407	19,740	7,089
	4,935	8,933	19,345	6,982
	4,465	9,964	21,122	6,678
L	5,107	5,613	22,340	5,356
	5,508	5,947	23,102	5,734
	4,743	5,161	21,446	4,965
W	6,807	12,243	28,560	9,803
	6,392	11,995	26,846	9,306
	7,208	12,974	30,559	10,233

TABLE 22.2 Transformed Data for the Code Size Study with Replications

Workload	W	X	Y	Z
I	3.8455	4.0807	4.4633	3.9958
	3.8191	4.0717	4.4321	3.9641
	3.8634	4.1164	4.4779	4.0015
J	3.5061	3.7095	3.9523	3.6184
	3.4598	3.7507	3.9066	3.6291
	3.5469	3.6635	3.9857	3.6091
K	3.6727	3.9735	4.2953	3.8506
	3.6933	3.9510	4.2866	3.8440
	3.6498	3.9984	4.3247	3.8246
L	3.7082	3.7492	4.3491	3.7288
	3.7410	3.7743	4.3636	3.7585
	3.6761	3.7127	4.3313	3.6959
M	3.8330	4.0879	4.4558	3.9914
	3.8056	4.0790	4.4289	3.9688
	3.8578	4.1131	4.4851	4.0100

fects in this case is similar to that in the analysis of two-factor design without replication. The means of all observations in each cell are used in the analysis, as shown in Table 22.3.

The results are interpreted as follows. An average workload on an average processor requires a log code size of 3.94 (8710 instructions). Processor W requires 0.23 less log code size (that is, a factor of 1.69 less) than an average processor. Processor X requires 0.02 more (a factor of 1.05 more) than an average processor, and so on. The difference of log code sizes of an average workload on processors W and X is 0.25 (a factor of 1.78).

TABLE 22.3 Computation of Effects for the Code Size Study with Replications

Workload	W	X	Y	Z	Row Sum	Row Mean	Row Effect
I	3.8427	4.0896	4.4578	3.9871	49.1315	4.0943	0.1520
J	3.5043	3.7079	3.9482	3.6188	44.3377	3.6948	−0.2475
K	3.6720	3.9743	4.3022	3.8397	47.3646	3.9470	0.0047
L	3.7084	3.7454	4.3480	3.7277	46.5887	3.8824	−0.0599
M	3.8321	4.0933	4.4566	3.9900	49.1163	4.0930	0.1507
Column sum	18.5594	19.6105	21.5128	19.1635	78.8463		
Column mean	3.7119	3.9221	4.3026	3.8327		3.9423	
Column effect	−0.2304	−0.0202	0.3603	−0.1096			

TABLE 22.4   Interactions in the Code Size Study with Replications

Workload	W	X	Y	Z
I	−0.0212	0.0155	0.0032	0.0024
J	0.0399	0.0333	−0.1069	0.0337
K	−0.0447	0.0475	−0.0051	0.0023
L	0.0564	−0.1168	0.1054	−0.0450
M	−0.0305	0.0205	0.0033	0.0066

The interactions (or cell effects) for the (i, j)th cell are computed by subtracting $\mu + \alpha_j + \beta_i$ from the cell mean $y_{ij\cdot}$. The mean interactions so computed are listed in Table 22.4. The computation can be verified by checking that the row as well column sums of interactions are zero.

The interactions are interpreted as follows. Workload I on processor W requires 0.02 less log code size than an average workload on processor W or equivalently 0.02 less log code size than that on an average processor. □

22.3   COMPUTATION OF ERRORS

The estimated response for all observations in the (i, j)th experiment is given by

$$\hat{y}_{ij} = \mu + \alpha_j + \beta_i + \gamma_{ij} = \overline{y}_{ij\cdot}$$

Thus, the error in the kth replication of the experiment is

$$e_{ijk} = y_{ijk} - \overline{y}_{ij\cdot}$$

Notice that this is simply the difference between the observation and the cell mean.

Example 22.2   For the data of Example 22.1, the cell mean for the cell $(1,1)$ is 3.8427. Thus, the errors in the three observations in this cell are $3.8455 - 3.8427 = 0.0028$, $3.8191 - 3.8427 = -0.0236$, and $3.8634 - 3.8427 = 0.0208$. We verify that the sum of the three errors is zero. The errors for other cells can be computed similarly. □

22.4   ALLOCATION OF VARIATION

The total variation of y can be allocated to the two factors, the interaction between them, and the experimental errors. To do so, we square both sides of the model equation and add across all observations. The cross-product terms cancel out, and we obtain

$$\sum_{ijk} y_{ijk}^2 = abr\mu^2 + br \sum_j \alpha_j^2 + ar \sum_i \beta_i^2 + r \sum_{ij} \gamma_{ij}^2 + \sum_{ijk} e_{ijk}^2$$

$$\mathrm{SSY} \;=\; \mathrm{SS0} \;+\; \mathrm{SSA} \;+\; \mathrm{SSB} \;+\; \mathrm{SSAB} \;+\; \mathrm{SSE}$$

where various sums of squares have been appropriately placed below their corresponding terms. The term SSAB is the variation explained by the interaction. The total variation (SST), as before, is

$$\mathrm{SST} = \mathrm{SSY} - \mathrm{SS0} = \mathrm{SSA} + \mathrm{SSB} + \mathrm{SSAB} + \mathrm{SSE}$$

Thus, the total variation can be divided into parts explained by factors A and B, the interaction AB, and an unexplained part due to experimental errors. This equation can also be used to compute SSE, since the other sums can be easily computed. The percentage of variation explained by a factor or interaction can be used to measure the importance of the corresponding effect.

Example 22.3 For the data of Example 22.1, various sums of squares are

$$\mathrm{SSY} = \sum_{i,j,k} y_{ijk}^2 = (3.8455)^2 + (3.8191)^2 + \cdots + (4.0100)^2 = 936.95$$

$$\mathrm{SS0} = abr\mu^2 = 4 \times 5 \times 3 \times (3.9423)^2 = 932.51$$

$$\mathrm{SSA} = br \sum_j \alpha_j^2 = 5 \times 3 \times [(-0.2304)^2 + (-0.0202)^2 + \cdots + (-0.1096)^2]$$

$$= 2.93$$

$$\mathrm{SSB} = ar \sum_i \beta_i^2 = 4 \times 3 \times [(0.1520)^2 + (-0.2475)^2 + \cdots + (0.1507)^2]$$

$$= 1.33$$

$$\mathrm{SSAB} = r \sum_{i,j} \gamma_{ij}^2 = 3 \times [(-0.0212)^2 + (0.0399)^2 + \cdots + (0.0200)^2] = 0.15$$

$$\mathrm{SST} = \mathrm{SSY} - \mathrm{SS0} = 936.95 - 932.51 = 4.44$$

The sum SSE can be obtained either by computing individual errors or more easily by using other sums of squares as follows:

$$\mathrm{SSE} = \mathrm{SSY} - \mathrm{SS0} - \mathrm{SSA} - \mathrm{SSB} - \mathrm{SSAB}$$

$$= 936.95 - 932.51 - 2.93 - 1.33 - 0.15$$

$$= 0.03$$

The percentage of variation explained by various factors are as follows:

$$\text{Explained by processors} = 100\frac{\text{SSA}}{\text{SST}} = 100 \times \frac{2.93}{4.44} = 65.95\%$$

$$\text{Explained by workloads} = 100\frac{\text{SSB}}{\text{SST}} = 100 \times \frac{1.33}{4.44} = 29.9\%$$

$$\text{Explained by Interactions} = 100\frac{\text{SSAB}}{\text{SST}} = 100 \times \frac{0.15}{4.44} = 3.48\%$$

$$\text{Unexplained} = 100\frac{\text{SSE}}{\text{SST}} = 100 \times \frac{0.03}{4.44} = 0.66\%$$

Since the model explains a total of 99.3% variation, it appears to be a good model. The interactions explain less than 5% variation and may be ignored. □

22.5 ANALYSIS OF VARIANCE

To statistically test the significance of a factor, we divide the sum of squares by their corresponding degrees of freedom (DF) to get mean squares. The degrees of freedoms for various sums are as follows:

$$\text{SSY} = \text{SS0} + \text{SSA} + \text{SSB} + \text{SSAB} + \text{SSE}$$
$$abr = 1 + (a-1) + (b-1) + (a-1)(b-1) + ab(r-1)$$

The errors have only $ab(r-1)$ degrees of freedom since only $r-1$ of the r errors in each cell can be independently chosen. The degrees of freedom for other sums can be similarly justified.

The mean squares are obtained by dividing the sums of squares by their respective degrees of freedom. The ratios MSA/MSE, MSB/MSE, and MSAB/MSE have $F[a-1, ab(r-1)]$, $F[b-1, ab(r-1)]$, and $F[(a-1)(b-1), ab(r-1)]$ distributions. A convenient tabular arrangement to conduct an Analysis Of Variance (ANOVA) for a two-factor design with replications is shown in Table 22.5.

Example 22.4 The ANOVA for the data of Example 22.1 is shown in Table 22.6. All three computed F-ratios are higher than the values from the table. Thus, all three effects are statistically significant at a significance level of 0.10. As the line under the table indicates, the standard deviation of the errors is 0.03. □

22.6 CONFIDENCE INTERVALS FOR EFFECTS

The variance of the model parameters can be obtained from that of the errors using expressions listed in Table 22.7. The confidence intervals for the effects can be computed using t-values read at $ab(r-1)$ degrees of freedom, which

TABLE 22.5 ANOVA Table for Two Factors with Replications

Component	Sum of Squares	Percentage of Variation	Degrees of Freedom	Mean Square	F-Computed	F-Table
y	$\text{SSY} = \sum y_{ij}^2$		abr			
$\bar{y}_{...}$	$\text{SS0} = abr\mu^2$		1			
$y - \bar{y}_{...}$	$\text{SST} = \text{SSY} - \text{SS0}$	100	$abr - 1$			
A	$\text{SSA} = br\sum \alpha_j^2$	$100\left(\dfrac{\text{SSA}}{\text{SST}}\right)$	$a - 1$	$\text{MSA} = \dfrac{\text{SSA}}{a-1}$	$\dfrac{\text{MSA}}{\text{MSE}}$	$F_{[1-\alpha;a-1,\,ab(r-1)]}$
B	$\text{SSB} = ar\sum \beta_i^2$	$100\left(\dfrac{\text{SSB}}{\text{SST}}\right)$	$b - 1$	$\text{MSB} = \dfrac{\text{SSB}}{b-1}$	$\dfrac{\text{MSB}}{\text{MSE}}$	$F_{[1-\alpha;b-1,\,ab(r-1)]}$
AB	$\text{SSAB} = r\sum \gamma_{ij}^2$	$100\left(\dfrac{\text{SSAB}}{\text{SST}}\right)$	$(a-1)$ $(b-1)$	$\text{MSAB} = \dfrac{\text{SSAB}}{(a-1)(b-1)}$	$\dfrac{\text{MSA}}{\text{MSE}}$	$F_{[1-\alpha,(a-1)\,(b-1),ab(r-1)]}$
e	$\text{SSE} = \text{SST}-$ (SSA + SSB +SSAB)	$100\left(\dfrac{\text{SSE}}{\text{SST}}\right)$	$ab(r-1)$	$\text{MSE} = \dfrac{\text{SSE}}{ab(r-1)}$		

$$s_e = \sqrt{\text{MSE}}$$

TABLE 22.6 ANOVA Table for the Code Size Study with Replications

Component	Sum of Squares	Percentage of Variation	Degrees of Freedom	Mean Square	F-Computed	F-Table
y	936.95					
$y_{..}$	932.51					
$y - y_{..}$	4.44	100.00	59			
Processors	2.93	65.96	3	0.9765	1340.01	2.23
Workloads	1.33	29.90	4	0.3320	455.65	2.09
Interactions	0.15	3.48	12	0.0129	17.70	1.71
Errors	0.03	0.66	40	0.0007		

$$s_e = \sqrt{\text{MSE}} = \sqrt{0.0008} = 0.03$$

are the degrees of freedom associated with errors. In the table, the estimates and variance for linear combination of effects, such as $\mu + \alpha_j$ and $\mu + \alpha_j + \beta_i$, are also shown along with those for contrasts of effects.

Example 22.5 For the data of Example 22.1, we know from Example 22.4 that $s_e = 0.03$.

The standard deviation of processor effects is

$$s_{\alpha_j} = s_e\sqrt{\frac{a-1}{abr}} = 0.03\sqrt{\frac{4-1}{4 \times 5 \times 3}} = 0.0060$$

TABLE 22.7 Parameter Estimation for Two Factors with Replications

Parameter	Estimate	Variance
μ	$\overline{y}_{...}$	s_e^2/abr
α_j	$\overline{y}_{i..} - \overline{y}_{...}$	$s_e^2(a-1)/abr$
β_i	$\overline{y}_{.j.} - \overline{y}_{...}$	$s_e^2(b-1)/abr$
γ_{ij}	$\overline{y}_{ij.} - \overline{y}_{i..} - \overline{y}_{.j.} + \overline{y}_{...}$	$s_e^2(a-1)(b-1)/abr$
$\sum h_j\alpha_j, \sum h_j = 0$	$\sum h_j\overline{y}_{.j.}$	$\sum h_j^2 s_e^2/br$
$\sum h_i\beta_i, \sum h_i = 0$	$\sum h_i\overline{y}_{i..}$	$\sum h_i^2 s_e^2/ar$
s_e^2	$\sum e_{ijk}^2/\{ab(r-1)\}$	

Degrees of freedom for errors $= ab(r-1)$

The error degrees of freedom are $ab(r-1) = 40$. Since the degrees are greater than 30, we can use the quantiles of a unit normal variate rather than the t-variate. The 0.95 quantile of unit normal $z_{0.95}$ from Table A.2 in the Appendix is 1.645. Thus, the 90% confidence interval for the effect of processor W is

$$\alpha_1 \mp ts_{\alpha_1} = -0.2304 \mp 1.645 \times 0.0060 = -0.2304 \mp 0.00987$$

$$= (-0.2406, -0.2203)$$

Since the confidence interval does not include zero, this effect is significant.

The confidence intervals for various processor and workload effects are listed in Table 22.8. The intervals are very narrow. This is because with

TABLE 22.8 Confidence Intervals for Effects in the Code Size Study with Replications

Parameter	Mean Effect	Standard Deviation	Confidence Interval
μ	3.9423	0.0035	(3.9364, 3.9482)
Processors			
W	−0.2304	0.0060	(−0.2406, −0.2203)
X	−0.0202	0.0060	(−0.0304, −0.0100)
Y	0.3603	0.0060	(0.3501, 0.3704)
Z	−0.1096	0.0060	(−0.1198, −0.0995)
Workloads			
I	0.1520	0.0070	(0.1402, 0.1637)
J	−0.2475	0.0070	(−0.2592, −0.2358)
K	0.0047	0.0070	(−0.0070, 0.0165)[a]
L	−0.0599	0.0070	(−0.0717, −0.0482)
M	0.1507	0.0070	(0.1390, 0.1624)

[a] Not significant.

TABLE 22.9 Confidence Intervals for Interactions in the Code Size Study with Replications

Work-load	W	X	Y	Z
I	(−0.0415, −0.0009)	(−0.0048, 0.0358)[a]	(−0.0171, 0.0236)[a]	(−0.0179, 0.0228)[a]
J	(0.0196, 0.0602)	(0.0130, 0.0536)	(−0.1272, −0.0865)	(0.0133, 0.0540)
K	(−0.0650, −0.0243)	(0.0271, 0.0678)	(−0.0254, 0.0152)[a]	(−0.0180, 0.0226)[a]
L	(0.0361, 0.0768)	(−0.1371, −0.0964)	(0.0850, 0.1257)	(−0.0654, −0.0247)
M	(−0.0508, −0.0101)	(0.0002, 0.0408)	(−0.0170, 0.0236)[a]	(−0.0137, 0.0270)[a]

[a] Not significant.

replications we have been able to isolate interactions from experimental errors. It turns out that in this case the experimental errors are very small, and thus, we can be very confident about the ranges of the effects. The confidence intervals for interactions are shown in Table 22.9.

As a final diagnostic check we also plot a scatter diagram of residuals versus the predicted responses in Figure 22.1. There is no visible trend in the magnitude or spread of the residuals. This verifies the assumption of independence of residuals and of their having an identical distribution (which implies the same variance for all values of the predictors).

A normal quantile-quantile plot of the residuals is shown in Figure 22.2. Notice the plot is approximately linear, and thus the assumption of normality is validated. ☐

The key results related to the analysis of two-factor full factorial designs with replications are summarized in Box 22.1.

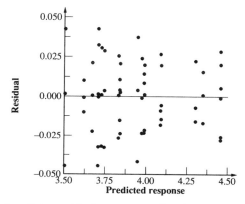

FIGURE 22.1 A plot of the residuals versus predicted response for the code comparison study with replications.

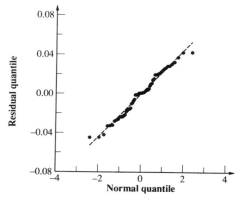

FIGURE 22.2 Normal quantile-quantile plot for the residuals of the code comparison study with replications.

Box 22.1 Analysis of Two-Factor Designs with Replications

1. Model: $y_{ijk} = \mu + \alpha_j + \beta_i + \gamma_{ij} + e_{ijk}$. Here, γ_{ij} is the interaction.
   $\sum_{j=1}^{a} \alpha_j = 0$; $\sum_{i=1}^{b} \beta_i = 0$; $\sum_{j=1}^{a} \gamma_{ij} = 0 \forall i$; $\sum_{i=1}^{b} \gamma_{ij} = 0 \forall j$;
   $\sum_{k=1}^{r} e_{ijk} = 0 \forall i, j$

2. Effects: $\mu = \bar{y}_{...}$, $\alpha_j = \bar{y}_{.j.} - \bar{y}_{...}$, $\beta_i = \bar{y}_{i..} - \bar{y}_{...}$,
   $\gamma_{ij} = \bar{y}_{ij.} - \bar{y}_{i..} - \bar{y}_{.j.} + \bar{y}_{...}$

3. Allocation of variation: SSE can be calculated after computing other terms below:

$$\sum_{ijk} y_{ijk}^2 = abr\mu^2 + br\sum_j \alpha_j^2 + ar\sum_i \beta_i^2 + r\sum_{ij} \gamma_{ij}^2 + \sum_{ijk} e_{ijk}^2$$

$$\text{SSY} \ = \ \text{SS0} \ + \ \ \text{SSA} \ \ + \ \ \text{SSB} \ + \ \text{SSAB} \ + \ \ \text{SSE}$$

4. Degrees of freedom:

$$\text{SSY} = \text{SS0} + \ \text{SSA} \ + \ \text{SSB} \ + \ \ \ \ \text{SSAB} \ \ \ + \ \ \text{SSE}$$

$$abr \ = \ \ 1 \ \ + (a-1) + (b-1) + (a-1)(b-1) + ab(r-1)$$

5. Mean squares: Divide the sums of squares by their respective degrees of freedom.

6. Analysis of variance: The ratios MSA/MSE, MSB/MSE, and MSAB/MSE have $F[a-1, ab(r-1)]$, $F[b-1, ab(r-1)]$, and $F[(a-1)(b-1), ab(r-1)]$ distributions.

(Continued)

Box 22.1   Continued

7. Standard deviation of effects:

$$s_\mu^2 = \frac{s_e^2}{abr}; \qquad s_{\alpha_j}^2 = \frac{s_e^2(a-1)}{abr};$$

$$s_{\beta_i}^2 = \frac{s_e^2(b-1)}{abr}; \qquad s_{\gamma_{ij}}^2 = \frac{s_e^2(a-1)(b-1)}{abr}$$

8. Contrasts:

For $\sum h_j \alpha_j$, $\sum h_j = 0$: mean $= \sum h_j \bar{y}_{.j.}$; variance $= \sum h_j^2 s_e^2 / br$

For $\sum h_i \beta_i$, $\sum h_i = 0$: mean $= \sum h_i \bar{y}_{i..}$; variance $= \sum h_i^2 s_e^2 / ar$

9. All confidence intervals are computed using $t_{[1-\alpha/2;ab(r-1)]}$.

10. Model assumptions:

   (a) Errors are IID normal variates with zero mean.
   (b) Errors have the same variance for all factor levels.
   (c) Effects of various factors and errors are additive.

11. Visual tests:

   (a) The scatter plot of errors versus predicted responses should not have any trend.
   (b) The normal quantile-quantile plot of errors should be linear.
   (c) Spread of y values in all experiments should be comparable.

   If any test fails or if the ratio y_{max}/y_{min} is large, multiplicative models or transformations should be investigated.

EXERCISE

22.1 Measured CPU times for three processors A1, A2, and A3 on five workloads B1 through B5 are shown in Table 22.10. Three replications of each experiment are shown. Analyze the data and answer the following:

   a. Are the processors different from each other at 90% level of confidence?

   b. What percentage of variation is explained by the processor-workload interaction?

   c. Which effects in the model are not significant at 90% confidence.

TABLE 22.10   Data for Exercise 22.1

	A1	A2	A3
B1	3,200	5,120	8,960
	3,150	5,100	8,900
	3,250	5,140	8,840
B2	4,700	9,400	19,740
	4,740	9,300	19,790
	4,660	9,500	19,690
B3	3,200	4,160	7,360
	3,220	4,100	7,300
	3,180	4,220	7,420
B4	5,100	5,610	22,340
	5,200	5,575	22,440
	5,000	5,645	22,540
B5	6,800	12,240	28,560
	6,765	12,290	28,360
	6,835	12,190	28,760

CHAPTER 23

GENERAL FULL FACTORIAL DESIGNS WITH k FACTORS

Work expands to fill the time available for its completion.
—C. Northcote Parkinson

The experimental designs analyzed so far are sufficient to solve problems encountered frequently. They can be easily extended to a larger number of factors. This chapter briefly describes the models used for such designs and illustrates it with a case study involving four factors. Three informal methods are then presented in Section 23.3 for analysis of experimental designs that can be used for larger number of factors as well as for designs discussed in earlier chapters.

23.1 MODEL

The model for a k-factor full factorial design contains $2^k - 1$ effects. This includes k main effects, $\binom{k}{2}$ two-factor interactions, $\binom{k}{3}$ three-factor interactions, and so on. For example, with three factors A, B, and C at $a, b,$ and c levels, respectively and r replications, the model is

$$y_{ijkl} = \mu + \alpha_i + \beta_j + \xi_k + \gamma_{ABij} + \gamma_{ACik} + \gamma_{BCjk} + \gamma_{ABCijk} + e_{ijkl}$$

$$i = 1,\ldots,a; \qquad j = 1,\ldots,b; \qquad k = 1,\ldots,c; \qquad l = 1,\ldots,r$$

where

y_{ijkl} =response (observation) in the lth replication of experiment with factors A, B, and C at levels i, j, and k,
respectively.

μ =mean response

α_i =effect of factor A at level i

and

β_j =effect of factor B at level j

ξ_k =effect of factor C at level k

γ_{ABij} =interaction between A and B at levels i and j.

γ_{ABCijk} =interaction between A, B, C at levels i, j, k.

and so on.

23.2 ANALYSIS OF A GENERAL DESIGN

The analysis of full factorial designs with k factors is similar to that with two factors presented earlier in Chapters 21 and 22. For example, the parameters can be estimated from means taken along various dimensions:

$$\mu = \overline{y}_{....}$$
$$\alpha_i = \overline{y}_{i...} - \overline{y}_{....}$$

The sums of squares, degrees of freedom, and F-test also extend as expected. The following case study illustrates the analysis of a general k-factor design.

Case Study 23.1   In a study to quantify the effect of various factors on the paging process, a full factorial $3 \times 3 \times 3 \times 3$ experimental design was used. The factors were main memory size, problem program, deck arrangement, and replacement algorithm. The effect of four factors each at three levels was used. The factors and their levels are listed in Table 23.1. The design

TABLE 23.1   Factors and Levels for Page Swap Study

Symbol	Factor	Level 1	Level 2	Level 3
A	Page replacement algorithm	LRUV	FIFO	RAND
D	Deck arrangement	GROUP	FREQY	ALPHA
P	Problem program	Small	Medium	Large
M	Memory pages	24P	20P	16P

TABLE 23.2 Total Number of Page Swaps

Algorithm	Program	GROUP			FREQY			ALPHA		
		24P	20P	16P	24P	20P	16P	24P	20P	16P
LRUV	Small	32	48	538	52	244	998	59	536	1,348
	Medium	53	81	1,901	112	776	3,621	121	1,879	4,639
	Large	142	197	5,689	262	2,625	10,012	980	5,698	12,880
FIFO	Small	49	67	789	79	390	1,373	85	814	1,693
	Medium	100	134	3,152	164	1,255	4,912	206	3,394	5,838
	Large	233	350	9,100	458	3,688	13,531	1,633	10,022	17,117
RAND	Small	62	100	1,103	111	480	1,782	111	839	2,190
	Medium	96	245	2,807	237	1,502	6,007	286	3,092	7,654
	Large	265	2,012	12,429	517	4,870	18,602	1,728	8,834	23,134

Data from Tsao and Margolin (1971). Reprinted with permission.

consisted of a total of 81 experiments for which the number of page swaps (PS) was measured. The measured values are listed in Table 23.2. It is seen from this table that the number of page swaps has a wide range, the ratio of y_{max}/y_{min} is 23134/32, or about 723. This suggests that we should try using a log transformation of the data. This is confirmed also by the observation that as a factor is changed from one level to the next, the change in response is approximately proportional to the response. A log transformation was therefore used. The transformed data, which was called log page swaps (LPS), is shown in Table 23.3. The effects of various factors and their interactions can be obtained by averaging along various axes. For example, the effect of algorithm (factor A) at level 1 is obtained as follows:

$$\alpha_1 = y_{1..} - y_{...} = 2.74 - 2.90 = -0.16$$

TABLE 23.3 Transformed Data for the Paging Study

Algorithm	Program	GROUP			FREQY			ALPHA		
		24P	20P	16P	24P	20P	16P	24P	20P	16P
LRUV	Small	1.51	1.68	2.73	1.72	2.39	3.00	1.77	2.73	3.13
	Medium	1.72	1.91	3.28	2.05	2.89	3.56	2.08	3.27	3.67
	Large	2.15	2.29	3.76	2.42	3.42	4.00	2.99	3.76	4.11
FIFO	Small	1.69	1.83	2.90	1.90	2.59	3.14	1.93	2.91	3.23
	Medium	2.00	2.13	3.50	2.21	3.10	3.69	2.31	3.53	3.77
	Large	2.37	2.54	3.96	2.66	3.57	4.13	3.21	4.00	4.23
RAND	Small	1.79	2.00	3.04	2.05	2.68	3.25	2.05	2.92	3.34
	Medium	1.98	2.39	3.58	2.37	3.18	3.78	2.46	3.49	3.88
	Large	2.42	2.30	4.09	2.71	3.69	4.27	3.24	3.95	4.36

Data from Tsao and Margolin (1971). Reprinted with permission.

TABLE 23.4 Main Effects in the Paging Study

Factor	Level 1	Level 2	Level 3
A	−0.16	0.02	0.14
D	−0.36	0.07	0.29
P	−0.47	−0.02	0.49
M	−0.69	−0.01	0.70

Other main effects are listed in Table 23.4. In addition to the main effect, there are six two-factor interactions, four three-factor interactions, and one four-factor interaction. The sum of squares of these effects and the percentage of variation explained by them is listed in Table 23.5.

Notice that most of the interactions are small. The only interaction that explained more than 1% variation is DM—the interaction between deck level and memory size. Therefore, all other interactions were considered negligible, and the following simplified model was used to represent the paging process:

$$y_{ijkl} = \mu + \alpha_i + \beta_j + \gamma_k + \delta_l + \xi_{jl}$$

TABLE 23.5 ANOVA Table for the Paging Study

Component	Sum of Squares	Percentage of Variation	Degrees of Freedom	Mean Square
y	730.01		81	
$\bar{y}$	681.21		1	
$y - \bar{y}_{....}$	48.80	100	80	
Main effects	45.80	93.85	8	5.7
A	1.30		2	
D	6.10		2	
P	12.30		2	
M	26.20		2	
First-order interactions	2.40	4.91	24	0.1
AD	0.07		4	
AP	0.02		4	
AM	0.03		4	
DP	0.15		4	
DM	1.96		4	
PM	0.14		4	
Second-order interactions	0.48	0.98	32	0.015
ADP	0.05		8	
ADM	0.13		8	
APM	0.04		8	
DPM	0.26		8	
Third-order interaction (ADPM)	0.07	0.14	16	0.004

Data from Tsao and Margolin (1971). Reprinted with permission.

TABLE 23.6   Interactions between Deck Arrangement and Memory Pages

	M1	M2	M3
D1	0.11	-0.30	0.19
D2	-0.05	0.09	-0.04
D3	-0.06	0.21	-0.15

where μ is the grand mean; α_i, β_j, γ_k, and δ_l are the main effects of factors A, D, P, and M, respectively; and ξ_{jl} is the interaction between D and M. The estimated values of these interactions at various combinations of factors D and M are shown in Table 23.6. The difference between the estimated response using the model and the measured response is the error. The errors in all 81 observations are shown in Table 23.7. A normal quantile-quantile plot of the residuals is shown in Figure 23.1. Notice that

TABLE 23.7   Errors in the Paging Study

		GROUP			FREQY			ALPHA		
Algorithm	Program	24P	20P	16P	24P	20P	16P	24P	20P	16P
LRUV	Small	0.18	0.08	-0.07	0.11	-0.04	-0.02	-0.05	-0.04	0.01
	Medium	-0.05	-0.13	0.04	0.01	0.02	0.10	-0.18	0.07	0.11
	Large	-0.13	-0.26	0.01	-0.14	0.04	0.03	0.22	0.04	0.04
FIFO	Small	0.17	0.04	0.09	0.11	-0.02	-0.07	-0.08	-0.04	-0.08
	Medium	0.05	-0.10	0.07	-0.02	0.04	0.05	-0.13	0.14	0.02
	Large	-0.10	-0.20	0.02	-0.00	0.00	-0.03	0.25	0.09	-0.02
RAND	Small	0.16	0.09	-0.06	0.14	-0.05	-0.07	-0.08	-0.08	-0.08
	Medium	-0.10	0.04	0.04	-0.02	0.00	0.01	-0.11	-0.02	-0.02
	Large	-0.17	0.44	0.04	-0.15	0.00	-0.01	0.16	-0.08	-0.01

Data from Tsao and Margolin (1971). Reprinted with permission.

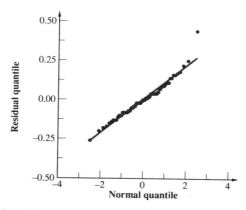

FIGURE 23.1   Normal quantile-quantile plot for the residuals of the paging study.

the plot is almost a straight line. There is one observation that is significantly away from the line followed by other points. This experiment was repeated to verify that it was not a mistake.

Thus, it was concluded that the observations do satisfy the following multiplicative model:

$$LPS = 2.90 + A \begin{cases} -0.16 \\ +0.02 \\ +0.14 \end{cases} + D \begin{cases} -0.36 \\ +0.07 \\ +0.29 \end{cases} + P \begin{cases} -0.47 \\ -0.02 \\ +0.49 \end{cases} + M \begin{cases} -0.69 \\ -0.01 \\ +0.70 \end{cases}$$

Log (pages	1. LRUV	1. GROUP	1. Small	1. 24P
swapped)	2. FIFO	2. FREQY	2. Medium	2. 20P
	3. RAND	3. ALPHA	3. Large	3. 16P

$$+ D \overbrace{\begin{cases} -0.27 & 1.40 & 1.30 \\ -0.60 & 0.80 & -0.20 \\ 3.30 & -2.20 & -1.10 \end{cases}}^{M} \pm 0.12$$

Notice that this is a good way to summarize the model.   □

23.3 INFORMAL METHODS

The analysis techniques presented so far produce the main effects, the interactions, and their confidence intervals. If the goal is simply to find the best combination of factor levels—the combination that produces the best performance—two much simpler techniques that are presented in this section can be used. These techniques are informal and their results can be easily explained to decision makers without getting into statistical details. Also, analysts may find these techniques useful for preliminary analysis before performing the analysis of variance. These techniques, known as observation method, ranking method, and range method are described next.

23.3.1 Observation Method

If the response variable is a HB (Higher is Better) or LB (Lower is Better) metric (defined in Section 3.4) and the goal is simply to find the combination of factor levels that produces the best response, then a simple look at the mean response column will suffice to find the answer. The experiment corresponding to the highest response (for an HB metric) or the lowest response (for an LB metric) is found, and its levels give the desired combination. If there are other responses, which are close to the best response, then the factor levels common to all such responses provide the desired answer.

TABLE 23.8   Measured Throughputs for Scheduler Design Study

Experiment No.	A	B	C	D	E	T_W	T_I	T_B
1	−1	−1	−1	−1	1	15.0	25.0	15.2
2	1	−1	−1	−1	−1	11.0	41.0	3.0
3	−1	1	−1	−1	−1	25.0	36.0	21.0
4	1	1	−1	−1	1	10.0	15.7	8.6
5	−1	−1	1	−1	−1	14.0	63.9	7.5
6	1	−1	1	−1	1	10.0	13.2	7.5
7	−1	1	1	−1	1	28.0	36.3	20.2
8	1	1	1	−1	−1	11.0	23.0	3.0
9	−1	−1	−1	1	−1	14.0	66.1	6.4
10	1	−1	−1	1	1	10.0	9.1	8.4
11	−1	1	−1	1	1	27.0	34.6	15.7
12	1	1	−1	1	−1	11.0	23.0	3.0
13	−1	−1	1	1	1	14.0	26.0	12.0
14	1	−1	1	1	−1	11.0	38.0	2.0
15	−1	1	1	1	−1	25.0	35.0	17.2
16	1	1	1	1	1	11.0	22.0	2.0

Example 23.1   Consider the scheduler design study of Case Study 19.2. The purpose of the study was to find the best factor levels that maximize the throughput for three classes of jobs, namely, word processing, interactive data processing, and background data processing. The factor levels in the 16 experiments used in the 2^{5-1} design and the throughputs obtained are listed again in Table 23.8. For simplicity, let us just consider the word processing jobs whose throughputs are listed in column labeled T_W. The maximum throughput is 28. The factor levels corresponding to this throughput have been circled in the table. The next highest throughput in the column is 27. The levels are circled in that row too. Notice that in both rows, factor A is at level −1, factor B is at level 1, and factor E is at level 1. The remaining two factors change their levels between these two values. One conclusion for this observation is that to get high throughput for word processing jobs, there should not be any preemption ($A = -1$), the time slice should be large ($B = 1$), and the fairness should be on ($E = 1$). The settings for queue assignment and requeueing do not matter.   □

23.3.2   Ranking Method

The ranking method is similar to the observation method except that the experiments are written in the order of increasing or decreasing responses so that the experiment with the best response is first and the worst response is the last. Now the factor columns are observed to find levels that consistently produce good or bad results. The following example provides further details of this method.

TABLE 23.9 Scheduler Design Study Data Sorted by Word Processing Throughput

Experiment No.	A	B	C	D	E	T_W	T_I	T_B
7	-1	1	1	-1	1	28.0	36.3	20.2
11	-1	1	-1	1	1	27.0	34.6	15.7
15	-1	1	1	1	-1	25.0	35.0	17.2
3	-1	1	-1	-1	-1	25.0	36.0	21.0
1	-1	-1	-1	-1	1	15.0	25.0	15.2
5	-1	-1	1	-1	-1	14.0	63.9	7.5
9	-1	-1	-1	1	-1	14.0	66.1	6.4
13	-1	-1	1	1	1	14.0	26.0	12.0
2	1	-1	-1	-1	-1	11.0	41.0	3.0
8	1	1	1	-1	-1	11.0	23.0	3.0
12	1	1	-1	1	-1	11.0	23.0	3.0
14	1	-1	1	1	-1	11.0	38.0	2.0
16	1	1	1	1	1	11.0	22.0	2.0
6	1	-1	1	-1	1	10.0	13.2	7.5
4	1	1	-1	-1	1	10.0	15.7	8.6
10	1	-1	-1	1	1	10.0	9.1	8.4

Example 23.2 The data of Example 23.1 is presented again in Table 23.9. The rows have been sorted in order of decreasing throughputs for the word processing jobs. Notice that in column A, all -1's are in the top half while the 1's are in the bottom half. Thus, it is clear that $A = -1$ (no preemption) is good for word processing jobs and also that $A = 1$ is bad. In column B, the top four rows are 1's. Thus, $B = 1$ (large time slice) is good for such jobs. Notice, however, that there is no corresponding pattern at the bottom of the table. Thus, no strong negative comment can be made about $B = -1$. Factor C has no pattern at the top. However, the bottom two values are -1. Thus, given a choice, C should be chosen at 1, that is, there should be two queues. Factor E has 1 in the top two rows, but the 1 also appears in the bottom four rows. Thus, the effect of E is no longer clear. If we have already chosen other factors at levels corresponding to the top rows, then $E = 1$ is a good choice. Thus, we see that the ranking method, in general, gives more information than the observation method. □

23.3.3 Range Method

One way to find out the importance of a factor in a model is to find the percentage of variation explained by the factor. Another simpler informal alternative is to find the average response corresponding to each level of the fac-

TABLE 23.10   Factor Averages and Range for the Paging Study

Factor	Level 1	Level 2	Level 3	Range of of Averages
Replacement algorithm	2056	2986	3781	1725
Deck arrangement	1584	2913	4326	2742
Problem program	592	2047	6185	5593
Memory size	305	2006	6512	6207

tor and find the difference between the maximum and the minimum of such averages. This difference is called the **range**. A factor with a large range is considered important. It is assumed, though, that the observations have been transformed into a scale for which arithmetic averaging makes sense.

Example 23.3   Consider the data of the paging study. The averages corresponding to the three levels of each of the four factors and their ranges are listed in Table 23.10. From the range column in the table, it can be seen that memory size is the most influential factor. Problem program, deck arrangement, and replacement algorithm are next in order. This, in fact, is also the order that would have been obtained from percentage of variation explained.   □

EXERCISES

23.1 Using the observation method on data of Table 23.8, find the factor levels that maximize the throughput for interactive jobs (T_I). Repeat the problem for background jobs (T_B).

23.2 Repeat Exercise 23.1 using the ranking method.

FURTHER READING FOR PART IV

The concepts of experimental design were developed for agriculture, and therefore, most of the examples in books on experimental design are from this field and not from computer science. It is therefore not surprising that this topic has been ignored in most textbooks on computer science performance analysis.

There are numerous books on design and analysis of experiments. In particular, see Mason, Gunst, and Hess (1989); Box, Hunter, and Hunter (1978); Dunn and Clark (1974); Hicks (1973); and Montgomery (1984). One of the recent developments in experimental design is the so-called *Taguchi method*. For details of this method see Ross (1988).

The scheduler design case study is from McHugh and Tzelnic (1981). The data for the code size comparison study of Examples 20.1 to 20.6 was adopted from that presented by Patterson and Sequin (1982). The data for Case Study 21.4 is from Hansen et al. (1982). The data as well as analysis for Case Study 23.1 is from Tsao and Margolin (1971).

PART V

SIMULATION

This part presents the key issues in simulation modeling. Following is a list of types of questions that you should be able to answer after reading this part:

- What are the common mistakes in simulation and why do most simulations fail?
- What language should you use for developing a simulation model?
- What are the different types of simulations?
- How should you schedule events in a simulation?
- How should you verify and validate a model?
- How should you determine that the simulation has reached a steady state?
- How long should you run a simulation?
- How should you generate uniform random numbers?
- How should you verify that a given random-number generator is good?
- How should you select seeds for a random-number generators?
- How should you generate random variables with a given distribution?
- What distributions should you use and when?

A knowledge of these issues will help you perform simulation correctly and successfully.

CHAPTER 24

INTRODUCTION TO SIMULATION

The best advice to those about to embark on a very large simulation is often the same as Punch's famous advice to those about to marry: Don't!
—Bratley, Fox, and Schrage (1986)

Simulation is a useful technique for computer systems performance analysis. If the system to be characterized is not available, as is often the case during the design or procurement stage, a simulation model provides an easy way to predict the performance or compare several alternatives. Further, even if a system is available for measurement, a simulation model may be preferred over measurements because it allows the alternatives to be compared under a wider variety of workloads and environments. Criteria for selecting among simulation, analytical modeling, and measurement have already been discussed in Section 3.1.

However, simulation models often fail; that is, they produce no useful results or misleading results. This is either because the model developers are proficient in software development but lack statistical background or because they are proficient in statistical techniques but are not aware of good software development techniques. More simulation efforts are terminated prematurely than completed. This is because simulation models take a long time to develop—much longer than initially anticipated.

This chapter therefore begins with a list of common mistakes in simulation. Techniques to overcome these mistakes are presented subsequently.

24.1 COMMON MISTAKES IN SIMULATION

1. *Inappropriate Level of Detail*: Simulation allows a system to be studied in more detail than analytical modeling. Analysis requires several simplifications and assumptions. In other words, an analytical model is less detailed. In a simulation model, the level of detail is limited only by the time available for simulation development. A more detailed simulation requires more time to develop. The likelihood of bugs increases and it becomes harder to spot them. The debugging time increases. A more detailed simulation also requires a greater computer time to run. This is particularly important for large simulations where the execution time may be of the order of several hours or days.

   It is generally assumed that a more detailed model is a better model, since it makes fewer assumptions. This is not always true. A detailed model may require more detailed knowledge of input parameters, which, if not available, may make the model inaccurate. For example, in simulating a timesharing system, suppose time spent in servicing disk requests needs to be simulated. One alternative is to generate it using an exponential distribution. A more detailed alternative is to simulate the head movement and disk rotation. If the second alternative is chosen, one would get more accurate results only if sector and track references are known. In an actual case study, an analyst chose the second alternative. However, since the sector reference information was not available for inputting into the model, the analyst then decided to generate exponentially distributed random sector numbers. The net result was that the service time came out exponentially distributed—an effect that could have been less expensively obtained with the first alternative.

   Another problem with detailed models is that they take too much time to develop. It is better to start with a less detailed model, get some results, study sensitivities, and introduce details in the areas that have the highest impact on the results.

2. *Improper Language*: The choice of the programming language has a significant impact on the timely development of the model. Special-purpose simulation languages require less time for model development and ease several common tasks such as verification (using traces) and statistical analysis. General-purpose languages, on the other hand, are more portable and provide more control over the efficiency and run time of the simulation. This issue is discussed further in Section 24.4.

3. *Unverified Models*: Simulation models are generally large computer programs, and unless special precautions are taken, it is possible to have several bugs or programming errors, which would make the conclusions meaningless. A number of techniques to verify simulation models are described in Section 25.1.

4. *Invalid Models*: Even if a simulation program has no errors, it may not represent the real system correctly because of incorrect assumptions

about the system's behavior. It is essential that the models be validated to ensure that the conclusion reached would be the same as those obtained from the real system. All simulation model results should be suspected until confirmed by analytical models, measurements, or intuition.

Techniques for model validation are described in Section 25.2.

5. *Improperly Handled Initial Conditions*: The initial part of a simulation trajectory is generally not representative of the system behavior in a steady state. The initial part should therefore be discarded. Several techniques for identifying the initial part are described in Section 25.3.

6. *Too Short Simulations*: Analysts often try to save their own time as well as the computer's time by running simulations that are too short. The results in such cases are heavily dependent on initial conditions and may not be representative of the real system. The correct length for simulations depends upon the accuracy (width of the confidence intervals) desired and the variance of the observed quantities.

Straightforward computation of variance from several values of a random variable does not produce a correct estimate of the variance in simulation models because of the correlation among the values. Several techniques for variance estimation are described in Section 25.5.

7. *Poor Random-Number Generators*: Simulation models require random quantities, and the procedures to generate the random numbers are called random-number generators. It is safer to use a well-known generator that has been extensively analyzed than to develop one's own. Even well-known generators have been known to have problems. This is discussed further in Chapter 26.

8. *Improper Selection of Seeds*: Random-number generators are computer procedures that given one random number generate another one. The first random number in the sequence is called the **seed** and has to be supplied by the analyst. The seed for different random-number streams should be carefully chosen to maintain independence among the streams. Often, analysts either share one stream among several different processes or use the same seed (generally initialized to zeros) for all streams. This introduces a correlation among various processes in the system and leads to conclusions that may not be representative of the real system. Guidelines for proper selection of seeds are presented in Section 26.7.

24.2 OTHER CAUSES OF SIMULATION ANALYSIS FAILURE

> *Any given program, when running, is obsolete.*
>
> *If a program is useful, it will have to be changed.*
>
> *Program complexity grows until it exceeds the capacity of the programmer who must maintain it.*
>
> —Datamation 1968

> *Adding manpower to a late software project makes it later.*
> —Fred Brooks

These quotations apply to all software development projects including simulation programs. Most simulation efforts become large projects that, unless managed properly, can fail. The following list of common causes of simulation failures is based largely on those pointed out by Annino and Russell (1979):

1. *Inadequate Time Estimate*: The first and foremost cause of failures of simulation models is that the model developers underestimate the time and effort required to develop a simulation model. It is common for simulation projects to start off as a "one-week" or "one-month" project and then continue for years. If a simulation is successful and provides useful information, its users want more features, parameters, and details to be added. On the other hand, if a simulation does not provide useful information, it is often expected that adding more features, parameters, and details will probably make it useful. In either case, the project continues far beyond initial projections.

   Among the three performance analysis techniques—modeling, measurement, and simulation—the simulation generally takes the longest time, particularly if a complete new model has to be developed from scratch. Time should also be allocated for model verification. Analysts new to the field underestimate the complexity of simulation development. For long simulation projects, provision should be made for incorporating changes in the system, which are inevitable over a long period.

2. *No Achievable Goal*: Simulation is a large complex project. Like any other project it should have a clearly specified set of goals that are specific, measurable, achievable, repeatable, and thorough (SMART) (see Section 3.5 for a discussion of SMART goals). The goals should be clearly written down and agreed to by the analysts and the end users of the results before beginning the model development.

   A common example of a goal that is not measurable is "to model X." It is possible to model several different characteristics of X at several different levels of detail. Without proper specification, it is impossible to tell whether the goal has been achieved. The projects without goals continue forever and are eventually terminated when the funding runs out.

3. *Incomplete Mix of Essential Skills*: A simulation project requires at least the following four areas of skills:

   (a) Project Leadership: The ability to motivate, lead, and manage the members of the simulation team.
   (b) Modeling and Statistics: The ability to identify the key characteristics of the system and model them at the required level of detail.

(c) Programming: The ability to write a readable and verifiable computer program that implements the model correctly.

(d) Knowledge of the Modeled System: The ability to understand the system, explain it to the modeling team, and interpret the modeling results in terms of their impact on the system design.

A simulation team should have members with these skills and be ideally led by a member who has some knowledge of all of the skills.

4. *Inadequate Level of User Participation*: It is essential that the modeling team and the user organizations meet periodically and discuss the progress, problems, and changes, if any, in the system. Most systems evolve or change with time, and a model developed without end user participation is rarely successful. The periodic meetings help point out the "modeling bugs" at an early stage and help keep the model in sync with changes in the system.

5. *Obsolete or Nonexistent Documentation*: Most simulation models evolve over a long period of time and are continuously modified as the system is modified or better understood. Documentation of these models often lags behind the development and, unless special care is taken to keep it up to date, it soon becomes obsolete. The best strategy is to include the documentation in the program itself and to use computer languages that are easier to read.

6. *Inability to Manage the Development of a Large Complex Computer Program*: A number of software engineering tools are available for management of large software projects. These tools help keep track of design objectives, functional requirements, data structures, and progress estimates. Also, a number of design principles, such as top-down design and structured programming, have been developed to help orderly development of large computer programs. Without the use of these tools and techniques, it is impossible to successfully develop a large simulation model.

7. *Mysterious Results*: Most mysterious results are due to bugs in the simulation program, invalid model assumptions, or lack of understanding of the real system. The model developers should therefore try to verify the model and, if the mysterious result still persists, bring it to the attention of the end users. It may provide a valuable insight into the system behavior or may point to the system features that need to be modeled in more detail.

The list of mistakes presented in Section 24.1 and the causes of simulation failures presented in this section lead to the checklist presented in Box 24.1. The questions in the list should all be anwered in the affirmative. The list consists of three sublists corresponding to the planning, development, and usage phases of a simulation project.

Box 24.1   Checklist for Simulations

1. Checks before developing a simulation:

    (a) Is the goal of the simulation properly specified?
    (b) Is the level of detail in the model appropriate for the goal?
    (c) Does the simulation team include personnel with project leader-
        ship, modeling, programming, and computer systems backgrounds?
    (d) Has sufficient time been planned for the project?

2. Checks during development:

    (a) Has the random-number generator used in the simulation been
        tested for uniformity and independence?
    (b) Is the model reviewed regularly with the end user?
    (c) Is the model documented?

3. Checks after the simulation is running:

    (a) Is the simulation length appropriate?
    (b) Are the initial transients removed before computation?
    (c) Has the model been verified thoroughly?
    (d) Has the model been validated before using its results?
    (e) If there are any surprising results, have they been validated?
    (f) Are all seeds such that the random-number streams will not over-
        lap?

    See also Box 2.1 for a checklist applicable to all performance evalua-
    tion projects.

24.3   TERMINOLOGY

There are a number of terms that are commonly used in modeling. To define
these terms, an example of simulating CPU scheduling is used in this section.
The problem is to study various scheduling techniques for given CPU demand
characteristics of jobs. Other components of the system, such as disks and
terminals, will be ignored for the moment.

- **State Variables:** The variables whose values define the state of the system are called *state variables*. If a simulation is stopped in the middle, it
  can be restarted later if and only if values of all state variables are known.
  In the CPU scheduling simulation, the state variable is the length of the
  job queue.

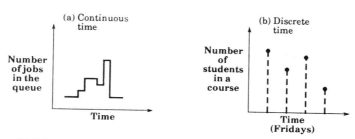

FIGURE 24.1   Continuous-time versus discrete-time models.

- **Event:** A change in the system state is called an *event*. In the CPU scheduling simulation, there are three events: arrival of a job, beginning of a new execution, and departure of a job.
- **Continuous-Time and Discrete-Time Models:** A model in which the system state is defined at all times is called a *continuous-time model*. The CPU scheduling model, for example, is a continuous-time model. If the system state is defined only at particular instants in time, the model is called a *discrete-time model*. As an example, consider a class that meets every Friday. Suppose, in a model, the state of the class is specified by the number of students who attend the class. Notice that the class size can be determined only on Fridays. On other days, the state of the class is not defined. This is therefore an example of a discrete-time model. Figure 24.1 shows these two types of models.
- **Continuous-State and Discrete-State Models:** A model is called *continuous-* or *discrete*-state model depending upon whether the state variables are continuous or discrete. Recall from Section 10.1 that the continuous variables can take uncountably infinite values. For example, if in a model of the weekly class, state is defined as the time spent by the students on the subject, it would be a continuous-state model. On the other hand, if the state is defined as the number of students, it would be a discrete-state model. In the CPU scheduling model, the state variable—the queue length—can assume only integer values. It is therefore also a discrete-state model, as shown in Figure 24.2. A discrete-state model is also called a **discrete-event model**. Similarly, a continuous-state model is called a **continuous-event model**.

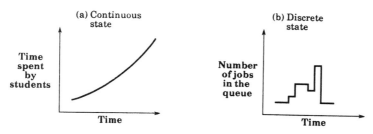

FIGURE 24.2   Continuous-state versus discrete-state models.

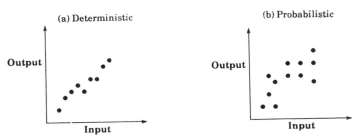

FIGURE 24.3 Deterministic and probabilistic models.

Notice that continuity of time does not imply continuity of state and vice versa. Thus, examples can be found for all four possible combinations: discrete state/discrete time, discrete state/continuous time, continuous state/discrete time, and continuous state/continuous time models.

- **Deterministic and Probabilistic Models**: If the output (results) of a model can be predicted with certainty, it is a *deterministic model*. A probabilistic model, on the other hand, gives a different result on repetitions for the same set of input parameters. This is shown in Figure 24.3. Figure 24.3b shows the results of a probabilistic model; multiple points along a vertical line represent different output possibilities for a given input. In Figure 24.3a, all repetitions with the same input produce the same output, and hence there is only one point along any vertical line.

- **Static and Dynamic Models**: A model in which time is not a variable is called *static*. If the system state changes with time, the model is *dynamic*. The CPU scheduling model, for example, is a dynamic model. An example of a static model is the following model of matter-to-energy transformation: $E = mc^2$.

- **Linear and Nonlinear Models**: If the output parameters are a linear function of the input parameter, the model is *linear*; otherwise it is *nonlinear*, as shown in Figure 24.4.

- **Open and Closed Models**: If the input is external to the model and is independent of it, it is called an *open model*. In a *closed model*, there is

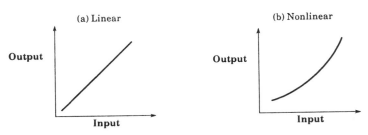

FIGURE 24.4 Linear and nonlinear models.

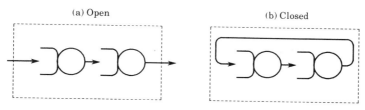

FIGURE 24.5 Open and closed models.

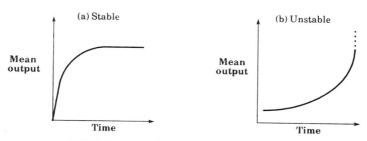

FIGURE 24.6 Stable and unstable models.

no external input. Figure 24.5 shows two queueing models of a computer system. In Figure 24.5b, the same jobs keep circulating in the model. A job departing the second queue reenters the first queue. This is therefore a closed model. Figure 24.5a shows an open model in which new jobs enter the model.

- **Stable and Unstable Models**: If the dynamic behavior of the model settles down to a steady state, that is, independent of time, it is called *stable*. A model whose behavior is continuously changing is called *unstable*. This is shown in Figure 24.6.

Computer system models are generally continuous time, discrete state, probabilistic, dynamic, and nonlinear. Some are open; others are closed. In addition, stable as well as unstable models of computer systems are used.

24.4 SELECTING A LANGUAGE FOR SIMULATION

Selecting a proper language is probably the most important step in the process of developing a simulation model. An incorrect decision during this step may lead to long development times, incomplete studies, and failures.

There are four choices: a simulation language, a general-purpose language, extension of a general-purpose language, and a simulation package (such as a network solver). Each choice has its own advantages and disadvantages.

Simulation languages such as SIMULA and SIMSCRIPT save the analyst considerable time when developing a simulation. These languages have built-in facilities for time advancing, event scheduling, entity manipulation, random-variate generation, statistical data collection, and report generation. They allow analysts to spend more time on issues specific to the system being modeled and not worry about issues that are general to all simulations. Also, these languages allow a very readable modular code with good error detection.

A general-purpose language such as Pascal or FORTRAN is chosen for simulation primarily because of an analyst's familiarity with the language. Most computer system designers and new analysts are not familiar with simulation languages. Also, deadline requirements do not allow time for them to learn a simulation language. Further, simulation languages are often not available on their computer systems. This is why most people write their first simulation in a general-purpose language.

Even for beginners, the time trade-off between a simulation language and a general-purpose language is really not what it appears. If they choose a simulation language, they have to spend time learning the language. In some cases, they may even have to install it on their computer system and see that no pieces are missing. If they choose a general-purpose language, they can get started right away. But they spend time developing routines for event handling, random-number generation, and so forth. Considerable time may be spent in learning about these issues and rediscovering known problems.

This is not to say that analysts should always use simulation languages. There are other considerations, such as efficiency, flexibility, and portability, which may make a general-purpose language the only choice. A model developed in a general-purpose language is more efficient and takes less CPU time. A general-purpose language gives analysts more flexibility by allowing them to take short cuts prohibited in a simulation language. Furthermore, a model developed in a general-purpose language can be easily converted for execution on different computer systems.

To make an objective choice between a simulation language and a general-purpose language, it is suggested that the analyst learn at least one simulation language so that other factors in addition to familiarity will help in the selection of the language.

An extension of a general-purpose language such as GASP (for FORTRAN) is another alternative. These extensions consist of a collection of routines to handle tasks that are commonly required in simulations. Their aim is to provide a compromise in terms of efficiency, flexibility, and portability.

Simulation packages such as QNET4 and RESQ allow the user to define a model using a dialog. The packages have a library of data structures, routines, and algorithms. Their biggest advantage is the time savings that they provide. Using a simulation package, for example, one could develop a model, solve it, and get results in one day. Developing a simulation using a language, on the other hand, may take several days (if not months) depending upon the complexity of the system.

The main problem with the simulation packages is their inflexibility. They provide only those flexibilities that were foreseen by their developers. In most practical situations, analysts run into one or another problem that cannot be modeled by the package. This may force an analyst to make simplifications. Nonetheless, it saves so much time that if a system cannot be modeled analytically, one should look at the possibility of using a simulation package before starting to develop a new simulation model.

Simulation languages can be classified into two categories, continuous simulation languages and discrete-event simulation languages, based on the types of events they simulate. Continuous simulation languages are designed to handle continuous-event models that are generally described by differential equations. Examples of such languages are CSMP and DYNAMO. These languages are popular in chemical system modeling. On the other hand, discrete-event simulation languages are designed to handle discrete-state changes. Two examples of these languages are SIMULA and GPSS. Some languages, such as SIMSCRIPT and GASP, allow discrete, continuous, as well as combined simulations. The latter four are the major languages used by computer systems performance analysts.

24.5 TYPES OF SIMULATIONS

Monte Carlo method [Origin: after Count Montgomery de Carlo, Italian gambler and random-number generator (1792-1838).] A method of jazzing up the action in certain statistical and number-analytic environments by setting up a book and inviting bets on the outcome of a computation.

—S. Kelly-Bootle
The Devil's DP Dictionary

Among the variety of simulations that are described in the literature, those that would be of interest to computer scientists are Emulation, Monte Carlo Simulation, Trace-Driven Simulation, and Discrete-Event Simulation.

A simulation using hardware or firmware is called **emulation**. A terminal emulator, for example, simulates one kind of terminal on another. A processor emulator emulates an instruction set of one processor on another. Even though emulation is a type of simulation, the design issues for emulation are mostly hardware design issues. Hence, emulation is not discussed any further.

The other three types of simulations are described next.

24.5.1 Monte Carlo Simulation

A static simulation or one without a time axis is called a Monte Carlo simulation. Such simulations are used to model probabilistic phenomenon that do not change characteristics with time. Like a dynamic simulation they require the generation of pseudo-random numbers. Monte Carlo simulations are also used for evaluating nonprobabilistic expressions using probabilistic methods. The following example illustrates one such application.

Example 24.1 The following integral is to be evaluated:

$$I = \int_0^2 e^{-x^2} dx$$

One way to evaluate this integral is to generate uniformly distributed random numbers x and for each number compute a function y as follows:

$$x \sim \text{Uniform}(0,2)$$

$$\text{Density function } f(x) = \tfrac{1}{2} \quad \text{iff} \quad 0 \le x \le 2$$

$$y = 2e^{-x^2}$$

The expected value of y is

$$E(y) = \int_0^2 2e^{-x^2} f(x) dx$$

$$= \int_0^2 2e^{-x^2} \tfrac{1}{2} dx$$

$$= \int_0^2 e^{-x^2} dx$$

$$= I$$

Thus, the integral can be evaluated by generating uniformly distributed random numbers x_i, computing y_i, and then averaging as follows:

$$x_i \sim \text{Uniform}(0,2)$$

$$y_i = 2e^{-x_i^2}$$

$$I = E(y) = \frac{1}{n} \sum_{i=1}^n y_i \qquad \square$$

24.5.2 Trace-Driven Simulation

A simulation using a trace as its input is a **trace-driven simulation**. A trace is a time-ordered record of events on a real system. Trace-driven simulations are quite common in computer system analyses. They are generally used in analyzing or tuning resource management algorithms. Paging algorithms, cache analysis, CPU scheduling algorithms, deadlock prevention algorithms, and algorithms for dynamic allocation of storage are examples of cases where trace-driven simulation has been successfully used and documented in the literature.

In these studies, a trace of the resource demand is used as input to the simulation, which models different algorithms. For example, in order to compare different memory management schemes, a trace of page reference patterns of key programs can be obtained on a system. This trace can then be used to find the optimal set of parameters for a given memory management algorithm or to compare different algorithms.

It should be noted that the traces should be independent of the system under study. For example, a trace of pages fetched from a disk depends upon the working set size and page replacement policy used. This trace could not be used to study other page replacement policies. For that, one would need a trace of pages referenced. Similarly, an instruction trace obtained on one operating system should not be used to analyze another operating system.

Sherman and Brown (1973) point out the following advantages of trace-driven simulations:

1. *Credibility*: The results of a trace-driven simulation are easy to sell to other members of the design team. A trace of page references, for example, has more credibility than references generated randomly using an assumed distribution.

2. *Easy Validation*: The first step in a trace-driven simulation is to monitor a real system to get the trace. During this monitoring, one can also measure performance characteristics of the system. By comparing the measured performance with that obtained by simulation, one can easily validate a trace-driven model.

3. *Accurate Workload*: A trace preserves the correlation and interference effects in the workload. No simplification, such as those needed in getting an analytical model of the workload, is required.

4. *Detailed Trade-offs*: Due to the high level of detail in the workload, it is possible to study the effect of small changes in the model or algorithms.

5. *Less Randomness*: A trace is a deterministic input. If the simulation is repeated again, the input trace is still the same but the output may be different due to randomness in other parts of the model. Overall, output of a trace-driven model has less variance, which means that a fewer number of repetitions are required to get a desired statistical confidence in the result. Also, if other parts of the system are not random, it is possible to get absolute results in one execution of the model.

6. *Fair Comparison*: A trace allows different alternatives to be compared under the same input stream. This is a fairer comparison than other simulation models in which input is generated from a random stream and is different for the various alternatives being simulated.

7. *Similarity to the Actual Implementation*: A trace-driven model is generally very similar to the system being modeled. Thus, when implementing it, one can get a very good feeling for the complexity of implementing a proposed algorithm.

The disadvantages of trace-driven simulations are as follows:

1. *Complexity*: A trace-driven model requires a more detailed simulation of the system. Sometimes, the complexity of the model overshadows the algorithm being modeled.
2. *Representativeness*: Traces taken on one system may not be representative of the workload on another system. Even on a single system workload may change with time, and thus traces become obsolete faster than other forms of workload models that can be adjusted with time.
3. *Finiteness*: A trace is a long sequence. A detailed trace of a few minutes of activity on a system may be enough to fill a disk pack. A result based on those few minutes may not be applicable to the activities during the rest of the day.
4. *Single Point of Validation*: While using traces for validation, one should be careful since the traces give only one point of validation each. An algorithm that is the best for one trace may not be the best for another. One should use a few different traces to validate the results.
5. *Detail*: The main problem with trace-driven simulation is the high level of detail. Traces are generally very long sequences that have to be read in from a disk and then computation has to be done for each element of the trace.
6. *Trade-off*: With traces, it is difficult to change workload characteristics. It is not possible to change a trace itself. In order to make conclusions about the impact of changes in workload, a trace for the changed workload is required. Similarly, if a trace contains resource demand characteristics of several jobs, it is difficult to study the effects on individual jobs.

24.5.3 Discrete-Event Simulations

A simulation using a discrete-state model of the system is called a discrete event simulation. This is opposite of continuous-event simulations in which the state of the system takes continuous values. The continuous-state models are used in chemical simulations where the state of the system is described by the concentration of a chemical substance. In computer systems, discrete-event models are used since the state of the system is described by the number of jobs at various devices. Notice that the term "discrete" does not apply to the time values used in the simulation. A discrete-event simulation may use discrete- or continuous-time values.

All discrete-event simulations have a common structure. Regardless of the system being modeled, the simulation will have some of the components described below. If a general-purpose language is used, all components have to be developed by the analyst. A simulation language provides some of the components and leaves others for the analyst. The components are as follows:

1. *Event Scheduler*: It keeps a linked list of events waiting to happen. The scheduler allows the events to be manipulated in various ways. Some of these manipulation activities are as follows:

   (a) Schedule event X at time T.
   (b) Hold event X for a time interval dt.
   (c) Cancel a previously scheduled event X.
   (d) Hold event X indefinitely (until it is scheduled by another event).
   (e) Schedule an indefinitely held event.

   Event scheduler is one of the most frequently executed components of the simulation. It is executed before every event, and it may be called several times during one event to schedule other new events. Since the event scheduling has a significant impact on the computational efficiency of a simulation, the topic is discussed further in Section 24.6.

2. *Simulation Clock and a Time-advancing Mechanism*: Each simulation has a global variable representing simulated time. The scheduler is responsible for advancing this *time*. There are two ways of doing this. The first way, called the **unit time** approach, increments time by small increment and then checks to see if there are any events that can occur. The second approach, called the **event-driven** approach, increments the time automatically to the time of the next earliest occurring event. The unit time approach is not generally used in computer simulations.

3. *System State Variables*: These are global variables that describe the state of the system. For example, in the CPU scheduling simulation, the system state variable is the number of jobs in the queue. This is a global variable that is distinct from local variables such as CPU time required for a job, which would be stored in the data structure representing the job.

4. *Event Routines*: Each event is simulated by its routine. These routines update the system state variables and schedule other events. For example, in simulating a CPU scheduling mechanism, one might need routines to handle the three events of job arrivals, job scheduling, and job departure.

5. *Input Routines*: These get the model parameters, such as mean CPU demand per job, from the user. It is better to ask for all input at the beginning of a simulation and then free the user, since simulations generally take a long time to complete. The input routines typically allow a parameter to be varied in a specified manner. For example, the simulation may be run with mean CPU demand varying from 1 to 9 milliseconds in steps of 2 milliseconds. Each set of input values defines one iteration that may have to be repeated several times with different seeds. Thus, each single execution of the simulation consists of several **iterations**, and each iteration consists of several **repetitions**.

6. *Report Generator*: These are the output routines executed at the end of the simulation. They calculate the final result and print in a specified format.

7. *Initialization Routines*: These set the initial state of the system state variables and initialize various random-number generation streams. It is suggested that there be separate routines to initialize the state at the beginning of a simulation, at the beginning of an iteration, and at the beginning of a repetition.

8. *Trace Routines*: These print out intermediate variables as the simulation proceeds. They help debug the simulation program. It is advisable that the trace have an on/off feature so that it can be turned off for final production runs of the model. A model may even allow the ability to interrupt the execution of the model from the keyboard and turn the trace on or off.

9. *Dynamic Memory Management*: The number of entities in a simulation changes continuously as new entities are generated and old ones are destroyed. This requires periodic garbage collection. Most simulation languages and many general-purpose languages provide this automatically. In other cases, the programmer has the burden of writing codes for dynamic memory management.

10. *Main Program*: This brings all the routines together. It calls input routines, initializes the simulation, executes various iterations, and finally, calls the output routines.

24.6 EVENT-SET ALGORITHMS

In discrete-event simulations, it is necessary to ensure that the events occur in the proper order and at the proper time. Most simulation languages provide facilities for this. However, for simulations written in general-purpose languages, the programmer must implement this facility. Sometimes, even while using a simulation language, analysts may prefer to use their own event-set algorithm. For example, efficient implementation of the event-set algorithm has resulted, in some cases, in as much as 30% savings in total processor time.

Event scheduling is usually done by keeping an ordered linked list of future event notices. Each notice contains the time at which the event should occur and a pointer to the code that must be executed at that time. There are two operations that are performed frequently on this set: one to insert new events in the set and one to find the next (earliest) event and remove it from the set. The choice of the data structure used to maintain this set affects the processor time required for the two operations. Some data structures have very little overhead for insertion but require considerable processing to find the next event. Other data structures do all the work at the time of insertion so that finding the next event is straightforward. The choice of the data structure is therefore based on the frequency of insertion and removals and on the average

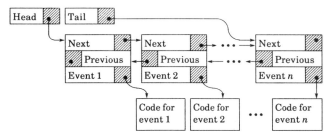

FIGURE 24.7   Doubly linked list.

number of events in the future set. Some of the data structures that have been proposed are as follows:

1. *Ordered Linked List*: The approach most commonly used in simulation languages such as SIMULA, GPSS, and GASP IV is that of keeping an ordered doubly linked list, as shown in Figure 24.7. The first entry in the list is the next earliest event. Thus, removal is straightforward. To insert a new event, the list is searched to find the right place for the new entry. A number of alternatives for search direction have been proposed. The most common method is to search backward from the highest time value. Alternately, the list could be searched forward from the first entry. Some have even tried keeping a pointer on the middle entry, first determining the half that would contain the right place and then searching forward or backward to determine the place.

2. *Indexed Linear List*: In this approach, the set of future events is divided into several subsets. Each subset spans a fixed interval Δt of the time interval and is maintained as a sublist, as shown in Figure 24.8. An array of indexes is kept such that the ith entry of the index points to the ith sublist that contains events scheduled for the interval $[(i-1)\Delta t, i\Delta t)$, that is, at or after time $(i-1)\Delta t$ but before time $i\Delta t$. Here, Δt is

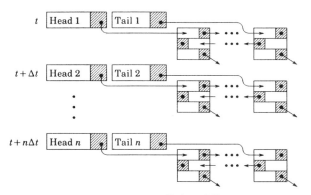

FIGURE 24.8   Indexed list.

an interval specified by the user. Thus, given a new event to be inserted, the required sublist can be determined without any search. The proper sublist is then searched backward to find the position of the new entry.

A number of variations to this approach have also been proposed based on the argument that the event-hold times (the time between scheduling an event and its occurrence) are not uniformly distributed. In one variation, an attempt is made to keep all lists of the same length, the interval covered by each index entry; that is, Δt is variable. Binary search is used to find the proper index entry. In another variation, only the first list is kept sorted; other lists are kept unsorted. A sublist is sorted only when it becomes the first sublist, thereby reducing the sorting overhead.

An interesting variation of this approach is called **calendar queues**. It is based on the desk calendars used by human beings to schedule events. A typical desk calendar has 365 pages—one page for each day of the year. All events for a single day are written down on the page corresponding to that day. The events for the same day of the next year can also be written on that page. This will not cause any confusion if the year of occurrence is also written down with the event and the events are deleted after they have taken place. This idea can be easily implemented using an indexed linear list. The interval Δt corresponds to a human day, and size of the index corresponds to the number of days in a year. Both these parameters should be carefully chosen so that the number of events per page is small (close to 0 or 1). A procedure to dynmically adjust these two parameters is described by Brown (1988) who also showed that the algorithm takes a fixed amount of time per event regardless of the number of events.

3. *Tree Structures*: Tree data structures have also been used for simulation event sets. Usually a binary tree is used. The time to search through n events is then $\log_2 n$.

A special case of the binary tree is the **heap**, where each event is stored as a node in the binary tree. Each node can have up to two children, and the event time for each node is smaller than that of its children, if any. This implies that the root always has the earliest event time. The advantage of heaps is that the tree can be stored in an array (as opposed to a linked list) by putting the root at position 1 of the array and its children at positions 2 and 3. The nodes at the next level are kept in array positions 4, 5, 6, 7, and so on, as shown in Figure 24.9. The traversal of a heap is simple because it is easy to find the parents and children of any particular node. The two children of the node in position i are in positions $2i$ and $2i + 1$. The parent of a node in position i is at the position $\lfloor i/2 \rfloor$. Here, $\lfloor \cdot \rfloor$ represents the truncation to the next lower integer. The array has to be rearranged partially after each insertion or removal.

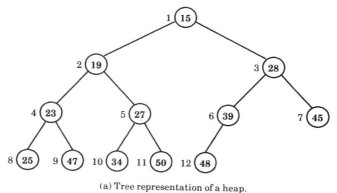

(a) Tree representation of a heap.

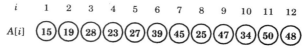

(b) Array representation of a heap.

FIGURE 24.9 A heap.

The heaps can be further extended to k-ary heaps that make use of k-ary trees in which each node has up to k children.

The choice of the proper data structure depends upon the distribution of event hold times and the number of events in the future event set. It also depends upon the ease with which various data structures can be implemented in the given programming language. In a study by Reeves (1984), the simple linked list was found to be the most efficient alternative if the number of events was small (less than 20 events). For event sets of sizes 20 to 120, index linear lists were the best, while for larger sets, heaps were found to be the most efficient. Similar conclusions were also drawn in an earlier study by McCormack and Sargent (1979).

EXERCISES

24.1 For each of the following models, identify all classifications that apply to it:

a. $y(t) = t + 0.2$

b. $y(t) = t^2$

c. $y(t + 1) = y(t) + \Delta$, Δ is not an integer.

d. $n(t + 1) = 2n(t) + 3$

e. $y(t) = \sin(wt)$

f. $\overline{y}(t + 1) = \overline{y}(t) + \Delta$

24.2 Which type of simulation would you use for the following problems:
  a. To model destination address reference patterns in a network traffic given that the pattern depends upon a large number of factors.
  b. To model scheduling in a multiprocessor system given that the request arrivals have a known distribution.
  c. To determine the value of π.

24.3 What is the unit time approach and why is it not generally used?

CHAPTER 25

ANALYSIS OF SIMULATION RESULTS

Always assume that your assumption is invalid.
—Robert F. Tatman

During the development of the simulation model, you must ensure that the model is correctly implemented and that it is representative of the real system. These two steps are called model verification and model validation, respectively. After the model development is compelete, the next two issues you will face are those of deciding how many of the initial observations should be discarded to ensure that the model has reached a steady state and how long to run the simulation. These issues are called transient removal and stopping criterion, respectively. These four issues are the main topics of this chapter.

25.1 MODEL VERIFICATION TECHNIQUES

The goodness of a simulation model is measured by the closeness of the model output to that of the real systems. Since a number of assumptions about the behavior of real systems are made in developing the model, there are two steps in measuring the goodness. The first step is whether the assumptions are reasonable, and the second step is whether the model implements those assumptions correctly. These two steps are called validation and verification, respectively. Validation is concerned with the representativeness of the assumptions, and verification is related to the correctness of the implementation. Verification can also be called debugging, that is, ensuring that the model does what it is intended to do.

Validation and verification are different concepts in that a model could be in any one of the four possible categories: invalid and unverified, invalid and verified, valid and unverified, or valid and verified. An invalid and verified model, for example, is one that correctly implements the assumptions, but the assumptions are far from reality. If the modeling and programming of a simulation model is being done by two separate persons (or teams), the modeling person would be responsible for validation and the programming person would be concerned with verification.

In the programming language literature, a number of techniques can be found for debugging. Any combination of these techniques can be used to verify the model. Some of these techniques, along with a few techniques applicable especially to simulation models, are described next.

25.1.1 Top-Down Modular Design

Simulation models are large computer programs. All techniques that help develop, debug, or maintain large computer programs are also useful for simulation models. Two important techniques are modularity and top-down design.

Modularity requires that the model be structured in modules that communicate with each other via well-defined interfaces. These modules are commonly called subroutines, subprograms, procedures, and so forth. The interface consists of a number of input and output variables or data structures. Once the interface and the function of a module have been specified, it can be independently developed, debugged, and maintained. Modularity thus allows the verification of the simulation to be broken down into smaller problems of verifying the modules and their interfaces.

Top-down design consists of developing a hierarchical structure for the model such that the problem is recursively divided into a set of smaller problems. First, the model is divided into a number of modules with different functions. Each of these modules is then further subdivided into modules. The process is repeated until the modules are small enough to be easily debugged and maintained.

The following example illustrates a sample top-down modular design.

Example 25.1   Figure 25.1 shows the modules for a computer network simulation developed for congestion control studies. The model simulates a network with a number of source nodes, a number of intermediate nodes, and a number of destinations, as shown in Figure 25.2. Packets start from the source nodes, travel through a number of prespecified intermediate nodes (called paths), and reach the destination. The packet sizes and service times at various nodes are randomly distributed. In Figure 25.2, S_i's are sources, R_i's are intermediate nodes, and D_i's are destinations. The model simulates n sources sharing a common path throught m intermediate nodes for any given n and m. This is equivalent to two local-area networks connected through m intermediate nodes.

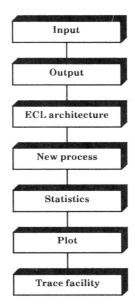

FIGURE 25.1 Layered structure of the congestion simulation model.

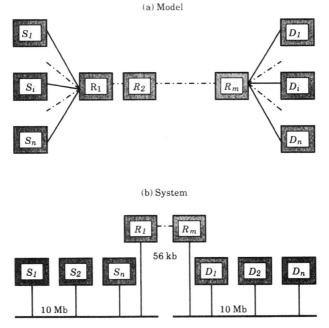

FIGURE 25.2 Model of two interconnected local-area networks.

The model consists of seven different modules, shown in Figure 25.1. Each module consists of several procedures and builds on the functionality provided by modules below it. The lowest layer is a general-purpose trace facility useful for debugging SIMULA programs. The plot module provides a general graph-plotting facility. A set of simple statistical routines to calculate, for example, the mean and variance forms the next layer. One problem that was encountered in using SIMULA was that the time variable cannot be reset to zero. The word length of the computer prevented us from running several iterations without time overflow. The fourth layer, labeled "new process" removes this restriction. It allows each iteration to reset a "new time" variable to zero and provides its own event-scheduling routines. The four layers discussed so far are very general and are not related to the problem being simulated.

The layer labeled "ECL architecture" contains all problem-specific routines. The output layer contains all the routines to produce intermediate and final results. Finally, the main program, initialization, and parameter input routines are part of the top layer.

The model is described in Jain (1986).   □

25.1.2 Antibugging

Antibugging consists of including additional checks and outputs in the program that will point out the bugs, if any. For example, if the probabilities for certain events are supposed to add up to 1, the program may check this and print an error message if the sum is not within a specified tolerance limit. Another example is that of counting the entities generated and served. In the computer network simulation, for example, the model counts the number of packets sent by a number of source nodes as well as the number received by the destination nodes. The number of packets lost on the route and the packets received should equal the number of packets sent. A nonzero difference would indicate a programming error. In fact, for each entity defined in the simulation, it is good practice to have a generate entity routine that counts the number of entities generated and to have an explicit destroy entity routine that decrements the number of entities before releasing their data structure for garbage collection. The numbers are maintained in a global (common) area, which is checked at the end of the simulation to see that all entities are properly accounted for. For example, in a network simulation, packets, nodes, and connections are counted when they are generated as well as destroyed. It is very useful since small changes in the model often result in bugs that are discovered by the entity accounting routine at the end of the simulation.

25.1.3 Structured Walk-Through

Structured walk-through consists of explaining the code to another person or a group. The code developer explains what each line of code does, which can be very helpful. It turns out that even if the listeners do not understand the model, the developers discover bugs simply by reading the code carefully, trying to explain it, and finding that the code does not exactly match the expectation.

25.1.4 Deterministic Models

The key problem in debugging simulation models is the randomness of variables. It is obvious that a deterministic program is easier to debug than a program with random variables. A common verification technique, therefore, is to allow the user to specify any distribution. Of course, the default parameter values should be set to represent the behavior in the real systems. But by specifying constant (deterministic) distributions, the user can easily determine output variables and thus debug the modules.

25.1.5 Run Simplified Cases

The model may be run with simple cases, for example, only one packet, or only one source, or only one intermediate node. These cases can be easily analyzed and the simulation results can be compared with the analysis. Of course, a model that works for simple cases is not guaranteed to work for more complex cases. Therefore, the test cases should be as complex as can be easily analyzed without simulation.

25.1.6 Trace

A trace consists of a time-ordered list of events and their associated variables. They may be presented at several levels of detail: events trace, procedure trace, or variables trace. The trace outputs are useful in debugging the model. Tracing causes additional processing overhead, and therefore, the model should have switches that allow the traces to be turned on and off.

A sample event trace for the computer network simulation is shown in Figure 25.3. The trace lists the time, event code, and various packet characteristics associated with the event. In the trace S_i, D_i, and R_i's are the ith source, ith destination, and ith intermediate node (router), respectively.

It is possible to have much more detail in a trace than exhibited in the sample trace of Figure 25.3. For example, the trace could show events and procedure names as well as values of the key variables. Each procedure's name could be printed as it is executed. The list is sometimes indented to indicate the call/return sequence. The trace statements explicitly put in the procedures print values of the key variables. The user should be able to select the level of detail in the trace, including no trace at all, which should be the default. The user may be allowed to trace only some selected events such as those belonging to a particular node in a computer network or a particular type of packet and so forth.

PKT=100 CR=4 #S=2 RS=2   ! This was a run with 100 packets, 4 credits per source, two sources. Router service time was twice that of the source.

Time	Node: Event	Pkt #/ Attempt	Sample Delay	Delay Estimate	
0.00:	S1: TIMR	1- 1			! Round trip delay-measuring stop watch started by source 1
	S1: SEND	1- 1/ 1			! Packet 1 sent by source 1
	S1: STRT				! Timeout alarm clock set by source 1
	S2: TIMR	2- 1			! Round trip delay-measuring stop watch started by source 2
	S2: SEND	2- 1/ 1			! Packet 1 sent by source 2
	S2: STRT				! Timeout alarm clock set by source 2
1.00:	R1: QUED	1- 1/ 1			! Packet 1 of source 1 was put into a queue at router 1
	R1: LOST!	2- 1/ 1			! Packet 1 of source 2 was lost due to lack of buffer at router 1
3.00:	D1: RECD	1- 1/ 1			! Packet 1 of source 1 was received at destination 1
	S1: ACKD	1- 1			! Acknowledgment for packet 1 was received at source 1
	S1: UPDT	1- 1	3.00	3.00	! Source 1 updated its estimate of round trip delay

FIGURE 25.3 Sample packet event-trace output from the simulation model.

25.1.7 On-Line Graphic Displays

Simulations take a long time to run. On-line graphic displays and traces help to keep the user informed of the status of the simulation. They also make the simulation interesting and are helpful in selling the simulation results to others. Most of all, the displays help debug the simulation; they can present the same information as in the trace but in a more comprehensive form. It is difficult to look at a long trace, while it is easy to inspect the display for the same period.

25.1.8 Continuity Test

Continuity tests consist of running the simulation several times for slightly different values of input parameters. For any one parameter, a slight change in input should generally produce only a slight change in the output. Any sudden changes in the output should be investigated. Often, they are due to modeling error.

An example of a continuity test is shown in Figure 25.4, which shows the response time for various values of an input parameter using an undebugged

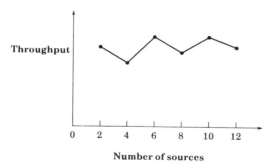

FIGURE 25.4   Discontinuities in the curve indicate the possibility of a programming error.

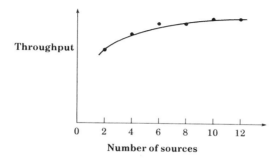

FIGURE 25.5   The curve after verification.

version of the simulation model. The output jumps caused us to carefully trace the code. The same graph from the verified version of the model is shown in Figure 25.5. Notice that the response time curve is now smooth.

25.1.9 Degeneracy Tests

Degeneracy tests consist of checking that the model works for extreme (lowest or highest allowed) values of system, configuration, or workload parameters. For example, a multi-CPU, multidisk workstation model should work for a single CPU without a disk (diskless) as long as these are valid system configurations. Although these extreme cases may not represent a typical case, they help discover bugs that the analyst would not have thought of otherwise. It is useful to incorporate checks for input parameter values and to verify that they are within the allowed bounds. The analyst should have verified that the model works for any combination of these allowed bounds.

   For example, the network simulation model works for a system with no sources, no routers, routers with zero service times, or sources with infinite flow control windows.

25.1.10   Consistency Tests

These tests consist of checking that the model produces similar results for input parameter values that have similar effects. For example, two sources with an arrival rate of 100 packets per second should load the network to approximately the same level as four sources with an arrival rate of 50 packets per second each. If the model output shows a significant difference, either the difference should be explainable or it could be due to programming errors.

The test cases used in continuity, degeneracy, and consistency tests should be saved in a test library so that whenever the model is changed, the tests can be repeated to verify the new model.

25.1.11   Seed Independence

The seeds used in random-number generation should not affect the final conclusion. Thus, the model should produce similar results for different seed values. The analyst should verify this by running the simulation with different seed values.

25.2   MODEL VALIDATION TECHNIQUES

Validation refers to ensuring that the assumptions used in developing the model are reasonable in that, if correctly implemented, the model would produce results close to that observed in real systems. The validation techniques depend upon the assumptions and, hence, on the systems being modeled. Thus, unlike verification techniques that are generally applicable, the validation techniques used in one simulation may not apply to another.

Model validation consists of validating the three key aspects of the model:

1. Assumptions
2. Input parameter values and distributions
3. Output values and conclusions

Each of these three aspects may be subjected to a validity test by comparing it with that obtained from the following three possible sources:

1. Expert intuition
2. Real system measurements
3. Theoretical results

This leads to nine possible validation tests. Of course, it may not be feasible to use some of these possibilities. For example, no real-system measurements may be available or no theoretical results may be available. In most real situations, in fact, none of the nine possibilities may be feasible. This is because simulation, being a time-consuming effort, is resorted to only if no other reliable means of finding the same information exist. In such cases, the analyst should at least validate the model for simple configurations.

The three sources of comparable information are described next.

25.2.1 Expert Intuition

Expert intuition is the most practical and common way to validate a model. A brainstorming meeting of the people knowledgeable with the system may be called. The people are drawn from those involved in the design, architecture, implementation, analysis, marketing, or maintenance of the system. Of course, the selection depends upon the life-cycle stage of the system being modeled. For systems already in use, field service and marketing people may have a better knowledge than implementors. The assumptions, input values and distributions, as well as outputs (if available) are presented and discussed in the meeting.

In practice, it is better to validate the three aspects—assumptions, input, and output—separately as the model progresses rather than waiting till the end. The assumptions of the model should be brainstormed as soon as a preliminary design of the simulation model has been prepared. The input values and distribution should be discussed and validated next during model development. The output should be validated as soon as an executable model exists and it has been verified.

One technique to judge the validity of outputs is to present the model results as well as the measurements from real systems to these experts and see if they can distinguish between them.

Expert analysts can point out errors in simulation by simply looking at the simulation outputs. To illustrate this and the use of expert intuition technique, we present, in Figure 25.6, a graph of network throughput as a function of probability of packet loss obtained from an invalid version of the network sim-

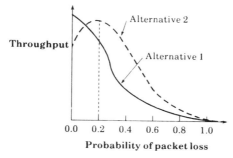

FIGURE 25.6 Example of problems caused by invalid assumptions that are easily detected by experts.

ulation model. Two different alternatives were simulated, and the normalized throughput for the two alternatives is shown separately in the figure. For alternative 1, the throughput drops as the probability of loss increases. For alternative 2, the throughput initially improves, reaches a maximum at a loss probability of 0.2, and then falls off. The results for alternative 2 are counterintuitive because, normally, packet loss leads to reduced throughput whereas the graph shows that for the best performance we ought to lose 20% of the packets. An expert in the field would wonder why the performance with no loss is worse than that for a 20% loss. This may be because alternative 2 was either not designed properly (algorithm design error) or not implemented properly (programming error). The two possibilities are related to validation and verification, respectively. In this particular instance, the problem was found to be an algorithm design error; an improved version of the alternative was later designed; this version behaved as expected.

25.2.2 Real-System Measurements

Comparison with real systems is the most reliable and preferred way to validate a simulation model. In practice, however, this is often unfeasible either because the real systems may not exist or because the measurements may be too expensive to carry out. Even one or two measurements add considerably to the validity of a simulation.

Assumptions, input values, output values, workloads, configurations, and system behavior should be compared with those observed in the real world. The statistical techniques described in Chapter 13 to test whether two systems are identical may be used to compare the simulation model and the measured data. Input distributions can be ascertained by statistical distribution fitting techniques or by using statistical tests (for example, a chi-square test). In trace-driven simulations, multiple traces obtained under different environments should be used to validate the model.

25.2.3 Theoretical Results

In some cases, it is possible to analytically model the system under simplifying assumptions. It may also be possible to analytically determine what the input distributions should be. In such cases, the similarity of theoretical results and simulation results is used to validate the simulation model. Similarly, in developing queueing system models of computer systems, analysts often find that the real-system behavior is too difficult to model exactly. In such cases, they develop an approximate technique and validate it by comparing the results with those obtained from a simulation.

Validation by comparing theoretical and simulation results should be used with care as both may be invalid in the sense that they both may not represent the behavior of a real system. Nonetheless, it is a useful technique provided a few points (of theory or simulation) have been validated using expert intuition or real-system measurements. Analytical modeling then allows validation for more complex cases. For example, a multiprocessor simulation model may be validated using a few real one- or two-processor systems, and then theory can be used to validate for a larger number of processors.

Before concluding this section on validation, we must point out that a "fully validated model" is a myth. In reality, it is only possible to show that the model is not invalid for some of the situations compared. To prove that the model produces the same result as the original system under all circumstances would generally require an inordinate amount of resources. The validation exercise is therefore limited to a few selected scenarios, and an attempt is made to cover all important cases. This helps increase the degree of confidence in the model results.

25.3 TRANSIENT REMOVAL

In most simulations, only the **steady-state performance**, that is, the performance after the system has reached a stable state, is of interest. In such cases, results of the initial part of the simulation should not be included in the final computations. This initial part is also called the transient state. The problem of identifying the end of the transient state is called **transient removal**.

The main difficulty with transient removal is that it is not possible to define exactly what constitutes the transient state and when that transient state ends. All methods for transient removal are therefore heuristic. There are six such methods:

1. Long runs
2. Proper initialization
3. Truncation
4. Initial data deletion
5. Moving average of independent replications
6. Batch means

25.3.1 Long Runs

The first method is simply to use very long runs; that is, runs that are long enough to ensure that the presence of initial conditions will not affect the result. There are two disadvantages to this method. First, it wastes resources; if resources are expensive, a simulation should not be run any longer than is absolutely necessary. Second, even if generating new observations does not consume any significant resources, it is difficult to ensure that the length of run chosen in long enough. For these two reasons, it is recommended that this method not be used.

25.3.2 Proper Initialization

Proper initialization requires starting the simulation in a state close to the expected steady state. For example, a CPU scheduling simulation may start with some jobs in the queue (rather than an empty queue) at the beginning. The number of jobs may be determined from previous simulations or by simple analysis. This method results in a reduction in the length of transient periods so that there is little effect on the overall computation.

25.3.3 Truncation

This and all subsequent methods are based on the assumption that the variability during the steady state is less than that during the transient state, which is generally true. In the trunctation method, the variability is measured in terms of range—the minimum and maximum of observations. If a trajectory showing successive observations is plotted on a graph paper, range of observations can often be seen to stabilize as the simulation enters the steady-state phase.

Given a sample of n observations $\{x_1, x_2, x_3, ..., x_n\}$, the truncation method consists of ignoring the first l observations and then calculating the minimum and maximum of the remaining $n - l$ observations. This step is repeated for $l = 1, 2, ..., n - 1$ until the $(l + 1)$th observation is neither the minimum nor maximum of the remaining observations. The value of l at this point gives the length of the transient state.

Example 25.2   Consider the following sequence of observations: 1, 2, 3, 4, 5, 6, 7, 8, 9, 10, 11, 10, 9, 10, 11, 10, 9, 10, 11, 10, 9, ...

Ignoring the first observation ($l = 1$), the range of the remaining observations is $(2, 11)$. Since the second observation is equal to the minimum, the transient phase is longer than 1.

Ignoring the first two observation ($l = 2$), the range of the remaining sequence is $(3, 11)$. Again, the next (third) observation is equal to the minimum; the truncation continues with $l = 3$ and so on.

Finally, at $l = 9$ the range of the remaining sequence is $(9, 11)$, and the tenth observation 10 is neither the minimum nor the maximum. The length of the transient interval is therefore 9, and the first nine observations are discarded.

A trajectory of this set of observations is shown in Figure 25.7. It is seen from the figure that the transient phase for this data does indeed end after nine observations.   □

Truncation method can sometimes give incorrect result as shown in Exercise 25.2.

25.3.4 Initial Data Deletion

Initial data deletion requires studying the overall average after some of the initial observations are deleted from the sample. During steady state, the average does not change much as the observations are deleted. However, the randomness in the observations does cause the averages to change slightly even during

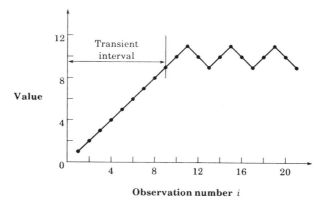

FIGURE 25.7 Plot of the data used in the truncation method example.

the steady state. To reduce the effect of randomness, the method requires first averaging across several replications. Each replication consists of a complete run of the simulation with no change in input parameter values. The replications differ only in the seed values used in the random-number generators. Averaging across the replications results in a smoother trajectory.

Suppose there are m replications of size n each. Let x_{ij} denote the jth observation in the ith replication. Notice that j varies from 1 to n along the time axis, while i varies from 1 to m across the replications. The method consists of the following steps:

1. Get a mean trajectory by averaging across replications:

$$\overline{x}_j = \frac{1}{m} \sum_{i=1}^{m} x_{ij}, \qquad j = 1, 2, \ldots, n$$

Figure 25.8a shows the trajectories of several replications, and an average trajectory is shown in Figure 25.8b.

2. Get the overall mean:

$$\overline{\overline{x}} = \frac{1}{n} \sum_{j=1}^{n} \overline{x}_j$$

Set $l = 1$ and proceed to the next step.

3. Assuming that the transient state is only l long, delete the first l observations from the mean trajectory and get an overall mean from the remaining $n - l$ values:

$$\overline{\overline{x}}_l = \frac{1}{n-l} \sum_{j=l+1}^{n} \overline{x}_j$$

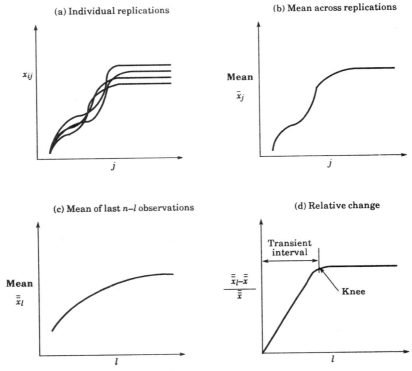

FIGURE 25.8   Initial data deletion method.

4. Compute the relative change in the overall mean:

$$\text{Relative change} = \frac{\overline{\overline{x}}_l - \overline{\overline{x}}}{\overline{\overline{x}}}$$

5. Repeat steps 3 and 4 by varying l from 1 to $n-1$. Plots of the overall mean and the relative change as functions of l are shown in Figure 25.8c and 25.8d. After a certain value of l, the relative change graph stabilizes. This point is known as the knee, and the value of l at the knee is the length of the transient interval.

25.3.5   Moving Average of Independent Replications

The method of moving averages of independent replications is similar to the initial data deletion. The key difference is that this method requires computing the mean over a moving time interval window instead of the overall mean.

Given m replications of size n each, again let x_{ij} denote the jth observation in the ith replication. The steps are as follows:

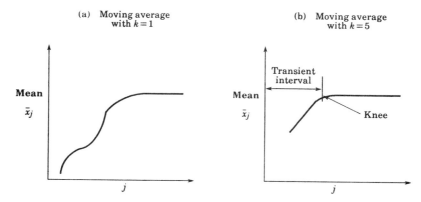

FIGURE 25.9   Moving average of independent replications.

1. Get a mean trajectory by averaging across replications:

$$\bar{x}_j = \frac{1}{m} \sum_{i=1}^{m} x_{ij}, \qquad j = 1, 2, \ldots, n$$

   Set $k = 1$ and proceed to the next step.

2. Plot a trajectory of the moving average of successive $2k + 1$ values:

$$\bar{\bar{x}}_j = \frac{1}{2k + 1} \sum_{l=-k}^{k} \bar{x}_{j+l}, \qquad j = k + 1, k + 2, \ldots, n - k$$

3. Repeat step 2, with $k = 2, 3, \ldots$ until the plot is sufficiently smooth.
4. Find the knee of the plot. The value of j at the knee gives the length of the transient phase.

Figure 25.9 shows two sample trajectories of moving averages. In the second trajectory, the plot is smooth and the knee can be easily identified.

25.3.6 Batch Means

The method of batch means requires running a very long simulation and later dividing it up into several parts of equal duration. Each part is called a **batch** or **subsample**. The mean of observations in each batch is called the **batch mean**. The method requires studying the variance of these batch means as a function of the batch size.

As shown in Figure 25.10, a long run of N observations can be divided into m batches of size n each, where $m = \lfloor N/n \rfloor$. Here, $\lfloor \cdot \rfloor$ is used to denote truncation to the lower integer value. Start with a small value for n, say, 2. Again, let x_{ij} denote the jth observation in the ith batch.

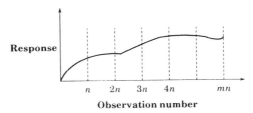

FIGURE 25.10   Transient removal by batch means requires dividing the data into m batches of size n each.

1. For each batch, compute a batch mean:

$$\overline{x}_i = \frac{1}{n} \sum_{j=1}^{n} x_{ij}, \qquad i = 1, 2, \ldots m$$

2. Compute the overall mean:

$$\overline{\overline{x}} = \frac{1}{m} \sum_{i=1}^{m} \overline{x}_i$$

3. Compute the variance of the batch means:

$$\mathrm{Var}(\overline{x}) = \frac{1}{m-1} \sum_{i=1}^{m} \left(\overline{x}_i - \overline{\overline{x}}\right)^2$$

Increase n and repeat steps 1 and 3, for $n = 3, 4, 5, \ldots$. Plot the variance as a function of batch size n. The length of the transient interval is the value of n at which the variance definitely starts decreasing.

The rationale behind this method is as follows. Suppose the length of the transient period is T. If the batch size n is much less than T, initial batches bring the overall mean toward the initial batch means and the variance is small. As the batch size is increased, the variance increases. At n larger than T, only the first batch mean is different; other batch means are approximately equal. This results in the decrease of the variance.

Note that in using this method, you should ignore those peaks on the variance curve that are followed by an upswing, as shown in Figure 25.11.

25.4 TERMINATING SIMULATIONS

Although a majority of simulations are such that steady-state performance is of interest, there are systems that never reach a steady state. These systems always operate under transient conditions. For example, if the network traffic consists of the transfer of small files (one to three packets), steady-state simulations using large files will give results of no interest to a typical user. In

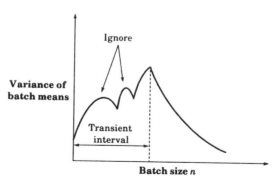

FIGURE 25.11 Transient removal by batch means.

such cases, it is necessary to study the system in a transient state. Such simulations are called **terminating simulations**. Other examples of terminating simulations are systems that shut down, for instance, at 5 PM every day, or systems that have parameters that change with time. Such simulations do not require transient removal.

Another related issue is that of **final conditions**—the conditions at the end of the simulation. The system state at the end of the simulation may not be typical of the steady state. In such cases, it is necessary to exclude the final portion of the response from the steady-state computations. The methods for this would be similar to those used for determining initial transient periods.

Finally, the analyst should be careful in handling the entities left at the end of the simulation. Consider the example of the CPU scheduling simulation. In computing mean service time, only those jobs that completed service must be included, that is,

$$\text{Mean service time} = \frac{\text{total service time}}{\text{number of jobs that completed service}}$$

In computing mean waiting time, only those jobs that completed waiting and started execution should be used, that is,

$$\text{Mean waiting time} = \frac{\text{sum of waiting time}}{\text{number of jobs that received service}}$$

If q_j is the queue length at the jth event that resulted in a queue length change, the average of q_j's does not give the mean queue length, that is,

$$\text{Mean queue length} \neq \frac{\sum_{j=1}^{n}(\text{queue length at event } j)}{\text{number of events } n}$$

Instead, a time average of the queue length process should be used, that is,

$$\text{Mean queue length} = \frac{1}{T} \int_0^T \text{Queue length}(t)\,dt$$

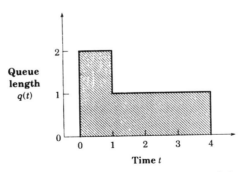

FIGURE 25.12   Mean queue length is time average of the queue length.

Example 25.3   Figure 25.12 shows the length of a hypothetical queue. Two jobs arrive at time $t = 0$. The first job departs at $t = 1$ and the second one departs at $t = 4$. There are three events—one arrival and two departures. The queue lengths at these events are 2, 1, and 0, respectively. The average queue length is not $(2 + 1 + 0)/3$, that is, 1. The area under the queue length curve is 5. Therefore, the correct average queue length is $\frac{5}{4}$, or 1.25.
□

25.5 STOPPING CRITERIA: VARIANCE ESTIMATION

It is important that the length of the simulation be properly chosen. If the simulation is too short, the results may be highly variable. On the other hand, if the simulation is too long, computing resources and manpower may be unnecessarily wasted. From the discussion in Section 13.9 on determining the sample sizes, it follows that the simulation should be run until the confidence interval for the mean response narrows to a desired width. If the sample mean is $\bar{x}$ and its variance is $\mathrm{Var}(\bar{x})$, a $100(1 - \alpha)\%$ confidence interval for the mean is given by

$$\bar{x} \pm z_{1-\alpha/2}\mathrm{Var}(\bar{x})$$

Recall that $z_{1-\alpha/2}$ is the $(1 - \alpha/2)$th quantile of a unit normal variate. Its values are listed in Table A.2 of the Appendix.

The variance of the sample mean of n *independent* observations can be obtained easily from the variance of the observations as follows:

$$\mathrm{Var}(\bar{x}) = \frac{\mathrm{Var}(x)}{n}$$

This formula is valid only if the observations are independent. Unfortunately, the observations in most simulations are *not* independent. For example, in a queueing simulation, if the waiting time for the ith job is large, the waiting time for the $(i + 1)$th job would be large too and vice versa. In this case, the successive waiting times are highly correlated, and the preceding formula cannot be used to estimate the variance of the mean waiting time. For correlated observations, the variance of the mean may be several times larger than that obtained from the formula. In one extreme case, the actual variance was 300 times that obtained computed using the formula. Ignoring this fact may result in narrow confidence intervals and premature termination of simulation.

Statisticians have developed a number of methods to correctly compute the variance of the mean of correlated observations. Three such methods are as follows:

- Independent replications
- Batch means
- Regeneration

Of these, the first two methods are similar to those described earlier under transient removal.

25.5.1 Independent Replications

Recall from Section 25.3 that replications are obtained by repeating the simulation with a different seed value. This method is based on the assumption that the means of independent replications are independent even though observations in a single replication are correlated.

The method consists of conducting m replications of size $n + n_0$ each, where n_0 is the length of transient phase. The first n_0 observations of each replication are discarded. The remaining steps are as follows:

1. Compute a mean for each replication:

$$\bar{x}_i = \frac{1}{n} \sum_{j=n_0+1}^{n_0+n} x_{ij}, \qquad i = 1, 2, \ldots, m$$

2. Compute an overall mean for all replications:

$$\bar{\bar{x}} = \frac{1}{m} \sum_{i=1}^{m} \bar{x}_i$$

3. Calculate the variance of replicate means:

$$\text{Var}(\bar{x}) = \frac{1}{m-1} \sum_{i=1}^{m} (\bar{x}_i - \bar{\bar{x}})^2$$

The confidence interval for the mean response is*

$$[\bar{\bar{x}} \mp z_{1-\alpha/2} \text{Var}(\bar{x})]$$

Notice that this method requires discarding mn_0 initial observations. Further, the confidence interval width is inversely proportional to $\sqrt{mn}$. Thus, a narrower confidence interval can be obtained equally well by increasing either

---

*Throughout this section, use $t_{[1-\infty/2;m-1]}$ in place of $z_{1-\infty/2}$ if m is less than 30 as explained in section 13.2

m or n. However, to reduce the waste (mn_0 initial observations), it is suggested that m be kept fairly small, for example, 10. The length of replications n should be increased to obtain the desired confidence.

25.5.2 Batch Means

The method of batch means, also called **method of subsamples**, consists of running a long simulation run, discarding the initial transient interval, and dividing the remaining observations run into several batches or subsamples.

Given a long run of $N + n_0$ observations, where n_0 is the number of observations that belong to the transient interval and are discarded, the remaining N observations are divided into $m = \lfloor N/n \rfloor$ batches of n observations each. Start with a small value of n, for example, $n = 1$, and proceed as follows:

1. Compute means for each batch:

$$\overline{x}_i = \frac{1}{n} \sum_{j=1}^{n} x_{ij}, \qquad i = 1, 2, \dots, m$$

2. Compute an overall mean:

$$\overline{\overline{x}} = \frac{1}{m} \sum_{i=1}^{m} \overline{x}_i$$

3. Calculate the variance of batch means:

$$\mathrm{Var}(\overline{x}) = \frac{1}{m-1} \sum_{i=1}^{m} \left(\overline{x}_i - \overline{\overline{x}}\right)^2$$

The confidence interval for the mean response is

$$\left[\overline{\overline{x}} \mp z_{1-\alpha/2} \mathrm{Var}(\overline{x})\right]$$

Notice that the computation is essentially the same as it is in the method of independent replications. However, the method of batch means incurs less waste. Only n_0 observations are discarded. The confidence interval width is again inversely proportional to $\sqrt{mn}$, and it can be reduced by increasing either the number of batches m or the batch size n. The batch size n must be large so that the batch means have little correlation. One way to find correct n is to compute the covariance of successive batch means:

$$\mathrm{Cov}(\overline{x}_i, \overline{x}_{i+1}) = \frac{1}{m-2} \sum_{i=1}^{m-1} (\overline{x}_i - \overline{\overline{x}})(\overline{x}_{i+1} - \overline{\overline{x}})$$

This quantity is also called the **autocovariance**. The prefix *auto* denotes that the fact that both random variables $\overline{x}_i$ and $\overline{x}_{i+1}$ are members of the same set.

The preceding analysis is repeated with increasing values of batch size n until the autocovariance of the batch means is small compared to their variance.

TABLE 25.1 Autocovariance and Variance for Various Batch Sizes

Batch Size	Autocovariance	Variance
1	−0.18792	1.79989
2	0.02643	0.81173
4	0.11024	0.42003
8	0.08979	0.26437
16	0.04001	0.17650
32	0.01108	0.10833
64	0.00010	0.06066
128	−0.00378	0.02992
256	0.00027	0.01133
512	0.00069	0.00503
1024	0.00078	0.00202

One alternative is to start with a small n, for instance, $n = 1$, and successively double n.

The following case study illustrates an application of this method.

Case Study 25.1 The performance of indirect binary n-cube networks, which are used for processor-memory interconnection, was analyzed by simulation. The method of batch means was used to decide when to stop the simulation. The batch size was successively doubled, and the variance of batch means and the autocovariance between successive batch means were computed. The results are shown in Table 25.1 for a two-stage network with full fanout.

Notice that the the autocovariance between successive batch means becomes less than 1% of the original sample variance at a sample size of 64 or more. Hence, the batch size for this simulation was selected to be 64. □

25.5.3 Method of Regeneration

To understand the concept of regeneration, consider the example of a single CPU scheduling simulation. Starting with an empty job queue, a possible trajectory of queue length as a function of time is shown in Figure 25.13. Notice that the system often returns to the initial state—the empty job queue. The trajectory, after returning to this state, does not depend upon the previous history. The waiting time for a job depends upon the CPU demands of previous jobs. However, for the job arriving after a CPU idle interval, the waiting time does not depend upon the prior jobs. In fact, the idle interval starts a new phase in which the waiting times of jobs that follow this interval do not depend upon anything that happened before the idle period. In a sense, the system takes a new birth totally independent of its previous life. Simulation experts call this phenomenon **regeneration**. The instant at which the system

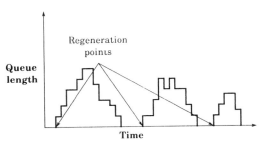

FIGURE 25.13   Regeneration points.

enters an independent phase is called the **regeneration point**. The duration between two successive regeneration points is called a **regeneration cycle**.

The trajectory shown in Figure 25.13 consists of three such cycles. Notice that the cycles are independent. The mean of the queue length in the second cycle is not correlated with that in the first cycle. The independence argument holds for variables other than the queue length as well.

A **regenerative system** (a system with regeneration cycles) can be analyzed using the method of regeneration. However, not all systems are regenerative. A system with two queues would regenerate when both queues are empty. As the number of queues increases, the regeneration points become rarer and regeneration cycles become longer. Some systems have long "memories" that make them **nonregenerative**.

The variance computation using regeneration cycles is a bit more complex than that in the method of batch means and the method of independent replications. This is because the regeneration cycles are of different lengths, whereas in the other two methods the batches or replications are all of the same length. In particular, the overall mean response cannot be obtained by averaging the mean responses of individual cycles. The cycle means are ratios with bases (cycle lengths) that are different. Recall from Section 12.7 that finding an average ratio requires special care.

Suppose you have a regenerative simulation consisting of m cycles of sizes $n_1, n_2, \ldots, n_m$, respectively. Cycle means are given by

$$\overline{x}_i = \frac{1}{n_i} \sum_{j=1}^{n_i} x_{ij}$$

However, the overall mean is not an arithmetic mean of cycle means:

$$\overline{\overline{x}} \neq \frac{1}{m} \sum_{i=1}^{m} \overline{x}_i$$

The correct procedure to compute the overall mean and its confidence interval is as follows:

1. Compute cycle sums:

$$y_i = \sum_{j=1}^{n_i} x_{ij}$$

2. Compute the overall mean:

$$\bar{\bar{x}} = \frac{\sum_{i=1}^{m} y_i}{\sum_{i=1}^{m} n_i}$$

3. Calculate the difference between expected and observed cycle sums:

$$w_i = y_i - n_i \bar{\bar{x}}, \qquad i = 1, 2, \ldots, m$$

4. Calculate the variance of the differences:

$$\mathrm{Var}(w) = s_w^2 = \frac{1}{m-1} \sum_{i=1}^{m} w_i^2$$

5. Compute the mean cycle length:

$$\bar{n} = \frac{1}{m} \sum_{i=1}^{m} n_i$$

The confidence interval for the mean response is given by

$$\bar{\bar{x}} \mp z_{1-\alpha/2} \frac{s_w}{\bar{n}\sqrt{m}}$$

Notice that unlike the previous two methods, the method of regeneration does not require removing transient observations. Thus, there is no waste. However, the method also has a number of disadvantages. First, the cycle lengths are unpredictable. It is not possible to plan the simulation time beforehand. Second, finding the regeneration point is not trivial. It may require a lot of checking after every event. Third, many of the variance reduction techniques such as common random streams or antithetic variables cannot be used due to the variable length of the cycles. Finally, the mean and variance estimators are biased in the sense that their expected values from a random sampling are not equal to the quantity being estimated.

A few other methods that have been developed for the purpose of variance computation are not discussed here due to their statistical sophistication. Two such methods are the autoregressive approach and spectral analysis. The first method involves fitting an autoregressive model to the observation sequence and then computing the variance from the variance of the residuals and coefficients of the autoregressive model. The spectral analysis approach is similar. It requires computing the spectral density from the coefficients of the autoregressive models. Neither of these methods is recommended for beginners.

25.6 VARIANCE REDUCTION

We have discussed many ways of getting maximum information with minimum effort. Proper experimental designs help us to analyze many factors with a minimum number of experiments. Variance estimation techniques discussed in Section 25.5 allow us to stop a simulation as soon as the desired confidence level is attained. Books on simulations have another set of techniques called variance reduction techniques that generally require controlling random-number streams to introduce correlation in successive observations such that the variance of the results is reduced. One problem with almost all such techniques is that their careless use may backfire, that is, lead to increased variance. These techniques have been developed by statisticians for use by statistically sophisticated analysts only. Their use by beginners is not recommended. Therefore, such techniques are not described here.

EXERCISES

25.1 Imagine that you have been called as an expert to review a simulation study. Which of the following simulation results would you consider nonintuitive and would want to carefully validate:

   a. The throughput of a system increases as its load increases.

   b. The throughput of a system decreases as its load increases.

   c. The response time increases as the load increases.

   d. The response time of a system decreases as its load increases.

   e. The loss rate of a system decreases as the load increases.

25.2 Find the duration of the transient interval for the following sample:

$$11, 4, 2, 6, 5, 7, 10, 9, 10, 9, 10, 9, 10, \ldots .$$

Does the method of truncation give the correct result in this case?

CHAPTER 26

RANDOM-NUMBER GENERATION

documentation *n.* [Latin *documentum* "warning"] **1** The promised literature that fails to arrive with the supporting hardware. **2** A single, illegible, photocopied page of proprietary caveats and suggested infractions.
3 The detailed, unindexed description of a superseded package.

—S. Kelly-Bootle
The Devil's DP Dictionary

One of the key steps in developing a simulation is to have a routine to generate random values for variables with a specified random distribution, for
example, exponential and normal. This is done in two steps. First, a sequence
of random numbers distributed uniformly between 0 and 1 is obtained. Then
the sequence is transformed to produce random values satisfying the desired
distribution. The first step is called random-*number* generation and the second
random-*variate* generation. We discuss the former in this chapter.

26.1 DESIRED PROPERTIES OF A GOOD GENERATOR

In order to understand why one random-number generator would be considered better than another, consider first how such generators operate. The most
common method is to use a recursive relation in which the next number in the
sequence is a function of the last one or two numbers, that is,

$$x_n = f(x_{n-1}, x_{n-2}, \ldots) \tag{26.1}$$

One such function is

$$x_n = 5x_{n-1} + 1 \bmod 16 \qquad (26.2)$$

Starting with $x_0 = 5$, we obtain x_1 as follows:

$$x_1 = 5(5) + 1 \bmod 16 = 26 \bmod 16 = 10 \qquad (26.3)$$

The first 32 numbers obtained by this procedure are 10, 3, 0, 1, 6, 15, 12, 13, 2, 11, 8, 9, 14, 7, 4, 5 10, 3, 0, 1, 6, 15, 12, 13, 2, 11, 8, 9, 14, 7, 4, 5.

The x's are integers between 0 and 15. By dividing x's by 16, we get a sequence of random numbers between 0 and 1. For this example, the numbers are 0.6250, 0.1875, 0.0000, 0.0625, 0.3750, 0.9375, 0.7500, 0.8125, 0.1250, 0.6875, 0.5000, 0.5625, 0.8750, 0.4375, 0.2500, 0.3125, 0.6250, 0.1875, 0.0000, 0.0625, 0.3750, 0.9375, 0.7500, 0.8125, 0.1250, 0.6875, 0.5000, 0.5625, 0.8750, 0.4375, 0.2500, 0.3125.

It is obvious that if the function f is known, we can regenerate the sequence any time provided the starting value x_0 is given. This value, which is used to begin the sequence, is called the **seed**.

An important observation about this example is that the function f is deterministic. Given the seed, we can tell with a probability of 1 what the numbers in the sequence would be. Yet the numbers are random in the sense that they would pass statistical tests for randomness. These numbers are therefore only partially random and are called **pseudo-random**. Such numbers are preferable to *fully random* numbers in simulation applications because it is often desirable to be able to repeat a simulation experiment exactly the way it was done before. Of course, if a different result is needed, we can change the seed before running the simulation. Thus, we have additional control over reproducibility of results.

Notice that in the preceding example, only the first 16 numbers are unique. The 17th number is the same as the first and the remaining sequence is simply a cyclic repetition of the first 16 numbers. In other words, this random-number generator has a **cycle length** of 16. Some generators do not repeat an initial part of the sequence. This part is called the **tail**. In such cases, the **period** of the generator is the sum of the tail length L and the cycle length C, as shown in Figure 26.1.

A performance analyst developing a simulation model has to select an appropriate value for seed and an appropriate generator function. The seed selection is discussed later in Section 26.7. Here, we concentrate on selecting the right generator function.

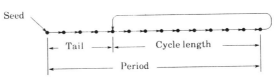

FIGURE 26.1   Cycle length, tail length, and period of a random-number generator.

The desired properties of the generator function are as follows:

1. *It should be efficiently computable.* Since simulations typically require several thousand random numbers in each run, the processor time required to generate these numbers should be small.
2. *The period should be large.* A small period may cause the random-number sequence to recycle, resulting in a repeated event sequence. This may limit the useful length of simulation runs.
3. *The successive values should be independent and uniformly distributed.* The correlation between successive numbers should be small. Correlation, if significant, indicates dependence.

While the first two properties are easy to establish, the third requires a battery of tests, which are discussed later in Chapter 27. Following are some of the types of random-number generators discussed in this chapter:

- Linear-congruential generators
- Tausworthe generators
- Extended Fibonacci generators
- Combined generators

A description of each of these approaches follows.

26.2 LINEAR-CONGRUENTIAL GENERATORS

In 1951, D. H. Lehmer discovered that the residues of successive powers of a number have good randomness properties. He obtained the nth number in the sequence by dividing the nth power of an integer a by another integer m and taking the remainder. That is,

$$x_n = a^n \bmod m$$

An equivalent expression used to compute x_n after computing x_{n-1} is

$$x_n = a x_{n-1} \bmod m$$

The parameters a and m are called **multiplier** and **modulus**, respectively. Lehmer's choices for these parameters were $a = 23$ and $m = 10^8 + 1$. These choices made it very easy to implement on ENIAC, which was an eight-digit decimal machine.

Many of the currently used random-number generators are a generalization of the Lehmer's proposal and have the following form:

$$x_n = a x_{n-1} + b \bmod m \qquad (26.4)$$

Here, the x_n's are integers between 0 and $m - 1$. Constants a and b are nonnegative.

These generators are popular because they can be analyzed easily, and certain guarantees can be made about their properties using the theory of congruences. For this reason, they are also called **Mixed Linear-Congruential Generators** or **Linear-Congruential Generators** (LCGs) for short. The word *mixed* implies using both multiplication by a and addition of b.

In general, the choice of a, b, and m affects the period and autocorrelation in the sequence. A number of researchers have studied such generators, and the results of their studies can be summarized as follows:

1. The modulus m should be large. Since all x's must be between 0 and $m - 1$, the period can never be more than m.
2. For mod m computation to be efficient, m should be a power of 2, that is, 2^k. In this case, mod m can be obtained by truncating the result to the right by k bits.
3. If b is nonzero, the maximum possible period m is obtained if and only if

   (a) integers m and b are relatively prime, that is, have no common factors other than 1;
   (b) every prime number that is a factor of m is also a factor of $a - 1$; and
   (c) $a - 1$ is a multiple of 4, if integer m is a multiple of 4.

Notice that all of these conditions are met if $m = 2^k$, $a = 4c + 1$, and b is odd. Here, c, b, and k are positive integers.

A generator that has the maximum possible period is called a **full-period** generator. All full-period generators are not equally good. Generators with lower autocorrelation between successive numbers are preferable. For example, both of the following two generators have the same full period, but the first one has a correlation of 0.25 between x_{n-1} and x_n, whereas the second one has a negligible correlation of less than 2^{-18}:

$$x_n = (2^{34} + 1)x_{n-1} + 1 \bmod 2^{35} \tag{26.5}$$

$$x_n = (2^{18} + 1)x_{n-1} + 1 \bmod 2^{35} \tag{26.6}$$

26.2.1 Multiplicative LCG

All the LCGs presented so far are mixed LCGs. If the increment b is zero, as was the case in Lehmer's original proposal, no addition is involved and the generator is called a **multiplicative LCG**. Such generators have the form

$$x_n = a x_{n-1} \bmod m$$

It is obvious that multiplicative LCGs are more efficient than the mixed LCGs in terms of processor time required for computation. Further efficiency can be obtained by choosing m to be a power of 2 so that the mod operation is trivial.

Thus, there are two types of multiplicative LCGs, those in which $m = 2^k$ and those in which $m \neq 2^k$.

26.2.2 Multiplicative LCG with $m = 2^k$

The key argument in favor of choosing $m = 2^k$ is the ease of the mod operation. However, such generators do not have a full period. The maximum possible period for a multiplicative LCG with modulus $m = 2^k$ is only one-fourth the full period, that is, 2^{k-2}. This period is achieved if the multiplier a is of the form $8i \pm 3$ and the initial seed is an odd integer.

Example 26.1 Consider the following multiplicative LCG:

$$x_n = 5x_{n-1} \bmod 2^5$$

Using a seed of $x_0 = 1$, we get the sequence 5, 25, 29, 17, 21, 9, 13, 1, 5,....
The period is 8, which is one-fourth the maximum possible 32. If we change the seed to $x_0 = 2$, the sequence is 10, 18, 26, 2, 10, ...
Here, the period is only 4. Thus, choosing an odd seed is important in this case. To see what happens if the multiplier is not of the form $8i \pm 3$, consider the LCG

$$x_n = 7x_{n-1} \bmod 2^5$$

Using a seed of $x_0 = 1$, we get the sequence 7, 17, 23, 1, 7, ...
Again, the period is only 4. Thus, both conditions are necessary to achieve the maximum period. ☐

Although the maximum period possible from a multiplicative LCG with $m = 2^k$ is only one-fourth the maximum possible, the resulting period may not be too small for many applications. In such cases, it may be more efficient to use a multiplicative generator than a mixed generator. It must be pointed out that low-order bits of random numbers obtained using multiplicative LCGs with $m = 2^k$ have a cyclic pattern, as discussed later in Section 26.8.

26.2.3 Multiplicative LCG with $m \neq 2^k$

A solution to the small-period problem is to use a modulus m that is a prime number. In this case, with a proper choice of the multiplier a, it is possible to get a period of $m - 1$, which is almost equal to the maximum possible length m. Notice that unlike a mixed LCG, x_n obtained from a multiplicative LCG can never be zero if m is prime. The values of x_n lie between 1 and $m - 1$, and any multiplicative LCG with a period of $m - 1$ is called a full-period generator.
Not all values of the multiplier are equally good. It can be shown that a multiplicative LCG will be a full-period generator if and only if the multiplier a is a *primitive root* of the modulus m. By definition, a is a primitive root of m if and only if $a^n \bmod m \neq 1$ for $n = 1, 2, ..., m - 2$.

Example 26.2 Consider the following multiplicative LCG:

$$x_n = 3x_{n-1} \bmod 31$$

Starting with a seed of $x_0 = 1$, the sequence is 1, 3, 9, 27, 19, 26, 16, 17, 20, 29, 25, 13, 8, 24, 10, 30, 28, 22, 4, 12, 5, 15, 14, 11, 2, 6, 18, 23, 7, 21, 1, ... The period is 30, so this is a full-period generator.

If we use a multiplier of $a = 5$ instead, we get the sequence 1, 5, 25, 1, ... The period is only 3.

Notice that the multiplier 3 is a primitive root of 31 since the smallest positive value for n for which $3^n \bmod 31 = 1$ is $n = 30$.

Also, 5 is not a primitive root of 31 since

$$5^3 \bmod 31 = 125 \bmod 31 = 1$$

Other primitive roots of 31 are 11, 12, 13, 17, 21, 22, and 24. □

The following multiplicative LCG is an example of a full-period generator:

$$x_n = 7^5 x_{n-1} \bmod(2^{31} - 1) \tag{26.7}$$

Notice that $2^{31} - 1 = 2,147,483,647$ is a prime number and 7^5 is one of its 534,600,000 primitive roots.

One of the important cautions in implementing LCGs is that the properties are guaranteed only if the computations are done exactly, without any round-off errors. This means that the computations should be done using integer arithmetic without overflow. In particular, the analyst should be careful in implementing such functions in languages like BASIC, in which all computation is done using real numbers. In such cases, truncation may cause the period to be reduced considerably.

The second problem in implementing LCGs is that the product ax_{n-1} can exceed the largest integer allowed on the system, causing integer overflow. One solution to this problem due to Schrage (1979) is based on the following identity:

$$ax \bmod m = g(x) + mh(x)$$

where

$$g(x) = a(x \bmod q) - r(x \text{ div } q)$$

and

$$h(x) = (x \text{ div } q) - (ax \text{ div } m)$$

Here, $q = m$ div a, $r = m \bmod a$. The operation A div B is equivalent to dividing A by B and truncating the result. It can be shown that for all x's in the range $1, 2, \ldots, m - 1$, the expressions involved in computing $g(x)$ are all less than $m - 1$. Also, if $r < q$, $h(x)$ is either 0 or 1 and can be inferred from $g(x)$; $h(x)$ is 1 if and only if $g(x)$ is negative. Thus, the operation ax, which could cause overflow, need not be executed. The following example illustrates the application of these implementation concepts.

Example 26.3 Consider the implementation of the multiplicative generator:

$$x_n = 7^5 x_{n-1} \bmod (2^{31} - 1)$$

or

$$x_n = 16{,}807 x_{n-1} \bmod 2{,}147{,}483{,}647$$

The product $a x_{n-1}$ can be as large as $16{,}807 \times 2{,}147{,}483{,}647 \approx 1.03 \times 2^{45}$. A straightforward implementation of the generator using integer arithmetic will produce integer overflow unless the machine supports 46 bits or larger integers.

In this case:

$$a = 16{,}807$$

$$m = 2{,}147{,}483{,}647$$

$$q = m \text{ div } a = 2{,}147{,}483{,}647 \text{ div } 16{,}807 = 12{,}773$$

$$r = m \bmod a = 2{,}147{,}483{,}647 \bmod 16{,}807 = 2{,}836$$

The Pascal routine shown in Figure 26.2 will correctly implement this generator on systems where the largest positive integer supported is $2^{31} - 1$ or larger. If the largest positive integer is smaller, a real version of the routine shown in Figure 26.3 can be used provided the reals are represented with a 32-bit or larger mantissa (including the sign bit). On many systems, this would require the use of double-precision real numbers.

One method to test whether an implementation of this generator is correct is to compute $x_{10{,}000}$ starting with $x_0 = 1$. For a correct implementation, the result would be 1,043,618,065. ☐

```
FUNCTION Random(VAR x:INTEGER) : REAL;

CONST
  a = 16807;        (* Multiplier *)
  m = 2147483647;   (* Modulus *)
  q = 127773;       (* m div a *)
  r = 2836;         (* m mod a *)

VAR
  x_div_q, x_mod_q, x_new: INTEGER;

BEGIN
  x_div_q := x DIV q;
  x_mod_q := x MOD q;
  x_new := a*x_mod_q - r*x_div_q;
  IF x_new > 0 THEN x := x_new ELSE x := x_new + m;
  Random := x/m;
END;
```

FIGURE 26.2 Random-number generator using integer arithmetic.

```
FUNCTION Random(VAR x:DOUBLE) : DOUBLE;

CONST
  a =   16807.0D0;        (* Multiplier *)
  m =  2147483647.0D0;   (* Modulus *)
  q =  127773.0D0;        (* m div a *)
  r =  2836.0D0;          (* m mod a *)

VAR
  x_div_q, x_mod_q, x_new: DOUBLE;

BEGIN
  x_div_q := TRUNC(x/q);
  x_mod_q := x-q*x_div_q;
  x_new := a*x_mod_q - r*x_div_q;
  IF x_new > 0.0D0 THEN x := x_new ELSE x := x_new + m;
  Random := x/m;
END;
```

FIGURE 26.3   Random-number generator using real arithmetic.

Exercises 26.6 and 26.7 show that Schrage's method cannot be used if the condition $r < q$ is not satisfied.

26.3   TAUSWORTHE GENERATORS

The interest in random-number generators has grown recently due to their use in cryptographic applications. In such applications, random numbers of long lengths are required. For example, a 64-byte (512-bit) long random key may be required to encode a message. Such large numbers are produced using a random sequence of binary digits (0 or 1) and then dividing the sequence into strings of desired length. Such generators were first proposed by Tausworthe (1965) and are named after him.

In general, a Tausworthe generator has the following form:

$$b_n = c_{q-1}b_{n-1} \oplus c_{q-2}b_{n-2} \oplus c_{q-3}b_{n-3} \oplus \cdots \oplus c_0b_{n-q} \tag{26.8}$$

where c_i and b_i are binary variables with values of 0 or 1 and $\oplus$ is the exclusive-or (mod 2 addition) operation. The generator uses the last q bits of the sequence. Therefore, it is called an *autoregressive sequence* of order q, or AR(q). An AR(q) generator can have a maximum period of $2^q - 1$.

If we use D to denote a delay operator such that $Db(n) = b(n + 1)$, Equation (26.8) can be written as

$$D^q b(i - q) = c_{q-1}D^{q-1}b(i - q) + c_{q-2}D^{q-2}b(i - q) + \cdots + c_0 b(i - q)\text{mod } 2$$

or

$$D^q - c_{q-1}D^{q-1} - c_{q-2}D^{q-2} - \cdots - c_0 = 0 \text{ mod } 2$$

Since in mod 2 arithmetic subtraction is equivalent to addition, the preceding equation is equivalent to

$$D^q + c_{q-1}D^{q-1} + c_{q-2}D^{q-2} + \cdots + c_0 = 0 \text{ mod } 2$$

The polynomial on the left-hand side of this equation is called a **characteristic** polynomial and is traditionally written using x in place of D:

$$x^q + c_{q-1}x^{q-1} + c_{q-2}x^{q-2} + \cdots + c_0 \tag{26.9}$$

The period of a Tausworthe generator depends upon the characteristic polynomial. In particular, the period is the smallest positive integer n for which $x^n - 1$ is divisible by the characteristic polynomial. The maximum possible period with a polynomial of order q is $2^q - 1$. The polynomials that give this period are called **primitive** polynomials.

The following example illustrates the generation of random bits using a primitive polynomial.

Example 26.4 Consider the following polynomial:

$$x^7 + x^3 + 1$$

Using the D operator in place of x, we get the following formula for generating the bit sequence:

$$D^7 b(n) + D^3 b(n) + b(n) = 0 \text{ mod } 2$$

or

$$b_{n+7} + b_{n+3} + b_n = 0 \text{ mod } 2, \qquad n = 0, 1, 2, \ldots$$

or using the exclusive-or operator in place of addition mod 2, we get

$$b_{n+7} \oplus b_{n+4} \oplus b_n = 0, \qquad n = 0, 1, 2, \ldots$$

or

$$b_{n+7} = b_{n+4} \oplus b_n, \qquad n = 0, 1, 2, \ldots$$

Substituting $n - 7$ for n,

$$b_n = b_{n-4} \oplus b_{n-7}, \qquad n = 7, 8, 9, \ldots$$

Starting with $b_0 = b_1 = \cdots = b_6 = 1$, we get the following bit sequence:

$$b_7 = b_3 \oplus b_0 = 1 \oplus 1 = 0$$
$$b_8 = b_4 \oplus b_1 = 1 \oplus 1 = 0$$
$$b_9 = b_5 \oplus b_2 = 1 \oplus 1 = 0$$
$$b_{10} = b_6 \oplus b_3 = 1 \oplus 1 = 0$$
$$b_{11} = b_7 \oplus b_4 = 0 \oplus 1 = 1$$

$$\vdots$$

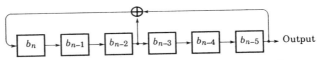

FIGURE 26.4 Linear-feedback shift-register implementation of a random-number generator using the polynomial $x^5 + x^3 + 1$.

The complete sequence is 1111111 0000111 0111100 1011001 0010000 0010001 0011000 1011101 0110110 0000110 0110101 0011100 1111011 0100001 0101011 1110100 1010001 1011100 0111111 1000011 1000000.

The first seven bits form the seed. Notice that the sequence starts repeating only after 127 bits; therefore, it has a period of 127, or $2^7 - 1$, bits. The polynomial $x^7 + x^3 + 1$ is therefore a primitive polynomial.   □

A Tausworthe sequence can be easily generated in hardware using Linear-Feedback Shift Registers (**LFSRs**). For example, the polynomial $x^5 + x^3 + 1$ results in the generator $b_n = b_{n-2} \oplus b_{n-5}$. This can be implemented using the LFSR shown in Figure 26.4. The circuit consists of six registers, each holding one bit. On every clock cycle, each register's content is shifted out, and the new content is determined by the input to the register. Figure 26.5 shows the circuit for the general Tausworthe sequence given by Equation (26.8) In practice, the AND gates shown are not required if values of the coefficients c_i are known. The feedback path consisting of the AND gates and the corresponding EXCLUSIVE-OR gates are omitted for those c_i's that are zero. For the remaining c_i's (which are 1), the AND gates are omitted and the outputs of the stages are connected directly to the respective EXCLUSIVE-OR gates.

From an AR(q)-bit sequence, we can get random integers of any desired length. Tausworthe proposed to construct l-bit random numbers x_n using the bit sequence b_n by dividing the sequence into successive groups of s bits and using the first l bits of each group as a binary fraction; that is,

$$x_n = 0.b_{sn}b_{sn+1}b_{sn+2}b_{sn+3}\ldots b_{sn+l-1}$$

or equivalently,

$$x_n = \sum_{j=1}^{l} 2^{-j} b_{sn+j-1} \qquad (26.10)$$

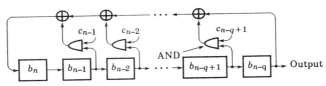

FIGURE 26.5 Feedback shift register implementation of a random-number generator using a general q-degree polynomial.

Here, s is a constant greater than or equal to l and is relatively prime to $2^q - 1$. The first restriction, $s \geq l$, ensures that x_n and x_j for $n \neq j$ have no bits in common. The second restriction of relative primeness guarantees a full period $2^q - 1$ for x_n. The following example illustrates this procedure for constructing l-bit words.

Example 26.5 Consider generation of 8-bit random numbers from the binary sequence of Example 26.4. The period $2^7 - 1 = 127$ is a prime number. Therefore, any value of i greater than or equal to $l = 8$ can be used. Using $s = 8$, the successive 8-bit random numbers obtained are as follows:

$$x_0 = 0.11111110_2 = 0.99219_{10}$$

$$x_1 = 0.00011101_2 = 0.11328_{10}$$

$$x_2 = 0.11100101_2 = 0.89453_{10}$$

$$x_3 = 0.10010010_2 = 0.29688_{10}$$

$$x_4 = 0.00000100_2 = 0.36328_{10}$$

$$x_5 = 0.01001100_2 = 0.42188_{10}$$

$$\vdots$$

The numbers in the middle are binary, and those on the right are the corresponding decimal numbers.   □

Tausworthe showed that the l-bit numbers generated using Equation (26.10) had the following property:

1. The mean of the sequence is $\frac{1}{2}$:

$$E[x_n] \approx \frac{1}{2}$$

2. The variance of the sequence is $\frac{1}{12}$:

$$\text{Var}[x_n] \approx \frac{1}{12}$$

3. The serial correlation is zero:

$$\text{Corr}[x_n, x_{n+s}] = 0 \quad \text{for} \quad 0 < |s| < \frac{2^q - 1 - l}{l}$$

4. The sequence is k distributed for all k's up to $\lfloor q/l \rfloor$. Briefly, this means that every k-tuple of l-bit numbers appears 2^{q-kl} times over the full period except the all-zero tuple, which appears one time less. The k-distributivity property is explained further in Section 27.5.

Using $k = 1$ and $l = 1$ in the last property, it follows that the complete period of the bit sequence contains 2^{q-1} ones and $2^{q-1} - 1$ zeros. Also, if a window of length q slides along the sequence, each of the $2^q - 1$ nonzero k-tuples appears exactly once in a complete period.

Most of the polynomials used for generating Tausworthe sequences are trinomials, that is, they have just three nonzero terms. In this case, generation of each new bit requires just one exclusive-or operation. For example, if only c_r and c_0 are 1 and all other c_i's are zero, then

$$b_n = b_{n-q+r} \oplus b_{n-q} \tag{26.11}$$

This makes the computation of bits b_i fast. However, to get random numbers, we still need to generate several bits. One way to simple random-number generation is to choose r and q such that $2r \le q$. In this case, one can generate successive q-bits by using the following shift and an exclusive-or sequence. The individual bits in a word are read from the right. For example, the seed word would be $b_{q-1}b_{q-2} \cdots b_0$.

1. Start with a q-bit seed Y_1.
2. Right shift Y_1 by r bits, filling with zeros on the left. Call the result Y_2.
3. Exclusive-or Y_1 and Y_2. Call the result Y_3. This completes the computation of the right $q - r$ bits.
4. Left shift Y_3 by $q - r$ bits, filling with zeros on the right. Call the result Y_4.
5. Exclusive-or Y_3 and Y_4. The result Y_5 is the new q-bit seed.

The following example illustrates the procedure.

Example 26.6   Consider the generation of 7-bit random numbers using the trinomial of Example 26.4:

$$x^7 + x^3 + 1$$

In this case, $r = 3$, $q = 7$, and $q - r = 4$. Therefore, we need a 3-bit right shift and a 4-bit left shift. Once again we start with a seed $X = 1111111$. The steps to generate the next 7 bits are as follows:

Step 1:   Copy seed, $Y_1 = X = 1111111$.

Step 2:   Right shift by 3, $Y_2 = 0001111$.

Step 3:   Exclusive-or, $Y_3 = Y_1 \oplus Y_2 = 1110000$.

Step 4:   Left shift by 4, $Y_4 = 0000000$.

Step 5:   Exclusive-or, $Y_5 = Y_3 \oplus Y_4 = 1110000$.

The next 7 bits (read from the right) are 0000111. The process can then be repeated:

Step 1: Copy seed, $Y_1 = X = 1110000$.

Step 2: Right shift by 3, $Y_2 = 0001110$.

Step 3: Exclusive-or, $Y_3 = Y_1 \oplus Y_2 = 1111110$.

Step 4: Left shift by 4, $Y_4 = 1100000$.

Step 5: Exclusive-or, $Y_5 = Y_3 \oplus Y_4 = 0011110$.

The next 7 bits (read from the right) are 0111100. As a check, we verify that the bit sequence is the same as that in Example 26.4. □

If q is equal to the number of bits in the computer word (not counting the sign bit), the generation of q-bit words using the word-wide shift and exclusive-or instructions is straightforward. For a large q, the shifting procedure can be implemented in hardware. A list of primitive trinomials of degree 31 or less is given in Table 26.1.

A disadvantage of Tausworthe generators is the observation by Tootill et al. (1971) that while the sequence may produce good test results over the complete cycle, it may not have satisfactory local behavior. In particular, it performed negatively on the runs up and down test. Although the first-order serial correlation is almost zero, it is suspected that some primitive polynomials may give poor high-order correlations. Later, in Section 27.5, it is shown that not all primitive polynomials are equally good.

To construct l-bit random numbers x_n from the binary sequence b_n, Lewis and Payne (1973) proposed a slightly different method than that proposed by Tausworthe. In this method, called the **Generalized Feedback Shift Register** (**GFSR**), an l-bit sequence x_n is generated from the binary sequence as follows:

$$x_n = 0.b_n b_{n+s} b_{n+2s} \cdots b_{n+(l-1)s}$$

Here, s is a "carefully selected delay." The key advantage of their idea is that the sequence x_n can be generated very efficiently using word-wide shift and

TABLE 26.1   List of Primitive Trinomials[a]

$x^2 + x + 1$	$x^3 + x + 1$	$x^4 + x + 1$	$x^5 + x^2 + 1$
$x^6 + x + 1$	$x^7 + x + 1$	$x^7 + x^3 + 1$	$x^9 + x^4 + 1$
$x^{10} + x^3 + 1$	$x^{11} + x^2 + 1$	$x^{15} + x + 1$	$x^{15} + x^4 + 1$
$x^{15} + x^7 + 1$	$x^{17} + x^3 + 1$	$x^{17} + x^5 + 1$	$x^{17} + x^6 + 1$
$x^{18} + x^7 + 1$	$x^{20} + x^3 + 1$	$x^{21} + x^2 + 1$	$x^{22} + x + 1$
$x^{23} + x^5 + 1$	$x^{23} + x^9 + 1$	$x^{25} + x^3 + 1$	$x^{25} + x^7 + 1$
$x^{28} + x^3 + 1$	$x^{28} + x^9 + 1$	$x^{28} + x^{13} + 1$	$x^{29} + x^2 + 1$
$x^{31} + x^3 + 1$	$x^{31} + x^6 + 1$	$x^{31} + x^7 + 1$	$x^{31} + x^{13} + 1$

[a] If $x^q + x^r + 1$ is listed, then $x^q + x^{q-r} + 1$ is also primitive.

exclusive-or instructions. However, it requires that an array of numbers be stored and that careful initialization of this array take place.

26.4 EXTENDED FIBONACCI GENERATORS

A Fibonacci sequence $\{x_n\}$ is generated by the following relationship:

$$x_n = x_{n-1} + x_{n-2}$$

The generation of random numbers can be attempted by using the following modification to the Fibonnaci sequence:

$$x_n = x_{n-1} + x_{n-2} \bmod m$$

However, this sequence does not have good randomness properties. In particular, it has a high serial correlation. An extension of this approach would be to combine, for instance, the fifth and seventeenth most recent values:

$$x_n = x_{n-5} + x_{n-17} \bmod 2^k$$

Marsaglia (1983) points out that this generator passes most statistical tests and recommends its implementation as follows using 17 storage locations $L[1], \ldots, L[17]$. During initialization, fill these locations with 17 integers, not all even, and set two pointers i and j to 17 and 5, respectively. On each successive call, the following procedure is executed, which returns the next random number and updates the pointers:

$$x := L[i] + L[j];$$

$$L[i] := x;$$

$$i := i - 1; \text{ IF } i = 0 \text{ THEN } i := 17;$$

$$j := j - 1; \text{ IF } j = 0 \text{ THEN } j := 17;$$

$$\text{Return } x;$$

The add operation in the first line of this generator is automatically mod 2^k in k-bit machines with 2's complement arithmetic. The period of the generator is $2^k(2^{17} - 1)$. For $k = 8, 16, 32$, this period is 1.6×10^7, 4.3×10^9, and 2.8×10^{14}, respectively. This is considerably longer than that possible with LCGs.

26.5 COMBINED GENERATORS

It is possible to combine two or more random generators to produce a "better" generator. Three such techniques are described next:

1. *Adding random numbers obtained by two or more generators.* If x_n and y_n are two random-number sequences in the range 0 and $m - 1$, they can be combined to produce $w_n = (x_n + y_n) \bmod m$. If the two sequences

have different periods and are obtained by different algorithms, this may considerably increase the period and randomness. For example, L'Ecuyer (1988) recommends combining the following two generators:

$$x_n = 40014x_{n-1} \bmod 2{,}147{,}483{,}563$$

$$y_n = 40692y_{n-1} \bmod 2{,}147{,}483{,}399$$

This would produce

$$w_n = (x_n - y_n) \bmod 2{,}147{,}483{,}562$$

This generator has a period of 2.3×10^{18}. Also, it does not have the problem of all points in the k-dimension falling on a small number of hyperplanes. For 16-bit computers, L'Ecuyer suggests combining the following three generators:

$$w_n = 157w_{n-1} \bmod 32{,}363$$

$$x_n = 146x_{n-1} \bmod 31{,}727$$

$$y_n = 142y_{n-1} \bmod 31{,}657$$

This would produce

$$v_n = (w_n - x_n + y_n) \bmod 32{,}362$$

This generator has a period of 8.1×10^{12}. Portable implementations of these combined generators can be found in L'Ecuyer (1988).

2. *Exclusive-or random numbers obtained by two or more generators.* This technique is similar to the previous one except that the arithmetic addition is replaced by bit-wise exclusive-or operation. Santha and Vazirani (1984) showed that the exclusive-or of several slightly random generators, each producing n-bit numbers, can be used to generate a more random sequence.

3. *Shuffle.* This technique, known as shuffling, uses one sequence as an index to decide which of several numbers generated by a second sequence should be returned. Many different shuffling procedures have been suggested in the literature. One popular technique, which is credited to Marsaglia and Bray (1964), is known as algorithm M. Here, an array of size 100, for instance, is filled with random numbers from a random sequence x_n. To generate a random number, generate a new y_n (between 0 and $m-1$) and scale it to obtain an index $i = 1 + 100y_n/m$. The value in the ith element of the array is returned as the next random number. A new value of x_n is generated and stored in the ith location. This generator is claimed to have better k-distributivity properties than the generators based on LFSRs.

One problem with shuffling is that it is not easy to skip a long subsequence as is usually required in multiple-stream simulations.

26.6 A SURVEY OF RANDOM-NUMBER GENERATORS

In this section, we describe a number of generators that have either been proposed in published literature or have been used in various simulation packages. In some cases, known problems and properties are also discussed. The list follows:

- A currently popular multiplicative LCG is

$$x_n = 7^5 x_{n-1} \mod(2^{31} - 1)$$

This generator is used in the SIMPL/I system (IBM 1972), the APL system from IBM (Katzan 1971), the PRIMOS operating system from Prime Computer (1984), and the scientific library from IMSL (1987). Since $2^{31} - 1$ is a prime number and 7^5 is a primitive root of it, this generator has the full period of $2^{31} - 2$. This generator has been extensively analyzed and shown to be good. Its low-order bits are uniformly distributed. It has reasonable randomness properties. This generator was highly recommended by Park and Miller (1988), and they called it the *minimal standard*. Pascal programs to implement this generator were presented earlier in Figures 26.2 and 26.3.

- Fishman and Moore (1986) conducted an exhaustive search of all full-period, multiplicative LCGs with modulus $m = 2^{31} - 1$ and compared them on the basis of implementation efficiency and randomness. Their conclusion was that the following two generators were the best:

$$x_n = 48,271 x_{n-1} \mod(2^{31} - 1)$$

$$x_n = 69,621 x_{n-1} \mod(2^{31} - 1)$$

- The following generator is used in SIMSCRIPT II.5 and in DEC-20 FORTRAN:

$$x_n = 630,360,016 x_{n-1} \mod(2^{31} - 1)$$

- The following multiplicative LCG, known as "RANDU" (IBM 1968), was very popular in the 1960s:

$$x_n = (2^{16} + 3) x_{n-1} \mod 2^{31}$$

The modulus and the multiplier were selected primarily to facilitate easy computation. Multiplication by $2^{16} + 3 = 65,539$ can be easily accomplished by a few shift and add instructions. This generator does not have a full period and has been shown to be flawed in many respects. Also, it does not have good randomness properties (Knuth, 1981). When the triplets of successive numbers generated by RANDU are plotted as points in a three-dimensional space, all the points lie on a total of 15 planes in the space. In other words, it has unsatisfactory three-distributivity (see Section 27.5 for k-distributivity). Also, like all LCGs with $m = 2^k$, the lower order bits of this generator have a small period, which is discussed later in Section 26.8. RANDU is no longer used.

- The following analog of RANDU is sometimes recommended for 16-bit microprocessors:

$$x_n = (2^8 + 3)x_{n-1} \bmod(2^{15})$$

This generator shares all known problems of RANDU. Also, this as well as any other generator with a period of only a few thousand numbers are not suitable for any serious simulation study.

- The following generator is used in the University of Sheffield Pascal system for Prime computers:

$$x_n = 16,807x_{n-1} \bmod 2^{31}$$

Since the multiplier 16,807 is not of the form $8i \pm 3$, this generator does not have the maximum possible period of 2^{31-2}. This generator is also used in the subroutine UNIFORM of the SAS statistical package. However, in this case, a shuffle technique is used to improve its randomness.

- SIMULA on UNIVAC uses the following generator:

$$x_n = 5^{13}x_{n-1} \bmod 2^{35}$$

Although this generator has the maximum possible period of 2^{33}, Park and Miller (1988) claim that it does not have good randomness properties.

- The UNIX operating system supports the following mixed LCG:

$$x_n = (1,103,515,245x_{n-1} + 12,345)\bmod 2^{32}$$

Like all LCGs with modulus $m = 2^k$, the binary representation of x_n's has a cyclic bit pattern. See Section 26.8 for further discussion on this issue.

Over the years, a number of random-number generators have been proposed in the literature. Most proposals start with a list of problems with the previously proposed generators. Thus, many generators that were considered good at one time are no longer considered good.

The purpose of the preceding list is to warn new analysts not to attempt inventing a new generator. Designing a new generator sounds trivial at first, but many generators proposed by expert statisticians have later been found to have undesirable properties. Therefore, *it is better to use an established generator that has been tested thoroughly than to invent a new one.*

26.7 SEED SELECTION

Ordinarily, the seed value used to initialize a random-number generator should not affect the results of the simulation. However, a wrong combination of a seed and a random generator may lead to erroneous conclusions. In this section we discuss some of the guidelines for proper selection of seeds.

If the generator has a full period and only one random variable is required, any seed value is as good as any other. However, considerable care is required in selecting seeds for simulations requiring random numbers for more than one variable. Such simulations are called **multistream simulations**. In fact, most simulations are multistream simulations. For example, a simulation of a single queue requires generating random arrival and random service times. This simulation would require two *streams* of random numbers: one for interarrival times and the other for service times. Most of the guidelines that follow are for multistream simulations. The first two apply to both single-stream and multistream simulations.

1. *Do not use zero*. Although a seed value of zero is fine for mixed LCGs, it would make a multiplicative LCG or a Tausworthe generator stick at zero.

2. *Avoid even values*. Even values are often as good as odd values. In fact, for full-period generators, all nonzero seed values are equally good. If a generator is not a full-period generator, for example, a multiplicative LCG with modulus $m = 2^k$, the seed should be odd. If possible, it is better to avoid generators that have too many conditions on seed values or whose performance (period and randomness) depends upon the seed value.

3. *Do not subdivide one stream*. Using a single stream for all variables is a common mistake. For example, if $\{u_1, u_2, \ldots\}$ is the sequence generated using a single seed u_0, the analyst may use u_1 to generate interarrival times, u_2 to generate service times, and so forth. This may result in a strong correlation between the two variables.

4. *Use nonoverlapping streams*. Each stream requires a separate seed. If the two seeds are such that the two streams overlap, there will be a correlation between the streams, and the resulting sequences will not be independent. Consider a trivial example of starting both streams for a single queue with the same seed values (a rather common mistake). The sequence of random numbers $\{u_1, u_2, \ldots\}$ used to generate the arrival and service times would be identical in this case, and values of u_n's that result in long interarrival times may also result in large service times. In other words, the service times and interarrival times may be positively correlated. This may lead to misleading conclusions.

    The right way to select a seed is to ensure that the sequences do not overlap at all. Thus, if $\{u_0, u_1, \ldots\}$ is the sequence of random numbers starting with u_0 and we need, for instance, 10,000 numbers for interarrival times and 10,000 for service times, we should select u_0 as the seed for the first stream, $u_{10,000}$ as the seed for the second stream, $u_{20,000}$ as the seed for the third stream, and so on. Random number u_n can be easily determined by writing a test program that calls the random-number generator n times starting with u_0. It is also possible to directly calculate the nth number in sequence without generating the intermediate values.

TABLE 26.2 Seeds for Generating Sequences 100,000 Apart for the LCG: $x_n = 7^5 x_{n-1} \bmod (2^{31} - 1)$

$x_{100,000i}$	$x_{100,000(i+1)}$	$x_{100,000(i+2)}$	$x_{100,000(i+3)}$
1	46,831,694	1,841,581,359	1,193,163,244
727,633,698	933,588,178	804,159,733	1,671,059,989
1,061,288,424	1,961,692,154	1,227,283,347	1,171,034,773
276,090,261	1,066,728,069	209,208,115	554,590,007
721,958,466	1,371,272,478	675,466,456	1,095,462,486
1,808,217,256	2,095,021,727	1769349045	904,914,315
373,135,028	717,419,739	881,155,353	1,489,529,863
1,521,138,112	298,370,230	1,140,279,430	1,335,826,707
706,178,559	110,356,601	884,434,366	962,338,209
1,341,315,363	709,314,158	591,449,447	431,918,286
851,767,375	606,179,079	1,500,869,201	1,434,868,289
263,032,577	753,643,799	202,794,285	715,851,524

The following formula can be used for mixed LCGs provided computation is done exactly:

$$ x_n = a^n x_0 + \frac{c(a^n - 1)}{a - 1} \bmod m $$

This formula also applies to multiplicative LCGs with $c = 0$.

Table 26.2 lists seeds that will produce sequences 100,000 apart for the generator:

$$ x_n = 7^5 x_{n-1} \bmod (2^{31} - 1) $$

The values of x_0, $x_{100,000}$, $x_{200,000}$, and so on are listed in the table. The values have to be read along rows. For example, $x_{100,000}$ is 46,831,694.

5. *Reuse seeds in successive replications.* If a simulation experiment is replicated several times, the random-number stream need not be reinitialized, and the seeds left over from the previous replication can continue to be used.

6. *Do not use random seeds.* Analysts often use random-seed values such as the time of day. This causes two problems: first, the simulation cannot be reproduced and, second, it is not possible to guarantee that the multiple streams will not overlap. Random-seed selection is therefore not recommended. In particular, do not use successive random numbers obtained from the generator as seeds.

26.8 MYTHS ABOUT RANDOM-NUMBER GENERATION

The following are myths that uninformed analysts may believe to be true.

1. *A complex set of operations leads to random results.* Early random-number generators were based on the belief that any set of operations whose

results could not be easily predicted would lead to random results. Using a sequence of operations where the final result is difficult to guess does not necessarily mean that the resulting sequence will pass the tests for uniformity and independence. In general, it is better to use simple operations that can be analytically evaluated for randomness.

2. *A single test such as the chi-square test is sufficient to test the goodness of a random-number generator.* The sequence $0, 1, 2, \ldots, m-1$ is obviously not random. However, it will pass the chi-square test with a perfect score but will fail the run test. Similarly, it is possible to write a sequence that will pass the run test but will fail the chi-square test. It is therefore necessary to use as many tests as possible. Some tests for randomness are discussed in Chapter 27. In general, it is better to avoid inventing new generators unless you are highly sophisticated statistically.

3. *Random numbers are unpredictable.* A truly random sequence should be completely unpredictable. For example, given the past history of the throws of a fair die, it is impossible to predict the result of the next throw. This is not the case with pseudo-random number generators. In fact, given a few successive numbers from an LCG, one can easily compute the parameters, a, c, and m and from then on predict the sequence forward or backward without any error. LCGs are therefore unsuitable for cryptographic applications where unpredictability is a desired goal. For a discussion on unpredictable pseudo-random number generators, see Vazirani and Vazirani (1984); Frieze, Kannan, and Lagarias (1984); Blum, Blum, and Shub (1986); and references cited there.

4. *Some seeds are better than others.* This may be true for some generators, for example,

$$x_n = (9806 x_{n-1} + 1) \bmod (2^{17} - 1)$$

The generator works correctly for all seeds except $x_0 = 37,911$. If by chance 37,911 is used as a seed, the generator will be stuck at $x_n = 37,911$ forever. Such generators should be avoided. To generate a single stream, any *nonzero* seed in the valid range should produce an equally good sequence. Some generators have an additional requirement that the seed should be odd. In general, generators whose period or randomness depends upon the seed should not be used, since an unsuspecting user may not remember to follow all the guidelines.

5. *Accurate implementation is not important.* The period and randomness properties of generators are guaranteed only if the generation formula is accurately implemented without any overflow or truncation. Overflows and truncations can suddenly change the path of a random-number generator and reduce the period. Neglecting overflows is a common mistake. For example, consider the generator

$$x_n = 1{,}103{,}515{,}245 x_{n-1} + 12{,}345 \bmod 2^{31}$$

This generator has been implemented in a popular operating system with the following FORTRAN statement:

$$x_n = (1103515245x_{n-1} + 12345).\text{AND.X}'7\text{FFFFFFF}'$$

The AND operation is used to clear the sign bit. It is clear that straight-forward multiplication above will produce overflow.

6. *Bits of successive words generated by a random-number generator are equally randomly distributed.* If an algorithm produces *l*-bit-wide random numbers, the randomness is guaranteed only when all *l* bits are used to form successive random numbers. Generally, any particular bit position or sequence of bit positions will not be equally random. The following example illustrates a case that is typical of all LCGs with modulus $m = 2^k$.

Example 26.7 Consider the generator

$$x_n = (25,173x_{n-1} + 13,849)\bmod 2^{16}$$

Starting with a seed of $x_0 = 1$, the first 20 numbers and their binary representations are listed in Table 26.3.

TABLE 26.3 Random Numbers Generated by the LCG: $x_n = 25,173x_{n-1} + 13,849 \bmod 2^{16}$

	x_n	
n	Decimal	Binary
1	25,173	01100010 01010101
2	12,345	00110000 00111001
3	54,509	11010100 11101101
4	27,825	01101100 10110001
5	55,493	11011000 11000101
6	25,449	01100011 01101001
7	13,277	00110011 11011101
8	53,857	11010010 01100001
9	64,565	11111100 00110101
10	1,945	00000111 10011001
11	6,093	00010111 11001101
12	24,849	01100001 00010001
13	48,293	10111100 10100101
14	52,425	11001100 11001001
15	61,629	11110000 10111101
16	18,625	01001000 11000001
17	2,581	00001010 00010101
18	25,337	01100010 11111001
19	11,949	00101110 10101101
20	47,473	10111001 01110001

Notice the following:

(a) Bit 1 (the least significant bit) is always 1.
(b) Bit 2 is always 0.
(c) Bit 3 alternates between 1 and 0; thus, it has a cycle of length 2.
(d) Bit 4 follows a cycle (0110) of length 4.
(e) Bit 5 follows a cycle (11010010) of length 8.

In general, the lth bit follows a cycle of length 2^{l-2} for $l \geq 2$. $\qquad\square$

The cyclic behavior of low-order bits illustrated in Example 26.7 is typical of all LCGs with modulus $m = 2^k$. This is true for both mixed as well as multiplicative LCGs.

For all multiplicative LCGs of the form $x_n = ax_{n-1} \bmod 2^k$, the least significant bit is either always 0 or always 1. The lth bit has a period at most 2^l. Here, bits are numbered such that $l = 1$ is the least significant bit. Similarly, for all mixed LCGs of the form $x_n = (ax_{n-1} + c) \bmod 2^k$, the lth bit has a period at most 2^l.

In general, the high-order bits are more randomly distributed than the low-order bits. Thus, if one wants an l-bit sequence, where l is less than the word width of the machine, it is better to take the high-order l bits than the low-order l bits.

EXERCISES

26.1 What is the maximum period obtainable from the following generator:

$$x_n = ax_{n-1} \bmod 2^4$$

What should be the value of a? What restrictions are required on the seed?

26.2 Determine $24^n \bmod 31$ for $n = 1, \ldots, 30$. Find the smallest n for which the mod operation's result is 1. Is 24 a primitive root of 31?

26.3 Determine all primitive roots of 11.

26.4 Compute the period of the following generator:

$$x_n = 13x_{n-1} \bmod 2311$$

26.5 Implement the following LCG using Schrage's method to avoid overflow:

$$x_n = 40{,}014x_{n-1} \bmod 2{,}147{,}483{,}563$$

Using a seed of $x_0 = 1$, determine $x_{10{,}000}$.

26.6 Implement the following LCG with and without the Schrage's method:

$$x_n = 11x_{n-1} \bmod 31$$

Are the sequences generated the same? If not, explain what is the problem.

26.7 Can you implement the following LCG using Schrage's method?

$$x_n = 24x_{n-1} \bmod 31$$

Write programs to implement the generator with and without Schrage's method and justify your answer.

26.8 Determine which of the following polynomials is a primitive polynomial:

a. $x^2 + x + 1$
b. $x^3 + x^2 + 1$
c. $x^4 + x^2 + 1$
d. $x^5 + x^2 + 1$

26.9 Determine the period of the Tausworthe sequence generated using each of the following characteristic polynomials:

a. $x^5 + x + 1$
b. $x^6 + x^3 + 1$
c. $x^8 + x + 1$
d. $x^{30} + x^{15} + 1$

26.10 Generate five 6-bit numbers using the Tausworthe method for the following characteristic polynomial starting with a seed of $x_0 = 0.111111_2$:

$$x^6 + x + 1$$

26.11 What is wrong with the parameters of the following two generators?

$$x_n = (40x_{n-1} + 3641) \bmod 729$$

$$x_n = (61x_{n-1} + 2323) \bmod 500$$

26.12 Generate 48 random numbers using a seed of $x_0 = 1$ in the following mixed LCG:

$$x_n = 13x_{n-1} + 11 \bmod 2^{16}$$

Find the period of the lth bit from the right for $l = 1, 2, \ldots, 5$.

CHAPTER 27

TESTING RANDOM-NUMBER GENERATORS

The man who does not read good books has no advantage over the man who can't read them.
—Mark Twain

Analysts using a simulation should ensure that the random-number generator used in the model produces a sufficiently random stream. The very first step in testing any random-number or random-variate generation algorithm is to plot and look at the histogram and cumulative frequency distributions. Quantile-quantile plots discussed in Chapter 12 may also be used. These often reveal gross programming errors, if any, in the implementation. The next step is to use as many of the tests described here as possible. In general, passing each test is only a necessary condition, not a sufficient condition. That is, if a generator fails a test, we can assume that the generator is bad. However, passing a test is no guarantee that the generator is good. It may fail the next test or may fail the same test for a different seed or segment of the cycle. As new tests are being introduced continually, many random-number generators that were initially considered good are no longer considered good on the basis of the new tests.

Although the purpose of this chapter is to describe tests for random numbers distributed uniformly, most of the tests described here can also be used to test random variates, that is, random variables with distributions that are not uniform.

27.1 CHI-SQUARE TEST

This is the most commonly used test to determine if an observed data set satisfies a specified distribution. The test is general and can be used for any distribution. It can be used for testing random numbers, that is, independently and identically distributed (**IID**) $U(0, 1)$, as well as for testing random-variate generators.

A histogram of the observed data is prepared, and the observed frequencies are compared with those obtained from the specified density function. Suppose the histogram consists of k cells, and o_i and e_i are the observed and expected frequencies for the ith cell. Then the test consists of computing

$$D = \sum_{i=1}^{k} \frac{(o_i - e_i)^2}{e_i}$$

For an exact fit, D should be zero. However, due to randomness, the D would be nonzero. It can be shown that D has a chi-square distribution with $k - 1$ degrees of freedom. The null hypothesis that the observations come from the specified distribution cannot be rejected at a level of significance α if the computed D is *less* than the $\chi^2_{[1-\alpha;k-1]}$ read from Table A.5 in the Appendix.

Example 27.1   One thousand random numbers were generated using the following generator with a seed of $x_0 = 1$:

$$x_n = (125x_{n-1} + 1)\text{mod}(2^{12})$$

The numbers so obtained were categorized in a histogram using 10 cells at intervals of 0.1, between 0 and 1. The data is presented in the first two columns of Table 27.1. At the $\alpha = 0.10$ level, can we say that the numbers are IID $U(0, 1)$?

TABLE 27.1   Chi-Square Test on 1000 Numbers

Cell	Observed	Expected	$\dfrac{(\text{Observed} - \text{Expected})^2}{\text{Expected}}$
1	100	100.0	0.000
2	96	100.0	0.160
3	98	100.0	0.040
4	85	100.0	2.250
5	105	100.0	0.250
6	93	100.0	0.490
7	97	100.0	0.090
8	125	100.0	6.250
9	107	100.0	0.490
10	94	100.0	0.360
Total	1000	1000.0	10.380

If the random numbers were IID $U(0,1)$, each of the 10 cells should have 1000/10, or 100, observations. The observed counts and the computation of the chi-square statistic is shown in the table.

From Table A.5 in the Appendix, we see that $\chi^2_{[0.9;9]}$ is 14.68. The observed difference, 10.380, is less than theoretically allowed. Therefore, at the 0.10 significance level, we accept that the random numbers generated are IID $U(0,1)$.   □

The chi-square test is not limited to uniform number. It can be used for any distribution. Notice, however, that in the equation, e_i appears in the denominator, and thus, errors in cells with a small e_i affect the chi-square statistic more than the errors in cells with a large e_i. The test works best when the cell sizes are chosen so that the expected probabilities e_i are all equal. In other words, an equiprobable histogram with variable cell sizes should be used rather than an equal-cell histogram. In order to get equiprobable cells, the expected frequencies of adjoining cells are combined so that the new cell probabilities are approximately equal.

In Example 27.1, it was assumed that none of the parameters of the hypothesized distribution were estimated from the sample. If that is not the case, then the number of degrees of freedom for the chi-square statistic should be reduced to $k - r - 1$ (in place of $k - 1$), where r is the number of parameters estimated from the sample.

Strictly speaking, the chi-square test is designed for discrete distributions and for large sample sizes only. For continuous distributions, a chi-square test is only an approximation. The specified level of significance applies only if the number of observations is infinite $(n \to \infty)$. With finite samples, the level of significance is slightly less. In particular, if the sample size is so small that some cells contain less than five observations, then a few neighboring cells should be combined so that each cell has at least five observations.

27.2 KOLMOGOROV-SMIRNOV TEST

This test is named after the statisticians A. N. Kolmogorov and N. V. Smirnov who developed it. An earlier version of this test was proposed by A. N. Kolmogorov in 1933. It was later modified by N. V. Smirnov in 1939. Like the chi-square test, the **K-S test** allows one to test if a given sample of n observations is from a specified continuous distribution. It is based on the observation that the difference between the observed CDF (Cumulative Distribution Function) $F_o(x)$ and the expected CDF $F_e(x)$ should be small. The symbols K^+ and K^- are used to denote the maximum observed deviations above and below the expected CDF in a sample of size n:

$$K^+ = \sqrt{n} \max_x [F_o(x) - F_e(x)]$$

$$K^- = \sqrt{n} \max_x [F_e(x) - F_o(x)]$$

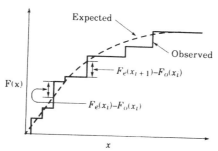

FIGURE 27.1 A K-S test requires measuring the maximum deviation of the observed CDF from the theoretical CDF.

Here, K^+ measures the maximum deviation when the observed CDF is above the expected CDF, and K^- measures the maximum deviation when the observed CDF is below the expected CDF. If the values K^+ and K^- are smaller than $K_{[1-\alpha;n]}$ listed in Table A.9 of the Appendix, the observations are said to come from the specified distribution at the α level of significance.

One common mistake in finding the K^- statistics is to compute the maximum of $F_e(x_i) - F_o(x_i)$. This is incorrect. Since F_o consists of a horizontal line segment at $F_o(x_i)$ in the interval $[x_i, x_{i+1})$, the maximum difference occurs just before x_{i+1}, as shown in Figure 27.1. Thus, $F_e(x_{i+1}) - F_o(x_i)$ is the correct difference to use in computing K^-.

For random numbers distributed uniformly between 0 and 1, the expected CDF is $F_e(x) = x$, and if x is greater than $j - 1$ other observations in a sample of n observations, then the observed CDF is $F_o(x) = j/n$. Therefore, to test whether a sample of n random numbers is from a uniform distribution, first sort the observations in an increasing order. Let the sorted numbers be $\{x_1, x_2, \ldots, x_n\}$ such that $x_{n-1} \leq x_n$. Then K^+ and K^- are computed as follows:

$$K^+ = \sqrt{n} \max_j \left(\frac{j}{n} - x_j \right)$$

$$K^- = \sqrt{n} \max_j \left(x_j - \frac{j-1}{n} \right)$$

By comparing the computed K's with the values listed in Table A.9, we can determine if the observations are uniformly distributed.

Example 27.2 Thirty random numbers were generated using a seed of $x_0 = 15$ in the following LCG:

$$x_n = 3x_{n-1} \bmod 31$$

The numbers are 14, 11, 2, 6, 18, 23, 7, 21, 1, 3, 9, 27, 19, 26, 16, 17, 20, 29, 25, 13, 8, 24, 10, 30, 28, 22, 4, 12, 5, 15.

The normalized numbers obtained by dividing the sequence by 31 are 0.45161, 0.35484, 0.06452, 0.19355, 0.58065, 0.74194, 0.22581, 0.67742,

0.03226, 0.09677, 0.29032, 0.87097, 0.61290, 0.83871, 0.51613, 0.54839, 0.64516, 0.93548, 0.80645, 0.41935, 0.25806, 0.77419, 0.32258, 0.96774, 0.90323, 0.70968, 0.12903, 0.38710, 0.16129, 0.48387.

Table 27.2 shows a sorted list of these numbers and differences. Using the maximum values obtained from the table, K-S statistics can be computed as follows:

$$K^+ = \sqrt{n}\max_j\left(\frac{j}{n} - x_j\right) = \sqrt{30} \times 0.03226 = 0.1767$$

$$K^- = \sqrt{n}\max_j\left(x_j - \frac{j-1}{n}\right) = \sqrt{30} \times 0.03226 = 0.1767$$

TABLE 27.2   Computation for the K-S Test Example

j	x_j	$\frac{j}{n} - x_j$	$x_j - \frac{j-1}{n}$
1	0.03226	0.00108	0.03226
2	0.06452	0.00215	0.03118
3	0.09677	0.00323	0.03011
4	0.12903	0.00430	0.02903
5	0.16129	0.00538	0.02796
6	0.19355	0.00645	0.02688
7	0.22581	0.00753	0.02581
8	0.25806	0.00860	0.02473
9	0.29032	0.00968	0.02366
10	0.32258	0.01075	0.02258
11	0.35484	0.01183	0.02151
12	0.38710	0.01290	0.02043
13	0.41935	0.01398	0.01935
14	0.45161	0.01505	0.01828
15	0.48387	0.01613	0.01720
16	0.51613	0.01720	0.01613
17	0.54839	0.01828	0.01505
18	0.58065	0.01935	0.01398
19	0.61290	0.02043	0.01290
20	0.64516	0.02151	0.01183
21	0.67742	0.02258	0.01075
22	0.70968	0.02366	0.00968
23	0.74194	0.02473	0.00860
24	0.77419	0.02581	0.00753
25	0.80645	0.02688	0.00645
26	0.83871	0.02796	0.00538
27	0.87097	0.02903	0.00430
28	0.90323	0.03011	0.00323
29	0.93548	0.03118	0.00215
30	0.96774	0.03226	0.00108
Maximum		0.03226	0.03226

From Table A.9 in the Appendix, the $K_{[0.9;n]}$ value for $n = 30$ and $\alpha = 0.1$ is 1.0424. Since the computed statistics K^+ and K^- are both less than the value from the table, the random-number sequence passes the K-S test at this level of significance. □

It is interesting to compare the K-S test with the chi-square test. The K-S test is specifically designed for small samples and continuous distributions. This is opposite of the chi-square test, which is designed for large samples and discrete distributions. The K-S test is based on the differences between observed and expected cumulative probabilities (CDFs) while the chi-square test is based on the differences between observed and hypothesized probabilities (pdf's or pmf's). The K-S test uses each observation in the sample without any grouping, while the chi-square test requires that the observations be grouped into a small number of cells. In this sense, a K-S test makes better use of the data. One of the problems in using the chi-square test is proper selection of the cell boundaries. The cell sizes affect the conclusion, but there are no firm guidelines for choosing the appropriate sizes. With the K-S test no such guidelines are required. A chi-square test is always approximate, while the K-S test is exact provided all parameters of the expected distributions are known.

27.3 SERIAL-CORRELATION TEST

One direct method to test dependence of two random variables is to see if their covariance is nonzero. If the covariance is nonzero, the variables are dependent. The inverse is not true, however. That is, if the covariance is zero, the variables may still be dependent.

Given a sequence of random numbers, one can compute the covariance between numbers that are k values apart, that is, between x_n and x_{n+k}. This is called **autocovariance** at **lag** k. Denoting this by R_k, the expression for computing it is

$$R_k = \frac{1}{n-k} \sum_{i=1}^{n-k} \left(U_i - \frac{1}{2} \right) \left(U_{i+k} - \frac{1}{2} \right)$$

For large n, R_k is normally distributed with a mean of zero and a variance of $1/[144(n-k)]$. The $100(1-\alpha)\%$ confidence interval for the autocovariance is

$$R_k \mp z_{1-\alpha/2} / \left(12\sqrt{n-k} \right)$$

If this interval does not include zero, we can say that the sequence has a significant correlation.

It must be pointed out that the preceding discussion applies only for $k \geq 1$. For $k = 0$, the computed value R_0 is the variance of the sequence and is expected to be $\frac{1}{12}$ for an IID $U(0,1)$ sequence.

TABLE 27.3 Autocovariances for the Random Sequence of Example 27.3

Lag k	Autocovariance R_k	Standard Deviation of R_k	90% Confidence Interval	
			Lower Limit	Upper Limit
1	−0.000038	0.000833	−0.001409	0.001333
2	−0.001017	0.000833	−0.002388	0.000354
3	−0.000489	0.000833	−0.001860	0.000882
4	−0.000033	0.000834	−0.001404	0.001339
5	−0.000531	0.000834	−0.001902	0.000840
6	−0.001277	0.000834	−0.002648	0.000095
7	−0.000385	0.000834	−0.001757	0.000986
8	−0.000207	0.000834	−0.001579	0.001164
9	0.001031	0.000834	−0.000340	0.002403
10	−0.000224	0.000834	−0.001595	0.001148

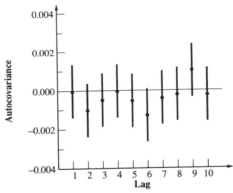

FIGURE 27.2 Plot of confidence intervals of the first 10 autocovariances.

Example 27.3 Again let us test the 10,000 random numbers generated by the following LCG with a seed of $x_0 = 1$:

$$x_n = 7^5 x_{n-1} \bmod (2^{31} - 1)$$

The autocovariance at lags 1 to 10 are shown in Table 27.3. The standard deviations and 90% confidence intervals are also shown in the table. The autocovariances are also plotted in Figure 27.2. We note that all confidence intervals include zero. All autocovariances can be assumed to be statistically insignificant at this confidence level. □

27.4 TWO-LEVEL TESTS

One problem with the empirical tests discussed so far is that if the sample size is too small, the test results may apply locally, but not globally to the complete cycle. Similarly, the results of a global test may not apply locally, and there may still be considerable nonrandomness in segments of the sequence. To overcome this problem, some researchers propose using two-level tests. For example, they use a chi-square test on n samples of size k each and then use a chi-square test on the set of n chi-square statistics so obtained. This is called a chi-square-on-chi-square test. Similarly, a K-S-on-K-S test has also been used. Some people have used this procedure to find a "nonrandom" segment of an otherwise random sequence.

27.5 k-DIMENSIONAL UNIFORMITY OR k-DISTRIBUTIVITY

The tests described in Sections 27.1 to 27.4 ensure that the numbers are uniformly distributed in one dimension. The concept of uniformity can be extended to k dimensions as follows.

Suppose u_n is the nth number in a random sequence that is uniformly distributed between 0 and 1. Given two real numbers a_1 and b_1, also between 0 and 1 such that $b_1 > a_1$, the probability that u_n lies in the interval $[a_1, b_1)$ is $b_1 - a_1$:

$$P(a_1 \leq u_n < b_1) = b_1 - a_1 \qquad \forall b_1 > a_1$$

This is known as the 1-distributivity property of u_n.

The 2-distributivity is a generalization of this property in two dimensions. It requires that the pairs of successive values u_{n-1} and u_n satisfy the following condition:

$$P(a_1 \leq u_{n-1} < b_1 \text{ and } a_2 \leq u_n < b_2) = (b_1 - a_1)(b_2 - a_2)$$

This is for all choices of a_1, b_1, a_2, b_2 in $[0, 1)$, $b_1 > a_1$ and $b_2 > a_2$. Finally, a sequence is called k distributed if

$$P(a_1 \leq u_n < b_1, \ldots, a_k \leq u_{n+k-1} < b_k) = (b_1 - a_1) \cdots (b_k - a_k)$$

This is for all choices of a_i, b_i in $[0, 1)$, with $b_i > a_i$, $i = 1, 2, ..., k$. Notice that a k-distributed sequence is always $k - 1$-distributed. The inverse is not true. A random-number sequence may be uniform in a lower dimension but may not be uniform in a higher dimension. Obviously, given a choice of several generators, the generator that produces most uniformity in the highest dimension is preferable.

In the next two sections we present two ways to check for k-distributivity:

- Serial test
- Spectral test

Before conducting these tests, it may be useful to visually check whether the sequence is uniform in two dimensions by looking at a plot of successive *overlapping* pairs of numbers in the sequence as points in a two-dimensional space. The following two examples illustrate this.

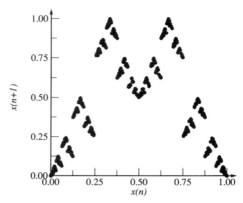

FIGURE 27.3   Plot of overlapping pairs from the Tausworthe generator $x^{15} + x + 1$.

Example 27.4   Consider the Tausworthe sequence generated by the following polynomial:

$$x^{15} + x + 1$$

This is a primitive polynomial. The resulting bit sequence has a full period of $2^{15} - 1$. A thousand 15-bit random numbers were generated using this polynomial. From the properties pointed out by Tausworthe, we know that the sequence is k distributed for k up to $\lceil q/l \rceil$, that is, $k = 1$. In other words, the numbers are uniformly distributed in one dimension. However, in two dimensions, the distribution is far from uniform. Figure 27.3 shows a plot of the successive overlapping pairs (x_n, x_{n+1}) in two dimensions. Notice the regularity in the plot. Not all possible subsets of the space are equally populated.   □

Example 27.5   Consider the polynomial

$$x^{15} + x^4 + 1$$

This is also a primitive polynomial. A thousand 15-bit random numbers were generated using this polynomial. Figure 27.4 shows a plot of the successive overlapping pairs (x_n, x_{n+1}) in two dimensions. This plot is less regular than the one in Figure 27.3.   □

27.6 SERIAL TEST

A serial test is used to test for uniformity in two dimensions or higher. In two dimensions, one divides the space between 0 and 1 into K^2 cells of equal area, as shown in Figure 27.5. Given n random numbers $\{x_1, x_2, \ldots, x_n\}$ between 0 and 1, we could count from $n/2$ *nonoverlapping* pairs $(x_1, x_2), (x_3, x_4), \ldots$ and count the points that fall in each of the K^2 cells. Ideally, one would expect

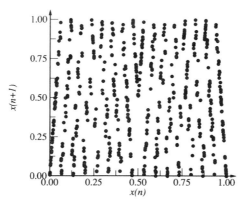

FIGURE 27.4   Plot of overlapping pairs from the Tausworthe generator $x^{15} + x^4 + 1$.

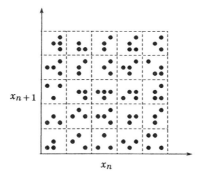

FIGURE 27.5   Two-dimensional uniformity requires that the the nonoverlapping pairs (x_n, x_{n+1}) fall uniformly on all square cells.

$n/(2K^2)$ points in each cell. A chi-square test can then be used to find the deviation of the actual counts from the expected counts. The degrees of freedom in this case are $K^2 - 1$. It is easy to see how this test can be extended to a k-dimension using k-tuples of nonoverlapping values.

It must be emphasized that for the serial test the pairs (or k-tuples) must be nonoverlapping. If overlapping pairs or tuples are used, the number of points in the cells are not independent and the chi-square test cannot be used. In the visual check of Section 27.5 as well as in the spectral test of Section 27.7, *overlapping* pairs and tuples are used. Given n numbers, there are $n - 1$ overlapping pairs, while there are only $n/2$ nonoverlapping pairs.

The dependence among successive numbers of a sequence shows up as nonuniformity in higher dimensions. For example, if the successive numbers have significant first-order negative correlation, a large x_n is more likely to be followed by a small x_n and vice versa. If we plot successive nonoverlapping pairs (x_{n-1}, x_n) as points on a scatter diagram, the points will tend to cluster more toward the right-bottom and left-top parts of the graph and will fail the chi-square test in two dimensions.

27.7 SPECTRAL TEST

Proposed by Conveyou and McPherson (1967), a spectral test determines how densely the k-tuples $\{x_1, x_2, \ldots, x_k\}$ can fill up the k-dimensional hyperspace. It was observed that the k-tuples from an LCG fall on a finite number of parallel hyperplanes. For example, if we plot successive pairs of numbers as points in two-dimensional space, all points would lie on a finite number of lines. In three dimensions, successive triplets lie on a finite number of planes. The following example illustrates this for a sample LCG.

Example 27.6   Consider the generator

$$x_n = 3x_{n-1} \bmod 31$$

Figure 27.6 shows the plot of overlapping pairs obtained from the LCG. It is shown that all the points lie on three straight lines. This is not a coincidence. By definition, the successive numbers obtained from the LCG are linearly related:

$$x_n = 3x_{n-1} \bmod 31$$

The equations of the straight lines are easily seen to be

$$x_n = 3x_{n-1}$$

$$x_n = 3x_{n-1} - 31$$

$$x_n = 3x_{n-1} - 62$$

or

$$x_n = 3x_{n-1} - 31k, \qquad k = 0, 1, 2 \tag{27.2}$$

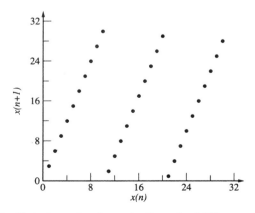

FIGURE 27.6   Plot of overlapping pairs from the LCG $x_n = 3x_{n-1} \bmod 31$.

Similarly, in three dimensions, the points (x_n, x_{n-1}, x_{n-2}) for the generator would lie on five planes given by

$$x_n = 2x_{n-1} + 3x_{n-2} - 31k, \qquad k = 0, 1, \ldots, 4$$

This equation is obtained by adding the following equation to Equation (27.2):

$$x_{n-1} = 3x_{n-2} - 31k_1, \qquad k_1 = 0, 1, 2$$

Note that $k + k_1$ will be an integer between 0 and 4. $\square$

Marsaglia (1968) has shown that successive k-tuples obtained from an LCG fall on, at most, $(k!m)^{1/k}$ parallel hyperplanes, where m is the modulus used in the LCG. For example, with $m = 2^{32}$, fewer than 2953 hyperplanes will contain all 3-tuples, fewer than 566 hyperplanes will contain all 4-tuples, and fewer than 41 hyperplanes will contain all 10-tuples. Thus, this is a weakness of LCGs.

The spectral test determines the maximum distance between adjacent hyperplanes. The larger this distance, the worse is the generator. For generators with a small period, the distance can be determined by complete enumeration as illustrated by the following example.

Example 27.7   Let us compare the following two generators:

$$x_n = 3x_{n-1} \bmod 31$$

$$x_n = 13x_{n-1} \bmod 31$$

Using a seed of $x_0 = 15$, we obtain the following sequence from the first generator: 14, 11, 2, 6, 18, 23, 7, 21, 1, 3, 9, 27, 19, 26, 16, 17, 20, 29, 25, 13, 8, 24, 10, 30, 28, 22, 4, 12, 5, 15, 14.

Using the same seed in the second generator, we obtain the following sequence: 9, 24, 2, 26, 28, 23, 20, 12, 1, 13, 14, 27, 10, 6, 16, 22, 7, 29, 5, 3, 8, 11, 19, 30, 18, 17, 4, 21, 25, 15, 9.

Notice that every number between 1 and 30 occurs once and only once in both sequences. Thus, both sequences will pass the chi-square test for uniformity. A plot of successive overlapping pairs of the first sequence is shown in Figure 27.6. We see that the points lie on 3 straight lines of positive slope or 10 lines of negative slope. Since the distance between the lines of positive slope is more, we consider only the lines with positive slope. Their equations are

$$x_n = 3x_{n-1}$$

$$x_n = 3x_{n-1} - 31$$

$$x_n = 3x_{n-1} - 62$$

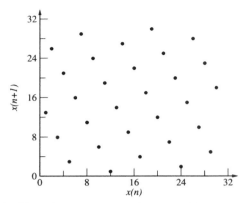

FIGURE 27.7   Plot of x_{n+1} versus x_n for the LCG $x_n = 13x_{n-1}$ mod 31.

The distance between two parallel lines $y = ax + c_1$ and $y = ax + c_2$ is given by $|c_2 - c_1|/\sqrt{1 + a^2}$. Thus, the distance between the lines is $31/\sqrt{10}$, or 9.80.

The plot of successive overlapping pairs of the second sequence is shown in Figure 27.7. In this case, all points fall on seven straight lines of positive slope or six straight lines of negative slope. The distance between lines of negative slope is larger than that between lines of positive slope, and therefore, for this generator, we will consider the set of lines with negative slopes. Their equations are

$$x_n = -\tfrac{5}{2}x_{n-1} + k\tfrac{31}{2}, \qquad k = 0, 1, \dots, 5$$

The distance between lines is $\tfrac{31}{2}/\sqrt{1 + (\tfrac{5}{2})^2}$, or 5.76.

Compared to the first generator, the second generator has a smaller maximum distance, and hence, the second generator has a better 2-distributivity.

It must be pointed out that in selecting between the sets of lines with positive and negative slopes, it is the set with a larger distance that is selected. This may not always be the set with fewer lines.   □

Notice that we used *overlapping* k-tuples in Example 27.7. Either overlapping or nonoverlapping k-tuples can be used. With overlapping k-tuples, we have k times as many points, which makes the graph visually more complete. The number of hyperplanes and the distance between them are the same with either choice. Thus, the result of the spectral test remains the same. This is not true for the serial test described in Section 27.6 where only nonoverlapping k-tuples should be used.

For generators with a large m and for higher dimensions, complete enumeration is not easy, and finding the maximum distance becomes quite complex. See Knuth (1981) for computing the maximum distance without complete enumeration.

EXERCISES

27.1 Generate 10,000 numbers using a seed of $x_0 = 1$ in the following generator:

$$x_n = 7^5 x_{n-1} \bmod (2^{31} - 1)$$

Classify the numbers into 10 equal-size cells and test for uniformity using the chi-square test at 90% confidence.

27.2 Generate 15 numbers using a seed of $x_0 = 1$ in the following generator:

$$x_n = (5x_{n-1} + 1) \bmod 16$$

Perform a K-S test and check whether the sequence passes the test at a 95% confidence level.

27.3 Generate 10,000 numbers using a seed of $x_0 = 1$ in the following LCG:

$$x_n = 48271 x_{n-1} \bmod (2^{31} - 1)$$

Perform the serial correlation test of randomness at 90% confidence and report the result.

27.4 Using the spectral test, compare the following two generators:

$$x_n = 7x_{n-1} \bmod 13$$

$$x_n = 11x_{n-1} \bmod 13$$

Which generator has a better 2-distributivity?

CHAPTER 28

RANDOM-VARIATE GENERATION

> *A man with one watch knows what time it is.*
> *A man with two watches is never sure.*
> —Segal's Law

There are a number of methods used to generate nonuniform variables. Each method is applicable only to a subset of the distribution. Also, for a particular distribution, one method may be more efficient than the others. In this chapter, some of the commonly used methods are described. Then, in Chapter 29, a list of distributions commonly used in computer systems modeling and their generation algorithms is presented.

28.1 INVERSE TRANSFORMATION

This method is based on the observation that given any random variable x with a CDF $F(x)$, the variable $u = F(x)$ is uniformly distributed between 0 and 1. Therefore, x can be obtained by generating uniform random numbers and computing $x = F^{-1}(u)$, as shown in Figure 28.1. Let us first prove this observation.

Proof 28.1   Given the distribution of a random variable x, it is possible to find the distribution of any nondecreasing function $g(x)$ of x as follows:

Let $y = g(x)$ so that $x = g^{-1}(y)$. Here $g^{-1}(\ )$ is the inverse function of $g(\ )$:

$$F_Y(y) = P(Y \le y) = P(x \le g^{-1}(y)) = F_X(g^{-1}(y))$$

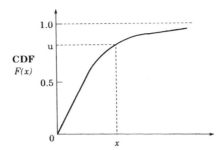

FIGURE 28.1   Inverse transformation of the CDF.

Now we select $g(\ )$ such that $g(x) = F(x)$, or $y = F(x)$, so that y is a random variable between 0 and 1 and its distribution is given by

$$F(y) = F(F^{-1}(y)) = y$$

and

$$f(y) = dF/dy = 1$$

That is, y is uniformly distributed between 0 and 1. $\square$

The preceding observation allows us to generate random variables with distributions for which F^{-1} can be determined either analytically or empirically. We present one example of each case.

Example 28.1   To generate exponential variates, proceed as follows:

- The pdf $f(x) = \lambda e^{-\lambda x}$.
- The CDF $F(x) = 1 - e^{-\lambda x} = u$ or $x = -\dfrac{1}{\lambda}\ln(1-u)$.

Thus, exponential variates x_i can be produced by generating a uniform variable u_i and by using the preceding equation to determine x_i. Since u is uniformly distributed between 0 and 1, $1-u$ is also uniformly distributed between 0 and 1. Therefore, the generation algorithm can be simplified to

$$x = -\frac{1}{\lambda}\ln(u)$$ $\square$

The next example illustrates the use of the inverse-transformation method for a case in which the inverse is found empirically.

Example 28.2 The packet sizes in computer networks were measured and found to be trimodal with the following probabilities:

Size (bytes)	Probability
64	0.7
128	0.1
512	0.2

The CDF for this distribution is

$$F(x) = \begin{cases} 0.0 & 0 \leq x < 64 \\ 0.7 & 64 \leq x < 128 \\ 0.8 & 128 \leq x < 512 \\ 1.0 & 512 \leq x \end{cases}$$

The inverse of the CDF is

$$F^{-1}(u) = \begin{cases} 64 & 0 < u \leq 0.7 \\ 128 & 0.7 < u \leq 0.8 \\ 512 & 0.8 < u \leq 1 \end{cases}$$

Thus, the packet sizes can be produced by generating a uniform random number between 0 and 1 and by comparing it with 0.7 and 0.8. If the number is less than or equal to 0.7, the packet size should be 64. If it is greater than 0.7 but less than or equal to 0.8, the packet size should be 128 bytes. If it is greater than 0.8, the packet size should be 512 bytes.   □

It should be pointed out that, by definition, the CDF is *continuous from the right*, that is, at any point where there is a discontinuity, the value on the right of the discontinuity is used. In Example 28.2, the CDF jumps from 0 to 0.7 at $x = 64$. The value at $x = 64$ is read as 0.7 (the value to the right of $x = 64$). Following this convention, the inverse function is *continuous from the left*. The inverse function is discontinuous at $u = 0.7$. However, if the random number generated comes out to be 0.7, the value of x to the left of $u = 0.7$, that is, $x = 64$, is used.

Inverse transformation is a powerful random-variate generation technique. Table 28.1 lists a number of distributions that can be generated using this technique. In each case, a $U(0,1)$ random number u is generated and the function listed under the "inverse" column is computed and returned as the desired variate. In the table, $\lceil \cdot \rceil$ is used to denote rounding up to the next integer.

28.2 REJECTION

A rejection technique can be used if another density function $g(x)$ exists so that $cg(x)$ *majorizes* the density function $f(x)$, that is, $cg(x) \geq f(x)$ for all

TABLE 28.1   Applications of the Inverse-Transform Technique

Distribution	CDF $F(x)$	Inverse
Exponential	$1 - e^{-x/a}$	$-a\ln(u)$
Extreme value	$1 - e^{-e^{(x-a)/b}}$	$a + b\ln\ln u$
Geometric	$1 - (1-p)^x$	$\left[\dfrac{\ln(u)}{\ln(1-p)}\right]$
Logistic	$1 - \dfrac{1}{1 + e^{(x-\mu)/b}}$	$\mu - b\ln\left(\dfrac{1}{u} - 1\right)$
Pareto	$1 - x^{-a}$	$1/u^{1/a}$
Weibull	$1 - e^{(x/a)^b}$	$a(\ln u)^{1/b}$

values of x. If such a function can be found, then the following steps can be used to generate random variate x with density $f(x)$:

1. Generate x with pdf $g(x)$.
2. Generate y uniform on $[0, cg(x)]$.
3. If $y \le f(x)$, then output x and return. Otherwise, repeat from step 1.

The algorithm continues *rejecting* the random variates x and y until the condition $y \le f(x)$ is satisfied; hence, the name of the technique.

The following example illustrates the rejection technique.

Example 28.3   Consider the beta $(2,4)$ density function

$$f(x) = 20x(1-x)^3, \qquad 0 \le x \le 1$$

The function is shown in Figure 28.2. It can be bounded inside a rectangle of height 2.11. Therefore, we can use $c = 2.11$, and

$$g(x) = 1, \qquad 0 \le x \le 1$$

The beta $(2,4)$ variates can be generated as follows:

1. Generate x uniform on $[0,1]$.
2. Generate y uniform on $[0, 2.11]$.
3. If $y \le 20x(1-x)^3$, then output x and return. Otherwise repeat from step 1.

Steps 1 and 2 generate a point (x, y) uniformly distributed over the rectangle shown in Figure 28.2. If the point falls above the beta density function $f(x)$, then step 3 rejects x.   □

The efficiency of the rejection technique depends upon the function $g(x)$ and how closely it envelopes $f(x)$. If there is a large area between $cg(x)$ and $f(x)$, then a large percentage of random variates generated in steps 1 and 2

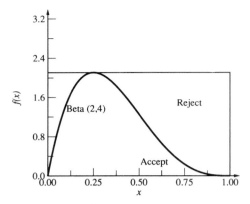

FIGURE 28.2 Generating a beta distribution.

are rejected. Similarly, if generation of random variates with $g(x)$ is complex, this method may not be efficient.

28.3 COMPOSITION

This technique can be used if the desired CDF $F(x)$ can be expressed as a weighted sum of n other CDFs $F_1(x), F_2(x), \ldots, F_n(x)$. That is,

$$F(x) = \sum_{i=1}^{n} p_i F_i(x)$$

Here, $p_i \geq 0$, $\sum_{i=1}^{n} p_i = 1$, and F_i's are distribution functions. The number of functions n can be finite or infinite. Thus, n CDFs are composed together to form the desired CDF; hence, the name of the technique. Another view of the same process is that the desired CDF is decomposed into several other CDFs. This is why the same technique is also called **decomposition**.

The technique can also be used if the density function $f(x)$ can be expressed as a weighted sum of n other density functions:

$$f(x) = \sum_{i=1}^{n} p_i f_i(x)$$

In either case, the steps to generate X are as follows:

1. Generate a random integer I such that

$$P(I = i) = p_i$$

   This can easily be done using the inverse-transformation method.
2. Generate x with the ith pdf $f_i(x)$ and return.

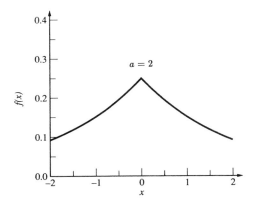

FIGURE 28.3 Laplace density function.

Example 28.4 The pdf for Laplace distribution is given by

$$f(x) = \frac{1}{2a}e^{-|x|/a}$$

A plot of the pdf with $a = 2$ is shown in Figure 28.3. The pdf is a composition of two exponential pdf's. The probability of x being positive is $\frac{1}{2}$. Similarly, the probability of x being negative is $\frac{1}{2}$.

Using the composition technique, Laplace variates can be generated as follows:

1. Generate $u_1 \sim U(0,1)$ and $u_2 \sim U(0,1)$.
2. If $u_1 < 0.5$, return $x = -a\ln u_2$; otherwise return $x = a\ln u_2$.

It must be pointed out that Laplace variates can be generated more efficiently using the inverse-transformation technique. □

28.4 CONVOLUTION

This technique can be used if the random variable x can be expressed as a sum of n random variables $y_1, y_2, \ldots, y_n$, that can be easily generated; that is,

$$x = y_1 + y_2 + \cdots + y_n$$

In this case, x can be generated by simply generating n random variate y_i's and then summing them.

If x is a sum of two random variables y_1 and y_2, then the pdf of x can be obtained analytically by a convolution of the pdf's of y_1 and y_2. This is why the technique is called convolution, although no convolution is required in random-number generation.

Notice the difference between composition and convolution. The former technique is used when the pdf or CDF can be expressed as a sum of other pdf's or CDFs. The latter technique is used when the random variable itself can be expressed as a sum of other random variables.

Some examples of applications of this technique are as follows:

- An Erlang-k variate is the sum of k exponential variates Thus, it can be obtained by generating k exponential variates and summing them.
- A binomial variate with parameters n and p is a sum of n Bernoulli variates with success probability p. Thus, a binomial variate can be obtained by generated n $U(0,1)$ random numbers and returning the number of random numbers that are less than p.
- The chi-square distribution with ν degrees of freedom is a sum of squares of ν unit normal $N(0,1)$ variates.
- The sum of two gamma variates with parameters (a,b_1) and (a,b_2) is a gamma variate with parameter $(a,b_1 + b_2)$. Thus, a gamma variate with a noninteger value of b parameter can be obtained by adding two gamma variates—one with integer b and the other with the fractional b.
- The sum of a large number of variates from any distribution has a normal distribution. This fact is used to generate normal variates by adding a suitable number of $U(0,1)$ variates.
- The sum of m geometric variates is a Pascal variate.
- The sum of two uniform variates has a triangular density.

28.5 CHARACTERIZATION

Special characteristics of some distributions allow their variates to be generated using algorithms specially tailored for them. All such algorithms are classified under the technique of **characterization**.

Examples of random-variate generation using characterization are as follows:

- If the interarrival times are exponentially distributed with mean $1/\lambda$, the number of arrivals n over a given period T has a Poisson distribution with parameter λT. Thus, a Poisson variate can be obtained by continuously generating exponential variates until their sum exceeds T and returning the number of variates generated as the Poisson variate.
- The ath smallest number in a sequence of $a + b + 1$ $U(0,1)$ uniform variates has a beta(a,b) distribution.
- The ratio of two unit normal variates is a Cauchy $(0,1)$ variate.
- A chi-square variate with even degrees of freedom $\chi^2(\nu)$ is the same as a gamma variate $\gamma(2,\nu/2)$.
- If x_1 and x_2 are two gamma variates $\gamma(a,b)$ and $\gamma(a,c)$, respectively, the ratio $x_1/(x_1 + x_2)$ has a beta(b,c) distribution.

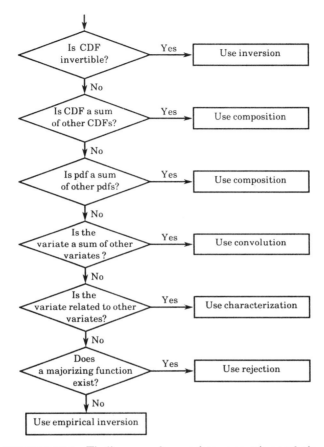

FIGURE 28.4   Finding a random-variate generation technique

• If x is a unit normal variate, $e^{\mu+\sigma x}$ is a lognormal (μ,σ) variate.

Figure 28.4 presents a flow chart that will help you decide which of the preceding techniques to use for a particular case. If the CDF is easily invertible, inverse transformation is the best choice. Otherwise, if either the CDF or pdf can be expressed as a sum of other CDFs or pdfs, the composition method can be used. If the variate can be expressed as a sum of other variates, use convolution. Characterization can be used if the distribution has some known properties that can be exploited for random-variate generation. Finally, if the pdf is such that a majorizing function can be found, the rejection technique can be used. If all else fails, you can always use empirical inverse transformation by numerically computing the distribution function and using it as illustrated earlier in Example 28.2.

EXERCISE

28.1 A random variate has the following triangular density:

$$f(x) = \min(x, 2 - x) \qquad 0 \leq x \leq 2$$

Develop algorithms to generate this variate using each of the following methods:

a. Inverse transformation

b. Rejection

c. Composition

d. Convolution

CHAPTER 29

COMMONLY USED DISTRIBUTIONS

> *Question: Why did you use the Gaussian assumption?*
>
> *Answer: Because it's the normal assumption!*
>
> *—Overheard at a conference.*
> —S. Pasupathy (1989)

This chapter describes the random-number generation algorithms for distributions commonly used by computer systems performance analysts. This chapter is organized in a manner convenient for future reference. The distributions are listed in an alphabetic order. For each distribution, the key characteristics are summarized, algorithms for random-number generation are presented, and examples of their applications are given.

29.1 BERNOULLI DISTRIBUTION

The Bernoulli distribution is the simplest discrete distribution. A Bernoulli variate can take only two values, which are usually denoted as failure and success or $x = 0$ and $x = 1$, respectively. If p denotes the probability of success, $1 - p$ is the probability of failure. The experiments to generate a Bernoulli variate are called **Bernoulli trials**.

The key characteristics of the Bernoulli distribution are summarized in Table 29.1. The Bernoulli distribution is used to model the probability of an

TABLE 29.1 Bernoulli Distribution Bernoulli(p)

---

1. Parameters: p = probability of success ($x = 1$), $0 \le p \le 1$
2. Range: $x = 0, 1$
3. pmf: $f(x) = \begin{cases} 1 - p & \text{if } x = 0 \\ p & \text{if } x = 1 \\ 0 & \text{otherwise} \end{cases}$
4. Mean: p
5. Variance: $p(1 - p)$

---

outcome having a desired class or characteristic, for example,

1. a computer system is up or down,
2. a packet in a computer network reaches or does not reach the destination, or
3. a bit in the packet is affected by noise and arrives in error.

The Bernoulli distribution and its derivative distributions can be used only if the trials are independent and identical so that the probability of success in each trial is p and is not affected by the outcomes of the past trials.

Using inverse transformation, Bernoulli variates can be generated as follows. Generate $u \sim U(0, 1)$. If $u \le p$, return 0. Otherwise, return 1.

29.2 BETA DISTRIBUTION

The beta distribution is used to represent random variates that are bounded, for instance, between 0 and 1. The key characteristics of the beta distribution are summarized in Table 29.2.

TABLE 29.2 Beta Distribution beta(a, b)

---

1. Parameters: a, b = shape parameters, $a > 0$, $b > 0$
2. Range: $0 \le x \le 1$
3. pdf: $f(x) = \dfrac{x^{a-1}(1 - x)^{b-1}}{\beta(a, b)}$

   $\beta(.)$ is the beta function and is related to the gamma function as follows:

   $$\beta(a, b) = \int_0^1 x^{a-1}(1 - x)^{b-1} dx = \frac{\Gamma(a)\Gamma(b)}{\Gamma(a + b)}$$

4. Mean: $a/(a + b)$
5. Variance: $ab/[(a + b)^2(a + b + 1)]$

The range of the beta variate as defined in Table 29.2 is $[0,1]$, that is, $0 \leq x \leq 1$. It can also be defined for any other range $[x_{min}, x_{max}]$ by substituting $(x - x_{min})/(x_{max} - x_{min})$ in place of x in the pdf specified.

The beta distribution is used to model random proportions, for example,

1. the fraction of packets requiring retransmissions or
2. the fraction of remote procedure calls (RPCs) taking more than a specified time.

Beta variates can be generated as follows:

1. Generate two gamma variates $\gamma(1,a)$ and $\gamma(1,b)$, and take the ratio:

$$\text{beta}(a,b) = \frac{\gamma(1,a)}{\gamma(1,a) + \gamma(1,b)}$$

2. If both parameters a and b are integers, the following algorithm by Fox (1963) can be used:

   (a) Generate $a + b + 1$ uniform $U(0,1)$ random numbers.
   (b) Return the ath smallest number as $\text{beta}(a,b)$.

3. If both a and b are less than 1, the following method by Jöhnk (1964) may be used:

   (a) Generate two uniform $U(0,1)$ random numbers u_1 and u_2.
   (b) Let $x = u_1^{1/a}$ and $y = u_2^{1/b}$. If $x + y > 1$, go back to the previous step. Otherwise, return $x/(x + y)$ as $\text{beta}(a,b)$.

4. If both a and b are greater than 1, an algorithm based on rejection techniques can be easily developed to generate beta variates.

29.3 BINOMIAL DISTRIBUTION

The number of successes x in a sequence of n Bernoulli trials has a binomial distribution. The key characteristics of the binomial distribution are summarized in Table 29.3.

TABLE 29.3 Binomial Distribution binomial(p,n)

1. Parameters: p = probability of success in a trial, $0 < p < 1$
   n = number of trials; n must be a positive integer
2. Range: $x = 0, 1, \ldots, n$
3. pdf: $f(x) = \binom{n}{x} p^x (1-p)^{n-x}$
4. Mean: np
5. Variance: $np(1-p)$

The binomial distribution is used to model the number of successes in a sequence of n independent and identical Bernoulli trials, for example,

1. the number of processors that are up in a multiprocessor system,
2. the number of packets that reach the destination without loss,
3. the number of bits in a packet that are not affected by noise, or
4. the number of items in a batch that have certain characteristics.

The variance of the binomial distribution is always less than the mean. For all the preceding applications, negative binomial or Poisson distributions can be used in place of a binomial distribution if the variance is greater than the mean or equal to the mean, respectively.

Binomial variates can be generated as follows:

1. Generate n $U(0,1)$ random numbers. The number of random numbers that are less than p is binomial(p,n). This is the composition method based on the observation that the sum of n Bernoulli variates has a binomial distribution.
2. For small p, a faster technique is as follows:

    (a) Generate geometric random numbers $G_i(p) = \lceil \ln(u_i)/\ln(1-p) \rceil$.
    (b) If the sum of geometric random numbers so far is less than or equal to n, go back to the previous step. Otherwise, return the number of random numbers generated minus 1. If $\sum_{i=1}^{m} G_i(p) > n$, return $m-1$.

3. Inverse transformation method: Compute the CDF $F(x)$ for $x = 0,1, 2,...,n$ and store in an array. For each binomial variate, generate a $U(0,1)$ variate u and search the array to find x so that $F(x) \le u < F(x+1)$; return x.

29.4 CHI-SQUARE DISTRIBUTION

The sum of squares of several unit normal variates has a distribution known as chi square. The distribution was first derived by Karl Pearson in 1900. In his original paper, Pearson used the symbol χ^2 for the sum. Since then statisticians have started referring to the distribution as the chi-square distribution. The key characteristics are summarized in Table 29.4.

The chi-square distribution is used whenever a sum of squares of normal variables is involved, for example, to model sample variances.

Chi-square variates can be generated as follows:

1. The following method is based on the observation that the chi-square distribution $\chi^2(\nu)$ is the same as the gamma distribution $\gamma(2,\nu/2)$. For

TABLE 29.4   Chi-Square Distribution $\chi^2(\nu)$

1. Parameters: ν = degrees of freedom, ν must be a positive integer
2. Range: $0 \leq x \leq \infty$
3. pdf: $f(x) = \dfrac{x^{(\nu-2)/2}e^{-x/2}}{2^{\nu/2}\Gamma(\nu/2)}$

   Here, $\Gamma(\cdot)$ is the gamma function defined as follows:

$$\Gamma(b) = \int_0^\infty e^{-x}x^{b-1}\,dx$$

4. Mean: ν
5. Variance: 2ν

ν even,

$$\chi^2(\nu) = -\frac{1}{2}\ln\left(\prod_{i=1}^{\nu/2} u_i\right)$$

For ν odd,

$$\chi^2(\nu) = \chi^2(\nu - 1) + [N(0,1)]^2$$

2. Generate ν $N(0,1)$ variates and return the sum of their squares.

29.5   ERLANG DISTRIBUTION

The Erlang distribution is commonly used in queueing models as an extension of the exponential distribution. The key characteristics of the Erlang distribution are summarized in Table 29.5.

The Erlang distribution is used as an extension to the exponential distribution if the coefficient of variation is less than 1, for example,

1. to model service times in a queueing network model [a server with Erlang(a, m) service times can be represented as a series of m servers

TABLE 29.5   Erlang Distribution Erlang(a, m)

1. Parameters: a = scale parameter, $a > 0$
   m = shape parameter; m is a positive integer
2. Range: $0 \leq x \leq \infty$
3. pdf: $f(x) = \dfrac{x^{m-1}e^{-x/a}}{(m-1)!a^m}$
4. CDF: $F(x) = 1 - e^{-x/a}\left[\sum_{i=0}^{m-1} \dfrac{(x/a)^i}{i!}\right]$
5. Mean: am
6. Variance: $a^2 m$

ponentially distributed service times] or
el time to repair and time between failures.

Erlang variates can be generated using convolution as follows. Generate m
$U(0,1)$ random numbers u_i, and then

$$\text{Erlang}(a,m) \sim -a \ln \left(\prod_{i=1}^{m} u_i \right)$$

29.6 EXPONENTIAL DISTRIBUTION

The exponential distribution is used extensively in queueing models. The key
characteristics of the distribution are summarized in Table 29.6.

TABLE 29.6   Exponential Distribution $\exp(a)$

1. Parameters: a = scale parameter = Mean, $a > 0$
2. Range: $0 \le x \le \infty$
3. pdf: $f(x) = \dfrac{1}{a} e^{-x/a}$
4. CDF: $F(x) = 1 - e^{-x/a}$
5. Mean: a
6. Variance: a^2

The exponential distribution is the only continuous distribution with the
memoryless property such that remembering the time since the last event does
not help in predicting the time till the next event. If the interarrival times of
jobs to a system are exponentially distributed, for instance, with mean $1/\lambda$,
the probability distribution function is

$$F(\tau) = P(\tau < t) = 1 - e^{-\lambda t}, \qquad t \ge 0$$

If we see an arrival and start our clock at $t = 0$, the mean time to the next
arrival is $1/\lambda$. Now suppose we do not see an arrival until $t = x$. The distribution of the time remaining until the next arrival is

$$P(\tau - x < t \mid \tau > x) = \frac{P(x < \tau < x + t)}{P(\tau > x)}$$

$$= \frac{P(\tau < x + t) - P(\tau < x)}{P(\tau > x)}$$

$$= \frac{(1 - e^{-\lambda(x+t)}) - (1 - e^{-\lambda x})}{e^{-\lambda t}}$$

$$= 1 - e^{-\lambda x}$$

This is identical to the situation at $t = 0$. In particular, the mean time to the next arrival is still $1/\lambda$. Thus, the expected time to the next arrival is always $1/\lambda$ regardless of the time since the last arrival. Remembering the past history does not help. A similar argument applies to any other exponential variate. This memoryless property, which considerably simplifies the analysis, is the main reason for the popularty of the exponential distribution.

The exponential distribution is used to model the time between successive events, particularly if the events are caused by a large number of independent factors, for example,

1. the time between successive request arrivals to a device or
2. the time between failures of a device.

The service times at devices are also modeled as exponentially distributed.

Exponential variates can be generate using inverse transformation. Generate a $U(0,1)$ random number u and return $-a\ln(u)$ as $\exp(a)$. This is based on the inverse transformation method.

29.7 F DISTRIBUTION

The ratio of two chi-square variates has an F distribution. The key characteristics of the F distribution are summarized in Table 29.7. Notice that the two parameters n and m of the F distribution are called numerator degrees of freedom and denominator degrees of freedom. The names of the parameters come from the fact that if we take two chi-square variates $\chi^2(n)$ and $\chi^2(m)$ with n and m degrees of freedom, then the ratio

$$\frac{[\chi^2(n)/n]}{[\chi^2(m)/m]}$$

has an $F(n,m)$ distribution.

TABLE 29.7 F Distribution $F(n,m)$

---

1. Parameters:
   n = numerator degrees of freedom; n should be a positive integer
   m = denominator degrees of freedom; m should be a positive integer
2. Range: $0 \le x \le \infty$
3. pdf: $f(x) = \dfrac{(n/m)^{n/2}}{\beta(n/2, m/2)} x^{(n-2)/2} \left(1 + \dfrac{n}{m} x\right)^{-(n+m)/2}$
4. Mean: $\dfrac{m}{m-2}$, provided $m > 2$
5. Variance: $\dfrac{2m^2(n+m-2)}{n(m-2)^2(m-4)}$, provided $m > 4$

The quantiles of the F distribution are listed in Tables A.6 to A.8 in the Appendix. These tables list only F_α values for α close to 1. From these values $F_{1-\alpha}$ can be computed using the following relationship:

$$F_{[1-\alpha;n,m]} = \frac{1}{F_{[\alpha;m,n]}}$$

For example, this relationship can be used to compute $F_{0.05}$ from the $F_{0.95}$ table.

The F distribution is used to model the ratio of sample variances, for example, in the F-test for regression and analysis of variance.

Using characterization, F-variates can be generated as follows. Generate two chi-square variates $\chi^2(n)$ and $\chi^2(m)$ and compute:

$$F(n,m) = \frac{\chi^2(n)/n}{\chi^2(m)/m}$$

29.8 GAMMA DISTRIBUTION

The Gamma distribution is a generalization of the Erlang distribution and allows noninteger shape parameters. Like exponential and Erlang distributions, it is used in queueing modeling. The key characteristics of the gamma distribution are summarized in Table 29.8.

TABLE 29.8   Gamma Distribution $\gamma(a,b)$

---

1. Parameters: a = scale parameter, $a > 0$
                   b = shape parameter, $b > 0$
2. Range: $0 \le x \le \infty$
3. pdf: $f(x) = \dfrac{(x/a)^{b-1}e^{-x/a}}{a\Gamma(b)}$
   $\Gamma(\cdot)$ is the gamma function.
4. Mean: ab
5. Variance: $a^2 b$

The gamma distribution is used to model service times of devices in queueing network models and for repair times in a manner similar to the Erlang distribution (See Section 29.5).

Gamma variates can be generated as follows:

1. If b is an integer, the sum of b exponential variates has a gamma distribution. This gives the following expression for generating gamma variates from $U(0,1)$ variates:

$$\gamma(a,b) \sim -a\ln\left[\prod_{i=1}^{b} u_i\right]$$

2. For $b < 1$, generate a beta variate $x \sim \text{BT}(b, 1 - b)$ and an exponential variate $y \sim \exp(1)$. The product axy has a $\gamma(a, b)$ distribution.

3. For other values of b, two gamma variates corresponding to the integer and fractional part of b can be added to give the desired gamma variate:

$$\gamma(a, b) \sim \gamma(a, \lfloor b \rfloor) + \gamma(a, b - \lfloor b \rfloor)$$

29.9 GEOMETRIC DISTRIBUTION

The distribution of number of trials up to and including the first success in a sequence of Bernoulli trials is called a geometric distribution. The key characteristics of the geometric distribution are summarized in Table 29.9.

TABLE 29.9 Geometric Distribution $G(p)$

1. Parameters: p = probability of success, $0 < p < 1$
2. Range: $x = 1, 2, \ldots, \infty$
3. pmf: $f(x) = (1 - p)^{x-1} p$
4. CDF: $F(x) = 1 - (1 - p)^x$
5. Mean: $1/p$
6. Variance: $\dfrac{1 - p}{p^2}$

The geometric distribution is a discrete equivalent of the exponential distribution. It is a memoryless distribution in the sense that remembering the results of past attempts does not help in predicting the future.

The geometric distribution is used to model the number of attempts between successive failures (or successes), for example,

1. the number of local queries to a database between successive accesses to the remote database,
2. the number of packets successfully transmitted between those requiring a retransmission, or
3. the number of successive error-free bits between in-error bits in a packet received on a noisy link.

Another common application of the geometric distribution is to model batch sizes with batches arriving in a Poisson stream. Under this condition, the arrivals remain memoryless and are easy to model.

Geometric variates can be easily generated using inverse transformation. Generate a $U(0, 1)$ random number u and compute

$$G(p) = \left\lceil \frac{\ln(u)}{\ln(1 - p)} \right\rceil$$

Here, $\lceil \cdot \rceil$ denotes rounding up to the next larger integer.

TABLE 29.10   Lognormal Distribution LN(μ, σ)

1. Parameters: μ = mean of $\ln(x)$, $\mu > 0$
   σ = standard deviation of $\ln(x)$, $\sigma > 0$
2. Range: $0 \leq x \leq \infty$
3. pdf: $f(x) = \dfrac{1}{\sigma x \sqrt{2\pi}} e^{-(\ln x - \mu)^2 / 2\sigma^2}$
4. Mean: $e^{\mu + \sigma^2/2}$
5. Variance: $e^{2\mu + \sigma^2}(e^{\sigma^2} - 1)$

29.10   LOGNORMAL DISTRIBUTION

The log of a normal variate has a lognormal distribution. In regression modeling and analysis of experimental designs, often log transformation is used. In
such cases, the response in the transformed model has a normal distribution
while the original response has a lognormal distribution. The key characteristics of a lognormal distribution are summarized in Table 29.10.

It must be noticed that μ and σ are the mean and standard deviation of
$\ln(x)$ and should not be confused with those for the lognormal variate x.

The product of a large number of positive random variables tends to have
an approximate lognormal distribution. It is therefore used to model errors
that are a product of effects of a large number of factors.

Lognormal variates can be generated using a log of a normal variate. Generate $x \sim N(0, 1)$ and return $e^{\mu + \sigma x}$.

29.11   NEGATIVE BINOMIAL DISTRIBUTION

In a sequence of Bernoulli trials, the number of failures x before the mth success has a negative binomial distribution. The key characteristics of a negative
binomial distribution are summarized in Table 29.11.

The negative binomial distribution is used to model the number of failures
before the mth success; for example:

TABLE 29.11   Negative Binomial Distribution NB(p, m)

1. Parameters: p = probability of success, $0 < p < 1$
   m = number of successes; m must be a positive integer
2. Range: $x = 0, 1, 2, \ldots, \infty$
3. pmf: $f(x) = \dbinom{m + x - 1}{m - 1} p^m (1 - p)^x = \dfrac{\Gamma(m + x)}{(\Gamma m)(\Gamma x)} p^m (1 - p)^x$
   The second expression allows a negative binomial to be defined for
   noninteger values of x.
4. Mean: $m(1 - p)/p$
5. Variance: $m(1 - p)/p^2$

1. Number of local queries to a database system before the mth remote query
2. Number of retransmissions for a message consisting of m packets
3. Number of error-free bits received on a noisy link before the m in-error bit

The variance of $NB(p,m)$ is greater than the mean for all values of p and m. Therefore, this distribution may be used in place of a Poisson distribution, which has a variance equal to the mean, or in place of a binomial distribution, which has a variance less than the mean.

Negative binomial variates can be generated as follows:

1. Generate $u_i \sim U(0,1)$ until m of the u_i's are greater than p. Return the count of u_i's less than or equal to p as $NB(p,m)$.
2. The sum of m geometric variates $G(p)$ gives the total number of trials for m successes. Thus, $NB(p,m)$ can be obtained from m geometric variates as follows:

$$NB(p,m) \sim \left(\sum_{i=1}^{m} G(p) \right) - m$$

3. The following composition method may be used for integer as well as noninteger values of m:

   (a) Generate a gamma variate $y \sim \Gamma(p/(1-p), m)$.
   (b) Generate a Poisson variate $x \sim \text{Poisson}(y)$.
   (c) Return x as $NB(p,m)$.

29.12 NORMAL DISTRIBUTION

Also known as Gaussian distribution, the normal distribution was actually discovered by Abraham De Moivre in 1733. Gauss and Laplace rediscovered it in 1809 and 1812, respectively. The normal distribution $N(0,1)$ with $\mu = 0$ and $\sigma = 1$ is called the **unit normal distribution** or **standard normal distribution**. The key characteristics of the normal distribution are summarized in Table 29.12.

TABLE 29.12 Normal Distribution $N(\mu, \sigma)$

1. Parameters: μ = mean
   σ = standard deviation $\sigma > 0$
2. Range: $-\infty \le x \le \infty$
3. pdf: $f(x) = \dfrac{1}{\sigma\sqrt{2\pi}} e^{-(x-\mu)^2/2\sigma^2}$
4. Mean: μ
5. Variance: σ^2

The normal distribution is used whenever the randomness is caused by several independent sources acting additively; for example:

1. Errors in measurement
2. Error in modeling to account for a number of factors that are not included in the model
3. Sample means of a large number of independent observations from a given distribution

Normal variates can be generated as follows:

1. *Convolution*: The sum of a large number of uniform $u_i \sim U(0,1)$ variates has a normal distribution:

$$N(\mu,\sigma) \sim \mu + \sigma \frac{(\sum_{i=1}^{n} u_i) - n/2}{(n/12)^{1/2}}$$

   Generally, $n = 12$ is used.

2. *Box-Muller Method* (Box and Muller (1958)): Generate two uniform variates u_1 and u_2 and compute two independent normal variates $N(\mu,\sigma)$ as follows:

$$x_1 = \mu + \sigma \cos(2\pi u_1)\sqrt{-2\ln(u_2)}$$
$$x_2 = \mu + \sigma \sin(2\pi u_1)\sqrt{-2\ln(u_2)}$$

   There is some concern that if this method is used with u's from an LCG, the resulting x's may be correlated. See Edgeman (1989).

3. *Polar Method* (Marsaglia and Bray (1964)):

   (a) Generate two $U(0,1)$ variates u_1 and u_2.
   (b) Let $v_1 = 2u_1 - 1$, $v_2 = 2u_2 - 1$, and $r = v_1^2 + v_1^2$.
   (c) If $r \geq 1$, go back to step 3a; otherwise let $s = [(-2\ln r)/r]^{1/2}$ and return:

$$x_1 = \mu + \sigma v_1 s$$
$$x_2 = \mu + \sigma v_2 s$$

   x_1 and x_2 are two independent $N(\mu,\sigma)$ variates.

4. *Rejection Method*:

   (a) Generate two uniform $U(0,1)$ variates u_1 and u_2.
   (b) Let $x = -\ln u_1$.
   (c) If $u_2 > e^{-(x-1)^2/2}$, go back to step 4a.
   (d) Generate u_3.
   (e) If $u_3 > 0.5$, return $\mu + \sigma x$; otherwise return $\mu - \sigma x$.

TABLE 29.13   Pareto Distribution Pareto(a)

1. Parameters: a = shape parameter, $a > 0$
2. Range: $1 \le x \le \infty$
3. pdf: $f(x) = a x^{-(a+1)}$
4. CDF: $F(x) = 1 - x^{-a}$
5. Mean: $\dfrac{a}{a-1}$, provided $a > 1$
6. Variance: $\dfrac{a}{(a-1)^2(a-2)}$, provided $a > 2$

29.13   PARETO DISTRIBUTION

The Pareto CDF is a power curve that can be easily fit to observed data. The key characteristics of Pareto distribution are summarized in Table 29.13.

Pareto distribution is useful to fit a distribution to observed data. Given a sample of n observations $\{x_1, x_2, \dots, x_n\}$, the maximum likelihood estimate of the parameter a is

$$a = \frac{1}{(1/n)\sum_{i=1}^{n} \ln x_i}$$

The inverse transformation method is the easiest way to generate Pareto variates. Generate $u \sim U(0,1)$ and return $1/u^{1/a}$.

29.14   PASCAL DISTRIBUTION

The Pascal distribution is an extension of the geometric distribution. In a sequence of Bernoulli trials, the number of trials up to and including the mth success has a Pascal distribution. The key characteristics of the Pascal distribution are summarized in Table 29.14.

The Pascal distribution is used to model the number of attempts to get a certain number of successes; for example:

1. Number of attempts to transmit an m-packet message
2. Number of bits to be sent to successfully receive an m-bit signal

TABLE 29.14   Pascal Distribution Pascal (p, m)

1. Parameters: p = probability of success, $0 < p < 1$
   m = number of successes; m should be a positive integer
2. Range: $x = m, m+1, \dots, \infty$
3. pmf: $f(x) = \dbinom{x-1}{m-1} p^m (1-p)^{x-m}$
4. Mean: m/p
5. Variance: $m(1-p)/p^2$

The attempts must be independent and identical as explained under "Bernoulli Distribution" in Section 29.1.

To generate Pascal variates, generate m geometric variates $G(p)$ and return their sum as Pascal(p, m).

29.15 POISSON DISTRIBUTION

The Poisson distribution is a limiting form of the binomial distribution, and it is used extensively in queueing models. The key characteristics of Poisson distribution are summarized in Table 29.15.

TABLE 29.15 Poisson Distribution Poisson(λ)

1. Parameters: λ = mean, $\lambda > 0$
2. Range: $x = 0, 1, 2, \ldots, \infty$
3. pmf: $f(x) = P(X = x) = \lambda^x \dfrac{e^{-\lambda}}{x!}$
4. Mean: λ
5. Variance: λ

The Poisson distribution is used to model the number of arrivals over a given interval; for example:

1. Number of requests to a server in a given time interval t
2. Number of component failures per unit time
3. Number of queries to a database system over t seconds
4. Number of typing errors per form

The Poisson distribution is particularly appropriate if the arrivals are from a large number of independent sources. Such arrival processes are also called **Poisson processes** and are discussed further in Chapter 30 on queueing theory.

See Section 29.3 for choosing among binomial, negative binomial, and Poisson distributions based on the relative magnitude of mean and variance.

Poisson variates can be generated as follows:

1. *Inverse Transformation Method*: Compute the CDF $F(x)$ for $x = 0, 1, 2, \ldots$ up to a suitable cutoff and store in an array. For each Poisson random variate, generate a $U(0,1)$ variate u, and search the array to find x such that $F(x) \le u < F(x + 1)$; return x.
2. Starting with $n = 0$, generate $u_n \sim U(0,1)$ and compute the product $\prod_{i=0}^{n} u_i$. As soon as the product becomes less than $e^{-\lambda}$, return n as the Poisson(λ) variate. Note that n is such that $u_0 u_1 \cdots u_{n-1} > e^{-\lambda} \ge$

$u_0 u_1 \cdots u_n$. On the average, $\lambda + 1$ uniform variates are required per Poisson variate.

29.16   STUDENT'S t DISTRIBUTION

This distribution was derived by W. S. Gosset (1876–1937), a statistician for a winery whose owner did not appreciate his publishing. Gosset, therefore, published his paper under the pseudonym Student. The symbol t was used to denote the variable and hence the name "Student's t distribution." The key characteristics of the t distribution are summarized in Table 29.16. If $x \sim N(0, 1)$ is a unit normal variate and $y \sim \chi^2(\nu)$ is a chi-square variate, the ratio $x/\sqrt{y/\nu}$ has a t distribution with ν degrees of freedom:

$$\frac{N(0, 1)}{\sqrt{\chi^2(\nu)/\nu}} \sim t(\nu)$$

The pdf of a t-variate is very similar to that of a unit normal. The distribution is bell shaped and is symmetrical about zero. For large degrees of freedom ($\nu > 30$), a t distribution can be approximated by a unit normal.

The t distribution is used whenever a ratio of a normal variate and the square root of a chi-square variable is involved and is commonly used in setting confidence intervals and in t-tests as discussed in Chapter 13.

The t-variates can be generated using characterization as follows. Generate $x \sim N(0, 1)$ and $y \sim \chi^2(\nu)$ and return $x/\sqrt{y/\nu}$ as $t(\nu)$.

TABLE 29.16   Student's t-Distribution t(ν)

1. Parameters: ν = degrees of freedom; ν must be a positive integer
2. Range: $-\infty \le x \le \infty$
3. pmf: $f(x) = \dfrac{\{\Gamma[(\nu + 1)/2]\} [1 + (x^2/\nu)]^{-(\nu+1)/2}}{(\pi\nu)^{1/2}\Gamma(\nu/2)}$
4. Variance: $\nu/(\nu - 2)$, for $\nu > 2$.

29.17   UNIFORM DISTRIBUTION (CONTINUOUS)

This is one of the simplest distributions to use. The key characteristics of the uniform distribution are summarized in Table 29.17.

A uniform distribution is commonly used if a random variable is bounded and no further information is available; for example:

1. Distance between source and destinations of messages on a network
2. Seek time on a disk

TABLE 29.17   Uniform Distribution (Continuous) $U(a,b)$

1. Parameters: a = lower limit
   $\qquad\qquad\quad b$ = upper limit, $b > a$
2. Range: $a \le x \le b$
3. pdf: $f(x) = \dfrac{1}{b-a}$
4. CDF: $F(x) = \begin{cases} 0 & \text{if } x < a \\ \dfrac{x-a}{b-a} & \text{if } a \le x < b \\ 1 & \text{if } b \le x \end{cases}$
5. Mean: $\dfrac{a+b}{2}$
6. Variance: $(b-a)^2/12$

To generate $U(a,b)$, generate $u \sim U(0,1)$ and return $a + (b-a)u$.

29.18   UNIFORM DISTRIBUTION (DISCRETE)

This is a discrete version of the uniform distribution. It takes a finite number of values, each with the same probability. The key characteristics of this distribution are summarized in Table 29.18.

The discrete uniform distribution is used when it is believed that the value is equally likely over a bounded interval; for example:

1. Track numbers for seeks on a disk
2. The I/O device number selected for the next I/O
3. The source and destination node for the next packet on a network

To generate $\mathrm{UD}(m,n)$, generate $u \sim U(0,1)$, return $\lfloor m + (n-m+1)u \rfloor$.

TABLE 29.18   Uniform Distribution (Discrete) $\mathrm{UD}(m,n)$

1. Parameters: m = lower limit; m must be an integer
   $\qquad\qquad\quad n$ = upper limit; n must be an integer greater than m
2. Range: $x = m, m+1, m+2, \ldots, n$
3. pmf: $f(x) = \dfrac{1}{n-m+1}$
4. CDF: $F(x) = \begin{cases} 0 & \text{if } x < m \\ \dfrac{x-m+1}{n-m+1} & \text{if } m \le x < n \\ 1 & \text{if } n \le x \end{cases}$
5. Mean: $(n+m)/2$
6. Variance: $\dfrac{(n-m+1)^2 - 1}{12}$

29.19 WEIBULL DISTRIBUTION

The Weibull distribution is commonly used in reliability analysis. The key characteristics of a Weibull distribution are summarized in Table 29.19. If $b = 3.602$, the Weibull distribution is close to a normal. For $b > 3.602$, it has a long left tail. For $b < 3.602$, it has a long right tail. For $b \leq 1$, the Weibull pdf is L shaped, and for $b > 1$, it is bell shaped. For large b, the Weibull pdf has a sharp peak at the mode.

The Weibull distribution is used to model lifetimes of components. For $b < 1$, the Weibull distribution gives a failure rate increasing with time. For $b > 1$, the failure rate decreases with time. At $b = 1$, the failure rate is constant and the lifetimes are exponentially distributed.

The inverse transformation technique can be used to generate Weibull variates. Generate $u \sim U(0,1)$ and return $a(\ln u)^{1/b}$ as Weibull(a,b).

TABLE 29.19 Weibull Distribution Weibull(a,b)

1. Parameters: a = scale parameter $a > 0$
   b = shape parameter $b > 0$
2. Range: $0 \leq x \leq \infty$
3. pdf: $f(x) = \dfrac{bx^{b-1}}{a^b}e^{-(x/a)^b}$
4. CDF: $F(x) = 1 - e^{-(x/a)^b}$
5. Mean: $\dfrac{a}{b}\Gamma(1/b)$
6. Variance: $\dfrac{a^2}{b^2}\left\{2b\Gamma(2/b) - [\Gamma(1/b)]^2\right\}$

29.20 RELATIONSHIPS AMONG DISTRIBUTIONS

Figures 29.1 and 29.2 summarize the relationships among various discrete and continuous distributions, respectively. In the figures, the relationships are indicated alongside the arrows between the distribution. A symbol x is used to denote variates of the distribution where the arrow starts. Thus, for example, the condition Σx alongside the arrow from the Bernouilli to the binomial distribution in Figure 29.1 indicates that the sum of Bernoulli variates has a binomial distribution. Similarly, as probability p tends to zero, the binomial distribution becomes close to a Poissson distribution, which for λ greater than 9 can be approximated by a normal distribution, and so on. Normal distribution, although not a discrete distribution, has been included in Figure 29.1 to provide a link between the discrete distributions of Figure 29.1 and the continuous distributions of Figure 29.2.

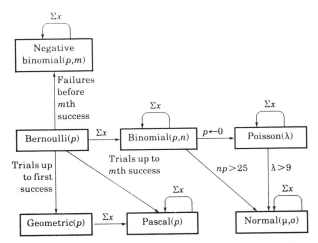

FIGURE 29.1   Relationships among discrete distributions.

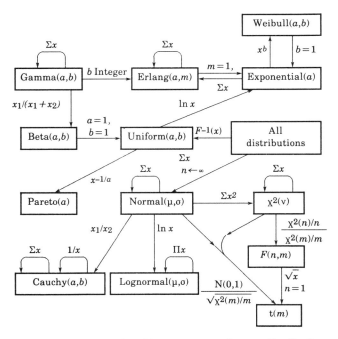

FIGURE 29.2   Relationships among continuous distributions.

EXERCISES

29.1 What distribution would you use to model the following?

  a. Number of requests between typing errors, given that each request has a certain probability of being in error.

  b. Number of requests in error among m requests, given that each request has a certain probability of being in error.

  c. The minimum or the maximum of a large set of IID observations.

  d. The mean of a large set of observations from a uniform distribution.

  e. The product of a large set of observatiosn from a uniform distribution.

  f. To empirically fit the distribution using a power curve for CDF.

  g. The stream resulting from a merger of two Poisson streams.

  h. Sample variances from a normal population.

  i. Ratio of two sample variances from a normal population.

  j. Time between successive arrivals, given that the arrivals are memoryless.

  k. Service time of a device that consists of m memoryless servers in series.

  l. Number of systems that are idle in a distributed system, given that each system has a fixed probability of being idle.

  m. Fraction of systems that are idle in a distributed system, given that each system has a fixed probability of being idle.

29.2 Let x, y, z, w be four unit normal variates. Find the distribution and 90-percentiles for the following quantities:

  a. $(x + y + z + w)/4$
  b. $x^2 + y^2 + z^2 + w^2$
  c. $(x^2 + y^2)/(z^2 + w^2)$
  d. $w/\sqrt{(x^2 + y^2 + z^2)/4}$

FURTHER READING FOR PART V

There are a number of good books and published papers on simulations. Law and Kelton (1982) and Bratley, Fox, and Schrage (1986) provide a good treatment of most topics discussed here. Lavenberg (1983) discusses transient removal, variance estimation, and random-number generation.

Several books cover individual simulation languages. For example, GPSS is explained by O'Donovan (1980) and Bobillier et al. (1976), SIMSCRIPT II by CACI (1983) and Markowitz et al. (1963), SIMULA by Birtwistle et al. (1973), Dahl et al. (1982), and by Franta (1977), and GASP by Pritsker and Young (1975).

Sherman and Browne (1973) discuss the advantages and disadvantages of trace-driven computer simulations.

Adam and Dogramaci (1979) include papers describing the simulation languages SIMULA, SIMSCRIPT, and GASP by their respective language designers. Bulgren (1982) discusses SIMSCRIPT and GPSS.

For discussions on event-set algorithms, see Franta and Maly (1977), Wyman (1975), and Vaucher and Duval (1975).

Crane and Lemoine (1977) explain regenerative simulations. Mitrani (1982) and Rubinstein (1986) provide a good discussion on variance reduction techniques. See Law (1983) for a survey of various simulation output analysis techniques.

Knuth (1981, Vol. 2) has a detailed discussion on random-number generation and testing. The idea of LCGs was first proposed by Lehmer (1951). The generators used in Equations (26.5) and (26.6) are from Greenberger (1961). The multiplicative LCG in Equation (26.7) was first proposed by Lewis, Goodman, and Miller (1969). Park and Miller (1988) provide an interesting discussion on its implementation. They also discuss problems with other popular generators as discussed in Section 26.6. The second generator of Exercise 26.11 is from Lamie (1987).

For additional discussions on generating q-bit words using generalized feedback shift registers and their properties see Bright and Enison (1979), Fushimi and Tezuka (1983), Fushimi (1988), and Tezuka (1987). For a detailed discussion of shift register sequences see Golomb (1982).

Kreutzer (1986) provides a number of ready-made Pascal routines for common simulation tasks such as event scheduling, time advancing, random-number generation, and others.

Hastings and Peacock (1975) list all the important formulas related to commonly used distributions, their generation, and their relationship to other distributions. See Pasupathy (1989) for an interesting discussion on normal distribution. Hastings, Jr. (1955) gives formulas for approximating normal quantiles.

The Society for Computer Simulations has published several compendiums of papers on distributed simulation and knowledge-based simulations. For example, see Unger and Fujimoto (1989) and Webster (1989).

CURRENT AREAS OF RESEARCH IN SIMULATION

Current areas of research in simulation include distributed simulations, knowledge-based simulations, simulations on microcomputers, object-oriented simulation, graphics and animation for simulations, and languages for concurrent simulations. Of these, the first two areas are highly active and are briefly described here.

The discrete-event simulations discussed in this book are sequential simulations because the events are processed sequentially. The events cannot be executed efficiently in parallel on multiprocessor systems because there are two global variables that are shared by all processes: the simulation clock and the event list. An alternative to parallel execution is to use the so-called **distributed simulation** approach, which does not use these global variables. In this approach, which is also known as **concurrent simulation** or **parallel simulation**, the global clock times are replaced by several (distributed) "channel clock values," and the events are replaced by messages that are sent between various processes via error-free channels. This allows a simulation to be split among an arbitrary number of computer systems or processors. However, it also introduces the problem of deadlock. A number of schemes for deadlock detection, deadlock recovery, and deadlock prevention have therefore been proposed. Readers interested in this topic are encouraged to read an excellent survey by Misra (1986) and to follow the references cited therein. See also Wagner and Lazowska (1989).

Another area of current research in simulation modeling is that of **knowledge-based simulation**. Techniques of artificial intelligence, in particular, the expert system, are being used for simulation modeling. These techniques allow the user to specify the system at a very high level and to ask questions that are interpreted intelligently by the simulation system, which carries out the required simulation experiments automatically. Attempts are underway to provide automatic verification and validation of simulation models, automatic design of experiments, as well as data analysis and interpretation. For examples of two such systems, see Ramana Reddy et al. (1986) and Klahr and Fought (1980).

PART VI

QUEUEING MODELS

Queueing theory is the key analytical modeling technique used for computer systems performance analysis. The literature on queueing theory is vast. Several hundred papers are published every year. Fortunately, a large percentage of day-to-day performance questions can be answered using only a few techniques. To begin with, you need a knowledge of the queueing notation and some results on single-queue systems. For systems with multiple queues, operational analysis, mean-value analysis, and convolution are very useful. In addition, the technique of hierarchical modeling is helpful in analyzing large systems. The discussion in this part has been limited to these techniques.

Following are examples of questions that you should be able to answer after reading this part:

1. What are the various types of queues?
2. What is meant by an M/M/m/B/K queue?
3. How should you obtain response time, queue lengths, and server utilizations?
4. How should you represent a system using a network of several queues?
5. How should you analyze simple queueing networks?
6. How should you obtain bounds on the system performance using queueing models?
7. How should you obtain variance and other statistics on system performance?
8. How should you subdivide a large queueing network model and solve it?

CHAPTER 30

INTRODUCTION TO QUEUEING THEORY

If the facts don't fit the theory, change the facts.
—Albert Einstein

In computer systems, many jobs share the system resources such as CPU, disks, and other devices. Since generally only one job can use the resource at any time, all other jobs wanting to use that resource wait in queues. Queueing theory helps in determining the time that the jobs spend in various queues in the system. These times can then be combined to predict the response time, which is basically the total time that the job spends inside the system. It is not, therefore, surprising that queueing models have become so popular among computer systems performance analysts.

30.1 QUEUEING NOTATION

Imagine yourself waiting in a queue with other computer science students at a typical computer terminal room, as shown in Figure 30.1. The service facility has a number of terminals to be used by students. If all terminals are busy, the arriving students wait in a queue. In queueing theory terms, the students would be called "customers." In order to analyze such a system, the following characteristics of the system should be specified:

1. *Arrival Process*: If the students arrive at times $t_1, t_2, \ldots, t_j$, the random variables $\tau_j = t_j - t_{j-1}$ are called the **interarrival times**. It is generally assumed that the τ_j form a sequence of Independent and Identically Distributed (IID) random variables. The most common arrival

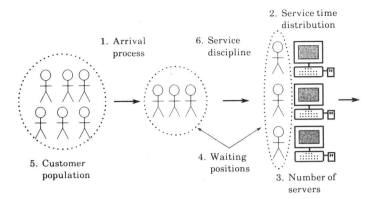

FIGURE 30.1   Basic components of a queue.

process is the so-called **Poisson arrivals**, which simply means that the interarrival times are IID and are exponentially distributed. Other distributions, such as the Erlang and hyperexponential, are also used. In fact, several queueing results are valid for all distributions of interarrival times. In such a case, the result is said to hold for a **general** distribution.

2. *Service Time Distribution*: We also need to know the time each student spends at the terminal. This is called the service time. It is common to assume that the service times are random variables, which are IID. The distribution most commonly used is the exponential distribution. Other distributions, such as the Erlang, hyperexponential, and general, are also used. Again the results for a general distribution apply to all service time distributions.

3. *Number of Servers*: The terminal room may have one or more terminals, all of which are considered part of the same queueing system since they are all identical, and any terminal may be assigned to any student. If all the servers are not identical, they are usually divided into groups of identical servers with separate queues for each group. In this case, each group is a queueing system.

4. *System Capacity*: The maximum number of students who can stay may be limited due to space availability and also to avoid long waiting times. This number is called the system capacity. In most systems, the capacity is finite. However, if the number is large, it is easier to analyze if infinite capacity is assumed. The system capacity includes those waiting for service as well as those receiving service.

5. *Population Size*: The total number of potential students who can ever come to the computer center is the population size. In most real systems, the population size is finite. If this size is large, once again, it is easier to analyze if we assume that the size is infinite.

6. *Service Discipline*: The order in which the students are served is called the service discipline. The most common discipline is First Come, First Served (FCFS). Other possibilities are Last Come, First Served (LCFS) and Last Come, First Served with Preempt and Resume (LCFS-PR). Computer system CPUs generally use Round-Robin (RR) with a fixed-size quantum. If the quantum size is small compared to average service time, it is called Processor Sharing (PS) since each of the n waiting jobs would then receive $1/n$th of the processor's time. A system with a fixed delay, for example, a satellite communication link, is called an **Infinite Server** (IS) or a **delay center**. Terminals in timesharing systems are usually modeled as delay centers.

Sometimes the scheduling is based on the service time required. Examples of such disciplines are Shortest Processing Time first (SPT), Shortest Remaining Processing Time first (SRPT), Shortest Expected Processing Time first (SEPT), and Shortest Expected Remaining Processing Time first (SERPT). In the real world, occasionally one may encounter Biggest In, First Served (BIFS) or Loudest Voice, First Served (LVFS).

To specify a queueing system, we need to specify these six parameters. Queueing theorists, therefore, use a shorthand notation called the **Kendall notation** in the form $A/S/m/B/K/SD$, where the letters correspond in order to the six parameters listed above. That is, A is the interarrival time distribution, S is the service time distribution, m is the number of servers, B is the number of buffers (system capacity), K is the population size, and SD is the service discipline.

The distributions for interarrival time and service times are generally denoted by a one-letter symbol as follows:

M	Exponential
E_k	Erlang with parameter k
H_k	Hyperexponential with parameter k
D	Deterministic
G	General

Exponential and Erlang distributions were defined earlier in Chapter 29. A deterministic distribution implies that the times are constant and there is no variance. A general distribution means that the distribution is not specified and the results are valid for all distributions.

Notice that an exponential distribution is denoted by M, which stands for *memoryless*. If the interarrival times are exponentially distributed, for instance, with mean $1/\lambda$, the expected time to the next arrival is always $1/\lambda$ regardless of the time since the last arrival (see Section 29.6 for a proof). Remembering the past history does not help. It is this unique memoryless property of exponential distribution that has led to its being called the **memoryless distribution**.

All of the preceding distributions assume individual arrivals or service. **Bulk arrivals** and **bulk service**, in which each arrival or service consists of a group of jobs,[1] is denoted by a superscript. For example, bulk Poisson arrivals or service are denoted by $M^{[x]}$. Here, x represents the group size, which is generally a random variable, and its distribution needs to be specified separately. Similarly, $G^{[x]}$ would represent a bulk arrival or service process with general intergroup times.

Example 30.1   M/M/3/20/1500/FCFS denotes a single-queue system with the following parameters:

1. The time between successive arrivals is exponentially distributed.
2. The service times are exponentially distributed.
3. There are three servers.
4. The queue has buffers for 20 jobs. This consists of three places for jobs being served and 17 buffers for jobs waiting for service. After the number of jobs reaches 20, all arriving jobs are lost until the queue size decreases.
5. There is a total of 1500 jobs that can be serviced.
6. The service discipline is first come, first served.   □

Unless explicitly specified, the queues are defined as having infinite buffer capacity, infinite population size, and an FCFS service discipline. Ordinarily, only the first three of the six parameters are sufficient to indicate the type of queue. The queue, G/G/1/∞/∞/FCFS, for example, is denoted as G/G/1.

Example 30.2   The term $M^{[x]}$/M/1 denotes a single server queue with bulk Poisson arrivals and exponential service times, whereas $M/G^{[x]}/m$ denotes a queue with Poisson arrival process, bulk service with general service time distribution, and m servers.   □

30.2 RULES FOR ALL QUEUES

In this section we introduce some of the key variables used in the analysis of single queues and discuss relationships among them. Figure 30.2 shows the key variables used in queueing analysis. These are

τ = interarrival time, that is, the time between two successive arrivals

---

[1]In computer systems, each device is usually modeled as a service center with a queue of jobs to be serviced. The customers in these queues are *jobs* that move from one device to the next. We therefore use the terms *jobs* and *customers* interchangeably. Similarly, the terms *device, service center,* and *queue* are also used synonymously. The term *buffer* is used for waiting positions for the jobs in the system.

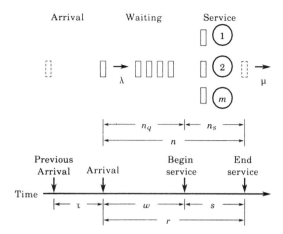

FIGURE 30.2   Common random variables used in analyzing a queue.

λ = Mean arrival rate = $1/E[\tau]$. In some systems, this can be a function of the state of the system. For example, it can depend upon the number of jobs already in the system.

s = service time per job.

μ = mean service rate per server, = $1/E[s]$. Total service rate for m servers is $m\mu$.

n = number of jobs in the system. This is also called **queue length**. Notice that this includes jobs currently receiving service as well as those waiting in the queue.

n_q = number of jobs waiting to receive service. This is always less than n, since it does not include the jobs currently receiving service.

n_s = number of jobs receiving service

r = response time or the time in the system. This includes both the time waiting for service and the time receiving service.

w = waiting time, that is, the time interval between arrival time and the instant the service begins

All of these variables except λ and μ are random variables. There are a number of relationships among these variables that apply to G/G/m queues. Since most of the queues that we discuss in this part are special cases of G/G/m, these apply to most of the queues that we will encounter.

1. *Stability Condition*: If the number of jobs in a system grows continuously and becomes infinite, the system is said to be unstable. For stability the mean arrival rate should be less than the mean service rate:

$$\lambda < m\mu$$

Here, m is the number of servers. This stability condition does not apply to the finite population and the finite buffer systems. In the finite population systems, the queue length is always finite; the system can never become unstable. Also, the finite buffer systems are always stable since the arrivals are lost when the number of jobs in the system exceeds the number of buffers, that is, the system capacity.

2. *Number in System versus Number in Queue*: The number of jobs in the system is always equal to the sum of the number in the queue and the number receiving service:

$$n = n_q + n_s$$

Notice that n, n_q, and n_s are random variables. In particular, this equality leads to the following relationship among their means:

$$E[n] = E[n_q] + E[n_s]$$

The mean number of jobs in the system is equal to the sum of the mean number in the queue and the mean number in service.

Further, if the service rate of each server is independent of the number in the queue, we have

$$\mathrm{Cov}(n_q, n_s) = 0$$

and

$$\mathrm{Var}[n] = \mathrm{Var}[n_q] + \mathrm{Var}[n_s]$$

That is, the variance of the number of jobs in the system is equal to the sum of the variance of the number of jobs in the queue and the variance of the number receiving service.

3. *Number versus Time*: If jobs are not lost due to insufficient buffers, the mean number of jobs in a system is related to its mean response time as follows:

Mean number of jobs in system = arrival rate × mean response time

$$(30.1)$$

Similarly

Mean number of jobs in queue = arrival rate × mean waiting time

$$(30.2)$$

Equations (30.1) and (30.2) are known as **Little's law**. We will give a general derivation of these in Section 30.3. In finite buffer systems, this law can be used provided we use effective arrival rate, that is, the rate of jobs actually entering the system and receiving service.

4. *Time in System versus Time in Queue*: The time spent by a job in a queueing system is, as shown in Figure 30.2, equal to the sum of the

time waiting in the queue and the time receiving service:

$$r = w + s$$

Notice that r, w, and s are random variables. In particular, this equality leads to the following relationship among their means:

$$E[r] = E[w] + E[s]$$

That is, the mean response time is equal to the sum of the mean waiting time and the mean service time.

If the service rate is independent of the number of jobs in the queue, we have

$$\text{Cov}(w,s) = 0$$

and

$$\text{Var}[r] = \text{Var}[w] + \text{Var}[s]$$

The variance of the response time is equal to the sum of the variances of the waiting time and that of the service time.

A few additional relationships are discussed later in Chapter 33. They apply to systems with single queues as well as to those with a network of several queues.

30.3 LITTLE'S LAW

One of the most commonly used theorems in queueing theory is Little's law, which allows us to relate the mean number of jobs in any system with the mean time spent in the system as follows:

Mean number in the system = arrival rate × mean response time

This relationship applies to all systems or parts of systems in which the number of jobs entering the system is equal to those completing service. Little's law, which was first proven by Little (1961), is based on a black-box view of the system, as shown in Figure 30.3. The law applies as long as the number of jobs entering the system is equal to those completing service, so that no new jobs are created in the system and no jobs are lost forever inside the system. Even in systems in which some jobs are lost due to finite buffers (see Section 31.4), the law can be applied to the part of the system consisting of the waiting and serving positions because once a job finds a waiting position (buffer), it is not lost. The arrival rate in this case should be adjusted to ex-

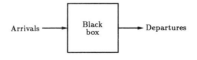

FIGURE 30.3 Black-box view of a system.

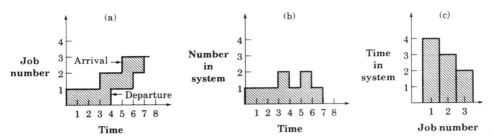

FIGURE 30.4 Three ways to plot the arrival and departure time data.

clude jobs lost before finding a buffer. In other words, the effective arrival rate of jobs entering the system should be used.

In this section we present a simple proof of the law.

Proof 30.1 Suppose we monitor the system for a time interval T and keep a log of arrival and departure times of each individual job. If T is large, the number of arrivals would be approximately equal to the departures. Let this number be N. Then

$$\text{Arrival rate} = \text{total arrivals/total time} = N/T$$

As shown in Figure 30.4, there are three ways to plot the data that we just gathered. Figure 30.4a shows the total number of arrivals and departures separately as a function of time. If at each time instant we subtract the departure curve from the arrival curve, we get the number of jobs in the system at that instant, as shown in Figure 30.4b. On the other hand, if we subtract the arrival time from departure time for each individual job, we get Figure 30.4c for time spent in the system. The hatched areas in the three parts of the figure represent total time spent inside the system by all jobs. Hence, all three hatched areas are equal. Let this area be J. From Figure 30.4c

$$\text{Mean time spent in the system} = J/N$$

From Figure 30.4b

$$\text{Mean number in the system} = \frac{J}{T}$$
$$= \frac{N}{T} \times \frac{J}{N}$$
$$= \text{arrival rate} \times \text{mean time spent in the system}$$

This is the Little's law. ☐

Notice that Little's law can be applied to any system or subsystem. For example, by applying it to just the waiting facility of a service center (see

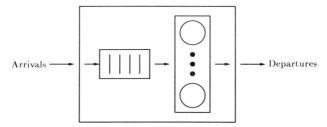

FIGURE 30.5   Little's law can be used for a system or any part of the system.

Figure 30.5), we get

Mean number in queue = arrival rate × mean waiting time

Similarly, for those currently receiving the service, we have

Mean number in service = arrival rate × mean service time

Example 30.3   A monitor on a disk server showed that the average time to satisfy an I/O request was 100 milliseconds. The I/O rate was about 100 requests per second. What was the mean number of requests at the disk server?

Using Little's law,

Mean number in the disk server = arrival rate × response time

$$= (100 \text{ requests/second}) \times (0.1 \text{ second})$$

$$= 10 \text{ requests} \qquad \square$$

30.4 TYPES OF STOCHASTIC PROCESSES

In analytical modeling, we use not only several random variables but also several different sequences or families of random variables that are functions of time. For example, let $n(t)$ denote the number of jobs at the CPU of a computer system. If we take several identical systems and observe the number of jobs at the CPU as a function of time, we would find that the number $n(t)$ is a random variable. To specify its behavior, we would need to specify the probability distribution functions for $n(t)$ at each possible value of t. Similarly, the waiting time in a queue $w(t)$ is a random function of time. Such random functions of time or sequences are called **stochastic processes**. Such processes are useful in representing the state of queueing systems. Some of the common types of stochastic processes used in queueing theory are explained next:

1. *Discrete-State and Continuous-State Processes*: A process is called **discrete or continuous state** depending upon the values its state can take.

If the number of possible values is finite or countable, the process is called a discrete-state process. For example, the number of jobs in a system $n(t)$ can only take discrete values $0, 1, 2, \ldots$. Therefore, $n(t)$ is a discrete-state process. The waiting time $w(t)$, on the other hand, can take any value on the real line. Therefore, $w(t)$ is a continuous-state process. A discrete-state stochastic process is also called a **stochastic chain**.

2. *Markov Processes*: If the future states of a process are independent of the past and depend only on the present, the process is called a **Markov process**. The Markov property makes a process easier to analyze since we do not have to remember the complete past trajectory. Knowing the present state of the process is sufficient. These processes are named after A. A. Markov, who defined and analyzed them in 1907.

A discrete-state Markov process is called a **Markov chain**.

Notice that to predict the future of a continuous-time Markov process, it is sufficient to know the current state. It is not necessary to know how long the process has been in the current state. This is possible only if the state time has a memoryless (exponential) distribution. This requirement limits the applicability of Markov processes.

As shown later in Section 31.3, M/M/m queues can be modeled using Markov processes. The time spent by a job in such a queue is a Markov process and the number of jobs in the queue is a Markov chain.

3. *Birth-Death Processes*: The discrete-space Markov processes in which the transitions are restricted to neighboring states only are called **birth-death processes**. For these processes, it is possible to represent states by integers such that a process in state n can change only to state $n+1$ or $n-1$. For example, the number of jobs in a queue with a single server and individual arrivals (not bulk arrivals) can be represented as a birth-death process. An arrival to the queue (a birth) causes the state to change by $+1$ and a departure after service at the queue (a death) causes the state to change by -1.

4. *Poisson Processes*: If the interarrival times are IID and exponentially distributed, the number of arrivals n over a given interval $(t, t+x)$ has a Poisson distribution, and therefore, the arrival process is referred to as a **Poisson process** or a **Poisson stream**. The Poisson streams are popular in queueing theory because the arrivals are then memoryless as the interarrival time is exponentially distributed. In addition, Poisson streams have the following properties:

(a) Merging of k Poisson streams with mean rate λ_i results in a Poisson stream with mean rate λ given by

$$\lambda = \sum_{i=1}^{k} \lambda_i$$

This is shown schematically in Figure 30.6a.

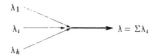

(a) Merging of Poisson streams results in a Poisson stream

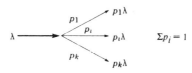

(b) Splitting of a Poisson stream results in Poisson streams

(c) Departures from an M/M/1 queue are a Poisson process

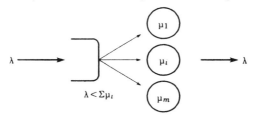

(d) Departures from an M/M/m queue are a Poisson process

FIGURE 30.6   Properties of Poisson processes.

(b) If a Poisson stream is split into k substreams such that the probability of a job going to the ith substream is p_i, each substream is also Poisson with a mean rate of $p_i\lambda$, as shown in Figure 30.6b.

(c) If the arrivals to a single server with exponential service time are Poisson with mean rate λ, the departures are also Poisson with the same rate λ, as shown in Figure 30.6c, provided the arrival rate λ is less than the service rate μ.

(d) If the arrivals to a service facility with m service centers are Poisson with a mean rate λ, the departures also constitute a Poisson stream with the same rate λ, provided the arrival rate λ is less than the total service rate $\sum_i \mu_i$. Here, the servers are assumed to have exponentially distributed service times. This is shown in Figure 30.6d.

The relationship among various types of stochastic processes is summarized in Figure 30.7.

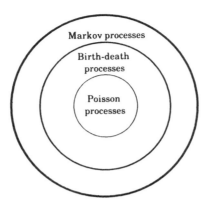

FIGURE 30.7   Relationship among various stochastic processes.

EXERCISES

30.1 What can you say about a queue denoted by $E_k/G^{[x]}/5/300/5000/$LCFS-PR?

30.2 Why is it not a good idea to have an $H_k/G/12/10/5/$LCFS queue?

30.3 Which queueing system would provide better performance: an M/M/3/300/100 system or an M/M/3/100/100 system?

30.4 During a 1-hour observation interval, the name server of a distributed system received 10,800 requests. The mean response time of these requests was observed to be one-third of a second. What is the mean number of queries in the server? What assumptions have you made about the system? Would the mean number of queries be different if the service time was not exponentially distributed?

30.5 When can the arrivals to an $E_k/M/1$ queue be called a Poisson process?

CHAPTER 31

ANALYSIS OF A SINGLE QUEUE

If it is fast and ugly, they will use it and curse you;
if it is slow, they will not use it.

—David Cheriton

The simplest queueing model is one that has only one queue. Such a model can be used to analyze individual resources in computer systems. For example, if all jobs waiting for the CPU in a system are kept in one queue, the CPU can be modeled using results that apply to single queues. This chapter presents results for several such queues. Many of these queues can be modeled as a birth-death process. Therefore, the chapter begins with a discussion of these processes in Section 31.1. The result obtained there is then used in the subsequent sections on various types of queues.

31.1 BIRTH-DEATH PROCESSES

As discussed in Section 30.4, a birth-death process is useful in modeling systems in which jobs arrive one at a time (and not as a batch). The state of such a system can be represented by the number of jobs n in the system. Arrival of a new job changes the state to $n + 1$. This is called a birth. Similarly, the departure of a job changes the system state to $n - 1$. This is called a death. The number of jobs in such a system can therefore be modeled as a birth-death process.

In this section, an expression for state probabilities (probability of having n jobs in the system) for a general birth-death process is derived. Later this

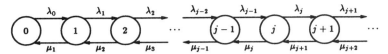

FIGURE 31.1   State transition diagram for a birth-death process.

result will be used to analyze queues in the form of $M/M/m/B/K$ for all values of m, B, and K.

The state transition diagram of a birth-death process is shown in Figure 31.1. When the system is in state n, it has n jobs in it. The new arrivals take place at a rate λ_n. The service rate is μ_n. We assume that both the interarrival times and service times are exponentially distributed.

The steady-state probability of a birth-death process being in state n is given by the following theorem.

Theorem 31.1   *The steady-state probability p_n of a birth-death process being in state n is given by*

$$p_n = \frac{\lambda_0 \lambda_1 \cdots \lambda_{n-1}}{\mu_1 \mu_2 \cdots \mu_n} p_0, \qquad n = 1, 2, \ldots, \infty \qquad (31.1)$$

Here, p_0 is the probability of being in the zero state.

Proof 31.1   Suppose the system is in state j at time t. There are j jobs in the system. In the next time interval of a very small duration Δt, the system can move to state $j - 1$ or $j + 1$ with the following probabilities:

$$P\{n(t + \Delta t) = j + 1 \mid n(t) = j\} = \text{probability of one arrival in } \Delta t$$

$$= \lambda_j \Delta t$$

$$P\{n(t + \Delta t) = j - 1 \mid n(t) = j\} = \text{probability of one departure in } \Delta t$$

$$= \mu_j \Delta t$$

If there are no arrivals or departures, the system will stay in state j, and thus,

$$P\{n(t + \Delta t) = j \mid n(t) = j\} = 1 - \lambda_j \Delta t - \mu_j \Delta t$$

Notice that we are assuming Δt to be so small that there is no chance (zero probability) of two events (two arrivals, two departures, or an arrival and a departure) occurring during this interval.

If $p_j(t)$ denotes the probability of being in state j at time t, we can write a set of linear equations as follows:

$$p_0(t + \Delta t) = (1 - \lambda_0 \Delta t)p_0(t) + \mu_1 \Delta t \, p_1(t)$$

$$p_1(t + \Delta t) = \lambda_0 \Delta t \, p_0(t) + (1 - \mu_1 \Delta t - \lambda_1 \Delta t)p_1(t) + \mu_2 \Delta t \, p_2(t)$$

$$p_2(t + \Delta t) = \lambda_1 \Delta t \, p_1(t) + (1 - \mu_2 \Delta t - \lambda_2 \Delta t)p_2(t) + \mu_3 \Delta t \, p_3(t)$$

$$\vdots$$

$$p_j(t + \Delta t) = \lambda_{j-1} \Delta t \, p_{j-1}(t) + (1 - \mu_j \Delta t - \lambda_j \Delta t)p_j(t) + \mu_{j+1} \Delta t \, p_{j+1}(t)$$

The jth equation can be written as follows:

$$\lim_{\Delta t \to 0} \frac{p_j(t + \Delta t) - p_j(t)}{\Delta t} = \lambda_{j-1}p_{j-1}(t) - (\mu_j + \lambda_j)p_j(t) + \mu_{j+1}p_{j+1}(t)$$

$$\frac{dp_j(t)}{dt} = \lambda_{j-1}p_{j-1}(t) - (\mu_j + \lambda_j)p_j(t) + \mu_{j+1}p_{j+1}(t)$$

Under steady state, $p_j(t)$ approaches a fixed value p_j, that is,

$$\lim_{t \to \infty} p_j(t) = p_j$$

and

$$\lim_{t \to \infty} \frac{dp_j(t)}{dt} = 0$$

Substituting these in the jth equation, we get

$$0 = \lambda_{j-1}p_{j-1} - (\mu_j + \lambda_j)p_j + \mu_{j+1}p_{j+1}$$

$$p_{j+1} = \left(\frac{\mu_j + \lambda_j}{\mu_{j+1}}\right) p_j - \frac{\lambda_{j-1}}{\mu_{j+1}}p_{j-1}, \qquad j = 1, 2, 3, \ldots$$

$$p_1 = \frac{\lambda_0}{\mu_1}p_0$$

The solution to this set of equations is

$$p_n = \frac{\lambda_0 \lambda_1 \cdots \lambda_{n-1}}{\mu_1 \mu_2 \cdots \mu_n} p_0$$

$$= p_0 \prod_{j=0}^{n-1} \frac{\lambda_j}{\mu_{j+1}}, \qquad n = 1, 2, \ldots, \infty \qquad \Box$$

Theorem 31.1 allows us to determine equilibrium probabilities p_n in terms of p_0, which in turn can be computed using the additional condition that the sum of all probabilities must be equal to 1. This gives

$$p_0 = \frac{1}{1 + \sum_{n=1}^{\infty} \prod_{j=0}^{n-1} [\lambda_j / \mu_{j+1}]} \qquad (31.2)$$

Once state probabilities have been determined using Equations (31.1) and (31.2), we can compute many other performance measures. We illustrate this for M/M/1 queues in the next section. Several other queues are also discussed later in this chapter.

31.2 M/M/1 QUEUE

An M/M/1 queue, which is the most commonly used type of queue, can be used to model single-processor systems or to model individual devices in a computer system. It is assumed that the interarrival times and the service times are exponentially distributed and there is only one server. There are no buffer or population size limitations and the service discipline is FCFS. To analyze this type of queue, we need to know only the mean arrival rate λ and the mean service rate μ.

The state of this queue is given by the number of jobs in the system. A state transition diagram for the system is shown in Figure 31.2. It is similar to that of the birth-death processes with the following correspondence:

$$\lambda_n = \lambda, \qquad n = 0, 1, 2, \ldots, \infty$$

$$\mu_n = \mu, \qquad n = 1, 2, \ldots, \infty$$

Theorem 31.1 gives us the following expression for the probability of n jobs in the system:

$$p_n = \left(\frac{\lambda}{\mu}\right)^n p_0, \qquad n = 1, 2, \ldots, \infty$$

The quantity λ/μ is called **traffic intensity** and is usually denoted by symbol ρ. Thus

$$p_n = \rho^n p_0$$

Since all probabilities should add to 1, we have the following expression for the probability of zero jobs in the system:

$$p_0 = \frac{1}{1 + \rho + \rho^2 + \cdots + \rho^\infty} = 1 - \rho$$

Substituting for p_0 in p_n, we get

$$p_n = (1 - \rho)\rho^n, \qquad n = 0, 1, 2, \ldots, \infty$$

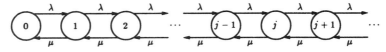

FIGURE 31.2 State transition diagram for an M/M/1 queue.

Notice that n is geometrically distributed. We can now derive many other properties of the M/M/1 queues. For example, the utilization of the server is given by the probability of having one or more jobs in the system:

$$U = 1 - p_0 = \rho$$

The mean number of jobs in the system is given by

$$E[n] = \sum_{n=1}^{\infty} n p_n = \sum_{n=1}^{\infty} n(1-\rho)\rho^n = \frac{\rho}{1-\rho} \qquad (31.3)$$

The variance of the number of jobs in the system is

$$\text{Var}[n] = E[n^2] - (E[n])^2 = \left(\sum_{n=1}^{\infty} n^2(1-\rho)\rho^n \right) - (E[n])^2 = \frac{\rho}{(1-\rho)^2}$$

The probability of n or more jobs in the system is

$$P(\geq n \text{ jobs in system}) = \sum_{j=n}^{\infty} p_j = \sum_{j=n}^{\infty} (1-\rho)\rho^j = \rho^n$$

The mean response time can be computed using Little's law, which states that

Mean number in system = arrival rate × mean response time

That is,

$$E[n] = \lambda E[r]$$

or

$$E[r] = \frac{E[n]}{\lambda} = \left(\frac{\rho}{1-\rho} \right) \frac{1}{\lambda} = \frac{1/\mu}{1-\rho}$$

The cumulative distribution function (CDF) of the response time can be shown to be

$$F(r) = 1 - e^{-r\mu(1-\rho)} \qquad (31.4)$$

Notice that the response time is exponentially distributed. From the distribution, we can also find out its percentiles. For example, the q-percentile of the response time can be computed as follows:

$$1 - e^{-r_q\mu(1-\rho)} = \frac{q}{100}$$

or

$$r_q = \frac{1}{\mu(1-\rho)} \ln\left(\frac{100}{100-q} \right)$$

Similarly, the CDF of the waiting time can be shown to be

$$F(w) = 1 - \rho e^{-w\mu(1-\rho)} \qquad (31.5)$$

This is a truncated exponential distribution. Its q-percentile is given by

$$w_q = \frac{1}{\mu(1-\rho)} \ln\left(\frac{100\rho}{100-q}\right)$$

This formula applies only if q is greater than $100(1-\rho)$. All lower percentiles are zero. This can be stated in one equation as follows:

$$w_q = \max\left\{0, \frac{E[w]}{\rho}\ln\left(\frac{100\rho}{100-q}\right)\right\}$$

The mean number of jobs in the queue is given by

$$E[n_q] = \sum_{n=1}^{\infty}(n-1)p_n = \sum_{n=1}^{\infty}(n-1)(1-\rho)\rho^n = \frac{\rho^2}{1-\rho}$$

When there are no jobs in the system, the server is said to be idle; at all other times the server is busy. The time interval between two successive idle intervals is called **busy period**. All results for M/M/1 queues including some for the busy period are summarized in Box 31.1. The following example illustrates the application of these results in modeling a network gateway.

Example 31.1   On a network gateway, measurements show that the packets arrive at a mean rate of 125 packets per second (**pps**) and the gateway takes about 2 milliseconds to forward them. Using an M/M/1 model, analyze the gateway. What is the probability of buffer overflow if the gateway had only 13 buffers? How many buffers do we need to keep packet loss below one packet per million?

Arrival rate $\lambda = 125$ pps

Service rate $\mu = 1/0.002 = 500$ pps

Gateway utilization $\rho = \lambda/\mu = 0.25$

Probability of n packets in gateway $= (1-\rho)\rho^n = 0.75(0.25)^n$

Mean number of packets in gateway $= \dfrac{\rho}{1-\rho} = \dfrac{0.25}{0.75} = 0.33$

Mean time spent in gateway $= \dfrac{1/\mu}{1-\rho} = \dfrac{1/500}{1-0.25} = 2.66$ milliseconds

Probability of buffer overflow $= P$(more than 13 packets in gateway)

$$= \rho^{13} = 0.25^{13} = 1.49 \times 10^{-8}$$

$$\approx 15 \text{ packets per billion packets}$$

To limit the probability of loss to less than 10^{-6},

$$\rho^n \le 10^{-6}$$

Box 31.1   M/M/1 Queue

1. Parameters:
   λ = arrival rate in jobs per unit time
   μ = service rate in jobs per unit time
2. Traffic intensity: $\rho = \lambda/\mu$
3. Stability condition: Traffic intensity ρ must be less than 1.
4. Probability of zero jobs in the system: $p_0 = 1 - \rho$
5. Probability of n jobs in the system: $p_n = (1 - \rho)\rho^n$, $n = 0, 1, \ldots, \infty$
6. Mean number of jobs in the system: $E[n] = \rho/(1 - \rho)$
7. Variance of number of jobs in the system: $\text{Var}[n] = \rho/(1 - \rho)^2$
8. Probability of k jobs in the queue:

$$P(n_q = k) = \begin{cases} 1 - \rho^2, & k = 0 \\ (1 - \rho)\rho^{k+1}, & k > 0 \end{cases}$$

9. Mean number of jobs in the queue: $E[n_q] = \rho^2/(1 - \rho)$
10. Variance of number of jobs in the queue:
    $\text{Var}[n_q] = \rho^2(1 + \rho - \rho^2)/(1 - \rho)^2$
11. Cumulative distribution function of the response time:
    $F(r) = 1 - e^{-r\mu(1-\rho)}$
12. Mean response time: $E[r] = (1/\mu)/(1 - \rho)$
13. Variance of the response time: $\text{Var}[r] = \dfrac{1/\mu^2}{(1 - \rho)^2}$
14. q-Percentile of the response time: $E[r]\ln[100/(100 - q)]$
15. 90-Percentile of the response time: $2.3E[r]$
16. Cumulative distribution function of waiting time:
    $F(w) = 1 - \rho e^{-\mu w(1-\rho)}$
17. Mean waiting time: $E[w] = \rho\dfrac{1/\mu}{1 - \rho}$
18. Variance of the waiting time: $\text{Var}[w] = (2 - \rho)\rho/[\mu^2(1 - \rho)^2]$
19. q-Percentile of the waiting time: $\max\left(0, \dfrac{E[w]}{\rho}\ln[100\rho/(100 - q)]\right)$
20. 90-Percentile of the waiting time: $\max\left(0, \dfrac{E[w]}{\rho}\ln[10\rho]\right)$
21. Probability of finding n or more jobs in the system: ρ^n
22. Probability of serving n jobs in one busy period:

$$\frac{1}{n}\binom{2n-2}{n-1}\frac{\rho^{n-1}}{(1+\rho)^{2n-1}}$$

(Continued)

Box 31.1   Continued

23. Mean number of jobs served in one busy period: $1/(1-\rho)$
24. Variance of number of jobs served in one busy period:
    $\rho(1+\rho)/(1-\rho)^3$
25. Mean busy period duration: $1/[\mu(1-\rho)]$
26. Variance of the busy period: $1/[\mu^2(1-\rho)^3] - 1/[\mu^2(1-\rho)^2]$

---

or

$$n > \log(10^{-6})/\log(0.25) = 9.96$$

We need about 10 buffers.

The last two results about buffer overflow are approximate. Strictly speaking, the gateway should actually be modeled as a finite buffer $M/M/1/B$ queue. However, since the utilization is low and the number of buffers is far above the mean queue length, the results obtained are a close approximation.   □

Figure 31.3 shows the response time as a function of the utilization at the gateway of Example 31.1. As the rate increases, the utilization approaches 1 and the number of jobs in the system and response time approach infinity. This infinite response time is the key reason for not subjecting a server to 100% utilization. For an $M/M/1$ queue to be stable, the traffic intensity ρ must be less than 1.

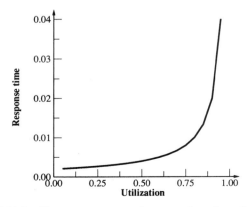

FIGURE 31.3   Gateway response time as a function of utilization.

31.3 M/M/m QUEUE

The M/M/m queue can be used to model multiprocessor systems or devices that have several identical servers and all jobs waiting for these servers are kept in one queue. It is assumed that there are m servers each with a service rate of μ jobs per unit time. The arrival rate is λ jobs per unit time. If any of the m servers are idle, the arriving job is serviced immediately. If all m servers are busy, the arriving jobs wait in a queue. The state of the system is represented by the number of jobs n in the system. The state transition diagram is shown in Figure 31.4. It is easy to see that the number of jobs in the system is a birth-death process with the following correspondence:

$$\lambda_n = \lambda, \qquad n = 0, 1, 2, \ldots, \infty$$

$$\mu_n = \begin{cases} n\mu, & n = 1, 2, \ldots, m - 1 \\ m\mu, & n = m, m + 1, \ldots, \infty \end{cases}$$

Theorem 31.1 gives us the following expression for the probability of n jobs in the system:

$$p_n = \begin{cases} \dfrac{\lambda^n}{n!\mu^n} p_0, & n = 1, 2, \ldots, m - 1 \\[3mm] \dfrac{\lambda^n}{m!m^{n-m}\mu^n} p_0, & n = m, m + 1, \ldots, \infty \end{cases}$$

In terms of the traffic intensity $\rho = \lambda/m\mu$, we have

$$p_n = \begin{cases} \dfrac{(m\rho)^n}{n!} p_0, & n = 1, 2, \ldots, m - 1 \\[3mm] \dfrac{\rho^n m^m}{m!} p_0, & n = m, m + 1, \ldots, \infty \end{cases}$$

Using this expression for p_n, other performance parameters for M/M/m queues can be easily derived. A summary of the results is presented in Box 31.2. Derivations of some of the results are given here. Readers who are not interested in the derivation may skip to the example following it.

Derivation 31.1 The probability of zero jobs in the system is computed by the relationship

$$\sum_{n=0}^{\infty} p_n = 1$$

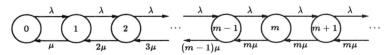

FIGURE 31.4 State transition diagram for an M/M/m queue.

Box 31.2   M/M/m Queue

1. Parameters:
   λ = arrival rate in jobs per unit time
   μ = service rate in jobs per unit time
   m = number of servers
2. Traffic intensity: $\rho = \lambda/(m\mu)$
3. The system is stable if the traffic intensity ρ is less than 1.
4. Probability of zero jobs in the system:

$$p_0 = \left[1 + \frac{(m\rho)^m}{m!(1-\rho)} + \sum_{n=1}^{m-1} \frac{(m\rho)^n}{n!} \right]^{-1}$$

5. Probability of n jobs in the system:

$$p_n = \begin{cases} p_0 \dfrac{(m\rho)^n}{n!}, & n < m \\[2ex] p_0 \dfrac{\rho^n m^m}{m!}, & n \geq m \end{cases}$$

6. Probability of queueing:

$$\varrho = P(\geq m \text{ jobs}) = \frac{(m\rho)^m}{m!(1-\rho)} p_0$$

In the remaining formulas below we will use ϱ as defined here.
7. Mean number of jobs in the system: $E[n] = m\rho + \rho\varrho/(1-\rho)$
8. Variance of number of jobs in the system:

$$\text{Var}[n] = m\rho + \rho\varrho \left[\frac{1 + \rho - \rho\varrho}{(1-\rho)^2} + m \right]$$

9. Mean number of jobs in the queue: $E[n_q] = \rho\varrho/(1-\rho)$
10. Variance of number of jobs in the queue:
    $\text{Var}[n_q] = \varrho\rho(1 + \rho - \varrho\rho)/(1-\rho)^2$
11. Average utilization of each server: $U = \lambda/(m\mu) = \rho$
12. Cumulative distribution function of response time:

$$F(r) = \begin{cases} 1 - e^{-\mu r} - \dfrac{\varrho}{1 - m + m\rho} e^{-m\mu(1-\rho)r} - e^{-\mu r}, \\[1ex] \hspace{6em} \rho \neq (m-1)/m \\[2ex] 1 - e^{-\mu r} - \varrho\mu r e^{-\mu r}, \\[1ex] \hspace{6em} \rho = (m-1)/m \end{cases} \quad r > 0$$

(**Continued**)

Box 31.2 Continued

13. Mean response time:

$$E[r] = \frac{1}{\mu}\left(1 + \frac{\varrho}{m(1-\rho)}\right)$$

14. Variance of the response time:

$$\mathrm{Var}[r] = \frac{1}{\mu^2}\left[1 + \frac{\varrho(2-\varrho)}{m^2(1-\rho)^2}\right]$$

15. Cumulative distribution function of waiting time:
$$F(w) = 1 - \varrho e^{-m\mu(1-\rho)w}$$

16. Mean waiting time: $E[w] = E[n_q]/\lambda = \varrho/[m\mu(1-\rho)]$

17. Variance of the waiting time: $\mathrm{Var}[w] = \varrho(2-\varrho)/[m^2\mu^2(1-\rho)^2]$

18. q-Percentile of the waiting time: $\max\left(0, \dfrac{E[w]}{\varrho}\ln\dfrac{100\varrho}{100-q}\right)$.

19. 90-Percentile of the waiting time: $\dfrac{E[w]}{\varrho}\ln(10\varrho)$

Once again, ϱ in these formulas is the probability of m or more jobs in the system: $\varrho = [(m\rho)^m/\{m!(1-\rho)\}]p_0$. For $m = 1$, ϱ is equal to ρ and all of the formulas become identical to those for M/M/1 queues.

This gives

$$p_0 + p_0 \sum_{n=1}^{m-1} \frac{(m\rho)^n}{n!} + p_0 \frac{(m\rho)^m}{m!} \sum_{n=m}^{\infty} \rho^{n-m} = 1$$

or

$$p_0 = \left[1 + \frac{(m\rho)^m}{m!(1-\rho)} + \sum_{n=1}^{m-1} \frac{(m\rho)^n}{n!}\right]^{-1}$$

The probability that an arriving job has to wait in the queue is denoted by ϱ and given by

$$\varrho = P(\geq m \text{ jobs}) = p_m + p_{m+1} + p_{m+2} + \cdots$$

$$= p_0 \frac{(m\rho)^m}{m!} \sum_{n=m}^{\infty} \rho^{n-m}$$

$$= p_0 \frac{(m\rho)^m}{m!(1-\rho)}$$

This is known as **Erlang's C formula**. This probability is an important performance parameter for M/M/m queues. It is convenient to compute ρ before proceeding to compute other parameters since ρ appears frequently in other expressions. Notice that for the single-server case ($m = 1$), the probability of queueing ϱ, or equivalently, the probability of all servers being busy, is equal to ρ.

Using the expression for p_n, the mean number of jobs in the queue $E[n_q]$ can be computed easily:

$$E[n_q] = \sum_{n=m+1}^{\infty} (n-m)p_n = p_0 \frac{(m\rho)^m}{m!} \sum_{n=m+1}^{\infty} (n-m)\rho^{n-m}$$

$$= p_0 \frac{(m\rho)^m \rho}{m!(1-\rho)^2} = \frac{\rho\varrho}{1-\rho}$$

The expected number of jobs in service is

$$E[n_s] = \sum_{n=1}^{m-1} np_n + \sum_{n=m}^{\infty} mp_n$$

$$= 1p_0 \frac{(m\rho)}{1!} + 2p_0 \frac{(m\rho)^2}{2!} + \cdots + (m-1)p_0 \frac{(m\rho)^{m-1}}{(m-1)!}$$

$$+ m(p_m + p_{m+1} + p_{m+2} + \cdots +)$$

$$= m\rho \left(p_0 + p_0 \frac{(m\rho)}{1!} + p_0 \frac{(m\rho)^2}{2!} + \cdots + p_0 \frac{(m\rho)^{m-2}}{(m-2)!} \right) + m\varrho$$

$$= m\rho(p_0 + p_1 + p_2 + \cdots + p_{m-2}) + m\varrho$$

$$= m\rho(1 - p_{m-1} - \varrho) + m\varrho$$

$$= m\rho - m\rho p_{m-1} + m\varrho(1-\rho)$$

$$= m\rho \qquad \text{since } m\varrho(1-\rho) = mp_m = m\rho p_{m-1}$$

The expected number of jobs in the system is

$$E[n] = E[n_q] + E[n_s] = m\rho + \frac{\rho\varrho}{1-\rho}$$

The variance of n and n_q can similarly be shown as

$$\text{Var}[n] = m\rho + \rho\varrho \left[\frac{1 + \rho - \rho\varrho}{(1-\rho)^2} + m \right]$$

$$\text{Var}[n_q] = \frac{\varrho\rho(1 + \rho - \varrho\rho)}{(1-\rho)^2}$$

If we observe the system for a long time, for instance, T seconds, the total number of jobs arriving and getting service will be λT. The total busy time of m servers to service these jobs will be $\lambda T/\mu$, and the utilization of each server will be

$$U = \frac{\text{busy time per server}}{\text{total time}} = \frac{(\lambda T/\mu)/m}{T} = \frac{\lambda}{m\mu} = \rho$$

The mean response time using Little's law is

$$E[r] = \frac{E[n]}{\lambda} = \frac{1}{\mu} + \frac{\varrho/m\mu}{1-\rho} = \frac{1}{\mu}\left(1 + \frac{\varrho}{m(1-\rho)}\right)$$

Similarly, the mean waiting time is

$$E[w] = \frac{E[n_q]}{\lambda} = \frac{\varrho}{m\mu(1-\rho)}$$

The probability distribution function of the response time can be shown as

$$F(r) = \begin{cases} 1 - e^{-\mu r} - \dfrac{\varrho}{1-m+m\rho}e^{-m\mu(1-\rho)r} - e^{-\mu r}, & \rho \neq (m-1)/m \\ & r > 0 \\ 1 - e^{-\mu r} - \varrho\mu r e^{-\mu r}, & \rho = (m-1)/m \end{cases}$$

$$(31.6)$$

Notice that the response time r is not exponentially distributed unless $m = 1$. In general, the coefficient of variation, that is, the ratio of the standard deviation to the mean, of r is less than 1.

Similarly, the probability distribution function of the waiting time is

$$F(w) = 1 - \varrho e^{-m\mu(1-\rho)w}$$

Since w has a truncated exponential distribution function, the q-percentile can be computed as follows:

$$w_q = \max\left\{0, \frac{1}{m\mu(1-\rho)}\ln\left(\frac{100\varrho}{100-q}\right)\right\}$$

If the probability of queueing ϱ is less than $1 - q/100$, the second term in the equation can be negative. The correct answer in those cases is zero.

□

Example 31.2 Students arrive at the university computer center in a Poisson manner at an average rate of 10 per hour. Each student spends an average of 20 minutes at the terminal, and the time can be assumed to be exponentially distributed. The center currently has five terminals. Some students have been complaining that waiting times are too long. Let us analyze the center usage using a queueing model.

The center can be modeled as an M/M/5 queueing system with an arrival rate of $\lambda = \frac{1}{6}$ per minute and a service rate of $\mu = \frac{1}{20}$ per minute.

Substituting these into the expressions previously used in this section, we get

$$\text{Traffic intensity } \rho = \frac{\lambda}{m\mu} = \frac{0.167}{5 \times 0.05} = 0.67$$

The probability of all terminals being idle is

$$p_0 = \left[1 + \frac{(5 \times 0.67)^5}{5!(1 - 0.67)} + \frac{(5 \times 0.67)^1}{1!} \right.$$

$$\left. + \frac{(5 \times 0.67)^2}{2!} + \frac{(5 \times 0.67)^3}{3!} + \frac{(5 \times 0.67)^4}{4!} \right]^{-1}$$

$$= 0.0318$$

The probability of all terminals being busy is

$$\varrho = \frac{(m\rho)^m}{m!(1 - \rho)} p_0 = \frac{(5 \times 0.67)^5}{5!(1 - 0.67)} \times 0.0318 = 0.33$$

Average terminal utilization is

$$\rho = 0.67$$

Average number of students in the center is

$$E[n] = m\rho + \frac{\rho\varrho}{1 - \rho} = 5 \times 0.67 + \frac{0.67 \times 0.33}{1 - 0.67} = 4.0$$

The average number of students waiting in the queue is

$$E[n_q] = \frac{\rho\varrho}{1 - \rho} = \frac{0.67 \times 0.33}{1 - 0.67} = 0.65$$

The average number of students using the terminals is

$$E[n_s] = E[n] - E[n_q] = 4 - 0.65 = 3.35$$

The mean and variance of the time spent in the center are

$$E[r] = \frac{1}{\mu} \left(1 + \frac{\varrho}{m(1 - \rho)} \right) = \frac{1}{0.05} \left(1 + \frac{0.33}{5(1 - 0.67)} \right) = 24$$

$$\text{Var}[r] = \frac{1}{\mu^2} \left(1 + \frac{\varrho(2 - \varrho)}{m^2(1 - \rho)^2} \right) = \frac{1}{0.05^2} \left(1 + \frac{0.33(2 - 0.33)}{5^2(1 - 0.67)^2} \right) = 479$$

Thus, each student spends an average of 24 minutes in the center. Of these, 20 minutes are spent working on the terminal and 4 minutes are spent waiting in the queue. We can further verify this using the formula for the mean waiting time:

$$E[w] = \frac{\varrho}{m\mu(1 - \rho)} = \frac{0.33}{5 \times 0.05 \times (1 - 0.67)} = 4$$

The 90-percentile of the waiting time is

$$\max\left\{0, \frac{E[w]}{\varrho}\ln(10\varrho)\right\} = \max\left\{0, \frac{4}{0.33}\ln(10 \times 0.33)\right\} = 14$$

Thus, 10% of the students have to wait more than 14 minutes.   □

Queueing models can be used not only to study the current behavior but also to predict what would happen if we made changes to the system. The following examples illustrate this.

Example 31.3   The students would like to limit their waiting time to an average of 2 minutes and no more than 5 minutes in 90% of the cases. Is it feasible? If yes, then how many terminals are required?

Let us analyze the system with $m = 6, 7, \ldots$ terminals while keeping the same arrival and service rates of $\lambda = 0.167$ and $\mu = 0.05$, respectively.

With $m = 6$ terminals, we have

$$\text{Traffic intensity } \rho = \frac{0.167}{6 \times 0.05} = 0.556$$

$$\text{Probability of all terminals being idle} = p_0 = 0.0346$$

$$\text{Probability of all terminals being busy} = \varrho = 0.15$$

$$\text{Average waiting time} = E[w] = 1.1 \text{ minutes}$$

The 90-percentile of waiting time is

$$\max\left\{0, \frac{1.1}{0.15}\ln(10 \times 0.15)\right\} = \max\{0, 3.0\} = 3.0$$

Thus, with just one more terminal we will be able to satisfy the students' demands.   □

One of the important decisions to be made when there is more than one identical server is whether to keep separate queues for each server or to keep just one queue for all servers. For Poisson arrivals and exponential service times, the first option of separate queues can be modeled using m M/M/1 queues, each with an arrival rate of λ/m. The second option of one queue can be modeled using an M/M/m queue with an arrival rate of λ. It is easy to show that the single-queue alternative is better. We illustrate this with an example.

Example 31.4   Consider what would have happened if the five terminals in Example 31.2 were located in five different locations on the campus, thereby needing a separate queue for each.

In this case, the system can be modeled as five separate M/M/1 queues. The arrival rate for each terminal would be one-fifth of the total arrival rate. Using $m = 1$, $\lambda = 0.167/5 = 0.0333$, and $\mu = 0.05$, we have

$$\text{Traffic intensity } \rho = \frac{0.0333}{0.05} = 0.67$$

The mean time spent in the terminal room is

$$E[r] = \frac{1/\mu}{1-\rho} = \frac{1/0.05}{1-0.67} = 60$$

The variance of the time spent in the terminal room is

$$\text{Var}[r] = \frac{1/\mu^2}{(1-\rho)^2} = \frac{1/0.05^2}{(1-0.67)^2} = 3600$$

Compare this to the mean of 24 minutes and a variance of 479 in Example 31.2 when all five terminals were located in one facility. It is clear that the single-queue alternative is better. In this example, we have ignored the difference in the walking time to the terminal room(s) from the dormitory. It is quite possible that having several terminal rooms distributed across the campus may reduce the walking time considerably and may become the preferred solution.   □

In general, if all jobs are identical, it is better to have just one queue than to have multiple queues. Of course, if some students need very short terminal sessions and others need very long sessions, this recommendation would not apply.

A special case of an M/M/m queue is the M/M/∞ queue with infinite servers. In such a queue, the jobs never have to wait. The response time is equal to the service time. The mean response time is equal to the mean service time regardless of the arrival rate. Such service centers are therefore also called **delay centers**. A delay center is used to represent dedicated resources, such as terminals in timesharing systems. Properties of such queues can be easily derived from those for M/M/m queues. Also results presented for M/G/∞ queues in Box 31.8 apply to delay centers as well.

31.4 M/M/m/B **QUEUE WITH FINITE BUFFERS**

An M/M/m/B queue is similar to the M/M/m queue except that the number of buffers B is finite. After B buffers are full, all arrivals are lost. We assume that B is greater than or equal to m; otherwise, some servers will never be able to operate due to a lack of buffers and the system will effectively operate as an M/M/B/B queue.

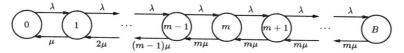

FIGURE 31.5 State transition diagram for an M/M/m/B queue.

The state transition diagram for an M/M/m/B queue is shown in Figure 31.5. The system can be modeled as a birth-death process using the following arrival and service rates:

$$\lambda_n = \lambda, \qquad n = 0, 1, 2, \ldots, B - 1$$

$$\mu_n = \begin{cases} n\mu, & n = 1, 2, \ldots, m - 1 \\ m\mu, & n = m, m + 1, \ldots, B \end{cases}$$

Theorem 31.1 gives us the following expression for the probability of n jobs in the system:

$$p_n = \begin{cases} \dfrac{\lambda^n}{n!\mu^n} p_0, & n = 1, 2, \ldots, m - 1 \\ \dfrac{\lambda^n}{m!m^{n-m}\mu^n} p_0, & n = m, m + 1, \ldots, B \end{cases}$$

In terms of the traffic intensity $\rho = \lambda/m\mu$, we have

$$p_n = \begin{cases} \dfrac{(m\rho)^n}{n!} p_0, & n = 1, 2, \ldots, m - 1 \\ \dfrac{\rho^n m^m}{m!} p_0, & n = m, m + 1, \ldots, B \end{cases}$$

The probability of zero jobs in the system is computed by the relationship

$$\sum_{n=0}^{B} p_n = 1$$

This gives

$$p_0 + p_0 \sum_{n=1}^{m-1} \frac{(m\rho)^n}{n!} + p_0 \frac{(m\rho)^m}{m!} \sum_{n=m}^{B} \rho^{n-m} = 1$$

or

$$p_0 = \left[1 + \frac{(1 - \rho^{B-m+1})(m\rho)^m}{m!(1 - \rho)} + \sum_{n=1}^{m-1} \frac{(m\rho)^n}{n!} \right]^{-1}$$

Using the expression for p_n, the mean number of jobs in the system $E[n]$ and the mean number of jobs in the queue $E[n_q]$ can be computed straightforwardly:

$$E[n] = \sum_{n=1}^{B} n p_n$$

$$E[n_q] = \sum_{n=m+1}^{B} (n - m) p_n$$

Variance and other statistics on n and n_q can be similarly computed.

All arrivals occurring when the system is in the state $n = B$ are lost. The rate of the jobs actually entering the system, called **effective arrival rate**, is

$$\lambda' = \sum_{n=0}^{B-1} \lambda p_n = \lambda \sum_{n=0}^{B-1} p_n = \lambda(1 - p_B)$$

The difference $\lambda - \lambda' = \lambda p_B$ represents the packet loss rate.

Since the jobs are not lost after entering the system, Little's law can be used to determine the mean response time:

$$E[r] = \frac{E[n]}{\lambda'} = \frac{E[n]}{\lambda(1 - p_B)}$$

Similarly, the mean waiting time is

$$E[w] = \frac{E[n_q]}{\lambda'} = \frac{E[n_q]}{\lambda(1 - p_B)}$$

If we observe the system for a long time, T seconds, for instance, the total number of jobs arriving and getting service will be $\lambda'T$. The total busy time of m servers to service these jobs will be $\lambda'T/\mu$, and the utilization of each server will be

$$U = \frac{\text{busy time per server}}{\text{total time}} = \frac{(\lambda'T/\mu)/m}{T} = \frac{\lambda'}{m\mu} = \rho(1 - p_B)$$

The probability of the full system is given by p_B. For a M/M/m/m system, the number of buffers is exactly equal to the number of servers, and the loss probability is

$$p_m = \frac{(m\rho)^m}{m!} p_0 = \frac{(m\rho)^m / m!}{\sum\limits_{j=0}^{m} [(m\rho)^j / j!]}$$

This formula is called **Erlang's loss formula**. It was originally derived by Erlang to compute the probability of lost phone calls at a telephone exchange. It turns out that the formula is valid not only for an M/M/m/m queue but also for M/G/m/m queues.

The results for the M/M/m/B queues are summarized in Box 31.3. For the special case of a single server, many of the results can be expressed in closed forms. This special case is summarized in Box 31.4. The following example illustrates the application of these results.

Example 31.5 Consider the gateway of Example 31.1 again. Let us analyze the gateway assuming it has only two buffers. The arrival rate and the service rate, as before, are 125 pps and 500 pps, respectively.
   In this case

$$\lambda = 125, \qquad \mu = 500, \qquad m = 1, \qquad B = 2$$

$$\text{Traffic intensity } \rho = \frac{\lambda}{m\mu} = \frac{125}{1 \times 500} = 0.25$$

For $n = 1, 2, \ldots, B$ are the p_n

$$p_1 = \rho p_0 = 0.25 p_0$$

$$p_2 = \rho^2 p_0 = 0.25^2 p_0 = 0.0625 p_0$$

Then p_0 is determined by summing all probabilities:

$$p_0 + p_1 + p_2 = 1 \Rightarrow p_0 + 0.25 p_0 + 0.0625 p_0 = 1 \Rightarrow p_0$$

$$= \frac{1}{1 + 0.25 + 0.0625} = 0.76$$

Substituting for p_0 in p_n, we get

$$p_1 = 0.25 p_0 = 0.19$$

$$p_2 = 0.0625 p_0 = 0.0476$$

The mean number of jobs in the system is

$$E[n] = \sum_{n=1}^{B} n p_n = 1 \times 0.19 + 2 \times 0.0476 = 0.29$$

The mean number of jobs in the queue is

$$E[n_q] = \sum_{n=m}^{B} (n - m) p_n = (2 - 1) \times 0.0476 = 0.0476$$

The effective arrival rate in the system is

$$\lambda' = \lambda(1 - p_B) = 125(1 - p_2) = 125(1 - 0.0476) = 119 \text{ pps}$$

and

$$\text{Packet loss rate } \lambda - \lambda' = 125 - 119 = 6 \text{ pps}$$

Box 31.3   M/M/m/B Queue (B Buffers)

1. Parameters:
   λ = arrival rate in jobs per unit time
   μ = service rate in jobs per unit time
   m = number of servers
   B = number of buffers, $B \geq m$

2. Traffic intensity: $\rho = \lambda/(m\mu)$

3. The system is always stable: $\rho < \infty$

4. Probability of zero jobs in the system:

$$p_0 = \left[1 + \frac{(1 - \rho^{B-m+1})(m\rho)^m}{m!(1-\rho)} + \sum_{n=1}^{m-1} \frac{(m\rho)^n}{n!}\right]^{-1}$$

   For $m = 1$:

$$p_0 = \begin{cases} \dfrac{1-\rho}{1-\rho^{B+1}}, & \rho \neq 1 \\[2mm] \dfrac{1}{B+1}, & \rho = 1 \end{cases}$$

5. Probability of n jobs in the system:

$$p_n = \begin{cases} \dfrac{1}{n!}(m\rho)^n p_0, & 0 \leq n < m \\[2mm] \dfrac{m^m \rho^n}{m!} p_0, & m \leq n \leq B \end{cases}$$

6. Mean number of jobs in the system: $E[n] = \sum_{n=1}^{B} n p_n$
   For $m = 1$:

$$E[n] = \frac{\rho}{1-\rho} - \frac{(B+1)\rho^{B+1}}{1-\rho^{B+1}}$$

7. Mean number of jobs in the queue: $E[n_q] = \sum_{n=m+1}^{B} (n-m) p_n$
   For $m = 1$:

$$E[n_q] = \frac{\rho}{1-\rho} - \rho\frac{1 + B\rho^B}{1-\rho^{B+1}}$$

8. Effective arrival rate in the system: $\lambda' = \sum_{n=0}^{B-1} \lambda p_n = \lambda(1 - p_B)$

9. Average utilization of each server: $U = \lambda'/(m\mu) = \rho(1 - p_B)$

10. Mean response time: $E[r] = E[n]/\lambda' = E[n]/[\lambda(1 - p_B)]$

11. Mean waiting time: $E[w] = E[r] - 1/\mu = E[n_q]/[\lambda(1 - p_B)]$

12. The loss rate is given by λp_B jobs per unit time.

13. For an M/M/m/m queue, the probability of a full system is given by

$$p_m = \frac{(m\rho)^m/m!}{\sum_{j=0}^{m} \dfrac{(m\rho)^j}{j!}}$$

Box 31.4 M/M/1/*B* Queue (*B* Buffers)

1. Parameters:
   λ = arrival rate in jobs per unit time
   μ = service rate in jobs per unit time
   B = number of buffers
2. Traffic intensity: $\rho = \lambda/\mu$
3. The system is always stable: $\rho < \infty$
4. Probability of zero jobs in the system:

$$p_0 = \begin{cases} \dfrac{1-\rho}{1-\rho^{B+1}}, & \rho \neq 1 \\[2ex] \dfrac{1}{B+1}, & \rho = 1 \end{cases}$$

5. Probability of n jobs in the system:

$$p_n = \begin{cases} \dfrac{1-\rho}{1-\rho^{B+1}}\rho^n, & \rho \neq 1 \\[2ex] \dfrac{1}{B+1}, & \rho = 1 \\[2ex] 0 & n > B \end{cases} \quad 0 \leq n \leq B$$

6. Mean number of jobs in the system:

$$E[n] = \frac{\rho}{1-\rho} - \frac{(B+1)\rho^{B+1}}{1-\rho^{B+1}}$$

7. Mean number of jobs in the queue:

$$E[n_q] = \frac{\rho}{1-\rho} - \rho\frac{1+B\rho^B}{1-\rho^{B+1}}$$

8. Effective arrival rate in the system: $\lambda' = \sum_{n=0}^{B-1}\lambda p_n = \lambda(1-p_B)$
9. Mean response time: $E[r] = E[n_q]/\lambda' = E[n]/[\lambda(1-p_B)]$
10. Mean waiting time: $E[w] = E[r] - 1/\mu = E[n_q]/[\lambda(1-p_B)]$

The mean response time is

$$E[r] = \frac{E[n]}{\lambda'} = \frac{0.29}{119} = 2.40 \times 10^{-3} \text{ second}$$

The mean time waiting in the queue is

$$E[w] = \frac{E[n_q]}{\lambda'} = \frac{0.0476}{119} = 4.0 \times 10^{-4} \text{ second}$$

The variance and other statistics for the number of jobs in the system can also be computed since the complete probability mass function p_n is known. For example,

$$\text{Var}[n] = E[n^2] - (E[n])^2 = (1^2 \times 0.19 + 2^2 \times 0.0476) - (0.29)^2 = 0.2963$$

□

31.5 RESULTS FOR OTHER QUEUEING SYSTEMS

A majority of queueing models used in computer systems performance analysis assume exponential interarrival times and exponential service times. Therefore, the M/M/m systems discussed so far cover a majority of cases. Also, systems with general arrivals or general service times are sometimes used. These include G/M/1, M/G/1, G/G/1, and G/G/m queueing systems. The key results for these systems and those for M/D/1 systems, which are a special case of M/G/1 systems, are summarized in Boxes 31.5 to 31.10. In particular, Box 31.10 for G/G/m systems summarizes the result presented earlier in Section 30.2. Readers interested in detailed derivation of results in other boxes should refer to one of several books devoted exclusively to queueing theory.

Box 31.5   M/G/1 Queue

1. Parameters:
   λ = arrival rate in jobs per unit time
   $E[s]$ = mean service time per job
   C_s = coefficient of variation of the service time
2. Traffic intensity: $\rho = \lambda E[s]$
3. The system is stable if the traffic intensity ρ is less than 1.
4. Probability of zero jobs in the system: $p_0 = 1 - \rho$
5. Mean number of jobs in the system: $E[n] = \rho + \rho^2(1 + C_s^2)/[2(1 - \rho)]$
   This equation is known as the Pollaczek-Khinchin (P-K) mean-value formula. Note that the mean number in the queue grows linearly with the variance of the service time distribution.
6. Variance of number of jobs in the system:

$$\text{Var}[n] = E[n] + \lambda^2 \text{Var}[s] + \frac{\lambda^3 E[s^3]}{3(1 - \rho)} + \frac{\lambda^4 (E[s^2])^2}{4(1 - \rho)^2}$$

7. Mean number of jobs in the queue: $E[n_q] = \rho^2(1 + C_s^2)/[2(1 - \rho)]$
8. Variance of number of jobs in the queue: $\text{Var}[n_q] = \text{Var}[n] - \rho + \rho^2$
9. Mean response time:
   $E[r] = E[n]/\lambda = E[s] + \rho E[s](1 + C_s^2)/[2(1 - \rho)]$

(Continued)

Box 31.5 Continued

10. Variance of the response time:
    $\text{Var}[r] = \text{Var}[s] + \lambda E[s^3]/[3(1-\rho)] + \lambda^2(E[s^2])^2/[4(1-\rho)^2]$
11. Mean waiting time: $E[w] = \rho E[s](1 + C_s^2)/[2(1-\rho)]$
12. Variance of the waiting time: $\text{Var}[w] = \text{Var}[r] - \text{Var}[s]$
13. Idle time distribution: $F(I) = 1 - e^{-\lambda I}$. The idle time is exponentially distributed.
14. Mean number of jobs served in one busy period: $1/(1-\rho)$
15. Variance of number of jobs served in one busy period:
    $\rho(1-\rho) + \lambda^2 E[s^2]/(1-\rho)^3$
16. Mean busy period duration: $E[s]/(1-\rho)$
17. Variance of the busy period: $E[s^2]/(1-\rho)^3 - (E[s])^2/(1-\rho)^2$

For last come, first served (LCFS) or service in, random order (SIRO), the expressions for $E[n]$ and $E[r]$ are the same as above for FCFS. The variance expressions are different:

$$\text{Var}[r_{\text{SIRO}}] = \text{Var}[s] + \frac{2\lambda E[s^3]}{3(1-\rho)(2-\rho)} + \frac{\lambda^2(2+\rho)(E[s^2])^2}{4(1-\rho)^2(2-\rho)}$$

$$\text{Var}[r_{\text{LCFS}}] = \text{Var}[s] + \frac{\lambda E[s^3]}{3(1-\rho)^2} + \frac{\lambda^2(1+\rho)(E[s^2])^2}{4(1-\rho)^3}$$

Notice that $\text{Var}[r_{\text{FCFS}}] \le \text{Var}[r_{\text{SIRO}}] \le \text{Var}[r_{\text{LCFS}}]$

Box 31.6 M/G/1 Queue with Processor Sharing (PS)

1. Parameters:
   λ = arrival rate in jobs per unit time
   $E[s]$ = mean service time per job
2. Traffic intensity: $\rho = \lambda E[s] < 1$
3. The system is stable if the traffic intensity ρ is less than 1.
4. Probability of n jobs in the system $p_n = (1-\rho)\rho^n$, $n = 0,1,\ldots,\infty$
5. Mean number in the system: $E[n] = \rho/(1-\rho)$
6. Variance of the number in system: $\text{Var}[n] = \rho/(1-\rho)^2$
7. Mean response time: $E[r] = E[s]/(1-\rho)$

Notice that the expressions given here are the same as those for the M/M/1 queue. The distributions are however different. Processor sharing approximates round-robin scheduling with small quantum size and negligible overhead.

Box 31.7   M/D/1 Queue

1. Parameters:

   λ = arrival rate in jobs per unit time

   $E[s]$ = service time per job, s is constant

   Substituting $E[s^k] = (E[s])^k$, $k = 2, 3, \ldots$, in the results for M/G/1, we obtain the results listed here for M/D/1.

2. Traffic intensity: $\rho = \lambda E[s]$

3. The system is stable if the traffic intensity is less than 1.

4. Probability of n jobs in system:

$$p_n = \begin{cases} 1 - \rho, & n = 0 \\ (1 - \rho)(e^\rho - 1), & n = 1 \\ (1 - \rho)\sum_{j=0}^{n} \dfrac{(-1)^{n-j}(j\rho)^{n-j-1}(j\rho + n - j)e^{j\rho}}{(n-j)!}, & n \geq 2 \end{cases}$$

5. Mean number of jobs in the system: $E[n] = \rho + \rho^2/[2(1-\rho)]$

6. Variance of number of jobs in the system:

   $\text{Var}[n] = E[n] + \rho^3/[3(1-\rho)] + \rho^4/[4(1-\rho)^2]$

7. Cumulative distribution function for response time:

$$F(r) = p_n \frac{(r - nE[s])}{E[s]} + \sum_{j=0}^{n-1} p_j, \qquad r \geq E[s] \text{ and } n = \left\lfloor \frac{r}{E[s]} \right\rfloor$$

8. Mean response time: $E[r] = E[s] + \rho E[s]/[2(1-\rho)]$

9. Variance of response time:

   $\text{Var}[r] = \rho(E[s])^2/[3(1-\rho)] + \rho^2(E[s])^2/[4(1-\rho)^2]$

10. Mean number of jobs in the queue:

$$E[n_q] = \rho^2/[2(1-\rho)]$$

11. Variance of number of jobs in the queue:

$$\text{Var}[n_q] = \rho^2 + \frac{\rho^2}{2(1-\rho)} + \frac{\rho^3}{3(1-\rho)} + \frac{\rho^4}{4(1-\rho)^2}$$

12. Mean waiting time: $E[w] = \rho E[s]/[2(1-\rho)]$

13. Variance of waiting time: $\text{Var}[w] = \text{Var}[r]$

14. Probability of serving n jobs in one busy period:

$$P(n) = \frac{(n\rho)^{n-1}}{n!} e^{-n\rho}$$

15. The cumulative distribution function of the busy period:

$$F(b) = \sum_{j=1}^{n} \frac{(j\rho)^{j-1}}{j!} e^{-j\rho}, \qquad n = \left\lfloor \frac{b}{E[s]} \right\rfloor$$

Here, $\lfloor x \rfloor$ is the largest integer not exceeding x.

Box 31.8 M/G/∞ Queue

1. Parameters:
   λ = arrival rate in jobs per unit time
   $E[s]$ = mean service time per jobs
2. Traffic intensity: $\rho = \lambda E[s]$
3. The system is always stable: $\rho < \infty$ is less than 1.
4. Probability of no jobs in the system: $p_0 = e^{-\rho}$
5. Probability of n jobs in the system: $p_n = (e^{-\rho}/n!)\rho^n$, $n = 0, 1, \ldots, \infty$
6. Mean number of jobs in the system: $E[n] = \rho$
7. Variance of number of jobs in the system: $\text{Var}[n] = \rho$
8. The number of jobs in the queue is always zero since there is no queueing. Thus, $E[n_q] = 0$.
9. Response time is equal to the service time. Therefore, it has the same distribution as the service time.
10. Mean response time: $E[r] = E[s]$

For the special case of the M/M/∞ queue, substitute $E[s] = 1/\mu$ in these results.

Box 31.9 G/M/1 Queue

1. Parameters:
   $E[\tau]$ = mean interarrival time
   μ = service rate in jobs per unit time
   If $L_\tau(\zeta)$ is the Laplace transform of the probability density function of the interarrival time τ, then let ϱ be the solution of the equation $\varrho = L_\tau(\mu - \varrho\mu)$.
2. Traffic intensity: $\rho = 1/(E[\tau]\mu)$
3. The system is stable if the traffic intensity ρ is less than 1.
4. Probability of zero jobs in the system: $p_0 = 1 - \rho$
5. Probability of n jobs in the system: $p_n = \rho\varrho^{n-1}(1 - \varrho)$, $n = 1, 2, \ldots, \infty$
6. Mean number of jobs in the system: $E[n] = \rho/(1 - \varrho)$
7. Variance of number of jobs in the system:
   $\text{Var}[n] = \rho(1 + \varrho - \rho)/(1 - \varrho)^2$
8. Cumulative distribution function of the response time:
   $F(r) = 1 - e^{(1-\varrho)\mu r}$, $r \geq 0$

(Continued)

Box 31.9   Continued

 9. Mean response time: $E[r] = 1/[\mu(1 - \varrho)]$
10. Variance of response time: $\text{Var}[r] = [1/\{\mu(1 - \varrho)\}]^2$
11. Probability distribution function of the waiting time:
    $F(w) = 1 - \varrho e^{(1-\varrho)\mu w}, \; w \geq 0$
12. Mean waiting time: $E[w] = \varrho/[\mu(1 - \varrho)]$
13. Variance of waiting time: $\text{Var}[w] = (2 - \varrho)\varrho/[\mu^2(1 - \varrho)^2]$
14. q-Percentile of the response time: $E[r]\ln[100/(100 - q)]$
15. 90-Percentile of the response time: $E[r]\ln[10] = 2.3E[r]$
16. q-Percentile of the waiting time: $\max(0, (E[w]/\varrho)\ln[100\varrho/(100 - q)])$.
    At low traffic intensities, the second term in this expression can be negative. The correct q-percentile for those cases is 0.
17. 90-Percentile of the waiting time: $\max(0, (E[w]/\varrho)\ln(10\varrho))$. At low traffic intensities, the second term in this expression can be negative. The correct 90-percentile for those cases is 0.
18. Probability of finding n or more jobs in the system: $\varrho^n(1 - p)/(1 - \varrho)$

For Poisson arrivals, $\varrho = p$, and all formulas become identical to those for M/M/1 queues.

Box 31.10   G/G/m Queue

1. Parameters:
   $E[\tau]$ = mean interarrival time
   λ = arrival rate, $= 1/E[\tau]$
   $E[s]$ = mean service time per job
   μ = service rate, $= 1/E[s]$
2. Traffic intensity: $\rho = \lambda/(m\mu)$
3. The system is stable if traffic intensity ρ is less than 1.
4. Mean number of jobs in service: $E[n_s] = m\rho$
5. Mean number of jobs in the system: $E[n] = E[n_q] + m\rho$
6. Variance of number of jobs in the system: $\text{Var}[n] = \text{Var}[n_q] + \text{Var}[n_s]$
7. Mean response time: $E[r] = E[w] + E[s]$. Alternately, $E[r] = E[n]/\lambda$
8. Variance of the response time: $\text{Var}[r] = \text{Var}[w] + \text{Var}[s]$
9. Mean waiting time: $E[w] = E[n_q]/\lambda$

EXERCISES

31.1 Consider a single-server system with discouraged arrivals in which the arrival rate is only $\lambda/(n+1)$ when there are n jobs in the system. The interarrival times, as well as the service time, are independent and identically distributed with an exponential distribution. Using a birth-death process model for this system, develop expressions for the following:

a. State probability p_n of n jobs in the system
b. State probability p_0 of the system being idle
c. Mean number of jobs in the system, $E[n]$
d. Effective arrival rate λ'
e. Mean response time $E[r]$

31.2 Consider an M/M/∞ system with an infinite number of servers. In such a system, all arriving jobs begin receiving service immediately. The service rate is $n\mu$ when there are n jobs in the system. Using a birth-death process model for this system, draw a state transition diagram for this system and develop expressions for the following:

a. State probability p_n of n jobs in the system
b. State probability p_0 of the system being idle
c. Mean number of jobs in the system, $E[n]$
d. Variance of number of jobs in the system, $\text{Var}[n]$
e. Mean response time $E[r]$

31.3 The average response time on a database system is 3 seconds. During a 1-minute observation interval, the idle time on the system was measured to be 10 seconds. Using an M/M/1 model for the system, determine the following:

a. System utilization
b. Average service time per query
c. Number of queries completed during the observation interval
d. Average number of jobs in the system
e. Probability of number of jobs in the system being greater than 10
f. 90-percentile response time
g. 90-percentile waiting time

31.4 A storage system consists of three disk drives sharing a common queue. The average time to service an I/O request is 50 milliseconds. The I/O requests arrive to the storage system at the rate of 30 requests per second. Using an M/M/3 model for this system, determine the following:

a. Average disk drive utilization
b. Probability of the system being idle, p_0
c. Probability of queueing, ϱ
d. Average number of jobs in the system, $E[n]$
e. Average number of jobs waiting in the queue, $E[n_q]$

f. Mean response time $E[r]$

g. Variance of the response time

h. 90-percentile of the waiting time

31.5 Complete Exercise 31.4 again assuming that a separate queue is maintained for each disk drive of the system. Also, assume the same total arrival rate.

31.6 Consider the problem of Example 31.3. The university is also considering the option to replace its computer system with a newer version that is twice as fast. The students will be able to finish their jobs within 10 minutes on an average. Would this system satisfy students' demands?

31.7 In the computer center problem of Example 31.3, space limitations do not allow more terminals to be installed at the current facility. If another identical computer facility is built in another part of the campus, will it help satisfy the students' requirements?

31.8 Assuming that there are only four buffers in the system of Exercise 31.4, determine the following:

a. Probability p_n of n jobs in the system for $n = 0, 1, \ldots, 4$

b. Mean number of jobs in the system, $E[n]$

c. Mean number of requests in the queue, $E[n_q]$

d. Variance of the number of jobs in the system, $\text{Var}[n]$

e. Effective arrival rate λ'

f. Request loss rate

g. Drive utilization

h. Mean response time $E[r]$

31.9 An M/M/m//K queue with a finite population of size K can be modeled as a birth-death process using the following arrival and service rates:

$$\lambda_n = (K - n)\lambda, \qquad n = 0, 1, 2, \ldots, K - 1$$

$$\mu_n = \begin{cases} n\mu, & n = 1, 2, \ldots, m - 1 \\ m\mu, & n = m, m + 1, \ldots, K \end{cases}$$

Derive an expression for the probability p_n of n jobs in the system, average throughput, and average response time of the system.

31.10 An M/M/m/B/K queue with B buffers and finite population of size K can be modeled as a birth-death process using the following arrival and service rates:

$$\lambda_n = (K - n)\lambda, \qquad n = 0, 1, 2, \ldots, B - 1$$

$$\mu_n = \begin{cases} n\mu, & n = 1, 2, \ldots, m - 1 \\ m\mu, & n = m, m + 1, \ldots, B \end{cases}$$

Derive an expression for the probability p_n of n jobs in the system, average throughput, and average response time of the system.

CHAPTER 32

QUEUEING NETWORKS

A problem well stated is a problem half solved.
—Charles F. Kettering

All the systems analyzed so far had only one queue. There are a number of systems that consist of several queues. A job may receive service at one or more queues before exiting from the system. Such systems are modeled by queueing networks. In general, a model in which jobs departing from one queue arrive at another queue (or possibly the same queue) is called a **queueing network**. This chapter presents several basic concepts about queueing networks. The techniques to solve the networks are described in Chapters 33 to 36.

32.1 OPEN AND CLOSED QUEUEING NETWORKS

Unlike single queues, there is no easy notation for specifying the type of queueing network. The simplest way to classify a queueing network is either open or closed. An **open queueing network** has external arrivals and departures, as shown in Figure 32.1. The jobs enter the system at "In" and exit at "Out." The number of jobs in the system varies with time. In analyzing an open system, we assume that the throughput is known (to be equal to the arrival rate), and the goal is to characterize the distribution of number of jobs in the system. A **closed queueing network** has no external arrivals or departures. As shown in Figure 32.2, the jobs in the system keep circulating from one queue to the next. The total number of jobs in the system is constant. It is possible to view a closed system as a system where the Out is connected back

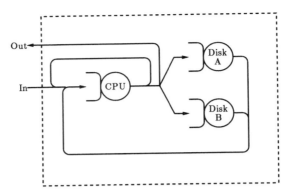

FIGURE 32.1 An open queueing network has external arrivals and departures.

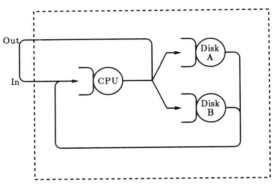

FIGURE 32.2 A closed queueing network has no external arrivals and departures.

to the In. The jobs exiting the system immediately reenter the system. The flow of jobs in the Out-to-In link defines the throughput of the closed system. In analyzing a closed system, we assume that the number of jobs is given, and we attempt to determine the throughput (or the job completion rate).

It is also possible to have **mixed queueing networks** that are open for some workloads and closed for others. Figure 32.3 shows an example of a mixed system with two *classes* of jobs. The system is closed for interactive jobs and is open for batch jobs. The term *class* refers to types of jobs. All jobs of a single class have the same service demands and transition probabilities. Within each class, the jobs are indistinguishable. The discussion here is limited to one class of jobs. Multiclass models are beyond the scope of the introductory treatment in this book.

32.2 PRODUCT FORM NETWORKS

The simplest queueing network is a series of M single-server queues with exponential service time and Poisson arrivals, as shown in Figure 32.4. The jobs

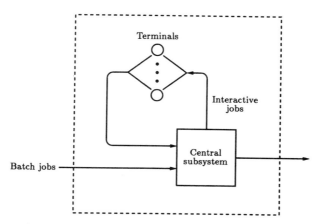

FIGURE 32.3   A mixed queueing network is open for some classes and closed for others.

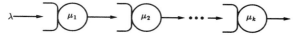

FIGURE 32.4   A simple queueing network consisting of k M/M/1 queues in series.

leaving a queue immediately join the next queue. It can be shown that each individual queue in this series can be analyzed independently of other queues. Each queue has an arrival as well as a departure rate of λ. If μ_i is the service rate for the ith server,

$$\text{Utilization of the }i\text{th server } \rho_i = \lambda/\mu_i$$

$$\text{Probability of }n_i\text{ jobs in the }i\text{th queue} = (1-\rho_i)\rho_i^{n_i}$$

The joint probability of queue lengths of M queues can be computed simply by multiplying individual probabilities; for example,

$$P(n_1, n_2, n_3, \ldots, n_M) = (1-\rho_1)\rho_1^{n_1}(1-\rho_2)\rho_2^{n_2}(1-\rho_3)\rho_3^{n_3}\cdots(1-\rho_M)\rho_M^{n_M}$$

$$= p_1(n_1)p_2(n_2)p_3(n_3)\cdots p_M(n_M) \tag{32.1}$$

This queueing network is therefore a **product form network.** In general, the term applies to any queueing network in which the expression for the equilibrium probability has the following form:

$$P(n_1, n_2, \ldots, n_M) = \frac{1}{G(N)}\prod_{i=1}^{M} f_i(n_i)$$

When $f_i(n_i)$ is some function of the number of jobs at the ith facility, $G(N)$ is a normalizing constant and is a function of the total number of jobs in the system.

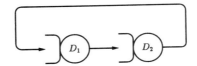

FIGURE 32.5   Closed network of two queues.

Example 32.1   Consider a closed system with two queues and N jobs circulating among the queues, as shown in Figure 32.5. Both servers have an exponentially distributed service time. The mean service times are 2 and 3, respectively.

Using the method discussed later in Chapter 35, the probability of having n_1 jobs in the first queue and $n_2 = N - n_1$ jobs in the second queue can be shown to be

$$P(n_1, n_2) = \frac{1}{3^{N+1} - 2^{N+1}} (2^{n_1} \times 3^{n_2})$$

In this case, the normalizing constant $G(N)$ is $3^{N+1} - 2^{N+1}$. The state probabilities are products of functions of the number of jobs in the queues. Thus, this is a product form network.   □

Product form networks are easier to analyze than nonproduct form networks. The set of networks that have a product form solution is continuously being extended by the researchers. First among these was Jackson (1963), who showed that the above method of computing joint probability is valid for any arbitrary open network of m-server queues with exponentially distributed service times (see Figure 32.6). In particular, if all queues are single-server queues, the queue length distribution is given by Equation (32.1). However, it is not correct to assume that each queue becomes an independent M/M/1 queue with a Poisson arrival process. In general, the internal flow in such networks is not Poisson. Particularly, if there is any feedback in the network, so that jobs can return to previously visited service centers, the internal flows are not Poisson. It is surprising that even though the flows are not Poisson,

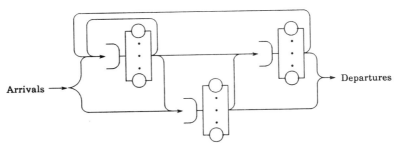

FIGURE 32.6   General open network of queues.

the queues are separable and can be analyzed as if they were independent M/M/*m* queues.

Jackson's results were later extended to closed networks by Gordon and Newell (1967). They showed that any arbitrary closed networks of *m*-server queues with exponentially distributed service times also have a product form solution.

Baskett, Chandy, Muntz, and Palacios (1975) showed that product form solutions exist for an even broader class of networks. This class consists of networks satisfying the following criteria:

1. *Service Disciplines*: All service centers have one of the following four types of service disciplines: First Come, First Served (FCFS), Processor Sharing (PS), Infinite Servers (ISs or delay centers), and Last Come, First Served Preemptive Resume (LCFS-PR).

2. *Job Classes*: The jobs belong to a single class while awaiting or receiving service at a service center but may change classes and service centers according to fixed probabilities at the completion of a service request.

3. *Service Time Distributions*: At FCFS service centers, the service time distributions must be identical and exponential for all classes of jobs. At other service centers, where the service times should have probability distributions with rational Laplace transforms, different classes of jobs may have different distributions.

4. *State-dependent Service*: The service time at a FCFS service center can depend only on the total queue length of the center. The service time for a class at PS, LCFS-PR, and IS centers can also depend on the queue length for that class, but not on the queue length of other classes. Moreover, the overall service rate of a subnetwork can depend on the total number of jobs in the subnetwork.

5. *Arrival Processes*: In open networks, the time between successive arrivals of a class should be exponentially distributed. No bulk arrivals are permitted. The arrival rates may be state dependent. A network may be open with respect to some classes of jobs and closed with respect to other classes of jobs.

Networks satisfying these criteria are referred to as **BCMP networks** after the authors of the criteria.

Denning and Buzen (1978) further extended the class of product form networks to non-Markovian networks with the following conditions:

1. *Job Flow Balance*: For each class, the number of arrivals to a device must equal the number of departures from the device.

2. *One-Step Behavior*: A state change can result only from single jobs entering the system, moving between pairs of devices in the system, or exiting from the system. This assumption asserts that simultaneous job moves will not be observed.

3. *Device Homogeneity*: A device's service rate for a particular class does not depend on the state of the system in any way except for the total device queue length and the designated class's queue length. This assumption implies the following:

   (a) *Single-Resource Possession*: A job may not be present (waiting for service or receiving service) at two or more devices at the same time.

   (b) *No Blocking*: A device renders service whenever jobs are present; its ability to render service is not controlled by any other device.

   (c) *Independent Job Behavior*: Interaction among jobs is limited to queueing for physical devices; for example, there should not be any synchronization requirements.

   (d) *Local Information*: A device's service rate depends only on local queue length and not on the state of the rest of the system.

   (e) *Fair Service*: If service rates differ by class, the service rate for a class depends only on the queue length of that class at the device and not on the queue lengths of other classes. This means that the servers do not discriminate against jobs in a class depending on the queue lengths of other classes.

   (f) *Routing Homogeneity*: The job routing should be state independent.

In the last condition, the term *routing* is used to denote a job's path in the network. The routing homogeneity condition implies that the probability of a job going from one device to another device does not depend upon the number of jobs at various devices.

The job flow balance assumption holds only in some observation periods. However, it is a good approximation for long observation intervals since the ratio of unfinished jobs to completed jobs is small.

32.3 QUEUEING NETWORK MODELS OF COMPUTER SYSTEMS

Two of the earliest queueing models of computer systems are the **machine repairman model** and the **central server model** shown in Figures 32.7 and 32.8, respectively. The machine repairman model, as the name implies, was originally developed for modeling machine repair shops. It has a number of working machines and a repair facility with one or more servers (repairmen). Whenever a machine breaks down, it is put in the queue for repair and serviced as soon as a repairman is available. Scherr (1967) used this model to represent a timesharing system with n terminals. Users sitting at the terminals generate requests (jobs) that are serviced by the system, which serves as

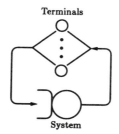

FIGURE 32.7 Machine repairman model of a computer system.

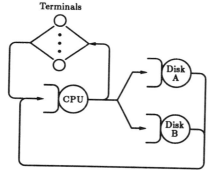

FIGURE 32.8 Central server model of a timesharing system.

a repairman. After a job is done, it waits at the user terminal for a random "think-time" interval before cycling again.

The central server model shown in Figure 32.8 was introduced by Buzen (1973). The CPU in the model is the "central server" that schedules visits to other devices. After service at the I/O devices, the jobs return to the CPU for further processing and leave it when the next I/O is encountered or when the job is completed.

In computer systems modeling, we encounter three kinds of devices. Most devices have a single server whose service time does not depend upon the number of jobs in the device. Such devices are called **fixed-capacity service centers**. For example, the CPU in a system may be modeled as a fixed-capacity service center. Then there are devices that have no queueing, and jobs spend the same amount of time in the device regardless of the number of jobs in it. Such devices can be modeled as a center with infinite servers and are called **delay centers** or **IS** (infinite server). A group of dedicated terminals is usually modeled as a delay center. Finally, the remaining devices are called **load-dependent service centers** since their service rates may depend upon the load or the number of jobs in the device. A M/M/m queue (with $m \geq 2$) is an example of a load-dependent service center. Its total service rate increases as more and more servers are used. A group of parallel links between two nodes in a computer network is an example of a load-dependent service center. Fixed-capacity centers and delay centers are considered in Chapters 34 and 35. Load-dependent centers are considered in Section 36.1. Unless specified otherwise, it is assumed that the service times for all servers are exponentially distributed.

In the next few chapters, we will describe a number of techniques to solve these queueing network models. The techniques are presented in the order of their complexity. The simplest technique is using operational analysis, and is presented in Chapter 33.

EXERCISE

32.1 Which product form condition is violated, if any, by the following system behaviors?

a. Jobs are lost if there are no buffers.

b. One job class has a priority over the other class.

c. Processes wait for fork and join primitives to complete.

d. A job intelligently chooses its path depending upon the congestion at the devices.

e. The system uses a back-pressure mechanism to avoid job loss when there are no buffer.

f. A job may execute while its I/O is proceeding.

g. The jobs are serviced in batches.

CHAPTER 33

OPERATIONAL LAWS

*All professional men are handicapped by not being
allowed to ignore things which are useless.*
—Johann Wolfgang von Goethe

A large number of day-to-day problems in computer systems performance analysis can be solved by using some simple relationships that do not require any assumptions about the distribution of service times or interarrival times. Several such relationships called **operational laws** were identified originally by Buzen (1976) and later extended by Denning and Buzen (1978).

The word *operational* means directly measured. Thus, *operationally testable* assumptions are the assumptions that can be verified by measurements. For example, it is easy to verify whether the assumption of number of arrivals being equal to the number of completions holds for a particular system. Therefore, this assumption, commonly called the **job flow balance** assumption, is operationally testable. On the other hand, one can never establish through measurement that a set of observed service times is or is not a sequence of independent random variables. Thus, the assumption of independence, although commonly used in stochastic modeling of queues, is not operationally testable.

The *operational quantities* are the quantities that can be directly measured during a finite observation period. For example, consider the black-box view of a device i shown earlier in Figure 30.3. If we observe the device for a finite time T, we can measure the number of arrivals A_i, the number of completions C_i, and the busy time B_i during this period. All of these are operational quantities. From these we can further derive the following operational quantities:

$$\text{Arrival rate } \lambda_i = \frac{\text{number of arrivals}}{\text{time}} = \frac{A_i}{T}$$

$$\text{Throughput } X_i = \frac{\text{number of completions}}{\text{time}} = \frac{C_i}{T}$$

$$\text{Utilization } U_i = \frac{\text{busy time}}{\text{total time}} = \frac{B_i}{T}$$

$$\text{Mean service time } S_i = \frac{\text{total time served}}{\text{number served}} = \frac{B_i}{C_i}$$

Notice that these operational quantities are *variables* that can change from one observation period to the next, but there are certain relationships that hold in every observation period. Such relationships are called **operational laws**. Several such laws are presented later in this chapter.

33.1   UTILIZATION LAW

Given the number of completions C_i and the busy time B_i of a device i during an observation period T, the following relationship holds among these variables:

$$U_i = \frac{B_i}{T} = \frac{C_i}{T} \times \frac{B_i}{C_i}$$

or

$$U_i = X_i S_i$$

This relationship is called the **utilization law.**

The utilization law, as well as other operational laws, is similar to the elementary laws of motion. For example, if a body starts at rest and accelerates at a constant acceleration a for an interval of time t, the distance traveled d is given by

$$d = \tfrac{1}{2}at^2$$

Notice that distance d, acceleration a, and time t are operational quantities. There is no need to consider them as expected values of random variables or to assume a probability distribution for them.

Example 33.1   Consider the network gateway problem of Example 31.1 again. The packets arrive at a rate of 125 packets per second (pps) and the gateway takes an average of two milliseconds to forward them.

$$\text{Throughput } X_i = \text{exit rate} = \text{arrival rate} = 125 \text{ pps}$$

$$\text{Service time } S_i = 0.002 \text{ second}$$

$$\text{Utilization } U_i = X_i S_i = 125 \times 0.002 = 0.25 = 25\%$$

Although this utilization is the same as that computed in Example 31.1, the key point to note is that while the result of Example 31.1 required assuming the interarrival times and service times to be IID random variables with exponential distribution, in this section we have made no such assumption, and the result is valid for any arrival or service process.   □

33.2 FORCED FLOW LAW

The forced flow law relates the system throughput to individual device throughputs. In an open model, the number of jobs leaving the system per unit time defines the system throughput. In a closed model, no job actually leaves the system. However, traversing the outside link (the link connecting "Out" to "In" in Figure 32.2) is equivalent to leaving the system and immediately reentering it, and the system throughput is defined as the number of jobs traversing this link per unit time.

If our observation period T is such that the number of job arrivals at each device is the same as the number of job completions, that is,

$$A_i = C_i$$

we can say that the device satisfies the assumption of job flow balance. If the observation period T is long, the difference $A_i - C_i$ is usually small compared to C_i. It will be exact if the initial queue length at each device is the same as the final queue length.

Suppose each job makes V_i requests for the ith device in the system, as shown in Figure 33.1. If the job flow is balanced, the number of jobs C_0 traversing the outside link and the number of jobs C_i visiting the ith device are related by

$$C_i = C_0 V_i \quad \text{or} \quad V_i = \frac{C_i}{C_0}$$

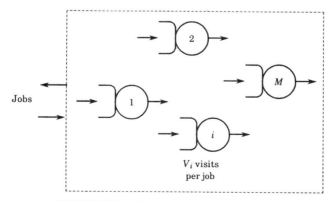

FIGURE 33.1 Internal view of the system.

Thus, the variable V_i is the ratio of visits to the ith device and the outside link. It is therefore called the **visit ratio**. The system throughput during the observation period is

$$\text{System throughput } X = \frac{\text{jobs completed}}{\text{total time}} = \frac{C_0}{T}$$

The throughput of the ith device and the system throughput are therefore related as follows:

$$\text{Device throughput } X_i = \frac{C_i}{T} = \frac{C_i}{C_0} \times \frac{C_0}{T}$$

In other words,

$$X_i = X V_i \tag{33.1}$$

This is the **forced flow law**. It applies whenever the job flow balance assumption is true.

It is clear that if the job flow balance is not true, then either there are some jobs that arrived during the observation period but did not leave or there were some jobs already in the system at the beginning of the observation period. In either case, it is possible that these jobs have not yet made all V_i visits to the ith device and $C_i \neq C_0 V_i$.

Combining the forced flow law and the utilization law, we get

$$\text{Utilization of the } i\text{th device } U_i = X_i S_i$$
$$= X V_i S_i$$

or

$$U_i = X D_i \tag{33.2}$$

Here $D_i = V_i S_i$ is the total service demand on the device for all visits of a job. Equation (33.2) states that the utilizations of various devices in the system are proportional to total demand D_i per job on the device. Hence, the device with the highest D_i has the highest utilization and is the **bottleneck device**. This result will be used later in Section 33.6.

Example 33.2 In a timesharing system, accounting log data produced the following profile for user programs. Each program requires 5 seconds of CPU time and makes 80 I/O requests to disk A and 100 I/O requests to disk B. The average think time of the users was 18 seconds. From the device specifications, it was determined that disk A takes 50 milliseconds to satisfy an I/O request and disk B takes 30 milliseconds per request. With 17 active terminals, disk A throughput was observed to be 15.70 I/O requests per second. We want to find the system throughput and device utilizations.

This system can be represented by the queueing network model shown earlier in Figure 32.8. Symbolically, we are given the following: $D_{\text{CPU}} =$

5 seconds, $V_A = 80$, $V_B = 100$, $Z = 18$ seconds, $S_A = 0.050$ second, $S_B = 0.030$ second, $N = 17$, and $X_A = 15.70$ jobs/second.

Since the jobs must visit the CPU before going to the disks or terminals, the CPU visit ratio is

$$V_{CPU} = V_A + V_B + 1 = 181$$

The first step in operational analysis generally is to determine total service demands D_i for all devices. In this case,

$$D_{CPU} = 5 \text{ seconds}$$

$$D_A = S_A V_A = 0.050 \times 80 = 4 \text{ seconds}$$

$$D_B = S_B V_B = 0.030 \times 100 = 3 \text{ seconds}$$

Using the forced flow law, the throughputs are

$$X = \frac{X_A}{V_A} = \frac{15.70}{80} = 0.1963 \text{ job/second}$$

$$X_{CPU} = X V_{CPU} = 0.1963 \times 181 = 35.48 \text{ requests/second}$$

$$X_B = X V_B = 0.1963 \times 100 = 19.6 \text{ requests/second}$$

Using the utilization law, the device utilizations are

$$U_{CPU} = X D_{CPU} = 0.1963 \times 5 = 98\%$$

$$U_A = X D_A = 0.1963 \times 4 = 78.4\%$$

$$U_B = X D_B = 0.1963 \times 3 = 58.8\% \qquad \square$$

Visit ratios are one way of specifying the routing of jobs in a queueing network. Another way is to specify the **transition probabilities** p_{ij} of a job moving to the jth queue after service completion at the ith queue. The visit ratios and transition probabilities are equivalent in the sense that given one we can always find the other. In a system with job flow balance,

$$C_j = \sum_{i=0}^{M} C_i p_{ij}$$

Here, subscript 0 is used to denote visits to the outside link. Thus, p_{i0} is the probability of a job exiting from the system after completion of service at the ith device. Dividing both sides of the equation by C_0, we get

$$V_j = \sum_{i=0}^{M} V_i p_{ij} \qquad (33.3)$$

Since each visit to the outside link is defined as the completion of the job, we have

$$V_0 = 1 \qquad (33.4)$$

Equations (33.3) and (33.4) are called **visit ratio equations** and can be used to get visit ratios from transition probabilities. A unique solution is always possible provided the network is operationally connected, that is, each device in the system is visited at least once by each job.

In central server models, after completion of service at every queue, the jobs always move back to the CPU queue:

$$p_{i1} = 1 \qquad \forall i \neq 1$$
$$p_{ij} = 0 \qquad \forall i, j \neq 1$$

These probabilities apply to the exit and entrance from the system $(i = 0)$ also. Therefore, the visit ratio equations become

$$1 = V_1 p_{10}$$
$$V_1 = 1 + V_2 + V_3 + \cdots + V_M$$
$$V_j = V_1 p_{1j} = \frac{p_{1j}}{p_{10}}, \qquad j = 2, 3, \ldots, M$$

Thus, we can find the visit ratios by dividing the probability p_{1j} of moving to the jth queue from the CPU by the exit probability p_{10}.

Example 33.3 Consider the queueing network of Figure 32.8. The visit ratios given in Example 33.2 are $V_A = 80$, $V_B = 100$, and $V_{\text{CPU}} = 181$.

It is easy to see in this case that after completion of service at the CPU, the probabilities of the job moving to disk A, disk B, or the terminals are $\frac{80}{181}$, $\frac{100}{181}$, and $\frac{1}{181}$, respectively. Thus, the transition probabilities are 0.4420, 0.5525, and 0.005525.

Given the transition probabilities, we can find the visit ratios by dividing these probabilities by the exit probability (0.005525):

$$V_A = \frac{0.4420}{0.005525} = 80$$
$$V_B = \frac{0.5525}{0.005525} = 100$$
$$V_{\text{CPU}} = 1 + V_A + V_B = 1 + 80 + 100 = 181 \qquad \square$$

33.3 LITTLE'S LAW

Little's law is also an operational law. In its derivation in Section 30.3, we used only operational (measurable) quantities. The only assumption required was that the number of arrivals is equal to the number of completions. This is the operationally testable assumption of job flow balance.

We can apply Little's law to relate queue length Q_i and response time R_i at the ith device:

Mean number in device = arrival rate × mean time in device

$$Q_i = \lambda_i R_i$$

If the job flow is balanced, the arrival rate is equal to the throughput, and we can write

$$Q_i = X_i R_i \tag{33.5}$$

It is this version of Little's law that we will use frequently hereafter. Notice that the queue length Q_i is synonymous with the number of jobs at the ith device. It includes not only the jobs waiting in the ith queue but also those getting service at the device.

Example 33.4 The average queue length in the computer system of Example 33.2 was observed to be 8.88, 3.19, and 1.40 jobs at the CPU, disk A, and disk B, respectively. What were the response times of these devices?

In Example 33.2, the device throughputs were determined to be

$$X_{\text{CPU}} = 35.48, \qquad X_A = 15.70, \qquad X_B = 19.6$$

The new information given in this example is

$$Q_{\text{CPU}} = 8.88, \qquad Q_A = 3.19, \qquad Q_B = 1.40$$

Using Little's law, the device response times are

$$R_{\text{CPU}} = Q_{\text{CPU}}/X_{\text{CPU}} = 8.88/35.48 = 0.250 \text{ second}$$

$$R_A = Q_A/X_A = 3.19/15.70 = 0.203 \text{ second}$$

$$R_B = Q_B/X_B = 1.40/19.6 = 0.071 \text{ second} \qquad \square$$

33.4 GENERAL RESPONSE TIME LAW

All timesharing systems can be divided into two subsystems: the terminal subsystem and the central subsystem consisting of the remaining devices including the CPU, as shown in Figure 33.2. There is one terminal per user and the rest of the system is shared by all users.

It is interesting to note that Little's law can be applied to any part of the system. The only requirement is that the job flow in that part be balanced. In particular, it can be applied to the central subsystem, which gives

$$Q = X R$$

Here, Q is the total number of jobs in the system, R is the system response time, and X is the system throughput. Given individual queue lengths Q_i at the devices, we can compute Q:

$$Q = Q_1 + Q_2 + \cdots + Q_M$$

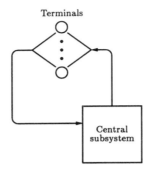

FIGURE 33.2 Two components of a timesharing system: terminals and the central subsystem.

Substituting for Q_i from Equation (33.5) yields

$$X R = X_1 R_1 + X_2 R_2 + \cdots + X_M R_M$$

Dividing both sides of this equation by X and using the forced flow law, we get

$$R = V_1 R_1 + V_2 R_2 + \cdots + V_M R_M$$

or

$$R = \sum_{i=1}^{M} R_i V_i \tag{33.6}$$

This is called the **general response time law**. It is possible to show that this law holds even if the job flow is not balanced. Intuitively, the law states that the total time spent by a job at a server is the product of time per visit and the number of visits to the server; and the total time in the system is equal to the sum of total times at various servers.

Example 33.5 Let us compute the response time for the timesharing system of Examples 33.2 and 33.4. For this system

$$V_{\text{CPU}} = 181, \qquad V_A = 80, \qquad V_B = 100$$

$$R_{\text{CPU}} = 0.250, \qquad R_A = 0.203, \qquad R_B = 0.071$$

The system response time is

$$R = R_{\text{CPU}} V_{\text{CPU}} + R_A V_A + R_B V_B$$

$$= 0.250 \times 181 + 0.203 \times 80 + 0.071 \times 100 = 68.6$$

The system response time is 68.6 seconds.   ☐

33.5 INTERACTIVE RESPONSE TIME LAW

In an interactive system, the users generate requests that are serviced by the central subsystem and responses come back to the terminal. After a think time Z, the users submit the next request. If the system response time is R, the total cycle time of requests is $R + Z$. Each user generates about $T/(R + Z)$ requests in time period T. If there are N users,

$$\text{System throughput } X = \frac{\text{total number of requests}}{\text{total time}}$$

$$= \frac{N[T/(R + Z)]}{T}$$

$$= \frac{N}{R + Z}$$

or

$$R = (N/X) - Z \qquad (33.7)$$

This is the **interactive response time law**.

Example 33.6 For the timesharing system of Example 33.2, we can compute the response time using the interactive response time law as follows:

$$X = 0.1963, \qquad N = 17, \qquad Z = 18$$

Therefore,

$$R = \frac{N}{X} - Z = \frac{17}{0.1963} - 18 = 86.6 - 18 = 68.6 \text{ seconds}$$

This is the same as that obtained earlier in Example 33.5. $\square$

33.6 BOTTLENECK ANALYSIS

One consequence of the forced flow law is that the device utilizations are proportional to their respective total service demands:

$$U_i \propto D_i$$

The device with the highest total service demand D_i has the highest utilization[1] and is called the **bottleneck device**. This device is the key limiting factor in achieving higher throughput. Improving this device will provide the highest payoff in terms of system throughput. Improving other devices will have little effect on the system performance. Therefore, *identifying the bottleneck device should be the first step in any performance improvement project.*

---

[1]Delay centers can have utilizations more than one without any stability problems. Therefore, delay centers cannot be a bottleneck device. Only queueing centers should be considered in finding the bottleneck or computing $D_{\max}$.

Suppose we find that the device b is the bottleneck. This implies that $D_b = D_{\max}$ is the highest among $D_1, D_2, \ldots, D_M$. Then the throughput and response times of the system are bound as follows:

$$X(N) \leq \min\left\{\frac{1}{D_{\max}}, \frac{N}{D+Z}\right\} \tag{33.8}$$

and

$$R(N) \geq \max\{D, ND_{\max} - Z\} \tag{33.9}$$

Here, $D = \sum D_i$ is the sum of total service demands on all devices except terminals. Equations (33.8) and (33.9) are known as **asymptotic bounds**. The proof follows.

Proof 33.1   The asymptotic bounds are based on the following observations:

1. The utilization of any device cannot exceed 1. This puts a limit on the maximum obtainable throughput.
2. The response time of the system with N users cannot be less than a system with just one user. This puts a limit on the minimum response time.
3. The interactive response time formula can be used to convert the bound on throughput to that on response time and vice versa.

We now derive the bounds using these observations. For the bottleneck device b we have

$$U_b = X D_{\max}$$

Since U_b cannot be more than 1, we have

$$X D_{\max} \leq 1$$

or

$$X \leq \frac{1}{D_{\max}} \tag{33.10}$$

With just one job in the system, there is no queueing and the system response time is simply the sum of the service demands:

$$R(1) = D_1 + D_2 + \cdots + D_M = D$$

Here, D is defined as the sum of all service demands. With more than one user there may be some queueing and so the response time will be higher. That is,

$$R(N) \geq D \tag{33.11}$$

Applying the interactive response time law to the bounds specified by Equations (33.10) and (33.11), we get

$$R(N) = \frac{N}{X(N)} - Z \geq ND_{\max} - Z$$

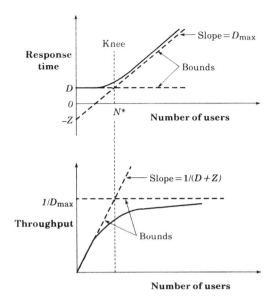

FIGURE 33.3   Typical asymptotic bounds.

and

$$X(N) = \frac{N}{R(N) + Z} \leq \frac{N}{D + Z}$$

Combining these bounds with Equations (33.10) and (33.11), we get the asymptotic bounds as specified in Equations (33.8) and (33.9).   □

Figure 33.3 shows asymptotic bounds for a typical case. As shown in the figure, both throughput and response time bounds consist of two straight lines. The response time bounds consist of a horizontal straight line at $R = D$ and a line passing through the point $(-Z, 0)$ at a slope of D_{max}. The throughput bounds consist of a horizontal straight line at $X = 1/D_{max}$ and a line passing through the origin at a slope of $1/(D + Z)$. The point of intersection of the two lines is called the **knee**. For both response time and throughput, the knee occurs at the same value of number of users. The number of jobs N^* at the knee is given by

$$D = N^* D_{max} - Z \quad \text{or} \quad N^* = \frac{D + Z}{D_{max}}$$

If the number of jobs is more than N^*, then we can say with certainty that there is queueing somewhere in the system.

The asymptotic bounds are useful in practice since they can be easily derived and explained to people who do not have any background in queueing theory or performance analysis.

The following examples illustrate the use of asymptotic bounds.

Example 33.7 For the timesharing system considered in Example 33.2:

$$D_{CPU} = 5, \qquad D_A = 4, \qquad D_B = 3, \qquad Z = 18$$

$$D = D_{CPU} + D_A + D_B = 5 + 4 + 3 = 12$$

$$D_{max} = D_{CPU} = 5$$

The asymptotic bounds are

$$X(N) \le \min\left\{ \frac{N}{D+Z}, \frac{1}{D_{max}} \right\} = \min\left\{ \frac{N}{30}, \frac{1}{5} \right\}$$

$$R(N) \ge \max\{D, ND_{max} - Z\} = \max\{12, 5N - 18\}$$

These bounds are shown by broken lines in Figure 33.4. The solid lines show the exact throughput and response times (obtained using the mean-value analysis to be discussed in Section 34.2). The knee occurs at

$$12 = 5N^* - 18$$

or

$$N^* = \frac{12 + 18}{5} = \frac{30}{5} = 6$$

Thus, if there are more than six users on the system, there will certainly be queueing in the system. $\square$

Example 33.8 How many terminals can be supported on the timesharing system of Example 33.2 if the response time has to be kept below 100 seconds?

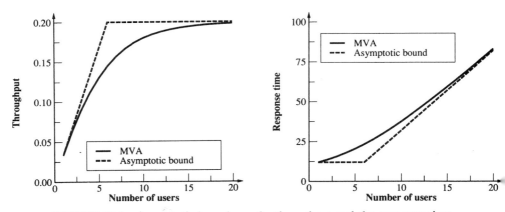

FIGURE 33.4 Asymptotic bounds on the throughput and the response time.

Using the asymptotic bounds on the response time, we get

$$R(N) \geq \max\{12, 5N - 18\}$$

The response time will be more than 100 if

$$5N - 18 \geq 100$$

That is, if

$$N \geq 23.6$$

the response time is bound to be more than 100. Thus, the system cannot support more than 23 users if a response time of less than 100 is required.

□

This completes the discussion on operational laws. A summary of all operational laws is presented in Box 33.1.

Box 33.1   Operational Laws

Utilization law	$U_i = X_i S_i = X D_i$
Forced flow law	$X_i = X V_i$
Little's law	$Q_i = X_i R_i$
General response time law	$R = \sum_{i=1}^{M} R_i V_i$
Interactive response time law	$R = N/X - Z$
Asymptotic bounds	$R \geq \max\{D, N D_{max} - Z\}$
	$X \leq \min\{1/D_{max}, N/(D + Z)\}$

Symbols:

D	Sum of service demands on all devices, $= \sum_i D_i$
D_i	Total service demand per job for the ith device, $= S_i V_i$
D_{max}	Service demand on the bottleneck device, $= \max_i\{D_i\}$
N	Number of jobs in the system
Q_i	Number in the ith device
R	System response time
R_i	Response time per visit to the ith device
S_i	Service time per visit to the ith device
U_i	Utilization of the ith device
V_i	Number of visits per job to the ith device
X	System throughput
X_i	Throughput of the ith device
Z	Think time

EXERCISES

33.1 During a 10-second observation period, 400 packets were serviced by a gateway whose CPU can service 200 pps. What was the utilization of the gateway CPU?

33.2 The throughput of a timesharing system was observed to be five jobs per second over a 10-minute observation period. If the average number of jobs in the system was four during this period, what was the average response time?

33.3 During a 10-second observation period, 40 requests were serviced by a file server. Each request requires two disk accesses. The average service time at the disk was 30 milliseconds. What was the average disk utilization during this period?

33.4 A distributed system has a print server with a printing speed of 60 pages per minute. The server was observed to print 500 pages over a 10-minute observation period. If each job prints five pages on the average, what was the job completion rate of the system?

33.5 For a timesharing system with two disks (user and system), the probabilities for jobs completing the service at the CPU were found to be 0.80 to disk A, 0.16 to disk B, and 0.04 to the terminals. The user think time was measured to be 5 seconds, the disk service times were 30 and 25 milliseconds, and the average service time per visit to the CPU was 40 milliseconds. Using the queueing network model shown in Figure 32.8, answer the following for this system:

a. For each job, what are the visit ratios for CPU, disk A, and disk B?

b. For each device, what is the total service demand?

c. If disk A utilization is 60%, what is the utilization of the CPU and disk B?

d. If the utilization of disk B is 10%, what is the average response time when there are 20 users on the system?

33.6 For the system of Exercise 33.5, answer the following:

a. What is the bottleneck device?

b. What is the minimum average response time?

c. What is the maximum possible disk A utilization for this configuration?

d. What is the maximum possible throughput of this system?

e. What changes in CPU speed would you recommend to achieve a response time of 10 seconds with 25 users? Would you also need a faster disk A or disk B?

    f. Write the expressions for asymptotic bounds on throughput and response time.

33.7 For the system of Exercise 33.6, which device would be the bottleneck if

    a. the CPU is replaced by another unit that is twice as fast?

    b. disk A is replaced by another unit that is twice as slow?

    c. disk B is replaced by another unit that is twice as slow?

    d. the memory size is reduced so that the jobs make 20 times more visits to disk B due to increased page faults?

CHAPTER 34

MEAN-VALUE ANALYSIS AND RELATED TECHNIQUES

The man who makes no mistakes does not usually make anything.
—Bishop W. C. Magee

This chapter extends the results presented in Chapter 33 on operational analysis of queueing networks. In particular, a popular technique known as mean-value analysis is presented. The technique allows analysis of computer systems that can be modeled as a closed queueing network. However, results on open queueing networks are presented first since they are easier to derive and since they help in understanding the results for closed systems.

34.1 ANALYSIS OF OPEN QUEUEING NETWORKS

Open queueing network models are used to represent transaction processing systems such as airline reservation systems or banking systems. In these systems, the transaction arrival rate is not dependent on the load on the computer system. The transaction arrivals are modeled as a Poisson process with a mean arrival rate λ. In this section, we present equations for an exact analysis of such systems. We assume that all devices in the computer system can be modeled as either fixed-capacity service centers (single server with exponentially distributed service time) or delay centers (infinite servers with exponentially distributed service time).

For all fixed-capacity service centers in an open queueing network, the response time is given by

$$R_i = S_i(1 + Q_i) \tag{34.1}$$

One easy way to understand this relationship is to consider a "tagged" job flowing through the system. On arrival at the ith device, the job sees Q_i jobs ahead (including the one in service) and expects to wait $Q_i S_i$ seconds. Including the service to itself, the job should expect a total response time of $S_i(1 + Q_i)$.

Notice that Equation (34.1) is not an operational law. It assumes that the service is memoryless, an assumption that is not operationally testable. To compute the response time of the tagged job without the memoryless assumption, we would also need to know the time that the job currently in service has already consumed.

Equation (34.1) along with the operational laws discussed earlier in Chapter 33 are sufficient to get mean values of system performance parameters, as shown next.

Assuming job flow balance, the throughput of the system is equal to the arrival rate:

$$X = \lambda$$

The throughput of the ith device using the forced flow law is

$$X_i = X V_i$$

The utilization of the ith device using the utilization law is

$$U_i = X_i S_i = X V_i S_i = \lambda D_i$$

The queue length of the ith device using Little's law is

$$Q_i = X_i R_i = X_i S_i(1 + Q_i) = U_i(1 + Q_i)$$

or

$$Q_i = \frac{U_i}{1 - U_i}$$

Notice that this equation for Q_i is identical to Equation (31.3) for M/M/1 queues. Substituting this expression for Q_i in Equation (34.1), the device response times are

$$R_i = \frac{S_i}{1 - U_i} \tag{34.2}$$

In delay centers, there are infinite servers, and therefore, the response time is equal to the service time regardless of the queue length. The queue length, in this case, denotes the number of jobs receiving service since there is no wait-

---

Box 34.1   Analysis of Open Queueing Networks

Inputs:

X = external arrival rate, system throughput
S_i = service time per visit to the ith device
V_i = number of visits to the ith device
M = number of devices (not including terminals)

Outputs:

Q_i = mean number of jobs at ith device
R_i = response time of the ith device
R = system response time
U_i = utilization of the ith device
N = mean number of jobs in the system

Total service demands: $D_i = S_i V_i$
Device utilizations: $U_i = X D_i$
Device throughputs: $X_i = X V_i$
Device response times:

$$R_i = \begin{cases} S_i/(1 - U_i) & \text{Fixed-capacity centers} \\ S_i & \text{Delay centers} \end{cases}$$

Device queue lengths:

$$Q_i = \begin{cases} U_i/(1 - U_i) & \text{Fixed-capacity centers} \\ U_i & \text{Delay centers} \end{cases}$$

System response time: $R = \sum_{i=1}^{M} R_i V_i$
Number of jobs in the system: $N = \sum_{i=1}^{M} Q_i$

---

ing required. Thus, the response time and queue length equations for delay centers are

$$R_i = S_i$$
$$Q_i = R_i X_i = S_i X V_i = X D_i = U_i$$

Notice that the utilization of the delay center represents the mean number of jobs receiving service and does not need to be less than 1.

All equations to analyze open systems are summarized in Box 34.1.

Example 34.1   Figure 32.1 shown earlier represents a queueing model of a file server consisting of a CPU and two disks, A and B. Measurements on a distributed system with six clients systems making requests to the file server produced the following data:

> Observation interval = 3600 seconds
>
> Number of client requests = 10,800
>
> CPU busy time = 1728 seconds
>
> Disk A busy time = 1512 seconds
>
> Disk B busy time = 2592 seconds
>
> Number of visits (I/O requests) to disk A = 75,600
>
> Number of visits (I/O requests) to disk B = 86,400

Based on these observations, we can compute the service demands and visit ratios as follows:

X = throughput = 10,800/3600 = 3 client requests per second

V_A = 75,600/10,800 = 7 visits per client request to disk A

V_B = 86,400/10,800 = 8 visits per client request to disk B

V_{CPU} = 1 + 7 + 8 = 16 visits per client requests to CPU

D_{CPU} = 1728/10,800 = 0.16 second of CPU time per client request

D_A = 1512/10,800 = 0.14 second of disk A time per client request

D_B = 2592/10,800 = 0.24 second of disk B time per client request

S_{CPU} = 0.16/16 = 0.01 second per visit to CPU

S_A = 0.14/7 = 0.02 second per visit to disk A

S_B = 0.24/8 = 0.03 second per visit to disk B

We now have all the input parameters required to analyze the system. Device utilizations using the utilization law are

$$U_{CPU} = X D_{CPU} = 3 \times 0.16 = 0.48$$

$$U_A = X D_A = 3 \times 0.14 = 0.42$$

$$U_B = X D_B = 3 \times 0.24 = 0.72$$

The device response times using Equation (34.2) are

$$R_{CPU} = S_{CPU}/(1 - U_{CPU}) = 0.01/(1 - 0.48) = 0.0192 \text{ second}$$

$$R_A = S_A/(1 - U_A) = 0.02/(1 - 0.42) = 0.0345 \text{ second}$$

$$R_B = S_B/(1 - U_B) = 0.03/(1 - 0.72) = 0.107 \text{ second}$$

Server response time $R = \sum V_i R_i = 16 \times 0.0192 + 7 \times 0.0345 + 8 \times 0.107$

$$= 1.406 \text{ seconds}$$

The model can be used to answer some of the typical questions. For example, we might want to quantify the impact of the following changes:

1. Increase the number of clients to 8.
2. Use a cache for disk B with a hit rate of 50%, although it increases the CPU overhead by 30% and the disk B service time (per I/O) by 10%.
3. Have a lower cost server with only one disk (disk A) and direct all I/O requests to it.

The first question can be answered if we assume that the new clients make requests similar to those measured. The request arrival rate will go up by a factor of $\frac{8}{6}$. Since the arrival rate was three requests per second, with more clients it will become four requests per second. The new analysis is as follows:

$$X = 4 \text{ requests/second}$$

$$U_{CPU} = X D_{CPU} = 4 \times 0.16 = 0.64$$

$$U_A = X D_A = 4 \times 0.14 = 0.56$$

$$U_B = X D_B = 4 \times 0.24 = 0.96$$

$$R_{CPU} = S_{CPU}/(1 - U_{CPU}) = 0.01/(1 - 0.64) = 0.0278 \text{ second}$$

$$R_A = S_A/(1 - U_A) = 0.02/(1 - 0.56) = 0.0455 \text{ second}$$

$$R_B = S_B/(1 - U_B) = 0.03/(1 - 0.96) = 0.75 \text{ second}$$

$$R = 16 \times 0.0278 + 7 \times 0.0455 + 8 \times 0.75 = 6.76 \text{ seconds}$$

Thus, if the number of clients is increased from 6 to 8, the server response time will degrade by a factor of $6.76/1.406 = 4.8$.

The second question requires changing V_B, S_{CPU}, and S_B as follows:

$$V_B = 0.5 \times 8 = 4$$

$$S_{CPU} = 1.3 \times 0.01 = 0.013 \Rightarrow D_{CPU} = 0.208 \text{ second}$$

$$S_B = 1.1 \times 0.03 = 0.033 \Rightarrow D_B = 4 \times 0.033 = 0.132 \text{ second}$$

The analysis of the changed systems is as follows:

$$U_{CPU} = XD_{CPU} = 3 \times 0.208 = 0.624$$

$$U_A = XD_A = 3 \times 0.14 = 0.42$$

$$U_B = XD_B = 3 \times 0.132 = 0.396$$

$$R_{CPU} = S_{CPU}/(1 - U_{CPU}) = 0.013/(1 - 0.624) = 0.0346 \text{ second}$$

$$R_A = S_A/(1 - U_A) = 0.02/(1 - 0.42) = 0.0345 \text{ second}$$

$$R_B = S_B/(1 - U_B) = 0.033/(1 - 0.396) = 0.0546 \text{ second}$$

$$R = 16 \times 0.0346 + 7 \times 0.0345 + 4 \times 0.0546 = 1.013 \text{ seconds}$$

Thus, if we use a cache for disk B, the server response time will improve by $(1.406 - 1.013)/1.406 = 28\%$.

The third question requires adjusting V_A and V_B. We assume that there is enough space on disk A to be able to accommodate all files on both disks. The analysis is as follows:

$$V_B = 0$$

$$V_A = 7 + 8 = 15$$

$$D_{CPU} = 0.16 \text{ second (as before)}$$

$$D_A = 15 \times 0.02 = 0.3 \text{ second}$$

$$U_{CPU} = XD_{CPU} = 3 \times 0.16 = 0.48$$

$$U_A = XD_A = 3 \times 0.3 = 0.90$$

$$R_{CPU} = S_{CPU}/(1 - U_{CPU}) = 0.01/(1 - 0.48) = 0.0192 \text{ second}$$

$$R_A = S_A/(1 - U_A) = 0.02/(1 - 0.90) = 0.2 \text{ second}$$

$$R = 16 \times 0.0192 + 15 \times 0.2 = 3.31 \text{ seconds}$$

Thus, if we replace the two disks by one, the server response time will degrade by a factor of $3.31/1.406 = 2.35$.   ☐

34.2   MEAN-VALUE ANALYSIS

Mean-Value Analysis (MVA) allows solving closed queueing networks in a manner similar to that used for open queueing networks in Section 34.1. As the name implies, it gives the mean performance. The variance computation is not possible using this technique. Mean-value analysis applies to networks with a variety of service disciplines and service time distributions. However, we will initially limit our discussion here to fixed-capacity service centers. Delay centers are considered later in this section. Load-dependent service centers are considered in Section 36.1.

Given a closed queueing network with N jobs, Reiser and Lavenberg (1980) showed that the response time of the ith device is given by

$$R_i(N) = S_i[1 + Q_i(N - 1)] \tag{34.3}$$

Here, $Q_i(N - 1)$ is the mean queue length at the ith device with $N - 1$ jobs in the network. Notice the similarity between this equation and Equation (34.1) for open queueing networks. As before, one way to explain this equation is to consider what happens when we add a tagged Nth job to the network with $N - 1$ jobs. On arrival at the ith service center, the tagged job sees $Q_i(N - 1)$ jobs ahead (including the one in service) and expects to wait $Q_i(N - 1)S_i$ seconds before receiving service. Including the service time for itself, the job should expect a total response time of $S_i[1 + Q_i(N - 1)]$.

It should be pointed out that Equation (34.3) is not an operational law. It assumes that the service is memoryless, an assumption that is not operationally testable.

Given the performance for $N - 1$ users, Equation (34.3), along with the operation laws discussed earlier in Chapter 33, is sufficient to allow us to compute the performance for N users. Since the performance with no users ($N = 0$) can be easily computed, performance for any number of users can be computed iteratively, as we show next.

Given the response times at individual devices, the system response time using the general response time law is

$$R(N) = \sum_{i=1}^{M} V_i R_i(N)$$

The system throughput using the interactive response time law is

$$X(N) = \frac{N}{R(N) + Z} \tag{34.4}$$

The device throughputs measured in terms of jobs per second are

$$X_i(N) = X(N)V_i \tag{34.5}$$

The device queue lengths with N jobs in the network using Little's law are

$$Q_i(N) = X_i(N)R_i(N) = X(N)V_i R_i(N) \tag{34.6}$$

The equations developed so far assumed all devices to be fixed-capacity queueing centers. If a device is a delay center (infinite servers), there is no waiting before service, and therefore, the response time is equal to the service time regardless of the queue length. As discussed earlier in Section 33.5, the queue length in this case denotes the number of jobs receiving service. Thus, the response time equation for delay centers is simply

$$R_i(N) = S_i \tag{34.7}$$

Box 34.2   MVA Algorithm

Inputs:

N = number of users

Z = think time

M = number of devices (not including terminals)

S_i = service time per visit to the ith device

V_i = number of visits to the ith device

Outputs:

X = system throughput

Q_i = average number of jobs at the ith device

R_i = response time of the ith device

R = system response time

U_i = utilization of the ith device

Initialization: FOR $i = 1$ TO M DO $Q_i = 0$

Iterations:

FOR $n = 1$ TO N DO

BEGIN

$$\text{FOR } i = 1 \text{ TO } M \text{ DO } R_i = \begin{cases} S_i(1 + Q_i) & \text{Fixed capacity} \\ S_i & \text{Delay centers} \end{cases}$$

$$R = \sum_{i=1}^{M} R_i V_i$$

$$X = \frac{N}{Z + R}$$

FOR $i = 1$ TO M DO $Q_i = X V_i R_i$

END

Device throughputs: $X_i = X V_i$

Device utilizations: $U_i = X S_i V_i$

Equations (34.5) and (34.6) for device throughputs and queue lengths apply to delay centers as well.

Equations (34.3) to (34.7) define one iteration of MVA. The procedure is initialized for $N = 0$ users as follows:

$$Q_i(0) = 0$$

The complete procedure is described in Box 34.2.

Example 34.2 Consider the queueing network model of Figure 32.8. Each user request makes ten I/O requests to disk A and five I/O requests to disk B. The service times per visit to disk A and disk B are 300 and 200 milliseconds, respectively. Each request takes 2 seconds of CPU time, and the user think time is 4 seconds. Let us analyze this system using MVA.

The system parameters are

$$S_A = 0.3, \quad V_A = 10 \Rightarrow D_A = 3$$
$$S_B = 0.2, \quad V_B = 5 \Rightarrow D_B = 1$$
$$D_{CPU} = 2, \quad V_{CPU} = V_A + V_B + 1 = 16 \Rightarrow S_{CPU} = 0.125$$
$$Z = 4, \quad N = 20$$

Initialization:

Number of users: $N = 0$

Device queue lengths: $Q_{CPU} = 0, \quad Q_A = 0, \quad Q_B = 0$

Iteration 1
Number of users: $N = 1$
Device response times:

$$R_{CPU} = S_{CPU}(1 + Q_{CPU}) = 0.125(1 + 0) = 0.125$$
$$R_A = S_A(1 + Q_A) = 0.3(1 + 0) = 0.3$$
$$R_B = S_B(1 + Q_B) = 0.2(1 + 0) = 0.2$$

System response time:

$$R = R_{CPU}V_{CPU} + R_A V_A + R_B V_B = 0.125 \times 16 + 0.3 \times 10 + 0.2 \times 5 = 6$$

System throughput:

$$X = N/(R + Z) = 1/(6 + 4) = 0.1$$

Device queue lengths:

$$Q_{CPU} = X R_{CPU}V_{CPU} = 0.1 \times 0.125 \times 16 = 0.2$$
$$Q_A = X R_A V_A = 0.1 \times 0.3 \times 10 = 0.3$$
$$Q_B = X R_B V_B = 0.1 \times 0.2 \times 5 = 0.1$$

Iteration 2
Number of users: $N = 2$
Device response times:

$$R_{CPU} = S_{CPU}(1 + Q_{CPU}) = 0.125(1 + 0.2) = 0.15$$
$$R_A = S_A(1 + Q_A) = 0.3(1 + 0.3) = 0.39$$
$$R_B = S_B(1 + Q_B) = 0.2(1 + 0.1) = 0.22$$

TABLE 34.1   MVA Results for Example 34.2

Iteration No.	Response Time				System Throughput	Queue Lengths		
	CPU	Disk A	Disk B	System		CPU	Disk A	Disk B
1	0.125	0.300	0.200	6.000	0.100	0.200	0.300	0.100
2	0.150	0.390	0.220	7.400	0.175	0.421	0.684	0.193
3	0.178	0.505	0.239	9.088	0.229	0.651	1.158	0.273
4	0.206	0.647	0.255	11.051	0.266	0.878	1.721	0.338
5	0.235	0.816	0.268	13.256	0.290	1.088	2.365	0.388
⋮	⋮	⋮	⋮	⋮	⋮	⋮	⋮	⋮
17	0.370	3.962	0.300	47.045	0.333	1.974	13.195	0.499
18	0.372	4.259	0.300	50.032	0.333	1.981	14.187	0.499
19	0.373	4.556	0.300	53.022	0.333	1.987	15.181	0.500
20	0.373	4.854	0.300	56.016	0.333	1.991	16.177	0.500

System response time:

$$R = R_{CPU}V_{CPU} + R_A V_A + R_B V_B = 0.15 \times 16 + 0.39 \times 10 + 0.22 \times 5 = 7.4$$

System throughput:

$$X = N/(R + Z) = 2/(7.4 + 4) = 0.175$$

Device queue lengths:

$$Q_{CPU} = X R_{CPU} V_{CPU} = 0.175 \times 0.15 \times 16 = 0.421$$

$$Q_A = X R_A V_A = 0.175 \times 0.39 \times 10 = 0.684$$

$$Q_B = X R_B V_B = 0.175 \times 0.22 \times 5 = 0.193$$

The iterations can be continued for higher values of N. They can be easily implemented using any spreadsheet software package. The response times, throughputs, and queue lengths at the end of these iterations are listed in Table 34.1.   □

Note that MVA is applicable only if the network is a product form network. This means that the network should satisfy the conditions of job flow balance, one-step behavior, and device homogeneity, as described in Section 32.2. In addition, the analysis, as presented here, assumes that all service centers are either fixed-capacity service centers or delay centers. In both cases, we assumed exponentially distributed service times.

34.3   APPROXIMATE MVA

Mean-value analysis is a recursive algorithm. Computation of performance with N jobs in the network requires knowledge of performance with $N - 1$

jobs. Since performance with $N = 0$ is trivially known, we always start the analysis with $N = 0$ and compute the performance for $N = 1, 2, \ldots$ successively. For small values of N, this procedure is not computationally too expensive. However, for large values of N, particularly if the performance for smaller values of N is not required, it would be preferable to avoid this recursion. Several approximate analysis techniques have been developed with this goal. Here we describe one such approximation technique known as **Schweitzer's approximation**. It avoids the recursion in MVA by appropriately estimating the queue lengths with N jobs and computing the response times and throughputs. The values so computed can be used to recompute the queue lengths, and if the previous estimate was good, the new computed value would be close to the estimate.

The approximation, due to Schweitzer (1979), is based on the assumption that as the number of jobs in a network increases, the queue length at each device increases proportionately. For example, doubling the number of jobs in the network will result in doubling the number of jobs at each device. Analytically:

$$\frac{Q_i(N)}{N} = a_i \text{ (constant)} \qquad \forall N$$

In particular, this implies

$$\frac{Q_i(N-1)}{N-1} = \frac{Q_i(N)}{N}$$

or

$$Q_i(N-1) = \frac{N-1}{N} Q_i(N)$$

The MVA equations can therefore be written as follows:

$$R_i(N) = \begin{cases} S_i(1 + \frac{N-1}{N} Q_i(N)) & \text{(fixed-capacity centers)} \\ S_i & \text{(delay centers)} \end{cases}$$

$$X(N) = \frac{N}{Z + \sum V_i R_i(N)}$$

$$Q_i(N) = X(N) V_i R_i(N)$$

Notice that the each iteration starts with some values for number of jobs $Q_i(N)$ at various devices and ends by recomputing new values for $Q_i(N)$. If the new values are not close to the values at the start of the iteration, we need to continue iterating. If they are sufficiently close, we stop. There is no guarantee that the successive iterations will converge. However, Bard (1979) tried several cases and found that it converges in almost all cases.

The initial values for queue lengths should not affect the final result, although they may affect the number of iterations required. One alternative is to start with all queue lengths being equal.

Box 34.3   MVA Algorithm Using Schweitzer's Approximation
Inputs:
N = number of users
Z = think time
M = number of devices (not including terminals)
S_i = service time per visit to the ith device
V_i = number of visits to the ith device
ϵ = maximum allowable error in queue length

Outputs:
X = system throughput
Q_i = average number of jobs at the ith device
R_i = response time of the ith device
R = system response time
U_i = utilization of the ith device

Initialization:
$X = 0$
FOR $i = 1$ TO M DO $Q_i = N/M$

Iteration:
WHILE $\max_i\{|Q_i - X R_i V_i|\} > \epsilon$ DO
BEGIN

$\quad$ FOR $i = 1$ TO M DO $R_i = \begin{cases} S_i\left(1 + \dfrac{N-1}{N}Q_i\right) & \text{Fixed capacity} \\ S_i & \text{Delay centers} \end{cases}$

$$R = \sum_{i=1}^{M} R_i V_i$$

$$X = \frac{N}{Z + R}$$

$\quad$ FOR $i = 1$ TO M DO $Q_i = X V_i R_i$

END

Device throughputs: $X_i = X V_i$
Device utilizations: $U_i = X S_i V_i$

The complete MVA algorithm using Schweitzer's approximation is summarized in Box 34.3.

Example 34.3   Consider again the timesharing system of Example 34.2. Let us analyze this model using Schweitzer's approximation when there are

20 users on the system. The stopping criterion is to stop when the maximum absolute change in every queue length is less than 0.01.

The system parameters are

$$S_A = 0.3, \qquad V_A = 10 \Rightarrow D_A = 3$$

$$S_B = 0.2, \qquad V_B = 5 \Rightarrow D_B = 1$$

$$D_{\text{CPU}} = 2, \qquad V_{\text{CPU}} = V_A + V_B + 1 = 16 \Rightarrow S_{\text{CPU}} = 0.125$$

$$Z = 4, \qquad N = 20$$

To initialize the queue lengths, we assume that the 20 jobs are equally distributed among the three queues of CPU, disk A, and disk B:

$$Q_{\text{CPU}} = Q_A = Q_B = \tfrac{20}{3} = 6.67$$

Iteration 1
Device response times:

$$R_{\text{CPU}} = S_{\text{CPU}}(1 + Q_{\text{CPU}}) = 0.125(1 + 6.77) = 0.92$$

$$R_A = S_A(1 + Q_A) = 0.3(1 + 6.77) = 2.20$$

$$R_B = S_B(1 + Q_B) = 0.2(1 + 6.77) = 1.47$$

System response time:

$$R = R_{\text{CPU}}V_{\text{CPU}} + R_A V_A + R_B V_B = 0.92 \times 16 + 2.20 \times 10 + 1.47 \times 5 = 44$$

System throughput:

$$X = N/(R + Z) = 20/(44 + 4) = 0.42$$

Device queue lengths:

$$Q_{\text{CPU}} = X R_{\text{CPU}} V_{\text{CPU}} = 0.42 \times 0.92 \times 16 = 6.11$$

$$Q_A = X R_A V_A = 0.42 \times 2.20 \times 10 = 9.17$$

$$Q_B = X R_B V_B = 0.42 \times 1.47 \times 5 = 3.06$$

Maximum absolute change in device queue lengths:

$$\Delta Q = \max\{|6.67 - 6.11|, |6.67 - 9.17|, |6.67 - 3.06|\}$$

$$= \max\{0.56, 2.5, 3.61\} = 3.61$$

Since the maximum absolute change in queue lengths is more than our stopping criterion of 0.01, we continue with the second iteration. In fact, it requires 16 iterations before satisfying the stopping criterion. The response times, throughputs, and queue lengths at the end of these iterations are listed in Table 34.2.

In this example, we used a stopping criterion of $\Delta Q \leq 0.01$. Other alternatives, although not as good, are to stop when the relative change in response time or throughput is below a certain threshold.   □

TABLE 34.2   Results for Example 34.3

Iteration No.	Response Time				System Throughput	Queue Lengths		
	CPU	Disk A	Disk B	System		CPU	Disk A	Disk B
1	0.92	2.20	1.47	44.00	0.42	6.11	9.17	3.06
2	0.85	2.91	0.78	46.64	0.39	5.38	11.50	1.54
3	0.76	3.58	0.49	50.46	0.37	4.49	13.14	0.90
4	0.66	4.05	0.37	52.83	0.35	3.70	14.24	0.65
5	0.56	4.36	0.32	54.23	0.34	3.10	14.97	0.56
6	0.49	4.57	0.31	55.08	0.34	2.67	15.45	0.52
7	0.44	4.70	0.30	55.62	0.34	2.37	15.78	0.50
8	0.41	4.80	0.30	55.97	0.33	2.17	16.00	0.49
9	0.38	4.86	0.29	56.20	0.33	2.04	16.15	0.49
10	0.37	4.90	0.29	56.35	0.33	1.94	16.25	0.48
11	0.36	4.93	0.29	56.45	0.33	1.88	16.31	0.48
12	0.35	4.95	0.29	56.52	0.33	1.84	16.35	0.48
13	0.34	4.96	0.29	56.57	0.33	1.82	16.38	0.48
14	0.34	4.97	0.29	56.59	0.33	1.80	16.40	0.48
15	0.34	4.97	0.29	56.61	0.33	1.79	16.41	0.48
16	0.34	4.98	0.29	56.63	0.33	1.78	16.42	0.48

The approximate analysis of queueing networks is an active area of research. The majority of new papers on queueing theory introduce approximations of one kind or another. Unfortunately, there are only a few approximation techniques that are used again by their inventors, and even fewer are used by people other than the inventors. Schweitzer's approximation discussed in this section is one of those exceptional approximation techniques that has been used and discussed by many researchers.

One of the common mistakes we find in papers proposing approximate queueing techniques is that the authors compare the results obtained from their technique and those from a simulation to show that the error in throughput is small. The fact, on the contrary, is that a small error in throughput does not imply that the approximation is satisfactory. The same applies to device utilizations and the system response time. In spite of a small error in any of these, the error in the device queue lengths may be quite large. It is easy to see this from Table 34.2. There we see that the throughput reaches close to its final value within five iterations, while the response time reaches close to its final value within six iterations. The queue lengths take the longest to stabilize.

Another way to understand the relative magnitude of errors in throughput, response time, and queue lengths is to look at Figures 34.1 and 34.2, which show the system throughput and the system response times as obtained from the Schweitzer approximation. The number of users is varied from 1 to 20, and in each case we start the iterations with queue lengths initialized at N/M and stop arbitrarily after five iterations. Also shown in the figures are the throughput and response time as obtained using the exact MVA. Finally, Figure 34.3

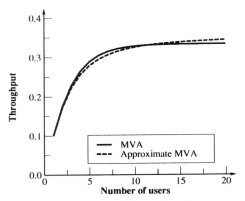

FIGURE 34.1   Throughput with exact MVA and five iterations of approximate MVA.

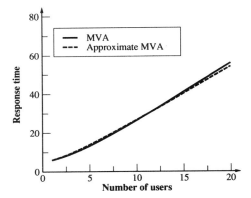

FIGURE 34.2   Response time with exact MVA and five iterations of approximate MVA.

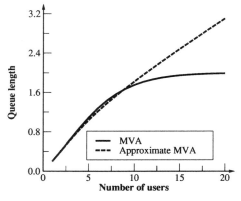

FIGURE 34.3   The CPU queue length with exact MVA and five iterations of approximate MVA.

shows the CPU queue length. Notice that for all values of N, the error in throughput is small, the error in response time is slightly larger, and the error in queue lengths is the largest. The error in queue lengths thus gives a better measure of the goodness of an approximation technique. For the same reason, a stopping criterion based on changes in queue lengths is better than one based on system throughput or response time.

34.4 BALANCED JOB BOUNDS

The asymptotic bounds presented earlier in Section 33.6 are applicable under very general conditions since very few assumptions are required for their derivation. However, they are only one sided in the sense that it is not possible to put a good lower bound on throughput or an upper bound on the response time. Zahorjan et al. (1982) derived a set of two-sided bounds based on the observation that a balanced system has a better performance than a similar unbalanced system. These bounds, called **balanced job bounds**, are presented in this section.

A system without a bottleneck device is called a **balanced system**. In such a system, total service time demands on all devices are equal. This is a preferable system in the sense that no single device is the bottleneck. An unbalanced system's performance can always be improved by replacing the bottleneck device with a faster device. As we improve the bottleneck device, the system performance improves until another device becomes a bottleneck. Based on this argument, the response time and throughput of a timesharing system can be bounded as follows:

$$\max\left\{ND_{\max} - Z, D + (N-1)D_{\text{avg}}\frac{D}{D+Z}\right\}$$

$$\leq R(N) \leq D + (N-1)D_{\max}\frac{(N-1)D}{(N-1)D+Z} \tag{34.8}$$

$$\frac{N}{Z + D + (N-1)D_{\max}\dfrac{(N-1)D}{(N-1)D+Z}}$$

$$\leq X(N) \leq \min\left\{\frac{1}{D_{\max}}, \frac{N}{Z + D + (N-1)D_{\text{avg}}\dfrac{D}{D+Z}}\right\} \tag{34.9}$$

Here, $D_{\text{avg}} = D/M$ is the average service demand per device. Equations (34.8) and (34.9) are known as **balanced job bounds**. These bounds are very tight in that the upper and lower bounds are very close to each other and to the actual performance.

For batch systems, the bounds can be obtained by substituting $Z = 0$ in Equations (34.8) and (34.9).

In this section we assume that all service centers except terminals are fixed-capacity service centers. Terminals are represented by delay centers. No other delay centers are allowed because the presence of delay centers invalidates several arguments related to D_{max} and D_{avg}.

Proof 34.1 The derivation of the balanced job bounds consists of the following steps:

1. Derive an expression for the throughput and response time of a balanced system.
2. Given an unbalanced system, construct a corresponding "best case" balanced system such that the number of devices is the same and the sum of demands is identical in the balanced and unbalanced systems. This produces the upper bounds on the performance.
3. Construct a corresponding "worst case" balanced system such that each device has a demand equal to the bottleneck and the number of devices is adjusted to make the sum of demands identical in the balanced and unbalanced systems. This produces the lower bounds on performance.

We now derive the bounds following these steps.

Any timesharing system can be divided into two subsystems: the terminal subsystem consisting of terminals only and the **central subsystem** consisting of the remaining devices. Consider a system whose central subsystem is balanced in the sense that all M devices have the same total service demand:

$$D_i = \frac{D}{M}$$

Here, D is the sum of total service demands on the M devices. The device response times using MVA (discussed in Section 34.2) are given by

$$R_i(N) = S_i\{1 + Q_i(N-1)\}, \qquad i = 1,2,\ldots,M$$

Since the system is balanced, all Q_i's are equal, and we have

$$Q_i(N-1) = \frac{Q(N-1)}{M}$$

Here, $Q(j)$ (without any subscript) denotes the total number of jobs in the central subsystem when there are j jobs in the system. The number of jobs in the terminal subsystem is $j - Q(j)$.

The system response time is given by

$$R(N) = \sum_{i=1}^{M} V_i R_i(N) = \sum_{i=1}^{M} \frac{D}{M}\left(1 + \frac{Q(N-1)}{M}\right)$$

or

$$R(N) = D + \frac{D}{M}Q(N-1)$$

A noniterative procedure to bound $Q(N)$ is based on the following arguments. If we replace the system with N workstations so that each user has
his/her own workstation and the workstations are identical to the original
system, then the new environment would have a better response time and
better throughput. As a result, the users will be spending less of their time
waiting for the response. The new environment consists of N single-user
systems and is therefore easy to model. Each user spends his/her time in
cycles consisting of Z units of time thinking and D units of time computing. Each job has a probability $D/(D+Z)$ of being in the central subsystem
(not at the terminal). Thus

$$\frac{Q(N)}{N} \geq \frac{D}{D+Z} \qquad (34.10)$$

Now consider another environment like the previous one except that each
user is given a workstation that is N times slower than the system being
modeled. This new environment has a total computing power equivalent to
the original system but there is no sharing. The users would be spending
more time in the central subsystem. That is,

$$\frac{Q(N)}{N} \leq \frac{ND}{ND+Z} \qquad (34.11)$$

Equations (34.10) and (34.11) combined together result in the following
bounds on the number of jobs at the devices:

$$\frac{D}{D+Z} \leq \frac{Q(N)}{N} \leq \frac{ND}{ND+Z}$$

or

$$(N-1)\frac{D}{D+Z} \leq Q(N-1) \leq (N-1)\frac{(N-1)D}{(N-1)D+Z}$$

In terms of response time, this results in the following bounds:

$$D + \frac{D}{M}(N-1)\frac{D}{D+Z} \leq R(N) \leq D + \frac{D}{M}(N-1)\frac{(N-1)D}{(N-1)D+Z}$$

This completes the first step of the derivation.

Suppose we have an unbalanced system such that the service demands
on the ith device is D_i. Without loss of generality, we can assume that
the devices in the central system are numbered such that the demands
$D_1, D_2, \ldots, D_M$ are in a nondecreasing order. In this case, the Mth device
is the slowest (bottleneck) device and the first device is the fastest device. We now perform the following experiment. We make the bottleneck
device slightly faster and the fastest device slightly slower. We reduce the

service time of the bottleneck device by a small amount ΔD and increase the service time of the fastest device by ΔD. The change in the bottleneck device improves the performance while that in the fastest device may degrade the performance slightly. Since the system performance is more sensitive to the bottleneck than any other device, the net effect should be an increase in performance. We continue this process until the bottleneck device's demand matches that of another device. At this point we will have two bottlenecks. We take the two fastest devices and two slowest devices in the system and continue reducing the service demands of bottlenecks while increasing the service demands of the fast devices. This will improve performance until a third device joins the bottleneck group. At this point, we add a third device to the "fast" group and keep the changes going. In the end we will have a balanced system with all devices having service demands $D_i = D_{avg}$, where

$$D_{avg} = \frac{1}{M} \sum_{i=1}^{M} D_i$$

This balanced system has a better performance (higher throughput and lower response time) than that of the original unbalanced system. This observation leads us to the following bounds on the performance of the unbalanced system:

$$R(N) \geq D + (N-1)D_{avg}\frac{D}{D+Z} \tag{34.12}$$

and

$$X(N) \leq \frac{N}{Z + D + (N-1)D_{avg}\dfrac{D}{D+Z}} \tag{34.13}$$

The expressions on the right-hand side are for the balanced system. This completes the second step of the derivation.

Now consider another experiment on the unbalanced system. All devices that have a demand equal to D_{max} (same as the bottleneck) are removed from the set of devices to be considered for change. From the remaining set, we take the fastest device and the slowest device. Let us say that these are the devices numbered 1 and k, respectively. Ordinarily, $k = M - 1$ unless $D_{M-1} = D_M$, in which case we take the highest k such that $D_k \neq D_M$. We reduce the service demand on the fastest device by a small amount ΔD and increase that on the kth device by the same amount. The change in the fastest device would improve the performance slightly, but the change in the kth device would degrade the performance considerably. The net effect would be a decrease in performance. We continue this process until either the service demand on the fastest device is reduced to zero or that of the kth device reaches D_{max}. Any device that has either zero demand or a demand equal to D_{max} is removed from the set of devices to be changed. We select the fastest and the slowest devices from the remaining set and continue the experiment. At the end, we would have a balanced system in which $M' = D/D_{max}$ devices have nonzero demands each equal to D_{max}; the remaining devices have zero demands and can therefore be deleted from the system. Since every change degraded the performance, the performance of this new balanced system should be worse than that of the original unbalanced system. In other words,

$$D + (N-1)D_{max}\frac{(N-1)D}{(N-1)D+Z} \geq R(N)$$

$$\frac{N}{Z + D + (N-1)D_{max}\dfrac{(N-1)D}{(N-1)D+Z}} \leq X(N)$$

The expressions on the left-hand side are for the balanced system.

Combining Equations (34.12), (34.13), (34.1), and (34.1) with asymptotic bounds we get the balanced job bounds.   □

The equations for the balanced job bounds are summarized in Box 34.4 and are illustrated by the following example.

Example 34.4 For the timesharing system of Example 34.2

$$D_{CPU} = 2, \qquad D_A = 3, \qquad D_B = 1, \qquad Z = 4$$

$$D = D_{CPU} + D_A + D_B = 2 + 3 + 1 = 6$$

$$D_{avg} = D/3 = 2, \qquad D_{max} = D_A = 3$$

The balanced job bounds (BJBs) are

$$\frac{N}{4 + 6 + (N-1)2\dfrac{6(N-1)}{6(N-1)+4}} \leq X(N) \leq \min\left\{\frac{1}{3}, \frac{N}{4 + 6 + (N-1)3\dfrac{6}{6+4}}\right\}$$

$$\max\left\{3N - 4, 6 + (N-1)3\frac{6}{6+4}\right\} \geq R(N) \leq 6 + (N-1)2\frac{6(N-1)}{6(N-1)+4}$$

The bounds are listed in Table 34.3 and are shown by broken lines in Figure 34.4. The exact throughputs and response times obtained in Example 34.2 are shown in the figures by solid lines.   □

Box 34.4   Balanced Job Bounds

Inputs:

N = number of users

Z = think time

M = number of devices (not including terminals)

S_i = service time per visit to the ith device

V_i = number of visits to the ith device

Outputs:

X_{min} = lower bound on system throughput

X_{max} = upper bound on system throughput

R_{min} = lower bound on system response time

R_{max} = upper bound on system response time

$X_{i,min}$ = lower bound on throughput of the ith device

$X_{i,max}$ = upper bound on throughput of the ith device

$U_{i,min}$ = lower bound on utilization of the ith device

$U_{i,max}$ = upper bound on utilization of the ith device

Initialization:

$D_{max} = \max_i\{D_i\}$

$D = \sum_{i=1}^{M} D_i$

$D_{avg} = D/M$

Iterations:

FOR $n = 1$ TO N DO

BEGIN

$$R_{min}(n) = \min\left\{ nD_{max} - Z, D + (n-1)\frac{D_{avg}}{1 + Z/D} \right\}$$

$$R_{max}(n) = D + (n-1)\frac{D_{max}}{1 + Z/[(n-1)D]}$$

$$X_{min}(n) = n/[Z + R_{max}(n)]$$

$$X_{max}(n) = n/[Z + R_{min}(n)]$$

  FOR $i = 1$ TO M DO

BEGIN

$$X_{i,min}(n) = X_{min}(n)V_i$$

$$X_{i,max}(n) = X_{max}(n)V_i$$

$$U_{i,min}(n) = X_{min}(n)D_i$$

$$U_{i,max}(n) = X_{max}(n)D_i$$

  END

END

TABLE 34.3 Balanced Job Bounds for the System of Example 34.4

	Response Time			Throughput		
N	Lower BJB	MVA	Upper BJB	Lower BJB	MVA	Upper BJB
1	6.000	6.000	6.000	0.100	0.100	0.100
2	7.200	7.400	7.800	0.169	0.175	0.179
3	8.400	9.088	10.500	0.207	0.229	0.242
4	9.600	11.051	13.364	0.230	0.266	0.294
5	11.000	13.256	16.286	0.246	0.290	0.333
⋮	⋮	⋮	⋮	⋮	⋮	⋮
15	41.000	41.089	46.091	0.299	0.333	0.333
16	44.000	44.064	49.085	0.301	0.333	0.333
17	47.000	47.045	52.080	0.303	0.333	0.333
18	50.000	50.032	55.075	0.305	0.333	0.333
19	53.000	53.022	58.071	0.306	0.333	0.333
20	56.000	56.016	61.068	0.307	0.333	0.333

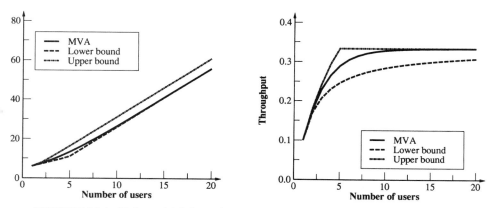

FIGURE 34.4 Balanced job bounds on the response time and the throughput.

EXERCISES

34.1 A transaction processing system can be modeled by an open queueing network shown in Figure 32.1. The transactions arrive at a rate of 0.8 transactions per second, use 1 second of CPU time, make 20 I/O's to disk A and 4 I/O's to disk B. Thus, the total number of visits to the CPU is 25. The disk service times are 30 and 25 milliseconds, respectively. Determine the average number of transactions in the system and the average response time.

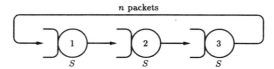

FIGURE 34.5   Model of a 2-hop computer network.

34.2 For the system of Exercise 33.6, use MVA to compute the system throughput and response time for $N = 1, \ldots, 5$ interactive users.

34.3 Repeat Exercise 34.2 using Schweitzer's approximation to MVA with $N = 5$ users. Use a starting value of $\frac{5}{3}$ for each of the three-device queue lengths and stop after five iterations.

34.4 A 2-hop computer network with a "flow control window size" of n is represented by the closed queueing network shown in Figure 34.5. Assuming that the network is balanced in that each computer takes the same service time S to process a packet and that each packet makes one visit to each queue, determine the network throughput and response time as a function of n for $n = 1, \ldots, 5$ using MVA. Write an expression for $X(n)$ and $R(n)$.

34.5 Repeat Exercise 34.4 for an h-hop computer network. Such a network will have $h + 1$ queues connected in a ring. Write an expression for "network power," which is defined as the ratio of throughput to the response time. Determine the window size n that gives the maximum network power.

34.6 Write the expressions for balanced bounds on the system throughput and response time of the system of Exercise 33.6 and compute the bounds for up to $N = 5$ users.

34.7 Consider a balanced, closed queueing network consisting of M fixed-capacity service centers (no terminals). The service demand on each center is $D_i = D/M$. For this system:

    a. Using MVA, develop an expression for the throughput and response time of the system as a function of the number of jobs N in the network.

    b. Write expressions for balanced job bounds on the system throughput and response times for this system.

    c. Verify that the bounds are tight in the sense that both upper and lower bounds are identical. Also, verify that the bounds are equal to the exact value obtained using MVA.

CHAPTER 35

CONVOLUTION ALGORITHM

Technology is dominated by two types of people: those who understand what they do not manage and those who manage what they do not understand.

—Archibald Putt

The mean-value analysis presented in Section 34.2 provides a simple algorithm for finding the average queue lengths and response times of various devices in computer systems. Although the average values are sufficient in many cases, sometimes one may want to find more detailed information, such as the distribution or variance of queue lengths and response times. For example, in a two-disk computer system, one may want to know what the probability is of both disks being busy at the same time or what the probability is of having more than five jobs at a disk. Such questions, which cannot be answered using MVA, can be answered using the convolution algorithm presented in this chapter. Although, historically, the convolution algorithm was discovered before MVA, in this book we present it after MVA since it is more complex and needs to be used only if MVA cannot provide the desired answer.

35.1 DISTRIBUTION OF JOBS IN A SYSTEM

The equations used in convolution algorithm are explained in two steps. Initially, all service centers in the closed queueing network are assumed to be load independent, that is, the service time per job does not depend upon the queue length. Thus, terminals are not allowed initially. They are considered in Section 35.4. For extensions to general load-dependent service centers, see Buzen (1973).

At any instant, the state of such a network is given by the number of jobs at various devices and is represented by the vector $\mathbf{n} = \{n_1, n_2, \ldots, n_M\}$. Here, n_i is the number of jobs at the ith device. Gordon and Newell (1967) showed that the probability of the system being in state $\mathbf{n}$ is

$$P(n_1, n_2, \ldots, n_M) = \frac{D_1^{n_1} D_2^{n_2} \cdots D_M^{n_M}}{G(N)} \tag{35.1}$$

Here, D_i is the total service demand per job for the ith device, $N = \sum n_i$ is the total number of jobs in the system, and $G(N)$ is a normalizing constant such that the probabilities for all states add to 1:

$$G(N) = \sum_{\mathbf{n}} \left(D_1^{n_1} D_2^{n_2} \cdots D_M^{n_M} \right) \tag{35.2}$$

One of the problems with this formula is that the value of $G(N)$ may become too large and may exceed the floating-point range of some computer systems. In some cases, it may become too small near the lower end of the floating-point range, causing significant errors in computation. Such overflow and underflow problems can be avoided by scaling all service demands D_i by a suitable constant α before computing $G(N)$. Let $y_i = \alpha D_i$ be the scaled service demand for the ith device. Then, Equations (35.1) and (35.2) become

$$P(n_1, n_2, \ldots, n_M) = \frac{y_1^{n_1} y_2^{n_2} \cdots y_M^{n_M}}{G(N)}$$

$$G(N) = \sum_{\mathbf{n}} \left(y_1^{n_1} y_2^{n_2} \cdots y_M^{n_M} \right)$$

When selecting scaling factors, the scaled values should neither be too large nor too small compared to 1. One such choice would be

$$\alpha = \frac{1}{(1/M) \sum_{i=1}^{M} D_i}$$

In any case, the choice of α should not affect the probabilities. The following example illustrates the use of α.

Example 35.1   Consider a batch computer system consisting of a processor and two disks. It can be represented by the closed central server model shown in Figure 32.2.

The service times are 39 milliseconds per visit to CPU, 180 milliseconds per visit to disk A, and 260 milliseconds per visit to disk B. Each batch job makes 13 I/O requests to disk A and 6 I/O requests to the disk B. We would like to compute the state probabilities when the multiprogramming level

TABLE 35.1 Computing System State Probabilities Using Gordon and Newell's Method

Number of Jobs at			Numerator,	
CPU	Disk A	Disk B	$\prod_i y_i^{n_i}$	Probability
0	0	3	8	0.089
0	1	2	12	0.133
0	2	1	18	0.200
0	3	0	27	0.300
1	0	2	4	0.044
1	1	1	6	0.067
1	2	0	9	0.100
2	0	1	2	0.022
2	1	0	3	0.033
3	0	0	1	0.011
			$G(N) = 90$	1.000

is 3:

Service times: $S_{CPU} = 0.039,$ $S_A = 0.18,$ $S_B = 0.26$

Visit ratios: $V_{CPU} = 13 + 6 + 1 = 20,$ $V_A = 13,$ $V_B = 6$

Total service demands are

$$D_{CPU} = 20 \times 0.039 = 0.78$$

$$D_A = 13 \times 0.18 = 2.34$$

$$D_B = 6 \times 0.26 = 1.56$$

For the scaling factor, we arbitrarily choose $\alpha = 1/0.78$. This results in $y_{CPU} = 1$, $y_A = 3$, and $y_B = 2$.

The system can be in any of the 10 states. These states and their probabilities are shown in Table 35.1. For each state, we first determine the product $\prod_i y_i^{n_i}$, add all the products to find $G(N)$, and divide each individual product by $G(N)$ to get the desired probability.   □

35.2 CONVOLUTION ALGORITHM FOR COMPUTING $G(N)$

The key problem with Gordon and Newell's method as illustrated by Example 35.1 is that the computation of the normalizing constant requires us to enumerate all possible states. For a system with N jobs and M devices, the number of states is given by

$$\binom{N + M - 1}{M - 1}$$

This number is of the order of N^{M-1} and is usually very large. Buzen solved this problem by devising a simple method to compute $G(N)$. This method is called **convolution** and is based on the following mathematical identity, which is true for all k and y_i

$$\sum_{\mathbf{n}} \prod_{i=1}^{k} (y_i)^{n_i} = \sum_{\mathbf{n}|n_k=0} \prod_{i=1}^{k} (y_i)^{n_i} + \sum_{\mathbf{n}|n_k>0} \prod_{i=1}^{k} (y_i)^{n_i} \tag{35.3}$$

$$= \sum_{\mathbf{n}|n_k=0} \prod_{i=1}^{k} (y_i)^{n_i} + y_k \sum_{\mathbf{n}^-} \prod_{i=1}^{k} (y_i)^{n_i} \tag{35.4}$$

Here, $\mathbf{n}$ is the set of all possible state vectors $\{n_1, n_2, \ldots, n_k\}$ such that $\sum_{i=1}^{k} n_i = n$; and $\mathbf{n}^-$ is the set of all possible state vectors such that $\sum_i n_i = n - 1$. Equation (35.3) simply breaks the sum into two sums—a sum belonging to states in which n_k is zero and a sum belonging to the remaining states. In Equation (35.4), the second sum is rewritten so that y_k, which is common to all terms in the second sum, is factored out.

Example 35.2 Consider the central server model of Example 35.1. To compute $G(N)$, we need to compute the following sum:

$$G(N) = y_1^0 y_2^0 y_3^3 + y_1^0 y_2^1 y_3^2 + y_1^0 y_2^2 y_3^1 + y_1^0 y_2^3 y_3^0 + y_1^1 y_2^0 y_3^2$$
$$+ y_1^1 y_2^1 y_3^1 + y_1^1 y_2^2 y_3^0 + y_1^2 y_2^0 y_3^1 + y_1^2 y_2^1 y_3^0 + y_1^3 y_2^0 y_3^0$$

The powers of y_i's in this sum correspond to the 10 states (specified by number of jobs at various devices) listed in Table 35.1. By separating out the terms containing y_3^0, the sum can be rewritten as follows:

$$G(N) = (y_1^0 y_2^3 y_3^0 + y_1^1 y_2^2 y_3^0 + y_1^2 y_2^1 y_3^0 + y_1^3 y_2^0 y_3^0)$$
$$+ (y_1^0 y_2^0 y_3^3 + y_1^0 y_2^1 y_3^2 + y_1^0 y_2^2 y_3^1 + y_1^1 y_2^0 y_3^2 + y_1^1 y_2^1 y_3^1 + y_1^2 y_2^0 y_3^1)$$

Since y_3 is common to all terms in the second part, the sum can also be written as

$$G(N) = (y_1^0 y_2^3 + y_1^1 y_2^2 + y_1^2 y_2^1 + y_1^3 y_2^0)$$
$$+ y_3(y_1^0 y_2^0 y_3^2 + y_1^0 y_2^1 y_3^1 + y_1^0 y_2^2 y_3^0 + y_1^1 y_2^0 y_3^1 + y_1^1 y_2^1 y_3^0 + y_1^2 y_2^0 y_3^0)$$

Notice that the first part contains terms corresponding to the states of a system with one less device (there is no y_3) and the terms inside the parantheses in the second part correspond to the states of a system with one less user (two users instead of three). This allows the problem of determining $G(N)$ to be divided into two smaller problems.   □

If we define an auxiliary function $g(n,k)$ as

$$g(n,k) = \sum_{\mathbf{n}} \prod_{i=1}^{k} y_i^{n_i}$$

the normalizing constant $G(N) = g(N,M)$ can be computed using a sequence of iterations as follows:

$$g(n,k) = g(n,k-1) + y_k g(n-1,k) \qquad (35.5)$$

The initial values for the auxiliary function are

$$g(n,0) = 0, \qquad n = 1,2,\ldots,N \qquad (35.6)$$

$$g(0,k) = 1, \qquad k = 1,2,\ldots,M \qquad (35.7)$$

The iterative relationship specified in Equation (35.5) together with the initial conditions given in Equations (35.6) and (35.7) give a simple algorithm for computing $g(N,M)$. A tabular representation of the algorithm is shown in Table 35.2. The table has $N+1$ rows and M columns. The rows are numbered 0 to N. The ith row corresponds to $n=i$ jobs in the system, and the jth column corresponds to the jth service facility. The (n,k)th entry in the table is $g(n,k)$. It is is obtained by adding together the value immediately to its left and the value immediately above multiplied by the corresponding column variable y_k. The service demands y_k are listed as column headings in the table. The first row corresponding to $n=0$ consists of all 1's, and the leftmost column consists of successive powers of y_1. Notice that the leftmost column will be correctly initialized if it is assumed that there is a column of zeros immediately to the left of that column at the start of the algorithm.

Generally, only the rightmost column values are of interest, and therefore, it is not necessary to store the complete table. It is sufficient to store just one column, $\{G[0], G[1],\ldots, G[N]\}$, and use the following algorithm:

FOR $k \leftarrow 1$ TO M DO
FOR $n \leftarrow 1$ TO N DO
$G[n] \leftarrow G[n] + y[k] \times G[n-1]$

TABLE 35.2 Convolution Algorithm

	y_1	y_2	$\cdots$		y_k	$\cdots$	y_M
0	1	1	$\cdots$		1	$\cdots$	1
1	y_1						
2	y_1^2						
3	y_1^3						
$\vdots$	$\vdots$				$g(n-1,k)$		
					$\downarrow \times y_k$		
n	y_1^n	$g(n,k-1) \longrightarrow$			$g(n,k)$		
$\vdots$	$\vdots$						
N	y_1^N						$g(N,M)$

When the algorithm terminates, the final values of $G[1],\ldots,G[N]$ correspond to the rightmost column of Table 35.2, that is, to $g(n,M)$ for $n = 1,2,\ldots,N$. Thus, the values of $G(1),\ldots G(N-1)$ are produced as a by-product of the computation of $G(N)$.

Note that each evaluation of $G[n]$ requires one addition and one multiplication and that $G[n]$ is evaluated a total of NM times. Thus, the algorithm requires NM additions and NM multiplications for computation of $G(N)$.

Example 35.3 Consider the central server model of Example 35.1 again. Using the convolution method, we can compute $G(N)$ as shown in Table 35.3. The first row of the table is initialized to all 1's. The first column consists of successive powers of y_1, which in this case happens to be 1. Each of the remaining entries is obtained using the entry to its left and the entry above it in Equation (35.5). For example, $1+3\times 1$ gives 4; $1+3\times 4$ gives 13; $1+3\times 13$ gives 40; $4+2\times 1$ give 6; and so on.   □

TABLE 35.3 Computing Normalizing Constant for Example 35.3

n	$y_{CPU}=1$	$y_A=3$	$y_B=2$
0	1	1	1
1	1	4	6
2	1	13	25
3	1	40	90

35.3 COMPUTING PERFORMANCE USING $G(N)$

Once the $G(1),\ldots,G(N)$ are known, other performance statistics can be computed as follows:

1. *Queue Length Distributions*: The probability of having j or more jobs at the ith device is given by:

$$P(n_i \geq j) = \sum_{n|n_i\geq j} \frac{y_1^{n_1}y_2^{n_2}\cdots y_M^{n_M}}{G(N)} = y_i^j \frac{G(N-j)}{G(N)}$$

The probability of exactly j jobs at the ith device is

$$P(n_i = j) = P(n_i \geq j) - P(n_i \geq j+1)$$

$$= \frac{y_i^j}{G(N)}[G(N-j) - y_i G(N-j-1)]$$

The mean number of jobs at the ith device, $E[n_i]$, is given by

$$Q_i = E[n_i] = \sum_{j=1}^{N} P(n_i \geq j) = \sum_{j=1}^{N} y_i^j \frac{G(N-j)}{G(N)}$$

The joint probability of having j or more jobs at the ith device and l or more jobs at the kth device is

$$P(n_i \geq j, n_k \geq l) = y_i^j y_k^l \frac{G(N-j-l)}{G(N)}$$

2. *Utilizations*: The device utilization is the same as the probability of having one or more jobs at the device:

$$U_i = P(n_i \geq 1) = y_i \frac{G(N-1)}{G(N)}$$

3. *Throughputs*: The device throughputs are given by the utilization law:

$$X_i = \frac{U_i}{S_i}$$

The system throughput is given by the forced flow law:

$$X = \frac{X_i}{V_i} = \frac{U_i}{D_i} = \alpha \frac{G(N-1)}{G(N)}$$

4. *Response Times*: The mean response time of a device is given by Little's law:

$$R_i = \frac{Q_i}{X_i} = \frac{Q_i}{XV_i}$$

The mean system response time is given by the general response time law:

$$R = \sum_{i=1}^{M} R_i V_i$$

We now illustrate the algorithm using an example.

Example 35.4 Once again, consider the central server model of Example 35.1. In Example 35.3, we computed the normalizing constants for this system. From Table 35.3 we know that $G(1) = 6$, $G(2) = 25$, and $G(3) = 90$.

1. *Queue Length Distributions*: The probability of having two or more jobs at disk A is

$$P(n_A \geq 2) = y_A^2 \frac{G(N-2)}{G(N)} = 3^2 \times \frac{6}{90} = 0.6$$

We can also obtain this probability from Table 35.1 by adding the probabilities for all states in which n_A is 2 or 3. There are three such states in the table, and their probabilities are 0.2, 0.3, and 0.1, which add up to 0.6, as already computed.

The probability of exactly one job at disk A is

$$P(n_A = 1) = \frac{y_A}{G(N)} \left(G(N-1) - y_A G(N-2) \right)$$

$$= \frac{3}{90}(25 - 3 \times 6) = \frac{21}{90} = 0.233$$

Again, from Table 35.1, we see that there are three states with $n_A = 1$; the sum of their probabilities is $0.133 + 0.067 + 0.033 = 0.233$.

The probability of exactly zero, two, and three jobs at disk A can be similarly computed:

$$P(n_A = 0) = \frac{y_A^0}{G(N)}[G(N-0) - y_A G(N-1)] = \frac{90 - 3 \times 25}{90} = 0.166$$

$$P(n_A = 2) = \frac{y_A^2}{G(N)}[G(N-2) - y_A G(N-3)] = 3^2 \times \frac{6 - 3 \times 1}{90} = 0.3$$

$$P(n_A = 3) = \frac{y_A^3}{G(N)}[G(N-3) - y_A G(N-4)] = 3^3 \times \frac{1 - 3 \times 0}{90} = 0.3$$

Now that we have a complete distribution of queue length at disk A, we can compute its mean, variance, and any higher order statistics:

$$E[n_A] = \sum_{j=1}^{N} jP(n_A = j) = 1 \times 0.233 + 2 \times 0.3 + 3 \times 0.3 = 1.733$$

$$E[n_A^2] = \sum_{j=1}^{N} j^2 P(n_A = j) = 1^2 \times 0.233 + 2^2 \times 0.3 + 3^2 \times 0.3 = 4.133$$

$$\text{Var}[n_A] = E[n_A^2] - (E[n_A])^2 = 4.133 - 1.733^2 = 1.13$$

The probability that both disks are busy is given by the joint probability of having one or more jobs at disk A and one or more jobs at disk B:

$$P(n_A \geq 1, n_B \geq 1) = y_A^1 y_B^1 \frac{G(N-2)}{G(N)} = \frac{3 \times 2 \times 6}{90} = \frac{36}{90} = 0.4$$

Again, this probability can be obtained from Table 35.1.

The mean queue lengths at the three service centers are

$$Q_{CPU} = \sum_{j=1}^{N} y_{CPU}^{j} \frac{G(N-j)}{G(N)} = \frac{1 \times 25 + 1^2 \times 6 + 1^3 \times 1}{90}$$

$$= \frac{25 + 6 + 1}{90} = \frac{32}{90} = 0.356$$

$$Q_A = \sum_{j=1}^{N} y_A^{j} \frac{G(N-j)}{G(N)} = \frac{3 \times 25 + 3^2 \times 6 + 3^3 \times 1}{90}$$

$$= \frac{75 + 54 + 27}{90} = \frac{156}{90} = 1.733$$

$$Q_B = \sum_{j=1}^{N} y_B^{j} \frac{G(N-j)}{G(N)} = \frac{2 \times 25 + 2^2 \times 6 + 2^3 \times 1}{90}$$

$$= \frac{50 + 24 + 8}{90} = \frac{82}{90} = 0.911$$

Notice that Q_A is the same as $E[n_A]$ computed earlier using queue length distribution. Also, as a check, note that the three queue lengths sum to 3, which is the total number of jobs in the system.

2. *Utilizations*: The CPU utilization is

$$U_{CPU} = P(n_{CPU} \geq 1) = y_{CPU} \frac{G(N-1)}{G(N)} = \frac{25}{90} = 0.278$$

3. *Throughputs*: The system throughput is

$$X = \alpha \frac{G(N-1)}{G(N)} = \frac{1}{0.78} \times \frac{25}{90} = 0.356 \text{ job/second}$$

The CPU throughput is

$$X_{CPU} = X V_{CPU} = 0.356 \times 20 = 7.12 \text{ jobs/second}$$

4. *Response Times*: The mean response times of the three devices are

$$R_{CPU} = \frac{Q_{CPU}}{X V_{CPU}} = \frac{0.356}{0.356 \times 20} = 0.05 \text{ second}$$

$$R_A = \frac{Q_A}{X V_A} = \frac{1.733}{0.356 \times 13} = 0.37 \text{ second}$$

$$R_B = \frac{Q_B}{X V_B} = \frac{0.911}{0.356 \times 6} = 0.43 \text{ second}$$

The mean system response time as given by the general response time law is

$$R = \sum_i R_i V_i = 0.05 \times 20 + 0.37 \times 13 + 0.43 \times 6 = 8.42 \text{ seconds}$$

As a check, we can use Little's law to find the mean number of jobs in the system:

$$N = XR = 0.356 \times 8.42 = 3 \qquad \square$$

35.4 TIMESHARING SYSTEMS

The convolution algorithm, as specified so far, applies only to networks of fixed-capacity service centers. It can be extended to networks of load-dependent service centers. While general load-dependent service centers are beyond the scope of this book, we do want to allow the possibility of the network having one set of terminals that are modeled as delay centers with think time Z. The easiest way to compute $G(N)$ in this case is to assume that the terminals are zeroth devices and the initialization Equation (35.6) is modified as follows:

$$g(n,0) = \frac{y_0^n}{n!}, \qquad n = 1,2,\ldots,N$$

Here, $y_0 = \alpha Z$ is the scaled value of the think time. The system state is now represented by a $(M + 1)$-component vector $\mathbf{n} = \{n_0, n_1, \ldots, n_M\}$, where n_i is the number of jobs at the ith device and n_0 is the number of jobs at the terminals. Obviously, all queue lengths n_i must be nonnegative ($n_i \geq 0$), and they should add to N ($\sum_{i=0}^{M} n_i = N$). The state probabilities are given by

$$P(n_0, n_1, \ldots, n_M) = \frac{y_0^{n_0} y_1^{n_1} y_2^{n_2} \cdots y_M^{n_M}}{n_0! G(N)} \qquad (35.8)$$

If there is more than one delay center in the network, they can all be combined into one service center by adding their total demands D_i to Z. The computed value of $G(N)$ is still correct, and n_0 now represents the sum of queue lengths at all delay centers. The mean queue lengths at individual delay centers are proportional to their service demands D_i.

The equations for system performance metrics given earlier in Section 35.3 are still valid. The queue length distribution formulas apply to devices other than terminals. Queue length distributions for terminals are somewhat difficult to compute and are not covered here. Interested readers may refer to Buzen (1973). The mean queue lengths and device utilizations for the terminals can be computed as follows:

1. *Mean Queue Length*: Using Little's law, the mean number of jobs at the terminals (or the number of thinking users) is given by

$$Q_0 = XZ$$

2. *Utilizations*: Using the utilization law, the average utilization of the terminal facility is

$$U_0 = XZ$$

This is the combined utilization of N terminals. Utilization of individual terminals is

$$U_Z = \frac{U_0}{N} = \frac{XZ}{N} = \frac{Z}{R+Z}$$

Example 35.5 Consider a timesharing system similar to the batch system of Example 35.1. The system consists of a central processor, two disks labeled A and B, and three terminals. It can be represented by the queueing network shown in Figure 32.8. An average user makes 13 I/O requests to disk A and 6 I/O requests to disk B. The service times per visit to the CPU, disk A, and disk B are 39, 180, and 260 milliseconds, respectively. The users have an average think time of 4.68 seconds.

For this system the service times are

$$S_{CPU} = 0.039, \qquad S_A = 0.18, \qquad S_B = 0.26$$

the visit ratios are

$$V_{CPU} = 13 + 6 + 1 = 20, \qquad V_A = 13, \qquad V_B = 6$$

total service demands are

$$D_{CPU} = 20 \times 0.039 = 0.78,$$

$$D_A = 13 \times 0.18 = 2.34,$$

$$D_B = 6 \times 0.26 = 1.56,$$

and $Z = 4.68$.

For the scaling factor, we once again choose $\alpha = 1/0.78$. This results in $y_0 = 6$, $y_{CPU} = 1$, $y_A = 3$, and $y_B = 2$. Computation of the normalizing constant is shown in Table 35.4. The tabular arrangement is identical to that of Table 35.3 except that a new column for the terminal has been added. The nth row of this column is $y_0^n/n!$. Computation of other columns is done as before.

From the last column of the table we can see that $G(0) = 1$, $G(1) = 12$, $G(2) = 79$, and $G(3) = 384$. The total number of system states is $\binom{3+4-1}{4-1}$, or 20. These 20 states and their probabilities, as computed using Equation (35.8), are listed in Table 35.5. From Table 35.5, we can compute any

TABLE 35.4 Computing the Normalizing Constant for Example 35.5

n	$y_0 = 6$	$y_{CPU} = 1$	$y_A = 3$	$y_B = 2$
0	1	1	1	1
1	6	7	10	12
2	18	25	55	79
3	36	61	226	384

TABLE 35.5   State Probabilities for Example 35.5

Term-inals	CPU	Disk A	Disk B	Probability
0	0	0	3	0.021
0	0	1	2	0.031
0	0	2	1	0.047
0	0	3	0	0.070
0	1	0	2	0.010
0	1	1	1	0.016
0	1	2	0	0.023
0	2	0	1	0.005
0	2	1	0	0.008
0	3	0	0	0.003
1	0	0	2	0.063
1	0	1	1	0.094
1	0	2	0	0.141
1	1	0	1	0.031
1	1	1	0	0.047
1	2	0	0	0.016
2	0	0	1	0.094
2	0	1	0	0.141
2	1	0	0	0.047
3	0	0	0	0.094
				1.000

(Note: header columns are "Number of Jobs at" — Terminals, CPU, Disk A, Disk B)

desired statistics on the queue length of any device including terminals. For example, the probability of two jobs at the terminals is $0.094 + 0.141 + 0.047 = 0.282$. Similarly, the probability of one job at disk A is $0.031 + 0.016 + 0.008 + 0.094 + 0.047 + 0.141 = 0.336$.

Without the table, the probability of one job at disk A can be computed as follows:

$$P(n_A \geq 1) = y_A^1 \frac{G(N-1)}{G(N)} = 3^1 \times \frac{79}{384} = 0.617$$

$$P(n_A \geq 2) = y_A^2 \frac{G(N-2)}{G(N)} = 3^2 \times \frac{12}{384} = 0.281$$

$$P(n_A = 1) = P(n_A \geq 1) - P(n_A \geq 2) = 0.617 - 0.281 = 0.336$$

Similarly, probabilities of 0, 2, and 3 jobs at disk A can be shown to be 0.383, 0.211, and 0.070. Using these values, the average queue length at disk A can be shown to be 0.97 and the variance of the queue length is 0.87.

The system throughput is

$$X = \alpha \frac{G(N-1)}{G(N)} = \frac{1}{0.78} \times \frac{79}{384} = 0.264$$

The device utilizations are

$$U_{CPU} = X D_{CPU} = 0.264 \times 0.78 = 0.206$$
$$U_A = X D_A = 0.264 \times 2.34 = 0.618$$
$$U_B = X D_B = 0.264 \times 1.56 = 0.412$$

The average number of jobs at the devices are

$$Q_{CPU} = \sum_j^N y_{CPU}^j \frac{G(N-j)}{G(N)} = \frac{1^1 \times 79 + 1^2 \times 12 + 1^3 \times 1}{384} = \frac{92}{384} = 0.240$$

$$Q_A = \sum_j^N y_A^j \frac{G(N-j)}{G(N)} = \frac{3^1 \times 79 + 3^2 \times 12 + 3^3 \times 1}{384} = \frac{372}{384} = 0.969$$

$$Q_B = \sum_j^N y_B^j \frac{G(N-j)}{G(N)} = \frac{2^1 \times 79 + 2^2 \times 12 + 2^3 \times 1}{384} = \frac{214}{384} = 0.557$$

$$Q_{term} = N - (Q_{CPU} + Q_A + Q_B) = 3 - (0.240 + 0.969 + 0.557) = 1.234$$

The device response times are

$$R_{CPU} = \frac{Q_{CPU}}{X V_{CPU}} = \frac{0.240}{0.264 \times 20} = 0.045 \text{ second}$$

$$R_A = \frac{Q_A}{X V_A} = \frac{0.969}{0.264 \times 13} = 0.283 \text{ second}$$

$$R_B = \frac{Q_B}{X V_B} = \frac{0.557}{0.264 \times 6} = 0.352 \text{ second}$$

The system response time is

$$R = \sum_i R_i V_i = 0.045 \times 20 + 0.283 \times 13 + 0.352 \times 6 = 6.694 \text{ seconds}$$

We can check the computation by computing the average number of jobs in the system:

$$N = X(R + Z) = 0.264(6.694 + 4.68) = 3 \qquad \square$$

The complete convolution algorithm is summarized in Box 35.1.

Box 35.1   Convolution Algorithm
Inputs:
α = scaling factor
N = number of users
Z = think time
M = number of devices (not including terminals)
S_i = service time per visit to the ith device
V_i = number of visits to the ith device

Outputs:
X = system throughput
Q_i = average number of jobs at the ith device
R_i = response time of the ith device
R = system response time
U_i = utilization of the ith device
$P(\mathbf{n})$ = probability of queue length vector being $\mathbf{n}$

Scaling: $y_0 = \alpha Z$
FOR $i = 1$ to M DO $y_i = \alpha S_i V_i$

Initialization:
$G(0) = 1$
FOR $n = 1$ TO N DO $G(n) = y_0^n / n!$

Compute G(N):
FOR $i = 1$ TO M DO
BEGIN

   FOR $n = 1$ TO N DO $G(n) = G(n) + y_i G(n-1)$

END

Compute performance metrics:
$X = \alpha \dfrac{G(N-1)}{G(N)}$
$U_i = X S_i V_i$
$Q_i = \sum_{j=1}^{N} y_i^j \dfrac{G(N-j)}{G(N)}$
$R_i = Q_i / (X V_i)$
$R = \sum_{i=1}^{M} R_i V_i$
Check: $N = X(R + Z)$

(Continued)

Box 35.1 Continued

State probabilities:

$$P(n_0, n_1, \ldots, n_M) = \frac{y_0^{n_0} y_1^{n_1} y_2^{n_2} \cdots y_M^{n_M}}{n_0! G(N)}$$

$$P(n_i \geq j) = y_i^j \frac{G(N-j)}{G(N)}, \quad i = 1, 2, \ldots, M$$

$$P(n_i = j) = \frac{y_i^j}{G(N)} [G(N-j) - y_i G(N-j-1)], \quad i = 1, 2, \ldots, M$$

$$P(n_i \geq j, n_k \geq l) = y_i^j y_k^l \frac{G(N-j-l)}{G(N)}, \quad i = 1, 2, \ldots, M$$

EXERCISES

35.1 Consider a batch system with two disks. Each job makes 20 visits to disk B and 4 visits to disk A. The service times per visit to the CPU, disk B, and disk A are 40, 30, and 25 milliseconds. The degree of multiprogramming is 3. Determine the distribution of the CPU queue length. Also, find the system throughput varying the degree of multiprogramming from 1 to 3.

35.2 Analyze the timesharing system of Exercise 33.6 using the convolution method with $N = 3$ users. Determine the distribution of the CPU queue length.

CHAPTER 36

HIERARCHICAL DECOMPOSITION OF LARGE QUEUEING NETWORKS

People would rather live with a problem they cannot solve than accept a solution they cannot understand.
—Woolsey and Swanson (1975)

The queueing network modeling techniques presented so far are sufficient to solve a large number of performance problems. One technique that is useful in modeling large systems but has not been covered is hierarchical decomposition. This technique, which is the main topic of this chapter, allows a large queueing network to be decomposed in smaller networks. Since the technique involves using load-dependent servers, an extension of MVA to handle such servers is presented first in Section 36.1. Hierarchical decomposition is explained in Section 36.2. Finally, Section 36.3 discusses current limitations of queueing theory as applied to computer systems modeling.

36.1 LOAD-DEPENDENT SERVICE CENTERS

A load-dependent service center is one whose service rate varies with the load, that is, the number of jobs in the center. For example, a disk subsystem with m disk drives sharing a single queue of requests may be represented by an m-server center whose service rate $\mu(n)$ varies with the number of requests n as follows:

$$\mu(n) = \begin{cases} \dfrac{n}{S}, & n = 1, 2, \ldots, m-1 \\ \dfrac{m}{S}, & n = m, m+1, \ldots, \infty \end{cases}$$

Here, S is the service time per request when there is only one request in the subsystem. This is similar to the M/M/m queue discussed earlier in Section 31.3 except that the arrivals may not be Poisson.

Mean-value analysis, as described earlier in Section 34.2, is applicable only for networks with fixed-capacity service centers and delay centers. (Strictly speaking, delay centers are also load dependent since their service rate is proportional to the number of jobs.) The analysis actually applies to a more general class of service centers and jobs. In particular, it can easily be extended to load-dependent service centers. Recall that MVA consists of three equations corresponding to computing the response time, throughput, and queue length. The throughput equation for a system with load-dependent service centers is identical to that presented earlier in Equation (34.4). The response time and queue length equations are different and are presented here.

For load-dependent service centers, the queue length distribution (rather than the mean queue length) is important since the service rate is a function of the queue length. Let $p_i(j \mid n)$ denote the probability of finding j jobs at the ith device when there are n jobs in the system. Let $\mu_i(j)$ be the service rate of the ith device when there are j jobs at the device. The response time at the device for a job arriving when there are already $j - 1$ jobs in the system (total j jobs including the one just arriving) is $j/\mu_i(j)$. The mean response time per visit is therefore given by

$$R_i(n) = \sum_{j=1}^{n} p_i(j - 1 \mid n - 1) \frac{j}{\mu_i(j)} \qquad (36.1)$$

The probability $p_i(j \mid n)$ of j jobs at the ith service center when there are n jobs in the system is computed as follows:

$$p_i(j \mid n) = \begin{cases} \dfrac{X(n)}{\mu_i(j)} p_i(j - 1 \mid n - 1), & j = 1, 2, \ldots, n \\[2mm] 1 - \displaystyle\sum_{k=1}^{n} p_i(k \mid n), & j = 0 \end{cases} \qquad (36.2)$$

The mean queue length $Q_i(n)$ at the ith device when there are n jobs in the system is given by

$$Q_i(n) = \sum_{j=1}^{n} j p_i(j \mid n)$$

It is easy to see that the preceding equations reduce to those for fixed-capacity service centers if we substitute $\mu_i(n) = 1/S_i$, where S_i is the service time per visit.

The complete MVA algorithm including fixed-capacity service centers, delay centers, and load-dependent service centers is summarized in Box 36.1.

Example 36.1 Consider the simple network of two service centers shown in Figure 36.1. The first service center, labeled "Disk B," is a fixed-capacity

---

Box 36.1   MVA Including Load-dependent Centers

Inputs:

Z = think time

S_i = service time per visit to the ith device

V_i = number of visits to the ith device

M = number of devices (not including terminals)

N = number of users

$\mu_i(j)$ = service rate of the ith center when there are j jobs in it

Outputs:

X = system throughput

Q_i = average number of jobs at the ith device

R_i = response time of the ith device

R = system response time

U_i = utilization of the ith device

$P_i(j)$ = probability of j jobs at the ith center

Initialization:

FOR i = 1 TO M DO $\begin{cases} Q_i = 0 & \text{Fixed capacity and delay centers} \\ P_i(0) = 0 & \text{General load-dependent centers} \end{cases}$

Iterations:

FOR n = 1 TO N DO

BEGIN

FOR i = 1 TO M DO $R_i = \begin{cases} S_i(1 + Q_i) & \text{Fixed capacity} \\ S_i & \text{Delay centers} \\ \sum_{j=1}^{n} P_i(j-1)\dfrac{j}{\mu_i(j)} & \text{Load dependent} \end{cases}$

$R = \sum_{i=1}^{M} R_i V_i$

$X = \dfrac{N}{Z + R}$

FOR i = 1 TO M DO

$\begin{cases} Q_i = XV_iR_i & \text{Fixed or delay} \\ \text{FOR } j = n \text{ TO 1 DO } P_i(j) = \dfrac{X}{\mu_i(j)}P_i(j-1) \\ P_i(0) = 1 - \sum_{j=1}^{n} P_i(j) \end{cases} \Bigg\} \text{Load dependent}$

END

FOR i = 1 TO M DO $X_i = XV_i$

FOR i = 1 TO M DO $U_i = \begin{cases} XS_iV_i & \text{Fixed capacity or delay centers} \\ 1 - P_i(0) & \text{Load dependent centers} \end{cases}$

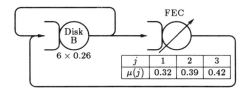

FIGURE 36.1   Queueing network model with a load-dependent server.

service center. The mean service time per visit for this center is 0.26 second and each job makes six visits to this center. The second center, labeled "FEC" (or **Flow-Equivalent Center**) is a load-dependent service center. It is visited once by each job. Its service rate $\mu(n)$, as a function of number of jobs n in the service center, is given by

$$\mu(1) = 0.32 \text{ job/second}$$

$$\mu(2) = 0.39 \text{ job/second}$$

$$\mu(3) = 0.42 \text{ job/second}$$

To analyze this network using MVA for load-dependent service centers, we proceed as follows:
Initialization:

$$Q_B(0) = 0, \qquad P(0 \mid 0) = 1$$

Iteration 1
Device response times:

$$R_B(1) = S_B[1 + Q_B(0)] = 0.26$$

$$R_{\text{FEC}}(1) = P(0 \mid 0)\frac{1}{\mu(1)} = 3.13$$

System response time:

$$R(1) = R_B(1)V_B + R_{\text{FEC}}(1)V_{\text{FEC}} = 0.26 \times 6 + 3.13 = 4.68$$

System throughput:

$$X(1) = N/R(1) = 1/4.68 = 0.21$$

Queue lengths and probabilities:

$$Q_B(1) = X(1)R_B(1)V_B = 0.21 \times 0.26 \times 6 = 0.33$$

$$P(1 \mid 1) = \frac{X(n)}{\mu(n)}P(0 \mid 0) = \frac{0.21}{0.32} \times 1 = 0.67$$

$$P(0 \mid 1) = 1 - P(1 \mid 1) = 1 - 0.67 = 0.33$$

Iteration 2
Device response times:

$$R_B(2) = S_B[1 + Q_B(1)] = 0.26(1 + 0.33) = 0.35$$

$$R_{\text{FEC}}(2) = P(0 \mid 1)\frac{1}{\mu(1)} + P(1 \mid 1)\frac{2}{\mu(2)}$$

$$= 0.33 \times \frac{1}{0.32} + 0.67 \times \frac{2}{0.39} = 4.46$$

System response time:

$$R(2) = R_B(2)V_B + R_{\text{FEC}}(2)V_{\text{FEC}} = 0.35 \times 6 + 4.46 = 6.54$$

System throughput:

$$X(2) = N/R(2) = 2/6.54 = 0.31$$

Queue lengths and probabilities:

$$Q_B(2) = X(2)R_B(2)V_B = 0.31 \times 0.35 \times 6 = 0.64$$

$$P(2 \mid 2) = \frac{X(2)}{\mu(2)}P(1 \mid 1) = \frac{0.31}{0.39} \times 0.67 = 0.52$$

$$P(1 \mid 2) = \frac{X(2)}{\mu(1)}P(0 \mid 1) = \frac{0.31}{0.32} \times 0.33 = 0.32$$

$$P(0 \mid 2) = 1 - P(1 \mid 2) - P(2 \mid 2) = 1 - 0.52 - 0.32 = 0.16$$

Iteration 3
Device response times:

$$R_B(3) = S_B(1 + Q_B(2)) = 0.26(1 + 0.64) = 0.43$$

$$R_{\text{FEC}}(3) = P(0 \mid 2)\frac{1}{\mu(1)} + P(1 \mid 2)\frac{2}{\mu(2)} + P(2 \mid 2)\frac{3}{\mu(3)}$$

$$= 0.16 \times \frac{1}{0.32} + 0.32 \times \frac{2}{0.39} + 0.52 \times \frac{3}{0.42} = 5.86$$

System response time:

$$R(3) = R_B(3)V_B + R_{\text{FEC}}(3)V_{\text{FEC}} = 0.43 \times 6 + 5.86 = 8.42$$

System throughput:

$$X(3) = N/R(3) = 3/8.42 = 0.36$$

Queue lengths and probabilities:

$$Q_B(3) = X(3)R_B(3)V_B = 0.36 \times 0.43 \times 6 = 0.91$$

$$P(3 \mid 3) = \frac{X(3)}{\mu(3)}P(2 \mid 2) = \frac{0.36}{0.42} \times 0.52 = 0.44$$

$$P(2 \mid 3) = \frac{X(3)}{\mu(2)}P(1 \mid 2) = \frac{0.36}{0.39} \times 0.32 = 0.29$$

$$P(1 \mid 3) = \frac{X(3)}{\mu(1)}P(0 \mid 2) = \frac{0.36}{0.32} \times 0.16 = 0.18$$

$$P(0 \mid 3) = 1 - P(1 \mid 3) - P(2 \mid 3) - P(3 \mid 3) = 1 - 0.44 - 0.29 - 0.18 = 0.09$$

The device throughputs with $N = 3$ are

$$X_B = XV_B = 0.36 \times 6 = 2.16 \text{ jobs/second}$$

$$X_{\text{FEC}} = XV_{\text{FEC}} = 0.36 \times 1 = 0.36 \text{ job/second}$$

The device utilizations with $N = 3$ are

$$U_B = XS_BV_B = 0.36 \times 0.26 \times 6 = 0.562$$

$$U_{\text{FEC}} = 1 - P(0 \mid 3) = 1 - 0.09 = 0.91$$

Thus, we can say the following about this system:

1. The system throughput is 0.21, 0.31, and 0.36 job/second with one, two, and three jobs in the system, respectively.
2. The system response time is 4.68, 6.54, and 8.42 seconds for $N = 1, 2, 3$, respectively.
3. The mean queue length for disk B with $N = 3$ is 0.91.
4. The mean response time for disk B with $N = 3$ is 0.43 second.
5. The utilization of disk B with $N = 3$ is 0.562.
6. The probabilities of zero, one, two, and three jobs in the second device with $N = 3$ are 0.09, 0.18, 0.29, and 0.44, respectively.

We will make use of these results later in Example 36.2.   □

36.2 HIERARCHICAL DECOMPOSITION

"Divide and conquer" is a well-known technique to solve complex problems. It requires breaking the complex problem into several smaller subproblems. An example of such a decomposition occurs with electrical circuits, where Norton's theorem allows any part of the circuit to be replaced by an equivalent current source with a resistance in parallel. For example, Figure 36.2a shows a sample electrical circuit. If we are interested in studying the behavior for

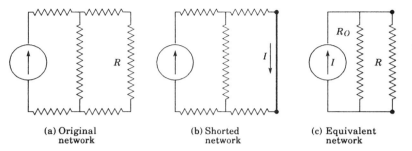

<table>
<tr><td>(a) Original
network</td><td>(b) Shorted
network</td><td>(c) Equivalent
network</td></tr>
</table>

FIGURE 36.2   Norton's theorem for electrical networks.

various values of resistor R, we can replace the remaining components by a current source whose current capacity is determined by shorting the "designated" resistor R and finding the current through the short circuit. The internal resistance R_0 of the current source is determined by the open-circuit voltage. Norton's theorem states that the current of the designated resistor R in the equivalent circuit is always the same as in the given circuit for all values of R.

Chandy, Herzog, and Woo (1975) discovered a similar method for queueing networks. They showed that if a queueing network satisfies certain conditions, it can be decomposed and solved in a manner very similar to that of applying Norton's theorem.

Consider, for example, the queueing network of Figure 36.3a. If we are interested in studying various alternatives for the ith device, we could replace the remaining network by a flow-equivalent center (**FEC**) as shown in Figure 36.3c. The FEC is a load-dependent service center, and its service rate $\mu(j)$ is a function of the number of jobs j present at this service center. The service rate $\mu(j)$ can be determined by short circuiting the ith device and solving the "shorted model" with j jobs circulating in it. The throughput $X(j)$ of the shorted model gives the service rate $\mu(j)$. In the equivalent network each job makes V_i visits to the ith device for each visit to the FEC. This is the reason for the link connecting the output of the ith device to its input

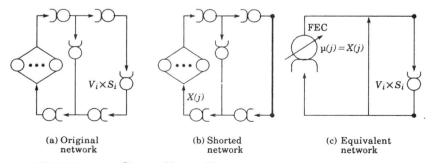

<table>
<tr><td>(a) Original
network</td><td>(b) Shorted
network</td><td>(c) Equivalent
network</td></tr>
</table>

FIGURE 36.3   Chandy-Herzog-Woo theorem for queueing networks.

in Figure 36.3c. Obviously, if $V_i = 1$, this link is not required. Many books on queueing theory do not explicitly show this link. However, if $V_i \neq 1$, the diagram will not correctly represent visit ratios, and the response times of individual devices will not be correctly computed.

In general, the portion of the network that can be isolated is not limited to a single queue. It can consist of any number of queues and is called the **designated subnetwork**. The remaining subnetwork is called the **aggregate subnetwork**. The **shorted model** is created by setting the service times of all service centers in the designated subnetwork to zero. The aggregate subnetwork can then be replaced by a single FEC to form an equivalent network. For any given number of jobs in the center, the service rate of the FEC is equal to the throughput of the shorted model with that many jobs circulating in the shorted model.

The hierarchical decomposition produces exact results for a large class of networks called BCMP networks, discussed earlier in Section 32.2. It is applicable to open as well as closed networks. However, for simplicity, we will limit our examples here to simple closed queueing networks consisting of fixed-capacity service centers, single classes of jobs, and fixed-transition probabilities that are independent of the state of the system.

Notice that the FEC is a load-dependent service center, and therefore, solution of the equivalent network requires using techniques that can handle such centers. The following theorem ensures that the results obtained for the equivalent network are valid for the original network as well.

Chandy-Herzog-Woo Theorem: *The queue length distribution for the designated subnetwork in the equivalent network is the same as in the original network.*

To summarize, the Chandy-Herzog-Woo decomposition method consists of the following steps:

1. Select a particular queue or set of queues to be studied in detail. These queues constitute the designated subnetwork. The remaining queues constitute the aggregate subnetwork.

2. Create a shorted model by setting the service times of all centers in the designated subnetwork to zero.

3. Solve the shorted model using MVA, convolution, or any other technique.

4. Replace the aggregate subnetwork by an FEC. This service center is a load-dependent service center whose service rate, when there are n jobs in it, is equal to the throughput of the shorted model with n jobs circulating in the shorted model.

5. Solve the equivalent network using techniques for load-dependent service centers. The performance metrics for service centers in the designated subnetwork, as obtained from the equivalent network, apply to the original network as well.

6. The performance metrics for service centers in the aggregate subnetwork are obtained by using conditional probabilities, as discussed next.

The statistics for service centers in the aggregate subnetwork are obtained using conditional probabilities as follows:

1. *Distribution of Number of Jobs*: The probability of finding j jobs at the ith device (in the aggregate subnetwork) is given by

$$P(n_i = j \mid N \text{ jobs in system}) = \sum_{n=j}^{N} [P(n_i = j \mid n \text{ jobs in aggregate})$$

$$\times P(n \text{ jobs in aggregate} \mid N \text{ jobs in system})]$$

$$= \sum_{n=j}^{N} [P(n_i = j \mid n \text{ jobs in aggregate})$$

$$\times P(n \text{ jobs in FEC} \mid N \text{ jobs in system})]$$

The mean number of jobs at the ith device is given by

$$Q_i(N) = \sum_{j=1}^{N} j P(n_i = j \mid N \text{ jobs in system})$$

2. *Throughput*: Throughputs of various devices are proportional to their visit ratios. Thus, the throughput of the ith device in the aggregate subnetwork and that of the jth device in the designated subnetwork are related as follows:

$$\frac{X_i}{V_i} = X = \frac{X_j}{V_j}$$

Here, X is the throughput of the combined system and V_i and V_j are the number of times a job visits service centers i and j, respectively.

3. *Response Time*: The response time can be computed using Little's law:

$$R_i = Q_i X_i$$

4. *Utilization*: The utilization can be computed using the utilization law:

$$U_i = X_i S_i = X D_i$$

Example 36.2 Consider the central server model of Examples 35.1, 35.3, and 35.4. Let us analyze this model using hierarchical techniques and verify that we obtain the same results. The model, shown again in Figure 36.4a, represents a batch computer system consisting of a processor and two disks. The degree of multiprogramming is 3.
The service times are

$$S_{\text{CPU}} = 0.039, \qquad S_A = 0.18, \qquad S_B = 0.26$$

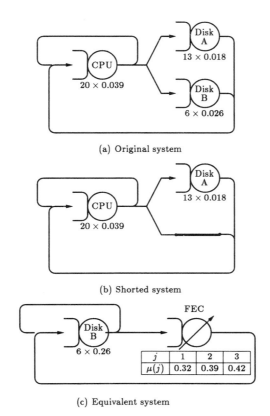

(a) Original system

(b) Shorted system

(c) Equivalent system

FIGURE 36.4 Hierarchical decomposition example.

The visit ratios are

$$V_{\text{CPU}} = 13 + 6 + 1 = 20, \qquad V_A = 13, \qquad V_B = 6$$

Total service demands are

$$D_{\text{CPU}} = 20 \times 0.039 = 0.78$$

$$D_A = 13 \times 0.18 = 2.34$$

$$D_B = 6 \times 0.26 = 1.56$$

Assuming that we are interested in studying several alternatives for disk B, we choose disk B as the designated subnetwork, set its service time to zero, and obtain the shorted model shown in Figure 36.4b. Although this shorted model can be easily solved using MVA, we will use a convolution algorithm instead so that we can study the distributions of queue lengths also.

TABLE 36.1   Computing $G(N)$ for the Shorted Model of Example 36.2

n	$y_{\text{CPU}} = 1$	$y_A = 3$
0	1	1
1	1	4
2	1	13
3	1	40

For the scaling factor, we arbitrarily choose $\alpha = 1/0.78$. This results in $y_{\text{CPU}} = 1$ and $y_A = 3$. The computation of the normalizing constant $G(N)$ is shown in Table 36.1.

From the table, we see that $G(0) = 1$, $G(1) = 4$, $G(2) = 13$, and $G(3) = 40$. The system throughputs for various degrees of multiprogramming are

$$X(1) = \alpha \frac{G(0)}{G(1)} = \frac{1}{0.78} \times \frac{1}{4} = 0.321$$

$$X(2) = \alpha \frac{G(1)}{G(2)} = \frac{1}{0.78} \times \frac{4}{13} = 0.394$$

$$X(3) = \alpha \frac{G(2)}{G(3)} = \frac{1}{0.78} \times \frac{13}{40} = 0.417$$

The probability of j jobs at disk A when there are n jobs in the shorted model is given by

$$P(n_A = j) = \frac{y_A^j}{G(N)} [G(N - j) - y_A G(N - j - 1)]$$

The probabilities so computed are listed in Table 36.2.

We replace the aggregate subnetwork by an FEC and obtain an equivalent network, as shown in Figure 36.4c. It consists of just two service centers: disk B and an FEC. The first service center has a service time of $S_B = 0.26$ second and a visit ratio of $V_B = 6$. The FEC is a load-dependent service center with a visit ratio of 1 and service rates identical to the throughputs of the shorted model. That is,

$$\mu(1) = 0.321, \qquad \mu(2) = 0.394, \qquad \mu(3) = 0.417$$

TABLE 36.2   Queue Length Probabilities for Disk A of Example 36.2

n	n_A 0	1	2	3
1	0.250	0.750		
2	0.077	0.231	0.692	
3	0.025	0.075	0.225	0.675

We have already solved this model in Example 36.1. The following results obtained for disk B (since it is in the designated subnetwork) and the system as a whole are still valid:

1. The system throughput is 0.21, 0.31, and 0.36 job/second with one, two, and three jobs in the system, respectively.
2. The system response times are 4, 68, 6.54, and 8.42 seconds for $N = 1, 2, 3$, respectively.
3. The mean queue length for disk B with $N = 3$ is 0.91.
4. The mean response time for disk B with $N = 3$ is 0.43 second.
5. The utilization of disk B with $N = 3$ is 0.562.

As a check, we verify that these are identical to those obtained for the original network in Example 35.4 without decomposition.

Obtaining performance statistics for queues in the aggregate subnetwork requires further work.

From Example 36.1, we know that when the degree of multiprogramming N is 3, the probabilities of zero, one, two, and three jobs at the FEC are 0.09, 0.18, 0.29, and 0.44, respectively. These values along with those listed in Table 36.2 allow us to compute the queue length distribution for disk A as follows:

$$
\begin{aligned}
P(n_A = 0 \mid N = 3) = {} & P(n_A = 0 \mid n = 0)P(n = 0 \mid N = 3) \\
& + P(n_A = 0 \mid n = 1)P(n = 1 \mid N = 3) \\
& + P(n_A = 0 \mid n = 2)P(n = 2 \mid N = 3) \\
& + P(n_A = 0 \mid n = 3)P(n = 3 \mid N = 3) \\
& = 1 \times 0.09 + 0.250 \times 0.18 + 0.077 \times 0.29 + 0.025 \times 0.44 \\
& = 0.166
\end{aligned}
$$

Similarly,

$$P(n_A = 1 \mid N = 3) = 0.750 \times 0.18 + 0.231 \times 0.29 + 0.075 \times 0.44 = 0.233$$
$$P(n_A = 2 \mid N = 3) = 0.692 \times 0.29 + 0.225 \times 0.44 = 0.3$$
$$P(n_A = 3 \mid N = 3) = 0.675 \times 0.44 = 0.3$$

Once again, we check that these probabilities are the same as those obtained in Example 35.4.

The mean number of jobs at disk A can be computed from the queue length distribution:

$$Q_A = \sum_{j=1}^{N} jP(n_A = j) = 1 \times 0.233 + 2 \times 0.3 + 3 \times 0.3 = 1.73$$

Similarly, Q_{CPU} can be shown to be 0.36 job.
The CPU and disk A throughputs using the forced flow law are

$$X_{CPU} = X V_{CPU} = 0.36 \times 20 = 7.2 \text{ jobs/second}$$

$$X_A = X V_A = 0.36 \times 13 = 4.68 \text{ jobs/second}$$

The CPU and disk A utilizations using the utilization law are

$$U_{CPU} = X D_{CPU} = 0.36 \times 0.78 = 0.281$$

$$U_A = X D_A = 0.36 \times 2.34 = 0.843$$

The CPU and disk A response times using Little's law are

$$R_{CPU} = Q_{CPU}/X_{CPU} = 0.36/7.2 = 0.05 \text{ second}$$

$$R_A = Q_A/X_A = 1.73/4.68 = 0.37 \text{ second}$$

Before leaving this example, we must remind the reader of the necessity of using the correct visit ratios $V_B = 6$ and $V_{FEC} = 1$. This is also the reason for the extra link around disk B in Figure 36.4c. Without this link, it is impossible for a job to make six visits to disk B while making just one visit to the FEC.   □

The technique of hierarchical decomposition produces exact results for networks with product form solutions. However, its real application is not for product form networks since the decomposition may turn out to be computationally more expensive than straightforward MVA for such networks. The real advantage of the hierarchical decomposition is in the fact that it can be used to approximately solve nonproduct form networks. The approximation is good if there are only a few components that do not satisfy the product form conditions and their interactions with the rest of the network is low. In such cases, the designated subnetwork consists of the nonproduct form components, and the remaining subnetwork is replaced by an FEC. Product form solution techniques can be used to solve the shorted model and find the service rates for the FEC. The equivalent network can then be solved by an appropriate nonproduct form technique or simulation. Since solving a nonproduct form network is computationally very expensive, the reduced number of service centers in the equivalent network considerably reduces the computation time.

36.3 LIMITATIONS OF QUEUEING THEORY

There are a number of real-life queueing behaviors that are not easily modeled by current queueing theory. If the system you are trying to model has any of the following behaviors, you may find it hard to model using queueing theory:

1. *Nonexponential Service Times*: Most of the results about queueing network models, with the clear exception of operational analysis, require

assuming exponential distribution of service times. Several studies, for example, Suri (1983), have shown that the results obtained are robust in the sense that a slight departure from the assumption does not make a significant difference in the result. Nonetheless, it must be pointed out that the error in predicted device utilizations is much less compared to that in response times and queue lengths. If accuracy in queue lengths is critical, one may have to use a simulation technique with the given service time distribution.

2. *Train Arrivals*: Bulk or group arrivals at a service center can be modeled under certain restricted conditions, for example, if the intergroup time is exponentially distributed. In computer networks, Jain and Routhier (1986) found the packet arrival pattern to follow a "train model" such that arrival of a packet makes the next packet more likely to appear shortly. This is different from group arrivals in the sense that there is a significant correlation between successive interarrival times that makes the problem difficult to model.

3. *Fork and Join*: Fork and Join primitives are used in computer systems to create and synchronize subprocesses. This causes the number of jobs in the system to change and also invalidates the assumption of independence among jobs. Queueing models are unsuitable for analyzing systems with such primitives.

4. *Load-dependent Arrivals*: Computer networks and distributed systems have intelligent load-balancing policies that cause new jobs or packets to go to one of a number of devices depending upon the load observed in the recent past. Such load-dependent arrivals are difficult to model.

5. *Blocking*: In computer systems, excessive queueing at a device may result in a "flow-off" signal, which results in blocking at other devices. Current queueing models cannot easily analyze such blocking.

6. *Transient Analysis*: Most of the queueing theory results are valid only during steady state. Many systems are so dynamic that they hardly ever reach a steady state. In such cases, a transient analysis would be more useful than steady-state analysis.

7. *Contention*: The service disciplines used in queueing models, such as first come, first served or last come, first served, are too simplistic to model some real systems. One example is that of service by contention, as in Ethernet local area networks, where several stations can attempt to use the medium and resolve the contention using a set of rules. Such service algorithms are not easy to model with queueing theory.

8. *Mutual Exclusion*: In distributed systems, several jobs attempting to use a resource have to follow a set of mutual exclusion rules. For example, two users attempting to read the same file can read it simultaneously, but two users attempting to read and write the same file cannot do so simultaneously. Such mutual exclusion rules are not easy to represent in queueing models.

9. *Response-dependent Arrivals*: If a packet or a request stays too long in a queue, it may be retransmitted by the source, thereby increasing the queue length even further. This is similar to the load-dependent arrivals except that the positive feedback resulting from more arrivals with longer queues may take the system to an unstable state such that a transient increase in response time leads to a continual increase in load and response time.

10. *Memory Modeling*: Memory is a resource that is shared among several jobs. The number of jobs is often limited by the available memory. Further, virtual memory allows a trade-off between available physical memory and the number of visits to the paging device. Such trade-offs are difficult to analyze with queueing models.

11. *Defections from the Queue*: One method used to avoid the instability caused by response-dependent arrivals in computer networks involves setting a maximum limit on the time a packet or request is allowed to stay in the queue. Thus, the packets that have been in the queue for a long time are dropped from the queue on the assumption that they may have already been retransmitted by higher protocol layers. Such defections from the queue are difficult to analyze using queueing models.

12. *Simultaneous Resource Possession*: In computer systems, a job may continue to compute while its I/O requests are progressing in parallel. Thus, the job may be simultaneously using two or more resources of the system. This phenomenon is similar to the fork and join discussed earlier and is difficult to analyze with queueing models.

13. *Think Time*: The time taken by a job waiting for human input is usually modeled as "think time." Modern computer systems have several new facilities, such as windows, type-a-head, mnemonic commands, and pull-down menus, which make the usual representation of the human as a delay center with think time invalid. Multiple windows make the human a resource with queueing; type-a-head results in overlap between computation and thinking; mnemonic commands have made the type-in part of the think time very small; and pull-down menus have further cut the time required to think about possible alternatives. These new behaviors require a new model for representing think times in computer systems.

In human life, customers have even more sophisticated behaviors than packets or requests that lead to such interesting but difficult to model phenomena as biggest first service, cheating and bribing for queue positions, balking before entering a queue, and jockeying among many queues.

EXERCISES

36.1 Determine the system throughput and response time for the system in Figure 36.5 using the load-dependent, MVA. The service rates $\mu(j)$ of

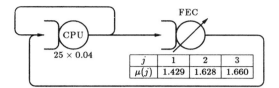

FIGURE 36.5 Queueing network model with a load-dependent server.

the load-dependent service center as a function of number of jobs j at the center are 1.429, 1.628, and 1.660, respectively, for $j = 1, 2, \ldots, 3$.

36.2 Use the hierarchical technique to analyze the system of Exercise 35.1. Use the CPU as the designated subsystem. Determine the throughput of the shorted system for $N = 1, \ldots, 3$ jobs in the system. Then use load-dependent MVA to analyze the equivalent system. Verify that the final results are the same as those obtained in Exercise 35.1.

FURTHER READING FOR PART VI

There are a number of good books on queueing theory. The classic book in this area is the first volume of Kleinrock (1975). Other good books for single queues are Gross and Harris (1985), Gelenbe and Pujolle (1987), and Cooper (1981).

Lazowska et al. (1984) provides an easy to understand treatment of queueing networks. Lavenberg (1983) provides a thorough treatment of the subject for a mathematically inclined reader. Leung (1987) provides case studies of queueing models of database and I/O subsystems. Agrawal (1985) discusses approximation techniques. Gelenbe and Mitrani (1980) and Kobayashi (1978) also discuss queueing theory and its application to computer systems.

For a derivation of Equation (31.6) for the cumulative distribution function of the response time, see Gross and Harris (1985).

A popular approximation to MVA called *Linearizer* is proposed by Chandy and Neuse (1982). Browne et al. (1975) discuss the application of hierarchical techniques.

SYMBOLS FREQUENTLY USED IN QUEUEING ANALYSIS

Symbol	Definition
b	Busy period duration for a server (a random variable)
B	Number of buffers (includes both waiting and serving positions)
C_x	Coefficient of variation of a random variable x
D	Total service demands on all service centers (except terminals)

D_i	Total service demand on the ith service center, $= V_i S_i$
$E[x]$	Mean of the random variable x
$f_i(x)$	Some arbitrary function of variable x
$f(x)$	Probability density function (pdf) of the random variable x
$F(x)$	Cumulative distribution function (CDF) of the random variable x
$g(n,m)$	Normalizing constant with n jobs and m service centers
$G(N)$	Normalizing constant with N jobs in the system, $= g(N,M)$
I	Idle time duration for a server (a random variable)
J	Sum of time spent by n jobs in the system
K	Population size
$L_x( )$	Laplace transform of the probability generating function of the continuous random variable x
m	Number of servers in a service center
m_i	Number of servers in the ith service center
M	Number of service centers in a queueing network
n	Number of jobs in the system (a random variable)
$\mathbf{n}$	Vector $\{n_1, n_2, \ldots, n_M\}$ indicating number of jobs at various service centers
n_i	Number of jobs in the ith service center
n_q	Number of jobs in the queue (a random variable)
n_s	Number of jobs receiving service (a random variable)
N	Number of jobs in a closed queueing network
p_n	Probability of n jobs in the system
p_{ik}	Probability of a job moving to the kth service center after service at the ith service center
$P(x)$	Probability of the event x
Q_i	Mean number of jobs at the ith service center
r	Response time or time in the system (a random variable)
R	Mean response time of a system
R_i	Response time of the ith service center
s	Service time (a random variable)
S_i	Mean service time per visit at the ith service center
t_j	Time of the jth state change
U_i	Utilization of the ith device
$\mathrm{Var}[x]$	Variance of the random variable x
V_i	Number of visits to service center i
w	Time spent waiting in the queue (a random variable)
$\bar{x}$	Mean of a random variable $x = E[x]$
X	System throughput
X_i	Throughput of the ith service center
Z	Average think time
β	Duration of busy interval for a server (a random variable)
λ	Arrival rate, $= 1/E[\tau]$
λ_j	Arrival rate when there are j jobs in the service center
μ	Service rate, $= 1/E[s]$

μ_j Service rate when there are j jobs in the service center

ρ Traffic intensity

ρ_i Traffic intensity at the ith service center

σ_x Standard deviation of the random variable x

τ Interarrival time (a random variable)

τ_j Time between the $(j-1)$th and jth arrival

ϱ Solution of the equation $\varrho = L_\tau(\mu - \varrho\mu)$ for G/M/1 queues or probability of queueing for M/M/m queues,
$$= [(m\rho)^m / \{m!(1-\rho)\}]p_0$$

APPENDIX A

STATISTICAL TABLES

A.1   Area of the Unit Normal Distribution
A.2   Quantiles of the Unit Normal Distribution
A.3   Commonly Used Normal Quantiles
A.4   Quantiles of the t Distribution
A.5   Quantiles of the Chi-Square Distribution
A.6   90-Percentiles of the $F(n, m)$ Distribution
A.7   95-Percentiles of the $F(n, m)$ Distribution
A.8   99-Percentiles of the $F(n, m)$ Distribution
A.9   Quantiles of the K-S Distribution
A.10 Approximation Formulas for Statistical Tables

A.1 AREA OF THE UNIT NORMAL DISTRIBUTION

Table A.1 lists area between 0 and z. For example, the area between $z = 0$ and $z = 1.03$ is 0.3485. Due to symmetry of the normal distribution, the area between $z = 0$ and $z = -1.03$ is also the same.

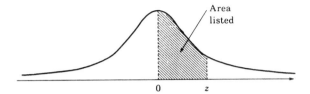

TABLE A.1   Area of the Unit Normal Distribution

z	0.00	0.01	0.02	0.03	0.04	0.05	0.06	0.07	0.08	0.09
0.0	0.0000	0.0040	0.0080	0.0120	0.0160	0.0199	0.0239	0.0279	0.0319	0.0359
0.1	0.0398	0.0438	0.0478	0.0517	0.0557	0.0596	0.0636	0.0675	0.0714	0.0753
0.2	0.0793	0.0832	0.0871	0.0910	0.0948	0.0987	0.1026	0.1064	0.1103	0.1141
0.3	0.1179	0.1217	0.1255	0.1293	0.1331	0.1368	0.1406	0.1443	0.1480	0.1517
0.4	0.1554	0.1591	0.1628	0.1664	0.1700	0.1736	0.1772	0.1808	0.1844	0.1879
0.5	0.1915	0.1950	0.1985	0.2019	0.2054	0.2088	0.2123	0.2157	0.2190	0.2224
0.6	0.2257	0.2291	0.2324	0.2357	0.2389	0.2422	0.2454	0.2486	0.2517	0.2549
0.7	0.2580	0.2611	0.2642	0.2673	0.2703	0.2734	0.2764	0.2794	0.2823	0.2852
0.8	0.2881	0.2910	0.2939	0.2967	0.2995	0.3023	0.3051	0.3078	0.3106	0.3133
0.9	0.3159	0.3186	0.3212	0.3238	0.3264	0.3289	0.3315	0.3340	0.3365	0.3389
1.0	0.3413	0.3438	0.3461	0.3485	0.3508	0.3531	0.3554	0.3577	0.3599	0.3621
1.1	0.3643	0.3665	0.3686	0.3708	0.3729	0.3749	0.3770	0.3790	0.3810	0.3830
1.2	0.3849	0.3869	0.3888	0.3907	0.3925	0.3944	0.3962	0.3980	0.3997	0.4015
1.3	0.4032	0.4049	0.4066	0.4082	0.4099	0.4115	0.4131	0.4147	0.4162	0.4177
1.4	0.4192	0.4207	0.4222	0.4236	0.4251	0.4265	0.4279	0.4292	0.4306	0.4319
1.5	0.4332	0.4345	0.4357	0.4370	0.4382	0.4394	0.4406	0.4418	0.4429	0.4441
1.6	0.4452	0.4463	0.4474	0.4484	0.4495	0.4505	0.4515	0.4525	0.4535	0.4545
1.7	0.4554	0.4564	0.4573	0.4582	0.4591	0.4599	0.4608	0.4616	0.4625	0.4633
1.8	0.4641	0.4649	0.4656	0.4664	0.4671	0.4678	0.4686	0.4693	0.4699	0.4706
1.9	0.4713	0.4719	0.4726	0.4732	0.4738	0.4744	0.4750	0.4756	0.4761	0.4767
2.0	0.4772	0.4778	0.4783	0.4788	0.4793	0.4798	0.4803	0.4808	0.4812	0.4817
2.1	0.4821	0.4826	0.4830	0.4834	0.4838	0.4842	0.4846	0.4850	0.4854	0.4857
2.2	0.4861	0.4864	0.4868	0.4871	0.4875	0.4878	0.4881	0.4884	0.4887	0.4890
2.3	0.4893	0.4896	0.4898	0.4901	0.4904	0.4906	0.4909	0.4911	0.4913	0.4916
2.4	0.4918	0.4920	0.4922	0.4925	0.4927	0.4929	0.4931	0.4932	0.4934	0.4936
2.5	0.4938	0.4940	0.4941	0.4943	0.4945	0.4946	0.4948	0.4949	0.4951	0.4952
2.6	0.4953	0.4955	0.4956	0.4957	0.4959	0.4960	0.4961	0.4962	0.4963	0.4964
2.7	0.4965	0.4966	0.4967	0.4968	0.4969	0.4970	0.4971	0.4972	0.4973	0.4974
2.8	0.4974	0.4975	0.4976	0.4977	0.4977	0.4978	0.4979	0.4979	0.4980	0.4981
2.9	0.4981	0.4982	0.4982	0.4983	0.4984	0.4984	0.4985	0.4985	0.4986	0.4986
3.0	0.4987	0.4987	0.4987	0.4988	0.4988	0.4989	0.4989	0.4989	0.4990	0.4990

A.2 QUANTITIES OF THE UNIT NORMAL DISTRIBUTION

Table A.2 lists z_p for a given p. For example, for a two-sided confidence interval at 95%, $\alpha = 0.05$ and $p = 1 - \alpha/2 = 0.975$. The entry in the row labeled 0.97 and column labeled 0.005 gives $z_p = 1.960$.

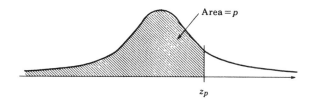

TABLE A.2   Quantiles of the Unit Normal Distribution

p	0.00	0.01	0.02	0.03	0.04	0.05	0.06	0.07	0.08	0.09
0.5	0.000	0.025	0.050	0.075	0.100	0.126	0.151	0.176	0.202	0.228
0.6	0.253	0.279	0.305	0.332	0.358	0.385	0.412	0.440	0.468	0.496
0.7	0.524	0.553	0.583	0.613	0.643	0.674	0.706	0.739	0.772	0.806
0.8	0.842	0.878	0.915	0.954	0.994	1.036	1.080	1.126	1.175	1.227

p	0.000	0.001	0.002	0.003	0.004	0.005	0.006	0.007	0.008	0.009
0.90	1.282	1.287	1.293	1.299	1.305	1.311	1.317	1.323	1.329	1.335
0.91	1.341	1.347	1.353	1.359	1.366	1.372	1.379	1.385	1.392	1.398
0.92	1.405	1.412	1.419	1.426	1.433	1.440	1.447	1.454	1.461	1.468
0.93	1.476	1.483	1.491	1.499	1.506	1.514	1.522	1.530	1.538	1.546
0.94	1.555	1.563	1.572	1.580	1.589	1.598	1.607	1.616	1.626	1.635
0.95	1.645	1.655	1.665	1.675	1.685	1.695	1.706	1.717	1.728	1.739
0.96	1.751	1.762	1.774	1.787	1.799	1.812	1.825	1.838	1.852	1.866
0.97	1.881	1.896	1.911	1.927	1.943	1.960	1.977	1.995	2.014	2.034
0.98	2.054	2.075	2.097	2.120	2.144	2.170	2.197	2.226	2.257	2.290

p	0.0000	0.0001	0.0002	0.0003	0.0004	0.0005	0.0006	0.0007	0.0008	0.0009
0.990	2.326	2.330	2.334	2.338	2.342	2.346	2.349	2.353	2.357	2.362
0.991	2.366	2.370	2.374	2.378	2.382	2.387	2.391	2.395	2.400	2.404
0.992	2.409	2.414	2.418	2.423	2.428	2.432	2.437	2.442	2.447	2.452
0.993	2.457	2.462	2.468	2.473	2.478	2.484	2.489	2.495	2.501	2.506
0.994	2.512	2.518	2.524	2.530	2.536	2.543	2.549	2.556	2.562	2.569
0.995	2.576	2.583	2.590	2.597	2.605	2.612	2.620	2.628	2.636	2.644
0.996	2.652	2.661	2.669	2.678	2.687	2.697	2.706	2.716	2.727	2.737
0.997	2.748	2.759	2.770	2.782	2.794	2.807	2.820	2.834	2.848	2.863
0.998	2.878	2.894	2.911	2.929	2.948	2.968	2.989	3.011	3.036	3.062
0.999	3.090	3.121	3.156	3.195	3.239	3.291	3.353	3.432	3.540	3.719

See Table A.3 for commonly used values.

A.3 COMMONLY USED NORMAL QUANTILES

Table A.3 lists commonly used normal quantiles. The confidence levels listed in the first column are for a two-sided confidence intervals. For example, for a two-sided confidence interval at 99%, $\alpha = 0.01$, $\alpha/2 = 0.005$ and $z_{0.995} = 2.576$. For a one-sided confidence interval at 99%, $\alpha = 0.01$, and $z_{1-\alpha} = 2.326$.

TABLE A.3 Commonly Used Normal Quantiles

Confidence Level (%)	α	$\alpha/2$	$z_{1-\alpha/2}$
20	0.8	0.4	0.253
40	0.6	0.3	0.524
60	0.4	0.2	0.842
68.26	0.3174	0.1587	1.000
80	0.2	0.1	1.282
90	0.1	0.05	1.645
95	0.05	0.025	1.960
95.46	0.0454	0.0228	2.000
98	0.02	0.01	2.326
99	0.01	0.005	2.576
99.74	0.0026	0.0013	3.000
99.8	0.002	0.001	3.090
99.9	0.001	0.0005	3.29
99.98	0.0002	0.0001	3.72

A.4   QUANTILES OF THE t DISTRIBUTION

Table A.4 lists $t_{[p;n]}$. For example, the $t_{[0.95;13]}$ required for a two-sided 90% confidence interval of the mean of a sample of 14 observation is 1.771.

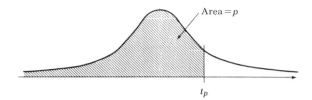

TABLE A.4   **Quantiles of the t Distribution**

n	0.6000	0.7000	0.8000	0.9000	0.9500	0.9750	0.9950	0.9995
1	0.325	0.727	1.377	3.078	6.314	12.706	63.657	636.619
2	0.289	0.617	1.061	1.886	2.920	4.303	9.925	31.599
3	0.277	0.584	0.978	1.638	2.353	3.182	5.841	12.924
4	0.271	0.569	0.941	1.533	2.132	2.776	4.604	8.610
5	0.267	0.559	0.920	1.476	2.015	2.571	4.032	6.869
6	0.265	0.553	0.906	1.440	1.943	2.447	3.707	5.959
7	0.263	0.549	0.896	1.415	1.895	2.365	3.499	5.408
8	0.262	0.546	0.889	1.397	1.860	2.306	3.355	5.041
9	0.261	0.543	0.883	1.383	1.833	2.262	3.250	4.781
10	0.260	0.542	0.879	1.372	1.812	2.228	3.169	4.587
11	0.260	0.540	0.876	1.363	1.796	2.201	3.106	4.437
12	0.259	0.539	0.873	1.356	1.782	2.179	3.055	4.318
13	0.259	0.538	0.870	1.350	1.771	2.160	3.012	4.221
14	0.258	0.537	0.868	1.345	1.761	2.145	2.977	4.140
15	0.258	0.536	0.866	1.341	1.753	2.131	2.947	4.073
16	0.258	0.535	0.865	1.337	1.746	2.120	2.921	4.015
17	0.257	0.534	0.863	1.333	1.740	2.110	2.898	3.965
18	0.257	0.534	0.862	1.330	1.734	2.101	2.878	3.922
19	0.257	0.533	0.861	1.328	1.729	2.093	2.861	3.883
20	0.257	0.533	0.860	1.325	1.725	2.086	2.845	3.850
21	0.257	0.532	0.859	1.323	1.721	2.080	2.831	3.819
22	0.256	0.532	0.858	1.321	1.717	2.074	2.819	3.792
23	0.256	0.532	0.858	1.319	1.714	2.069	2.807	3.768
24	0.256	0.531	0.857	1.318	1.711	2.064	2.797	3.745
25	0.256	0.531	0.856	1.316	1.708	2.060	2.787	3.725
26	0.256	0.531	0.856	1.315	1.706	2.056	2.779	3.707
27	0.256	0.531	0.855	1.314	1.703	2.052	2.771	3.690
28	0.256	0.530	0.855	1.313	1.701	2.048	2.763	3.674
29	0.256	0.530	0.854	1.311	1.699	2.045	2.756	3.659
30	0.256	0.530	0.854	1.310	1.697	2.042	2.750	3.646
60	0.254	0.527	0.848	1.296	1.671	2.000	2.660	3.460
90	0.254	0.526	0.846	1.291	1.662	1.987	2.632	3.402
120	0.254	0.526	0.845	1.289	1.658	1.980	2.617	3.373

A.5 QUANTILES OF THE CHI-SQUARE DISTRIBUTION

Table A.5 lists $\chi^2_{[p;n]}$. For example, the $\chi^2_{[0.95;13]}$ required for a chi-square test at 95% confidence using 14 cells is 22.362.

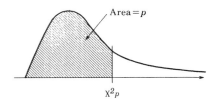

TABLE A.5   Quantiles of the Chi-Square Distribution

n	0.005	0.010	0.050	0.100	0.200	0.500	0.800	0.900	0.950	0.990	0.995
1	a	b	c	d	0.064	0.455	1.642	2.706	3.841	6.635	7.879
2	0.010	0.020	0.103	0.211	0.446	1.386	3.219	4.605	5.991	9.210	10.596
3	0.072	0.115	0.352	0.585	1.005	2.366	4.642	6.253	7.817	11.356	12.861
4	0.207	0.297	0.711	1.064	1.649	3.357	5.989	7.779	9.488	13.277	14.861
5	0.412	0.554	1.145	1.610	2.343	4.351	7.289	9.236	11.071	15.086	16.750
6	0.676	0.872	1.635	2.204	3.070	5.348	8.558	10.645	12.592	16.812	18.548
7	0.989	1.239	2.167	2.833	3.822	6.346	9.803	12.017	14.067	18.475	20.278
8	1.344	1.646	2.733	3.490	4.594	7.344	11.030	13.362	15.507	20.090	21.955
9	1.735	2.088	3.325	4.168	5.380	8.343	12.242	14.684	16.919	21.666	23.589
10	2.156	2.558	3.940	4.865	6.179	9.342	13.442	15.987	18.307	23.209	25.188
11	2.603	3.053	4.575	5.578	6.989	10.341	14.631	17.275	19.675	24.725	26.757
12	3.074	3.571	5.226	6.304	7.807	11.340	15.812	18.549	21.026	26.217	28.300
13	3.565	4.107	5.892	7.041	8.634	12.340	16.985	19.812	22.362	27.688	29.820
14	4.075	4.660	6.571	7.790	9.467	13.339	18.151	21.064	23.685	29.141	31.319
15	4.601	5.229	7.261	8.547	10.307	14.339	19.311	22.307	24.996	30.578	32.801
16	5.142	5.812	7.962	9.312	11.152	15.339	20.465	23.542	26.296	32.000	34.267
17	5.697	6.408	8.672	10.085	12.002	16.338	21.615	24.769	27.587	33.409	35.719
18	6.265	7.015	9.390	10.865	12.857	17.338	22.760	25.989	28.869	34.805	37.156
19	6.844	7.633	10.117	11.651	13.716	18.338	23.900	27.204	30.144	36.191	38.582
20	7.434	8.260	10.851	12.443	14.578	19.337	25.038	28.412	31.410	37.566	39.997
21	8.034	8.897	11.591	13.240	15.445	20.337	26.171	29.615	32.671	38.932	41.401
22	8.643	9.542	12.338	14.041	16.314	21.337	27.301	30.813	33.924	40.289	42.796
23	9.260	10.196	13.090	14.848	17.186	22.337	28.429	32.007	35.172	41.638	44.181
24	9.886	10.856	13.848	15.659	18.062	23.337	29.553	33.196	36.415	42.980	45.559
25	10.520	11.524	14.611	16.473	18.940	24.337	30.675	34.382	37.653	44.314	46.928

a 3.93×10^{-5}
b 1.57×10^{-4}
c 3.93×10^{-3}
d 1.58×10^{-2}

(Continued

TABLE A.5 (Continued)

n	0.005	0.010	0.050	0.100	0.200	0.500	0.800	0.900	0.950	0.990	0.995
26	11.160	12.198	15.379	17.292	19.820	25.336	31.795	35.563	38.885	45.642	48.290
27	11.808	12.878	16.151	18.114	20.703	26.336	32.912	36.741	40.113	46.963	49.645
28	12.461	13.565	16.928	18.939	21.588	27.336	34.027	37.916	41.337	48.278	50.993
29	13.121	14.256	17.708	19.768	22.475	28.336	35.139	39.088	42.557	49.588	52.336
30	13.787	14.953	18.493	20.599	23.364	29.336	36.250	40.256	43.773	50.892	53.672
31	14.458	15.655	19.281	21.434	24.255	30.336	37.359	41.422	44.985	52.191	55.003
32	15.134	16.362	20.072	22.271	25.148	31.336	38.466	42.585	46.194	53.486	56.328
33	15.815	17.073	20.866	23.110	26.042	32.336	39.572	43.745	47.400	54.776	57.649
34	16.501	17.789	21.664	23.952	26.938	33.336	40.676	44.903	48.602	56.061	58.964
35	17.192	18.509	22.465	24.797	27.836	34.336	41.778	46.059	49.802	57.342	60.275
36	17.887	19.233	23.269	25.643	28.735	35.336	42.879	47.212	50.998	58.619	61.581
37	18.586	19.960	24.075	26.492	29.635	36.336	43.978	48.363	52.192	59.893	62.883
38	19.289	20.691	24.884	27.343	30.537	37.335	45.076	49.513	53.384	61.162	64.181
39	19.996	21.426	25.695	28.196	31.440	38.335	46.173	50.660	54.572	62.428	65.476
40	20.706	22.164	26.509	29.050	32.345	39.335	47.269	51.805	55.759	63.691	66.766

A.6   90-PERCENTILES OF THE $F(n, m)$ DISTRIBUTION

Table A.6 lists $F_{[0.90;n,m]}$. For example, the $F_{[0.90;9,18]}$ required for an F-test at 90% confidence level is 2.00.

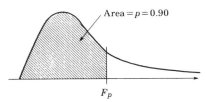

TABLE A.6   90-Percentiles of the $F(n, m)$ Distribution

	Numerator Degrees of Freedom n									
m	1	2	3	4	5	6	7	8	9	10
1	39.86	49.50	53.59	55.83	57.24	58.20	58.90	59.44	59.86	60.19
2	8.53	9.00	9.16	9.24	9.29	9.33	9.35	9.37	9.38	9.39
3	5.54	5.46	5.39	5.34	5.31	5.28	5.27	5.25	5.24	5.23
4	4.54	4.32	4.19	4.11	4.05	4.01	3.98	3.95	3.94	3.92
5	4.06	3.78	3.62	3.52	3.45	3.40	3.37	3.34	3.32	3.30
6	3.78	3.46	3.29	3.18	3.11	3.05	3.01	2.98	2.96	2.94
7	3.59	3.26	3.07	2.96	2.88	2.83	2.78	2.75	2.72	2.70
8	3.46	3.11	2.92	2.81	2.73	2.67	2.62	2.59	2.56	2.54
9	3.36	3.01	2.81	2.69	2.61	2.55	2.51	2.47	2.44	2.42
10	3.29	2.92	2.73	2.61	2.52	2.46	2.41	2.38	2.35	2.32
12	3.18	2.81	2.61	2.48	2.39	2.33	2.28	2.24	2.21	2.19
14	3.10	2.73	2.52	2.39	2.31	2.24	2.19	2.15	2.12	2.10
16	3.05	2.67	2.46	2.33	2.24	2.18	2.13	2.09	2.06	2.03
18	3.01	2.62	2.42	2.29	2.20	2.13	2.08	2.04	2.00	1.98
20	2.97	2.59	2.38	2.25	2.16	2.09	2.04	2.00	1.96	1.94
25	2.92	2.53	2.32	2.18	2.09	2.02	1.97	1.93	1.89	1.87
30	2.88	2.49	2.28	2.14	2.05	1.98	1.93	1.88	1.85	1.82
35	2.85	2.46	2.25	2.11	2.02	1.95	1.90	1.85	1.82	1.79
40	2.84	2.44	2.23	2.09	2.00	1.93	1.87	1.83	1.79	1.76
500	2.72	2.31	2.09	1.96	1.86	1.79	1.73	1.68	1.64	1.61

	Numerator Degrees of Freedom n									
m	12	14	16	18	20	25	30	35	40	500
1	60.70	61.07	61.35	61.56	61.74	62.05	62.26	62.41	62.53	63.26
2	9.41	9.42	9.43	9.44	9.44	9.45	9.46	9.46	9.47	9.49
3	5.22	5.20	5.20	5.19	5.18	5.17	5.17	5.16	5.16	5.13
4	3.90	3.88	3.86	3.85	3.84	3.83	3.82	3.81	3.80	3.76
5	3.27	3.25	3.23	3.22	3.21	3.19	3.17	3.16	3.16	3.10
6	2.90	2.88	2.86	2.85	2.84	2.81	2.80	2.79	2.78	2.72
7	2.67	2.64	2.62	2.61	2.59	2.57	2.56	2.54	2.54	2.47
8	2.50	2.48	2.45	2.44	2.42	2.40	2.38	2.37	2.36	2.29
9	2.38	2.35	2.33	2.31	2.30	2.27	2.25	2.24	2.23	2.16
10	2.28	2.26	2.23	2.22	2.20	2.17	2.16	2.14	2.13	2.06
12	2.15	2.12	2.09	2.08	2.06	2.03	2.01	2.00	1.99	1.90
14	2.05	2.02	2.00	1.98	1.96	1.93	1.91	1.90	1.89	1.80
16	1.99	1.95	1.93	1.91	1.89	1.86	1.84	1.82	1.81	1.72
18	1.93	1.90	1.87	1.85	1.84	1.80	1.78	1.77	1.75	1.66
20	1.89	1.86	1.83	1.81	1.79	1.76	1.74	1.72	1.71	1.61
25	1.82	1.79	1.76	1.74	1.72	1.68	1.66	1.64	1.63	1.52
30	1.77	1.74	1.71	1.69	1.67	1.63	1.61	1.59	1.57	1.46
35	1.74	1.70	1.67	1.65	1.63	1.60	1.57	1.55	1.53	1.41
40	1.71	1.68	1.65	1.62	1.61	1.57	1.54	1.52	1.51	1.38
500	1.56	1.52	1.49	1.46	1.44	1.39	1.36	1.33	1.31	2.16

A.7   95-PERCENTILES OF THE $F(n, m)$ DISTRIBUTION

Table A.7 lists $F_{[0.95;n,m]}$. For example, the $F_{[0.95;9,14]}$ required for an F-test at 95% confidence level is 2.70.

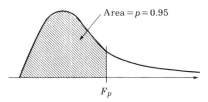

Area $= p = 0.95$

F_p

TABLE A.7   95-Percentiles of the $F(n, m)$ Distribution

	Numerator Degrees of Freedom n									
m	1	2	3	4	5	6	7	8	9	10
1	161.45	199.50	215.70	224.57	230.15	233.97	236.76	238.87	240.53	241.87
2	18.51	19.00	19.16	19.25	19.30	19.33	19.35	19.37	19.38	19.40
3	10.13	9.55	9.28	9.12	9.01	8.94	8.89	8.85	8.81	8.79
4	7.71	6.94	6.59	6.39	6.26	6.16	6.09	6.04	6.00	5.96
5	6.61	5.79	5.41	5.19	5.05	4.95	4.88	4.82	4.77	4.74
6	5.99	5.14	4.76	4.53	4.39	4.28	4.21	4.15	4.10	4.06
7	5.59	4.74	4.35	4.12	3.97	3.87	3.79	3.73	3.68	3.64
8	5.32	4.46	4.07	3.84	3.69	3.58	3.50	3.44	3.39	3.35
9	5.12	4.26	3.86	3.63	3.48	3.37	3.29	3.23	3.18	3.14
10	4.96	4.10	3.71	3.48	3.33	3.22	3.14	3.07	3.02	2.98
12	4.75	3.89	3.49	3.26	3.11	3.00	2.91	2.85	2.80	2.75
14	4.60	3.74	3.34	3.11	2.96	2.85	2.76	2.70	2.65	2.60
16	4.49	3.63	3.24	3.01	2.85	2.74	2.66	2.59	2.54	2.49
18	4.41	3.55	3.16	2.93	2.77	2.66	2.58	2.51	2.46	2.41
20	4.35	3.49	3.10	2.87	2.71	2.60	2.51	2.45	2.39	2.35
25	4.24	3.39	2.99	2.76	2.60	2.49	2.40	2.34	2.28	2.24
30	4.17	3.32	2.92	2.69	2.53	2.42	2.33	2.27	2.21	2.16
35	4.12	3.27	2.87	2.64	2.49	2.37	2.29	2.22	2.16	2.11
40	4.08	3.23	2.84	2.61	2.45	2.34	2.25	2.18	2.12	2.08
500	3.86	3.01	2.62	2.39	2.23	2.12	2.03	1.96	1.90	1.85

	Numerator Degrees of Freedom n									
m	12	14	16	18	20	25	30	35	40	500
1	243.90	245.35	246.45	247.31	248.00	249.25	250.09	250.68	251.13	254.05
2	19.41	19.42	19.43	19.44	19.45	19.46	19.46	19.47	19.47	19.49
3	8.74	8.71	8.69	8.67	8.66	8.63	8.62	8.60	8.59	8.53
4	5.91	5.87	5.84	5.82	5.80	5.77	5.75	5.73	5.72	5.63
5	4.68	4.64	4.60	4.58	4.56	4.52	4.50	4.48	4.46	4.36
6	4.00	3.96	3.92	3.90	3.87	3.83	3.81	3.79	3.77	3.67
7	3.57	3.53	3.49	3.47	3.44	3.40	3.38	3.36	3.34	3.23
8	3.28	3.24	3.20	3.17	3.15	3.11	3.08	3.06	3.04	2.93
9	3.07	3.03	2.99	2.96	2.94	2.89	2.86	2.84	2.83	2.71
10	2.91	2.86	2.83	2.80	2.77	2.73	2.70	2.68	2.66	2.54
12	2.69	2.64	2.60	2.57	2.54	2.50	2.47	2.44	2.43	2.30
14	2.53	2.48	2.44	2.41	2.39	2.34	2.31	2.28	2.27	2.13
16	2.42	2.37	2.33	2.30	2.28	2.23	2.19	2.17	2.15	2.01
18	2.34	2.29	2.25	2.22	2.19	2.14	2.11	2.08	2.06	1.92
20	2.28	2.22	2.18	2.15	2.12	2.07	2.04	2.01	1.99	1.84
25	2.16	2.11	2.07	2.04	2.01	1.96	1.92	1.89	1.87	1.71
30	2.09	2.04	1.99	1.96	1.93	1.88	1.84	1.81	1.79	1.62
35	2.04	1.99	1.94	1.91	1.88	1.82	1.79	1.76	1.74	1.56
40	2.00	1.95	1.90	1.87	1.84	1.78	1.74	1.72	1.69	1.51
500	1.77	1.71	1.66	1.62	1.59	1.53	1.48	1.45	1.42	2.21

A.8 99-PERCENTILES OF THE $F(n, m)$ DISTRIBUTION

Table A.8 lists $F_{[0.99;n,m]}$. For example, the $F_{[0.99;6,12]}$ required for an F-test at 99% confidence level is 4.82.

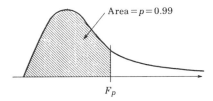

Area $= p = 0.99$

F_p

TABLE A.8   99-Percentiles of the $F(n, m)$ Distribution

	Numerator Degrees of Freedom n									
m	1	2	3	4	5	6	7	8	9	10
1	4052.18	4999.50	5403.05	5624.30	5763.37	5858.71	5928.09	5980.80	6022.21	6055.58
2	98.50	99.00	99.17	99.25	99.30	99.33	99.36	99.37	99.39	99.40
3	34.12	30.82	29.46	28.71	28.24	27.91	27.67	27.49	27.34	27.23
4	21.20	18.00	16.69	15.98	15.52	15.21	14.98	14.80	14.66	14.55
5	16.26	13.27	12.06	11.39	10.97	10.67	10.46	10.29	10.16	10.05
6	13.75	10.92	9.78	9.15	8.75	8.47	8.26	8.10	7.98	7.87
7	12.25	9.55	8.45	7.85	7.46	7.19	6.99	6.84	6.72	6.62
8	11.26	8.65	7.59	7.01	6.63	6.37	6.18	6.03	5.91	5.81
9	10.56	8.02	6.99	6.42	6.06	5.80	5.61	5.47	5.35	5.26
10	10.04	7.56	6.55	5.99	5.64	5.39	5.20	5.06	4.94	4.85
12	9.33	6.93	5.95	5.41	5.06	4.82	4.64	4.50	4.39	4.30
14	8.86	6.51	5.56	5.04	4.69	4.46	4.28	4.14	4.03	3.94
16	8.53	6.23	5.29	4.77	4.44	4.20	4.03	3.89	3.78	3.69
18	8.29	6.01	5.09	4.58	4.25	4.01	3.84	3.71	3.60	3.51
20	8.10	5.85	4.94	4.43	4.10	3.87	3.70	3.56	3.46	3.37
25	7.77	5.57	4.68	4.18	3.85	3.63	3.46	3.32	3.22	3.13
30	7.56	5.39	4.51	4.02	3.70	3.47	3.30	3.17	3.07	2.98
35	7.42	5.27	4.40	3.91	3.59	3.37	3.20	3.07	2.96	2.88
40	7.31	5.18	4.31	3.83	3.51	3.29	3.12	2.99	2.89	2.80
500	6.69	4.65	3.82	3.36	3.05	2.84	2.68	2.55	2.44	2.36

	Numerator Degrees of Freedom n									
m	12	14	16	18	20	25	30	35	40	500
1	6106.06	6142.42	6169.85	6191.28	6208.48	6239.57	6260.40	6275.32	6286.53	6359.26
2	99.42	99.43	99.44	99.44	99.45	99.46	99.47	99.47	99.47	99.50
3	27.05	26.92	26.83	26.75	26.69	26.58	26.50	26.45	26.41	26.12
4	14.37	14.25	14.15	14.08	14.02	13.91	13.84	13.79	13.75	13.46
5	9.89	9.77	9.68	9.61	9.55	9.45	9.38	9.33	9.29	9.02
6	7.72	7.60	7.52	7.45	7.40	7.30	7.23	7.18	7.14	6.88
7	6.47	6.36	6.28	6.21	6.16	6.06	5.99	5.94	5.91	5.65
8	5.67	5.56	5.48	5.41	5.36	5.26	5.20	5.15	5.12	4.86
9	5.11	5.01	4.92	4.86	4.81	4.71	4.65	4.60	4.57	4.31
10	4.71	4.60	4.52	4.46	4.41	4.31	4.25	4.20	4.17	3.91
12	4.16	4.05	3.97	3.91	3.86	3.76	3.70	3.65	3.62	3.36
14	3.80	3.70	3.62	3.56	3.51	3.41	3.35	3.30	3.27	3.00
16	3.55	3.45	3.37	3.31	3.26	3.16	3.10	3.05	3.02	2.75
18	3.37	3.27	3.19	3.13	3.08	2.98	2.92	2.87	2.84	2.57
20	3.23	3.13	3.05	2.99	2.94	2.84	2.78	2.73	2.69	2.42
25	2.99	2.89	2.81	2.75	2.70	2.60	2.54	2.49	2.45	2.17
30	2.84	2.74	2.66	2.60	2.55	2.45	2.39	2.34	2.30	2.01
35	2.74	2.64	2.56	2.50	2.44	2.35	2.28	2.23	2.19	1.89
40	2.66	2.56	2.48	2.42	2.37	2.27	2.20	2.15	2.11	1.80
500	2.22	2.12	2.04	1.97	1.92	1.81	1.74	1.68	1.63	2.30

A.9 QUANTILES OF THE K-S DISTRIBUTION

Table A.9 lists quantiles $K_{[p;n]}$ of the K-S distribution. For example, the $K_{[0.99;12]}$ required for a K-S test at 99% confidence level is 1.4521.

TABLE A.9   Quantiles of the K-S Distribution

					p						
n	0.00	0.01	0.05	0.10	0.20	0.50	0.80	0.90	0.95	0.99	0.995
1	0.0050	0.0100	0.0500	0.1000	0.2000	0.5000	0.8000	0.9000	0.9500	0.9900	0.9950
2	0.0067	0.0135	0.0673	0.1296	0.2416	0.5176	0.7818	0.9670	1.0980	1.2728	1.3142
3	0.0081	0.0162	0.0792	0.1471	0.2615	0.5147	0.8187	0.9783	1.1017	1.3589	1.4359
4	0.0093	0.0186	0.0879	0.1590	0.2726	0.5110	0.8248	0.9853	1.1304	1.3777	1.4685
5	0.0103	0.0207	0.0947	0.1675	0.2793	0.5245	0.8277	0.9995	1.1392	1.4024	1.4949
6	0.0113	0.0226	0.1002	0.1739	0.2834	0.5319	0.8343	1.0052	1.1463	1.4144	1.5104
7	0.0121	0.0243	0.1048	0.1787	0.2859	0.5364	0.8398	1.0093	1.1537	1.4246	1.5235
8	0.0130	0.0259	0.1086	0.1826	0.2874	0.5392	0.8431	1.0135	1.1586	1.4327	1.5324
9	0.0137	0.0275	0.1119	0.1856	0.2881	0.5411	0.8455	1.0173	1.1624	1.4388	1.5400
10	0.0145	0.0289	0.1147	0.1880	0.2884	0.5426	0.8477	1.0202	1.1658	1.4440	1.5461
11	0.0151	0.0303	0.1172	0.1900	0.2883	0.5439	0.8498	1.0225	1.1688	1.4484	1.5512
12	0.0158	0.0314	0.1193	0.1916	0.2879	0.5453	0.8519	1.0246	1.1714	1.4521	1.5555
13	0.0164	0.0324	0.1212	0.1929	0.2903	0.5468	0.8537	1.0265	1.1736	1.4553	1.5593
14	0.0171	0.0333	0.1229	0.1940	0.2925	0.5486	0.8551	1.0282	1.1755	1.4581	1.5626
15	0.0176	0.0342	0.1244	0.1948	0.2944	0.5500	0.8564	1.0298	1.1773	1.4606	1.5655
16	0.0182	0.0351	0.1257	0.1955	0.2961	0.5512	0.8576	1.0311	1.1789	1.4629	1.5681
17	0.0188	0.0359	0.1269	0.1961	0.2975	0.5523	0.8587	1.0324	1.1803	1.4649	1.5704
18	0.0193	0.0367	0.1280	0.1965	0.2987	0.5532	0.8597	1.0335	1.1816	1.4667	1.5725
19	0.0198	0.0374	0.1290	0.1968	0.2998	0.5540	0.8607	1.0346	1.1828	1.4683	1.5744
20	0.0203	0.0381	0.1298	0.1971	0.3007	0.5547	0.8616	1.0355	1.1839	1.4699	1.5761
21	0.0208	0.0387	0.1306	0.1973	0.3015	0.5554	0.8624	1.0365	1.1850	1.4712	1.5777
22	0.0213	0.0394	0.1313	0.1974	0.3023	0.5561	0.8631	1.0373	1.1859	1.4725	1.5792
23	0.0217	0.0400	0.1320	0.1974	0.3030	0.5567	0.8639	1.0381	1.1868	1.4737	1.5806
24	0.0221	0.0405	0.1326	0.1974	0.3035	0.5573	0.8645	1.0388	1.1876	1.4748	1.5816
25	0.0225	0.0411	0.1331	0.1974	0.3041	0.5579	0.8651	1.0395	1.1884	1.4758	1.5829
26	0.0228	0.0416	0.1336	0.1977	0.3046	0.5585	0.8657	1.0402	1.1891	1.4768	1.5840
27	0.0231	0.0421	0.1340	0.1985	0.3050	0.5590	0.8663	1.0408	1.1898	1.4777	1.5850
28	0.0235	0.0426	0.1344	0.1992	0.3054	0.5595	0.8668	1.0414	1.1905	1.4786	1.5860
29	0.0238	0.0431	0.1348	0.2000	0.3058	0.5600	0.8673	1.0419	1.1911	1.4794	1.5869
30	0.0241	0.0435	0.1351	0.2006	0.3062	0.5605	0.8678	1.0424	1.1916	1.4801	1.5878

A.10 APPROXIMATION FORMULAS FOR STATISTICAL TABLES

In computer programs, the following approximate formulas may be used in place of statistical tables:

1. *Area Under the Normal Distribution*: The area under the unit normal pdf between 0 and z is given approximately by (Hastings, Jr. (1955)):

$$p = \tfrac{1}{2} - \tfrac{1}{2}(1 + 0.196854z + 0.115194z^2 + 0.000344z^3 + 0.019527z^4)^{-4}$$

Given z_α, this formula can be used to find α ($\alpha = 0.5 + p$).

2. *Unit Normal Quantiles*: The unit normal quantile z_p for a given p can be calculated approximately by the following formula (Hastings, Jr. (1955)):

$$z_p = \eta - \frac{2.515517 + 0.802853\eta + 0.010328\eta^2}{1 + 1.432788\eta + 0.189269\eta^2 + 0.001308\eta^3}$$

where

$$\eta = \sqrt{\ln\left(\frac{1}{(1-p)^2}\right)}, \qquad 0.5 < p \le 1$$

A simpler but more approximate formula is

$$z_p = 4.91[p^{0.14} - (1-p)^{0.14}]$$

3. *Chi-Square Quantiles*: For large degrees of freedom, the $\chi^2(\nu)$ quantiles can be calculated approximately from the unit normal quantiles z_α as follows:

$$\chi^2_{[\alpha;\nu]} = \tfrac{1}{2}\left(\sqrt{2\nu - 1} + z_\alpha\right)^2$$

Given a χ^2_α value, this formula can also be used to compute z_α and hence the significance α.

4. *F-Quantiles*: For large degrees of freedoms, the following approximation can be used to compute F_α from z_α:

$$F_{[\alpha;n,m]} = \frac{m}{m-2} + z_\alpha\left[\frac{m}{m-2}\sqrt{\frac{2(n+m-2)}{n(m-4)}}\right]$$

Again, given an F_α value, this formula can also be used to to compute z_α and hence the significance α.

SOLUTIONS TO SELECTED EXERCISES

1.1 System A is better if B is used as a base and vice versa.

6.1 The correlation between CPU time (t_{CPU}) and number of I/O's ($n_{I/O}$) is 0.663. The principal factors y_1 and y_2 are

$$\begin{bmatrix} y_1 \\ y_2 \end{bmatrix} = \begin{bmatrix} \dfrac{1}{\sqrt{2}} & \dfrac{1}{\sqrt{2}} \\ \dfrac{1}{\sqrt{2}} & -\dfrac{1}{\sqrt{2}} \end{bmatrix} \begin{bmatrix} \dfrac{t_{CPU} - 7.43}{4.69} \\ \dfrac{n_{I/O} - 454.0}{1009.3} \end{bmatrix}$$

The first factor explains 83% of total variation.

6.2 There is no unique solution to this exercise. Depending upon the choice of outliers, scaling technique, or distance metric, different results are possible, all of which could be considered correct. One solution using no outliers, range normalization to (0,1), and Euclidean distance starts with the the normalized values shown in the following:

Program	CPU time	I/O's
TKB	1.00	1.00
MAC	0.92	0.09
COBOL	0.54	0.01
BASIC	0.38	0.01
Pascal	0.38	0.00
EDT	0.23	0.03
SOS	0.00	0.01

BASIC, Pascal, EDT, COBOL, SOS, MAC, and TKB join the dendrogram at distances of 0.01, 0.15, 0.21, 0.38, 0.63, and 1.14, respectively.

Other possibilities are to discard TKB and MAC as outliers, normalize using the mean and standard deviation, and transform I/O's to a logarithmic scale. All these and similar alternatives should be considered correct provided a justification is given for the choice.

10.1   **a.** Bar

      b. Line

      c. Bar

      d. Line

10.4   FOM=73

11.1   Each of the three systems can be shown to be the best by taking an average of the ratios with respect to its execution times.

12.1   **a.** $\frac{1}{3}$

      b. $\frac{2}{3}$

      c. 0

      d. $\frac{2}{3}$

      e. $\frac{1}{9}$

      f. $1/3^9$

12.2   Mean $= 1/p$, variance $= (1-p)/p^2$, standard deviation $= \sqrt{(1-p)}/p$, C.O.V. $= \sqrt{1-p}$

12.3   Mean $= \lambda$, variance $= \lambda$, C.O.V. $= \lambda^{-1/2}$

12.4   **a.** 2λ

      b. 2λ

      c. 0

      d. 2λ

      e. $-\lambda$

      f. $5\lambda^{-1/2}$

12.5 $f(x) = \dfrac{x^{m-1}e^{-x/a}}{(m-1)!a^m}$,

      mean $= am$, variance $= a^2m$, mode $= a(m-1)$, C.O.V. $= 1/\sqrt{m}$

12.6 $f(x) = ax^{-(a+1)}$; mean $= a/(a-1)$ provided $a > 1$; variance $= a/[(a-1)^2(a-2)]$ provided $a > 2$; C.O.V. $= [a(a-2)]^{-1/2}$; mode $= 0$

12.7   **a.** 0.2742

      b. 0.5793

      c. 0.2348

      d. 6.644 seconds

12.8   **a.** Mean
     b. Mean
     c. Median
     d. Mode

12.9   **a.** Mode
     b. Median
     c. Mode
     d. Median
     e. Median

12.10   Since the ratio of maximum to minimum is very high, use the median. The geometric mean can also be used if a logarithmic transformation can be justified based on physical considerations.

12.11   Arithmetic mean since the data is very clustered together (not skewed) and y_{max}/y_{min} ratio is small.

12.13   Use SIQR since the data is skewed.

12.14   Use the coefficient of variation (or standard deviation) since the data is not skewed.

12.15   The normal quantile-quantile plot for this data is shown in Figure 20.2. From the plot, the errors do appear to be normally distributed.

13.1   **a.** $N(\mu, 1/\sqrt{n})$
     b. $N(0, 2/\sqrt{n})$
     c. $N(2\mu, 2/\sqrt{n})$
     d. $N(\mu, 1/\sqrt{2n})$
     e. $\chi^2(n)$
     f. $\chi^2(2n)$
     g. $F(n, n)$
     h. $t(n)$

13.2   **a.** 14 and 38
     b. 26.91
     c. (24.18, 29.64)
     d. 0.485, (0.342, 0.628)
     e. (24.79, 26.91) or (26.91, 29.03)

13.3   (−223.92, 4943.92), (−337.53, 4821.31), (−118.89, 2961.08), (43.77, 2593.10), and (−9.75, 2554.76). The processors are not different.

14.2   **a.** Only b_1 is significant.
     b. 97%
     c. 160.55

d. (139.50, 181,60)

e. (141.45, 179.66)

14.3 CPU time in milliseconds $= -0.2556 + 0.0512 \times$ (memory size in kilobytes); $R^2 = 0.972$; the 90% confidence intervals of b_0 and b_1 are $(-1.9532, 1.4421)$ and $(0.0433, 0.0591)$; the intercept is zero but the slope is significant.

14.4 Elasped time $= 0.196$ (number of days) $+ 0.511$; the 90% confidence intervals for the regression coefficients are $(0.36, 0.66)$ for the intercept and $(0.18, 0.21)$ for the slope; both are significant.

14.5 Elapsed time $= 0.635 + 0.063 \times$ (number of keys); $R^2 = 0.943$; the confidence intervals of the coefficients are $(0.461, 0.809)$ and $(0.042, 0.084)$, respectively.

14.6 Number of disk I/O's $= -3.875 + 6.625 \times$ (number of keys); $R^2 = 0.846$; the 90% confidence intervals for the coefficients are $(-35.627, 27.877)$ and $(2.78, 10.47)$; b_0 is not significant.

14.7 Time $= -15315.96 + 49.557$ (record size); $R^2 = 0.744$. Both parameters are significant. However, the scatter plot of the data shows a nonlinear relationship. The residuals versus predicted estimates show that the errors have a parabolic trend. This indicates that the errors are not independent of the predictor variables and so either other predictor variables or some nonlinear terms of current predictors need to be included in the model.

15.1 **a.** 90.25%

b. Yes

c. x_4

d. x_2

e. All

f. Multicollinearity possible

g. Compute correlation among predictors and reduce the number of predictors.

15.2 $\log(\text{time}) = -3.738 + 2.690 \log(\text{key size}) - 0.152 x_2$, where $x_2 = 1 \Rightarrow$ multiprocessor and $x_2 = 0 \Rightarrow$ uniprocessor; $R^2 = 0.9981$. The confidence intervals of the coefficients are $(-4.01, -3.46)$, $(2.58, 2.80)$, and $(-0.22, -0.08)$.

16.1 **a.** 27

b. 9

c. 7

17.1 **a.** $q_0 = 48.13$, $q_A = 1.88$, $q_B = -13.13$, $q_C = -21.88$, $q_{AB} = -1.88$, $q_{AC} = 1.88$, $q_{BC} = 26.88$, and $q_{ABC} = 8.13$

b. 0.24%, 11.88%, 33.01%, 0.24%, 0.24%, 49.82%, 4.55%

c. BC, C, B, ABC, A, AB, AC

18.1 The effects are 50.67, 4.46, -0.89, and -6.19. The effect of workloads is not significant. Interactions explain 62.67% of the variation.

19.1 **a.** $q_0 + q_{ACD} = 48.13$, $q_A + q_{CD} = 1.88$, $q_B + q_{ABCD} = -13.13$, $q_C + q_{AD} = -21.88$, $q_{AB} + q_{BCD} = -1.88$, $q_{AC} + q_D = 1.88$, $q_{BC} + q_{ABD} = 26.88$, and $q_{ABC} + q_{BD} = 8.13$

b. 0.24%, 11.88%, 33.01%, 0.24%, 0.24%, 49.82%, 4.55%

c. BC, C, B, BD, A, AB, D. Higher order interactions are assumed smaller.

d. See **a** above. The generator is $I = -ACD$.

e. $I = ABCD$ may be better.

f. R_{III}

19.2 Yes, $I = ABC$; yes, $I = AB$; yes, $I = ABCD$.

20.1

$$a_{ikj} = \begin{cases} \dfrac{1}{r} - \dfrac{1}{ra}, & k = j \\ \dfrac{1}{ra}, & \text{otherwise} \end{cases}$$

$$\sigma^2_{e_{\alpha j}} = \left[r \left(\frac{1}{r} - \frac{1}{ra} \right)^2 + (ar - r) \left(\frac{1}{ra} \right)^2 \right] \sigma^2_e = \frac{(a-1)\sigma^2_e}{ar}$$

21.1 The confidence intervals for the differences are $(-29.5632, 1.5016)$, $(-18.8270, 12.2378)$, and $(-4.7962, 26.2686)$.

21.3 After logarithmic transformation:

a. 1.18% variation is explained by the processors.

b. 96.10% variation is due to workloads.

c. Yes, several processor pairs are significantly different at 90% confidence level.

21.4 **a.** 1.65% variation is explained by the processors.

b. 96.04% variation is due to workloads.

c. Yes, several processor pairs are significantly different at 90% confidence level.

22.1 **a.** Yes. All processors are significantly different from each other.

b. 16.8%

c. All effects and interactions are significant.

23.1 T_i is high for $A = -1$, $B = -1$, and $E = -1$; T_B is high for $A = -1$, $B = 1$, and $D = -1$.

23.2 T_i is high for $A = -1$, $B = -1$, and $E = -1$; T_B is high for $A = -1$, $B = 1$, and $D = -1$.

24.1
  a. Continous state, deterministic, dynamic, linear, and unstable
  b. Continuous state, deterministic, dynamic, nonlinear, and unstable
  c. Discrete time, continuous state, deterministic, dynamic, linear, and unstable
  d. Discrete time, deterministic, dynamic, linear, and unstable
  e. Continuous time, continuous state, dynamic, nonlinear, and stable
  f. Discrete time, continuous state, probabilistic, dynamic, linear, and unstable

24.2
  a. Trace-driven simulation
  b. Discrete-event simulation
  c. Monte Carlo simulation

25.1
  a. This is expected when the system is underloaded.
  b. This is quite common when the system is overloaded.
  c. This is expected.
  d. This is uncommon and would require validation.
  e. This is rare and would require serious validation effort.

25.2 The transient interval using the truncation method is 1, since 4 is neither the maximum nor the minimum of the remaining observations. However, this is incorrect.

26.1 Maximum period is $2^{4-2} = 4$; a must be 5 or 11. The seed must be odd.

26.2 The values of $24^n \bmod 31$ for $n = 1,\ldots,30$ are 24, 18, 29, 14, 26, 4, 3, 10, 23, 25, 11, 16, 12, 9, 30, 7, 13, 2, 17, 5, 27, 28, 21, 8, 6, 20, 15, 19, 22, 1. The smallest n that results in 1 is 30. Yes, 24 is a primitive root of 31.

26.3 2, 6, 7, 8

26.4 1155

26.5 $x_{10,000} = 1,919,456,777$

26.6 $r = 9$, $q = 2$. The condition $r < q$ is not satisfied.

26.7 No, because $q = 1$ and $r = 7$, thus, r is not less than q.

26.8
  a. Primitive
  b. Primitive
  c. Not primitive
  d. Primitive

26.9 **a.** 21

   b. 9

   c. 63

   d. 45

26.10 0.000001_2, 0.000011_2, 0.000101_2, 0.001111_2, 0.010001_2.

26.11   In both cases, the additive paħameter c should be replaced by c mod m.

26.12   The period of the lth bit is 2^l.

27.1   The computed statistic is 6.690. The 0.9-quantile of a chi-square variate with nine degrees of freedom is 14.68. The sequence passes the test at 90%.

27.2 $K^+ = 0.2582$, $K^- = 0.2259$. Both values are less than $K_{[0.95;15]} = 1.1773$. The sequence passes the test.

27.3   The confidence intervals for the serial autocovariances at lags 1 to 10 are $(-0.003067, -0.000325)$, $(-0.000942, 0.001800)$, $(-0.001410, 0.001332)$, $(-0.001592, 0.001151)$, $(-0.000036, 0.002706)$, $(-0.001791, 0.000951)$, $(-0.000516, 0.002227)$, $(-0.000741, 0.002002)$, $(-0.002476, 0.000267)$, and $(-0.000407, 0.002336)$. One autocovariance is significant.

27.4   The pairs generated by the first generator lie on the following two lines with a positive slope:

$$x_n = \tfrac{1}{2}x_{n-1} + \tfrac{13}{2}k, \qquad k = 0,1$$

The distance between the lines is $13/\sqrt{5}$. The pairs generated by the second generator lie on the following two lines with a negative slope:

$$x_n = -2x_{n-1} + 13k, \qquad k = 1,2$$

The distance between the lines is $13/\sqrt{5}$. Both generators have the same 2-distributivity.

28.1   **a.** Inverse transformation: Generate $u \sim U(0,1)$. If $u < 0.5$, then $x = \sqrt{2u}$; otherwise $x = 2 - \sqrt{2(1-u)}$.

   b. Rejection: Generate $x \sim U(0,2)$ and $y \sim U(0,1)$. If $y \le \min(x, 2 - x)$, then output x; otherwise repeat with another pair.

   c. Composition: The pdf $f(x)$ can be expressed as a weighted sum of a left triangular density and a right triangular density.

   d. Convolution: Generate $u_1 \sim U(0,1)$ and $u_2 \sim U(0,1)$. Return $u_1 + u_2$.

29.1   **a.** Geometric

   b. Negative binomial

   c. Logistic

   d. Normal

   e. Lognormal

   f. Pareto

    g. Poisson

    h. Chi square

    i. F

    j. Exponential

    k. Erlang-m

    l. Binomial

    m. Beta

29.2 **a.** $N(0,1)$, 1.281

    b. $\chi^2(4)$, 7.779

    c. $F(2,2)$, 9.00

    d. $t(3)$, 1.638

30.1 Erlang-k arrivals, general bulk service, five servers, 300 waiting positions, 5000 population size, and last come, first served preemptive resume service.

30.2 Because it provides 10 waiting positions for a population of only 5. Also, two servers have no waiting positions.

30.3 Both will provide the same performance. Increasing buffers beyond the population size has no effect.

30.5 If $k = 1$.

31.1 **a.** $p_n = \dfrac{\rho^n}{n!} p_0$, where $\rho = \dfrac{\lambda}{\mu}$

    b. $p_0 = e^{-\rho}$

    c. $E[n] = \rho$

    d. $\lambda' = \dfrac{\lambda}{\rho}(1 - e^{-\rho})$

    e. $E[r] = \dfrac{E[n]}{\lambda'} = \dfrac{\rho^2}{\lambda(1 - e^{-\rho})}$

31.2 **a.** $p_n = \dfrac{\rho^n}{n!} p_0$, where $\rho = \dfrac{\lambda}{\mu}$

    b. $p_0 = e^{-\rho}$

    c. $E[n] = \rho$

    d. $\mathrm{Var}[n] = \rho$

    e. $E[r] = \dfrac{E[n]}{\lambda} = \dfrac{1}{\mu}$

31.3 **a.** $\rho = \frac{5}{6}$

    b. $E[s] = 1/\mu = E[r](1 - \rho) = 0.5$ second

    c. $\lambda = \mu\rho = 10/6 \Rightarrow 60(10/6) = 100$ queries per minute

    d. $E[n] = \dfrac{\rho}{1 - \rho} = 5$

    e. $P(n > 10) = \rho^{11} = 0.135$

f. $r_{90} = E[r]\ln[10] = 6.9$ seconds

g. $w_{90} = E[r]\ln[10\rho] = 6.36$ seconds

30.4 $E[n] = \lambda E[r] = \dfrac{10{,}800}{3600} \times \dfrac{1}{3} = 1$. Job flow balance was assumed. Service time distribution has no effect.

31.4
a. $\rho = \dfrac{30}{3 \times (1/0.05)} = 0.5$

b. $p_0 = 0.21$

c. $\varrho = 0.24$

d. $E[n] = 1.7$

e. $E[n_q] = 0.25$

f. $E[r] = 0.0579$ second

g. $\mathrm{Var}[r] = 0.00296$ second^2

h. $w_{90} = 0.0287$ second

31.5
a. $\lambda = \frac{30}{3} = 10 \Rightarrow \rho = 0.5$

b. $p_0 = 0.50$

c. $\varrho = 0.50$

d. $E[n] = 1$ request per drive

e. $E[n_q] = 0.5$ request per drive

f. $E[r] = 0.1$ second

g. $\mathrm{Var}[r] = 0.01$ second^2

h. $w_{90} = 0.16$ second

31.6 Yes. With the new system, the 90-percentile of the waiting time will be zero.

31.7 Yes, since with $\lambda = 0.167/2 = 0.0833$, average waiting time is 0.18 minute and the 90-percentile of waiting time is zero.

31.8
a. $p_0 = 0.22$, $p_1 = 0.34$, $p_2 = 0.25$, $p_3 = 0.13$, $p_4 = 0.0629$

b. $E[n] = 1.5$ requests

c. $E[n_q] = 0.0629$ request

d. $\mathrm{Var}[n] = 1.3$

e. $\lambda' = 28$ requests per second

f. Loss rate$=1.9$ requests per second

g. $U = \rho(1 - p_B) = 0.5(1 - 0.0629) = 0.47$

h. $E[r] = 0.0522$ second

31.9

$$
p_n = \begin{cases} p_0(m\rho)^n \dbinom{K}{n}, & 0 \le n < m \\[2ex] p_0\rho^n \dbinom{K}{n} \dfrac{n!}{m!} m^m, & m \le n \le K \end{cases}
$$

where $\rho = \dfrac{\lambda}{m\mu}$

Average throughput $\lambda' = \sum_{n=0}^{K-1}(K-n)\lambda p_n = \lambda(K - E[n])$

$U = \dfrac{\lambda'}{m\mu} = \rho(K - E[n])$

$E[r] = \dfrac{E[n]}{\lambda'} = \dfrac{E[n]}{\lambda(K - E[n])}$

31.10

$$p_n = \begin{cases} \dbinom{K}{n}(m\rho)^n p_0, & 0 \le n < m \\[2ex] \dbinom{K}{n}\dfrac{n!(\rho)^n m^m}{m!}p_0, & m \le n \le B \end{cases}$$

where $\rho = \dfrac{\lambda}{m\mu}$

Average throughput $\lambda' = \lambda(K - E[n] - (K - B)p_B)$
where p_B is the probability of B jobs in the system.

$U = \dfrac{\lambda'}{m\mu} = \rho(K - E[n] - (K - B)p_B)$

$E[r] = \dfrac{E[n]}{\lambda'} = \dfrac{E[n]}{\lambda(K - E[n] - (K - B)p_B)}$

32.1 **a.** Job flow balance
   b. Fair service
   c. Single resource possession
   d. Routing homogeneity
   e. No blocking
   f. Single resource possession
   g. One-step behavior

33.1 $X = 400/10 = 40$, $S = 1/200$, $U = XS = 40/200 = 20\%$

33.2 $n = 4$, $X = 5$, $n = XR \Rightarrow R = \frac{4}{5}$ second

33.3 $X = \frac{40}{10} = 4$, $V_{\text{disk}} = 2$, $X_{\text{disk}} = XV_{\text{disk}} = 8$, $S_{\text{disk}} = 0.030$, $U_{\text{disk}} = X_{\text{disk}}S_{\text{disk}}$
   $= 0.24 \Rightarrow 24\%$

33.4 $X_{\text{printer}} = 500/10 = 50$, $V_{\text{printer}} = 5$, $X = X_{\text{printer}}/V_{\text{printer}} = 10$ jobs/minute

33.5 **a.** 25, 20, and 4
   b. $D_1 = 1$, $D_2 = 0.6$, $D_3 = 0.1$
   c. $U_k = XD_k \Rightarrow X = 0.6/0.6 = 1$; $U_{\text{CPU}} = 1$, $U_B = 0.1$
   d. $U_k = XD_k \Rightarrow X = 0.1/0.1 = 1$; $R = N/X - Z = 20/1 - 5 = 15$ seconds

33.6 a. CPU

    b. $R_{min} = D_1 + D_2 + D_3 = 1.7$

    c. 60%

    d. $D_{max} = 1$, $U_k = X D_k \Rightarrow X \leq 1$ job/second

    e. $R \geq \max\{D, N D_{max} - Z\} \Rightarrow D_{max} \leq \dfrac{R + Z}{N} = 0.6$. We need at least a 40% faster CPU; disk A would be just OK.

    f. $D = 1.7$, $\ D_{max} = 1$, $\ Z = 5$, $\ \Rightarrow X \leq \min\left\{\dfrac{N}{6.7}, 1\right\}$, $\ R \geq \max\{1.7, N - 5\}$

33.7 a. $D_1 = 0.5 \Rightarrow$ disk A

    b. $D_2 = 1.2 \Rightarrow$ disk A

    c. $D_3 = 0.2 \Rightarrow$ CPU

    d. $D_3 = 2 \Rightarrow$ disk B

34.1 $\sum_i Q_i = 5.01$, $R = 6.26$ seconds

34.2

	Response Time			System	Queue Lengths		
N	CPU	Disk A	Disk B	System	Throughput	CPU	Disk A	Disk B
1	0.040	0.030	0.025	1.700	0.149	0.149	0.090	0.015
2	0.046	0.033	0.025	1.904	0.290	0.333	0.189	0.029
3	0.053	0.036	0.026	2.149	0.420	0.559	0.299	0.043
4	0.062	0.039	0.026	2.443	0.537	0.838	0.419	0.056
5	0.074	0.043	0.026	2.795	0.641	1.179	0.546	0.068

34.3

Itera-tion No.	Response Time			System	Queue Lengths		
	CPU	Disk A	Disk B	System	Throughput	CPU	Disk A	Disk B
1	0.293	0.220	0.183	12.467	1.145	8.397	5.038	0.840
2	0.359	0.174	0.045	12.629	1.135	10.185	3.939	0.204
3	0.427	0.142	0.030	13.640	1.073	11.454	3.053	0.128
4	0.475	0.117	0.028	14.334	1.034	12.291	2.421	0.116
5	0.507	0.099	0.028	14.767	1.012	12.826	2.003	0.112

34.4 $R = (n + 2)S$, $X = \dfrac{n}{(n + 2)S}$, $n \geq 1$

34.5 $R = (n + h)S$, $X = \dfrac{n}{(n + h)S}$, Power X/R is maximum at $n = h$.

34.6 The balanced job bounds are

$$\frac{N}{5 + 1.7 + (N-1)0.57\dfrac{1.7(N-1)}{1.7(N-1)+5}}$$

$$\le X(N) \le \min\left\{1, \frac{N}{5 + 1.7 + (N-1)\dfrac{1.7}{1.7+5}}\right\}$$

$$\max\left\{N-5, 1.7 + (N-1)\frac{1.7}{1.7+5}\right\}$$

$$\ge R(N) \le 1.7 + (N-1)0.57\frac{(N-1)1.7}{(N-1)1.7+5}$$

	Response Time			Throughput		
	Lower		Upper	Lower		Upper
N	BJB	MVA	BJB	BJB	MVA	BJB
1	1.700	1.700	1.700	0.149	0.149	0.149
2	1.844	1.904	1.954	0.288	0.290	0.292
3	1.988	2.149	2.510	0.399	0.420	0.429
4	2.131	2.443	3.215	0.487	0.537	0.561
5	2.275	2.795	4.005	0.555	0.641	0.687
6	2.419	3.213	4.848	0.609	0.731	0.809
7	2.563	3.706	5.726	0.653	0.804	0.926
8	3.000	4.278	6.629	0.688	0.862	1.000
9	4.000	4.930	7.549	0.717	0.906	1.000
10	5.000	5.658	8.483	0.742	0.938	1.000

34.7 **a.** $X = \dfrac{NM}{D(M+N-1)}$, $R = \dfrac{D(M+N-1)}{M}$

b. Substituting $D_{avg} = D_{max} = D/M$ and $Z = 0$ in Equations (34.8) and (34.9), we get the same expressions as in Exercise 34.6 for balanced job bounds.

35.1 $P(Q_{CPU} = n \mid N = 3)$ for $n = 0, 1, 2, 3$ are 0.108, 0.180, 0.293, and 0.419, respectively. The $X(N)$ for $N = 1, 2, 3$ are 0.588, 0.798, and 0.892, respectively.

35.2 $P(Q_{CPU} = n \mid N = 3)$ for $n = 0, 1, 2, 3$ are 0.580, 0.298, 0.103, and 0.018, respectively.

36.1 $X = 0.588$, 0.796, and 0.892 for $N = 1, 2, 3$, respectively; $R = 1.700$, 2.506, 3.365 for $N = 1, 2, 3$, respectively.

36.2 The service rates of the FEC are 1.429, 1.628, and 1.660, respectively, for one through three jobs at the service center.

REFERENCES

Adam, N. R. and Dogramaci, A., Eds. (1979). *Current Issues in Computer Simulation*, Academic Press, New York.

Agrawal, S. C. (1985). *Metamodeling: A Study of Approximations in Queueing Models*, MIT Press, Cambridge, MA.

Agrawala, A. K., Mohr, J. M., and Bryant, R. M. (1976). An Approach to the Workload Characterization Problem, *Computer*, 9(6), 18–31.

Agrawala, A. K. and Mohr, J. M. (1977). Some Results on the Clustering Approach to Workload Modeling, Proc. CPEUG'77, New Orleans, LA, 23–38.

Annino, J. S. and Russell, E. C. (1979). *The Ten Most Frequent Causes of Simulation Analysis Failure*, CACI, Los Angles, CA, Report 7.

Anonymous et al. (1985). A Measure of Transaction Processing Power, *Datamation*, 31(7), 112–118.

Artis, H. P. (1978). Capacity Planning for MVS Computer Systems, in D. Ferrari, Ed., *Performance of Computer Installations*, North-Holland, Amsterdam, 25–35.

Bahr, D. (1975). A Note on Figures of Merit, *Performance Evaluation Review*, 4(3), 1–3.

Bard, Y. (1979). Some Extensions to Multiclass Queueing Network Analysis, in Arato, M., Butrimenko, A., and Gelenbe, E., Eds., *Performance of Computer Systems*, North-Holland, Amsterdam.

Barnes, M. F. (1979). *Measurement and Modelling Methods for Computer System Performance*, Input Two-Nine, Surrey, U.K.

Baskett, F., Chandy, K. M., Muntz, R. R. and Palacios, F. G. (1975). Open, Closed, and Mixed Networks of Queues with Different Classes of Customers, *Journal of the ACM*, 22(2), 248–260.

Bentley, J. L. (1982). *Writing Efficient Programs*, Prentice-Hall, Englewood Cliffs, NJ.

Birtwistle, G., Dahl, O.-J., Myhrhaug, B. and Nygaard, K. (1973). *SIMULA Begin*, Auerbach, Philadelphia, PA.

Blum, L., Blum, M. and Shub, M. (1986). A Simple Pseudo-Random Number Generator, *SIAM Journal on Computing*, **15**(2), 364–383.

Bobillier, P. A., Kahan, B. C. and Probst, A. R. (1976). *Simulation with GPSS and GPSS V*, Prentice-Hall, Englewood-Cliffs, NJ.

Bouhana, J. P. (1979). Using Accounting Log Data in Performance Reporting, Proc. CPEUG'79, San Diego, CA, 241–243.

Box, G. E. P. and Muller, M. E. (1958). A Note on the Generation of Random Normal Deviates, *Annals of Mathematical Statistics*, **29**, 610–611.

Box, G. E. P., Hunter, W. G. and Hunter, J. S. (1978). *Statistics for Experimenters*, Wiley, New York.

Bratley, P., Fox, B. L. and Schrage, L. E. (1986). *A Guide to Simulation*, Springer-Verlag, New York.

Bright, H. S. and Enison, R. L. (1979). Quasi-Random Number Sequences from a Long-Period TLP Generator with Remarks on Application to Cryptography, *ACM Computing Surveys*, **11**, 357–370.

Brown, R. (1988). Calendar Queues: A Fast O(1) Priority Queue Implementation for the Simulation Event Set Problem, *Communications of the ACM*, **31**(10), 1220–1227.

Browne, J. C., Chandy, K. M., Brown, R. M., Keller, T. W., Towsley, D. F. and Dizzly, C. W. (1975). Hierarchical Techniques for the Development of Realistic Models of Complex Computer Systems, *Proceedings of IEEE*, **62**(6), 966–975.

Buchholz, W. (1969). A Synthetic Job for Measuring System Performance, *IBM Systems Journal*, **8**(4), 309–318.

Bulgren, W. G. (1982). *Discrete System Simulation*, Prentice-Hall, Englewood Cliffs, NJ.

Buzen, J. P. (1973). Computational Algorithms for Closed Queueing Networks with Exponential Servers, *Communications of the ACM*, **16**(9), 527–531.

Buzen, J. P. (1976). Fundamental Laws of Computer System Performance, Proc. SIG-METRICS'76, Cambridge, MA, 200–210.

CACI (1983). *SIMSCRIPT II.5 Programming Language*, CACI, Los Angeles, CA.

COMTEN, Inc. (1977). *DYNAPROBE D-7900 User's Guide*, COMTEN, Inc., St. Paul, MN.

Calcagni, J. M. (1976). Shape in Ranking Kiviat Graphs, *Performance Evaluation Review*, **5**(1), 35–37.

Calzarossa, M. and Ferrari, D. (1986). A Sensitivity Study of the Clustering Approach to Workload Modeling, *Performance Evaluation*, **6**, 25–33.

Chambers, J. M., Cleveland, W. S., Kleiner, B. and Tukey, P. A. (1983). *Graphical Methods for Data Analysis*, Wadsworth International Group, Belmont, CA and Duxbury Press, North Scituate, MA.

Chandy, K. M., Herzog, U. and Woo, L. (1975). Parametric Analysis of Queueing Networks, *IBM Journal of Research and Development*, **19**(1), 36–42.

Chandy, K. M. and Neuse, D. (1982). Linearizer: A Heuristic Algorithm for Queueing Network Models of Computing Systems, *Communications of the ACM*, **25**(2), 126–134.

Conveyou, R. R. and McPherson, R. D. (1967). Fourier Analysis of Uniform Random Number Generators, *Journal of the ACM*, **14**, 100–119.

Cooper, R. (1981). *Introduction to Queueing Theory*, North-Holland, New York.

Crane, M. A. and Lemoine, A. J. (1977). *An Introduction to the Regenerative Method for Simulation Analysis*, Springer-Verlag, New York.

Curnow, H. J. and Wichmann, B. A. (1975). A Synthetic Benchmark, *The Computer Journal*, **19**(1), 43–49.

Dahl, O.-J., Myhrhaug, B. and Nygaard, K. (1982). *SIMULA 67: Common Base Language*, Norwegian Computing Center, Oslo, Norway.

Das, M. N. and Giri, N. C. (1986). *Design and Analysis of Experiments*, Wiley, New York.

Datametrics Systems Corp. (1983). Capacity Planning: A State of the Art Survey, National Bureau of Standards, Washington, DC, Report No. NBS-GCR-83-440.

Denning, P. J. and Buzen, J. P. (1978). The Operational Analysis of Queueing Network Models, *Computing Surveys*, **10**(3), 225–261.

Dongarra, J. J. (1983). Performance of Various Computers Using Standard Linear Equations Software in a FORTRAN Environment, *Computer Architecture News*, **11**(5). Recent updates to this article can be obtained from the author.

Dunn, O. J. and Clark, V. A. (1974). *Applied Statistics, Analysis of Variance and Regression*, Wiley, New York.

Edgeman, R. L. (1989). Random Number Generators and the Minimal Standard, *Communications of the ACM*, **32**(8), 1020–1021.

Everitt, B. (1974). *Cluster Analysis*, Heinemann Educational Books, London.

Ferrari, D. (1972). Workload Characterization and Selection in Computer Performance Measurement, *Computer*, **5**(7), 18–24.

Ferrari, D. (1978). *Computer Systems Performance Evaluation*, Prentice-Hall, Englewood Cliffs, NJ.

Ferrari, D., Serazzi, G. and Zeigner, A. (1983). *Measurement and Tuning of Computer Systems*, Prentice-Hall, Englewood Cliffs, NJ.

Finehirsh, S. (1985). Effective Service Level Reporting, Proc. CMG'85, Dallas, TX, 505–509.

Fishman, G. S. and Moore, L. R. (1986). An Exhaustive Analysis of Multiplicative Congruential Random Number Generators with Modulus $2^{31} - 1$, *SIAM Journal on Scientific and Statistical Computing*, **7**, 24–45.

Fleming, P. J. and Wallace, J. J. (1986). How Not to Lie with Statistics: The Correct Way To Summarize Benchmark Results, *Communications of the ACM*, **29**(3), 218–221.

Fox, B. L. (1963). Generation of Random Samples from the Beta and F distributions, *Technometrics*, **5**, 269–270.

Franta, W. R. (1977). *The Process View of Simulation*, North-Holland, New York.

Franta, W. R. and Maly, K. (1977). An Efficient Data Structure for the Simulation Event Set, *Communications of the ACM*, **20**(8), 596–602.

Frieze, A. M., Kannan, R., and Lagarias, J. C. (1984). Linear Congruential Generators Do Not Produce Random Sequences, Proc. 25th Symp. on Foundations of Computer Sci., Boca Raton, FL, 480–484.

Fushimi, M. and Tezuka, S. (1983). The k-Distribution of Generalized Feedback Shift Register Pseudorandom Numbers, *Communications of the ACM*, **26**(7), 516–523.

Fushimi, M. (1988). Designing a Uniform Random Number Generator Whose Subsequences are k-Distributed, *SIAM Journal on Computing*, **17**(1), 89–99.

Gelenbe, E. and Mitrani, I. (1980). *Analysis and Synthesis of Computer Systems*, Academic Press, London.

Gelenbe, E. and Pujolle, G. (1987). *Introduction to Queueing Networks*, Wiley, New York.

Gibson, J. C. (1970). *The Gibson Mix*, IBM Systems Development Division, Poughkeepsie, NY, Report No. TR 00.2043.

Gilbreath, J. (1981). A High-Level Language Benchmark, *Byte*, **6**(9), 180–198.

Glasser, N. E. (1987). *The Remote Channel System*, M. S. Thesis, Dept. of Electrical Engineering and Computer Science, MIT, Cambridge, MA.

Goldstein, S. (1988). Storage Benchmarking—Traps, Pitfalls, and Swindles, Proc. CMG'88, Dallas, TX, 1058–1063.

Golomb, S. W. (1982). *Shift Register Sequences*, Aegean Park Press, Laguna Hills, CA.

Gordon, W. J. and Newell, G. F. (1967). Closed Queueing Systems with Exponential Servers, *Operations Research*, **15**(2), 254–265.

Greenberger, M. (1961). An A Priori Determination of Serial Correlation in Computer Generated Random Numbers, *Mathematics of Computation*, **15**, 383–389.

Gross, D. and Harris, C. (1985). *Fundamentals of Queueing Theory*, Wiley, New York.

Gross, T., Hennessy, J., Przybylski, S. and Rowen, C. (1988). Measurement and Evaluation of the MIPS Architecture and Processor, *ACM Transaction on Computer Systems*, **6**(3), 229–257.

Haack, D. G. (1981). *Statistical Literacy: A Guide to Interpretation*, Duxbury Press, North Scituate, MA.

Hansen, P., Linton, M., Mayo, R., Murphy, M. and Patterson, D. A. (1982). A Performance Evaluation of the Intel iAPX432, *Computer Architecture News*, 10(4), 17–26.

Harman, H. H. (1976). *Modern Factor Analysis*, University of Chicago Press, Chicago, IL.

Hastings, C. Jr., (1955). *Approximations for Digital Computers*, Princeton University Press, Princeton, NJ.

Hastings, N. A. J. and Peacock, J. B. (1975). *Statistical Distributions*, Wiley, New York.

Hicks, C. R. (1973). *Fundamental Concepts in the Design of Experiments*, Holt, Rinehart, & Winston, New York.

Holmes, N. (1984). *Designer's Guide to Creating Charts & Diagrams*, Watson-Guptill Publications, New York.

Hooke, R. (1983). *How to Tell the Liars From the Statisticians*, Marcel Dekker, New York.

Houghton, R. C. Jr., (1982). Program Instrumentation Techniques, Proc. CPEUG'82, Washington, DC, 195–202.

Howard, P. C., Ed., (1983). *The EDP Performance Management Handbook*, Vol. 2: *Tools and Techniques*, Applied Computer Research, Phoenix, AZ.

Huff, D. (1954). *How to Lie with Statistics*, Norton, New York.

Hughes, J. H. (1980). Diamond—A Digital Analyzer and Monitoring Device, Proc. Performance'80, Toronto, Canada, published as *Performance Evaluation Review*, **9**(2), 27–34.

IBM (1968). *System/360 Scientific Subroutine Package, Version III, Programmer's Manual*, IBM, White Plains, NY, p. 77.

IBM (1972). *SIMPL/1 Program Reference Manual*, Publication SH19-5060-0, IBM, New York.

IMSL (1987). *IMSL Stat/Library User's Manual*, International Mathematical and Statistical Libraries, Houston, TX, 947–951.

Jackson, J. R. (1963). Jobshop-Like Queueing Systems, *Management Science*, **10**(1), 131–142.

Jain, R. and Turner, R. (1982). Workload Characterization Using Image Accounting, Proc. CPEUG'82, Washington, DC, 111–120.

Jain, R., Chiu, D. M. and Hawe, W. (1984). *A Quantitative Measure of Fairness and Discrimination for Resource Allocation in Shared Systems*, Digital Equipment Corporation, Littleton, MA, Technical Report DEC-TR-301.

Jain, R. (1985). Using Simulation to Design a Computer Network Congestion Control Protocol, Proc. Sixteenth Annual Pittsburgh Conf. on Modeling and Simulation, Pittsburgh, PA, 987–993.

Jain, R. and Chlamtac, I. (1985). The P^2 Algorithm for Dynamic Calculation of Quantiles and Histograms without Storing Observations, *Communications of the ACM*, **28**(10), 1076–1085.

Jain, R. (1986). A Timeout-based Congestion Control Scheme for Window Flow-controlled Networks, *IEEE Journal on Selected Areas in Communications*, **SAC-4**(7), 1162–1167.

Jain, R. and Routhier, S. (1986). Packet Trains: Measurements and a New Model for Computer Network Traffic, *IEEE Journal on Selected Areas in Communications*, **SAC-4**(6), 986–995.

Jöhnk, M. D. (1964). Erzeugung von Betaverteilten und Gammaverteilten Zufallszahlen, *Metrika*, **8**, 5–15.

Joyce, J., Lomow, G., Slind, K. and Unger, B. (1987). Monitoring Distributed Systems, *ACM Transactions on Computer Systems*, **5**(2), 121–150.

Katzan, H. Jr., (1971). *APL User's Guide*, Van Nostrand Reinhold, New York.

Kelly-Bootle, S. (1981). *The Devil's DP Dictionary*, McGraw-Hill, New York.

King, R. S. and Julstrom, B. (1982). *Applied Statistics Using the Computer*, Mayfield Publishing, Palo Alto, CA.

Klahr, P. and Fought, W. S. (1980). Knowledge-based Simulation, Proc. First Conf. AAAI, Stanford, CA, 181–183.

Kleinrock, L. (1975). *Queueing Systems*, Vol. 1, *Theory*, Wiley, New York.

Knuth, D. E. (1981). *The Art of Computer Programming*, Vol. 2: *Seminumerical Algorithms*, Addison-Wesley, Reading, MA.

Kobayashi, H. (1978). *Modelling and Analysis: An Introduction to System Performance Analysis*, Addison-Wesley, Reading, MA.

Kolence, K. W. (1973). The Software Empiricist, *Performance Evaluation Review*, **2**(2), 31–36.

Kolence, K. W. and Kiviat, P. J. (1973). Software Unit Profiles and Kiviat Figures, *Performance Evaluation Review*, **2**(3), 2–12.

Koopman, B. O. (1956). Fallacies in Operations Research, *Operations Research*, **4**(4), 422–426.

Kreutzer, W. (1986). *System Simulation Programming Styles and Languages*, Addison-Wesley, Reading, MA.

L'Ecuyer, P. (1988). Efficient and Portable Combined Random Number Generators, *Communications of the ACM*, **31**(6), 742–774.

Lamie, E. L. (1987). *Pascal Programming*, Wiley, New York, 150.

Lavenberg, S. S., Ed. (1983). *Computer Performance Modeling Handbook*, Academic Press, New York.

Law, A. M. and Kelton, W. D. (1982). *Simulation Modeling and Analysis*, McGraw-Hill, New York.

Law, A. M. (1983). Statistical Analysis of Simulation Output, *Operations Research*, **19**(6), 983–1029.

Lazowska, E. D., Zahorjan, J., Graham, S. G. and Sevcik, K. C. (1984). *Quantitative System Performance: Computer System Analysis Using Queueing Network Models*, Prentice-Hall, Englewood Cliffs, NJ.

Leavitt, D. (1986a). Modeling and Simulation: Keys to Capacity Planning, *Software News*, **6**(1), 55–57.

Leavitt, D. (1986b). Software Monitors Help Pinpoint Resource Usage, *Software News*, **6**(11), 42–46.

Lefferts, R. (1981). *How to Prepare Charts and Graphs for Effective Reports*, Barnes and Noble, New York.

Lehmer, D. H. (1951). Mathematical Methods in Large-Scale Computing Units, *Harvard University Computation Laboratory Annals*, **26**, 141–146.

Leung, C. H. C. (1987). *Quantitative Analysis of Computer Systems*, Wiley, Chichester, U.K.

Levin, R. I. (1981). *Statistics for Management*, Prentice-Hall, Englewood Cliffs, NJ.

Levy, H. and Clark, D. (1982). On the Use of Benchmarks for Measuring System Performance, *Computer Architecture News*, **10**(6), 5–8.

Lewis, P. A., Goodman, A. S. and Miller, J. M. (1969). A Pseudo-Random Number Generator for the System/360, *IBM Systems Journal*, **8**(2), 136–146.

Lewis, T. G. and Payne, W. H. (1973). Generalized Feedback Shift Register Pseudo-Random Number Algorithm, *Journal of ACM*, **20**(3), 456–468.

Little, J. D. C. (1961). A Proof for the Queueing Formula: $L = \lambda W$, *Operations Research*, **9**(3), 383–387.

Lucas, H. C. Jr., (1971). Performance Evaluation and Monitoring, *Computing Surveys*, **3**(3), 79–91.

McCormack, W. M. and Sargent, R. G. (1979). Comparison of Future Event Set Algorithms for Simulations of Closed Queueing Systems, in Adam, N. R. and Dogramaci, A., Eds., *Current Issues in Computer Simulation*, Academic Press, New York, 71–82.

McGalliard, J. and Thareja, A. (1988). Remote Workstation Emulation and Other Alternatives to RTE, Proc. CMG'88, Dallas, TX, 401–406.

McHugh, E. F. and Tzelnic, P. (1981). Using Fractional Factorial Design to Examine Scheduling Policies, Proc. CMG'81, New Orleans, LA, 130–135.

McKerrow, P. (1987). *Performance Measurement of Computer Systems*, Addison-Wesley, Reading, MA.

MacKinnon, D. R. (1987). Is a Picture Always Worth a Thousand Words? Proc. CMG'87, Orlando, FL, 272–278.

McMahon, F. H. (1986). *Livermore FORTRAN Kernels: A Computer Test of the Numerical Performance Range*, Lawrence Livermore National Laboratories, Livermore, CA.

Majone, G. and Quade, E. S. (1980). *Pitfalls of Analysis*, Wiley, Chichester, U.K.

Mamrak, S. A. and Amer, P. D. (1977). A Feature Selection Tool for Workload Characterization, Proc. SIGMETRICS'77, Washington, DC, 113–120.

Markowitz, H. M., Hausner, B. and Karr, H. W. (1963). *SIMSCRIPT: A Simulation Programming Language*, Prentice-Hall, Englewood Cliffs, NJ.

Marsaglia, G. and Bray, T. A. (1964). A Convenient Method for Generating Normal Variables, *SIAM Review*, **6**, 260–264.

Marsaglia, G. (1968). Random Numbers Fall Mainly in the Planes, *Proceedings of the National Academy of Science*, **60**(5), 25–28.

Marsaglia, G. (1983). Random Number Generation, in Ralston, A. and Reilly, E. D. Jr., Eds., *Encyclopedia of Computer Science and Engineering*, Van Nostrand Reinhold, New York, 1260–1264.

Mason, R. L., Gunst, R. F. and Hess, J. L. (1989). *Statistical Design and Analysis of Experiment*, Wiley, New York.

Merrill, H. W. B. (1974). A Technique for Comparative Analysis of Kiviat Graphs, *Performance Evaluation Review*, **3**(1), 34–39.

Merrill, H. W. B. (1975). Further Comments on Comparative Evaluation of Kiviat Graphs, *Performance Evaluation Review*, **4**(1), 1–10.

Misra, J. (1986). Distributed Discrete-Event Simulation, *ACM Computing Surveys*, **18**(1), 39–66.

Mitrani, I. (1982). *Simulation Techniques for Discrete-Event Systems*, Cambridge University Press, London.

Molloy, M. K. (1989). *Fundamentals of Performance Modeling*, Macmillan, New York.

Montgomery, D. C. (1984). *Design and Analysis of Experiments*, Wiley, New York.

Morris, M. F. (1974). Kiviat Graphs—Conventions and Figure of Merit, *Performance Evaluation Review*, **3**(3), 2–8.

Morris, M. F. and Roth, P. F. (1982). *Tools and Techniques: Computer Performance Evaluation for Effective Analysis*, Van Nostrand Reinhold, New York.

Natrella, M. G. (1966). *Experimental Statistics*, National Bureau of Standards, Washington, DC, Handbook 91.

Nutt, G. J. (1975). Tutorial: Computer System Monitors, *Computer*, **8**(11), 51–61.

Nutt, G. J. (1979). *A Survey of Remote Monitoring*, National Bureau of Standards, Washington, DC, Special Publication 500-42.

O'Donovan, T. M. (1980). *GPSS Simulation Made Simple*, Wiley, Chichester, U.K.

Oed, W. and Mertens, B. (1981). Characterization of Computer Systems Workload, *Computer Performance*, **2**(2), 77–83.

Papoulis, A. (1965). *Probability, Random Variables, and Stochastic Processes*, McGraw-Hill, New York.

Park, S. K. and Miller, K. W. (1988). Random Number Generators: Good Ones Are Hard to Find, *Communications of the ACM*, **31**(10), 1192–1201.

Pasupathy, S. (1989). Glories of Gaussianity, *IEEE Communications Magazine*, **27**(8), 37–38.

Patterson, D. A. (1982). A Performance Evaluation of the Intel 80286, *Computer Architecture News*, **10**(5), 16–18.

Patterson, D. A. and Sequin, C. H. (1982). A VLSI RISC, *Computer*, **15**(9), 8–21.

Pinkerton, T. B. (1977). Techniques for Software Monitoring, in *System Tuning*, InfoTech International, Maidenhead, U.K., 347–358.

Plattner, B. and Nievergelt, J. (1981). Monitoring Program Execution: A Survey, *Computer*, **14**(11), 76–93.

Powell, C. (1988). A Passion for Graphics Excellence, Proc. CMG'88, Dallas, TX, 761–765.

Power, L. R. (1983). Design and Use of a Program Execution Analyzer, *IBM Systems Journal*, **22**(3), 271–294.

Prime Computer (1984). *Subroutines Reference Guide*, 3rd ed., Prime Computer, Framingham, MA, p. 12.45.

Pritsker, A. and Young, R. E. (1975). *Simulation with GASP-PL/I: A PL/I Based Continuous/Discrete Simulation Language*, Wiley-Interscience, New York.

Proppe, M. and Wallack, B. (1982). The Design and Application of a Remote Terminal Emulator, Proc. CPEUG'82, Washington, DC, 409–413.

Ramage, I. L. (1977). The Design of Software Monitors, in *System Tuning*, InfoTech International, Maidenhead, U.K., 359–372.

Ramana-Reddy, Y. V., Fox, M. S., Husain, N. and McRoberts, M. (1986). The Knowledge-Based Simulation System, *IEEE Software*, **3**(2), 26–37.

Reeves, C. M. (1984). Complexity Analyses of Event Set Algorithms, *The Computer Journal*, **27**(1), 72–79.

Reichmann, W. J. (1961). *Use and Abuse of Statistics*, Oxford University Press, New York.

Reiser, M. and Lavenberg, S. S. (1980). Mean-Value Analysis of Closed Multichain Queueing Networks, *Journal of the ACM*, **27**(2), 313–322.

Ross, P. J. (1988). *Taguchi Techniques for Quality Engineering*, McGraw-Hill, New York.

Rubinstein, R. Y. (1986). *Monte Carlo Optimization, Simulation and Sensitivity of Queueing Networks*, Wiley, New York.

Runyon, R. P. (1977). *Winning with Statistics: A Painless First Look at Numbers, Ratios, Percentages, Means, and Inference*, Addison-Wesley, Reading, MA.

Santha, M. and Vazirani, U. V. (1984). Generating Quasi-Random Sequences from Slightly Random Sources, Proc. 25th Symp. on Foundations of Computer Science, Boca Raton, FL, 434–440.

Sauer, C. H. and Chandy, K. M. (1981). *Computer Systems Performance Modelling*, Prentice-Hall, Englewood Cliffs, NJ.

Scherr, A. (1967). *An Analysis of Timeshared Computer Systems*, MIT Press, Cambridge, MA.

Schmid, C. F. and Schmid, S. E. (1979). *Handbook of Graphic Presentation*, Wiley, New York.

Schmid, C. F. (1983). *Statistical Graphics*, Wiley, New York.

Schrage, L. E. (1979). A More Portable FORTRAN Random Number Generator, *ACM Transactions on Mathematical Software*, **5**(2), 132–138.

Schweitzer, P. (1979). Approximate Analysis of Multiclass Closed Networks of Queues, International Conf. on Stochastic Control and Optimization, Amsterdam.

Serazzi, G. (1981). A Functional and Resource-Oriented Procedure for Workload Modeling, Proc. Performance'81, Amsterdam, North-Holland, Amsterdam, 345–361.

Serazzi, G. (1985). Workload Modeling Techniques, in Abu El Ata, N., Ed., *Modelling Techniques and Tools for Performance, Analysis*, North-Holland, Amsterdam, 13–27.

Sherman, S. W. and Browne, J. C. (1973). Trace-Driven Modeling: Review and Overview, Proc. Symp. on Simulation of Computer Systems, 201–207.

Smith, J. E. (1988). Characterizing Computer Performance with a Single Number, *Communications of the ACM*, **31**(10), 1202–1206.

SPEC (1990). SPEC Benchmark Suite Release 1.0, *SPEC Newsletter* **2**(2), 3–4. Available from Waterside Associates, Fremont, CA.

Spiegel, M. G. (1980). RTE's- Past is Prologue, Proc. CPEUG'80, Orlando, FL, 303–310.

Sreenivasan, K. and Kleinman, A. J. (1974). On the Construction of a Representative Workload, *Communications of the ACM*, **17**(3), 127–133.

Stevens, B. A. (1975). A Note on Figure of Merit, *Performance Evaluation Review*, **4**(1), 11–19.

Strauss, M. J. (1981). *Computer Capacity: A Production Control Approach*, Van Nostrand Reinhold, New York.

Suri, R. (1983). Robustness of Queueing Network Formulas, *Journal of the ACM*, **30**(3), 564–594.

Svobodova, L. (1976). *Computer Performance Measurement and Evaluation Methods: Analysis and Applications*, Elsevier, New York.

Tanenbaum, A. (1988). *Computer Networks*, Prentice-Hall, Englewood Cliffs, NJ.

Tausworthe, R. C. (1965). Random Numbers Generated by Linear Recurrence Mod Two, *Mathematics of Computation*, **19**, 201–209.

Tezuka, S. (1987). Walsh-Spectral Test for GFSR Pseudorandom Numbers, *Communications of the ACM*, **30**(8), 731–735.

Tolopka, S. (1981). An Event Trace Monitor for the VAX 11/780, Proc. SIGMETRICS'81, Las Vegas, NV, 121–128.

Tootill, J. P. R., Robinson, W. D. and Adams, A. G. (1971). The Runs Up and Down Performance of Tausworthe Pseudo-Random Number Generators, *Journal of the ACM*, **18**, 381–399.

Transaction Processing Performance Council (TPC) (1989). *TPC Benchmark A*, Draft 5E (Edited) Proposed Standard. Available from ITOM International Co., Los Altos, CA.

Trehan, V. (1978). Problems in Remote Terminal Emulation, Proc. CPEUG'78, Boston, MA, 37–61.

Trivedi, K. S. (1982). *Probability and Statistics with Reliability Queueing and Computer Science Applications*, Prentice-Hall, Englewood Cliffs, NJ.

Tsao, R. F. and Margolin, B. H. (1971). A Multifactor Paging Experiment: II Statistical Methodology, in Freiberger, W., Ed., *Statistical Computer Performance Evaluation*, Academic Press, New York, 135–162.

Unger, B. and Fujimoto, R., Eds. (1989). *Distributed Simulation*, The Society for Computer Simulation, San Diego, CA, 1989.

Vaucher, J. G. and Duval, P. (1975). A Comparison of Simulation Event List Algorithms, *Communications of the ACM*, **18**(4), 223–230.

Vazirani, U. V. and Vazirani, V. V. (1984). Efficient and Secure Pseudo-Random Number Generation, Proc. 25th Symp. on Foundations of Computer Science, Boca Raton, FL, 458–463.

Wagner, D. B. and Lazowska, E. D. (1989). Parallel Simulation of Queueing Networks: Limitations and Potentials, Proc. SIGMETRICS'89, Berkeley, CA, 146–155.

Watkins, S. W. and Abrams, M. D. (1977a). *Survey of Remote Terminal Emulators*, National Bureau of Standards, Washington, DC, Special Publication 500-4.

Watkins, S. W. and Abrams, M. D. (1977b). Remote Terminal Emulation in the Procurement of Teleprocessing Systems, Proc. NCC'77, Dallas, TX, 723–727.

Webster, W., Ed. (1989). *Simulation and AI*, Society for Computer Simulations, San Diego, CA, 1989.

White, J. V. (1984). *Using Charts and Graphs: 1000 Ideas for Visual Persuasion*, Bowker, New York.

Wichmann, B. A. (1976). Ackermann's Function: A Study in the Efficiency of Calling Procedures, *BIT*, **16**, 103–110.

Wight, A. S. (1981). Cluster Analysis for Characterizing Computer System Workloads—Panacea or Pandora? Proc. CMG'81, New Orleans, LA, 183–189.

Woolsey, R. E. D. and Swanson, H. S. (1975). *Operations Research for Immediate Applications*, Harper & Row, New York.

Wright, L. S., Kohler, W. H. and Zahavi, W. Z. (1989). The Digital DebitCredit Benchmark: Methodology and Results, Proc. CMG'89, Reno, NV, 84–92.

Wyman, F. P. (1975). Improved Event Scanning Mechanisms for Discrete-Event Simulation, *Communications of the ACM*, **18**(6), 350–353.

Zahorjan, J., Sevcik, K. C., Eager, D. L. and Galler, B. (1982). Balanced Job Bound Analysis of Queueing Networks, *Communications of the ACM*, **25**(2), 134–141.

AUTHOR INDEX

Abrams, M. D., 176, 660
Adam, N. R., 502, 651, 656
Adams, A. G., 659
Agrawal, S. C., 624, 651
Agrawala, A. K., 175, 651
Amer, P. D., 175, 657
Anderson, A., xi
Annino, J. S., 396, 651
Anonymous, 56, 651
Arato, M., 651
Artis, H. P., 175, 651
Ayers, A., xi

Bahr, D., 176, 651
Bard, Y., 580, 651
Barnes, M. F., 176, 651
Baskett, F., 551, 651
Bentley, J. L., 176, 651
Birtwhistle, G., 502, 652
Bloch, A., 293, 314
Blum, L., 456, 652
Blum, M., 456, 652
Bobillier, P. A., 502, 652
Bouhana, J. P., 176, 652
Box, G. E. P., 494, 652
Bratley, P., 393, 502, 652
Bray, T. A., 451, 494, 657
Bright, H. S., 503, 652
Brooks, F., 396
Brown, R., 410, 652
Brown, R. M., 652

Browne, J. C., 405, 624, 652, 659
Bryant, R. M., 651
Bucher, I., 111
Buchholz, W., 50, 652
Bulgren, W. G., 502, 652
Butrimenko, A., 651
Buzen, J. P., 551, 553, 555, 595, 596, 602,
    652, 653

CACI, 502, 652
Calcagni, J. M., 176, 652
Calzarossa, M., 175, 652
Carroll, L., 60
Chambers, J. M., 272, 652
Chandy, K. M., 44, 551, 614, 624, 651, 652,
    658
Cheriton, D., 519
Chiu, D. M., 44, 655
Chlamtac, I., 196, 655
Clark, D., 175, 656
Clark, V. A., 390, 653
Cleveland, W. S., 652
COMTEN, 175, 652
Conveyou, R. R., 470, 653
Cooper, R., 624, 653
Crane, M. A., 502, 653
Curnow, H. J., 55, 653

Dahl, O.-J., 652, 653
Das, M. N., 272, 653
Datametrics, 176, 653

Denning, P.J., 551, 555, 653
Devil's DP Dictionary, The, 30, 47, 403, 437.
  See also, Kelly-Bootle, S.,
Dizzly, C. W., 652
Dogramaci, A., 502, 651, 656
Dongarra, J. J., 55, 653
Dunn, O. J., 390, 653
Duval, P., 502, 660

Eager, D. L., 660
Edgeman, R. L., 494, 653
Einstein, A., 343, 507
Enison, R. L., 503, 652
Everitt, B., 175, 653

Ferrari, D., 44, 175, 176, 652, 653
Finehirsh, S., 176, 653
Fishman, G. S., 452, 653
Fleming, P. J., 272, 653
Fought, W. S., 504, 655
Fox, B. L., 393, 652, 653
Fox, M. S., 658
Franta, W. R., 502, 653
Frieze, A. M., 456, 653
Fujimoto, R., 503, 660
Fushimi, M., 503, 654

Galler, B., 660
Galton, F., 179
Gates, W. I. E., 192
Gelenbe, E., 44, 624, 651, 654
Gibson, J. C., 48, 175, 654
Gilbreath, J., 175, 654
Giri, N. C., 272, 653
Glasser, N. E., 28, 654
Goethe, J. W. von, 555
Goldstein, S., 176, 654
Golomb, S. W., 503, 654
Goodman, A. S., 503, 656
Gordon, W. J., 551, 594, 654
Gosset, W. S., 497
Graham, S. G., 656
Greenberger, M., 503, 654
Gross, D., 624, 654
Gross, T., 272, 654
Gunst, R. F., 390, 657

Haack, D. G., 272, 654
Hansen, P. M., 175, 390, 654
Harman, H. H., 77, 654
Harris, C., 624, 654
Hastings, C., Jr., 503, 638, 654
Hastings, N. A. J., 503, 654
Hausner, B., 657

Hawe, W., 44, 655
Hennessy, J., 654
Herzog, U., 614, 652
Hess, J. L., 390, 657
Hicks, C. R., 390, 654
Holmes, N., 176, 654
Hooke, R., 272, 654
Houghton, R. C., Jr., 176, 654
Howard, P. C., 44, 175, 654
Hsu, S., xi
Huff, D., 272, 654
Hughes, J. H., 101, 175, 655
Hunter, J. S., 390, 652
Hunter, W. G., 390, 652
Husain, N., 658

IBM, 452, 655
IMSL, 452, 655

Jackson, J. R., 551, 655
Jain, R., 44, 175, 176, 196, 416, 621, 655
Jöhnk, M. D., 485, 655
Joyce, J., 176, 655
Julstrom, B., 272, 655

Kahan, B. C., 652
Kannan, R., 456, 653
Karr, W., 657
Katzan, H., Jr., 452, 655
Keller, T. W., 652
Kelly-Bootle, S., 655. *See also* Devil's DP
  Dictionary, The
Kelton, W. D., 502, 656
Kettering, C. F., 547
King, R. S., 272, 655
Kipling, R., 3
Kiviat, P. J., 139, 153, 176, 655
Klahr, P., 504, 655
Kleiner, B., 652
Kleinman, A. J., 175, 659
Kleinrock, L., 624, 655
Knuth, D. E., 452, 472, 502, 655
Kobayashi, H., 44, 624, 655
Kohler, W. H., 175, 660
Kolence, K. W., 176, 655, 656
Koopman, B. O., 44, 656
Kreutzer, W., 503, 656

Lagarias, J. C., 456, 653
La Guardia, F., 203
Lamie, E. L., 503, 656

Lang, A., 244
Lavenberg, S. S., 44, 502, 576, 624, 656, 658
Law, A. M., 502, 656
Lazowska, E. D., 44, 503, 624, 656, 660
Leavitt, D., 175, 176, 656
L'Ecuyer, P., 451, 656
Lefferts, R., 176, 656
Lehmer, D. H., 439, 440, 502, 656
Lemoine, A. J., 502, 653
Leung, C. H. C., 44, 624, 656
Levin, R. I., 272, 656
Levy, H., 175, 656
Lewis, P. A., 503, 656
Lewis, T. G., 449, 656
Linton, M., 654
Little, J. D. C., 513, 656
Lomow, G., 655
Lucas, H. C., Jr., 175, 656

McCormack, W. M., 411, 656
McGalliard, J., 176, 656
McHugh, E. F., 390, 657
McKerrow, P., 44, 176, 657
MacKinnon, D. R., 176, 657
McMahon, F. H., 56, 657
McPherson, R. D., 470, 653
McRoberts, M., 658
Magee, W. C., 570
Majone, G., 44, 657
Maly, K., 502, 653
Mamrak, S. A., 175, 657
Margolin, B. H., 390, 660
Markowitz, H. M., 502, 657
Marsaglia, G., 450, 451, 470, 494, 657
Mason, R. L., 390, 657
Mayo, R., 654
Merrill, H. W. B., 155, 176, 657
Mertens, B., 175, 657
Miller, J. M., 503, 656
Miller, K. W., 452, 453, 503, 658
Misra, J., 503, 657
Mitrani, I., 44, 502, 624, 654, 657
Mohr, J. M., 175, 651
Molloy, M. K., 44, 657
Montgomery, D. C., 390, 657
Moore, L. R., 452, 654
Morris, M. F., 176, 657
Mousley, K., xi
Muller, M. E., 494, 652
Muntz, R. R., 551, 651
Murphy, M., 654
Myhrhaug, B., 652, 653

Natrella, M. G., 272, 657
Neuse, D., 624, 652
Newell, G. F., 551, 594, 654
Nievergelt, J., 176, 658
Nutt, G. J., 175, 657
Nygaard, K., 652, 653

O'Donovan, T. M., 502, 657
Oed, W., 175, 657

Palacios, F. G., 551, 651
Papoulis, A., 272, 658
Park, S. K., 452, 453, 503, 658
Parkinson, C. W., 381
Pasupathy, S., 483, 503, 658
Patterson, D. A., 166, 175, 176, 390, 654, 658
Payne, W. H., 449, 656
Peacock, J. B., 503, 654
Pinkerton, T. B., 175, 658
Plattner, B., 176, 658
Powell, C., 176, 658
Power, L. R., 176, 658
Prime Computer, 452, 658
Pritsker, A., 502, 658
Probst, R., 652
Proppe, M., 176, 658
Przybylski, S., 654
Pujolle, G., 624, 654
Putt, A., 139, 593

Quade, E. S., 44, 657

Ramage, I. L., 175, 658
Ramana Reddy, Y. V., 504, 658
Reeves, C. M., 411, 658
Reichmann, W. J., 272, 658
Reiser, M., 576, 658
Restivo, J. P., xi
Robinson, W. D., 659
Ross, P. J., 390, 658
Roth, P. F., 176, 658
Routhier, S., 621, 655
Rowen, C., 654
Rubinstein, R. Y., 502, 658
Runyon, R. P., 272, 658
Russell, E. C., 396, 651

Santha, M., 451, 658
Sargent, R. G., 411, 656
Sauer, C. H., 44, 658
Scherr, A., 552, 658
Schmid, C. F., 176, 659

Schmid, S. E., 176, 659
Schrage, L. E., 393, 442, 502, 652, 659
Schweitzer, P., 580, 659
Sequin, C. H., 166, 176, 390, 658
Serazzi, G., 44, 175, 176, 653, 659
Sevcik, K. C., 656, 660
Sherman, S. W., 405, 502, 659
Shub, M., 456, 652
Slind, K., 655
Smith, J. E., 272, 659
SPEC, 58, 659
Spiegel, M. G., 176, 659
Sreenivasan, K., 175, 659
Stevens, B. A., 176, 659
Strauss, M. J., 176, 659
Suri, R., 621, 659
Svobodova, L., 175, 659
Swanson, H. S., 608, 660

Tanenbaum, A., 63, 659
Tatman, R. F., 413
Tausworthe, R. C., 444, 446, 447, 449, 468, 659
Tezuka, S., 503, 654, 659
Theraja, A., 176, 656
Tolopka, S., 96, 659
Tootill, J. P. R., 449, 659
Towsley, D. F., 652
Transaction Processing Performance Council, 58, 659
Trehan, V., 176, 659
Trivedi, K. S., 272, 660
Tsao, R. F., 390, 660
Tukey, P. A., 652

Turner, R., 175, 176, 655
Twain, M., 460
Tzelnic, P., 390, 657

Unger, B., 503, 655, 660

Vaucher, J. G., 502, 660
Vazirani, U. V., 451, 456, 658, 660
Vazirani, V. V., 456, 660

Wagner, D. B., 503, 660
Wallace, J. J., 272, 653
Wallace, J. M., 71
Wallack, B., 176, 658
Wang, J., xi
Wanuga, T., xi
Watkins, S. W., 176, 660
Webster, W., 503, 660
Weicker, R., 55
Wells, H. G., 14
White, J. V., 176, 660
Wichmann, B. A., 54, 55, 653, 660
Wight, A. S., 175, 660
Woo, L., 614, 652
Woolsey, R. E. D., 608, 660
Wright, L. S., 175, 660
Wu, H., xi
Wyman, F. P., 502, 660

Young, R. E., 502, 658

Zahavi, W. Z., 175, 660
Zahorjan, J., 585, 656, 660
Zeigner, A., 44, 176, 653

SUBJECT INDEX

2^k experimental designs, 280, 283–292
2^{k-p} experimental designs, 314–326
$2^k r$ experimental designs, 293–313
$2^2 r$ experimental designs, 293–308
6502 processor, xxvii, 166
68000 processor, xii, 275, 276, 281, 282, 359, 360, 361, 365, 367
Z8002 processor, 167, 360, 361, 365
8080 processor, 16, 276
8086 processor, xii, 275, 281, 282, 359
80286 processor, 282

Abnormal events monitoring, 97–98
Absolute deviation, mean, 193, 194, 197
Accounting logs, 114, 116–121, 176
  analysis of, 117–119
  data recorded in, 117–119
  interpretation of, 117–119
  use of, 119–121
  workload characterization using, 121
Accuracy vs. correctness, 32
Ackermann benchmark, 50, 53, 167, 358, 359, 360, 361, 365
  SIMULA listing of, 53
ACM, 8, 9
Ada, 359
Addition instruction, 48
Additive model, 303–306
Advertising, by monitors, 105
AFIPS, 9
Agglomerative clustering techniques, 87

Aggregate subnetwork, 614, 615, 618
Airline reservation systems, 570
ALGOL-like languages, 53
ALGOL programs, 54
Algorithm(s):
  convolution, 590, 593–607
  correlation, 606–607
  event-set, 408
  page replacement, 382
  paging, 404
Allocation of variation, 226–228, 295–298, 331–332, 372–374
Alternatives comparison:
  several, 327
  two, 208–209, 218
ALU (arithmetic logic units), 23, 61, 62, 66
Amdahl's law validation, 257, 258
American Federation of Information Processing Societies, see AFIPS
Analysis, 106
  bottleneck, 563–568
  cache, 404
  complex, 19
  coverage, 112
  data, 97, 102
  factor, 77
  mean value, 570, 575–579
  principal-component, 76–80
  stress-load, 132
  user participation in, 397
Analysis rat holes, 161

665

Analysis tools, commercial, 175
Analytical modeling, when to use, 31
Analyzer, in monitors, 106
ANOVA (analysis of variance), 250-253, 332-334, 374
ANOVA table:
  one-factor designs, with equal sample sizes, 333
  for simple linear regression, 252
  for two-factor design, without replication, 374
  two-factor designs, with replication, 334
Antibugging, 416
Application benchmarks, 51-52
Applied Computer Research, 10
Approximate MVA, 579-585
Approximation:
  for chi-square quantiles, 638
  for F-quantiles, 638
  for normal quantiles, 198, 638
  for statistical tables, 638
Arc sine transformation, 261
ARGUS operating system, 230-232, 239, 240, 256
Arithmetic logic units, *see* ALU
Arithmetic mean, 70, 73, 188, 305
Arrival rate, effective, 512, 513-514, 536-537, 538, 539
Arrivals, 507-508, 510, 513-515, 551
  bulk Poisson, 510
  discouraged, 540
  Poisson, 508
  response-dependent, 621
  train, 621
Artifact, 94
Art of:
  data presentation, 139-163
  performance evaluation, 7
  workload selection, 60-69
Assertion checking, 112
Assumptions' validation, 421
Asymmetric plot, 199, 200
Asymptotic bounds, 564-567
Autocovariance, 432, 465-466
Autoregressive sequence, 444
Availability, 34, 40, 43
Averaging, 73, 182
  queue length, 429-430
  utilization, 190
  waiting time, 429-430

Balance, job flow, 551
Balanced job bounds, 585-591
Balanced system, 585

Bandwidth, 39
Banking systems, 56-57, 570
Bar chart, 140, 144
Baseline validation, 126
Base system for ratio games, 165-167
Batch computer systems, 594
Batches, 427-428
Batch means, 427-428, 431, 432
Batch monitors, 95
BCMP networks, 551
Benchmark(s), 47, 52 *See also* Workload
  Ackermann, 50, 53, 167, 358, 359, 360, 361, 365
  application, 51-52
  debit-credit, 57, 175
  Dhrystone, 55, 345, 346, 357
  Doduc, 58
  eqntott, 58
  espresso, 58
  fpppp, 59
  GCC, 58
  LINPACK, 55
  LISP interpreter, 58
  matrix, 58
  NASA7, 58
  puzzle, 50, 167, 359, 360, 361, 365
  sieve, 50, 52, 175, 345, 346, 357, 359
  SPEC, 58
  spice, 58
  tomcatv, 59
  towers of Hanoi, 167, 360, 361, 365
  TPC, 58
  Whetstone, 54, 55
Benchmarking, 52
  games, 130-131
  mistakes in, 127-130
Bernoulli distribution, 483-484, 499, 500
  use of, 483-484
  variate generation, 480, 483-484
Bernoulli trials, 483
Beta distribution, 484-485
  use of, 484
  variate generation, 480, 485
Biased goals, 15
Bimodal distributions, 183
Binary n-cube networks, 433
Binomial distribution, 485-486, 499, 500
  use of, 486, 492-493
  variate generation, 480, 486
Birth-death processes, 516, 519-522
Bits, random, 457
Blocking, 552, 621
Bottleneck analysis, 563-568
Bottleneck device, 34, 558, 563

Bounds:
  asymptotic, 564–567
  balanced job, 585–591
Box-Cox transformations, 262–263, 264
Box-Mueller method, 494
bps (bits per second), 38
Broken scales in column charts, 149
Buckets, *see* Cells or buckets, in histograms
Buffers, 509
  in monitors, 96, 128
  in queues, 534–540
Bulk arrivals, 510
  Poisson, 510
Bulk service, 510
Busy period, 524

Cache(s):
  analysis, 404
  comparison, 345–347
  design alternatives, 352
  disk, 574
  hit ratios, 187
  miss ratios, 187
  in multiprocess environment, 353
Caching effects, 128
CACI, 502
Calendar queues, 410
Capacity, 39
  knee, 39, 125
  nominal, 39, 125
  usable, 125
Capacity management, 123
Capacity planning, 123–127, 176
  commercial products, 176
  problems in, 125
  steps in, 124
Categorical predictors in regression models, 254–257
Categorical variables, *see* Qualitative variables
Cauchy variate, 480
CDF, *see* Cumulative Distribution Function
Cells or buckets, in histograms, 75
  size, 149, 197–198
Central limit theorem, 182
Central processing unit (CPU), 4
Central server model, 552
Central subsystem, 586
Central tendencies, indices of, 183
Certification, component, 132
Chandy-Herzog-Woo theorem, 615
Channels, 26
Characteristic polynomial, 445

Characterization method, 480–481
Chart(s):
  Gantt, 149–152, 163
  graphic, 140, 141–145, 176
    bar, 140
    column, 140, 145
      broken scales in, 149
    guidelines for preparing, 141
    line, 140
      misuse of, 145
    mistakes in, 163
    mistakes in preparing, 144–145
    Schumacher, 160
Checklist:
  for avoiding mistakes, in evaluation, 22
  graphic charts, 143
  for regression analysis, 269–270
  for simulations, 398
Chi-square distance, 86
Chi-square distribution, 486–487
  quantiles of, 632–633
    approximation for, 638
  use of, 486
  variate generation, 480, 486–487
Chi-square test, 461–462
CISC (Complex Instruction Set Computer), 16
Classes of jobs, 548, 551
Clock, simulation, 503
Clock-advancing mechanisms, 407
Closed models, 400–401
Closed queueing networks, 547–548
Clustering analysis, 83–86, 175
  agglomerative techniques, 87
  divisive techniques, 87
  interpretation, 90
  problems with, 90–91, 175
CMG (Computer Measurement Group), 10, 176
Code:
  optimization, 114, 120
  restructuring, 120
Code size comparison study, 167, 329, 365, 390
Coefficient:
  of correlation, 267
  of determination, 227, 240, 246, 267
  of multiple correlation, 246, 249
  of skewness, 197
Coefficient of Variation (C.O.V.), 74, 181, 197
Collinearity, 253–254
Column chart, 140, 144, 145
  broken scales in, 149

Commercial products:
for capacity planning, 176
for monitoring, 175
for performance analysis, 175
Comparators, 98
Comparison of systems, 203–220
several, 327
two, 211, 218, 327
Completeness, of metrics, 35
Complex analysis, 19
Component certification, 132
Components, principal, 77
Component under study (CUS), 61, 62
Composition method, 493. *See also*
Decomposition method
Compression, data, 97
Computation of errors, 372
Computer network(s):
combining performance of layers, 187
comparison of algorithms, 218
comparison of architectures, 168
congestion control, 35, 414, 415
flow control, 592
gateway, 524, 556, 568
Kiviat graphs for, 159
local area, 39, 415, 621
metrics for, 35, 159
power, 592
queueing models for, 592
requirement specification, 42
simulation, 414–415
workload for, 63–65, 77, 82, 621
COMTEN, 175
Conclusion validation, 421
Concurrent simulation, 503
Conferences, performance, 8
Confidence coefficient, 204
Confidence interval(s), 147, 204, 219
for mean, 204–207
one-sided, 219
two-sided, 219
meaning of, 206
for model parameters, 229–232, 298–299,
335–337, 351–353, 374–379
for model predictions, 232–234, 299–301
one-sided, 213–215
for proportions, 215–216
one-sided, 219
two-sided, 219
for regression parameters, 267
vs. hypothesis testing, 213
Confidence level, 204
choosing a value for, 212
Configuration monitoring, 108

Configuration summarizing, 202
Confirmation experiment, 300
Confounding, 318–320
algebra of, 320–321
Congestion control:
metrics selection, 35
simulation model, 414, 415
Consistency tests, 420
Console, 102–103
functions, 109
Constant standard deviation of errors, 237
Contention, server, 621
Continuity test, 418–419
Continuous distributions, relationship
among, 500
Continuous-event models, 399
Continuous simulation languages, 403
Continuous-state models, 399
Continuous-state processes, 515–516
Continuous-time models, 399
Continuous variables, 140
Contrasts, 285, 299, 301, 336
Convolution, 596
Convolution algorithm, 590, 593–607
Convolution method, 479–480
Correctness *vs.* accuracy, 32
Correlated observations, variance of the
mean, 430–431
Correlated predictor variables, 268
Correlation, 181
coefficient of multiple, 246
Correlation coefficient, 181
Cost/performance ratio, 40
Counters, 97
overflow, 97
C.O.V., *see* Coefficient of Variation
Covariance, 181, 465
Coverage analysis, 112
CPM operating system, 282
CPU, *see* Central processing unit
CPU keelboat Kiviat graph, 155
CPU scheduling, 404
simulation, 398, 407, 423–424, 428–430,
433
Crashes, time between system, 214
Crossbar interconnection networks, 289–290
C/70 processor, 167, 360, 361, 365
CSMP, 403
Cumulative distribution function (CDF), 180.
See also Distributions; *particular
distributions*
Curvilinear regression, 257
CUS (component under study), 61, 62
Customers, in a queue, 507, 510

Cycle, regeneration, 434
Cycle length, 438

Databases, Kiviat graphs for, 159
Database systems, 6, 12, 201, 242, 545
Data deletion, initial, 424–425
Datametrics, 176
Data presentation, 20, 25, 102, 106–108,
    139–163
Data structures:
  calendar queues, 410
  heap, 410, 411
  indexed linear list, 409
  ordered linked list, 409
  tree, 410, 411
dB (decibels), 262
Deadlock, 503
Deadlock prevention algorithms, 404
Debit-credit benchmark, 57, 175
  pseudocode, 57
Decibels (dB), 262
Deciles, 194
Decision maker, 17
Decision makers' games, 162
Decomposition, hierarchical, 608, 613–620
Decomposition method, 478–479
Defections from a queue, 622
Degeneracy tests, 419
Degrees of freedom, 194, 228, 250, 299, 300,
    332, 348, 374, 489
Delay center, 509, 534, 551, 553, 563, 576,
    586, 602
Deletion, initial data, 424–425
Demands, skewness of, 128
Dendrogram, 89
Density function, probability, 180
Design, resolution, 321–326
Designated subnetwork, 615
Destination, 35
Detail, level of, 18, 66–67, 394
Determination, coefficient of, 240
Deterministic distribution, 509
Deterministic models, 400
  for verification, 417
Deviation, mean absolute, 193, 194, 197
Device, 510
  bottleneck, 558, 563
Device demands, skewness of, 128
Device homogeneity, 552
Dhrystone benchmark, 55–56, 345, 346, 357
DIPS (Dhrystone instructions per second),
    55
Discouraged arrivals, 540

Discrete distributions, relationship among,
    500
Discrete event:
  models, 399
  simulation, 406–408
    components of, 407–408
    languages, 403
Discrete state:
  models, 399
  processes, 515–516
Discrete uniform distribution, 498
  use of, 498
  variate generation, 498
Discrete variables, 140
Disk cache, modeling effect of, 574
Dispersion, indices of, 193
  selecting, 195–196
Displays, graphic, 418
Distance metrics, 86
  chi-square, 86
  Euclidean, 86
Distributed simulation, 503
Distributed-system monitors, 101–109
Distributed systems, 101–109, 200, 568
Distribution of data, determining, 196–199
Distribution function, cumulative, 180
Distributions:
  asymmetric, 199, 200
  commonly used, 483–501
    Bernoulli, 483–484, 499, 500
      use of, 483–484
      variate generation, 480, 483–484
    beta, 484–485
      use of, 484
      variate generation, 480, 485
    binomial, 485–486, 499
      use of, 492–493
      variate generation, 480, 486
    chi-square, 486–487
      approximation for, 638
      quantiles of, 632–633
      use of, 486
      variate generation, 480, 486–487
    deterministic, 509
    Erlang, 201, 487–488, 509
      use of, 487
      variate generation, 488
    exponential, 488–489, 509, 510
      truncated, 523–524, 531
      use of, 488
      variate generation, 475, 477, 489
    extreme value, 477
    F, 489–490
      approximation for, 638

Distributions (*Continued*)
  percentiles of, 636
  use of, 490
  variate generation, 490
  gamma, 490–491
  use of, 490
  variate generation, 480, 490
  general, 509
  geometric, 200, 491
  use of, 491
  variate generation, 477, 491
  hyperexponential, 509, 510
  K-S (Kolmogorov-Smirnov), quantiles of, 637
  Laplace, variate generation, 480
  logistic, variate generation, 477
  lognormal, 492
  use of, 492
  variate generation, 480, 492
  negative binomial, 492–493
  use of, 486, 492–493
  variate distribution, 493
  variate generation, 493
  normal, 493–494, 499, 500
  approximation for, 198–199, 638
  area under, 628, 638
  quantiles of, 629, 630
  standard, 181–182, 493
  test for, 237, 302
  unit, 181–182, 493
  use of, 494
  variate generation, 480, 494
  Pareto, 201, 495
  use of, 495
  variate generation, 477, 495
  Pascal, 495–496
  use of, 495
  variate generation, 480, 496
  Poisson, 201, 499, 500
  use of, 486, 493, 496
  variate generation, 480, 496
  relationships among, 500
  t, 497
  quantiles of, 631
  variate generation, 497
  triangular, variate generation, 480
  uniform (continuous), 497–498
  use of, 497
  variate generation, 498
  uniform (discrete), 498
  use of, 498
  variate generation, 498
  Weibull, 499
  use of, 499
  variate generation, 477, 499
Distributivity, *k*, 452, 467–470
Divisive clustering techniques, 87
Documentation, 397, 437
Doduc benchmark, 58
Domain of monitors, 94
Double-whammy graph, 147
Doubly-linked list, 409
Downtime, 40
Drivers, load, 132
Dynamic allocation of storage, 404
Dynamic memory management, 408
Dynamic models, 400
DYNAMO, 403

Editing sessions, 74, 122
EDP performance review, 10, 176
Educational environments, program usage in, 74
Effective arrival rate, 512, 513–514, 536–537, 538, 539
Effects:
  computation of, 285–286, 294, 328–329, 369–372
  confidence intervals for, 335–337, 351–353
Efficiency, programs, improvement of, 176
Efficiency of multiprocessor systems, 39
8080 processor, 166, 276
8086 processor, xii, 275, 281, 282
80286 processor, 282
Empirical distributions, generation, 475–476
Emulation, 403
  keyboard monitor, 176
  remote terminal, *see* Remote-terminal emulator
  workstation, 138
Encryption, performance of, 243, 271
End systems, 35
Eqntott benchmark, 58
Erlang distribution, 201, 487–488, 509
  use of, 487
  variate generation, 480, 488
Erlang's C formula, 530
Erlang's loss formula, 536
Erroneous analysis, 18, *See also* Games; Mistakes; Misuses
Error, 34, 222
  standard, 205, 219
Error-free seconds, 40
Error monitoring, 108
Errors, computation of, 372
Errors in input, 19

Espresso benchmark, 58
Euclidean distance, 86
  weighted, 86
Evaluation:
  mistakes in, 14–22
  performance, 8, 10, 16
    avoiding mistakes in, 22
    checklist, 22
    systematic approach to, 22–26
  technique(s), 16
    selection of, 24, 30–33
Event, 94
  notices, 408
  routines, 407
  scheduling, 407, 503
  trace, 418
Event-driven monitors, 95
Event-driven simulation, 407
Events, independent, 179
Event-set algorithms, 408, 502
Exclusion, mutual, 621
Executable workload, 67
Execution profile, 112
Exerciser loops, 50–51
Expected value, 180
Experimental design, 273–282
  mistakes in, 277, 278–279
  terminology, 275–278
Experimental designs, types of, 279–282
  fractional factorial, 18, 25, 281
  full factorial, 18, 280, 343–367
  half-replicate, 314
  k factor, 381–389
  one-factor, 327, 337–342
  two-factor:
    multiplicative models for, 353–359
    with replications, 368–380
    without replications, 343–367
  2^k factorial, 280, 283–292
  $2^k r$ factorial, 293–313
  2^2 factorial, 284–285
  $2^2 r$ factorial, 293–308
  2^{k-p} fractional factorial, 314–326
Experimental errors, 222, 278
  estimation of, 294–295, 346, 372
  estimation of SSE, 329–330
  standard deviation of, 228
  test for independence, 234, 235, 237, 302, 324
Experimental unit, 277
Expert intuition, 421
Explicit instrumenting, 104
Exponential distribution, 488–489, 509, 510

  truncated, 523–524, 531
  use of, 488
  variate generation, 475, 476, 489
Extended Fibonacci generators, 450
Extreme value distribution, 476

Factor analysis, 77
Factors, 17, 24, 77, 221, 276
  principal, 77–81
  selection of, 24
Fairness index, 36
FCFS (first come, first served), 509, 541, 551
F distribution, 489–490
  approximation for, 638
  percentiles of, 636
  use of, 490
  variate generation, 490
FEC (Flow-Equivalent Center), 611
Feedback shift register(s)
  generalized, 449, 503
  linear, 446
Fibonacci generators, 450
FIFO (first in, first out), 382, 383, 385
Figure of merit, 155, 157–158
File servers, 200, 568, 572–573
Filters, 104
Final conditions, 429
Finite buffer systems, 534–540
Firmware monitors, 100–101
First come, first served (FCFS), 509, 541, 551
Fixed-capacity service centers, 553, 570, 575, 576, 609
Flow balance, job, 551, 555
Flow control in computer networks, 592
Flow-Equivalent Center (FEC), 611
Flow law, forced, 557–560
FOM, see Figure of merit
Forced flow law, 557–560
Fork and join, 621
FORTRAN, as a simulation language, 402
Fpppp benchmark, 59
Fractile, 194
Fractional factorial designs, 25, 281, 314–326
Freedom, degrees of, 228, 332, 374, 489
F-test, 251, 267, 298, 333
Full factorial design, 280, 281
Function:
  Ackermann's, 50, 53
  cumulative distribution, 180
  probability density, 180
  probability mass, 180

Games:
  benchmarking, 130–131
  decision makers', 162
  percentage, 169–170
  pictorial, 146
  ratio, 8, 165–174
  winning, 170–173
Gamma distribution, 490–491
  use of, 490
  variate generation, 480, 490
Gantt charts, 149–152, 163
Garbage collection, 263, 311–313
GASP, 402, 403, 409, 502
Gateway response time, 527
Gateways, in networks, 524, 556, 568
Gaussian, see Normal distribution
GCC benchmark, 58
Generalized feedback shift register (GFSR),
  449, 503
Generator polynomial, 320
Generators, load, 4
Geometric distribution(s), 200, 491
  use of, 491
  variate generation, 477, 491
Geometric mean, 187, 197, 271
GFSR (generalized feedback shift register),
  449, 503
G/G/m queueing system, 544
Gibson instruction mix, 48, 49, 175
Global metrics, 34
G/M/1 queueing system, 543–544
Goals, 14–15
  biased, 15
  setting, 15
  SMART, 42
Gordon and Newell's method, 595
GPSS, 403, 409, 502
Grand mean, 328
Graphic charts, 140, 141–145, 176
  checklist for, 143
  guidelines for, 141
  mistakes in, 163
Graphic displays, 418
Graphs:
  double-whammy, 147
  Kiviat, 153–159
Grid lines, 145

Half-replicate design, 314
Hanoi, towers of, benchmark, 167, 360, 361, 365
Hardware mapping, 98
Hardware monitors, 98
  vs. software monitors, 98–100, 101
Harmonic mean, 188–189, 197

HB (higher is better) metric, 40, 153, 154,
  168, 171, 172, 386
Heap, 410, 411
Hierarchical decomposition, 608, 613–620
Histogram, 144
  broken scales in, 149
  bucket (cell) sizes, 147
  multiparameter, 76, 175
  single-parameter, 75
Hit ratios, cache, 187
Homogeneity:
  device, 552
  routing, 552
Homoscedasticity, 237, 261
HP9000/840 processor, 354
Hybrid monitor, 101, 103, 175
Hyperexponential distribution, 509
Hypothesis testing, 213

iAPX 432, Intel, processor, 358, 359
IBM, 452
IBM PC, 69, 109
IBM PCjr, 69
Idle time, 39
IEEE, 8, 11
IFIP working group, 9
IID (independent and identically
  distributed), 241, 247, 461, 501, 507,
  508, 516, 557
Implicit spying, 104
IMSL, 452
Independent and identically distributed
  (IID), see IID
Independent errors, test for, 234, 235, 237,
  302
Independent events, 179
Independent job behavior, 552
Independent replications, 426–427, 431
Indexed linear list, 409
Indices of central tendencies, 183
Indices of dispersion, 193, 194, 195–196
Indirect binary n-cube networks, 433
Individual metrics, 34
Infinite servers (IS), 509, 551, 553
Informal methods, 386–389
Information systems, 242
INFORS, 10
Inherited time, 113
Initial conditions, 129, 395
Initial data deletion, 424–425
Initialization:
  proper, 423–424
  test for incorrect, 236

Input:
errors, 19
rate, 94
routine, 407
width, 94
Institute of Electrical and Electronic
Engineers (IEEE), 8, 11
Instruction mix, 48–49
Gibson, 48, 49
Instrumentation mechanisms, 113
Instrumentation of programs, 175
Integration of systems, 132
Intel iAPX 432 processor, 358, 359
Intensity, traffic, 522
Interacting factors, 279
Interaction, 277, 279
Interactive response time law, 563
Interarrival times, 507
Interconnection networks:
comparison of, 289–290
Crossbar, 289–290
memory, 289–290
Omega, 289–290
simulation, 433
Intergroup variance, 87
Intermediate systems, 35
Internal driver, 132
International Federation for Information
Processing (IFIP), 9
International Federation of Operational
Research Societies
(INFORS), 10
Interpretation:
of accounting logs, 117–119
of clustering results, 90
of data, 25, 102
of monitor results, 109
of normal quantile-quantile plots, 199, 200
Interquartile range, 194
Intragroup variance, 87
Intuition, expert, 421
Invalid models, 394–395
Inverse transformation, 474–476
I/O-arrow Kiviat graph, 155, 156
I/O-bound programs, 120
I/O optimization, 114
I/O-wedge Kiviat graph, 155
IS (infinite servers), 509, 551, 553

Jackson networks, 551
Job behavior, independent, 552
Job bounds, balanced, 585–591, 590
Job flow balance, 551, 555

Jobs, 510
classes of, 548, 551
in a system, distribution of, 593–595, 616,
619
Join and fork, 621
Journals, performance, 8, 9, 10

k-dimensional uniformity, 452, 467–470
k-distributivity, 452, 467–470
Keelboat Kiviat graph, CPU, 155
Kendall notation, 509
Kernels, 49–50, 175
2^k experimental design, 280, 283–292
Keyboard emulation monitor, 176
k factor experimental designs, 381–389
Kilo Whetstone Instructions Per Second
(KWIPS), 55
Kiviat graphs, 153–159, 176
for computer networks, 159
CPU-keelboat, 155
for databases, 159
I/O-arrow, 155, 156
I/O-wedge, 155
shapes of, 155–159
Knee, 565
capacity, 39, 125
Knowledge-based simulation, 503, 504
Kolmogorov-Smirnov test, see K-S test
2^{k-p} experimental design, 314–326
sign table for, 316–317
$2^k r$ experimental design, 293–313
K-S (Kolmogorov-Smirnov) distribution,
quantiles of, 637
K-S (Kolmogorov-Smirnov) test, 462–465
comparison with chi-square test, 465
KWIPS, 55

Lagrange multiplier technique, 241
Languages, for monitors, 97
LAN (local area network), 415, 621
Laplace distribution, variate generation, 480
Last Come, First Served (LCFS), with
Preempt and Resume, 509, 551
LaTex, 322
Law(s):
Amdahl's, 257, 258
forced flow, 557–560
Little's, 512, 513–515, 560
operational, 555–568
definition, 556
response time:
general, 561–562
interactive, 563

Law(s) (*Continued*)
  of slow creation, 121
  utilization, 556
Lawrence Livermore loops, 56
LB (lower is better) metric, 40, 153, 154, 168, 171, 172, 386
LCFS (Last Come, First Served), 509, 541
LCFS-PR (with Preempt and Resume), 509, 551
LCG, *see* Linear-congruential generators
Least-squares criterion, 223
Left-skewed pdf, *see* Skewed distribution
Legend box, 141
Length of simulation, 429–430
Level(s), 24, 255, 276
  of accuracy, 32
  of confidence, 204, 212–213
  of detail, 18, 66–67, 394
  of loading, 69
  of significance, 204
LFSR (linear-feedback shift register), 446
Libraries, probe-point, 98
Limitations, of queueing theory, 620–622
Limit theorem, central, 182
Linear-congruential generators, 439–440
  mixed, 440
  multiplicative, 441–444
    with $m = 2^k$, 441
    with $m \neq 2^k$, 441
Linear-feedback shift register, *see* LFSR
Linearizer algorithm, 624
Linear list, indexed, 409
Linear models, 400
Linear regression models, 221–243
  multiple, 244, 245–250
  simple, 221–243
Linear relationship, 266
  test for, 235
Line chart, 140, 144, 145
  misuse of, 145
Lines, grid, 145
Linked list:
  doubly, 409
  ordered, 409
LINPACK benchmark, 55
LISP interpreter benchmark, 58
Little's law, 512, 513–515, 560
Live operators, 132
Livermore loops, Lawrence, 56
Load:
  drivers, 132
  generators, 4
Load-dependent:
  arrivals, 621
  service center, 554, 608–613

Loading level, 69, 77, 128
Local area network (LAN), 39, 415, 621
Local information, 552
Locality of reference, 120
Logic elements, 98
Logistic distribution, variate generation, 477
Lognormal distribution, 492
  use of, 492
  variate generation, 480, 492
Log transformation, 260–261
Long runs, 423
Loops, Lawrence Livermore, 56
Loss formula, Erlang's, 536
Lottery, 212

Machine repairman model, 552
Macintosh, 69
Magnetic tape backup systems, 65–66
Majorizing function, 476
Management of capacity, 123
  steps in, 124
Management of systems, 103
Manager, system, 103
Many-to-many mapping, 103
Mapping hardware, 98
Markoff, *see* Markov *entries*
Markov chain, 516
Markov models, 81–82
Markov processes, 516
Mass function, probability, 180
Matrix:
  benchmark, 58
  transition, 81–82
M/D/1 queue, 542–543
Mean, 180, 183
  arithmetic, 73, 188, 197
  confidence interval for, 204–207
  geometric, 187, 191, 197
  harmonic, 188–189, 197
  misuses of, 186
  of ratio, 189–192
  relationship to median, mode, 183–186
  sample size for determining, 216–217
  selecting median, mode, and, 183–186
  standard error of, 205, 219
  of sums, 181
  testing for zero, 207–208, 216
Mean absolute deviation, 193, 194, 197
Mean arithmetic, 305
Mean queue length, 429–430, 602
Mean square of errors, 251, 299. *See also* MSE (mean squared error)
Mean time to failure (MTTF), 40

Mean-value analysis, 570, 575–579
    approximate, 579–585
    with load-dependent centers, 608–613
    Schweitzer's approximation, 580, 581
Mean waiting time, 429
Measure, when to, 30
Measured data:
    for simulation validation, 422
    summarizing, 179, 182–183
    validation of, 32, 129
Measurement techniques, program, 113
Median, 181, 197
    relationship to mean, mode, 183–186
    selecting mean, mode, and, 183–186
Memoryless distribution, 488–489, 509
Memory management, dynamic, 408
Memory management systems, 311, 622
Method of subsamples, *see* Batch means
Metrics, 4, 23
    commonly used, 36
    for computer networks, 159
    distance, 86
    global, 34
    HB (higher is better), 40, 153, 154, 168, 386
    individual, 34
    LB (lower is better), 40, 153, 154, 168, 386
    mistake in selecting, 16
    NB (nominal is best), 40
    selection, 33–37, 61
    utility classification of, 40
MFLOPS, 38, 49, 56
M/G/1 queue, 540–541
M/G/∞ queue, 543
Millions of Floating-point Operations Per
    Second, *see* MFLOPS
Millions of Instructions per Second, *see*
    MIPS
Minimal standard random number generator,
    452
Minimum spanning tree method, 87
MIPS, 16, 38, 49
    averaging, 188
Missing observations, 360–366
Miss ratios, cache, 187
Mistakes:
    in benchmarking, 127–130
    in charts, 144–145
    in evaluation, 14–22
        how to avoid, 14–29
    in experimental design, 277, 278–279
    in model validation, 583
    in queueing approximations, 583
    in regression, 266–269

in selecting metrics, 16
in simulation, 393–397
Misuses:
    of line charts, 145
    of means, 186
    of percentages, 170
    of statistics, 271
Mixed linear-congruential generators, 440
Mixed queueing networks, 548
M/M/m/B queue, 534–540
M/M/m queue, 527–534
M/M/∞ queue, 540
M/M/1 queue, 522–526
Mode, 181, 197
    relationship to mean, median, 183–186
    selecting mean, median, and, 183–186
Modeling error, *see* Error
Model parameter estimation, 223–226, 284–
    285, 294, 328, 344–346, 370
Model(s):
    additive, 303–306
    central server, 552
    definition of a good, 222–223
    deterministic, 400, 417
    for experimental designs, 327, 344–346,
        368–369, 381–382
    linear and nonlinear, 400
    linear regression, 221–243
        multiple, 244, 245–250
        simple, 221–243
    machine-repairman, 552
    Markov, 81–82
    multiplicative, 303–308, 353–359
    open and closed, 400–401
    probabilistic, 400
    queueing network, 553
    stable and unstable, 401
    static and dynamic, 400
    stochastic, 10
Model validation, 413–414
    mistakes in, 583
    techniques, 420
Model verification, 413–414
Modular design, 414–416
Modularity, 414
Modulus, 439
Monitor(s), 4, 93–110, 175
    accounting logs as, 114, 116–121
    activation mechanisms for, 95–96
    advertising by, 105
    buffer size in, 96
    data collection in, 105
    priority, 97
    soliciting by, 105

Monitor(s) (*Continued*)
  terminology, 94
  types of, 94–95
    commercially available, 175
    distributed system, 101–109
    hardware, 98
    keyboard emulation, 176
    program execution, 111–114
    software, 95, 175
Monitoring:
  abnormal events, 97–98
  on-off switch for, 97
  overhead, 129
  reasons for, 93
Monitor languages, 97
Monte Carlo simulation, 403
Moving average method, 427
MSA (Mean Square of A), 333
MS-DOS, 70, 282
MSE (mean squared error), 229, 246, 251,
    299, 333, 348
MSR (mean squared residual), 246, 251
MTTF, *see* Mean time to failure
Multicollinearity, 253–254
Multiparameter histograms, 76, 175
Multiple correlation coefficient, 246, 249
Multiple linear regression, 244, 245–250,
    266. *See also* Linear regression models
Multiplicative linear-congruential generator,
    440–444
  with $m \neq 2^k$, 441
Multiplicative models
  for 2^2r experiments, 303–308
  for two-factor experiments, 353–359
Multiplier, 439
Multiprocessor systems, 527
Multistream simulations, 454
Myths, random number generation, 455–458

Name server, 518
NASA7 benchmark, 58
NB (nominal is best) metric, 40
Negative binomial distribution, 492–493
  use of, 486, 492–493
Nominal capacity, 38, 125
Nondistributed systems, 101
Nonexecutable workload, 67
Nonexponential service times, 620–621
Noninteracting factors, 279
Nonlinear models, 400
Nonproduct form networks, 620
Nonredundancy of metrics, 35
Nonregenerative simulation, 434
Nonzero origins in charts, 146

Normal distribution, 181–182, 493–494, 499,
    500
  approximation for, 198–199, 638
  area under, 628, 638
  quantiles of, 629, 630
  standard, 181–182, 493
  test for, 237, 302
  unit, 182, 493
  use of, 494
  variate generation, 480, 494
Normalization (for clustering):
  percentile, 86
  range, 85–86
  variance, 85
  weight, 85
Normalizing constant, 603
Normal quantile-quantile plot, 198, 237, 303,
    305, 307, 335, 350, 356, 363, 364, 366,
    378, 385
  interpretation of, 199, 200
Norton's theorem, 614
Notices, event, 408
Number of jobs in a queue, 511
  vs. in system, 511
  vs. system, distribution of, 619
  vs. time in system, 512

Observation method, 386–387
Observations:
  correlated, 430–431
  missing, 360–366
  in monitors, 104–105
  paired, 209
  system, 102
  unpaired, 209–210
Observer, 102
Omega interconnection networks, 289–290
Omega transformation, 261
One-factor-at-a-time designs, 279
One-factor experimental designs
  with equal sample sizes, 327–341
    ANOVA table for, 333
  with unequal sample sizes, 337–342
    ANOVA table for, 338, 340
One-sided confidence intervals, 213–215
  for means, 219
  for proportions, 219
One-step behavior, 551
On-line graphic displays, 418
On-line monitors, 95
Open models, 400–401
Open queueing networks, 547–548, 551
  analysis of, 570, 572, 575–579

Operating systems:
    ARGUS, 230–232, 239, 240, 256
    CPM, 282
    MS-DOS, 70, 282
    PRIMOS, 452
    UNIX, xii, 230, 231, 256, 282, 359
    VMS, 359
    WANG VS, 324
Operational laws, 555–568
    definition, 556
Operationally testable assumptions, 555
Operational quantities, 555
Operations Research Society of America
    (ORSA), 10
Operators, live, 132
Optimization:
    of code, 114, 120
    of I/O, 114
    of paging, 114
Optimizer, program, 192
Ordered linked list, 409
Ordered qualitative variable, 140
Organizations, professional, 8
ORSA, 10
Orthogonal vectors, 77, 288
Outliers, 19, 83, 85, 183, 193, 194, 265
Output analysis techniques for simulations,
    502
Overflow counter, 97
Overflow of buffers in monitors, 97
Overhead, monitor, 94
Overlapping pairs, 468–472

Page faults, 120
Paging
    algorithms, 382, 404
    optimization, 114
    performance, 383–385
    study, 382–385, 389
Paired observations, 209
P^2 algorithms for percentiles, 196
Parallelism
    in space, 354
    in time, 354
Parallel simulation, 504
Parameters, 17, 23, 204–207
    confidence intervals for, 229–232, 240,
        241, 246, 249, 298–299, 335–337, 351–
        353, 374–379
    estimation, 223–226, 284–285, 294, 328,
        346, 370
    regression, 223
    validation, 421
    for workloads, 83

Pareto distribution, 201, 495
    use of, 495
    variate generation, 477, 495
Partial factorial designs, 18
Pascal, 359
    program for random number generation,
        443
    program for sieve benchmark, 53
    routines for simulation, 503
    as a simulation language, 402
Pascal distribution, 495–496
    use of, 495
    variate generation, 480, 496
pdf, see Probability density function (pdf),
    skewed
PDF, see Probability distribution function
PDP-11/70 processor, xii, 167, 361, 365
Percentages, ratio games with, 169–170
Percentile normalization, 86
Percentiles, 194, 195, 197
Performance:
    conferences, 8
    evaluation, see Evaluation
    journals, 8–9, 10
    projects, 11
    requirements, setting, 40–43
    tuning, 123
Performance evaluation
    art of, 7
    mistakes in, 14–29
Performance Evaluation Review, 8
Performance monitoring, 108
Period of generators, 438
Pictograms, 148
Pictorial games, 146–149
Pie chart, 144, 146
Pipes, remote, 25–27
Plotting random quantities, 147–148
pmf, see Probability mass function
Poisson arrivals, 508
    bulk, 509
Poisson distributed variable, 261
Poisson distribution, 201, 496
    use of, 486, 493, 496
    variate generation, 480, 496
Poisson processes/streams, 201, 496, 516–
    517
    properties of, 517
Polar method, 494
Pollaczek-Khinchin (P-K) mean value
    formula, 541
Polynomial:
    characteristic, 445
    generator, 320

Polynomial (*Continued*)
  primitive, 445, 468
Population size, 508
Possession, single resource, 552
Power, metric, 36
Power transformation, 262
PPS (packets per second), 38, 524
Predictability of random numbers, 456
Predicted responses, confidence intervals for, 232–234, 240, 241, 246, 250, 299–301
Prediction beyond measured range, 268
Predictors, 221, 276
  categorical, 254–257
  correlated, 268
  too many, 268–269
Preempt and Resume, Last Come First Served, 509, 551
Presentation of data, 20, 25, 102, 106–108, 139–163
Price-performance ratio, 58
Primary factors, 276
Primitive polynomials, 445, 449, 459, 468
Primitive trinomials, 449
PRIMOS operating system, 452
Principal-component analysis, 76–80, 175
Principal factor, 77
Print server, 568
Probabilistic models, 400
Probability density function (pdf), 180, 181. *See also* Distributions; *particular distributions*
  skewed, 186
Probability distribution function (PDF), 180, 181. *See also* Distributions; *particular distributions*
Probability mass function (pmf), 180. *See also* Distributions; *particular distributions*
Probability theory, 179
Probe points, 98, 104
Probing, 104
Problem(s):
  in capacity planning, 125
  with clustering, 90–91, 175
  of multicollinearity, 253–254
Procedure call, remote, 26, 230–232
Processes:
  arrival, 507–508, 551
  birth-death, 516, 519–522
  continuous-state, 515–516
  discrete state, 515–516
  Markov, 516
  Poisson, 201, 496, 516–517
  relationship among, 517
  stochastic, 515–517

types of, 515–517
Processing kernel, 50
Z80 Processor, xii, 275, 276, 279, 281
Z8002 Processor, 167, 360, 361, 365
68000 Processor, xii, 275, 276, 281, 282, 359, 360, 361, 365, 367
8080 Processor, 166, 276
8086 Processor, xii, 275, 281, 282, 359
80286 Processor, 282
Processor comparison study, 357
Processors:
  68000, xii, 275, 276, 281, 282, 359, 360, 361, 365, 367
  8080, 166, 276
  8086, xii, 275, 281, 282, 359
  80286, 282
  C/70, 167, 360, 361, 365
  HP9000/840, 354
  Intel iAPX 432, 358, 359
  PDP-11/70, xii, 167, 360, 361, 365
  RISC-I, 167, 360, 361–365
  VAX-11/780, xii, 167, 359, 360, 361, 365
  Z80, xii, 275, 276, 279, 281
  6502, xxvii, 166
  Z8002, 167, 360, 361, 365
Processor sharing, 509, 551
Product-form networks, 548–552
Productivity metrics, 34
Professional organizations, *see* Organizations, professional
Profile:
  execution, 113
  resource usage, 68
Profile report, 113
Program(s):
  efficiency of, 115, 120
  execution monitors, 111–114
    design, 112
  instrumentation, 113, 175
  measurement techniques, 113
  optimizer, 191, 192
  performance improvement, 114, 115–116
  synthetic, 50–51
  text formatting, 322
  usage in educational environments, 74
Program execution, monitor design, 112
Projection validation, 126
Projects, performance, 11
Proportions, 215
  confidence intervals for, 215–216
  sample size for determining, 217–218
Pseudo-random numbers, 438
PS (processor sharing), 551
Puzzle benchmark, 50, 167, 359, 360, 361, 365

QNET4, 402
Qualitative variables, 140
    ordered, 140
    unordered, 140
Quantile(s), 181. *See also* Percentiles
    of chi-square distribution, 632–633, 638
    of F distribution, 634, 638
    of K-S (Kolmogorov-Smirnov) distribution, 637
    of normal distribution, 198, 629, 630, 638
    of t distribution, 631
Quantile-quantile plots, 198, 202, 271
Quantitative variables, 140
    continuous, 140
    discrete, 140
Quartiles, 194
Queue(s), 509
    analysis of, 519–546
    calendar, 410
    components of, 508
    $G/G/m$, 544
    $G/M/1$, 543–544
    $M/D/1$, 542–543
    $M/G/\infty$, 543
    $M/G/1$, 540–541
    $M/M/\infty$, 540
    $M/M/1$, 522–526
    $M/M/1/B$, 533, 539
    $M/M/m$, 527–534
    $M/M/m/B$, 534–540
    $M/M/m/B/K$, 546
    $M/M/m/K$, 546
    notation, 507–510
    rules for all, 509
Queueing analysis, symbols, 624–626
Queueing approximations, mistakes in, 583
Queueing network(s), 547–554
    BCMP, 551
    closed, 547–548
    large, 608–620
    mixed, 548
    models of computer systems, 553
    nonproduct form, 620
    open, 547–548, 551
        analysis of, 570, 572, 575–579
    product form, 548–552
Queueing notation, 507–510
Queueing theory:
    introduction to, 507–518
    limitations of, 620–622
Queue length, 511
    distribution of, 599–600, 601, 609, 619
    mean computation, 430

Random number, 82
Random-number generation, 437–458, 502, 503
    nonoverlapping streams, myths, 454
Random-number generators
    combined, 451–453
    desired properties of, 437–439
    Fibonacci, 450
    implementing, 456
    linear-congruential, 439–440
        Pascal code for, 443
    myths about, 455–458
    poor, 395
    RANDU, 452
    survey of, 452–453
    Tausworthe, 444–450
    testing, 456, 460–472, 502
    in UNIX, 453
Random numbers, 395
    bits of, 457
        predictability of, 456
    nonoverlapping pairs, 468, 469
    nonoverlapping streams, 454
Random variable, 179
Random-variate generation, 474–482. *See also* Distributions; *particular types of distributions*
    technique, finding, 481
RANDU, 452
Range, 193, 197, 389
Range method, 388–389
Range normalization, 85–86
Ranking method, 387
Rat holes, 162
Ratio(s):
    cost/performance, 40
    hit, 187
    mean of, 189–192
    miss, 187
    reads to writes, 121
    visit, 558, 560
Ratio games, 8, 165–174
    with percentages, 169–170
    relative performance enhancement, 168
    strategies for winning, 170–173
Ratio metrics, 35, 168
Reaction time, 38
Reads to writes, ratio of, 121
Real measurements, 422
Real variables, 140
Real workload, 47, 128
Reduced Instruction Set Computer, *see* RISC
Reduction techniques, variance, 436, 502
Reference, locality of, 120

Regeneration, 433–435
  cycle, 434
  method of, 434
  point, 434
Regenerative simulations, 502
Regenerative system, 434
Regression analysis, 221, 244–271
  assumptions, 234
    visual tests for, 234–241, 266
  checklist for, 269–270
  mistakes in, 266–269
Regression models, 221–243, 244–271
  with categorical predictors, 254–257
  curvilinear, 257
  good and bad, 222
  linear, 221, 241
    multiple, 244, 245–250
    simple, 221
  other, 244–271
  over partial range, 268–269
  predictions, confidence intervals for, 232–234
  transformations for, 259
Regression parameters, 223
  confidence intervals for, 229–232, 267
  estimation of, 223–226, 241, 246
  numerical values of, 266
Regression testing, 132
Rejection method, 476, 494
Reliability, 34, 40, 42
Remote pipes, 25–27
Remote procedure call, 26, 230–232, 239, 256
Remote-terminal emulation, 132–133
Remote-terminal emulator (RTE), 4, 132–138, 176
  components emulated by, 133
  components of, 134
  output, 135
Repairman model, machine, 552
Repeatability of workloads, 69
Repetitions, 407
Replacement algorithm, 382
Replication(s), 276
  $2^k r$ factorial designs with, 294
  moving average of independent, 426–427
  two-factor designs with, 368–380
Report, profile, 113
Report generator, 408
Representativeness, 67
Requirements, setting, 40–43
Reservation systems, airline, 570
Residual, see Error
Resolution:

design, 321–326
  monitor, 94
Resource possession:
  simultaneous, 622
  single, 552
Resource usage profile, 68
Response(s), 276
Response-dependent arrivals, 621
Response time, 4, 30, 37, 601, 616
  variability of, 36
Response time law:
  general, 561–562
  interactive, 563
Response variable, 221, 276
  confidence intervals for, 232–234, 250, 299–301
Responsiveness, 34
resq, 402
Results:
  presentation of, 20
  reasons for not accepting, 161–162
  saleability of, 32
$2^2 r$ experimental designs, 293–308
  multiplicative model for, 303–308
RISC, 12, 16, 354–356
RISC architecture (Scheme and Spectrum), 354–356
RISC-I code size study, 167, 329, 365, 390
RISC-I processor, 166, 167, 360, 361, 365
Round-robin (RR), 509
Routines
  event, 407
  input, 407
  trace, 408
Routing homogeneity, 552
RPC (remote procedure call), 26, 230–232, 239, 256
RTE, see Remote-terminal emulator
Run length, 432
Runs, long, 423

Saleability of results, 32
Sample, 203–207
  mean, 183
  median, 183
  mode, 183
  standard deviation, 193, 197
  vs. population, 203–204
Sample data:
  comparing systems using, 203
  summarizing, 179
Sample size:
  for comparing two alternatives, 18

for determining mean, 216–217
for determining proportions, 217–218
Sample variance, 193, 197
Sampling, 84, 113, 128
Sampling monitors, 95
SAS statistical package, 453
Scale:
  in histograms, broken, 149
  ranges, selection of, 145
Scaling, data, 85
Scaling factor, 594, 595
Scatter diagram(s), 76, 77, 224, 230, 231,
  235, 236, 237, 238, 257, 260, 267, 303,
  335, 350, 469
Scatter plots, see Scatter diagram(s)
Scenario, 133
Scheduler design study, 325, 387, 390
Scheduling:
  CPU, 404
    simulation of, 407, 423–424, 428–430,
      433
  events, 503
Scheme RISC architecture, 354–356
Schrage's method, 442, 444
Schumacher charts, 160, 176
Schweitzer's approximation, 580, 581, 583
Script, 133
SCS, see Society for Computer Simulations
Secondary factors, 276
Seed(s), 395, 438
  independence, 420
  selection of, 395, 453–455, 456
  table of, 455
Self-time, 113
Semi-Interquartile Range (SIQR), 194–195,
  197
Sequence:
  Fibonacci, 450
  Tausworthe, 444, 446
Serial-correlation test, 465
Serial test, 468–470
Server(s):
  central, 552
  file, 200, 568, 572–573
  infinite, 551
  print, 568
Service center(s), 509
  fixed-capacity, 553, 570, 575, 576, 577,
    609
  flow equivalent, 611
  load-dependent, 554, 608, 609, 610
Service discipline(s), 509, 551
  fair, 552
  first come, first served (FCFS), 509, 541,
    551

  last come, first served (LCFS), 509
    with preempt and resume (LCFS-PR),
      509, 551
  processor sharing (PS), 551
  in random order (SIRO), 541
Services, 23, 26, 62
Service times:
  distribution, 509, 551
  nonexponential, 620–621
  state-dependent, 551
Shift register(s):
  generalized feedback, 448–449, 503
  linear feedback, 446
Shorted model, 614, 615, 618
SIAM, 9, 10
Sieve benchmark, 50, 52, 175, 345, 346, 357,
  359
  Pascal listing for, 53
SIGMETRICS, 8
Signaling theory, 262
Significance level, 204–207
Sign table, 286, 292
  for 2^{k-p} experimental design, 316–317
SIGSIM, 9
Simple designs, 18, 279–280
Simple linear regression, 221
SIMPL/I system, 452
SIMSCRIPT, 402, 403, 452, 502
SIMULA, 402, 403, 409, 416, 453, 502
  listing of Ackermann's function, 53
Simulation:
  of computer networks, 414–415
  of CPU scheduling, 433
  types of, 403–408
    concurrent, 503
    continuous, 403
    discrete event, 403, 406–408
    emulation, 403
    event driven, 403, 407
    knowledge-based, 503, 504
    Monte Carlo, 403
    multistream, 454
    nonregenerative, 434
    parallel, 503
    regenerative, 434, 502
    static, 403–404
    terminating, 428–430
    trace driven, 404–406, 502
Simulation analysis, 393–412, 413–436
  failure, causes of, 395–397
  mistakes in, 393–395
  when to use, 31
Simulation books, 502–503

Simulation clock, 407
Simulation language(s), 401–403, 416, 502
  CSMP, 403
  DYNAMO, 403
  FORTRAN as a, 402
  GASP, 402, 403, 409, 502
  GPSS, 402, 409, 502
  Pascal as a, 402
  selection of, 401–403
  SIMSCRIPT, 402, 403, 452, 502
  SIMULA, 402, 403, 409, 453, 502
Simulation length, 395, 430
Simulation output analysis, 413, 502
Simulation packages, 402
  QNET4, 402
  RESQ, 402
Simulation team, 397
Simultaneous resource possession, 622
Sine transformation, arc, 261
Single-parameter histogram, 75
Single-resource possession, 552
SIQR (Semi-Interquartile Range), 194–195,
  197
SIRO (service in, random order), 541
6502 processor, xxvii, 166
68000 processor, xii, 275, 276, 280, 359, 360,
  361, 366, 367
Sizing, system, 124–125
Skewed distribution, 183, 185, 186
  left-, 183
  right-, 183
Skewness, 185
  coefficient of, 197
  of device demands, 128
Skills:
  for simulation, 397
  social, 20–21
  substantive, 20–21
Slow creation, law of, 121
SMART goals, 42, 396
Social skills, 20–21
Society for Computer Simulations (SCS), 9,
  503
Society for Industrial and Applied
  Mathematics, *see* SIAM
Software monitors, 95, 175
  vs. hardware monitors, 98–100, 101
Soliciting, by monitors, 105
Spanning tree method, minimum, 87
SPEC benchmark suite, 58
SPECmark, 59
SPECthruput, 59
Spectral test, 470–472
Spectrum RISC architecture, 354–356

Speed, 34, 42
Spice benchmark, 58
Square criterion, least, 223
Square-root transformation, 259
Squares, sum of, 226, 287
SSE (sum of squared errors), 223, 225, 228,
  295, 296, 297, 299, 331–332, 348, 373
SS0, 227, 297, 331–332, 348, 373
SSR, 227
SST (sum of squares total), 226–227, 287,
  296, 297, 331–332, 348, 373
SSY, 227, 297, 331–332, 348, 373
Stability condition, 511
Standard deviation, 180, 193, 197
  vs. hardware monitors
    errors, 228
    test for constant, 238
  of parameters, 246
Standard error, 205
  of sample mean, 219
Standard normal distribution, 181
State:
  continuous, 399
  discrete, 399
  steady, 129–130, 395, 401, 413, 423, 428,
    520, 621
  transient, 129–130, 423
State-dependent service, 551
State probabilities, 595, 604, 607
State transition diagram, 81
  for birth-death processes, 520
  for M/M/m/B queues, 535
  for M/M/m queues, 527
  for M/M/1 queues, 522
Static models, 400
Static simulation, 403–404
Statistical package, SAS, 453
Statistical tables, 627–638
  approximation formulas for, 638
Statistics, 204–207
  basic concepts, 179
  misuse of, 271
Steady state, 395, 520
Steady-state performance, 423
Steady-state probability, of birth-death
  process, 520
Stochastic model, 10
Stochastic processes, 515–517
  relationship among, 518
Stopping criteria, 430–431
Storage, dynamic allocation of, 404
Storage systems, benchmarking, 176
Strategies, ratio game, 170–173

Streams:
nonoverlapping, 454
Poisson, 201
Stress-load analysis, 132
Stretch factor, 38
Structured walk-through, 416–417
Student's *t* distribution, *see t* distribution
Subsample, 427
Substantive skills, 20–21
data, 179, 182, 197
variability, 192
Sum of squared errors, *see* SSE
Sum of squares total, *see* SST
SUT (system under test), 61, 62, 133
Symbols, queueing analysis, 624–626
Symbols in charts, 144
Synthetic programs, 50–51
Synthetic workload, 47
System, 4
balanced, 585
end, 35
finite buffer, 534–540
finite population, 546
intermediate, 35
vs. queue, 511, 512
regenerative, 434
System capacity, 509
System console, 102–103
System crashes, time between, 214
System integration, 132
System management, 103
System observation, 102
System parameters, 17, 23
System performance evaluation cooperative
(SPEC), 58
Systems:
airline reservation, 570
banking, 56–57, 570
batch, 594
comparison of, 203–220
several, 327
two, 18, 208–209
database, 6, 12, 201, 242
distributed, 101–109, 200, 568
information, 242
magnetic tape, 65–66
memory management, 311, 622
multiprocessor, 40, 527
storage, 176
text formatting, 322
timesharing, 62, 568, 602–607
transaction processing, 569, 570, 591
word processing, 388
System sizing, 124–125

System under test (SUT), 61, 62, 133

Table(s):
seeds, 455
sign-, 286, 292, 316–317
statistical, 627–638
approximation formulas for, 638
Taguchi method, 390
Tail, 438
Tape backup system, magnetic, 65–66
Tausworthe generators, 444–450
disadvantage of, 449
Tausworthe sequence, 468
t distribution, 497
quantiles of, 631
use of, 497
variate generation, 497
Terminating simulations, 428–430
Terminology:
experimental design, 275–278
workload characterization, 71–90
Test(s):
chi-square, 461–462
consistency, 420
for constant variance, 237, 302
continuity, 418–419
for correct initialization, 236
degeneracy, 419
F, 251, 298, 333
hypothesis, 213
for independent errors, 235, 302, 324
K-S (Kolmogorov-Smirnov), 462–465
for linear relationship, 235
for normality, 237, 302
for random-number generators, 456, 460
serial, 468–470
serial-correlation, 465
spectral, 470–472
statistical, 271
t-test, 209–211
two-level, 466–467
for zero mean, 207–208, 216
Testing:
hypothesis, 213
regression, 132
Test workload, 47, 128, 175
Text formatting programs, 322
Theorems:
central limit, 182
Chandy-Herzog-Woo, 615
Norton's, 614
Think time, 134, 553, 622
Three-quarter high rule, 146
Throughput, 38, 616

Time:
  inherited, 113
  vs. number in queue, 512–513
  parallelism in, 354
  between system crashes, 214
Time-advancing mechanisms, 407, 503
Time in queue, *vs.* time in system, 512–513
Timeliness, 68
Time-rate-resource metrics, 34
Timer interrupt, 96
Timesharing systems, 62, 568, 602–607
Time to failure, 40
Tomcatv benchmark, 59
Top-down design, 414–416
Towers of Hanoi benchmark, 167, 360, 361, 367
TPC benchmark, xii, 58
TPC (Transaction Processing Performance Council), xii, 58
TPS (transactions per second), 4, 38, 57
Trace, 67, 94, 404, 417
  event, 418
  mode, 96
  routines, 408
Trace-driven simulations, 404–406, 502
  advantages of, 405
  disadvantages of, 406
Tracing, 111, 113
Trade-off evaluation, 31
Traffic intensity, 522
Train arrivals, 621
Transaction Processing Performance Council (TPC), xii, 58
Transaction processing systems, 569, 570, 591
Transactions per second, *see* TPS
Transformation(s), 83, 84, 259–265, 271
  determining, 260
  inverse, 474–476
  log, 260–261
  omega, 261
  power, 262
  square-root, 259, 261
  to stabilize the variance, 262
Transient:
  performance, 129–130
  removal, 423
Transient analysis, 621
Transient state, 130, 423
Transition probability matrix, 81, 82, 559
Trap instruction, 96
Treatment, 276
Tree, minimum spanning, 87
Tree structures, 410, 411
Triangular distribution, 480

troff, 322
TRS-80, 109
Truncated exponential distribution, 523–524, 531
Truncation method, 424
t-test:
  paired, 209
  unpaired, 210
Tuning, performance, 111, 123
Turnaround time, 38
Two-factor experimental designs
  multiplicative models for, 353–359
  with replications, 368–380
    ANOVA table, 374
  without replications, 343–367
    ANOVA table, 349
2^k experimental designs, 280, 283–292
2^{k-p} experimental designs, 314–326
$2^k r$ experimental designs, 293–313
$2^2 r$ experimental designs, 293, 309
Two-level tests, 466–467

Uniform distribution (discrete)
  use of, 498
  variate generation, 498
Uniformity, k-dimensional, 467–470
Unimodal distributions, 183
Unit-time approach, 407
UNIX operating system, xii, 230–232, 256, 282, 359
  random number generator, 453
Unordered qualitative variables, 140
Unpaired observations, 209–210
Unrepresentative workload, 16
Unstable model, 401
Unverified models, 394
Uptime, 40
Usable capacity, 39, 125
User participation in analysis, 397
Users, 125
Utility classification of metrics, 40
Utilization, 34, 39, 601, 602, 603, 606, 616
  law, 556
  use for validation, 130

Validation
  of Amdahl's law, 257, 258
  of assumptions, 421
  baseline, 126
  of conclusions, 421
  of measured data, 32, 130
  of parameters, 421
  projection, 126
  rules for, 32

Validation (*Continued*)
  of simulation models, 420–421
  using utilization, 130
Variability, 19
  of metrics, 35
  of response time, 36
  summarizing, 192
Variables, types of, 140
  continuous, 140
  discrete, 140
  predictor, 221, 269
  qualitative, 140
  quantitative, 140
  random, 179
  response, 221
Variance, 180, 193, 197, 287
  intergroup, 87
  intragroup, 87
  of queue length, 593
  of sample mean, 181, 430–431
  of sums, 181
  test for constant, 302
Variance estimation, 430–431
Variance normalization, 85
Variance reduction, 436, 502, 503
Variate, 437
Variate generation, 474–482
Variation, 226, 286–291
  allocation of, 226–228, 295–298, 331–332,
    347–348, 372–374
  coefficient of, 181, 197
  difference from variance, 287
VAX-11/780 processor, xii, 167, 359, 365
Vectors, orthogonal, 77
Verification, of models, 413–414
Visit ratio, 558, 560
Visual tests:
  for confidence intervals, 211–212
  for equality, 211–212

for experimental designs, 302–303, 309,
    334, 366, 379
  for regression, 234–241, 266
VMS operating system, 359

Waiting time, mean, 429
Walk-through, structured, 416–417
WANG VS operating system, 324
Weibull distribution, 498
  use of, 498
  variate generation, 477, 499
Weighted Euclidean distance, *see* Euclidean
    distance
Weight normalization, 85
Whetstone benchmark, 54, 55
Word processing systems, 388
Workload, 4, 24
  characterization, 71–90, 175
    using accounting logs, 121
    using average values, 74
  component, 72
  for computer networks, 63–65
  features, 72
  loading level of, 69
  parameters, 17, 23, 72
  real, 128
  selection, 60–69
  test, 128
  types of, 47, 48–52
Workload unit, 72, 125
Workstation
  design, 275–276
  emulation, 138, 176
Writes, ratio of reads to, 121

Zero mean, testing for, 207–208
Z80 processor, xii, 275, 276, 279, 281
6502 processors, 166
Z8002 processor, 167, 360, 361, 365